Papers from the 24th AIA Conference

Challenges for the 21st Century:
Dilemmas, Ambiguities, Directions

VOLUME I

Literary Studies
Edited by
ROSY COLOMBO, LILLA MARIA CRISAFULLI, FRANCA RUGGIERI

Cultural Studies
Edited by
RICHARD AMBROSINI, ALESSANDRA CONTENTI, DANIELA CORONA

Challenges for the 21st Century: Dilemmas, Ambiguities, Directions.
Papers from the 24th AIA conference.
Volume I. Literary Studies (edited by R. Colombo, L.M. Crisafulli, F. Ruggieri);
Cultural Studies (edited by R. Ambrosini, A. Contenti, D. Corona).

La pubblicazione di questo volume è stata finanziata dal Rettorato e dai dipartimenti di Letterature Comparate, Linguistica e Studi Internazionali della Università degli Studi Roma Tre, Roma.

Edizioni Q - Roma
info@edizioniq.it

I edizione: ottobre 2011.

ISBN: 978-88-903969-8-4

Revisione: Ilenia Cassetta, Andrea Ciccioli, Alessandro Di Menno di Bucchianico, Paola Vinesi.

Elaborazione grafica dell'immagine in copertina: Mario Crosara.

Impaginazione e stampa:
Grafiche VD srl - Città di Castello (PG)
grafichevd@gmail.com

Front cover image from:
Laurence Sterne, *The Life and Opinions of Tristram Shandy, Gentleman*, 1761;
Penguin 2003, vol. VI, Chapter Forty, p. 454.

By which it appears, that except at the curve, marked A, where I took a
trip to Navarre, – and the indented curve B, which is the short airing
when I was there with the Lady Baussiere and her page, - I have not taken
the least frisk of a digression, till John de la Casse's devils led me the
round you see marked D – for as for C C C C C they are nothing but
parentheses, and the common ins and outs incident to the lives of the
greatest ministers of state; and when compared with what men
have done , – or with my own transgressions at the letters A B D – they
vanish into nothing.

To Giorgio Melchiori

*In memory of a lifelong contribution
to English studies*

Contents

Part 1

$\mathcal{L}$ITERARY STUDIES

1. Origin and Identity

2. The Languages of Literature

3. Literature and the Media

4. Past and New Directions

Part 2

$\mathscr{C}$ULTURAL STUDIES

Introduction

1. Cultural Translation: New Theories and Practices

2. Community and Nation: Hybrid Identities, Reinvented Traditions (I)

3. Community and Nation: Hybrid Identities, Reinvented Traditions (II)

4. Travelling Concepts, Transforming Bodies

5. Postcolonial London

6. Representations of Antinormative Sexual Identities

7. New Challenges for Drama Studies and Cultural Theory

8. Visual and Media Studies

Foreword

The 24th Conference of the *Associazione Italiana di Anglistica* (AIA) was held on October 1-3, 2009, hosted by the Faculty of *Lettere e Filosofia* of Roma Tre University. The Conference title, "Challenges for the 21st Century: Dilemmas, Ambiguities, Directions", was decided upon by the Board of the Association at that time and by the Anglicists from Roma Tre, working in different Departments. The Conference attracted more than 300 participants, among whom the vast majority were young researchers, to whom AIA Conferences are traditionally addressed. More than 200 AIA members presented their contributions in the 39 parallel sessions or in the Poster sessions, and all AIA areas – Literary Studies, Cultural Studies and Language Studies – also attracted contributions from senior scholars.

Due to editorial constraints and the large number of papers accepted for publication, the Editors decided to divide contributions into two volumes: volume one includes contributions in the areas of Literary Studies (Part 1) and Cultural Studies (Part 2); volume two is made up of contributions in the area of Language Studies. Each volume has been jointly edited by the Convenors of the Conference sessions, who summarize contributions and explain the logic behind their sequencing in greater detail in their Introductions to Part 1 and Part 2 of volume one and to volume two.

The two volumes do not constitute the complete Proceedings of the Conference: some contributors at the Conference did not submit their papers for publication. The Editors have followed the thematic sequencing of the original sessions as far as possible, on occasion re-grouping contributions to offer a more cohesive presentation of the various research topics investigated from a number of different perspectives, and to highlight convergences and divergences. They hope that readers will find the sequencing helpful and that individual authors will feel rewarded for their efforts.

The Editors

Acknowledgements

As coordinator of the Scientific Committee and of the Organising Committee of the 24th AIA (*Associazione Italiana di Anglistica*) Conference "Challenges for the 21st Century: Dilemmas, Ambiguities, Directions", I wish to express my gratitude to all those who have helped turn the original proposal put forward by the AIA Board at the time into a major event and who have made the publication of these two volumes possible.

My first thanks go to AIA President, Giuseppina Cortese, and to the other members of the Board – Carlo Bajetta, John Douthwaite, Oriana Palusci, Rita Salvi, Maristella Trulli, Marina Vitale – for inviting me and Roma Tre Anglicists to take on the daunting task of organizing the national Conference. The Conference organization appeared at first to be a real challenge and perhaps not by chance the word "challenge" played a major role when the Board and the organisers discussed the Conference title and eventually became a key word in its theme.

I also wish to extend warm thanks to all the members of the Scientific Committee (Richard Ambrosini, Rosy Colombo, Alessandra Contenti, Daniela Corona, Lilla Maria Crisafulli, Gabriella Di Martino, Linda Lombardo, Marinella Rocca Longo, Franca Ruggieri) and of the local organising committee (Patrick Boylan, Adriano Elia, Paola Faini, Liz Glass, Enrico Grazzi, David Hart, Lucilla Lopriore, Patrizia Pierini, Tania Zulli) for their invaluable help and suggestions at all stages of this initiative.

The Conference was made possible thanks to the financial, administrative and logistic support of Roma Tre Rectorate, of the Faculty of *Lettere e Filosofia*, and of the Departments of *Letterature Comparate*, *Linguistica* and *Studi Internazionali*, that actively contributed to its organization before, during and after the Conference itself. Special thanks go to the Rector, Prof Guido Fabiani, and the Administrative Director Dr Pasquale Basilicata; the Dean of the Faculty, Prof Francesca Cantù, and her administrative staff; the Department Heads, Professors Otello Lottini, Franca Orletti and Annunziata Nobile, and their administrative staffs.

I also wish to thank the British Council, in particular the former Director Paul Docherty, the current Director Christine Melia, and the Deputy Director Kevin Mackenzie: they gave their enthusiastic support to the Conference from the very beginning and made it possible for the organisers to invite John Simpson, OED Chief Editor, as plenary speaker. Christine Melia also attended the inaugural session, and her illustration of British Council activities was well received by the audience.

The plenary session devoted to institutional matters, a novelty in AIA Conferences, was most stimulating and special thanks go to the Head of CUN, Prof Andrea Lenzi and to CUN Member Prof Simona Costa, for readily agreeing to take part in this very important moment of the conference and for their insights into the global and local trends in the reorganization of the macro-areas representing AIA members' academic, scientific and didactic activities.

On behalf of the Organisers I express special gratitude to Prof Fernando Galvan, ESSE President, for accepting the invitation to attend the Conference and for his insightful comments on various topics.

Specific appreciation must be expressed to the Convenors of the three main AIA Conference areas – to Franca Ruggieri, Rosy Colombo and Lilla Maria Crisafulli for Literary Studies; to Richard Ambrosini, Alessandra Contenti and Daniela Corona for Cultural Studies; and to Linda Lombardo and Gabriella Di Martino who worked with me for Language Studies – for their commitment and involvement both before the Conference as members of the Scientific Committee and afterward as editors of these volumes. I am personally indebted to the local Convenors of Literary and Cultural Studies, Franca Ruggieri and Richard Ambrosini, for the numerous meetings I have asked them to attend and the innumerable email messages we have exchanged from the conference planning stage to the final editorial summing up. I am also personally indebted to my co-convenors, Linda Lombardo and Gabriella Di Martino, for their active participation in all stages of the editorial process, always in a friendly and collaborative way, which was especially gratifying. Thank you Linda, thank you Gabriella.

Special thanks go also to the Chairs of the Plenary sessions, Prof Barbara Arnett and Prof Giuseppina Cortese, and to the Chairs of the parallel sessions, too many to name them all here.

All my Faculty Colleagues were very patient during the days of the Conference, and the entire University staff, in particular the technicians, were especially cooperative and helpful. My personal thanks go to them all.

A special mention must go to the agency Prestige Italy and to all their staff for attending to both the organisational and administrative aspects of the Conference, from the social dinner to welcoming participants and catering for their needs, from coffee breaks to printing and distributing programmes.

A final word concerns the gratitude that AIA in its entirety owes to its co-founder and first President, Giorgio Melchiori, for his internationally renowned achievements and for his academic, scientific and didactic commitment. It is to him that the volumes containing the papers from the 24th Conference, the first since he sadly passed away, are dedicated in fond memory.

Stefania Nuccorini

Part 1
Literary Studies

Introduction

Part 1 of the first volume of the Conference Proceedings collects the contributions presented in the Literary Studies section of the 24th AIA Conference.

The Conference opened with JOHN SIMPSON's inaugural talk entitled "Watching The Cars Go By or Directing the Traffic? Literature, Language, and Culture in the 21st Century". His role as Chief Editor of the *OED* allowed him, as a plenary speaker addressing scholars in the fields of Literary, Cultural and Language Studies, to give an overview from a privileged position of the relations between the way the English language has developed, the linguistic and cultural networks of which words are a part, their communicative role therein, their contribution to 'great' literature or to literature in the sense of "anything that has been committed to paper". He discussed extensively the concept and role of authoritativeness which people tend to attribute to the dictionary and lexicographers' commitment to the analysis of data. He remarked that: "people require authority – something to rely on. In order to obtain this from a reference work, they turn dictionaries into their authorities". He reflected on the place the *OED* occupies in this context, and stressed that its aim is to monitor the language and report back on findings. His analysis of the meanings of the word *cell* and of the word *radical* showed how words are often 'on the move', and he concluded, by way of explaining both the title and the metaphor it conveys, that "the typical speaker of English may not know who is directing the traffic, but he or she gets to their destination in the end".

As the table of contents indicates, the present organization of the volume reflects the actual grouping of the twelve literature workshops organised throughout the conference sessions. The editors have chosen a formal division of the essays on the basis of the four main thematic groupings: "Origin and Identity"; "The Languages of Literature"; "Literature and the Media"; "Past and New Directions".

The essays provide a lively picture of 'the state of the art' of English literature studies in Italy. The contributors are mostly young scholars from all over the country, as their university affiliations demonstrate. The contributions testify to a lively variety of critical approaches; taken as a whole, they give an indication of a great wealth of research interests, with topics ranging from the Renaissance to Postmodern Age.

During the Conference an interesting Round Table was held on "Literary History and Its Problems" on the occasion of the publication of the book *Manuale di Letteratura e Cultura Inglese*, edited by Lilla Maria Crisafulli and Keir Elam. Both editors participated in the event.

Literature Workshop A, "Origin and Identity": in "One Life, Many Languages, Multilingualism in Hugo Hamilton's *The Speckled People* (2003) and Charlotte Williams's *Sugar and Slate* (2002)", ELISA ARMELLINO focuses on multilinguism. She highlights a number of linguistic choices and their cultural implications inside the "speckled" mixture of English-German-Irish-Welsh languages at work in the two texts analysed.

ELISA BOLCHI's "Look into My I. Narrating Subjects, Identity and Gender in Jeanette Winterson's Fiction" is a well argued paper exploring Jeanette Winterson's fiction and providing interesting insights into intertextual relationships with Virginia Woolf's writings.

LISANNA CALVI's article, "Jane Barker's *Exilius* as Jacobite Fiction in Exile", is an engaging comparison between the Jacobite Aeneid: *Exilius, or The Banish'd Roman*, read as a politically encoded romance, and the epic of Jacobite experience and cause.

MARIA MICAELA COPPOLA, in "Dead Eye. Dead I: Telling Stories at the End in Ali Smith's *Hotel World*", provides a convincing analysis of Ali Smith's novel, backed by an appropriate theoretical framework.

LAURA GIOVANNELLI's "J.M. Coetzee's *Diary of a Bad Year* and the Risky Challenge of Cultivating Strong Opinions" is a profound and documented analysis of Coetzee's *Diary of a Bad Year* within a literal, critical and ethical context: the author provides a well written and well argued reading of Coetzee's "diary" as well as of the author's inner conflicts as an internationally acclaimed writer burdened with a postcolonial legacy.

FABIO LIBERTO's "Poor Susans!": Wordsworth and the "Single(s) in the Wide Waste" is an excellent study of Wordsworth's complex relationship with urban experience, filtered by the eye of imagination. Particular emphasis is laid on the issue of individuality: quotations are selected with intelligence and the Wordsworth canon is well assimilated.

PIERPAOLO MARTINO's contribution, *"The Importance of Being Oscar*: Performance, Performativity and Identity in Wilde", takes its cue from the theoretical frame of performance studies. He shows how Wilde's self-conscious construction of identity and his performance of an ironic masculinity have become sources of inspiration for twenty first century artists. The essay offers an enthusiastic comment on Oscar Wilde as a cultural icon, a clever construction of his image as a "pop idol".

FRANCESCO MINETTI's study on "White Negroes and Irish Brigades in Joseph O'Connor's *Redemption Falls*", is a descriptive analysis of O'Connor's historical novel about the role of the Irish in the American Civil war: the novel's rescuing of atrocious stories of Irish American workers from oblivion can be read as a disrespectful rewriting of Irish memory, which desacralizes the biographical traits and political plans of a prominent nationalist leader.

In "Careless Talk Costs Lives: War Propaganda and Wartime Fiction in Elizabeth Bowen's *The Heat of the Day*", STEFANIA PORCELLI focuses on the relevance of the slogans of war propaganda in Bowen's fiction of the 1940s. She argues that propaganda works as an ideologically-laden interpretative frame, which disturbs self-perception. A well organized historical contextualization of Elizabeth Bowen's wartime fiction.

PAOLA DANIELA SMECCA's "The Role of Memory in Ian McEwan's *Atonement*" is a perceptive paper, intelligently argued, on MacEwan's narrative exploration of the traumatic impact of war on individual lives and memory, taking into account the novel's multi-layered handling of individual, collective and meta-literary stances.

With "A Portrait of a Poet as an Exile: the Case of Philip Larkin" ANNA ENRICHETTA SOCCIO, proposes a passionate, competent textual analysis, that focuses on the condition of exile and estrangement as dramatized in Larkin's poetry, regarded as conducive to a heightened, poetic view of everyday life, as well as to an intense experience of knowledge and compassion.

STEFANIA STERLECCHINI, the author of "When Memory and Exile Intertwine. Brian Friel's Theatre", concentrates on Brian Friel's dramatic corpus, mainly on three plays. She highlights the theatrical devices through which Friel stages his complex sense of what it means to be Irish, looking at Ireland with a blend of irony and affection.

In an interesting, competent article, "A Kind of Medical Chaucer: Testimony, Storytelling and Caregiving in Ian McEwan's *Atonement*", MARIA VACCARELLA reads Ian McEwan's novel as a meditation on the ethical significance of caregiving and on the value of testimony. With a self-reflexive gesture, Vaccarella argues, McEwan extends such meditation to the prerogatives of literature itself.

MASSIMO VERZELLA's "The Paradoxical Vision: Samuel Butler's Use of Ambiguity in *Erewhon*" is an original paper. Well argued and well written, supported by a good bibliography, it proposes a deconstructive reading of Samuel Butler's *Erewhon*, seen as an attempt to undermine metaphysical master plots.

Literature Workshop B, "The Languages of Literature": GIOIELLA BRUNI ROCCIA presents an excellent contribution. Her "Writing, When Properly Managed, Is But a Different Name for Conversation: *Tristram Shandy* and the Ethics of Reading", interprets Sterne's masterpiece as a magnificent example of the interaction of writing and reading as a an ethical issue. It is an innovative reading of the singularity of a literary work, based on the creative transformation of the reader's habits, expectations, and visions of the world. Shaftesbury's influence on Sterne is the most original aspect of the essay, a new perspective on 18th century studies.

SONIA BUTTINELLI's "The Art-Work of the Future: from Wagner to Joyce", analyses Joyce's early work in the light of the deep connection between drama and art on one side, and everyday human life on the other. Tracing its source in Richard Wagner's essays, the article opens new perspectives in the complex field of Wagnerian echoes at work in Joyce's early writing.

RICCARDO CAPOFERRO's paper, "Apparition Narratives and the Style of the Fantastic", proposes an original interpretation of the coexistence of empirical reality with non-empirical issues in 18th century novels. It challenges the conventional categories of "realism" and "romance" and displays a strong epistemological commitment to the theory of the novel, with new insights into 18th century narrative.

IVANA DIPIETRO's "Bodies in Change: Lewis Carroll's *Alice in Wonderland* and Salman Rushdie's *The Firebird's Nest*" focuses on the image and concept of the body, tracing the possible development line from bodies that change size in *Alice* to bodies which can 'be written' or 'burn like paper' in Rushdie's short story. Supported by a scholarly background, the paper is an ambitious reading of Rushdie' s rewriting of *Alice in Wonderland* stressing the centrality of Alice's metamorphosis as a dream of rebellion.

CARLOTTA FARESE's paper, "Unlike Emma. Mary Elizabeth Braddon's Response to Bovarism in *The Doctor's Wife*", illustrates the centrality and uses of the figure of the woman reader in the nineteenth-century artistic and literary imagination. Its analysis of Braddon's subtle reworking of Flaubert's *Madame Bovary* stresses the positive and constructive value of female reading.

C. MARIA LAUDANDO's "The Joint Venture of Tim Crouch's Performance Between Visual Art, Theatre and Education", focuses on the experimental work of the "theatre-maker" Tim Crouch, highlighting the intriguing and playful interrogation of the audience's agency within the de-materialized space of theatre. A provocative interdisciplinary approach supports a well organized, persuasive article.

FABIO LUPPI's "John Keats's First Poems According to Gaston Bachelard's *Poetics of Space* (A Modern Reading for an Old Theme)", is a well written paper. It draws on psychological theories to discuss the problematic significance of the artistic creation in a protective, familiar space: Luppi works on the 'nest' as a symbolic recurrent image in Keats's poetry.

MARIA DOMENICA MANGIALAVORI: "Music, Painting and Memory in Virginia Woolf's *To the Lighthouse*", explores the ways in which motives, tropes and formal conventions of painting and musical genres, such as the sonata, entwine in the rhythms of Woolf's writing, stirring action in the reader's memory. The analysis of each section of the novel is beautifully argued and sustained by a good selection of critical references. The reading of the novel in the form of a sonata is fascinating.

MARIA GRAZIA NICOLOSI's "Re-membering the Past in Adam Thorpe's War Novels" is a sophisticated reading of Adam Thorpe's novels specifically dealing with the war theme. Supported by a good theoretical bibliography, the essay addresses the question of the fictional space of historical memory and re-writing, together with the cultural and literary myths of the Great War; it represents an interestingly eccentric intervention in the field.

Literature Workshop C, "Literature and the Media": ROBERTA BORGNA's paper "Is Life in the 21st Century "A Long Way Down"? Thematic and Linguistic Issues from One of Nick Hornby's Latest Novels" is an analysis of Nick Hornby's novel *A Long Way Down* as constructed by intertwined monologues: the characters, coming from very different milieux and experiences, paradoxically create new and complex relationships, through which some of them attain a kind of new awareness.

ILARIA ODDENINO's "Ern Malley: Contemporary Perspectives on Australia's Bogus Bard" is an interesting and well written research, though most of it is devoted to the description of the Malley affair, rather than to a critical analysis of the text. It deals with the literary and critical questions arising from a notorious hoax played on an Australian avant-garde critic, showing how a poetic text, composed as a joke out of disparate materials, succeeded in capturing the spirit of modernist issues like intentionality, death of the author, canonicity.

Literature Workshop D, "Past and New Directions": MARIJA BERGAM's "Robinson Crusoe's Sea-Change: Caribbean Transformations" examines from new perspectives the character of Robinson Crusoe, ever considered an icon of colonial venture. The paper explores in fact the transformations of the Crusoe figure in Derek Walcott's poems, and in Sam Selvon's novel *Moses Ascending*.

VALENTINA CASTAGNA's "Reading *The Book of Margery Kempe* in the 21st Century: Gender, Authorship and Performance" is an interesting paper, backed by a wide ranging critical bibliography, that shows evidence of her long-standing research on the topic. The essay focuses on the reception history of *The Book of Margery Kempe*, from the beginning of the 15th century down to contemporary rewritings of the text as radio play and novel.

FRANCA DELLAROSA's "Connecting Across Centuries: Memory, Displacement, and Exile in Caryl Phillips' Stage Plays" proposes an original reading of Caryl

Phillips as a playwright, engaged in the challenge of writing plays about black subjects. It explores theoretical and ethical issues concerning the nature and role of public memory in relation to the debate on the abolition of the slave trade. The result is a piece of excellent critical writing.

PAOLA D'ERCOLE's "A Migration of Dreams and Ideas: from Books to Bricks and Mortar", inspired by Walter Besant's novel *All Sorts and Conditions of Men*, is an original exploration of the urbanistic, social and cultural development of East London in the late nineteenth century and the following migration of ideas from the oral and written culture to the actual construction of buildings.

MARIA LUISA DE RINALDIS's "Walter Pater's Venus and Pre-cinematographic Reproduction of the Human Body" is an interesting paper on Pater's construction of modernity, in the light of Pater's dematerialized perception of the human body. Within a frame of appropriate contextualization, well informed on recent visual studies, the author investigates the representation of Venus in Walter Pater's essay *Sandro Botticelli* from a post-cinematographic perspective.

SAURO FABI's contribution, "*How* is Poetry Going?: Bottlenecks and New Paths for a Seemingly Marginal Art", opens with a survey of the widening gap between poetry and mass audience in the course of the twentieth century, whereby poetry has become a somewhat marginal art. It subsequently examines promising new poetic forms that might bridge the gap during the 21st century.

GIAN PIETRO LEONARDI's "Gay and After: Notes Towards a Definition of the Post-Gay Novel" voices a serious approach to some issues of gay studies from the point of view of the radical post-gay novel. Well written, the paper assumes however an ideological rather than a critical stance. In the process, he provides a thought-provoking reading of Alan Hullinghurst's much acclaimed *The Line of Beauty*.

VALENTINA PONTOLILLO D'ELIA's "A Madman Shakes a Dead Geranium: T.S. Eliot Updated for Our Times?" highlights the relationship between Eliot's early work, especially the posthumous volume *The Inventions of the March Hare*, and his later output, arguing that Eliot's early poetry is not inconsistent with his more canonical texts and deserves closer critical attention.

MARIANNA PUGLIESE's paper, "Antigone in Liz Lochhead's *Thebans*: the Structure, the Character and the Language", investigates the role of the mythical Greek heroine in Liz Lochhead's *Thebans*, focusing on the ways in which the playwright rearticulates ancient tragedy for contemporary Scottish audiences, with particular reference to her use of dialectal and regional phonetic forms. The article is a thorough and persuasive critical reading of Liz Lochhead's work in the wider context of contemporary adaptations of classical mythological themes.

ANNAMARIA SPORTELLI's paper "I Am Often Asked Whether There Can Be a Long Imagist or Vorticist Poem: Evolution or Involution of Epic in Modernist

Poetics" is an engaged and engaging critical contribution by a distinguished scholar. After a thoughtful and thorough survey of the debate on epic from the Romantics to E. Pound and T.S. Eliot, the author analyses how changing outlooks on epics brought about a re-modulation of the genre in Modernist poetics.

Rosy Colombo
(Sapienza – Università di Roma)

Lilla Maria Crisafulli
(Università di Bologna)

Franca Ruggieri
(Università Roma Tre)

JOHN SIMPSON

Chief Editor, *Oxford English Dictionary*

"Watching the Cars Go By or Directing the Traffic?"
Literature, Language, and Culture in the 21st Century

Dictionaries are generally regarded as authorities, and yet much of the information they contain cannot be regarded as representing 'absolute' authority. There is an element of illusion in the dictionary. The comments which follow look at this issue from the point of view of historical dictionaries, but the issues raised are relevant to monolingual dictionaries generally.

The appearance of freedom in society

A common perception of Britain is of a society which is largely free of authoritarian control. There is no written constitution; there is a free press. Society has the freedom to do what it wishes: its citizens can more or less write what they want; they can more or less go where they want; they can more or less live how they like.

Much the same can be said of the English language. No one is in control of it. There is no academy to tell people what they can or cannot say. There are no committees in charge of planning new words. In some contexts (such as text messaging) spelling is not always rule-bound. This is quite at odds with the situation in some other countries, where the state takes a controlling interest in the use of language in the media, in education, and in many other areas of society.

On the political level, the simplistic picture is that authority derives from legislation and common practice. A network of laws is enacted and amended over time, and society operates within this legal framework. This framework of legislation appears to reside in the background – leaving citizens free to do more or less what they like. But there are a surprising number of restrictions.

The borderline between an enabling social restriction and one that curbs our personal freedom is a hard one to draw. The list of these social restrictions is surprisingly large: seat belts (1968 onwards), speed limits (introduced early on in the life of the motor car), recycling requirements (now prevalent almost everywhere), tax legislation, libel laws: the list could be extended considerably.

Language: the impression of freedom

Does the same state of affairs apply in the field of language? There is no state authority for language in Britain: the language develops as it wants. New words come and go: some remain and some disappear. The most useful ones survive – by a process akin to the survival of the fittest. People are free to select their own words, to order them how they like, and use them to communicate in everyday social discourse, or to create great literature, or pot-boiling commercial successes, or estate agents' particulars.

Freedom for the Oxford English Dictionary (OED)

What is the place of the *Oxford English Dictionary* in this linguistic environment? It is not under state control: the dictionary is entirely funded by the Oxford University Press, which is itself a part of the University of Oxford. The dictionary's aim is to monitor the language, and to report back on what it finds. This has been its role for over 120 years. It does not report back just on *contemporary* English; it takes out its rear-view mirror and surveys the English language of the past, right back to the earliest times. It does this not only in Britain, but wherever English is spoken.

The *OED* is free to choose how it observes the English language, and it is free to report on its findings – which it does every three months by updating its online database at oed.com. The current revision of the dictionary – the first for a hundred years – saw its first instalment published in the year 2000, and at present editorial work is approximately a quarter complete. The words updated so far include many which are central to the language. It is an interesting exercise to take some of these and to see how they have changed since the days of the first edition of the *OED* a century ago: words like *cultural, identity, language, literature, memory, myth, narrative, photorealist, post-modern,* and *realism*.

The *OED*, then, does not legislate; it is not an official authority. Its objective is to monitor the language from the earliest times up to the present day, and to report back on its findings.

Different attitudes to authority

But people's attitudes to authority differ. Some people want to rely on an official authority, and constantly seek security in a framework of rules. For others the idea of an overriding authority is anathema. Everybody fits along the spectrum between these two extremes. People write to the *OED* from time to time and ask the dictionary to use its apparent influence to ban certain words (such as the sentence-adverb use of *hopefully*, or the verb *to access*): they write to complain that inclusion in the dictionary gives validity to a usage they detest, and demand that their pet hate be struck out. Others want the dictionary to introduce new words which the language, in their view, desperately needs. Such correspondents do not realize that the language already 'lacks' more words than it contains, because there is not a one-to-one (or a many-to-one) relationship between things in the real world and words used to refer to them. In many cases correspondents would find that their meaning could easily be expressed in ways that do not require the coining of a new term.

Between these two ends of the spectrum there are many people who take a general interest in language, who pick up new words and new usages as they come along, and who even send to the dictionary offices evidence for these neologisms just to ensure that they are registered somewhere.

So as far as the language is concerned, we can identify numerous intersecting axes of interest. These include the authority/anarchy axis; the descriptive/prescriptive axis; the generational axis (different generations have different expectations of language); the chronological axis (words come with a weight of history); and doubtless many more.

Similar axes are present in our culture itself, and this is hardly surprising, as the language reflects contemporary societal concerns. There is a constant tension between authority and freedom, like and dislike, black and white, and all of the shades in between.

How authoritative is a dictionary?

In Britain dictionaries monitor and describe the traffic of words. They do not set themselves up as authorities. Scholarly investigation into language is objective, and may report a trend which some people find disconcerting. But many people require authority – something to rely on. In order to obtain this from a reference work, they turn dictionaries into their authorities. Everyone will be familiar with the unfounded assertion: "It must be a word because it's in the dictionary".

But there are, in fact, very few categories of information in a dictionary that are 'absolute'. In most cases this tag can be applied to the spelling of the headword. There is in general a consensus across dictionaries about how most words are spelt. Exceptions include the use of *judgement* and *disc* in specific contexts; varietal differences between, for example, *honour* and *honor*, *catalogue* and *catalog*. But the ground is far less certain in the area of pronunciation. Dictionaries have various schemes for representing pronunciation, but requirements of space mean that they only reflect one or two generalized realizations – sometimes subtly at variance with the gradations of sound by which these words are spoken in the real world. The stress and vowel quality of, for example, the word *pronunciation* itself can be variable.

The area of definitions is also problematic. There is an unlimited number of ways of describing the meaning of a term – the choice of words which a dictionary selects for its definitions is based on its size, its intended audience, maybe sometimes the subjective bias of the lexicographer. Just because the *OED* defines culture (in one sense) as "the distinctive ideas, customs, social behaviour, products, or way of life of a particular society, people, or period", this does not mean that there are not many other ways of expressing the same concept.

There are similar problems in the case of etymology. The idea that there is a science of etymology, that it is possible to plot accurately the development of words from the earliest times right up to the present day, is a comforting one. But at the root of almost every etymology is a black hole, a vanishing point beyond which it is impossible to delve with any certainty. The original motivating factors for the creation of words are lost in the mists of time. Linguists do not know how the first words were created. Authoritative etymology can only aspire to establish an accurate analysis from the time of written records. Since the *OED*'s entry for *monkey* was revised and published in September 2002 new information has become available which shifts the balance of likelihood for its etymology, and in December 2009 a substantively revised etymology for this term was published by the dictionary. Any word is subject to change if new findings and better analyses come to light.

Lexicographers present the most reliable information that they can, in the absence of full and accurate information. Just as contemporary language changes and the speech patterns of the past shift subtly into those of today, so our knowledge of English in past centuries changes. We make discoveries – sometimes thousands of little discoveries a year – and the apparently reliable picture we have of the English language in the past shifts.

But there is some continuity. Our core vocabulary carries on more or less regardless. Today most literature (including within the term 'literature' anything that has been committed to paper) back to the mid eighteenth century can be read without any significant problem. Before the mid eighteenth century, the situation for the modern reader becomes more problematic. He or she starts to read modern meanings into old words, to reinterpret the past in the light of the present, whether we want to or not.

The following quotation shows a use of the verb "to purvey" in the late seventeenth century. The modern reader would probably assume that the word here has something to do with the provision of food or other goods. But documentary evidence shows that this is one of the final recorded occurrences of an old, broader sense "to arrange in advance; to prepare or plan", typically followed by an infinitive or *that*-clause:

1683 I. WALTON *Chalkhill's Thealma & Clearchus* 118 They reach the Land at length, their Food grew scant, And now they purvey to supply their want.

The case for achronology is highlighted by televised historical documentaries. These present a view of the past filtered by the values of the modern day. The modern observer does not view the past objectively, but shapes it according to his or her knowledge and taste.

The lexicographer (and the scholar in general) seeks to overcome this bias by working with raw data which has been acquired neutrally. This reaches to the heart of the *OED*'s linguistic philosophy. This is not, as noted above, to tell people how to use the English language. And despite the propaganda, it is not simply to monitor the way language has changed over the centuries and to report back objectively on this. It is to interpret objective lexical data analytically so that the underlying patterns emerge.

The *OED* is seeking to record the English language on the presumption that it is evolving (and has evolved) in a logical and patterned way. This can be regarded dismissively as a Victorian preoccupation with classification. But it is not as simplistic as this. Language is analysed as if it were a Darwinian genus, or an exploding universe. The historical lexicographer identifies a particular word, recorded as being used with a particular set of meanings in, say, 1650. By a process which involves analysing lexical data over a long time-frame, the lexicographer is then able to identify the set of meanings that this same word possessed two hundred years later. In this case, some of the old meanings from 1650 will have been retained, but in all probability these will have been enhanced by a new set of meanings which have arisen out of the word's involvement with its environment (and especially with evolving societies) in the following two hundred years.

What the historical lexicographer is trying to show is that there are reasons for the evolution of the meaning set (say, of the word *repulse* or *retire*) of 1650 into the meaning set of 1850, and that there will be reasons for the evolution of the meaning set of the same word into those that will be current in 2050.

The lexicographer's view of language

For the historical lexicographer, continuity and moderate change are more important than authority, and this helps to reinforce the idea that the analysis contained in a historical dictionary is not entirely an illusion. But even in this analysis, there are times when the documentary evidence available for a particular word does not easily fit a coherent, logical progression. In these instances the lexicographer will argue that: a) the documentary evidence is not yet complete, and if it were it would fall in line with the principle of coherence, or b) that some external factor is responsible – that there must be something in the existing network of words, or in the changing culture within which they exist and develop, that is responsible for an apparent disjunction in the steady progression of meaning. Each such discontinuity becomes the subject of further research and discussion. A clear example of this occurs with the word *milksop*. The earliest records for this word appear in the thirteenth century, where it is used as a surname (e.g. *Rogerus Milksoppe*). By the late fourteenth century the lexicalized use is found: "a feeble, timid, or ineffectual person, *esp.* a man or boy who is indecisive, effeminate, or lacking in courage". It is not until the late fifteenth century that an isolated 'literal' use occurs:

> *a*1475 *Liber Cocorum* 53 Melle white brede in dysshes...Powre in wellyd mylke…
> þat called is mylke soppys.

The reader, and the lexicographer, is challenged to consider why the 'transferred' use precedes the literal one.

The popular stereotypical conception of the historical dictionary is of a text which presents a sequence of entries in the form of a ledger or book of accounts, as the lexicographer works painstakingly through the alphabet recording in detail how individual words have developed over the centuries. Some lexicographers never get beyond this simplistic view of their work.

Words as individuals and words as part of a society or network of communicative tools

But one of the many things that it takes time for new historical lexicographers to appreciate is that when they are working on the meaning, etymology, or history of a particular word, they need to step back and see how their word fits into the language as a whole. Lexicographers have various devices to help them achieve this, such as text corpora, which can show hundreds of examples of their word in context. But the network of words requires more than this.

The word *cell* offers a convenient insight into parts of this network. *Cell* has been used in English from the Anglo-Saxon period, though it derives from a Romance rather than a Germanic base. That itself is a minor puzzle that the lexicographer (or etymologist) needs to explain. At present the word *cell* has, according to the *OED*, 34 different meanings in English, including "a dwelling consisting of a single chamber inhabited by a hermit or anchorite", a monastery or nunnery, a small room for a monk or nun, a small room for an inmate in a prison, a compartment of the brain, any of the typically hexagonal wax compartments in a honeycomb, the basic unit of a battery, the region within which a mobile phone can be used, the fundamental (usually microscopic) structural and functional unit of all living organisms, a location in a matrix-like diagram, and a small group of people working within a larger organization as a nucleus of political, esp. revolutionary, activity.

So when speakers of English use the word *cell* they are calling on a vast palimpsest of meanings, all united semantically in some way, with a progression which moves hand in hand with the cultural concerns of the day. The earliest meanings in this case are religious, and date from the Old English period – and several of these senses remain in use today. As usage of the word moves into the eighteenth century, speakers start to make the connection between the monk spending days in his monastic cell with the prisoner confined for years in one of the spartan rooms of a prison. This sense gained a stronghold at a time when early prison reformers were creating large prison structures in which the individual rooms might well be described as cells within a larger institution.

Earlier, in the Middle Ages, people had likened the solitary retreat of the monk to the organic structures which they were discovering or hypothesizing in the human body – the brain cells, for example: again all small units in a larger structure. In an agricultural and agrarian society it became obvious that *cell* could similarly describe the structural units within a honeycomb. As society basks in a technological age speakers have discovered new uses of the word in designating the unit of memory in a computer, or any of the restricted areas in which short-range signals can be sent to and from mobile phones.

The expanding network of language

But in order to appreciate this lexical network it is necessary to look further afield than the simple word *cell* itself. The word belongs to a much larger network. It can come packaged in compounds of which it is the final element, such as *blood cell, brain cell, padded cell, prison cell, stem cell*. And it can be the initial element of other compounds: *cell biologist, cell mate, cell phone, cell wall*, and many more. It (or related terms in other languages) forms the base of still more words: *celliform, cellular* (and *acellular*), *celluloid, cellulose*, and others. Further afield, it interacts over history with other words from the same semantic neighbourhood: the *OED* contains nearly 1,500 words for which 'cell' appears in the definition. The set of links which can be established with other terms and phrases in the early twentieth century are different from those it enjoyed two hundred years ago, and those in turn are quite different from its associations two hundred years before that. These sets of associations can also depend on the evolving senses of the equivalent word in other languages (in the case of English, typically with other European languages).

From time to time this wider cultural perspective is observed by others. It seems difficult to write about convincingly, and it is certainly difficult to portray through the broadcast media. The *OED* was recently involved in a BBC2 television series in which the public was presented with a series of modern words (mostly from the area of slang) and were asked to contribute documentary information which improved the dictionary's coverage by providing earlier attestations. The programme (*Balderdash and Piffle*) had a small and devoted audience, and it brought the dictionary some very useful information about a small range of terms, but it could not compete in the ratings war against racy crime drama or sport on the other channels. The whole concept that it is possible to improve the dictionary seemed almost too hard for many people to imagine. How can an 'authority' be improved upon?

Attempts to apply a coherent narrative to a network of words

One book which did make a successful attempt to explain the wider network of lexical usage was Raymond Williams's celebrated *Keywords*, published in 1976. This text goes some way towards placing key cultural words in their wider context, but even Williams tends to restrict his horizon to close semantic neighbourhoods. The language is even more interconnected than this. A typical entry in *Keywords* is the article on the word *radical*, both as an adjective and as a noun. Williams based much of his analysis on what was available to him through the pages of the *OED*, and his treatment of *radical* holds closely to his source text. His broad sweep, in which *radical* moves from a word principally associated with its etymological sense of 'root', expressing, as he says, "an inherent and fundamental quality", to more general meanings from the sixteenth century onwards covers nicely the coherent narrative of radicalism in English over its period of use.

Since Williams wrote *Keywords* in 1976, the *OED*'s entry has been revised, making use of new information not available to the original compilers. The dictionary now provides earlier evidence for 27 of its 46 meanings, and a further 7 new meanings have been added. Most significantly, the crucial modern sense of the adjective "progressive, unorthodox, or innovative in outlook, conception, design, etc." (*radical artist*, for example) now dates from 1869, not 1907. This new information adjusts our perception of the word *radical* in the late 19th century – where previously its major cultural meaning related to politics.

The new etymology does not provide a new origin for the established term, but emphasizes the continuity of development of the English word alongside, for example, its French equivalent from the Middle Ages onwards.

Perhaps the best 'alternative' view of the word *radical* can be taken by examining not just the basic meanings themselves, but the dates at which it spawned compounds (when a word is "on the move").

For *radical* the first compounds appear in the study of linguistics, in the late 16th and early 17th century: *radical letter* and *radical word*. Later in the 17th century mathematics offers *radical sign*, the root symbol; in the 18th century linguistics reappears, with *radical sound*. In 1766 the science of chemistry starts to refer to *radical vinegar*. From this point *radical* moves into politics, and lives there pretty happily up to the present day. The latter end of the 18th century sees *radical reform* and *radical reformer*. 1870 marks the earliest recorded use of the *radical left* (followed fifty years later by the *radical right*). More politics in the early twentieth century, with *radical pluralism* and *radical pluralist*, and – at a date that seems early now – *radical feminist* (1905) and *radical feminism* 1921). It was not until 1970 that one of the last major lexical innovations emerges: *radical chic*. At each point the emergence of compounds mirrors the emergent cultural perspectives of their time. No one is legislating on the vocabulary – words simply arise to meet society's needs.

Each word in the language – in any language – is, therefore, the midpoint of its own set of references, and is an outlier in the set of references based on other words. It is not surprising that language is not easily susceptible to authority.

Popular links between culture and language

The link between everyday culture and language is brought out interestingly in what has come to be known as 'forensic linguistics': the use of linguistic analysis to investigate documents associated with crime. One of the *OED*'s first encounters with this methodology occurred about fifteen years ago when the dictionary received some correspondence relating to the famous 'Jack the Ripper' murders in London in late 1888. The *OED*'s correspondent was planning to write a book about the murders, and wanted to know whether a letter – purportedly from the Ripper – was genuine.

It was the *OED*'s basic assumption that the text of the 'Ripper' letter had to fit the era of the crimes both in terms of cultural reference and linguistic usage. Cultural reference is reasonably easy to simulate in a short letter; even the type of paper and ink used can be replicated. But what the writer was less able to do – and the letter was indeed a later forgery – was to use syntax and vocabulary in ways that were consistent with the time of the murders. Any terminology that first recorded after 1888 lent credence to the belief that the letter was a later creation.

In general, non-linguists are aware that the language of the 1880s differs from the language spoken today. But they fall back on stereotypical ideas when attempting to represent this on paper. The purported murderer had not fallen into any of the obvious traps, but he had used the expression 'one-off' as an adjective, in a way that was (according to the lexical evidence) at least fifty years too early. Coupled with other minor problems, the *OED* was able to conclude that the letter did not derive from the 1880s, but was in all likelihood a modern forgery.

Similar tests have been applied to supposedly early poems. From time to time 'new' Shakespeare poems are found, and it is possible to apply the same sort of analysis to these. The *OED* is a touchstone for historical usage, but nowadays there are also large-scale databases of historical texts against which to test potential forgeries. Sometimes these may be historical forgeries – created at some point between the date of supposed creation and the present day. But the same logic applies. In each case there must be a match between the text and its cultural references and historical English usage. If no match can be found, then the text is probably not genuine.

Viewing the past through the eyes of the present

It is quite normal for non-linguists to rely on their stereotypes of historical language use. This is a pervasive notion, and one by which most people view the past through the eyes of the present. Many years ago a staff member of the *OED* dreamed of spending her retirement working steadily through the scripts of the American TV show *M*A*S*H* against the lexical records presented by the *OED*, to show that the writers of the television show had created a clever replica of Korean War army usage, but not the real thing. Sadly she never found time to complete her project, being distracted by too many other avenues of historical research for the *OED* – such as tracking down the origin of the term *nachos*.

This paper asks whether lexicographers, or historians of language, are concerned with observing and monitoring change, or whether they are in some way controlling what was happening. The typical response from historical lexicographers comes in the form of the lexicographical commonplace that they simply describe what they see, that they just watch the traffic to see how it is moving.

But language does not exist in a vacuum. Whenever it is used, both in the present and in the past, it is profoundly influenced by the environment in which it is used. So who is directing the traffic?

Pressure towards conformity

There is, of course, enormous social pressure towards conformity. Language is only useful if it facilitates communication, and communication is not possible without conformity to established practice. It often surprises non-linguists that new words are normally old words repackaged in a new form (new senses, new compounds from existing elements, verbs from existing nouns – for example). Fewer than 1% of new words are entirely new to the language: nouns become verbs, adjectives nouns, compounds are readily formed from existing terms, and so on. Words which are quite new pose communication difficulties, and so are seldom encountered.

So the words people use and the grammatical structures they put them in are largely the established ones that seem to work for the purpose of communication. But ever since the circulation of printed texts became a regular phenomenon in the sixteenth century there have been written models that tend towards standardization and conformity. When Dr Johnson published his celebrated dictionary in 1755 he was not (as is often popularly supposed) laying down the law on how words should be spelt, but in almost all cases he was simply reflecting the models that society had taught him. As far as dictionaries are concerned, he was a great assimilator of previous ideas and customs.

But what acts in the background as a restrictive framework?

There are several major influences:

The media. It is a commonplace to consider the mid eighteenth century as the time when English became 'standardized'. But society had been edging towards this emerging standard for many years before this. External influences included local newspapers – again beginning to become established features of life in the eighteenth century. The media today are some of the greatest purveyors of the conformity of language. It may seem strange that although there is no national authority for language in Britain, newspapers always seem to spell the same words in the same way.

Education. Perhaps the other great force towards conformity is the educational system. The national curriculum in British schools presents material to students in a predigested and regular format. Teachers reinforce spelling patterns and syntactical structures. And they often do this by recourse to dictionaries – which, as noted above, are describing what they find. There is of course a circularity to this argument. But in fact it seems to be this very circularity that holds things together. Very little is based in absolute fact, but the illusion of authority is established by conformity to generally accepted rules.

Academy. And what effect might a language academy have in Britain? In fact, in Britain an academy would find it difficult to become accepted as an authority, and would represent yet another in a series of choices offered to the language user (American English, European English, World English). And yet there are many people who would welcome 'rules'. It is a dichotomy that, it seems, will never be resolved.

Wikis (and especially Wikipedia) offer models in which knowledge is in a continual state of refinement – but not necessarily improvement: in the context of computer software, Version 2 is often worse than Version 1.

We see similar potential models in other spheres: the Internet offers the opportunity for people to develop new modes of speech and writing, as does texting (or SMSing) on mobile phones. The varieties of English around the world offer further models of choice. Broadcasting, for example, also presents alternative models of pronunciation. Sometimes there seems to be so much choice that English is spiralling into a period of decadence in which there are no rules.

But perhaps the choices offered by these alternative models simply strengthen the system. Given that language changes, education, the media, and other authoritative streams offer access to new modes of communication which revitalize rather than destroy the language. It becomes important now to be able to recognize different modes of accepted discourse – much more so than it was a hundred years ago. Our response to language is becoming more complex as more and more choices become available. It will be one of the challenges of the twenty-first century to inculcate this realistic view of authority generally.

The *OED* is still piecing together a coherent narrative from the results of this choice-laden linguistic landscape. Writers are tussling with choices as they re-express the present in the discourse modes that surround them. Society is evolving by fits and starts in response to this constant struggle between change and conformity.

There are aspects of both authority and illusion in our response to language. The *OED* is interested in observing and monitoring change, but does not set itself up as an authority. But there are hidden persuaders within language and society which tend towards conformity, while still accepting gradual change. It is perhaps this *appearance* of authority that holds things together without an externally imposed authority, and allows a coherent narrative to emerge from a system which is both beset by the centrifugal potential for over-regulation, decadence, and chaos and yet is bound together by history, by associative networks, by self-regulation, and by illusion. The typical speaker of English may not know who is directing the traffic, but he or she gets to their destination in the end. That is reassuring, but we will continue to live with the dichotomy by which the experts know that this 'truth' is fiction, and the non-specialist hopes the fiction is 'truth'.

Section 1
Origin and Identity

ELISA ARMELLINO

Università di Torino

One Life, Many Languages, Multilingualism in Hugo Hamilton's *The Speckled People* (2003) and Charlotte William's *Sugar and Slate* (2002)

The themes of origin and identitity by which several of the AIA conference workshops are inspired are the perfect opportunity for discussing two remarkable 'marginal' writers active now in the UK: the half Irish, half German Hugo Hamilton and the half Caribbean, half Welsh Charlotte Williams. Both trace back their steps to the past by shaping their personal life stories through words. They do this through a rich intertwining of different languages in the same text, using English as their main narrative tool but often switching to Welsh and Guyanese (Charlotte Williams) and to Irish and German (Hugo Hamilton). Their objective is not only to achieve an effect of realism; all the languages they use are inscribed in their life-stories. What I am going to present are some of the most significant linguistic items in the two memoirs. Through them, it will be easier to understand the way language and identity are interconnected in the two works.

I will focus now on *The Speckled People* by Hamilton, whose literary production often revolves around the characters' search for a sense of belonging. His memoir is told through the eyes of his childhood self, and the way he sees the world reveals all the conflicts and contradictions in it. The narrator is essentially concerned with the way people around him make him and his family feel out of place and different. As Hamilton states in an interview: "When I was growing up – in the sixties – it was very unusual in Ireland to belong to a mixed cultural family. We were a peculiarity. We were constantly made fun of or ridiculed". The narrator is sensed as an outsider because he is German, and the German words in the story reveal that this language has a double significance in his life. On the one hand, German is linked to the figure of his mother, Irmgard Kaiser, who came from Kempen, in Germany, where she suffered terribly under the Nazi regime, before going to Ireland on a pilgrimage to forget the horrors of the war (she was to meet her future husband there). The German language she passes on to her children is the language of love and affection, as expressions like *Mein Schätzchen* ("my sweety"), *Wie schön, wie schön warm* ("oh lovely and cosy and warm") reveal. On the other hand, it is the language of discrimination as this is used by Irish boys to insult the narrator by calling him a Nazi (*Donner und Blitzen*, lit. "thunder and lightning", *Sieg Heil*). The Irish language is the language of his father, Jack Hamilton, a militant Irish nationalist who strictly forbids all use of English at home, beating his children violently when they do not respect the rule. His motto is: "Your language is your home and your country is your language and your language is your flag" (Hamilton 2003, 3). Finally, there is English, the forbidden language – the language of guilt and oppression according to Jack Hamilton, and the language of the world existing outside home boundaries, since, as the narrator says: "Everything inside is Irish and outside is English" (Hamilton 2003, 10). However, not to speak English means to be cut off from the rest of the world, at a time, as the author said in an interview, when British and American culture were spreading widely in Ireland.

The idea which best represents the Hamilton children's condition is conveyed through the Irish word *brack*. This word is used by Mr. Hamilton when he explains to his children that they are the new Irish: "Partly from Ireland and partly from somewhere else, half-Irish and half-German. We're the speckled people, he says, the 'brack' people, which is a word that comes from the Irish language, from Gaelic". As the narrator explains: "[Brack] means speckled, dappled, flecked, spotted, coloured" (Hamilton 2003, 7).

The fact that Mr. Hamilton chooses a word from Gaelic suggests how strong is his desire to inscribe his children deeply inside the core of Irish culture. Interestingly, *brack* is also a term which was preserved in spite of British colonisation, being used by Irish people while they were "crossing over into the English language". In the *Oxford English Dictionary*, the word *brack* is also given together with the word *barm*: "1. Barm brack: n − s [IrGael bairghean breac, lit., speckled cake, from bairghean cake, loaf (from OIr bairgen bread) + breac speckled, from OIr brecc" (Weiner and Simpson 1989, 78). A *barm brack* is also mentioned in the memoir: "A trout is brack and so is a speckled horse. A barm brack is a loaf of bread with raisins in it and was borrowed from the Irish words bairín breac" (Hamilton 2003, 7). This image of the barm brack is exploited by the narrator to convey the sense of his speckled identity: "So we are the speckled-Irish, the brack-Irish. Brack home-made Irish bread with German raisins" (Hamilton 2003, 8).

Another interesting example of an Irish word which is linked to the Hamilton children's identities is *ciotóg*. This word means left-handed and it is used by the teacher at school for the narrator's brother:

> Franz can only eat with his left hand and write with his left hand. He is a
> ciotóg, the master says. My mother has to go into school and tell the master
> Onkel Ted was a ciotóg, too, and now is a Jesuit. But that makes no difference
> and the master ties Franz's hand behind his back to make sure he can only
> write with his right hand. All that comes out on the page is a scribble. I want

to help him, because the master laughs and says it looks like a snail has crossed the page with ink (Hamilton 2003, 46).

Then, quite unexpectedly, the topic changes: "I know what it's like to lose, because I'm Irish and I'm German. My mother says we shouldn't be afraid of losing. Winning makes people mean" (Hamilton 2003, 246). By association, the discourse has shifted from the description of his brother's painful experience as a *ciotóg* at school to the idea of losing and being a loser, which is so much a part of the characters' story.

With quite a different meaning but still linked to the opposed ideas of success and failure, we find the word *dána* (*dona*), which means "bold". It is taken from a children's song that the narrator remembers he was taught at school: "'Maidirín a rua, 'tá dána', we all sing together. The little red fox is bold" (Hamilton 2003, 69). Then, an event makes the importance of this word even stronger – that is when the narrator remembers slapping his teacher in the face for scolding him while she was repeating: "bold, bold, bold; dána, dána, dána". For slapping his teacher in the face, his mother, as he says, felt proud of him, since according to her: "You can't be afraid of anyone. You can't let anyone make you small, because that's what they tried to do with Onkel Gerd" (Hamilton 2003, 70). A digression about Onkel Gerd's life as the Lord Mayor of Kempen is now made. For refusing to accept orders from the Nazis, who began to interfere more and more often with his work, he was sent away and replaced by a more obedient Bürgermeister (Lord Mayor). This is why, like *ciotóg*, *dána* is a word that is remembered in association with a far wider range of meanings than those which can be inferred at first – through these words, the author recalls more than just episodes in his life; he recalls the sense of failure in his family, together with their desire for revolt and hopes for a better future.

There are also words which are repeated in different languages in the memoir, and the way they are used suggests a mechanical, not a harmonious, switching from one to the other. Even the simple action of counting stairs is taught to Hamilton at two different times and by two different people, his mother and a susbtitute for his mother, Aine, their Irish nanny. This is not so surprising if one thinks that even bilingual children do not necessarily mix languages, but in Hamilton's case the father's imposition of Irish makes the children's linguistic behavior particularly unnatural and artificial. At the end of the memoir, the narrator somehow manages to cope with his split sense of identity. He decides not to run away any more from the children who call him a Nazi. As he says: "I am not afraid anymore of being German or Irish or anywhere in between" (Hamilton 2003, 295). To be speckled is not a disgrace any longer, the original meaning of *brack* being also that of perfect beauty as this results from the encounter of all colours, the perfect spectrum of all different shades.

As far as Charlotte Williams's memoir is concerned, what can be said is that it has much in common with Hugo Hamilton's in that it presents a quest for identity by someone, the narrator, who is divided between a double cultural and linguistic identity. For *Sugar and Slate*, this Welsh-Guyanese author (a lecturer in Social Work at the University of Wales, Bangor) won the Welsh Book of the Year Award in 2003. Her father, Denis Williams, came to England in 1946 on a scholarship from his native country, Guyana, and became a famous painter and writer. Her mother, Catherine Alice, was born in a small Welsh slate quarry community, Bethesda. With her sisters, Charlotte Williams spent part of her childhood in Nigeria and Sudan after moving back to Wales, where they found that they were regarded by the community there as a kind of 'peculiarity'. As she says: "There are no brown skins in this place. Peanut brown we are. Roasted peanut from another land. In Africa we were white and in Wales we weren't". The impression of having lost her pathway in life prompts her into searching for her roots in the Caribbean. As she realizes: "The truth was I was history-less, an unclaimed orphan of some 'elsewhere' place of which I had no first hand nor second hand knowledge" (Williams 2002, 101).

I will focus now on the functions of Welsh in her memoir. Like German in Hugo Hamilton's text, Welsh is the language linked to the narrator's mother. The linguistic items in Welsh carry deep emotional meanings and define the narrator and her family as strongly related to Wales. For example, the author uses Welsh to describe and define "her small family" when embarking for Africa: "Just Ma and four small girls made our family then; teulu (teili) bach. Just a small cargo on a big ship" (Williams 2002, 5). As Charlotte Williams pointed out when I interviewed her:

> I think this was a conscious strategy to inscribe myself in the cultures. By using popular parlance you can signal a sense of ownership of that culture and also signal something about a rejection of social statuses. The term *teulu bach* for example, "small family" in Welsh, is used by the common people and is not high class Welsh.

Another interesting term is the adjective *cariad*, which means "sweetheart", "darling", and which is used by the narrator's mother when addressing her daughters: "We were cariad" (Williams 2002, 24). As Charlotte Williams says: "It was Ma who shaped our cultural memory, passed to us in her stories and her way of telling them; in the songs of her childhood that reached out to us and formed us. We were cariad" (*ibidem*). By calling her children "cariad", their mother inscribes them in the Welsh world to which she belongs and passes her language to them, together with family history. As in Hamilton, the mother, the female has a constructive role.

However, Welsh is also the language through which the world and other cultures are seen and defined. Thus, black people are *pobbl du* and the

Reverend prays for them and praises the missionary zeal which is bringing them to Christianity. Then, there are "Y (e) plant duon", the black children. As the narrator writes, remembering her childhood: "We collect every week in the box to help y plant duon in Africa" (Williams 2002, 19). The expression is in Welsh again – it belongs to the Welsh and to Welsh culture, because it is from there that black people are looked at and defined, exactly as happens in the children's song the author recollects from her memories: "[I] hear Miss Thomas say, / God's children, / plentyn bach, plentyn du, / they are really all the same to me / they just blend in like milk and tea" (Williams 2002, 40). There are several other examples like this in the text, such as the children's poem *King of the Cannibals*, which, as Charlotte Williams explains, appeared in children's books until recently.

When the author moves to the Caribbean in order to find her forgotten roots and to feel that she belongs somewhere, she senses the language spoken there as foreign and she cannot feel at ease with the new culture. Language and the world she has fallen into seem to her like surreal dimensions in which all which is known turns into the unknown and everything seems to be upside-down, as when a preacher transforms her name into Sharla, a friend asks her to buy "sharts" meaning "shorts" and "shirts" meaning "shorts". The author is defined by others as a "Neva see com fo see" (Williams 2002, 150), a popular Guyanese expression, commonly used as a noun today to describe an unaccomplished, very naive person, and in the end she decides to go back to Wales. However, this is another Wales. As she explains: "I began to imagine Wales as my own. It wasn't the same Wales as before though [...]. It wasn't to do with the Wales of my childhood, nice as that was in so many ways" (Williams 2002, 177). The author can come to this new awareness after discovering that Welsh and Caribbean people share the same destiny of exploitation and subjugation. In the area of Wales near Bethesda from which her ancestors come, there used to be the largest slate quarries in the world. They were run by Lord Penrhyn, who had made a huge fortune thanks to his sugar plantations in Africa. As the author explains:

It was the cruelly driven slaves; men, women and children who toiled and sweated for the huge sugar profits that built the industries in Wales. Out of the profits of slave labour in one Empire, he built another on near-slave labour. The plantocracy sponsored the slateocracy in an intimate web of relationships where sugar and slate were the commodities and brute force and exploited labour were the building blocks of the Welsh Empire (Williams 2002, 175).

At the end of the book, after describing the poor living conditions of Welsh people and of her own ancestors, who worked in the slate quarries, Charlotte Williams addresses them in her mind and says: "We meet with the legacy of these two intertwined histories and struggles over freedom and identity and in my split memory we speak the same language". In this way, the author seems to vindicate her right to be Welsh just as she is, a medley of cultures. Like Hamilton, she accepts 'speckledness' but, at the same time, and unlike him, she chooses to belong – she is and feels Welsh, though she can state this only after re-constructing her Welsh identity. In both memoirs, language is embedded in memories exactly as memories are brought back through language, and the co-existence of words from different languages is a means through which hybrid identities are re-valued and reconciled. Even though Hamilton and Williams do not praise God for speckledness as Gerard Manley Hopkins does in his poem *Pied Beauty*, there is certainly a strong sense of victory over the attempt at levelling differences – both cultural and linguistic. English, in this respect, is used by them as a lingua franca which allows them to speak and mediate between their different identities, being, in the case of Hamilton, real evidence of self-fulfilment and freedom against the initial limits imposed on him in the first part of his life.

References

Auer P. (ed.) 1999. *Code-Switching in Conversation: Language, Interaction and Identity*. New York: Routledge.

Cenoz J., Hufeisen B., Jessner U. (eds.) 2001. *Looking Beyond Second Language Acquisition.*: Tübingen: Stauffenburg.

Edwards J. 1995. *Multilingualism*. London: Penguin.

Hamilton H. 2003. *The Speckled People*. London: Harper.

Hamilton H. 2007. "Speaking to the Walls in English". In Hamilton H. *Original Essays*. Cleveland: Powell Books; see http://www.powells.com/essays/hamilton.html (last accessed August 2011).

Hopkins G.M. 1986. "Pied Beauty". In Phillips C. (ed.) *Gerard Manley Hopkins*. New York: Oxford University Press.

Milroy L., Muysken P. 1995. *One Speaker, Two Languages: Cross-disciplinary Perspectives on Code-switching*. Cambridge: Cambridge University Press.

Sanchez Camara F., Ayala F. 1979. *Concepts for Communication and Development in Bilingual-bicultural Communities*. Mouton: The Hague.

Weiner E., Simpson J. (eds.) 1989. *The Oxford English Dictionary*. Oxford: Clarendon Press.

Williams C. 2002. *Sugar and Slate*. Aberystwyth: Planet.

Elisa Bolchi

Università Cattolica del Sacro Cuore, Milano

Look into My I.
Narrating Subjects, Identity and Gender
in Jeanette Winterson's Fiction

"Two things significantly distinguish human beings from the other animals: an interest in the past and the possibility of language. Brought together they make a third: Art" (Winterson 1995, 137). This is a quotation from *Art & Lies*, Winterson's fifth novel, and it is a clear declaration of the writer's three greatest passions: the past – both in its time and in its literary tradition implications – language and art. I will start from this declaration to illustrate Winterson's making of characters, to show how she starts from these three elements to build her narrating subjects, and I will focus on language, first.

Almost all of Jeanette Winterson's novels are written in the first person, a person narrating his or her life, but none of her novels is to be considered an autobiography, not even *Oranges Are Not the Only Fruit*, which tells about the early life of the writer, since she often explained how the very fact that the events she narrates are the exact description of her life is not enough to call that work an autobiography.[1] "There's no such thing as autobiography there's only art and lies" she writes in her novel *Art & Lies* (Winterson 1995, 69), and in her essay *Testimony Against Gertrude Stein* she explains how "like Stein" she prefers herself "as a character" in her own fiction and, "like Stein and Woolf" what concerns her is language (Winterson 1996a, 53). What Winterson is trying to say, and to prove with her novels, is that it is *in* and *through* language that a human being becomes a subject, because it is only language that creates a concept of *I* inside reality.

The idea is not a new one. The linguist Ferdinand de Saussure and then the psychoanalyst and philosopher Jacques Lacan explained how we are born into language and how it is through language that we become speaking subjects and shape ourselves into society.

---

[1] The matter is amply discussed in Maria Micaela Coppola's "Soggetti d'arte e di scambio. La semiotica del sé nei saggi di Jeanette Winterson" (Bottalico and Chialant 2005, 283-294, containing other interesting essays exploring autobiography issues).

Self and subjectivity themselves have become problematic issues since psychology split and shattered the idea of person at the beginning of last century, and this new concept of subject found its representation in the so called psychological novels of James Joyce, Virginia Woolf and Marcel Proust, to mention the most important names. Modernist writers in particular rejected the old and stable realistic *self* and their characters appeared to be aware of their multiplicity.

According to Linda Hutcheon (1988, 158-178), the instability of the modernist point of view is mainly displayed in two ways. First, the narrator becomes a problematic issue. Modernist writers want their narrator to force the reader to think and to cooperate, a technique that would lead to the narrator-interlocutor in Postmodernism. In Postmodernist fiction, in fact, not only the narrator winks at the reader, but s/he also speaks directly to her/him (let's just think of Margaret Drabble's *The Waterfall* or John Fowles's *The French Lieutenant's Woman*). But instability is also represented in Modernist fiction by the multitude of points of view. There is not, in modernist fiction, a single perspective but a myriad of voices, a pluralizing multivalence of points of view. Postmodern fiction transformed it into a narration carried on by several subjects: different narrators, through their own fragmented self, try to create a unified narrating identity. This very idea is well described by Jeanette Winterson in *Sexing the Cherry*, where she writes that

> the inward life tells us that we are multiple not single, and that our one existence is really countless existences holding hands like those cut-out paper dolls, but unlike the dolls never coming to an end (Winterson 1989, 90).

The reason I have been focusing on Modernist points of view so far is that Winterson never takes distance from the past which is, as I said, one of her three main interests. On the contrary, she considers literary tradition and what came before her essential for her writing and she wishes her work to be a continuation of Modernists' path. "The true artist is connected", she writes in her essay *Art Objects*, "the true artist studies the past" (Winterson 1996b, 12), and she adds, in *Testimony against Gertrude Stein*,

> A writer is a raider and whatever has been made possible in the past must be gathered up by her, melted down, and re-formed differently. As she does that, she makes out of her own body a connection to what has gone before and her skull becomes a stepping stone to what will follow (Winterson 1996a, 53-54).

Let's see, then, *how* she makes her skull a stepping stone connected to the past, and specifically to Modernism, which is known to be a movement deeply interested in the rediscovery and reuse of the past, through a comparison with Virginia Woolf, who is one of Winterson's favourite writers and represents a great source of inspiration for her. In *A Room of One's Own* Woolf points out how it is necessary to be able to narrate with as many voices as possible, and to think of ourselves as more than a single subject (Woolf 2000). She realizes this ideal in her novel *The Waves*, where a multitude of voices creates a unique music and rhythm and almost represents, one could say, the stream of consciousness of a single identity.

In some way this same multiplicity of voices and consciousness can be found in Winterson's work, and above all in *Art & Lies*, where she writes that "language is rich when it is fed from difference. Where there is no difference there is no richness" (Winterson 1995, 64). Probably helped by her being homosexual, Winterson seems to be particularly inclined to represent poliedric personalities, which fragment a language otherwise complementary, so that a new and experimental subject is created where the opposites melt together. The best example of this tendency is, no doubt, the protagonist and narrator of *Written on the Body*, probably the most postmodern of Winterson's characters. That narrator is different characters at the same time: Greta Garbo, Alice in Wonderland, Lothario or "Socrate infelice" (Winterson 1996c, 13). This character is never described, the reader doesn't even know his or her gender. The narrating subject as an identifiable identity has disappeared. But, although Winterson's character is not a definite subject, s/he is not looking for his/her own identity. It is simply a narrating identity and as such it could be anyone – a concept which reminds us not only of the Medieval *Everyman*, but also, or even more so, of the "ordinary mind on an ordinary day" (Woolf 1966, 106). The idea in *Written on the Body* is that Jeanette Winterson wants to erase all the specific characteristics of gender and offer the reader a character with a mask of a gender-free identity. About this experiment Winterson herself comments in her website:

> All my work is experimental, in that it plays with form, refuses a traditional narrative line, and includes the reader as a player. By that I mean that the reader has to work with the book. In the case of *Written on the Body*, the narrator has no name, is assigned no gender, is age unspecified, and highly unreliable. I wanted to see how much information I could leave out – especially the kind of information that is routine – and still hold a story together (http://www.jeanettewinterson.com/pages/content/index. asp?PageID=13 – last accessed August 2011).

Does not this declaration remind us of Woolf's note in her diary, on 5 September 1923: "Directly you specify hair, age etc. something frivolous, or irrelevant gets into the book" (Woolf 1982, 92)? In Winterson's fiction even gender becomes "something frivolous, or irrelevant." But, even though Winterson's choice seems, if not derived, at least inspired by the same ideas as Woolf's, this lack of characteristics is quite relevant in a comparison between *Written on the Body* and *Orlando*, a novel which cannot but be taken into consideration when speaking of androgynous subjects. *Orlando* is widely considered Woolf's try to represent an androgynous subject, or at least a subject containing both sexes in one person. But Orlando is always characterized by male and female characteristics at a time so that his sex, or her sex after Chapter III, is always clearly identified. Winterson's novel takes place at the end of XX century, when women and men can dress in the same way so that references to trousers, coats and shoes are of no help to identify the gender, while in *Orlando* clothes are fundamental: "they change our view of the world" Woolf writes "and the world's view of us" (Woolf 1993, 170). In Winterson's novel, on the contrary, not even love stories solve our doubts but increase them.[2] An emblematic passage is a dialogue between the narrator and his/her lover Louise where she addresses to him/her by saying: "when I first saw you two years ago I thought you were the most beautiful creature, male or female, I had ever seen" (Winterson 1996c, 84). It may sound forced as a love declaration but that is what Jeanette Winterson wanted to do in this novel: deconstruct all the *clichés* about love – "it is the clichés that cause the trouble" (Winterson 1996c, 155), she writes – and deconstruct all the behaviour codes specific to men and women. We could almost say that in this novel Winterson tries to comply with Woolf's statement: "it is fatal to be a man or a woman pure and simple; one must be woman-manly or man-womanly" (Woolf 2000, 94). Not only Winterson's voice is not typically womanly, but not even her characters' life is either female or male.

Winterson's choice to give no gender to the protagonist and narrator of her novel also allows her to question the canonical roles of men and women in a sentimental relationship. For many years women were represented only as the lovers of men, an accusation also proposed by Woolf in *A Room of One's Own*, where she accuses the representation of women of having been much too simple and much too monotonous, imagining how boring it would have been if "men were only represented in literature as the lovers of women, and were never the friends of men, soldiers, thinkers, dreamers" (Woolf 2000, 75). In *Written on the Body*, not only Winterson deconstructs the classic idea of subjectivity, but she creates an identity only through a relationship with a woman, overturning the literary tradition which always imposed to women to be described through their men. It is in fact the protagonist's relationship with Louise the only element allowing us to know who is telling the story we are reading, and so it is through this relationship that Winterson gives her protagonist a voice.

Of course there are characters in Woolf's fiction who act in a similar way, trying to find a new way to build their identity outside fixed gender parameters. Lily Briscoe is an example: she is the only character in *To the Lighthouse* to wonder on male and female roles and if she acts according to conventions she just does it because she is forced to it by 'good manners'. Another of Woolf's characters

---

[2] At the beginning of the novel, in fact, we are led to think that the narrator is a man, as he speaks about his love stories with women, but then the narrator suddenly speaks of his relationship with a boy who looks like the typical macho: a giant almost two meters high, with rings on his nipples held together by a golden chain. What we understand here is that we are in front of a bisexual narrator but we have no clue of his or her gender.

offering this construction of identity through male or female language is Bernard, the main narrator of *The Waves*. In this novel language is a fundamental element and learning both male and female language means learning to be both a man and a woman. Woolf's character who most resembles the narrator of *Written on the Body* is, however, Rhoda. Rhoda, in *The Waves*, likes ambiguity as it allows her multiplicity, difference and variety. She represents Woolf's concept of modern subject, made of single parts not forming a whole (Harris 2000). The modern subject, in fact, not only lacks a unified identity but also doubts the existence of such an identity. In *The Waves* Woolf anticipates the postmodern moment when "the subject as a self-identical entity is no more" (Butler 1993, 230). Rhoda's entity can be found, I think, also in Winterson's *Art & Lies*. Here we have three narrating characters, all telling themselves in the first person and, like as the six characters of *The Waves*, they weave together their stories to create one narration. The concept is more or less the same as Woolf's: the self is made of different subjects that, on their own, do not form a whole, but together form one voice and one identity. The single entities are fully aware of themselves, question themselves, question their existence, like the protagonists of *The Waves*. And in *Art & Lies*, too, the boundaries between male and female seem to disappear: one character is a man, and two of them are women, or are they? The man is Handel, but he is a half man: a castrated boy who lacks his manly identity and, like Bernard in *The Waves*, becomes a "differently gendered being, one in whom masculine and feminine coexist" (Harris 2000, 59). One of the two women is Picasso, bearing a name which has nothing feminine, described throughout her path to the discovery of her lesbianism and the third is Saffo, the Greek poetess famous for her homosexuality. Saffo is the incarnation of language, and she is the clearest example of how Winterson models the identities of her characters and of her narrating subjects through language. Saffo is "bone and black ink" (Winterson 1995, 72) and she is "the boy-daughter, the girl-son, the union of language and lust" (Winterson 1995, 74), the incarnation of all identities and all genders because not only is she *language*, she is *art language*. And so here we come to the last of Jeanette Winterson's greatest interests: art. Saffo says in the novel: "The lines around my eyes are in terza rima, three above, three below. There is a quatrain at my chin and a sonnet on each breast, Villanelle is the poise of my hands" (Winterson 1995, 63). Even her love relationship is shaped out of art language: "Aren't we a couplet?" she asks "two successive lines of verse that rhyme with each other?" (74). It is most significant that Winterson chooses the poetess Saffo to create a character completely made out of poetic language, as Saffo complains in the novel that "she is an apocrypha. She has become a book of tall stories, none of them written by herself. Her name has passed into history. Her work has not. Her island is known now, her work is not" (Winterson 1995, 69). Saffo is Winterson's try to shape an identity only through language, she clearly represents an experiment in language, and as the writer says in her essay *Writer, Reader,*

Words: "if we want a living language [...] then we need men and women whose whole self is bound up in [a] work with words" (Winterson 1996d, 36). Winterson creates such men and women, and it is through her passion for language, for art and for literary past, through her "new way with words" (Winterson 1996a, 53), to quote the author one last time, that she creates her new way with identity.

References

Bottalico M., Chialant M.T. (eds.) 2005. *L'impulso autobiografico. Inghilterra, Stati Uniti, Canada... e altri ancora*. Napoli: Liguori.

Butler J. 1993. *Bodies That Matter: On the Discursive Limits of Sex*. New York: Routledge.

Coppola M.M. 2005. "Soggetti d'arte e di scambio. La semiotica del sé nei saggi di Jeanette Winterson". In Bottalico M., Chialant M.T. (eds.) *L'impulso autobiografico. Inghilterra, Stati Uniti, Canada... e altri ancora*. Napoli: Liguori, 283-294.

Drabble M. 1971. *The Waterfall*. London: Penguin.

Fowles J. 2004. *The French Lieutenant's Woman*. London: Vintage.

Harris A.L. 2000. *Other Sexes. Rewrinting Difference from Woolf to Winterson*. Albany: State University of New York Press.

Hutcheon L. 1988. *A Poetics of Postmodernism. History, Theory, Fiction*. London: Routledge.

Winterson J. 1985. *Oranges Are Not the Only Fruit*. London: Pandora Press.

Winterson J. 1989. *Sexing the Cherry*. London: Vintage.

Winterson J. 1995. *Art & Lies*. London: Vintage.

Winterson J. 1996a. "Testimony Against Gertrude Stein". In Winterson J. *Art Objects*. London: Vintage 45-60.

Winterson J. 1996b. "Art Objects". In Winterson J. *Art Objects*. London: Vintage 3-21.

Winterson J. 1996c. *Written on the Body*. London: Vintage.

Winterson J. 1996d. "Writer, Reader, Words". In Winterson J. *Art Objects*. London: Vintage 25-44.

Winterson J. 1996e. *Art Objects*. London: Vintage.

Woolf V. 1966. "Modern Fiction". In Woolf V. *Collected Essays. Vol II*. London: The Hogarth Press, 103-110.

Woolf V. 1982. *A Writer's Diary*. London: Harcourt Inc.

Woolf V. 1993. *Orlando*. London: Penguin.

Woolf V. 1993. *The Waves*. Oxford-Cambridge: Blackwell.

Woolf V. 1994. *To the Lighthouse*. Ware: Wordsworth.

Woolf V. 2000. *A Room of One's Own*. London: Penguin.

LISANNA CALVI

Università di Verona

Jane Barker's *Exilius* as Jacobite Fiction in Exile

In a late 1680s miscellaneous and allegedly unauthorized publication of some early Jane Barker's poetry, entitled *Poetical Recreations*, we find, together with her own, which fill up the first section of the volume, a number of poems attributed to "several gentlemen of the Universities" (Barker 1688), as the title-page styles them. They belonged indeed to a circle of amateur poets probably from Oxford or Cambridge the then thirty-five-year-old Jane was in contact with. We cannot claim masterpiece status for these coterie verses, but it is interesting to single out three compositions, one of which written by the publisher of the collection, a Benjamin Crayle, all referring to "Mrs Barker's Excellent Romance of Scipina" (Barker 1688, II, 29) and announcing it as forthcoming. The three of them especially praise the supposed 'Englishness' of Barker's work whose publication would refresh what they describe as an uncreative literary panorama crowded with dull translations of French romances.

Despite such commendatory introduction, *Scipina* did not see the light and its failed appearance remains a mystery to this day (although I assume the swift political changes of 1688-89 contributed to halt the publishing). Yet Barker apparently kept working on the manuscript and a "new romance", as she subtitled it, eventually came out of the press as late as 1714.[1] And this is *Exilius: or, the Banish'd Roman*. Although Benjamin Crayle's poetical appraisal had deemed Barker's "Virgin *Muse*" (Barker 1688, II, 196) far superior to "*Dedalean Scuddery*" (Barker 1688, II, 196), *Exilius* presents in fact a labyrinthine network of interrelated narratives opportunely seasoned with shipwrecks, abductions, attempted rapes, incestuous desires and virginal

---

[1] As a matter of fact the title-page of the first edition reads 1715, although Barker's "new romance" appeared in August 1714; the indication of a subsequent date was a commercial strategy commonly used by Edmund Curll, the publisher, in order to prolong the work's currency on the book market (King 2000, 150 ff.). A second edition was issued in 1719 with a dedication to Elizabeth Cecil, Countess of Exeter, and a third one appeared posthumously in 1736.

vows and, of course, unravelling final agnitions, which eventually lead the reader – not without some effort – to a general happy ending for the seven pairs of at times united at times divided lovers of whom the eponymous hero, Exilius, is one.

Their adventures are set against the backdrop of republican Rome at the time of the Scipiones and it is the characters themselves who build up the action by delivering their own "histories" (Barker 1715, I, 3 *et passim*) to different listeners, which allows the protagonists, especially women, to recollect their experiences and draw some moral teachings out of them. This wholly responds to Barker's intentions, especially directed towards the education of younger readers, as she explains in the *Preface*:

> '[T]is to be hoped, that a View of those worthy Characters which *Romances* represent, might assist them to avoid such dangerous Naufrages, and fix their Affections where Duty and Merit require (Barker 1715, A2).

This is by all means remindful of what bishop Pierre-Daniel Huet recommended (and applauded) in his 1670 *Traité de l'origine des romans* (first translated into English in 1672) in which, along with a learned disquisition on the genre's origins in classical antiquity, he describes contemporary romances as "Fictions of Love-Adventures, writ in Prose with Art, for the delight and Instruction of the readers" (Huet 1715, A2); such description perfectly suits Barker's *Exilius*, which ultimately turns out to be an imitation of French heroic romances, as Mary Anne Schofield rather disappointedly remarks in her study of eighteenth-century feminine fiction, *Masking and Unmasking the Female Mind* (Schofield 1990); apparently Schofield ignores the 1680s 'Scipina precedent', from which, despite Barker's friends early protestations of originality, may derive the work's *cliché* "Love-Adventures". Although I may share in Schofield's critical amazement in dealing with such a belated option, Barker's choice of genre deserves indeed some further attention as her preference for romance (definitely out of fashion at the beginning of the eighteenth century) apparently conveys not only nostalgia for long forgotten values of fidelity and love as moral guidance for young people, but also – as I will try to point out later – the speculation on contemporary Jacobite stance.

In the dedication to the Countess of Exeter, Barker begs her to:

> [R]aise my Exilius from his Dust, and make him live; live in Hearts of all the Fair, and in the Esteem of all his own Sex, 'till they make his unfashionable Constancy become the newest Mode, [...] and restore heroic Love to its ancient Jurisdiction (Barker 1719, 4).

Exilius and his fellow-lovers actually display adamant faithfulness to a staunch moral code and relentlessly follow the paths of unyielding virtue, even in front of enticing prospects. Among the others, the foundling Ismenus scorns

Carthaginian princess Emelia's proffer of sexual favours to him, while being someone else's wife:

> These Words were so amazing, and so contradictory to that Virtue I so much value in the Sex, that [...] my Soul was seiz'd with such a secret Disgust, that all her Charms had not the Power to fix one tender Thought in me towards her, so as to make her grateful to my Senses (Barker 1715, I, 61-62).

Those who have been separated by fate or malice are eventually brought together, but the longing for reunion does not hinder the expression of shared feelings of admiration and reverence for social retreat or seclusion (be it in prison or in a hermitage), even when this means the renunciation of marriage, at which the young lovers aim as the supreme social realization. Exilius himself, who already spent his childhood and young age as an exile on an island with his father, the Roman Catullus, tests his virtue while imprisoned because of his rivalry with the king of Egypt for beautiful Scipiana's love; there he becomes "a Pattern of Patience" (Barker 1715, I, 149), completely devoted to his own true love, a steadfast commitment he carries on even after he has been marooned in a remote cave (transformed into a sort of 'chapel' dedicated to the same Scipiana) and in which he spends his days practising "Humility and Self-Denyal [...] in Perfection" (Barker 1715, I, 69). Even the fair Cordiala, banished by her adoptive mother because she refuses to marry a lewd suitor, disguises herself as a boy and, after a few more incidents, joins a house of votaries of Apollo, finding there "much Happiness and Tranquillity" (Barker 1715, II, 12). Yet, after a young girl, the temple steward's daughter, has fallen in love with 'him', she is forced to abandon the sanctuary and looks for comfort into "a solitary Grove" (Barker 1715, II, 17), where a chapel dedicated to Diana has been erected. There she is given an oracular piece of advice, which once again exalts patience, endurance, and faith:

> Those, who on Providence depend,
> And patiently its Will attend,
> Shall be rewarded in the End. [...]
> Griefs to Heav'n's Favourites are sent,
> To purify the Penitent,
> And justify the Innocent (Barker 1715, II, 18).

Once more Scipio Asiaticus and Clarinthia, a noble damsel he has rescued from a brutal assault performed by a disguised aggressor who turns out to be the girl's own father, come to a hermit's cave and there sojourn for some time, much revering this retreat, whose conditions of life lead to perfection. Again, after he has been separated from Clarinthia (who in her turn believes him dead and therefore vows perpetual virginity), Asiaticus seeks for seclusion into Mount Atlas and there entertains in long hours of meditation:

I look'd down upon all moral Vertues, as Steps by which I had ascended to this Happiness of Mind; I almost bless'd those Misfortunes that had thus brought me to know the Feebleness and Instability of all earthly Persuits and Acquests, and chiefly that I had truly learnt to know and contemn myself, and, for the Love of the Gods, long'd to be freed from this mortal Being (Barker 1715, II, 59).

Through the exercise of virtue and the contemplation of past adversities, Asiaticus engages in a sort of mystical heightening which leads him to discard earthly cares towards the ultimate and longed for reunion with the divine, after the loss of his beloved.

The motif of the 'lost lover' is therefore united to that of withdrawal into prayer and meditation. Although it may sound rather conventional in a 'heroic' scenario, such thematic pairing calls for some further attention if one considers that Barker's romance appeared in 1714, just a few days after the death of the last Stuart reigning monarch, Queen Anne. None of the Queen's children had survived infancy and, despite the Act of Settlement had set the crown on the Protestant Hanoverian line since 1701, and actual negotiations with the exiled James Edward Stuart had broken down in March 1714, the moment was laden with dynastic tension, especially on the part of those who supported the claims of the Queen's half-brother, the Old Pretender. Among these stood Jane Barker. A Catholic convert some time after 1685, she had followed James II to Saint-Germain-en-Laye in 1689 and had remained there until probably 1704.

The topic of exile (straightforward from the very title, *Exilius: or, the Banish'd Roman*) becomes therefore, together with the theme of the 'lost lover', which recurred in Jacobite poems and popular songs throughout the eighteenth century, politically relevant.[2] Still, the meditative shade the fictional lovers constantly attach to it builds up yet another and more intriguing connection with the court in exile. The insistence on the value of patience and sufferance is remindful of James II's own spiritual writings. During his second exile on the Continent James authored a number of devotional papers meant to circulate among the Saint-Germain court; there he repeatedly exalted the redemptive significance of suffering and the importance of composing one's thoughts into quiet and holy preparation for a 'happy death'. He writes: "[I]f it be the will of God we remaine

---

[2] James Edward Stuart (1688-1766), the Old Pretender, and later on his son, Charles Edward (Bonnie Prince Charlie, 1720-1788), were celebrated and sung in popular Jacobite literature as the good kings who would one day return and restore social harmony or as the longed-for absent lovers who would eventually respond to and fulfil the erotic nostalgia of their beloved (nation). The discourse of the 'lost lover' actually aimed at replacing feelings of bereavement with passion and yearning but, as Murray Pittock points out, after the Jacobite army, led by Charles Edward Stuart, was definitely crushed at the Battle of Culloden (1746), the "substitution of loss by desire was no longer so practical when the desire's fulfilment (the return of the Jacobite leader) had led to further loss" (Pittock 1994, 175).

in this world, we aught not only to be content to suffer, but desire it, since tis by suffrings (if we make the right of them) we are to attaine everlasting glory" (James II 1925, 89). The exiled king shapes his figure and role in moral teachings and devout warnings thus bequeathing a spiritual guidance and testament to a generation of followers. Patience is likewise extolled, this time particularly in a meditative booklet James supposedly penned (or at least authorized) back in 1692. Under the title of *Imago Regis*, in imitation of the Carolean 'best-seller' *Eikon Basilike*, the king praises patience and resignation to a superior will as "the noblest Victory over my self and my Enemies" (James II 1692, 92) because it is thanks to patience that "whatsoever Adversity or Affliction, we shall more easily bear" (James II 1692, 99). Such calling to endurance and self-discipline – "I will suffer Patiently whatsoever can happen" (James II 1692, 92), writes James – is met by Barker's protagonists and their heroism finds expression in patience rather than in bravery and dauntlessness; indeed, the qualities Exilius and the others exercise are those of "passive Courage" (Barker 1715, I, 149), which significantly echoes the 'passive obedience' attitude adopted by those who, after the Glorious Revolution, kept their allegiance to the 'king over the water'.[3] The exiled Catullus, Exilius's father, who is eventually restored to his house, friends and family, might actually recall the figure of James II as it emerges from his writings, where he displays a Christ-like attitude of resignation and forgiveness.[4] Back from exile, Catullus likewise protests his innocence but shows a compassionate attitude towards those who banished him: "I accepted willingly my Sufferings, and with Pleasure begg'd Pardon of the Gods for those that had been my Persecutors" (Barker 1715, II, 139).

Intertextual resonance with James's writings and moral kindredness with Jacobite stance undoubtedly help place Barker's work into its proper historical context, but also frame a code of conduct to which the characters must comply

---

[3] Staunch Jacobites maintained downright loyalty to James and refused to take the oath to William III, but after the Glorious Revolution, it was common practise to "swear allegiance to William and Mary as *de facto* rulers, whilst still recognising James II as King *de jure*" (Harris 1993, 138). This allowed to remain faithful to the principles of 'passive obedience' and 'non-resistance', according to which kings were accountable to God alone, and could not be resisted by subjects. For many Tories, who had supported the accession of James Stuart back in 1685, this became in fact the only conscience-appeasing solution for having turned their backs on the lawful, if Catholic, King of England.

[4] In particular, the eight meditations of which *Imago Regis* is composed trace a sort of spiritual progression that leads to the recognition of pain and distress as means of grace through the adherence to the example of Christ. The text engages into a journey that guides its protagonist, as well as the reader, towards a broadened perspective of universal Providence, which transcends the concern for individual security, and looks to suffering as a promise of redemption in afterlife. However, *Imago Regis* also reveals a political subtext, which parallels its more evident spiritual itinerary, in that the *private* dimension of James as believer is readily complemented by the *public* status of James II, his royal trust and moral legacy, which he deciphered in terms of Stuart kingship (Calvi 2009).

in order to attain not only a morally but also socially rewarding finale, when separated lovers and exiled friends are reunited, legitimate children are recognized and restored to their loving fathers and a promising future of glorious deeds is announced for the next generation. The final restoration shows romance features, such as what, in his *The Secular Scripture*, Northrop Frye calls "talismans of recognition" (Frye 1976, 145), which assist the regeneration of a disrupted familial and social order. Scipio jr, known by the name of Ismenus, turns out to be Publius Scipio's long lost son, now recognized because of an eagle-shaped mark on his chest. The young Cordiala is discovered to be Catullus's daughter (again a red heart on the girl's arm proves it) and her newly acquired noble status allows a socially appropriate marriage with Scipio jr (which had been earlier forbidden because of the bride's inferior rank).

The final settlement gives back a positive outlook on the rewarding pursuit of "unfashionable Constancy" (Barker 1719, 4) and at the same time envisages an optimistic urge towards the restitution of past ideals of "heroic Love" (Barker 1719, 4), but also of political allegiance, to their proper "ancient Jurisdiction" (Barker 1719, 4).

We are therefore presented with romance reinterpreted into Jacobite experience of exile and this choice of genre may be justified both by Barker's revising of an earlier version of the text (the "excellent romance of Scipina") and perhaps by her willingness to resume the tradition of seventeenth-century romance as a model for aristocratic morality (which she re-writes from a Stuart perspective). Still, we might also suppose that, although probably unawares, she saw in this bygone literary genre a fit emblem for the ideals of Jacobitism which, despite the feelings of anticipation that surrounded the succession to the throne in the summer of 1714, were doomed to find their fulfilment only in the distant and never fading world of romance. Unlike "these noble Romans and young Lovers" (Barker 1715, II, 142) the Stuarts were not rewarded with a "happy Conclusion" (Barker 1715, II, 142), but if marvellous and supernatural elements are virtually absent from *Exilius*, one wonders if its complicated mechanics and 'romantic' ending may have repaid in idealization and make-believe what history would deny.

References

Barker J. 1688. *Poetical Recreations: Consisting of Original Poems, Songs, Odes, & c. with Several New Translations: in two parts. Part I, occasionally written by Mrs. Jane Barker, Part II, by several Gentlemen of the Universities, and Others.* London: Printed for Benjamin Crayle, at the Peacock and Bible, at the West-end of St. Pauls.

Barker J. 1715. *Exilius: or, The Banish'd Roman. A New Romance*. London, Printed for E. Curll, at the Dial and Bible against St. Dunstan's Church in Fleetstreet [reprinted in 1973, New York & London: Garland Publishing].

Barker J. 1719. *Exilius: or, The Banish'd Roman. The Second Edition To which is added, The Amours of Bosvil and Galesia*. London: Printed for E. Curll in Fleetstreet.

Calvi L. 2009. *La corona e la Croce. Gli scritti dell'esilio di Giacomo II Stuart (1688-1701)*. Pisa: ETS.

Frye N. 1976. *The Secular Scripture. A Study of the Structure of Romance*. Cambridge, Massachusetts: Harvard University Press.

Harris T. 1993. *Politics Under the Later Stuarts. Party Conflict in a Divided Society 1660-1715*. London: Longman.

Huet P.D. 1715. *The History of Romances. An Enquiry into their Original; Instructions for Composing them; an Account of the most Eminent Authors; With Characters, and Curious Observations upon the Best Performances of that Kind*. London: Printed for J. Hooke, at the Flower-de-Luce, and T. Caldecott, at the Sun; both against St. Dunstan's Church in Fleetstreet.

James II & VIII 1692. "Imago Regis: or, The Sacred Image of His Majesty in his Solitudes and Sufferings, Written during his Retirements in France". In *Royal Tracts*. Paris: Imprinted for Estiene Lucas.

James II & VIII 1925. *Papers of Devotion of James II*, ed. by G. Davies. Oxford: Oxford University Press.

King K. 2000. *Jane Barker, Exile. A Literary Career 1675-1725*. Oxford: Clarendon Press.

Pittock M.G. H. 1994. *Poetry and Jacobite Politics in Eighteenth-Century Britain and Ireland*. Cambridge: Cambridge University Press.

Schofield M.A. 1990. *Masking and Unmasking the Female Mind. Disguising Romances in Feminine Fiction, 1713-1799*. Newark: University of Delaware Press.

MARIA MICAELA COPPOLA

Università di Trento

"Dead Eye. Dead I":
Telling Stories at the End in Ali Smith's *Hotel World*

A li Smith (Inverness, 1962) could be described as a writer of paradoxes and broken boundaries: she is a Scottish writer who lives and works in England (Cambridge) and who draws on European cultural tradition (including Pier Paolo Pasolini and Italo Calvino); she explicitly locates herself as a lesbian artist, but often lesbianism and lesbian identity are an undercurrent in her stories more than their core themes, and she has been acclaimed by critics and readers both inside and outside the mainstream; she has published novels (*Like*, 1997; *Hotel World*, 2001; *The Accidental*, 2004; *Girl Meets Boy*, 2007) made up of several dissonant voices, and short stories that intermingle as fragments of the same tale (*Other Stories and Other Stories*, 1999; *The Whole Story and Other Stories*, 2003; *The First Person and Other Stories*, 2008); her language is at once hyperbolic and exact, ironic and direct. This paper aims at exploring the contradictory nature of Ali Smith's fiction by focusing in particular on *Hotel World*, where, while facing issues such as the power of storytelling, fate, and death, Smith raises dilemmas and exposes ambiguities rather than providing answers and certainties.

1. Dying to tell

The title of *Hotel World* invites the reader into the Global Hotel, in a city that is peculiar and unique (and Scottish), with its "historic buildings and its modern developments teetering on top of medieval sewers" (Smith 2002, 45), but also globalised and anonymous (or British), with its restaurants, banks, Marks & Spencer, and hotel chains encompassing a whole world. The hotel and the city constitute the framework of the stories of five women: an old beggar whose favourite spot is just outside the hotel, the hotel director who invites her to spend one night (just one night) in, a journalist, an adolescent, and her dead sister. These women are drawn together as if by chance. A metaphor for society and for storytelling (Smith and Ciavarella 2007), the Global Hotel offers hospitality to these very different women, of different social classes, backgrounds and ages, and with different tales to tell – tales of life and of death.

In this context, two elements hold the narrative structure together: the above-mentioned Global Hotel, and the ghost of a young, lesbian waitress. On the one hand, the microcosm of the hotel and of the city encircles characters and stories from the outside. Within its perimeters, chance happenings, random meetings, meaningless events, and small changes take place, extend their boundaries, and acquire new meanings. On the other hand, a curious yet fortuitous deadly incident connects these stories, as if cutting across them: a young waitress dies falling down (ironically) the shaft of a dumb waiter. However, death is not seen as the end of a life story but as the beginning of new stories, of the past and of the present, since it spurs and tacks together the other women's narratives. So, we can say that the story starts at the end, with the waitress's death, without which the other tales would not exist.

Moreover, the girl's fall down the shaft is portrayed from her point of view. That is, the *eye* that has witnessed its own experience of dying is transformed into the *I* that witnesses for it.

> Woooooooo-
> hooooooo what a fall what a soar what a plummet what a dash into dark
> into light what a plunge what a glide thud crash what a drop what a rush
> what a swoop what a fright what a mad hushed skirl what a smash mush
> mash up broke and gashed what a heart in my mouth what an end.
> What a life.
> What a time.
> What I felt. Then. Gone (Smith 2002, 3).

This incipit introduces us to a dying but also dead story-teller, who is eager to remember and to capture with words the exact moment of her passing. Following her stream of words, first we are pushed forward, or better, downward, together with her body. Then, the word "end", a series of full stops, short sentences and new paragraphs, and the use of past tenses mark the abrupt interruption of this flow, and seem to anticipate the ultimate silence. Indeed, the story and the novel begin at this point, unravelling around the postponement of compulsory speechlessness by means of compulsory storytelling.

Having introduced Smith as a writer of paradoxes, it is not surprising to see in *Hotel World* a sort of narrative broadening of the fleeting moment of intersection between living and passing. As we can read in Goodwin and Bronfen's *Death and Representation*, death can be described as "a site of paradoxes, referring to more than one state" (Goodwin and Bronfen 1993, 4). Over the centuries, its inescapability has inspired and haunted the work of artists, intellectuals, and ordinary people. Furthermore, the experience of deceiving is subjectively unrepresentable, since, as Virginia Woolf noted in her diary (1926), for her as a writer, death is "the one experience I shall never describe" (Enright 1983, 35). But exactly for this reason death has constituted a challenge for novelists and poets. In particular, Goodwin and Bronfen highlight the difficulty in determining and representing the moment when human life ends. They reflect: "When does a body become a corpse? And who or what represents the corpse?" (Goodwin and Bronfen 1993, 6). In my opinion, through the pages of *Hotel World* we can glimpse at that state of transition between the living and the dead. However, this is portrayed not as a *state* but as a *process*.

Particularly in the initial chapter, we can find descriptions of the passage from body to corpse; a passage that shows many facets. Firstly, the process of shifting from the material to the spiritual sphere is not one-way and obvious in its conclusion. As a matter of fact, we can notice that Ali Smith depicts her protagonist as an extremely 'carnal' ghost: she is concerned with her bodily and earthly life, she is made as much of flesh as of spirit. This is evident when, on the verge between the material and the spiritual realms, unable to feel her own body, the girl is eventually able to capture the essence of her carnal existence:

> now that I'm nearly gone, I'm more here than I ever was. Now that I'm nothing but air, all I want is to breathe it. Now that I'm silent forever, haha, it's all words words words to me. Now that I can't just reach out and touch, it's all I want to do (Smith 2002, 5-6).

Lack and desire foster her (and our) inner knowledge of the multiple dimensions of life. Once she is deprived of feelings but also of small, material experiences, this ghost longs for dust in her mouth, a stone in her shoe, "some itching detail" (Smith 2002, 4). So, an incorporeal and dying/dead being reveals what it means to live in the flesh.

Secondly, the novel's dead protagonist struggles to recover her bodily sensations by resorting to imagination and words. Thus, we can say that the process of transition from body to corpse is also represented as the crossover of the experience of life and of its narrative representation. We can observe a young woman, physically dead and spiritually entering into another dimension, as she strives to grasp the meaning of her life and to find the words she needs to tell it. As Goodwin and Bronfen have noted, a meaningless life and a meaningless death can be transformed into something meaningful, when they are turned into a narrative moment: "To give voice to the corpse, to represent the body, is in a sense to return it to life: the voice represents not so much the dead as the once living, juxtaposed with the needs of the yet living" (Goodwin and Bronfen 1993, 7). From this point of view, the protagonist of this novel longs for remembering her life and her death – no matter how meaningless the former and inglorious the latter – but also for telling them with her own voice, because words seem to be the only link that connects her to the earthly world and to the living.

However, as she tries to speak in the first person, words elude her. Establishing another paradox, Smith gives voice to a narrator whose ability to tell her own story is progressively and inexorably failing her: "I am hanging falling breaking between this word and the next" (Smith 2002, 31), she realises. Before the reader's eyes, the narrator is losing sight, smell, memory of her body: she is losing touch with the material world and she is losing words. Indeed, the narrative is continuously interrupted by the sudden lack of the right term.

> If I could feel it again, how I hit it, the basement, from floor floors up, from toe to head, dead. Dead leg. Dead arm. Dead hand. Dead eye. Dead I, four floors between me and the world, that's all it took to take me, that's the measure of it, the length and death of it, the short goodb– (Smith 2002, 4).

If we analyse this passage, we can see how single words become tricky and display their ambiguous and musical nature. Moreover, the process of dying seems to follow the rhythm of each uttered item. The eye/I who is witnessing this process is dead whenever a syllable is missed, only to come to life again when the ability to utter a word is restored. In this way, the transition from life to death is portrayed as the resistance to speechlessness of a compulsory storyteller.

Progressively, sentences become immaterial and incorporeal, but also less obvious and, thus, more evocative, as in the following extract:

> remember
> you
> must
> live
>
> remember
> you
> most
> love
>
> remainder
> you
> mist
> leaf
>
> Wooooo-
>   hooooooo
>   oo
>   o (Smith 2002, 237-238).

Eventually, as the body is dragged down and ends its living experience, the voice is lifted up and moves forward into another, unknown, realm. It is not surprising that one of Ali Smith's favourite books is *Lezioni americane* (*Six Memos for the Next Millennium*; Calvino 1988). In fact, the first word that Calvino brings into the new millennium is 'lightness', meant as absence of gravity and weight; and absence of gravity and weight characterize the musical, poetical, ironic language in this novel (Smith and Ciavarella 2007).

2. The collective experience of (telling) death

As we have underlined, in *Hotel World* death is imagined as trespassing the boundaries between the material and the spiritual, between speaking and silence. As we will see, death also bridges the distance between the subject and the others, the survivors, since individual death gives rise to collective narratives.

From the passages we have examined, it is clear that the urge to tell death is at the core of this novel. The relevance given to death and to its representation contrasts with what Philippe Ariès, in his seminal work *Western Attitudes toward Death from the Middle Ages to the Present*, defines as the "procedure of hushing-up", which, he claims, is typical of our days and of Western culture. According to Ariès, whereas in the past death was omnipresent, familiar, and overtly and collectively confronted by the mourners, then it has become a shameful, forbidden, and individual experience (Ariès 1974, 85). Ariès describes this new attitude towards death, characteristic of modernity, as follows:

> one must avoid – no longer for the sake of the dying person, but for society's sake, for the sake of those close to the dying person – the disturbance and the overly strong and unbearable emotion caused by the ugliness of dying and by the very presence of death in the midst of a happy life, for it is henceforth given that life is always happy or should always seem to be so (Ariès 1974, 87).

In this view, individual death has been culturally interdicted in order to preserve collective happiness, seen as a moral duty and a social obligation. Referring to Geoffrey Gorer and his *Death, Grief and Mourning in Contemporary Britain*, Ariès concludes that the taboo of the twentieth century is no longer sex but death (Ariès 1974, 92-94).

Taking into consideration these approaches toward death, we could state that in *Hotel World* dying is depicted both as an individual experience and as a collective one. While the first pages are centred on the dying-I of the main protagonist, the novel as a whole bears witness to the dramatic impact of death on the yet living, and it shows different ways to mourn, or not to. Some survivors are muted in their pain, like the dead girl's father described in the passage below:

> A wall crept inches higher from his shoulders round his head: every time I came he added a new layer of bricks to the top of it. By autumn the wall was way past the top of his head, swaying, badly bricklayed and dangerously unbalanced, nearly up to the ceiling in the living room where it knocked against the lampshade and sent light and shadow spinning every time he crossed the room (Smith 2002, 13).

Other survivors are helplessly isolated from the outer world, engulfed in their feelings. This fictional society seems to mirror our death-avoiding society, where the dying person is often isolated, and 'proper' forms of mourning are desperately personal and mute.

However, here death acquires a collective reality, for the reader, who is directly addressed by the narrator, and who can observe different approaches to death, different ways of dying, of mourning, and of telling death. Thus, the experience of passing ceases to be perceived as an abstraction, and it becomes real (at least from a narrative point of view): a space-bound reality (connected to the pages of the novel), and a time-bound reality (connected to the act of storytelling).

3. The socially dead eye/I

After having analysed how in *Hotel World* the 'dead-eyed' narrator witnesses her own death, in this last section I would like to focus on who this 'dead I' is. To put it in a nutshell, we could say that she is a waitress, a young woman, and a lesbian. I would argue that these characteristics make of Ali Smith's protagonist a common and yet original literary ghost.

In *Over Her Dead Body. Death, Femininity and the Aesthetic*, Elisabeth Bronfen explores the connection between death and representation, seeing them in relation to femininity. Reflecting on why representations of death have been so common and pleasing in our culture and over the centuries, she concludes:

> because they occur in a realm clearly delineated as not life, or not real, even as they refer to the basic fact of life we know but choose not to acknowledge too overtly. They delight because we are confronted with death, yet it is the death of the other. [...] The aesthetic representation of death lets us repress our knowledge of the reality of death precisely because here death occurs *at* someone else's body and *as* an image (Bronfen 1992, x).

In this view, the portrayal of a dead body would enable the viewer to observe and face death, while avoiding personal involvement.

Often, in literature and in figurative arts, the image of this dead body, of this corpse that reminds individuals of their finitude – but with the necessary distance and detachment – has been the corpse of the socially dead, that is, not only of women but also of sexual and class minorities. John Stephenson echoes this vision of death and representation, and writes:

> The social existence of the majority, of those white, male bodies that supposedly matter, is conditioned by a certain disavowal and projection of the body's finitude. The socially dead are thus made to stand in for the death that haunts each and every life (Stephenson 1985, 157).

Since our patriarchal, capitalist and heterosexist culture has been denying death, the socially dead have born this culture's burden, and have served as its images. Regarding woman as a socially dead figure, Bronfen reports a letter addressed to a woman by Thomas de Quincey, which epitomises this attitude:

> Yet, sister woman, though I cannot consent to find a Mozart or a Michael Angelo in your sex, cheerfully, and with the love that burns in depths of admiration, I acknowledge that you can do one thing as well as the best of us men – a greater thing than even Milton is known to have done, or Michael Angelo: you can die grandly, and as goddesses would die, were goddesses mortal (Bronfen 1992, ii).

This approach was by no means restricted to early XIX century intellectuals. And it does not regard gender or class minorities only. Innumerable other examples could be mentioned. As far as the protagonist of this novel is concerned, the Lesbian has often represented another socially dead body too. Historians and critics of lesbian literature have pointed out that she is a common figure in mainstream canonical literature, but traditionally she is present as a mere ghost, a fading presence, visible only through specific lenses and between the lines (see in particular Castle 1993).

To conclude, we could say that in *Hotel World* another social, woman, lesbian ghost can be tracked. As a waitress, as a woman, and as a lesbian, Ali Smith's phantom embodies a multifaceted minority body; a body that historically has been subjected to erasure, invisibility, and social and material death. The protagonist's life seemed to anticipate her death: she was invisible and powerless as far as class, gender, and sexual orientation were concerned. Likewise, this working-class lesbian does not die grandly, as a goddess (as De Quincey envisioned). Nonetheless, her body refuses to stay in "the passive, horizontal position" that was typical of women's or lesbian corpses in literary and artistic representations of the past (Bronfen 1992, 65). She is not merely the image of death for the yet living, since she gives voice to her own corpse, and, in doing so, she strains to touch and feel it. With her, Ali Smith has created a social ghost who strives to resist disappearance by speaking for herself, for her life, and for her death.

References

Ariès P. 1974. *Western Attitudes toward Death from the Middle Ages to the Present.* Translated by Patricia M. Ranum. Baltimore and London: The John Hopkins University Press.

Bronfen E. 1992. *Over Her Dead Body. Death, Femininity and the Aesthetic.* Manchester: Manchester University Press.

Calvino I. 1988. *Lezioni americane. Sei proposte per il nuovo millennio.* Milano: Garzanti.

Castle T. 1993. *The Apparitional Lesbian. Female Homosexuality and Modern Culture.* New York: Columbia University Press.

Enright D.J. 1983. *The Oxford Book of Death.* Oxford: Oxford University Press.

Goodwin S.W., Bronfen E. (eds). 1993. *Death and Representation.* Baltimore and London: The John Hopkins University Press.

Smith A. 2002. *Hotel World.* London: Penguin Books.

Smith A. 2004. *Other Stories and Other Stories.* London: Penguin Books.

Smith A. 2004. *The Whole Story and Other Stories.* London: Penguin Books.

Smith A. 2005. *Free Love and Other Stories.* London: Virago Press.

Smith A. 2005. *Like.* London: Virago Press.

Smith A. 2006. *The Accidental.* London: Penguin Books.

Smith A. 2007. *Girl Meets Boy.* Edinburgh: Canongates Books.

Smith A. 2008. *The First Person and Other Stories.* London: Penguin Books.

Smith A., Ciavarella A. 2007. "Ali Smith. Intervista di Antonia Ciavarella", available at http://www.soggettiva.it/edizione2007/i_alismith.html (last accessed August 2011), also published in *Cassero*, VI, no. 2, 2007.

Stephenson J.S. 1985. *Death, Grief, and Mourning. Individual and Social Realities.* New York: The Free Press.

LAURA GIOVANNELLI

Università di Pisa

J.M. Coetzee's *Diary of a Bad Year*
and the Risky Challenge of Cultivating Strong Opinions

An aptest introduction to Coetzee's polyphonic *Diary of a Bad Year* is provided by one of the last sections of the text itself through the narrative voice of young Anya, a sexy Philippine-Australian girl whose vanity, arrogance and bimbo pose shall gradually leave room for genuine sympathy and affection as her relationship with the alleged author of the diary takes on more humane, intimate tones:

> Sometimes I blush when I think of the comments I made about your opinions – you were the world-famous author, after all, and I was just the little secretary – but then I think to myself, *Maybe he appreciated having a perspective from below, so to speak, an opinion of his opinions.* Because I did feel that you were taking a risk, being so isolated, so out of touch with the modern world [...]. It is a pity you are so alone in the world. We can all do with someone by our side, to help us (Coetzee 2007, 196-197).

Isolation, alienation, the half-stifled crowing over a victory (that of literary achievement and world-wide fame) which doesn't seem to score so high in the end, to say nothing of the humiliating infirmities of old age and illness, are all elements inherent in the tragicomic subtext underpinning *Diary of a Bad Year*. Far from coming unheralded upon any practised reader of the latest Coetzee, this web of kernel themes and moods has been spinning out since the late 1990s, from the Costello 'performances' to the stream of *bathos* flowing through *Slow Man*, where elderly and invalid Paul Rayment finds himself tenderly falling in love with Marijana Jokić, his dependable nurse. A Croatian woman who has settled in Australia with her husband and children, she sets out to look after her maimed patient, a helpless prisoner in his Adelaide apartment because of a leg-amputation, until this philanthropic romance is broken off by the intrusive play of Elizabeth Costello, the pestering would-be author of Paul's story.

Both physically and emotionally 'slow', Paul seems to be rescued from the abyss of depression by the palpable presence and statuesque beauty of

Marijana, on whom he is ready to lavish all the moral and financial support he can, as if trying to make up for his spiritually wasted existence. A divorced man, he bitterly regrets having no offspring and leaving no trace behind, sliding through life invisibly and listlessly, with the fatal accident on the road (a sort of trivialized way to Damascus for a secular St. Paul) 'freezing' him in the state of "a half-man, an after-man, like an after-image; the ghost of a man looking back in regret on time not well used" (Coetzee 2006, 33-34).

Somewhere in-between the effete sentimentality and religious humanism of Rayment and the lofty intellectualism of David Lurie in *Disgrace* (the academic who eventually endorses the zero-degree task of the 'dog man'), the variously called "JC", "Juan" and "Señor C" in *Diary* appears to be a more factual stand-in for Coetzee himself, whose ideological stances, aesthetic principles and obsessive questionings can be easily detected behind the postmodern sleight of hand. An ageing South African professor and novelist now living in Australia, allegedly born in 1934 (instead of 1940) and suffering from Parkinson's disease, the writer of this hybrid diary, where a sequence of thirty-one thought-pieces entitled "Strong Opinions" (12 September 2005-31 May 2006) is followed by a more intimate "Second Diary", locates himself in many ways within the bio-bibliographical frame of his twin in the flesh.

Besides the clue supplied by his name initials – Anya hardly succeeds in distracting us by lending him a South American identity – we learn that this low-spirited, sometimes peevish and cynical Señor is an internationally famous novelist, laden with literary awards; that he is the author of *Waiting for the Barbarians* and a number of essays on censorship (hence the connection with *Giving Offence: Essays on Censorship*, 1996); that as a boy he attended a Catholic high school in Cape Town and his father's name began with "Z" (for Zacharias Coetzee). Still more revealing are JC's disenchanted comments on the conflictual relationship with "Z", an attorney who went through financial troubles, shunned political commitment and never seemed to be a model for the introverted and self-centred child. In "My Father", the third section of his undated "Second Diary" – what Anya calls a concoction of "Soft Opinions" (Coetzee 2007, 193) – the man's character is just sketched in through some biting understatements which are soon counterbalanced by the speaking I's scathing self-anatomy:

> one who, not industrious by nature – *easygoing* might be the kindest word – nevertheless resigned himself from his middle years to a round of dull toil with little variety. One of the generation whom apartheid was designed to protect and benefit; yet how slight was his gain from it! It would take a hard heart indeed, on the Day of Judgment, to consign him to the pit of hell reserved for the slavedrivers and exploiters.
> Like me, he disliked friction, flare-ups, displays of anger, preferred to get along with everyone. He never told me what he thought of me. But in his secret heart I am sure he had no very high opinion. A selfish child, he must

have thought, who has turned into a cold man; and how can I deny it? (Coetzee 2007, 166).

This is one of the passages where, looking back on the interviews collected in *Doubling the Point*, Coetzee can be seen as approaching his deeper self, betraying a yearning for high goals and a Calvinistic fear of indolence or easy compromise, but also highlighting the paralysing effects of violence, the poignant motifs of coldness and self-restraint and the difficulties he usually meets with taking strong positions. The young historical Coetzee had portrayed himself as "[s]ympathetic to the human concerns of the left", though "alienated, when the crunch comes, by its language" as well as by any "language that lays down the law, that is not provisional, that does not as one of its habitual motions glance back skeptically at its premises" (Coetzee 1992, 394). JC, his fictitious acronym, feels equally uneasy about the irrefutability of authority and the aggressiveness or overpowering emotions of crowds, and finds a detrimental connection between his sheltered life and disengaged art.

Such pronouncements should on the one hand be read as a tight-lipped answer to certain cursory evaluations and received views about Coetzee's novels, like their assumed evasiveness and escapist vein. Right at the beginning, for instance, JC welcomes the opportunity offered to him by Mittwoch Verlag – contributing to a volume in which six eminent writers are called upon to express their 'strong opinions' on contemporary society and its evils – as a chance to "grumble in public [...] to take magic revenge on the world for declining to conform to my fantasies" (Coetzee 2007, 23). On the other hand, we feel that the failing argumentative strength of JC, a worn-out man, assailed by doubts about his work and public figure's role, only too aware that to "write a novel you have to be like Atlas, holding up a whole world on your shoulders" (Coetzee 2007, 54), does need room for debate, for a dialogic and hopefully refreshing confrontation with a newborn, transnational alterity, no matter how shallow and lacking in wit this interlocutor might be.

Not forgetting T.S. Eliot's lessons of 'invisibility' (especially the 'symphonic' assimilation and transcendence of autobiographical references in *Four Quartets*), Coetzee appears to stage an interweaving of discourses, each of them embodied by a *persona*, where the amplified solo voice of JC the intellectual – resonating in the magisterial, mainly political (left-leaning, anarchist) and philosophical essays fittingly contained in the *top* section of each page – is countervailed or temporarily held at bay by a chorus of other voices recorded in a single and then, from the sixth 'strong opinion' onward, double narrative strip covering the second half of the page.

This flaunted structural device, through which running black lines divide the book's contents into two and later three independent tiers, also allows for variations in rhythm and intensity. Starting from the bottom section of the very first page, the reader is in fact gradually ushered into JC's inner world via his chance meeting with a twenty-nine-year old neighbour in the laundry room of his apartment building in Sydney. This exotic, dark-haired nymph suddenly awakens a flash of desire in his feeble body ("As I watched her an ache, a metaphysical ache, crept over me that I did nothing to stem", Coetzee 2007, 7),[1] and he hastens to engage the girl, with no secretarial experience and a poor cultural background, to type his thought-pieces. Like a prelude, that 'itch' ignites an introspective process which will be tracked down in the central narrative portion of the book, characterized by passing comments, reported speech and painful moments of insight. Yet, this middle subtext also includes blanks (the emotional side of JC doesn't utter a word all through the first four sections of "Second Diary") and interpolations, since in the last thirty pages Anya's voice shall unexpectedly take over by means of a letter that she is said to have sent from Brisbane.

In other terms, the female narrator eventually 'jumps' from the third (bottom) section of the page to the second one, according to a metamorphic script which halfway through "Second Diary" lends ear to a third personification, particularly hostile to the old-generation man of letters: Anya's boyfriend, a yobbish, greedy go-getter in the frantic "new economy" world and an elated advocate of the modern "managerial state" (Coetzee 2007, 95). An epitome for the "hard certainties" side *vs* the intellectual's "hard opinions" (Coetzee 2007, 109), this investment consultant with a degree in business and a firm belief in goal-directed activities will even plant spyware on the hard drive of JC's computer with a view to making illegal profits out of the man's bank accounts.

Since initials and abbreviations are always connoted in Coetzee's narrative, we can hardly overestimate the fact that the name of this dissonant figure should begin as well with the letter "A": the man in question is *Australian Alan*, and one wonders whether this might mischievously hint at the Alans, the barbarian people of Persian origin who penetrated into the Roman Empire and whose legacy would now press on the exhausted author of *Waiting for the Barbarians*. By calling him "Mr Aberdeen" or simply "Mr A", JC picks instead on the opponent's Celtic pallor, ginger hair and freckled skin to play down his own jealousy for the lucky fellow.

"Alan and Anya, A&A" (Coetzee 2007, 19), to echo the writer's dig at commercial companies, ironically convey the flicker of a new beginning enciphered in the very first letter of their names, and could be compared to

---

[1] Mantel (2008) certainly strikes home when recording a mischievous and comic undertone here.

a couple of crass *a*gents (*a*ngels?)[2] bringing about a shock of recognition in JC's secluded life in his ground-floor apartment of Sydenham Towers. If his dwelling symbolizes a foundation stone, everything about A&A's location tells of something new, a recently established order: they have in fact occupied since January (the *first* month of the year) "a *prime* unit on the *top floor* of this same *North* Tower" (Coetzee 2007, 9; my italics).

Stepping further into the onomastic path, one notes that the two letters which "Alan" and "Anya" do not share, "l" and "y", sound like the word "lie", as though unveiling the functional nature of these characters, not so much rounded-off personalities as devices or, picking up the metaphor of the musical score, instruments eliciting different kinds of 'vibrations' (sympathetic, prickly, melodramatic) when performing their often discordant pieces. While most reviewers have so far shown mixed feelings towards the cumbersome architecture of the novel – comparing it to "one of those segmented children's books in which you end up with the head of a gorilla, the torso of a policeman and the legs of a ballerina" (Lowry 2007, 2), or conceding that by means of "annoying jump cuts [...] Coetzee allows the didactic, erotic and criminal elements of his story to echo and even melt into one another" (Jones 2007) – some have grasped the communicative potentialities stemming from the three-voiced interplay among 'sameness' and different degrees of 'alterity'. Taking his cue from the second-last 'soft opinion' on Bach, whose music is hailed by JC as "a gift, unearned, unmerited, for free" (Coetzee 2007, 221), Andrew Riemer argues that

> *Diary of a Bad Year* is laid out like a three-part musical score in which the notation for each 'voice' is printed on a separate staff, though in performance all are sounded simultaneously. Bach's music is famously contrapuntal: each strand is separate, distinct, yet enters into intricate relationships with its companions. If only it were possible to take in the constituent parts of Coetzee's book in one glance, as it were, in the way musicians read a score. Then we might relish fully the nuances, anticipations and echoes, assonances and dissonances as the strands intertwine, one rising above the others at times, then falling silent for a while (Riemer 2007, 2).

---

[2] There are at least two passages where Anya is portrayed with angelic traits, be they the features of the "Angel of Death" or of the "angel-like woman" (Coetzee 2007, 59-61, 190). What should be kept in mind about the *Diary*'s texture of resonances concerning names is the teasing blurring of identities that we occasionally come across: Anya's final recognition of JC as "one of the best, class AA" (Coetzee 2007, 221) leads us double-edgedly back to the writer's guarded approach to A&A, the uninhibited couple, whereas "Anya" could be split into "Any A", virtually embracing any embryonic identity in contrast with the unrecoverable 'seniority' of Senior C, whose shoulders were once as strong as *Atlas*'s. There are also a series of hot epithets being exchanged between Alan and Anya, while the former eventually addresses JC as "Juan", perhaps snickering at Byron's epic satire *Don Juan* alongside Mozart's opera (consider Donna *Anna*'s crucial role in Lorenzo Da Ponte's libretto).

If in this case we cannot speak of a 'right' tonality but of an alternation between tuneful and diaphonic moments, on the semantic level we are similarly prevented from getting at an axiomatic truth. Neither indisputable nor conceived to pave any epistemological royal road, JC's opinions lend themselves to additions and revisions: the author sardonically ensures that this is made clear via Anya, who proceeds to 'edit' the texts if only to trivialize or distort their meaning. JC's utterances are in short *propositions* soliciting an answer, half-truths articulated within a counterpoint framework allowing for areas of overlap and bifurcation: for a language – to quote again the passage from *Doubling the Point* – that privileges provisionality and the act of "glancing back skeptically at its premises".

We therefore need to draw attention to the Dostoevskian and Bakhtinian imprint of *Diary*, with its ingrained dialogic nature and lack of finalism,[3] and also notice how the awkward hovering between the academic and journalistic field, the diaristic mode and the fictional realm of criminal/erotic intrigue metonymically incorporates change and the search for new directions both within the novel genre and the socio-cultural sphere. By having his book 'walk the tightrope', Coetzee manages to see through the cracks of globalization and carve out a space for diasporic subjects: as had been the case with French Paul and Croatian Marijana in *Slow Man*, Australia becomes a kind of free zone for South African JC and Anya, who "likes to present herself as a Filipina, a little Filipina guest-worker. In fact she has never lived in the Philippines" (Coetzee 2007, 70).

Besides the erotic urge at play, Anya's captivatingly delicate features and polemical remarks against paedophilia and pornographic filming even smack of a debased Nabokovian tradition, with its capitalizing on the Medusa-like potential of the girl-child. Albeit the author of a series of 'strong opinions' (Nabokov wrote a volume of interviews with the same title) and a diary, JC is however miles away from devious and hysterically elated Humbert Humbert. An ironic twist is seemingly introduced to pin down that difference, since the inflamed words uttered by H. H. at the beginning of the novel, with their hypnotic puns – "Lo-lee-ta: the tip of the tongue taking a trip of three steps down the palate to tap, at three, on the teeth. Lo. Lee. Ta" (Nabokov 1980, 9) – are echoed here by the girl herself: "At first I was just supposed to be his

---

[3] In this perspective "ideas, like the characters themselves, are in constant circulation and mutual qualification [...] with a character's inconsistencies and illogicalities and unreason" (Wood 2007, 3). We also realize that *Diary* has been provided with a suitable background via such 'truthful fictions' as *Elizabeth Costello*. Indeed, what we encounter "are not these characters' beliefs, but their believings; we undergo their speeches and arguments as events, and we share, momentarily, the process of articulating feelings and ideas", since the emphasis is laid on "the event – literary and ethical at the same time – of storytelling, of testing, of self-questioning, and not the outcome" (Attridge 2004, 205).

segretaria, his secret aria, his scary fairy" and again "I was his secret aria [...]. If I had cared to listen in on a warm spring night, I am sure I would have heard him crooning his love song up the lift shaft. Him and the magpie. Mr Melancholy and Mr Magpie, the amoro-dolorous duo" (Coetzee 2007, 28, 225).

The musical innuendo leads us back full circle to the contrapuntal framework of voices, moods and motifs we have been speaking of. There is now little doubt that Anya should be performing the author's long suppressed (or forgotten) sensual *aria*, an *allegro* giving free rein to an unruly feminine side. By the same token, we may conjecture that the "Second Diary" appendage works as a slackened coda recording JC's *softer* tunes: the more personal opinions that are not due to appear in the Verlag volume, but which hold nevertheless a significant place in Coetzee's finished text, where they look like a present for Anya, the tangible evidence of JC's efforts to try out a less irksome route, as she had suggested to him. These twenty-four reflections are spelled out along a zig-zag path, touching on such manifold themes as dreams, fan mail, mass emotion and, with a resonant rising in pitch, Bach and Dostoevsky, to whose glorious memory JC and Coetzee – here palpably at one – sing a consecrating hymn.

JC and Anya end up cooperating to the creation of *Diary*, where several rich semantic implications are brought into being by their dialectical wrestling. She will drop her loutish jargon and common-or-garden reflections to embody a caring Muse and model reader for her exhausted employer, going so far as to consider having children with her new boyfriend.[4] Correspondingly, JC acknowledges that what "has begun to change since I moved into the orbit of Anya is not my opinions themselves so much as my opinion of my opinions" (Coetzee 2007, 136): hence his agreeing to the plan of a "Second Diary" collection.

The third band of the book's last page leaves us with a peaceful sense of reconciliation: Anya is intoning a melancholy air, a sweet 'nocturne' in which she imagines herself holding the hand and kissing the brow of a dying Señor C. In spite of this, we feel that the *Diary*'s 'consort' does not quite add up to a whole, since a number of sore points have been touched and then surreptitiously dropped. If mean and duly stifled, it is the mordant voice of Alan the 'sham villain' and Darwinian fraud that won't let us overlook JC's and, self-evidently, Coetzee's inner conflicts as an internationally acclaimed writer burdened with a (post)colonial legacy. The antagonist features the Señor as an "old-fashioned free-love, free-speech sentimental hippie socialist", mentally stuck to Africa but leaning on old Europe for "the kind of hearing [he] won't get at home" (Coetzee

---

[4] This is where Anya enters the Christian region inhabited by Marijana – the phonetic correspondences between their names are worth noting – whom Paul describes as a "woman built for motherhood", while trying his hand at a Nabokovian spell: "[Paul] has no reservations about calling her 'Marijana'. He likes the name, with its four full, uncompromising syllables" (Coetzee 2006, 34, 30).

2007, 92, 213). In this grim portrayal, nothing could be farther from action and risk than the vagueness of opinions and vicarious experience of literary activity, rooted in the fanciful and crudely laughed off:

> You put yourself forward as a lone voice of conscience speaking up for human rights and so forth, but I ask myself, If he really believes in these human rights, why isn't he out in the real world fighting for them? What is his track record? And the answer, according to my researches, is: His track record is not so hot. In fact his track record is virtually blank (Coetzee 2007, 197).[5]

In the end, the sliest challenge that the learned humanist and morally-committed intellectual is asked to face in our world is seemingly objectified by the market-trusting, cheatingly optimistic assault of the Philistine.

References

Università di Roma Attridge D. 2004. *J. M. Coetzee and the Ethics of Reading: Literature in the Event*. Chicago and London: The University of Chicago Press.

Coetzee J. M. 1992. *Doubling the Point: Essays and Interviews*, ed. by D. Attwell. Cambridge, Massachusetts and London: Harvard UP.

Coetzee J. M. 2006 [2005]. *Slow Man*. London: Vintage.

Coetzee J. M. 2007. *Diary of a Bad Year*. London: Harvill Secker.

Jones L. 2007. "Strong Opinions Abound". In *Telegraph.co.uk*, August 24, available at http://www.telegraph.co.uk/culture/books/fictionreviews/3667470/Strong-opinions-abound.html (last accessed August 2011).

Lowry E. 2007. "J. M. Coetzee's Ruffled Mirrors". In *Times Online*, August 28, 1-5, available at http://entertainment.timesonline.co.uk/tol/arts_and_entertainment/the_tls/article2322205.ece (last accessed August 2011).

Mantel H. 2008. "The Shadow Line". In *The New York Review of Books*, January 17, 55, 1, 1-6, available at http://www.powells.com/review-a-day/the-shadow-line-by-review-a-day/(last accessed August 2011).

---

[5] In the complex fabric of the book's statements and counterstatements, this 'move' had been studiously anticipated by JC, who proves to be more far-sighted than people like Alan might conjecture: "My mother's generation had a distinctly pre-modern attitude to the market: it was a creation of the devil; only the wicked prospered in the market [...]. Hence the stupid doggedness with which I pursue my little projects, even today. Stubbornly I believe that labour is in itself good, whether or not it achieves measurable results. Looking over the record of my life, an economic rationalist would smile and shake his head" (Coetzee 2007, 118).

Nabokov V. 1980 [1955]. *Lolita*. Harmondsworth: Penguin.

Riemer A. 2007. *Diary of a Bad Year*, The Sydney Morning Herald, August 25, 1-2, available at http://www.smh.com.au/news/book-reviews/diary-of-a-bad-year/2007/08/24/1187462503346.html (last accessed August 2011).

Wood J. 2007. "Squall Lines". In *The New Yorker*, December 24, 1-4, available at http://www.newyorker.com/arts/critics/books/2007/12/24/071224crbo_books_wood (last accessed August 2011).

FABIO LIBERTO

Università di Bologna

"Poor Susans!":
Wordsworth and the "Single(s) in the Wide Waste"

William Wordsworth is often considered and referred to as a "nature poet" whose sentimental and poetical education took place in the region of the Lakes. Recent studies, however, hint with increasing interest at the relationship between the poet and the urban environment, and particularly at his ambivalent opinions on the city of London, which, at that time, was one of the most astounding symbols of the outcomes of the Industrial Revolution. The relation between Wordsworth and the city is broad and very complex, as the poet's ever-changing approaches to the urban throughout his literary career cannot be easily summarized in schematic axioms. In this paper, therefore, we will consider, thorough a chronological prospect, some major characters that appear in Wordsworth's poems who are suitable epitomes of "single(s) in the wide waste" (Wordsworth 1979, VII, l. 76).[1]

One of the main problems connected to the experience of the city is the potential of the urban environment to deny the individual his most important constitutive part, namely his individuality. According to the sociologist Georg Simmel, the "deepest problems of modern life derive from the claim of the individual to preserve the autonomy and individuality of his existence in face of the overwhelming social forces" (Simmel 1964, 409). William Wordsworth deeply felt the problem of individuality as connected to the urban experience. His description of London in Book 7 of *The Prelude* is probably the most astonishing representation of the city that he ever wrote: the account of the "din / Barbarian and infernal", that "hell / For eyes and ears", and that all-embracing "blank confusion" (Wordsworth 1979, VII, ll, 659-660; 658-659; 695) are undoubtedly memorable representations of the endless "hubbub" (Wordsworth 1979, l. 227) of the urban reality, whose characterization seems to rely mostly on the Miltonic representation of Hell in *Paradise Lost*. Among the "weary throng" (Wordsworth 1979, l. 171) of the city, however, the reader can occasionally catch glimpses of

---

[1] The quoted passages from *The Prelude* are from the 1805 version.

minor figures, aliens among the urban who, in one way or another, try to put an
end to the anonymity that the "Monstrous" city imposes upon them.

The first of these alienated characters (following a chronological order
of composition) is the protagonist of "Poor Susan"[2] (1797), a poem in which
imagination is represented as a faculty that acts in joined force with recollection.
This binomial force, typical in Wordsworth, is essential for the protagonist, who
uses it in order to escape from the prosaic and dim reality of the city. The poem
tells the story of Susan who, walking down the street, encounters a singing
thrush:

> At the corner of Wood Street, when daylight appears,
> Hangs a Thrush that sings loud, it has sung for three years:
> Poor Susan has passed by the spot, and has heard
> In the silence of morning the song of the Bird.
> 'Tis a note of enchantment; what ails her? She sees
> A mountain ascending, a vision of trees;
> Bright volumes of vapour through Lothbury glide,
> And a river flows on through the vale of Cheapside
> (Wordsworth 1979, ll. 1-8)

The setting of the poem is that of the city, but the landscape depicted is that
of the country: even though Susan clearly "sees" the topographical structure of
London (Wood Street, Lothbury, and Cheapside), the song of the bird acts on
her mind so that the real landscape is mystified with the recollection of "The
only dwelling on earth that she loves" (Wordsworth 1979, l. 12). The song of the
bird opens for Susan the doors of memory allowing her to experience a genuine
wood rather than "Wood Street", namely its grotesque urban equivalent.
However, the ecstatic recollection is brief, and soon the vision fades for, as the
poet relates, "the colours have all passed away from her eyes!":

> She looks, and her heart is in heaven: but they fade,
> The mist and the river, the hill and the shade:
> The stream will not flow, and the hill will not rise,
> And the colours have all passed away from her eyes!
> (Wordsworth 1979, ll. 13-16)

From the beginning of the poem, it is quite clear that Susan is a luminal
figure that does not fit anywhere: we meet her at a "corner", *between* two streets,
and the name of one of these designates a context that is *between* a country
("wood") and city ("street"). Susan's necessity to rely on a reverie further reveals
her condition of universal outcast: she is an outcast from the city, whose scenery

---

[2] All quotations from Wordsworth's poems are from *Poetical Works*, 1969.

she tries to ignore; from nature, as she left her father's house in the country; and also from her own reverie, which eventually abandons her.

In "Poor Susan" the description of the city is carefully avoided, not only because the "beauty of the morning"[3] mitigates the vision, but also because the intervention of imagination enacts a transformation of reality. In "The Farmer of Tilsbury Vale" (1800) Wordsworth depicts Susan's counterpart in reality,[4] but goes further with his argument and introduces, even if in a restricted perspective, "London's Wide Town" (Wordsworth 1979, l. 5). The poem tells the story of a farmer who, after experiencing economic difficulties, decides to move to London: "a sad emigration I ween", comments the narrator. As soon as Adam arrives in London, he is depicted as being in utter solitude and "As lonely he stood as a crow on the sands" (Wordsworth 1979, l. 48). Just like Susan, Adam is able to rely on his recollection of the country in order to escape mentally from the scenery of the city, but he succeeds more effectively than Susan. The vision for Adam is frequent ("Full ten times a day", Wordsworth 1979, l. 64) and it does not vanish. This, however, does not mean that Adam is "able to reconcile himself to life in the city", as David Simpson suggests (Simpson 1986, 602). On the contrary, Adam refuses the urban setting, and almost ignores it. His only relation to the city is limited to his search for those natural elements that could encourage his imagination:

'Mid coaches and chariots, a waggon of straw,
Like a magnet, the heart of old Adam can draw;
With a thousand soft pictures his memory will teem,
And his hearing is touched with the sounds of a dream.
Up the Haymarket hill he oft whistles his way,
Thrusts his hands in a waggon, and smells at the hay;
He thinks of the fields he so often hath mown,
And is happy as if the rich freight were his own.
(Wordsworth 1979, ll. 77-81)

While Susan's imagination was enacted accidentally by the song of the bird, here Adam himself actively searches for natural elements within the urban environment. The real city, however, remains alien to the old man: "In the throng of the town like a stranger is he, / Like one whose own country's far over the sea" (Wordsworth 1979, ll. 61-62).

Both the farmer of Tilsbury Vale and Susan are outcasts who are equally separated from the city *and* from reality. In *The Prelude*, where the description of London is instead real[5] and often realistic, as Timothy Webb remarks (Webb

---

[3] As the poet observes in "Composed Upon Westminster Bridge", in *The Prelude*, l. 5.

[4] "With this picture, which was taken from real life, compare the imaginative one of 'The Reverie of Poor Susan'" (Wordsworth 1969, 726).

[5] The poet announces the separation from the imaginary scene with which Book 7 begins by remarking: "And now I looked upon the real scene" (Wordsworth 1979, l, 139).

2002, 54), such figures, that in former poems were in the foreground, fade into the background. Probably this shift in perspective was due to Wordsworth's deeper fascination with the city and what it represented.[6] Speaking about the capability of the mind to be excited "without the application of gross and violent stimulants", Wordsworth remarks:

> [...] a multitude of causes, unknown to former times, are now acting with a combined force to blunt the discriminating powers of the mind, and, unfitting it for all voluntary exertion, to reduce it to a state of almost savage torpor. The most effective of these causes are the great national events which are daily taking place, and the increasing accumulation of men in cities, where the uniformity of their occupations produces a craving for extraordinary incident, which the rapid communication of intelligence hourly gratifies (Wordsworth 1969, 735).

This often-quoted passage from the Preface to the second edition of *Lyrical Ballads* (1801) is crucial to understand Wordsworth's change in perspective, as some of the keywords ("discriminating powers", "uniformity" and "extraordinary") reveal the poet's growing problematization of the urban experience. People, according to what Wordsworth writes, are accumulated in cities and rendered uniform by their occupations; this causes them to crave for extraordinary events in order to satisfy their minds which, being at this point only used to uniformity, are no longer able to discriminate. This passage anticipates some of the twentieth-century most important theorizations on the effects of the urban experience upon the mind. Georg Simmel, in his seminal study on the experience of the urban, remarks in an extremely similar way that the "essence of the blasé attitude consists in the blunting of discrimination" (Simmel 1964, 414): thence, within the city, the mind would no longer be able to discern.

On this very belief is grounded the description of London in *The Prelude*. Here the city is described as a spectacle that offers the observer real "extraordinary" incidents, and Bartholomew's Fair, in its exceptional spectacularity, is consequently presented as "a type not false / Of what the mighty City is itself" (Wordsworth 1979, VII, ll. 695-696). However, as Wordsworth himself observes in the Preface, the massive presence of *extra-ordinary* renders the overall vision extremely *ordinary*: the "discriminating powers" of the poet/observer necessarily fails and, paradoxically, everything seems to be "melted and reduced / To one identity, by differences" (Wordsworth 1979, ll. 702-703). Wordsworth's portrayal of London is chaotic and people are often reduced to lists of names deprived of the distinctiveness of the description. Thus, these figures can only find

---

[6] Four years had elapsed between the composition of "The Farmer of Tilsbury Vale" and Book 7 of *The Prelude*.

personality by converging into the single, flattening identity that the narrator's poetics of the catalogue and his list-making obsession offer. This modality of artistic representation dispossesses the observed subjects/objects of their "stories", so that they can only find a unifying character in the very narrative device of the catalogue employed by Wordsworth.

At times, the poet's attention is directed to some solitary individual that he meets along the way, but he rarely ventures into a close-up, as his capability of distinguishing people proves to be ineffective. One example of his quick glances is the "travelling cripple":

> As on the broadening Causeway we advance,
> Behold a face turned up toward us, strong
> In lineaments, and red with over-toil;
> 'Tis one perhaps, already met elsewhere,
> A travelling cripple, by the trunk cut short,
> And stumping with his arms.
> (Wordsworth 1979, ll. 215-220)

The depicted image of the man is jarring and realistic, but in the urban environment a character as such is far too common to obtain a privileged place in the observer's memory. Therefore, the only comment that the poet is able to make is that, probably, he had already met the travelling cripple somewhere else. The poet continues with his walk and the cripple remains there, alone among the crowd. More specific attention is paid to some other characters, since, according to the observer, they do not deserve to be "left behind" in memory (Wordsworth 1979, l. 365). One of these remarkable characters is the "rosy babe" that the poet meets, significantly, in a theatre and who is left by his mother among "dissolute men / And shameless women" (Wordsworth 1979, ll. 384-385):

> 'Twas at a Theatre
> That I beheld this Pair; the Boy had been
> The pride and pleasure of all lookers-on
> In whatsoever place; but seemed in this
> A sort of alien scattered from the clouds
> (Wordsworth 1979, ll. 373-377)

The babe immediately becomes an attraction for the crowd that observes him, and even though he is *surrounded* by many "chance spectators" (Wordsworth 1979, l. 836), he is described as both alienated and abandoned. His characterization as a "cottage-child" (Wordsworth 1979, l. 381) seems to distance him even more from the urban, suggesting that the babe belongs to a different context, as the other singles "in the wide waste". In this particular case, the alienation of the character is ultimate and so absolute as to break even the strongest of ties, namely that between mother and son: the child is "placed" upon a "board" and abandoned by his mother in a guise of stage where he entertains his audience.

Moving on in his promenade among the London streets, the poet arrests his glance upon another solitary figure: the blind beggar. Just before introducing the beggar, however, the poet notably remarks that the "face of everyone / That passes by me is a mystery", yet states his firm resolution to "look" (Wordsworth 1979, ll. 599-603):

> And once, far travelled in such mood, beyond
> The reach of common indications, lost
> Amid the moving pageant, 'twas my chance
> Abruptly to be smitten with the view
> Of a blind beggar, who, with upright face,
> Stood propped against a wall, upon his chest
> Wearing a written paper, to explain
> The story of the man, and who he was.
> My mind did at this spectacle turn round
> As with the might of waters, and it seemed
> To me that in this label was a type,
> Or emblem, of the utmost that we know,
> Both of ourselves and of the universe;
> And, on the shape of the unmoving man,
> His fixèd face and sightless eyes, I looked
> As if admonished from another world
> (Wordsworth 1979, ll. 608-623)

The blind beggar is the only character, among those we have met so far, that the narrator defines as a "type" and an "emblem"[7] and is possibly the most alienated too. Whereas the travelling cripple's handicap did not totally exclude him from his environment (with which he interacted by "stumping with his arms"), the blindness of the beggar is arguably the most alienating of the physical conditions. The beggar's actions (or rather *inactions*) are radically opposed to the urban incidents: while the city is connoted by an incessant "hubbub" and "Babel din", the beggar is silent, and writes, rather than tells, his story; while the city is a "quick dance" (Wordsworth 1979, l. 156), the beggar is "unmoving", keeping a "fixèd face"; and while the city presents "a hell / For eyes and ears" (Wordsworth 1979, ll. 659-660), the beggar has "sightless eyes". Thence, for the blind beggar, just like for the poet, the face of every one that passes by him "is a mystery".

---

[7] Although, probably, he is not the only one, and as Lindeberger remarks, in Book 7 the city, and I add, the characters, assumes a "consciously symbolic role" (Lindenberger 1963, 241).

Whether Wordsworth wanted the blind beggar to represent the most alienated "type" in the city, rather than the child, is hard to tell, but there is certainly another person in Book 7, who could rightly be regarded as the most alienated. So far, this character has been partially left aside, in the background, since we need to consider him also in the light of the characters mentioned above. The missing character is, obviously, Wordsworth. Up to now, Wordsworth has been the focal point of our observation, the narrator who has provided the reader with his point of view on the various "poor Susans". But the dual nature of *The Prelude* both as autobiography and epic, leads us to consider Wordsworth also as the author and the protagonist: the author who, like the blind beggar, writes his own story on "paper", and the protagonist who, like the child, is on a stage both to be observed and to observe (as he is simultaneously the narrator).

The blind beggar is indeed a "type" of Wordsworth as the author of both an "internalized" (Webb 2002, 54) and "national" (Butler 1982, 67) epic. In this characterization, two different *personae* are involved: the first is the author, external to the text, who writes his own story, like the beggar; the second is the epic protagonist who performs within the text his own story, which is *personal* but tending towards the *universal* (as the epic experience requires). In György Lukács theorization, lyricism, namely the subjective expression, becomes "all-embracing message only when the event, in its epic objectivation, becomes the vehicle and symbol of unbounded feeling" (Lukács 1978, 52). In other words, the story of the beggar, which is an emblem of the knowledge "Both of ourselves and of the universe", is as epic as Wordsworth's, since both, despite being lyrical, "Carr[y] within [them] the ultimate meaning of life" (Lukács 1978, 52).

The analogy with the child, on the other hand, emphasises Wordsworth as a character, or rather the poet's literary transition from narrator/observer to protagonist/observed subject. We have noticed that the child is placed in a theatrical context and becomes a spectacle to the men as much as the men become a spectacle to the child. A similar convergence of roles involves also the protagonist who, towards the end of the book, obtains an ambiguous vantage point:

> For once the Muse's help will we implore,
> And she shall lodge us, wafted on her wings,
> Above the press and danger of the Crowd,
> Upon some Showman's platform: what a hell
> For eyes and ears! what anarchy and din
> Barbarian and infernal!
> (Wordsworth 1979, ll. 656-660)

Wordsworth places himself onto an ambivalent "Showman's platform", becoming at the same time the observer and the observed, spectator and actor. This convergence of roles reveals the reader the ambiguity of the Wordsworthian *I*. If up to this moment the *I* of the narrator was the same as the reader's (as narrator and reader are both tied by identical pronouns and points of view) his position on the platform separates him from all that surrounds him. In addition, his invocation of the muse, which is a classical *topos*, manifestly collides with the register maintained up to this moment by the narrator, as to differentiate further the literary *personae*, via different registers. However, standing on the platform chiefly means to be physically alone. If throughout Book 7 the poet maintained a "psychological" alienation from the city, as many other characters in the book, now his isolation is also physical and final. If, as Johnston suggests, the city is made up of two parallel realities, the moral and the physical (Johnston 1984, 4), the poet, at the end of Book 7, chooses to separate himself from both.

The poet who through the eyes of Susan and Adam looks at the city and sees nature gives up his visionary undertaking in Book 7. In the great city "The whole creative powers of man [lay] asleep" (Wordsworth 1979, l. 654), meaning that the poet, unlike Susan or Adam, is unable to apply the "colouring of imagination" to the urban, so that all that he can see is an infernal world. By placing himself on the platform, the protagonist represents the decision of the individual who is aware of his estrangement from the external world.[8] Furthermore, the platform is the only device for the poet to alienate himself from a crowd that is both factual and symbolic, as it is the emblem of anarchy, loss of identity and, probably, brings with it the dreadful shadow of the French Revolution.

This conclusion only aims to offer a selected perspective on Wordsworth's relation to the urban. The question is more complex than that, as a deep ambiguity connotes the poet's vision of the city. Elsewhere, as in the sonnet "Composed Upon Westminster Bridge", where London is immersed in the "beauty of the morning" (Wordsworth 1979, l. 5), Wordsworth will be able to find his "Wood Street" even in the urban reality. However, that disquieting "still" with which the poem ends (which functions both as a substantive and an adverb)[9] reminds the reader of Wordsworth's ambiguous and ever-changing perception of the city. Wordsworth's London is characterised by overwhelming forces that make the city constantly shift between a temporary threatening hell and a transient peaceful paradise.

---

[8] The epic individual, according to Lukács, is precisely "the product of estrangement from the outside world" (Lukács 1978, 66).

[9] "Dear God! the very houses seem asleep;/And all that mighty heart is lying still" (Wordsworth 1969, ll. 13-14).

References

Butler M. 1982. *Romantics Rebels and Reactionaries*. New York: Oxford University Press.

Johnston J.H. 1984. *The Poet and the City: A Study in Urban Perspectives*. Athens (Ga.): University of Georgia Press.

Lindenberger H. 1963. *On Wordsworth's Prelude*. Princeton: Princeton University Press.

Lukács G. 1978. *The Theory of the Novel: A Historico-Philosophical Essay on the Forms of Great Epic Literature*. London: Merlin Press.

Newlyn L. "'In City Pent': Echo and Allusion in Wordsworth, Coleridge and Lamb, 1797-1801". *In The Review of English Dtudies* 32, 128, 408-428.

Simmel G. 1964. "The Metropolis and Mental Life". In Wolff K.H. (ed.) *The Sociology of Georg Simmel*. London: Collier-Macmillan, 409-424.

Simpson D. 1986. "What Bothered Charles Lamb about Poor Susan?". In *Studies in English Literature, 1500-1900*, 26, 4, 589-612.

Webb T. 2002. "Dangerous Plurals: Wordsworth's Bartholomew Fair and the challenge of an Urban Poetics". In Onega S., Stotesbury J.A. (eds.) *London in Literature: Visionary Mappings of the Metropolis*. Heidelberg: Universitätsverlag Winter, 53-82.

Williams R. 1973. The Country and the City. London: Chatto & Windus.

Wordsworth W. 1969. *Poetical Works*. London: Oxford University Press.

Wordsworth W. 1979. *The Prelude, 1799, 1805, 1850*. New York: Norton & Company.

PIERPAOLO MARTINO

Università di Bari Aldo Moro

The Importance of Being Oscar:
Performance, Performativity and Identity in Wilde

Oscar Wilde has achieved iconic status in contemporary popular culture, and within the fields of English literary and cultural studies; the secret of his success is given by the artist's capacity of translating his life into a form of writing and his writing into a vital gesture which articulates a complex critique of late Nineteenth Century English society. According to cultural critic Michael Bracewell (1997), Wilde stands as the first pop star of British history, a pop idol, a cultural icon who, notoriously, put all his genius in his life and only his talent in his work, in the desperate and yet successful attempt to turn his life into a work of art.

Interestingly, a 1998 film, Todd Haynes' *Velvet Goldmine*, establishes a very strong connection between Wilde's life (and art) and Pop culture. The film features two kinds of Wildean performance: the character of Oscar Wilde (as played by a very young actor) as well as a number of other male characters, moving within the world of 1970s British pop and in particular glam culture who – because of their interest in artifice, self-construction, and gender bending – are, as Francesca Coppa observes, "of the Oscar Wilde sort" (Coppa 2004, 89). In the film the infant Wilde is brought to earth on a glittering spaceship that moves like a shooting star, for Haynes, indeed, Wilde's genius is so otherworldly it could only be extraterrestrial. Significantly in the Victorian school scene, each boy announces what he wants to be when he grows up and then the young Wilde stands a declares "I want to be a Pop Idol".

It can be argued that Wilde's iconicity implies a kind of double articulation based on a complex dialogism involving past and present. As Kaye observes in his own time Wilde was "the most self-conscious marketer of his own image" (Kaye 2004, 193) that is, like many contemporary pop stars, he carefully constructed his status within society with the intention of selling, himself and translate his art and life into economic success. Wilde's iconicity, however, also relates to the author's after-life. According to the Oxford English Dictionary, a (cultural) icon "is a person or thing regarded as a representative symbol or as worthy of veneration" (1999, 704). Undoubtedly, there is something religious about Wilde's iconicity, which today brings admirers to worship both his image and the world connected to that image (to the extent that we can speak of a Wilde cult, his image and his epigrams are everywhere on T-shirts, album covers, posters). Interestingly, during the last years of his life in the long confessional letter *De Profundis* the author described himself in terms of a Christ-like figure, it is significant, moreover, that Terry Eagleton entitled a play in which he focuses on the life of the Anglo-Irish writer *Saint Oscar* (1997), a title which also makes reference to a trend in gay studies and in gay culture in general to see Wilde as the first homosexual martyr of history.

In order to fully understand Wilde's contemporary iconic status it is necessary to analyse the man in his time or rather the many men, the many roles played by Wilde in his lifetime. In this sense, Waldrep observes how:

> Wilde's trajectory was not toward some ultimate being, but the beginning in earnest of a system of becoming, that left any belief that there could be a natural, stable Oscar Wilde. Wilde's legacy as both a writer and a literary figure of social, political and cultural significance is such that Wilde the man cannot be readily separated by Wilde the careerist. His roles, as aesthete, lecturer, businessman, family man, poet, editor, playwright, seducer, prisoner and exile are part of a broader role of writer as performer that he used self-consciously in an attempt to destroy the binary opposition, separating art and life (Waldrep 2004, xiii).

In this perspective, Wilde's life can be usefully analyzed through the theoretical frame offered by performance studies. According to Coppa:

> Peformance studies recognizes that behavior, as well as speech, is a language that has rules and is structured by a grammar, and, as with any other language, comprehension depends on re-cognition or knowing something again when we see it (Coppa 2004, 73).

In this sense, performing doesn't simply mean doing, but "showing-doing", in short "staging" behavior. All human behavior is learned and then put on some sort of display. Wilde's capacity of self-fashioning his identities owes much to his very peculiar background, in which a key role is played, in my opinion, by his childhood, by his Oxford/early London years and by his tour of the United States.

Much has been written about the connection between Wilde's homosexuality and his mother's influence on him, however what was even more important is, the fact that Oscar inherited his mother's tendency to romantic self-invention. As Wilde's biographer, Richard Ellmann, observes:

> Lady Wilde had a sense of being destined for greatness, and imparted it [...]. She had always been uneasy about her first name, which was Jane,

and had modified her second name almost certainly Frances into Francesca, regarding the new name as a brilliant vestige of the Elgee family's origins in Italy, where […] they had been called Algiati (Ellmann 1987, 5)

which to her ears sounded as a corruption of Alighieri. It must also be stressed how little Oscar had access to *Lady Speranza*'s discussions – Speranza being Lady Wilde's correspondence forename – with her guests at tea time, even though he would not speak, he became acquainted with the art of conversation, which was to prove of paramount importance in the construction of his Oxford and London personae. He was practically watching, listening and studying what later he would be seen *showing-doing*.

Wilde made a very good impression at Oxford with his beautiful figure, elegance of manners and brilliant conversation. At Oxford he performed the role of the Englishman, as Sloan observes, "Wilde's lifelong performance was actually that of an Oxonian, which meant a distinct feeling of cultural superiority to the rest of society". Wilde adopted an Oxford accent, developing "his own languid, melodic version, of the intonations of his Oxford friends" (Sloan 2003, 6). This transformation at the prosodic level was also accompanied by interesting visual developments. Besides adopting a dandified look and way of dressing, with long hair and velvet suits, Wilde started decorating his Magdalen rooms with blue vases filled with lilies, the recognized symbol of the then fashionable Pre-Raphaelites.

When Wilde came down from Oxford to London in 1879 he self-designated himself on his visiting cards as "professor of aesthetics". Now Wilde had not only to reinvent himself but to make his way in the commercial world. In this world the press played a crucial role. As Sloan observes,

the production and underconsumption of new commodities initiated the modern techniques of advertising. The process also absorbed and assimilated the artist turning the earlier image of the artist as hero and critic of society into the commodified image of the artist as colorful personality (Sloan 2003, 10).

And yet Wilde used the new methods of advertising "in order to oppose the culture in which they were taking root" (*ibidem*). Wilde was also taking advantage of the mixing of higher and middle classes which offered opportunities for mobility. In this sense, his visibility was also given by the capacity of being everywhere offering his precious epigrams and observations and mixing with celebrities such as Lillie Langtry.

Wilde's became a global celebrity during his Tour of the United States; as any contemporary pop star in order to become a proper celebrity he had first to be *big* in America. The chance was given by the success of Gilbert and Sullivan's operetta, *Patience or Bunthorne's Bride* which focused on the look and manner of the aesthete in the character of Bunthorne. Richard D'Oyly Carte, the show's producer, offered Wilde a series of promotional lectures to offer American audiences the chance to see a real life aesthete, a similar practice was to become quite popular in the 1960s with British rock and pop artists, such as the Beatles, promoting their albums in long American tours. Interestingly Wilde didn't link his name with opera as a form of high art but with operetta as a form of low culture entertainment. In America, Wilde gave lectures such as "the English Renaissance of art" and "The Decorative arts" and hundreds of photographs were shot of the aesthete in his poses, like the famous Sarony photos which perfectly capture Wilde's look and capacity for self-promotion. On his arrival in New York a customer official asked him if he had anything to declare, Wilde promptly answered "I have nothing to declare except my genius" (Ellmann 1987, 152). Wilde's notorious epigram is a sign of his astonishing linguistic and conversative skills;

> in an attempt to transcribe his unique style of lecturing, one American Journalist went so far as to devise a system of diactrical marks to represent the elaborate pauses and inflections that Wilde would use to manipulate his audience (Waldrep 2004, 66).

In a sense Wilde's was speech as music, he was a great improviser who knew that basically society is, as Schutz (1976) puts it, playing music together. In this musical performance – in which he mixed different genres (stories, philosophy, wit) – very often form becomes more relevant then content. Wilde's epigrams, which he would easily enunciate in his speeches with the same elegance and stillness of his characters, were in a sense evergreen melodies on which he improvised in different contexts. Indeed Wilde used to recycle his epigrams in plays, essays and everyday conversation. In this sense one might create a link between Wilde and a great American icon, Andy Warhol, himself "of the Wilde sort", who based much of his art on seriality and who, like Wilde, treated trivial things as the most important of things and vice versa.

Wilde's performance was part of his "self-promotion, which fed his professionalism, but his conversation as performance was also a type of self-writing in which he constantly invented and reinvented himself for different purposes" (Waldrep 2004, 68). In short, Wilde was at once director and actor of himself in that complex and charming play which became his life. Wilde had a theatrical sense of life, his was a dialogical interiority in which, as in a play, different personae spoke to each other without ever reaching a fixed, immutable truth (or identity).

The author chose London as the main stage for the performance of the most important of his plays *Oscar Wilde*; it is not a chance that theatre – as a space in which the literary word is enacted and trough which literature becomes a source of entertainment for the audience – gave him world-wide fame. Wilde's most successful play of the 1890s was *The Importance of Being Earnest* which, in a sense, reflects *Oscar Wilde* as a living play with its focus on masks, double identities, inversion of gender roles and verbal complexities. Since its very title the play refers to the very idea of performance, to the importance of being, playing, performing someone else in particular contexts. Yet this is also a permanent condition, we are the differences, the different roles which we enact every day, in this sense the play exceeds the page and the (theatrical) stage: the importance of being Earnest turns into the importance of being Oscar which again becomes the symbol of life as theatre and of an ironic approach to identity. According to Waldrep:

> The play, like the post prison work has a typological function only to the extent to which it acts as an expression of Wilde's own interest of discovering the possibilities in himself. If *Dorian Gray* represented in the characters of Basil, Harry and Dorian – the splitting of his consciousness into three separate versions of himself, then Earnest carries his self into the arena of pure concept. It represents a world where queer space is not merely hinted but explicitly defined (Waldrep 2004, 60).

The queerness at the heart of Earnest (and indirectly) Wilde has sometimes been *over-simplified*. The play, according to some readings, contains a clear homosexual politics and subtext. Sloan notes how:

> Jack and Algernoon both pretend to be Earnest in order to maintain a double life. Algernoon's special term for this – 'Bunburying' – has also been credited as another coded word for homosexual desire, a play on the slang word 'bun' for 'buttocks' (Sloan 2003, 118).

Even without taking in account such readings, the relevance of the play still lies in the subversion of rigidly conventional Victorian attitudes to gender and sexuality, an attitude which is exemplified by the character of Gwendolen who often acts and speaks against accepted norms concerning female behaviour. In short, as Waldrep puts it, "*Earnest* is a performance about performance, as it is only by performing a gender – or a sexuality – via the use of masks and language that one can begin the manipulate and change the status quo" (Waldrep 2004, 59). And this bring us to the complex issue of Wilde's personal performance of gender.

There has been a general trend in Twentieth century criticism, as we have seen, to consider Wilde as the first gay martyr, in this sense, for many, the trials which found Wilde guilty and gave him two years of hard labor coincided with the advent of a public homosexuality. In truth, Wilde's was an attempt to construct an alternative discourse on masculinity, which sharply contrasted with the normative, imperial one so fashionable in Victorian England. According to Alan Sinfield:

Wilde's principal male characters do look and sound like the mid-twentieth century stereotype of the queer man. They are effete, camp, leisured or aspiring to be, aesthetic, amoral, witty, insouciant, charming, spiteful dandified. If these characters are not offered as homosexual (and generally they are pursuing women characters), the whole ambience reeks, none the less, of queerness. Or rather, it does for us. And so does Wilde himself (Sinfield 1994, vi).

Sinfield, in his study *The Wilde Century. Effeminacy, Oscar Wilde and the Queer Moment*, notes how Wilde's contemporaries "didn't see queerness in the way we have come to see it [...] Wilde was perceived as effeminate, to be sure; but not thereby as queer" (Sinfield 1994, vii). The term effeminacy up until Wilde, meant not being womanish, and consequently desiring men, but rather spending too much time *on* and *with* women, and consequently not being sufficiently occupied with proper manly pursuits. Wilde was, for sure, obsessed with fashion and interior design and he adored stars such as Sarah Bernhardt and Lilly Langtree, who, in their time, were the equivalent of today's pop celebrities; most importantly, in 1887 Wilde became editor of *The Woman's World* which thanks to contributions from prominent women writers, activists and actresses tried to change conventional attitudes to women's history and women's life. In short Wilde was displaying and supporting effeminacy in ways potentially threatening to the establishment.

In an article entitled "the Bi-social Oscar Wilde and 'Modern' Women" Stetz (2001) shows how Wilde was capable of moving freely between male and female environments, he regularly attended universities, offices, clubs but also women's drawing rooms and workplaces. Wilde's most interesting feature is, as queer theorists have shown, his liminality, his capacity of never taking sides, of rejecting a fixed, predictable, centralizing frame of mind, and so in his resistance to the irreconcilability of contradictory, even opposite realities.

In *Masculinity and Culture* John Beynon, dealing with masculinity in the Victorian age, contrasts Wilde with Eugene Sandow who in 1890s began to publish books on physical training which attracted a considerable readership; whereas Sandow "stood for normal masculinity and the improvement of the national and racial stock Wilde represented the abnormal and was the living embodiment of the debauched" (Beynon 2002, 44). In this sense, Wilde's humiliation was often considered as a victory for Imperial masculinity and, by implication, for national and imperial health. Yet the twentieth century will witness the crisis of the British empire and of the kind of masculinity associated with it. Paradoxically the defeat of Wilde implies the defeat of the Empire and the success of Wilde's performative paradigm of masculinity as something absolutely escaping. In the Twentieth and in the Twenty-First Century, Wilde's self-conscious construction of his identity and his performance of an ironic masculinity have become sources of inspiration for many artists such as Truman Capote, Andy Warhol, Stephen Fry (who played Oscar in Gilbert's 1997 film *Wilde*), David Bowie, Russell Brand, Pete Doherty and Morrissey in key fields such as music, literature, cinema and television, showing how the strength of Wilde's life and work also resides in its capacity of easily translating into non-literary modes.

Music and in particular popular music seems to be the discursive mode in which Wilde's performative paradigm seems to be more easily translatable. I opened this discussion with Todd Haynes' film which investigates the link between Wilde and glam rock; I'd like to close it by making reference to a singer by many considered the late twentieth century Wilde, namely Morrissey, solo artist and leader of the 1980s cult band The Smiths. Morrissey shares Wilde's love for flowers, his capacity of transcending genders, his conversational skill, in particular his taste for epigrams, and an iconoclastic stance on which the Smiths' masterpiece *The Queen is Dead* (1986) is based. Morrissey's awareness of the Importance of being Oscar, of playing Oscar, in Margaret Thatcher's repressive Britain, reminds us that Wilde is a subversive, critical, intelligent role that any of us might successfully perform and make our own in a world more and more de-humanizing.

References

Beynon J. 2002. *Masculinities and Culture*. Buckingham and Philadelphia: Open UP.

Bracewell M. 1997. *Oscar*. BBC documentary.

Coppa F. 2004. "Performance Theory and Performativity". In Roden F.S. (ed.) *Palgrave Advances in Oscar Wilde Studies*. Basingstoke: Palgrave Macmillan, 72-95.

Eagleton T. 1997. *Saint Oscar and Other Plays*. Oxford: Blackwell.

Ellmann R. 1987. *Oscar Wilde*. London: Penguin.

Haynes T. 1998. *Velvet Goldmine*. DNC home Entertainment (DVD).

Kaye R.A. 2004. "Gay Studies/Queer Theory and Oscar Wilde". In Roden F.S. (ed.) *Palgrave Advances in Oscar Wilde Studies*. Basingstoke: Palgrave Macmillan, 189-223.

Pearsall J. (ed.) 1999. *Oxford English Dictionary* (Concise). Oxford: Oxford University Press.

Schutz A. 1976. "Fragments on the Phenomenology of Music" in Smith F.J. (ed.) *In Search of Musical Method*. New York: Gordon and Breach Science Publishers, 23-49.

Sinfield A. 1994. *The Wilde Century: Effeminacy, Oscar Wilde and the Queer Moment*. London: Cassell.

Sloan J. 2003. *Oscar Wilde*. Oxford: Oxford University Press.

Smiths The. 1986. *The Queen is Dead*. London: Rough Trade (audio CD).

Stetz M.D. 2001. "The Bi-Social Oscar Wilde and 'Modern' Women". *Ninenteenth Century Literature*, Vol. 55, Issue 4, 515-537.

Waldrep S. 2004. *The Aesthetics of Self-Invention. Oscar Wilde to David Bowie*. Minneapolis: University of Minnesota Press.

FRANCESCO MINETTI

Università del Salento

White Negroes and Irish Brigades
in Joseph O'Connor's *Redemption Falls*

In his recent historical fiction, Joseph O'Connor combines a third-person narration with letters and newspaper cuttings, diaries and ballads, photos and cartoons, which help to recognize how deeply the main character, James O'Keefe, draws on personality traits and political choices of one of the most prominent nineteenth-century Irish nationalist leaders. The identity will come to light not only when O'Keefe is hounded down by a British spy in a remote village up in Montana, Redemption Falls:

> 'General O'Keefe, sir?' I asked.
> He gave me a meaning look. 'Who wants to know it?' came the sullen rejoinder. Here loomed before me 'O'Keefe the Blade' Old England's sworn foe; Young Ireland's banished hero (O'Connor 2007, 292).

The 'Blade' adjunct is consistently metamorphosed through puns and typographic ploys in reference to a fiery speech, which Thomas Francis Meagher delivered in Dublin to repeal the Act of Union as a source of national weakness: "To be strong a people must be self-reliant, self-ruled, self-sustained" (Griffith 1916, 29). After his arrest in 1848, Meagher challenged his jurors stating that the Young Irelanders' armed uprising "loses all its guilt, is sanctified as a duty, will be enobled as a sacrifice" (Cavanagh 1892, 294); and, with apparently similar feelings, the novelistic double covets his death for hanging, drawing and quartering at Bridewell Gaol:

> Revile the rapier? I shall never, sirs: Never. It will slash the slaver's knot which binds us to an alien crown, which strangles my countrymen in the chokehold of hunger. I kiss its redeeming hilt and touch it to this unworthy breast. Come: you may now slaughter me; but you will never be rid of me (O'Connor 2007, 18).

Yet, the retouch-job desacralizes the patriot's warlike and parochial mind revising the years after his capital sentence was commuted into a transportation to Tasmania. O'Connor drafts a plot of "elapsed, inconvenient, embarassing" exposures (O'Connor 2007, 78), which enlarges on a few fleeting hints that one of the prisoners of the penal colony dropped in his journal at "the lady of this sylvan hermitage" married by Meagher "some time before his escape" (Lyons 1886, 70, 64). Indeed, the desertion is not only meant to invest with iconoclastic irony a public oration, which the itinerant exile addressed to the New York City Coucil once arrived in America, when he declined any honour in recollection of his countrymen's captivity: "My heart is with them at this hour, and shares the solitude in which they dwell" (Meagher 1853, 315). O'Connor's protagonist, though feeling guilty and being brutalized with alchol, will send a letter to his Aborigenal son which urges him rather falsely to defend his coloured skin against abuses: "Any person that uses the term 'half-breed' about his fellow human being requires our prayers and our pity, for he is a failure". Readers are led to recall that the sender has railed at an Irish-American soldier, accusing him precisely of being an "half-breed" who disgraces "the name of IRELAND by claiming ancestry there". All the letter exemplifies therefore how Meagher's consciousness of being Irish superimposed his mythic primacy of blood affiliation upon a complex of ethnies, dialects and cultural sensibilities which collectively embodied the diaspora in America. The patriot counterfeits his beliefs: "I myself have Caribbean blood, from an ancestor who was once established at Jamaica", and likens himself implausibly to his son's visage: "So you see, dearest Robert, I am myself of 'the Negro race', whatever those words might signify" (O'Connor 2007, 195, 411).

Here as elsewhere in the novel, the tight weave of literary allusions exhumes a vituperative comparison which Thomas Carlyle drew between Irishmen and blacks in "Occasional Discourse on the Nigger Question". The essayst regretted in 1853 that in the West Indies the emancipated people were ruining the planters' sugar-crops in consequence of their innate laziness: "sitting yonder with their beautiful muzzles up to the ears in pumpkins, imbibing sweet pulps and juices", and yet he warned that Irish famine posed a more serious threat to the British rule, because among "that group of unsold, unbought, unmarketable Irish free citizens" there were "divine missionaries" who did not settle for humanitarian help. Carlyle unified the dangers of the Irish independence and slavery abolition, divulging a suasive stereotype of the white Negroes:

> To have "emancipated" the West Indies into a *Black Ireland*; "free" indeed, but an Ireland, and Black! The world may yet see prodigies; and reality be stranger than a nightmare dream. Our own white or sallow Ireland, sluttishly starving from age to age on its act-of-parliament "freedom", was hitherto the flower of mismanagement among the nations: but what will this be to a Negro Ireland, with pumpkins themselves fallen scarce like potatoes (Carlyle 1864, 3, 26, 5).

The creole image is variously recycled by O'Connor to blame all his expatriate characters for not feeling any sympathy with blacks in the United States. He intrudes into his story disputing, for instance, with Eliza Mooney and insinuating that her young brother is too brownish:

> You can be Irish and colored together, Eliza, that don't mean shit. Better to put black and white. But he aint a buckin zebra. Then 'Negro' and 'White'. But Jeddo don't look mulatto, so why mention that at all? Christ's sake, the ignorant melon-head thinks he's Mexicano. But who told him such a gum? You did, you liar (O'Connor 2007, 197-198).

As is signalled by the chapter-title of "The Fause Knight On The Road", he plays the part of a devil who in the medieval ballad incites a schoolboy to sail "in the wild sea" (Child 1866, 269), and amplifies the hellish suggestion narrating that Eliza hears an unintelligible song: "O I am a gallant blah blah blah, now that's just what I blah / For the United States of Tyranny, I do not give one blah". Eliza's thoughts erase the singer's blackness: "Colored. What does it mean? Does any one not have a color?". She wishes all people had a filmy skin like a jellyfish with "their innards and bones on display" and copes with the unavoidable difference imagining that in the world malignant faeries use to replace white newborns with black ones: "A changeling you'd be, and the world terrified to vex you". Her devotion to the Celtic heritage will prove fatal very soon, when she falls prey to Irish soldiers and is repeatedly raped:

> 'You are Irish', she continued quietly. 'I am Irish, too. My people come from Galway. Let me go and I won't tell. Your own mother come from Galway, I heard you say that before. I never even see you, I swear it'. 'Never even seed me?'. 'I swear to the Virgin'. 'You never heared lyin's a sin, girl?'. 'I'll do anythin you want. Only let me go away'. 'You'll do anythin I want, cause you don't got no choice, bitch'.

And, although the gang leader eventually marries Eliza to legitimate her son, O'Connor will mock dually at the law of honour, because one of his ballads makes things clearer declaiming that the groom has readily given up his prior black love:

> She wept for her outlaw, turned weeping away
> Then ghostly she vanished, that ebony phantom
> As shadows of night at the dawn of the day
> (O'Connor 2007, 199; 214, 224).

Among these characters' irrational fear, a fugitive slave is entitled to witness that racism derives from a vulnerability of social standing which might align black victims with Irish people: "Nigger ain no color, it the place you put to stand. I seen slaves white as milk". Elizabeth Longstreet's idiom is recorded to contest a nascent Irish-American organization, the Fenian Brotherhood, urging its members to understand that their dream of freedom does not prevent them from adopting other western masters' behaviours and interests:

> Mastuh a Irishman. O'Hara his name [...] Wolf got more nature than O'Hora [...] Do ever thing but kill you [...] Cause he paid for you, see. You a dollar to O'Hora. You was livestock [...] Want you in his lust; pick his harvest; tend his children; rawhide lash for the rest of it [...] Yes, his wife mustof knowed. Knowed ever thing he done [...] Then ride along to chapel on his chestnut bay. And his "Glory Be to Jesus" and his "Holy Queen Mary". Any of his kin gets [to] hear what he done, then bow their head for disgrace (O'Connor 2007, 105, 45).

Indeed, the report frames differently a tour of American cities, which Meagher made as "the Darling of Erin" in 1850s; a window bill of the travel plugs his arrival at Macon, Georgia, and notifies graphically with a pointing finger that "No Negroes" are admitted to listen to "his bravest hopes for our Motherland". But the novel is stuffed with clues which very timidly suggest and stigmatize Meagher's supposed racial prejudice. His black cook is compelled to live in a ghetto: "Miss O'Keefe come up an she an the General not too quiet. An it come to where I couldn abide the house no more", and these words are twisted in order to bare the patriot's fixed idea: "He was an odd fish for sure. Think too much on a thing". He is concerned only with renaming streets at Redemption Falls:

> The signs became contentious, were often torn down or altered to read obscenely. His deputies raised them again, made them larger, more solid. Some they surrounded with trenches and cut-wire. He was ordered to come to the courthouse and explain his decision; he refused to be summoned, claimed such a writ was illegal; were it repeated, he threatened, he would arrest the judge and declare martial law the width of the Territory. The streets would be named for the patriots of his homeland. If anyone couldn't live with it, let him go someplace else (O'Connor 2007, 47-48, 105, 162, 96).

Meagher would have act as a governor in Montana to present petitions, which asked that all Irish emigrants were allowed to settle in the newly-formed state, although they had fought during the Civil War in opposed trenches:

> KNOW THAT I, James O'Keefe, de facto Governor of this Territory, do hereby raise a PETITION TO THE UNITED STATES CONGRESS, to wit, that the name of this Territory shall henceforth be "NEW IRELAND" & that the place styled at present REDEMPTION FALLS, Territorial Capital and Administrative Seat, henceforth be incorporated and styled "DUBLIN CITY" & that Irish-born veterans of the lately defeated Confederacy be also permitted, with their dependants, to apply, so that a new dispensation may be fostered in the Republic with the TERRITORY OF NEW IRELAND its exemplar (O'Connor 2007, 96).

If readers give weight to these half-serious historical paradoxes, the very issue of Irish racism will appear to be raised in the novel mainly to question Meagher's political charisma. Actually, he revealed what slavery meant for him promulgating at the outbreak of the war that the preservation of the Republic was "the duty of us Irish citizens, who aspire to establish a similar form of government in our native land". He raised an ethnically based volunteer infantry regiment in the hope of being endorsed by the Congress in a future military action against Britain: "We could not hope to succeed in our effort to make Ireland a Republic without the moral and material aid of the liberty-loving citizens of these United States" (Cavanagh 1892, 369). In April 1861, this mere ambition was share by some New York ladies who embodied their dual loyalties to Ireland and to President Lincoln, presenting the soldiers both with a stars & stripes flag and a Fenian green one "having in the centre a richly embroidered Irish harp, with a sunburst above it and a wreath of shamrock beneath" (Conyngham 1867, 56). Conversely, in the novel the parade along Great Jones Street is described by a disaffected bystander, who stresses how the mob recruited by Meagher follow him "under a banner few had previously seen" and are led to death:

> Their leader had on a uniform of his own design – dark green, Bolivarian, Celtic harps on the epaulettes, a sash of golden braid, *caballero*'s boots. It would have been easy, as you observed from your drawing-room window, to have been amused by the sight of this felon and his rabble, for there was something of comic operetta in his appearance that morning, but more in the mien of his followers. The poor, about to die in an uncountable numbers, while you gorged behind the glass of your ironies (O'Connor 2007, 154).

The witness deplores thousands of Irish aliens, "the nobodies penciled as monkeys and monsters in the journals", who are all at once judged on the *Tribune* "with surprising sobriety" because they take arms "for the country that had spat on their children" (O'Connor 2007, 154). Particularly, he refers to to the Enrollment Act lines which, some years after the New York parade, stated that all male adults of "foreign birth" who had declared "their intention to become citizens" were forced to fill the ranks of the Federal Army. A glance at Irish volunteers' letters in 1863 can better help to understand that the conscription law was perceived as an unbearable cunning, which shattered not only Meagher's nationalist plans but also his soldiers' hard-headed hope of receiving the American citizenship in return for their service; for instance, Thomas Jones wrote from Fort Pulaski, Georgia, to his sister:

> The men are all discouraged and down-hearted; they feel themselves duped. I will tell you why. The army that is now in the field came out to put down the rebellion. Now they are fighting on a different scale than when the war first started. If they wanted an army to free the slaves I think they would have gotten a very small army (Macdonald 2007, 460).

As a result of his disappointment the soldier prognosticated an escalation of racist violence, ascribing it implicitly to Congressmen:

> [...] they say they will hang out to the last minute before they will give up the negro. They say that it is all we are fighting for. It is too bad that so many brave men have to sacrifice their lives for the sake of freeing the blacks and after it is accomplished, if it ever is, who is to thank the soldier for what he has suffered and endured since the war commenced? And still the cry is to free the nigger and let the cost be what it may to liberate no less than four million slaves and spread them all over the United States. Times are hard but they would be harder then. A nigger is more respected here now than the soldier is (Trimble 2000, 43-44).

In the same year various groups of aliens, many of them Irish-American workers, unleashed their anger in a great number of northern cities; in the State of New York, Governor Horatio Seymour issued an address to the people which seemed to exonerate the rioters: "I know that many of those who have participated in these proceedings would not have allowed themselves to such extremes of violence" and he advised them to get even with the Enrollment Act without vile attacks against property: "such persons are reminded that the only opposition to the conscription which can be allowed is an appeal to the courts" (Carey 1868, 347). As a matter of fact, a detailed account drawn up by the Metropolitan Police warned that "the evidences of violence were gathering apace; every unfortunate negro who appeared was chased and beaten"; blacks were not only lynched in the slums between Five Points and the present-day West Village; at the docks, policemen found "two negroes, one with his head terribly cut and his arm broken, the other only suffering from body bruises", and the Colored Orphan Asylum on 5th Avenue was besieged and assaulted: a portion of the five hundred children "escaped from their home by the rear as the dastardly and infamous mob forced an entrance in front and fired the building". A man returning from a bakery was hung to a lamp-post: "His body was left suspended for several hours. A fire was made underneath him and he was literally roasted"; some weeks later, two women were mourning for the dead when the widow, Mary Jones, identified him as her husband thanks to a surviving chunk of bread (Barnes 1863, 21, 24, 70, 115).

These stories are fully forgotten in *Redemption Falls*. O'Connor regrets that they have not yet become a subject of popular literature: "One of the most shameful atrocities in the history of Irish-America, it does not feature, to my knowledge, in Irish balladry", and, even though resorting to his mazy texture of narrating voices and forged documents, he stresses how a Southern editorial praises the New York hostilities and attributes them to Meagher: "he has raised the average intelligence of that CONFEDERATE city so that it approaches the national norm" (O'Connor 2007, 97). But more influential and moderate Irish speakers added fuel to the fire even before the Enrollment Act. An Irish-born judge, Charles Patrick Dale, informed his wife in 1862 that "recruiting was difficult enough now because of the everlasting Negro question" (Lydig Daly 2000, 177). In the same year, the first Archbishop of New York thundered in a letter to Union Secretary of War Cameron that the Irish troops "have not the slightest idea of carrying on a war, that costs so much blood and treasure, just to gratify a clique of Abolitionists" (Hassard 1866, 437).

References

Barnes D.M. (ed.) 1863. *The Draft Riots in New York, July 1863. The Metropolitan Police: Their Services During Riot Week, Their Honorable Record*. New York: Barker.

Carey M. (ed.) 1868. *The Democratic Speaker's Hand-book*. Cincinnati: Miami Public Company.

Carlyle T. 1864. *Collected Works*, Vol. XIII. London: Chapman.

Cavanagh M. 1892. *Memoirs of Gen. Thomas Francis Meagher, Comprising the Leading Events of His Career Chronologically Arranged, with Selections from His Speeches, Lectures and Miscellaneous Writings, Including Personal Reminiscence*. Worcester (Mass.): Messenger Press.

Child F.J. (ed.) 1866. *English and Scottish Ballads*, Vol. VIII. Boston: Little.

Conyngham D.P. 1867. *The Irish Brigade and its Campaigns*. New York: McSorley.

Griffith A. (ed.) 1916. *Meagher of the Sword. Speeches of Thomas Francis Meagher in Ireland 1846-1848*. Dublin: Gill.

Hassard J. 1866. *Life of the Most Reverend John Hughes, D.D.: First Archbishop of New York, with extracts from his private correspondence*. New York: Appleton.

Lydig Daly M. 2000. *Diary of a Union Lady, 1861-1865*. Lincoln: University of Nebraska Press.

Lyons W.F. 1886. *Brigadier-General Thomas Francis Meagher. His Political and Military Career*. New York: Sadlier.

Macdonald W. (ed.) 2007. *Documentary Source Book of American History 1606-1898*. New York: Macmillan.

Meagher T.F. 1853. *Speeches on the Legislative Independence of Ireland*. New York: Redfield.

O'Connor J. 2007. *Redemption Falls*, London: Harvill Secker.

Trimble R. (ed.) 2000. *The Civil War Letters of William, Thomas, and Maggie Jones 1861-1865*. Macon: Mercer U.P.

STEFANIA PORCELLI

Sapienza – Università di Roma

"Careless Talk Costs Lives": War Propaganda and Wartime Fiction in Elizabeth Bowen's *The Heat of the Day*

Elizabeth Bowen is one the writers that most poignantly convey the atmosphere of London during the Second World War (Wilson 1999, 7). As Heather Bryant Jordan puts it, "very little that marked wartime life escaped Bowen's pencil" (1992, 148). The aim of this paper is to investigate to what extent the slogans of war propaganda feature in Elizabeth Bowen's fiction of the Forties, in order to illuminate her complex attitude towards the great demands of WWII upon individual lives. Elizabeth Bowen questions home front propaganda at a linguistic level, the level at which she also interrogates her own works. I will take into consideration Bowen's prominent war novel, *The Heat of the Day* (1949), but I will also refer to one of her wartime short stories, "Careless Talk" (1945). Firstly, I would like to show that her narrative overtly or indirectly refers to war posters issued by the Ministry of Information during the war years. Secondly, I will analyse two key episodes in the novel, which focus on the different response of two female characters to war propaganda.

Like many British civilians, Bowen suffered the Blitz, and worked as an air raid warden. Yet, she also accepted to work for the Ministry of Information, writing confidential reports on the Irish attitude to the war. The Ministry, which – after a short activity in WWI – was re-established at the outbreak of WWII (MacLaine 1979, 12), was also in charge of co-ordinating domestic war propaganda in Britain. Its function was to sustain civilian morale through "weapons on the wall" (Vysny 2000) as they were sometimes called.[1] As means of propaganda, posters added to films, radio broadcasts, pamphlets, and newspaper or magazine articles. All this material enters Bowen's fiction, which turns out to be a place of intersection of literature and other forms of

---

[1] "Weapons on the Wall: British Propaganda Posters of the Second World War" is a website devised by Paul Vysny, available from http://www.st-andrews.ac.uk/~pv/pv/courses/posters/index.html (last accessed August 2011). All the posters I refer to in this paper can be found at this website. I will refer to the numeration given to them by Vysny.

communication, the product of a strong inter-textual and intermedial operation. Yet, while in *The Heat of the Day* Louie's wireless is said to be "by this time dead out, finished" (Bowen 1998, 147), I argue that posters and newspapers, i.e. printed propaganda, play a major role in Bowen's representation of wartime London.

Bowen's narrator overtly refers to war posters, especially to the anti-gossip campaign "Careless Talk Costs Lives".[2] "Careless Talk" is also the title of one of Bowen's short stories in the 1945 collection *The Demon Lover and Other Stories*, which suggests that secrecy takes top priority in wartime. War propaganda conveyed this idea in at least two ways: through humorous sketches or by means of threatening images. Posters by Fougasse (pen-name of Cyril Kennet Bird), for example, were drawn a funny cartoons rather than realistic images. Other posters dealing with the same issue were intended to induce a sense of guilt in the population: this is the case of Abram Games's posters (for instance "Your Talk May Kill Your Comrades" and "Talk Kills"; see Vysny 2000, 4.4 and 4.5) and of posters carrying the same caption as Fougasse's, but warning women with a reproachful, patronizing tone (among others, the 1940 poster "She Talked… This Happened"; see Vysny 2000, 4.13). Indeed, as Petra Rau remarks, women have no tenable position in relation to the propaganda discourse: "whether they talk too much, not at all or to the wrong people" (2005, 36).

Bowen's short story maintains the same tone as Fougasse's posters. In "Careless Talk", as Phyllis Lassner summarizes, "two men and two women at a fashionable restaurant try to understand the war by exchanging names of people they assume one another know" (Lassner 1991, 39). The situation clearly resembles one of Fougasse's pictures, namely the poster depicting a couple talking over a meal in a restaurant, while a Hitler figure eavesdrops from under the table (Vysny 2000, 4.11). One of the last sentences in Bowen's story even conveys the hope that "it doesn't matter my having told you that" (Bowen 1999a, 670), thus recalling the poster's ironic statement "of course there's no harm in your knowing".

The same phrase "careless talk" appears in *The Heat of the Day*, where Bowen refers either to Fougasse's series or to her own story. In the following passage, the protagonists Stella and Robert are questioning the identity of a third character, known by his surname Harrison:

> "My still having no idea who he is. He doesn't sound like anyone very special. I know you said he wasn't a commercial traveller, but I can't remember what you said he was."

---

[2] From February 1940 on, 2.5 million posters with the caption "Careless Talk Costs Lives" were distributed. However, this campaign concerned also British cinema, as many critics have shown. See, for example, Aldgate and Richards (1994); Chapman (1998).

"I think I just said he was not a commercial traveller... yes, he's always about."
"Perhaps he listens for careless talk." Robert yanked himself out of the deep armchair [...].
She answered: "Why – who's been talking carelessly?"
"Everyone, I imagine. You know how *I* talk" (Bowen 1998, 101, emphasis in the text).

Although the novel's characters think that "conversations are the leading thing in this war" (Bowen 1998, 63), they are quite conscious that "you never know [...] who may pick up what" (Bowen 1998, 62), as Roderick – Stella's son – states. The same warning appears in Fougasse's bus poster, warning that "you never know who's listening" (Vysny 2000, 4.7). Moreover, "Conversations at No. 10" (Bowen 1998, 153), which are held in Chilcombe Street between the subplot's characters Louie and Connie, are a clear parody of the far more important conversations at No. 10, Downing Street, where Churchill had to make decisions about the war. Thus, Bowen depicts war as a discursive, as well as a material activity.

When posters physically appear in the narration, they refer to other campaigns as well, mainly those belonging to the category "Savings and Austerity", according to Paul Vysny's categorization:[3]

[T]he fruiterer filled a longstanding void with fans of cardboard bananas and *a "Dig for Victory" placard*; the greengrocer's crates had been emptied of all but earth by those who had somehow failed to dig hard enough. The butcher flaunted unknown joints of purplish meat in the confidence that these could not be bought; the diary restricted itself to a china cow; the grocer, with costless courage, kept intact his stocks of dummy boxes of chocolate among flyblown cut-outs of pre-war blondes. Newsagents without newspapers gave out in angry red chalk that they had no matches either. Pasted *inside a telephone booth, a notice asked one to telephone less* (Bowen 1998, 73, emphasis added).

While the "Dig for Victory" campaign spurs people to do as much as possible, other campaigns ask for savings:

Stella kept glancing about at the other platforms, the shabby initialled seats, rusting enamelled advertisements which must have been here since Robert's boyhood, and *the new posters up to discourage travel*. Laudably little travel was on her conscience (Bowen 1998, 104, emphasis added).

---

[3] Vysny divides propaganda posters into six key themes and a general seventh category: specialist recruiting, industrial production, maintaining morale, security concern, saving and austerity, health and safety, and miscellaneous. Other categorizations are possible: e.g. one group could include posters referring to religious themes. Yet, it seems to me that all the themes of home front propaganda feature in Elizabeth Bowen's wartime fiction, except maybe the religious one (the idea that God was behind the British).

As Paul Vysny puts it:

The cost of waging total war imposed severe strains on Britain's limited economic resources, leading to appeals for public co-operation in financing the effort. This resulted not only in posters stressing the need for increased savings but also in campaigns against waste and unnecessary consumption, for the recycling of scarce materials, and for boosting food production from gardens and allotments (Vysny 2000, 5).

In order to convince the British people of the necessity of totally committing themselves to the sacrifices imposed upon them by the war, propaganda suggests a strong dichotomy between "us" and "them", as enacting the eternal struggle between good and evil. A famous poster hanging in the Imperial War Museum's section dedicated to WWII encourages civilians to save food by visually setting Churchill against Hitler and by means of a linguistic pun: "Better Pot-Luck with Churchill Today that Humble Pie under Hitler tomorrow. Don't waste Food!" (Vysny 2000, 5.11). The use of two different prepositions envisages the individual as part of a community in the first case ("with"), and as a slave in the other ("under"). Still, civilians have to play their part (i.e. not to waste food), if they want to keep their political freedom. As another of Fougasse's posters shows – "Waste the Food and Help the Hun" (Vysny 2000, 5.4), again about the restriction on food –, the idea is that those who do not actively help their country are in fact collaborating with the enemy.

Everybody is thus made responsible for every act they perform and for every word they utter. The anti-gossip campaign "Careless Talk Costs Lives" was specifically aimed at preventing the exchange of information of possible value to the enemy (MacLaine 1979, 82). In order to discourage this, the domestic propaganda also made up the existence of a Fifth Column, that was supposed to be everywhere and to have helped Hitler in the conquest of the continent (74). Spies, basically, that would pass information on to the Germans. On this idea of a leakage of information hinges *The Heat of the Day*, a novel that draws on Bowen's direct experience of the city under siege, as many critics have noticed. Yet, as Andrew Bennet and Nicholas Royle have argued, "the life of the novel is blotted out by the focus on the life of the author" (Bennet and Royle 1995, 15). In line with their suggestion that "Bowen's novels present dissolutions at the level of personal identity, patriarchy, social conventions and language itself – up to and including the language of fiction and criticism" (Bennet and Royle 1995, xix), I'd like to insist that the language of propaganda stands among the linguistic levels she questions. And to quote Catherine Belsey "it is in language that the ideology inscribed in the language can be challenged" (2002, 41).

According to these premises, I will now propose my reading of the two female characters' attitude towards the language of propaganda, and of their different perceptions of themselves in relation to the British population at war.

The first character I will focus on is Stella, the novel's protagonist. One of the first pieces of information about her is that Stella is a mother, and that her son has joined the army. The first chapters of the novel, thus, emphasise her duty as a citizen and as a woman towards the State, represented by the army and by Harrison, who will turn out to be a counter spy. The latter, however, is soon described as resembling "a German in Paris" (Bowen 1998, 44), that is like the enemy, by means of a simile that blurs the abovementioned contraposition between "us" and "them".[4] Stella stands apart from the conventional role of the proud mother of a British soldier, by creating a linguistic distance with regard to the army. In no way does Stella adhere to the linguistic dichotomy at the basis of (every) war propaganda.[5] Confronted with Harrison's blackmail, she states: "You have bludgeoned me with your perpetual 'we' – your 'we' is my 'they': what view would 'they' take of that?" (Bowen 1998, 40, emphasis added). Stella resists identification by questioning Harrison's use of pronouns. The use of the generic "they" eventually yields to the passive construction in relation to Roderick's enlistment: "whatever happened, whatever *was done* to him" (Bowen 1998, 48-49, emphasis added). Stella stands linguistically apart from Harrison, the army and war propaganda. Stella – the novel's main character – fears "dissolution never to be repaired" (Bowen 1998, 49) in the life of her son, after he has joined the army. Rather than military defeat or slavery under Hitler's regime, dissolution is her main concern.

Through Stella, the novel raises doubts about the possibility of any linguistic identification of the individual with others in a common "we". Identification would lead to the dissolution of the subject's individuality. On the contrary, working class Louie – the protagonist of *The Heat of the Day*'s subplot – strives to construct an identity of her own that would "fit into the paper's picture". The following passage from chapter n. 8 is revealing:

> Dark and rare were the days when she failed to find on the inside page of her paper an address to or else account of herself. Was she not a worker, a soldier's lonely wife, a war orphan, a pedestrian, a Londoner, a home- and animal-lover, a thinking democrat, a movie-goer, *a woman of Britain*, a letter writer, a fuel saver, and a housewife? She was *not a mother*, a knitter, a gardener, a foot-sufferer, or a sweetheart – at least not rightly. Louie now felt bad only about any part of herself which in any way *did not fit into the paper's picture*; she could not have survived their disapproval (Bowen 1998, 152, emphasis added).

---

[4] If so, however, Bowen fails to distinguish between Germans and Nazis, an identification which was, according to MacLaine, the essence of the so-call Anger Campaign started in 1940 and of domestic propaganda for the rest of the war (MacLaine 1979, 146ff).

[5] Writing before the war, Hans Speier stated in "Morale and Propaganda": "In modern war, in which mass opinions count, the enemy has to be wholly identified [...] with the principle of evil, so that one can mobilize the power of right for one's own cause" (qtd in MacLaine 1979, 137).

A "woman of Britain" like Stella, Louie is nevertheless Stella's counterpart, since she is not a mother. Not only does she need the newspapers' words to perceive that "she *had* got a point of view, and not only a point of view but the right one" (Bowen 1998, 152, Bowen's emphasis), but she also speaks the language of propaganda:

> Still, you'd surely not rather be like the Germans, Conny? I was told how they swallow anything they are told. I know I saw where it said how they do have papers, but not like our ones with ideas. It said how to get *them* through the war they have to kid them along, but how the war makes us think (Bowen 1998, 154, Bowen's emphasis).

While insisting, on a surface level, on the difference between "us" and "them", Louie links the two populations by using the same verb in the passive form ("I was told", "they are told"). Yet, at least superficially Louie's speech mirrors the Anti-German campaign, along with the Ministry's campaign sustaining civilian morale. The pronoun "we" has already reappeared in this chapter:

> She did not rally till next evening, when her paper came out strongly in favour of non-standoffishness – it appeared that *we* were becoming less standoffish; the Americans had been agreeably surprised. *War now made us one big family...* she was reinstated; once again round her were the everlasting arms (Bowen 1998, 152-153, emphasis added).

In her love for newspapers, in her conviction that "Britain could always, in default of anything else, face facts" (Bowen 1998, 151), Louie is the literary personification of the sentiment expressed in a pamphlet – issued by the Ministry of Information and called *Eve in Overalls* – on the contribution of women to the war effort: "Private interests [...] are giving way more and more to those of the community. There is no longer room for privilege and class interest" (qtd in MacLaine 1979, 154). This idea of the blurring of the barriers between classes and individuals emerges both in Bowen's autobiographical essays (for instance, in "London, 1940") and throughout *The Heat of the Day* (Bowen 1998, 92 and 195). However, it's Louie who states: "we women are all in the same boat" (Bowen 1998, 237), ultimately referring the communal "we" to the community of the women. Louie, unlike Stella, seems to be the perfect addressee of war propaganda.

References

Aldgate A., Richards J. 1994. *Britain Can Take It: The British Cinema in the Second World War*. Edinburgh: Edinburgh University Press.

Belsey C. 2002. *Critical Practice*. London: Routledge.

Bennet A., Royle N. 1995. *Elizabeth Bowen and the Dissolution of the Novel*. London: Macmillan.

Bowen E. 1945. *The Demon Lover and Other Stories*. London: Jonathan Cape.

Bowen E. 1998. *The Heat of the Day*. London: Vintage.

Bowen E. 1999a. *The Collected Stories of Elizabeth Bowen*. London: Vintage.

Bowen E. 1999b. "London, 1940". In Lee H. (ed.) *The Mulberry Tree, Writings of Elizabeth Bowen*. London: Vintage, 21-25.

Chapman J. 1998. *The British at War: Cinema, State and Propaganda, 1939-45*. London-New York: IB Tauris.

James D., Thomson R. (2007) *Poster and Propaganda in Wartime* (in asociation with the Imperial War Museum). London-Sidney: Franklin Watts.

Jordan H.B. 1992. *How Will the Heart Endure? Elizabeth Bowen and the Landscape of War*. Ann Arbor: University of Michigan Press.

Lassner Ph. 1991. *Elizabeth Bowen: A Study of the Short Fiction*. New York: Twayne.

MacLaine I. 1979. *Ministry of Morale: Home Front Morale and the Ministry of Information in World War II*. London: George Allen & Unwin.

Rau P. 2005. "The Common Frontier: Fictions of Alterity in Elizabeth Bowen's *The Heat of the Day* and Graham Greene's *The Ministry of Fear*". In *Literature and History*, 14, 1, 31-55.

Vysny P. 2000. "Weapons on the Wall: British Propaganda Posters of the Second World War", available at http://www.st-andrews.ac.uk/~pv/pv/courses/posters/index.html (last accessed August 2011).

Wilson A. 1999. "Introduction". In Bowen E. *The Collected Stories of Elizabeth Bowen*. London: Vintage.

PAOLA DANIELA SMECCA

Università di Catania

The Role of Memory in Ian McEwan's *Atonement*

Ian McEwan's *Atonement* is perhaps a contemporary British novel in which historical and private experiences are most convincingly combined. The main plot – Briony's attempt to undo the evil she had unwillingly inflicted when she was a thirteen-year-old child – intertwines with the history of World War II and of one of the most painful national wounds, i.e. the British retreat to Dunkirk in May and June 1940.

Memory is one of the keywords of this novel. In fact, different levels of memory overlap in *Atonement*: the literary memory of British fiction from Jane Austen onwards, the historical memory of a military disaster during the Second World War, and the individual character's family memory recollecting a sequence of events dating back sixty-four years.

The parallelisms with literature are suggested by the epigraph of the novel, where McEwan quotes from Austen's *Northanger Abbey* (1818). As the author himself acknowledged, his source of inspiration for his protagonist Briony Tallis was Austen's heroine, Catherine Morland, who is guilty of distorting the reality around her with her hyperactive imagination nurtured on literature (Gothic fiction in Catherine's case). Yet, while Catherine's mistakes are comical and do not bring about tragic consequences for others, Briony's deluded perceptions have terrible effects on two of the other characters' lives: her sister Cecilia and their cleaning lady's son, Robbie Turner. Unlike Austen, however, McEwan does not focus on the crime in itself, but rather on its consequences and on the following desire for atonement Briony believes she can achieve through writing, by telling her own story and giving it a happy ending.

Briony's perception, which gives origin to the terrible *dénouement* of the events, is distorted by two concomitant circumstances: on the one hand, her fondness of literature and her reading of folktales and romances, in which there is always a villain who attempts to destroy the heroine's virtue and is doomed to be condemned; on the other, her youth, which prevents her from having a full understanding of "the ways of the world" (McEwan 2002, 6). Her ignorance of adult behaviour eventually leads her to draw erroneous conclusions and to commit her crime: her lie when she accuses the innocent Robbie of sexually assaulting her cousin Lola.

Intertextual connections are not limited to the epigraph however, but are scattered throughout the novel and engage the reader's literary memory. McEwan himself defined *Atonement* his "Jane Austen novel" and, besides *Northanger Abbey*, there are several elements drawn from *Mansfield Park* (1814): for example, the country house setting, the rehearsal of a play that is not performed in the end, and the sexual predator from London. Moreover, the extensive use of free indirect speech in order to reproduce the consciousness of the characters is a narrative device pioneered by Jane Austen and brought to perfection by modernist writers.

In the opening pages, Briony devotes herself to the rehearsal of a play she has written in honour of her brother Leon, entitled *The Trials of Arabella*. This youthful work, clearly influenced by traditional folktales and melodrama, is an optimistic play in rhymed couplets in imitation of Shakespeare's comedies, with a moralistic tone and a final happy ending brought about by the heroine's amendment (she abandons her family to run off with her beloved but wicked count against her parents' will; then she is abandoned by him and falls into poverty and despair before meeting a prince who will marry her and restore love and happiness).

The quarrel between Cecilia and Robbie over the vase near the Italianate fountain recalls the love scene at the Italian fountain in Evelyn Waugh's *Brideshead Revisited* (1945). This is the climactic scene of the novel, when the series of misunderstandings begin. Through a window of the nursery room, Briony sees (or rather, believes she sees) Robbie imperiously ordering Cecilia to remove her clothes and dive in the fountain. The narrator soon clarifies that it was easy for the girl to get everything wrong and that this dumb show "survived in memory, in three separate and overlapping memories" (McEwan 2002, 41). The episode is, in fact, seen from three different points of view in the novel. The scene was first seen from Cecilia's point of view and conveyed quite a different interpretation: her actions were not the result of Robbie's command, but her reaction to the offer of masculine help and her desire to affirm her independence and superiority. As Robbie was responsible for breaking the vase although he wanted to help her fill it with water, she decided that by "denying his help, any possibility of making amends, was his punishment" (McEwan 2002, 30). Thus it was she who wanted to humiliate him! Although Cecilia did not know why she was so angry with him, Robbie was more aware of his feelings and had already understood his awkwardness was a consequence of his being in love with her.

Yet literature is not only a source for inter-textual parallelisms, but also a theme. After the unsuccessful rehearsals of her play with her cousins, Briony ponders the advantages and drawbacks of writing drama and recognizes she would do better to dedicate herself to fiction:

> She felt the attraction of the neat, limited and controllable form she had left behind when she decided to write a play. A story was direct and simple, allowing nothing to come between herself and her reader – no intermediaries with their private ambitions or incompetence, no pressures of time, no limits on resources. In a story you only had to wish, you only had to write it down and you could have the world; in a play you had to make do with what was available: no horses, no village streets, no seaside. No curtain. […] A story was a form of telepathy. By means of inking symbols onto a page, she was able to send thoughts and feelings from her mind to her reader's (McEwan 2002, 37).

Briony naively deems writing and reading fiction as a magical process where symbols can be understood easily. Before becoming aware of the multiple points of view which make reality multi-faceted and difficult to categorize, one of her faults is due to her eagerness for control, her sense for order and her wish to classify things, which can be seen in her search for the proper definition.

Later, she would turn to modernist techniques when, at the age of eighteen, she would write a fictionalised account of that fountain episode which marked the starting point of the tragedy caused by her misinterpretation. This was the novella entitled *Two Figures by a Fountain* which she sent to Cyril Connolly, editor of the literary journal *Horizon*. The critic judged the story to be too much in imitation of Virginia Woolf, but placed her in the tradition of British female fiction of the 1930s. In the long letter which accompanies his restitution of the draft, he informs her that another writer, Elizabeth Bowen, liked her short story and found some similarities with Rosamond Lehmann's *Dusty Answer* (1927). Lehmann was a successful author in the interwar period and was loosely associated with the Bloomsbury group. In this novel, which was also her first, the protagonist Judith quite provocatively goes to study at Cambridge. This element, which connects Judith with the character of Cecilia in *Atonement*, is also autobiographical, because Lehmann studied English at Girton and this was considered daring and unusual in the Twenties.

In his introduction to a recent edition of *Dusty Answer*, the contemporary critic Jonathan Coe suggested that Lehmann's prose style, an alternation of memories and facts mainly rendered through the stream-of-consciousness technique, affected teenagers with its "concentrated mixture of embarrassment and pleasure" (Coe 2000). This comment could fit Briony, as she was eighteen years old at that time. Moreover, Briony acknowledges her debt to Virginia Woolf, because not only did she read *The Waves* three times but also, aware of the great transformations in human life, she became convinced that:

> only fiction, a new kind of fiction, could capture the essence of the change. To enter a mind and show it at work, or being worked on, and to do this within a symmetrical design – this would be an artistic triumph (McEwan 2002, 282).

Literature is also discussed by the other two main characters, Cecilia and Robbie, who study at Cambridge and openly comment on literary matters: Cecilia is engaged in the reading of Richardson's *Clarissa* which she finds so boring while she would rather read Fielding any day; Robbie disagrees with Leavis' conception of literature as "the core" of existence. To him, "the study of English literature seemed in retrospect an absorbing parlour game, and reading books and having opinions about them, the desirable adjunct to a civilised existence". Yet, it was not "the most vital pursuit of an enquiring mind"; so, in order to develop skills far more elaborate than the ones required in literary criticism, he decided to become a doctor, aware of the fact that "he would be a better doctor for having read literature" (McEwan 2002, 91-92).

With a more practical approach, Emily Tallis believes literature is useless in life and a vain subject at university. She thus criticises her daughter Cecilia, who "had lolled about for three years at Girton with the kind of books she could equally have read at home – Jane Austen, Dickens, Conrad, all in the library downstairs, in complete sets", and exclaims: "How had that pursuit, reading the novels that others took as their leisure, let her think she was superior to anyone else?" (McEwan 2002, 152). She approved of Paul Marshall who had a degree in chemistry and had invented a chocolate bar without cocoa butter, which would make him a millionaire.

After Briony's indictment and Robbie's imprisonment, the two lovers use quotes from famous British writers and literary characters as codes in their letters: Robert refers to Prometheus, "chained to a rock, his liver devoured daily by a vulture" (McEwan 2002, 204), while Cecilia quotes from W. H. Auden's 1939 poem *In Memory of W. B. Yeats* and identifies with the patient Griselde, but also compares her unhappy love with those of Tristan and Isolde, the Duke Orsino and Olivia, Troilus and Criseyde, Mr Knightley and Emma, Venus and Adonis.

Part Two describes the British soldiers hurrying to Dunkirk from 24 May to 4 June 1940, after the German invasion of the Netherlands and the collapse of Belgium. This section consists in a novel within a novel, as it is a realistic portrait of the British troops fleeing through the French countryside, and it is connected to the previous part of the novel only by the character of Robbie Turner.

Here, where the great memory of the war alternates with memories of an individual soldier's past, his presence allows the fictional story to develop: through Robbie's memory readers learn what happened after Briony's lie. The events are made more dramatic by the perception that soldiers were not an impersonal group fighting for their mother-country, but had single, private stories and lives. This awareness is also attributed by McEwan to Bernard, one of the main characters in *Black Dogs*, who saw the recently concluded war not as a historical, geopolitical fact but as a multiplicity, a near-infinity of private sorrows, as a boundless grief minutely subdivided without diminishment among individuals who covered the continent like dust (McEwan 1992, 140).

As in *The Innocent*, McEwan portrays here "how private lives are worked out against the backdrop of world historical events" (Gussow 2002). Individual memories are contrasted with the manipulations of historical memories made by single individuals, such as biographers and realist writers, and by the institutions which tend to construct a mythologized (and therefore fake) version of 'the history'. The evacuation from Dunkirk was a military failure transformed by the government and newspapers into a successful strategy. What was factually a disaster was changed in the national memory into the turning point which led the British people to react, fight on and upturn the destiny of the war. As the critic Dominic Head points out:

> McEwan's portrayal of the retreat to Dunkirk as a hellish ordeal puts a different perspective on a historical event usually viewed, through a patriotic lens, as a rescue of heroic proportions (Head 2007, 156).

The historical memory may be altered by two filters: the historians' voluntary intentions and the individuals' unconscious deformation of events. Robbie's memory, which seems to be the source of all information in Part 2, fails near the end and, as a consequence of shell shock, he begins to suffer from amnesia:

> Periodically, something slipped. Some everyday principle of continuity, the humdrum element that told him where he was in his own story, faded from his use, abandoning him to a waking dream in which there were thoughts, but no sense of who was having them. No responsibility, no memory of the hours before, no idea of what he was about, where he was going, what his plan was. And no curiosity about these matters (McEwan 2002, 246).

The Imperial War Museum in London is the repository of British national memory. In his *Acknowledgements*, McEwan declared he searched in its archives for "unpublished letters, journals and reminiscences of soldiers and nurses serving in 1940", and borrowed other details from Gregory Blaxland's *Destination Dunkirk* (1973), Walter Lord's *The Miracle of Dunkirk* (1982), and Lucilla Andrews' *No Time for Romance* (1977). While Blaxland's is a history book from which McEwan took the logistic information about the evacuation, the other two works are chronicles rich in autobiographical anecdotes. Lord's book was McEwan's source for the attack on the RAF man who is charged with being responsible for the absence of RAF cover during the retreat, even though he is a simple clerk. He risks being lynched and is saved by Robbie and his two companions. This episode allows McEwan, as usual in his narrative production, to analyse man's behaviour when facing a moment of crisis and to focus on the aggressiveness of human impulses.

Andrews' autobiography provides him with the descriptions of Briony's nursing activities at St. Thomas's Hospital in Part 3. It is the source for both the account of removing pieces of shrapnel from a soldier's body and Briony's talk with a dying soldier (including the subtle revelations, such as her naivety as she does not grasp he is going to die from the Sister's instruction not to wear a mask).

This transformation of private memories into fictional accounts raises a moral question about the writer's right to exploit other people's lives for his/her own literary ambitions. Symmetrically, within the narrative, the protagonist (and fictional author) Briony confesses she drew the information for writing Part 2 from the soldiers' letters found in the Imperial War Museum. In order to make Robbie's experience more credible and accurate, however, she maintains she also relied on the direct account provided by Corporal Nettle, one of Robbie's companions during his march to Dunkirk. To recount these events, McEwan also drew on his own family memory, as his father took part in the retreat: he was a dispatch rider on a motorbike when he got his legs shot up. This autobiographical episode is included in the novel.

Nothing is left to the imagination in the description of the war scenes in France and at St. Thomas's Hospital in London. The coldness and detached hyper-realism with which they are narrated are typical of McEwan's prose style and link *Atonement* to his previous literary outcomes, above all to *The Innocent*. The precise details of Briony nursing the casualties in the retreat and her descriptions of the wounds and the amputations in the soldiers' bodies do not attempt to raise any sentimentalism or compassion in the reader.

To question the difference between what is real and what is imaginary, McEwan has Robbie's memory fail in the end. Before dying, due to a fever, Robbie is overcome by delirium. This weakness of the human mind establishes a parallelism with Briony's character who longs to finish her novel before vascular dementia causes the loss of her memory. The loss of memory, in fact, implies a loss of identity and it is paradoxical that the greater awareness reached with maturity should give way to loss of memory while ageing. The illness adds to the importance bestowed on memory and represents a kind of retaliation for having spent her whole life revisiting such a crucial day in her past.

As in fancy, truth does not exist in memory. Memory is a fluid thing which can easily be manipulated. The power of the imagination not only alters perceptions but also modifies the interpretations of past actions. Therefore, a single episode may be seen in different ways from different perspectives and according to one's mood. An example is Briony's diving into the swimming pool when she was ten, which is interpreted by Robbie first as a reckless act, a "stupid thing"(McEwan 2002, 231), later as evidence of her crush on him. Briony, on the contrary, considers it as a spontaneous action soon forgotten, but can the reader trust her? If the narrator sees events through tinted glasses, then the reader can count on nothing.

The three levels of memory (literary, historical and individual) are connected in the afterword, headed "London, 1999", when the historical memory mixes with private memories and triggers a meta-narrative debate which connects this novel to the British literary tradition with its several fictional strands. In fact, the novel draws from the British literary tradition its postmodernist structure and metafictional frame. I agree with the literary critic David Lodge when he points out that it is the last section which makes *Atonement* a postmodernist work, with its introduction of the first-person narrator (Lodge 2002, 87). Besides being an instance of postmodernist metafiction (as the narrator is a writer who describes the most significant event in her life and discusses the ethics of writing), the novel also revisits all the literary genres in Western culture (from folktales to drama, from realism to modernism). The metafictional frame indicates the novel is Briony's final draft completed in London 1999 and to be published in 2001 after her death.

The afterword also adds a second ending: while Part Three ends with the imagined re-union of the two lovers, the afterword reveals that the two lovers "actually" died during the war (Robbie from septicaemia and Cecilia during the bombing at Balham tube station). This double ending confirms the moral question about the writer's right to manipulate real life events. Like Briony, McEwan is also guilty of exploiting other people's misfortune as useful material for his novels. Yet, for McEwan there is no possibility of consolation: Briony will not find atonement through storytelling.

The novel ends with Briony's grand-children who for her birthday perform her old play, *The Trials of Arabella*, in the old Tallis' country-house, now changed into Tilney's Hotel (again echoing *Northanger Abbey*). This play makes the structure of the novel recursive, as it pretends to end as it had begun with fundamental variations in-between: a new generation acting the play, a whole life (64 years) lived in the meanwhile, and two people dead because of someone's actions.

With this novel, McEwan manages to achieve two goals: on the one hand, he exposes the mechanisms of construction of fake national myths and of private family histories; on the other, he ensures his place in the British literary tradition.

References

Andrews L. 1977. *No Time for Romance: An Autobiographical Account of a Few Moments in British and Personal History*. London: Harrap.

Coe J. 2000. "Introduction". In Lehmann R. *Dusty Answer* [1927]. London: Virago.

Gussow M. 2002. "A Cool Writer Warms Up: Ian McEwan's Latest Novel Charts an Emotional Journey". In *The New York Times*, April 23.

Head D. 2007. *Ian McEwan*. Manchester: Manchester University Press.

Lodge D. 2002. *Consciousness and the Novel*. London: Secker & Warburg.

Lord W. 1998. *The Miracle of Dunkirk* [1982]. Ware: Wordsworth Editions.

McEwan I. 1992. *Black Dogs*. London: Jonathan Cape.

McEwan I. 2002. *Atonement*. London: Vintage.

ANNA ENRICHETTA SOCCIO

Università Gabriele d'Annunzio, Chieti-Pescara

A Portrait of a Poet as an Exile: the Case of Philip Larkin

> I don't want to go around pretending to be me.
> Philip Larkin, *Required Writings* (1983)

1. Eager to define the new relationships amongst literature, readers and criticism, the poet Laura Riding Jackson bravely discussed the state of twentieth-century poetry in an article that appeared in *PN Review* in 1987. She argued that, in our contemporary world, literary thinking requires new definitions of the ideas of "poetry" and "poet" since literature itself no longer belongs to the area of human understanding. Rather, it has been reduced to "a historical backdrop against which to set up the special case of the immediate twentieth-century human being" (Riding Jackson 1987, 71). As a consequence,

> the poet no longer represents, in his intensities of care in word-choice, a common impulse to a high degree of achievement in truth of utterance. He represents the individual human being as desiring to give forceful expression to the individual sense he makes of existence in his heightened consciousness of himself as a modern human being: the sense he makes of existence is the sense he makes of *his* existence (Riding Jackson 1987, 71).

Despite its being almost entirely based on the different idea of human person that was originated by intellectual modernism, Riding Jackson's analysis quite interestingly describes the transformation of human identity "as collectively identified in men" into "concrete individuality of men" (Riding Jackson 1987, 76). That is to say, the poet would speak only *of* and *for* himself, and poetry would be a mythology of private personality.

On a first reading Philip Larkin's poetry can be taken for the tangible, unambiguous manifestation of an eccentric, even paranoid existence of a desperately cynical, nihilistic, and half-frustrated middle-class librarian. His most famous verse – "They fuck you up your mom and dad" ("This be the Verse"), "When I see a couple of kids / And guess he's fucking her [...]" ("High Windows"),

"Books are a load of crap" ("A Study of Reading Habits") – are ascribed to his notion that life is something essentially elusive, dull and unsatisfactory. For this reason, Larkin's poetry has often been regarded as a matter of "private personality". Indeed, if on the one hand it somehow mirrors the poet's life, on the other hand the many comments scattered throughout his non-poetical writings often enhance the sensation that literary product and real experience are perversely intertwined.

Still, a closer analysis reveals that autobiography and authorial opinions ought not to be taken into too great a consideration when looking at the poetic text itself. This approach will open a completely different world in which hermeneutic complexity and technical virtuosity emerge as more than mere aesthetic artifices. Characteristically, instead, these artifices loom in Larkin's macrotext as distinctive features that allow the poet to be constructed on the artistic plane. Yet, along with craftsmanship lies Larkin's notorious minimalism – both formal and imaginative. In a 1979 interview, he tersely said: "[...] there is not much to *say* about my work. When you've read a poem, that's it, it's all quite clear what it means" (Larkin 1983, 53-54, emphasis in the text). Although his main concern is to write about everyday human experience in the simplest and most straightforward words, one cannot escape the feeling that Larkin is not writing about himself (the man and/ or the poet) but about the condition of being a Poet.

After publishing *The North Ship* in 1945, his intensely subjective and Yeats-inspired first collection, Larkin was in search of a more distinctive voice. In 1982 he confessed: "After finishing my first books, say by 1945, I thought I had come to an end. [...] My personal life was rather harassing. Then in 1950 I went to Belfast, and things reawoke somehow" (Larkin 1983, 68). Interestingly enough, the process of finding his own way implied isolation and loneliness that he experienced in a voluntary exile to Northern Ireland where, between 1950 and 1955, he held the post of sub-librarian at Queen's University, Belfast. Despite the uncomfortable sense of separateness from home, those years were very prolific and definitely speeded that process (Larkin 1983, 58). The Northern Irish adventure originated some memorable poems in the typical Larkinian manner. In this phase, the semantic nuclei of his poetics are already fully disclosed: failure, death, boredom, the fragility of ordinary humanity, and the universality of human misery find aesthetic meaning in the framework of conventional poetic structures. Most revealing of all is "The Importance of Elsewhere", written three months after his returning to England. It is a poem which gives the poet's account of what exile meant for him:

"The Importance of Elsewhere"

Lonely in Ireland, since it was not home,
Strangeness made sense. The salt rebuff of speech,
Insisting so on difference, made me welcome:
Once that was recognised, we were in touch.

Their draughty streets, end-on to hills, the faint
Archaic smell of dockland, like a stable,
The herring-hawker's cry, dwindling, went
To prove me separate, not unworkable.

Living in England has no such excuse:
These are my customs and establishments
It would be much more serious to refuse.
Here no elsewhere underwrites my existence
(Larkin 1988, rev. edn 2003, 105).

As can be noticed, the traditional three-stanza structure appears perfectly functional to convey the poet's sense of loneliness and strangeness in a foreign country – in order to emphasise its foreignness, Belfast synecdochically stands for Ireland, and equally Ireland, being "not home", stands for "elsewhere". Although with a note of nostalgia (Swarbrick 1995, 94), the poem explores the feelings of an exile who seeks to grasp the essence of his sense of belongingness. Sound patterning, and in particular the alternation of perfect and imperfect rhymes (*home/welcome, speech/touch, faint/went*), sound repetition, and symmetry in phrasing – provide the necessary rhythm to configure the poet who is seen in the attempt to describe his relationship with the place in which he is living. But, however strange and unfamiliar that "elsewhere" can appear, loneliness is not regarded as a negative condition. Surprisingly, it is a pre-existent condition that allows the speaker to be aware of his own identity. As John Goodby aptly notes, "[...] it is feeling 'lonely' there which makes 'sense' of the poet's felt 'strangeness', a condition which he implies existed before his move" (Goodby 1989, 133). Line 2 is self-evident: "Strangeness made sense", that is to say, only exile can reveal the secrets of our inner selves. Therefore, "The Importance of Elsewhere" is not a poem on the Irish/English antithesis, rather it paints a transnational landscape where familiar and unfamiliar, home and exile become original concepts whose respective definitions are largely mixed and confused.

That "place is contingent" (Booth 2005, 138) is further confirmed in the last stanza which is, from the viewpoint of the formal composition, quite the reversal of the first stanza, as a series of binary oppositions makes clear:

$_1$ Lonely in Ireland	*vs.*	$_9$ Living in England
$_2$ Strangeness	*vs.*	$_{10}$ my customs and establishments
$_3$ welcome	*vs.*	$_{11}$ refuse

These pairings emphasise the antithesis here/there, but the poet recognizes with contempt that "here", namely "home-England", may equally be regarded as an "elsewhere" that cannot "underwrite [his] existence". There is neither difference nor point of intersection between the opposites, since exile can be experienced at home as well as elsewhere. In the last line, which sounds almost like a verdict on and from the speaker, loneliness becomes the most suitable condition for the poet who, no matter the place or time, feels the collision between the self and the others.

From a sort of exilic island, the poet builds his own world, so admirable in its being marginalized yet pluralistic since it combines two kinds of experience, two distinct cultures. In this sense, Larkin's dualism is ontologically remarkable because it entails a sense of the self and of humanity as made of "difference". It suggests, moreover, that (spiritual) isolation is a privileged condition to which the Poet has to aspire if he/she wants to be endowed with space enough for the full expression of his/her individuality. Whatever place the Poet chooses, then, the acceptance of differences allows him/her to grasp the ungraspable, in moments of visions that generate art: "The sense of exclusion is turned into the reward of art" (Bayley 1988, 205).

2. That Larkin, in the form of his characters who are recurrently outsiders, has been exploring the conflicts between personal identity and community is even more explicitly dramatized in "Places, Loved Ones", written one year earlier in Belfast. This is another poem that tackles the poet's sense of an "elsewhere":

"Places, Loved Ones"

No, I never found
The place where I could say
This is my proper ground,
Here I shall stay;
Nor met that special one
Who has an instant claim
On everything I own
Down to my name;

To find such seems to prove
You want no choice in where
To build, or whom to love;
You ask them to bear
You off irrevocably,
So that it's not your fault
Should the town turn dreary,
The girl a dolt.

Yet, having missed them, you're
Bound, none the less, to act
As if what you settled for
Mashed you, in fact;
And wiser to keep away
From thinking you still might trace

Uncalled-for to this day
Your person, your place
(Larkin 1988, rev. edn 2003, 46)

Underlying the speaker's voluntary loneliness is the idea that free will is the only way towards self-definition. Not only does it permit the individual to protect himself from hostile, indifferent society, but it also minimizes the danger of deception and suffering. In Larkin's *Weltanschauung*, this sense of autonomy and selfhood can be expressed, as Lolette Kuby's astutely suggests, "only as a negative" (Kuby 1974, 61). Indeed, the prevailing isotopy of negation – we cannot help noticing the recurrence of negative lexemes ($_1$ *No*, $_1$ *never*, $_5$ *Nor*, $_7$ *no*, $_{11}$ *not*, $_{14}$ *none*) – conveys the notion that the choice of loneliness and, therefore, detachment from the ordinary habits of society is a direct consequence of one's freedom of action. Further, the poem's tripartite structure draws our attention to different stages of the dilemma (Osborne 2008, 109):

STANZA 1 = the speaker has found neither a place to put down roots nor a person with whom to share his life
STANZA 2 = the speaker rejects any responsibility in case of failure whenever the choice is made
STANZA 3 = the speaker realizes that life, as ironic intertwining of the comic and the tragic, imposes its rules, whatever the individual may desire or do.

This is Larkin at his best. Just as Thomas Hardy combines the two views of humanity as both responsible for its fortune and victim of blind fate, so Larkin depicts his characters as trapped in the conflict between the ideal and the real, what they would like to be and what they really are. For this reason, choosing to live forever in an "elsewhere" (that is, in other words, a "no-where") appears a comfortable, yet vulnerable condition for the poet who, poised in a spiritual limbo, can more easily distance himself from the emotional implications of the reality he observes around him. The extreme self-consciousness gained from the reflection on the world from the angle of an outsider allows both poet and reader to overcome the limits of disappointment and frustration. On the other hand, this "defensive" strategy entails grasping fragments of reality only with an ample load of irony as well as empathy.

In such a privileged intersection between "here" and "there", once the difference between "I" and "they" is recognized, epiphanic visions follow. This happens, for example, in one of the most anthologized yet remarkable poems written by Larkin, "Here". It is the record of a train journey from the south to the north of England where country landscape, cityscape and seascape assume a life of their own becoming, thus, highly symbolic in their simple reality. After twenty-four descriptive lines, the traveller arrives at a place

> [...] where removed lives
> Loneliness clarifies. Here silence stands
> Like heat. Here leaves unnoticed thicken,
> Hidden weeds flower, neglected waters quicken,
> Luminously-peopled air ascends;
> And past the poppies bluish neutral distance
> Ends the land suddenly beyond a beach
> Of shapes and shingle. Here is unfenced existence:
> Facing the sun, untalkative, out of reach
> (Larkin 1988, rev. edn 2003, 79-80)

Although it is tempting to identify the poem's "here" with the north-west coast of England[1] as the real destination and end of the journey, we realize that this ultimate end is not real at all. *Here* "silence stands / Like heat"; *here* is "bluish neutral distance"; *here* is "unfenced existence"; and finally, *here* is "untalkative, out of reach". To put it in other words, the place cannot be described nor specified by clear and unambiguous acts of speech since it is a place of the imagination and a symbolic destination which transcends reality. In order to understand and enjoy moments of vision like this, utter isolation plays a fundamental role. By adopting a metonymic strategy, the poet is trying to make silence speak, to define the indefinite, to reach what is beyond human observation and understanding. In this respect, the "elsewhere" to which the poet aspires appears as a positive non-human dimension that, paradoxically once more, can be described only by negatives ($_{25}$*loneliness*, $_{25}$*silence*, $_{26}$*unnoticed*, $_{27}$*neglected*, $_{31}$*unfenced*, $_{32}$*untalkative*, $_{32}$*out of reach*). Replying to Neil Powell who asked him why his first collection "seem[ed] to be a book with a lot of negatives in it", Larkin said:

> [...] People say I'm very negative, and I suppose I am, but the impulse for producing a poem is never negative; the most negative poem in the world is a very positive thing to have done. The fact that a poem makes a reader want to lie down and die rather than get up and sock somebody is irrelevant. Perhaps my negation is my subject-matter: it doesn't seem like negation to me, but like daffodils to Wordsworth (Larkin 2001, 31).

The reference to Wordsworth's daffodils is important and must be read as a synecdochic allusion to Larkin's full participation in the great tradition of the British poetry.[2]

---

[1] Larkin himself admitted "the poem is about the part of England I live in" in the comment on the poem in his recording of the entire collection (Larkin 1965).

[2] See Barker (2005, 228-229).

References

Barker J. 2005. *Wordsworth. A Life*. New York and London: Harper.

Bayley J. 1988. "Too Good for This World". In Hartley G. (ed.) *Philip Larkin, 1922-1985: A Tribute*. Hull: The Marvell Press, 198-212.

Booth J. 2005. *Philip Larkin: the Poet's Plight*. Basingstoke: Palgrave Macmillan.

Goodby J. 1989. "'The Importance of Being Elsewhere', or 'No Man is an Ireland': Self, Selves and Social Consensus in the Poetry of Philip Larkin". In *Critical Survey*, vol. 1, n. 2, 131-138.

Kuby L. 1974. *An Uncommon Poet for the Common Man. A Study of Philip Larkin's Poetry*. The Hague, Paris: Mouton.

Larkin P. 1965. *Philip Larkin reads "The Whitsun Weddings"*. Listen cassettes. Hessle: The Marvell Press.

Larkin P. 1983. *Required Writing. Miscellaneous Pieces 1955-1982*. London: Faber.

Larkin P. 1988, revised edition 2003. *Collected Poems*. Thwaite A. (ed.) Victoria (Australia): The Marvell Press; London: Faber.

Larkin P. 2001. *Further Requirements. Interviews, Broadcasts, Statements, and Book Reviews 1952-1985*. Thwaite A. (ed.) London: Faber.

Osborne J. 2008. *Larkin, Ideology and Critical Violence. A Case of Wrongful Conviction*. Basingstoke: Palgrave Macmillan.

Riding Jackson L. 1987. "Twentieth-Century Change in the Idea of Poetry, and of the Poet, and of the Human Being". In *PN Review*, 14 suppl. 1, 71-88.

Swarbrick A. 1995. *Out of Reach. The Poetry of Philip Larkin*. Basingstoke and London: Macmillan.

STEFANIA STERLECCHINI

Università di Teramo

When Memory and Exile Intertwine. Brian Friel's Theatre

> [...] the purpose of playing, whose end, both
> at the first and now, was and is, to hold, as
> 'twere, the mirror up to Nature; to show
> virtue her own feature, scorn her own image,
> and the very age and body of the time his
> form and pressure.
> W. Shakespeare, *Hamlet*, III, ii, vv. 21-24.[1]

As it is well known, in his famous dialogue with the players who arrive in Elsinore, Prince Hamlet explains his idea of theatre as a way of representing life: a mirror that reflects the times while showing the audience its good and bad qualities. He, thus, exposes what he thinks are the dynamics and aesthetics of drama (Barranger 2005). If this idea of theatre can be accepted, as claimed by some critics such as Desmond Ernest Stewart Maxwell, Richard Kearney and Margaret Llewellyn-Jones, then it can be stated that the Irish theatre is no exception at all, with its rootedness in its national, historical and cultural context. More specifically, quoting the title of a very famous book on the matter, that is *Twentieth Century Irish Drama, Mirror Up To Nation* by Irish scholar Christopher Murray, we could say that Irish theatre *mirrors up* the nation itself, as at the end of the XIX century the Irish stage started being the privileged place where the audience could experience all those ideals of unity and freedom, and all those feelings strictly linked to their Irishness.

For these reasons, a key feature of contemporary Irish drama is the exploration of the themes of exile and homecoming, which are both strongly connected to Irish history and culture, and it is not astonishing that the drama critic Fintan O'Toole described his own homeland Erin as an *ex-isle*, underlying

---

[1] Well S., Taylor G. (eds.) 1994. *The Oxford Shakespeare. The Complete Works*. Oxford: Oxford University Press, 671.

the link between the green island and the complex phenomenon of migration in the Irish history and lore (O'Toole 1996).

Some of the most important scholars in the field of XX century Irish drama, such as Nicholas Grene, Anthony Roche and Richard Kearney, agree that the thematic path drawn by these topics are particularly present in the works of two major playwrights, Brian Friel and Tom Murphy, mainly because of two reasons: they both tap into the Irish cultural tradition and, most important of all, they began writing drama when the migration rate reached the highest level since 1880s, sharply nourishing the question. Tom Murphy dealt with the disenchantment of exile in many of his plays, but above all in *A Whistle in the Dark* (1961), *A Crucial Week in the Life of a Grocer's Assistant* (1969) and *Conversations on a Homecoming* (1986), where he explored the fate of Irish emigrants and showed that emigration was not a solution. In all these plays exile is seen through the lens of the disillusioned author, and as it is assumed by Murray, "the returned emigrant is a kind of ghost, whose incomplete knowledge acts as a device to define or re-define 'home truths'" (Murray 1997, 168).

Brian Friel has used the *topoi* of migration and exile with a constant and profound intensity over the years, intertwining them with an acute use of memory. More than once the playwright has stated that life is subjective, and so is drama, and he has stressed that however much we aspire to the certainties of objectivity, reality is the individuality of each person's experience. Furthermore, at the level of individual perception and memory, Friel dissolves the traditional distinction between *fact* and *fiction* mostly because in his opinion facts themselves can be considered fictitious. He once explained this idea in the following terms: "a fact is something that happened to me or something I experienced. It can also be something I thought happened to me, something I thought I experienced" (Pine 1999, 50).

This paper will investigate three of Friel's works belonging to different periods of his career. They are very diverse in style and tone but are all characterised by the lingering presence of memory and exile.

Philadelphia, Here I come! (1964) is the story of a young man, Gar O'Donnell, who is to leave for the United States of America in search of a better life than the one his native Donegal has to offer. This is why this play – that Richard Pine has labelled as the starting point for contemporary Irish drama (Pine 1990, 1) – is on exile: Gar gathers up all the doubts and contrasting feelings of those Irish emigrants who were forced to leave, and were divided between the excitement of going away and the fear of loosing their roots, therefore their identities. This emigrant's dilemma is made clear by Friel through the brilliant expedient of splitting the character into two: Private Gar and Public Gar, played by two different actors. The former addresses only to Public Gar and to the audience, and represents the most intimate part of the character, clearly expressing his own frustrations and fears; the latter interacts with the other characters, without showing off his real feelings about what is going to happen. Because of his doubled personality, Gar has often been considered an *alter-ego* of the playwright, who said of himself "Perhaps I'm twins" (Pine 1999, 41). Also Friel's wife Anne stressed this remarkable similarity between Gar and Friel, as expressed by Mel Gussow: "For her, her husband has something of a split personality, combining the utmost seriousness with great humour. He is, she says, like the doubled character, the private and public man, in *Philadelphia, Here I Come!*" (Gussow 2000b, 209).

As Neil Corcoran once said, "the two Gars, Public and Private, are certainly a way of dramatising Gar's alienation, the virtual schizophrenia of character and reaction into which he is forced by his cultural and domestic circumstances" (Corcoran 1993, 15). This oppressive uncertainty is summarised by Gar's final words:

> PRIVATE: God, Boy, why do you have to leave? Why? Why?
> PUBLIC: I don't know. I – I – I don't know (Friel 1985, 99).[2]

Throughout the play, the theme of exile is always blended with memory; this creates an atmosphere of misery, or, as Tony Coult put it, a feeling of "angry despair that refocuses attention on the culture of contemporary Ireland" (Coult 2003, 35). Private Gar often reminds himself and the audience some episodes of his life in Ballybeg, the imaginative town where some of Friel's plays take place, but talks as if he were already far away, and uses words full of sad nostalgia:

> PRIVATE GAR: No one will ever know or understand the fun there was; for there was fun and there was laughing – foolish, silly fun and foolish, silly laughing; but what it was all about you can't remember, can you? Just the memory of it – that's all you have now – just the memory; and even now, even so soon, it is being distilled of all its coarseness; and what's left is going to be precious, precious gold (Friel 1985, 77).

What is left is only memory, but that memory is as precious as gold to Gar's eyes.

Friel leaves the ending open, without resolving any of Gar's hesitations. The 'oppressive uncertainty' which has been mentioned earlier is almost obvious here. As Nicholas Grene put it, "*Philadelphia* affirms for emigrants the rightness of the decision to emigrate [...]. Yet the art of the play can allow also the luxury of enhanced memory of what has been abandoned" (Grene 1999, 205).

Faith Healer (1979) deals with the complicated relationship with Ireland, and of the necessity of going away, of being exiled. Frank Hardy, the faith healer, and his wife Grace decided to leave Ireland behind, began wandering from England

---

[2] This quotation and all the following from *Philadelphia, Here I come!* are from *Selected Plays* (Friel 1985).

to Scotland and Wales; he used his presumed healing touch to eke out a living. The couple shared this experience with Teddy, Frank's manager. In a dramatic structure which has been often compared to the one used by William Faulkner in *The Sound and the Fury* (1929), the three characters in four separate monologues remember their lives together, using their own divergent memories to recollect significant episodes. Elmer Andrews assumed that "[...] there is no single event which forms the undisputed common point of reference for all other events in the lives of the three characters. Each character, that is, has a different centre of meaning, and so produces a different version of the past" (Andrews 1993, 45).

In other words, the only truth available is the one created by the characters' deepest needs, by their private images of the past (McGrath 1997, 5-6). The audience is given the duty to follow the different monologues up to the end of the play, when the three protagonists finally put an end to their exiles and find their way home to Ballybeg. This is the episode of their return as narrated by Frank, who came home after losing his gift in search of restoration:

> FRANK: Twelve years later I was back in Ireland again; with Teddy and Grace. [...] I was heartsick of Wales and Scotland as they were. [...] And there we got lodgings in a pub, a lounge bar, really, outside a village called Ballybeg, not far from Donegal Town. There was no sense of homecoming. I tried to simulate it but nothing stirred. Only few memories, wan and neutral. [...] Maybe one or two memories. They evoked nothing (Friel 1985, 338-339).[3]

At first, it seems that Frank has no feelings toward his native land because he feels no sense of homecoming at all. But as soon as he has the chance, he realises that his touch is lost forever, thus understanding with cold certainty "that nothing was going to happen. Nothing at all" (Friel 1985, 375), accepting this condition and undergoing his gloomy fate in Ireland. As Coult put it, "[...] in the end, Frank returns to his home town and knowingly sacrifices himself to the primitive faith of his audience. Knowing that [...] the penalty for failure is to be murdered by brutal local men drunk on ignorance and blind faith, he goes to his death with a terrible fatalism" (Coult 2003, 69).

And that is the very moment when he ultimately feels at home:

> FRANK: And as I moved across that yard towards them and offered myself to them, then for the first time I had a simple and genuine sense of home-coming. Then for the first time there was no atrophying terror; and the maddening questions were silent (Friel 1985, 376).

The message Friel wants to convey to his audience seems to be that while in exile there is safety, returning home means danger, or even death.

---

[3] This quotation and all the following from *Faith Healer* are from *Selected Plays* (Friel 1985).

Seamus Deane explained this idea very clearly when he said that the first impression you have of *Faith Healer* is that "it shows a man creating his own death by coming home out of exile" (Deane 1985, 173). But is it really so? Is this Friel's ultimate conviction? If we consider Friel's biography and concentrate on the fact that he almost never left Ireland, we could say that the answer to the question is no. Over the years Friel has moved a lot around Ireland and England to promote his own productions, but always feeling out of place when away. His friend Mel Gussow said that "the longer he is away from Donegal, the more unsettled he feels. For all his talk of exile-at-home, he is rock-rooted and as indigenous as his art. His home is his refugee" (Gussow 2000b, 209). And when in 1991 he was asked why he had always remained homebound, Friel candidly replied as follows: "I think exile can be acquired sitting in the same place for the rest of your life. Physical exile is not necessary" (Gussow 2000a, 143). This is the main reason why the explanation for Frank's death should be searched somewhere else. Critics tend to explain this highlighting the universally recognised contradictory character of Friel's art, so that, as Grene wrote, *Faith Healer* has been read as "[...] a dramatic enactment of the fictions of memory, as a portrait of the artist as a charlatan / miracle worker, as a parable of Irish exile and return, as a secular theatrical recreation of religious rites: all true, or at least valid, illuminating readings" (Grene 2006, 53).

So, the final sequence of the play is considered one of the most mysterious passages in Friel's dramatic artistry, and maybe this is the reason why the play is still so appealing to the audience and to Friel's scholars after so many years from its first performance. There seems to be no ending line, no definite conclusion, because even if we face Frank's death, we cannot completely grab its most profound meaning.

As quoted before, in 1991 Friel expressed his idea that to feel exiled you do not have to be physically away from home, thus anticipating the main topic of his 1994 masterpiece, *Molly Sweeney*. Molly, the eponymous character, has often been described by many scholars (Pine 1999) as being Friel's most successful and touching representation of Ireland, and so once again the Irish nation takes life on stage. To understand how the playwright transposed his idea of 'mental exile' into the play – using Molly's pilgrimage into madness – its plot will be briefly summarised. Molly has been blind since she was ten months old. She has married Frank Sweeney, a nice guy who has no sympathy for work, and who is much concerned about his wife's recovery. For this reason, he takes her to Mr. Rice, a fallen-from-grace ophthalmologist who would do anything to prove that he is still a good doctor. The two men seem to persuade Molly to have an operation, but the audience know that she is not happy with this choice. She cries her heart out expressing her feelings in the following passage:

MOLLY: And then with sudden anger I thought: why am I going for this operation? None of this is my choosing. Then why is this happening to me? I am being used. [...] And have I anything to gain? Anything? Anything? And then I knew, suddenly I knew why I was so desolate. It was the dread of exile, of being sent away. It was the desolation of homesickness (Friel 1999, 473).[4]

Some of the words that appear in this monologue are very interesting for what it is being discussed here, but *exile* and *homesickness* are undoubtedly the keywords. Molly is divided between her own sentiments and those of others, who want her to be different. For this reason Peter Brook, who used the adjective 'magnificent' for *Molly Sweeney*, underlined the similarities between Molly and Gar O'Donnell:

> I recognize in both *Philadelphia, Here I Come!* and *Molly Sweeney* the fusion and yet the separation of inner and outer man, the outer man whose behaviour is bound by the rule of everyday life [...] and the inner man, whose anarchy and poetry is usually expressed only in his words (Pine 1999, 34).

Molly is perfectly aware that if she accepted their proposal, she would be exiled in another world where she does not belong. The space which Molly occupies before having the operation is a sort of *in-between space*, an interstitial place where, as Homi Bhabha said, "identity becomes 'split' or estranged from itself in the process of being examined and reconstituted" (Pine 1999, 26).

In the end Molly accepts the operation, but soon after she lives her own personal drama, feeling a total sense of failure which brings her to a psychological collapse and, finally, to a state of *blindsight*, the state in which the patient sees but actually decides not to see. Practically, she becomes mad, getting deeper and deeper into depression and folly.

Unexpectedly, from this complex state of mind that she has chosen to fall into, Molly recovers herself thanks to the memories that link her to her beloved lost mother, who died when Molly was a just baby. Her mother's ghost comes into Molly's room like a timely reminder that love is still possible:

> MOLLY: Mother comes in occasionally, in her pale blue headscarf and muddy wellingtons. Nobody pays much attention to her. She just wanders through the wards. [...] She doesn't talk much – she never did. But when she sits uneasily on the edge of my bed, as if she were waiting to be summoned, her face always frozen in that nervous half smile, I think I know her better than I ever knew her, and I begin to love her all over again (Friel 1999, 508).

Molly will finally be at peace with the world, feeling absolutely at ease exiled in her inner space together with the memories her mind creates.

---

[4] This quotation and all the following from *Molly Sweeney* are from *Plays 2* (Friel 1999).

MOLLY: I think I see nothing at all now. But I'm not absolutely sure of that. Anyhow my borderline country is where I live now. I'm at home there. Well... at ease there. It certainly doesn't worry me any more that what I think I see may be fantasy or indeed what I take to be imagined may very well be real [...]. Real – imagined – fact – fiction – fantasy – reality – there it seems to be. And it seems to be all right (Friel 1999, 509).

The touching words that end Molly's last monologue seem to remind the audience, once and for all, about Friel's decisive vision. Memory and its contrasting versions can be either useful or misleading, helping us to reach that place called *home* – wherever it is – to completely feel ourselves. And this is the final expression of the myth Friel has been narrating through all these years, and which takes his audience and readers to "the point of eternal renewal and confident departure", as discussed by Seamus Heaney (Heaney 1993, 228).

References

Andrews E. 1993. "The Fifth Province". In Peacock A. (ed.) *The Achievement of Brian Friel.* Gerrards Cross: Colin Smythe, 29-48.

Barranger M. 2005. *Theatre: a Way of Seeing.* Belmont (Ca.): Wadsworth Publishing, 6th ed.

Corcoran N. 1993. "The Penalties of Retrospect: Continuities in Brian Friel". In Peacock A. (ed.) *The Achievement of Brian Friel.* Gerrards Cross: Colin Smythe, 14-28.

Coult T. 2003. *About Friel, the Playwright and the Work.* London: Faber & Faber.

Deane S. 1985. *Celtic Revivals. Essays in Modern Irish Literature, 1880-1980.* London: Faber & Faber.

Delaney P. (ed.) 2000. *Brian Friel in Conversation.* Ann Arbor (Mi.): University of Michigan Press.

Friel B. 1985. *Selected Plays. With an Introduction by Seamus Deane.* Gerrards Cross: Colin Smythe.

Friel B. 1999. *Plays 2. With an Introduction by Christopher Murray.* London: Faber & Faber.

Grene N. 1999. *The Politics of Irish Drama. Plays in Context from Boucicault to Friel.* Cambridge: Cambridge University Press.

Grene N. 2006. "Five ways of looking at 'Faith Healer'". In Roche A. (ed.) *The Cambridge Companion to Brian Friel.* Cambridge: CUP, 53-65.

Gussow M. 2000a. "In Interview with Mel Gussow". In Murray C. (ed.) *Brian Friel: Essays, Diaries, Interviews, 1964–1999.* London: Faber & Faber, 139-149.

Gussow M. 2000b. "From Ballybeg to Broadway". In Delaney P. (ed.) *Brian Friel in Conversation*. Ann Arbor (Mi.): University of Michigan Press, 202-212.

Heaney S. 1993. "For Liberation: Brian Friel and the Use of Memory". In Peacock A. (ed.) *The Achievement of Brian Friel*. Gerrards Cross: Colin Smythe, 229-240.

McGrath F.C. 1997. "Brian Friel and the Irish Art of Living". In Kerwin W. (ed.) *Brian Friel. A Casebook*. New York/London: Garland Press, 3-12.

Murray C. 1997. *Twentieth-Century Irish Drama: Mirror up to Nation*. Manchester: Manchester University Press.

Murray C. (ed.) 2000. *Brian Friel: Essays, Diaries, Interviews, 1964–1999*. London: Faber & Faber.

O'Toole F. 1996. *The Ex-Isle of Erin: Images of a Global Ireland*. Dublin, New Island.

Pine R. 1990. *Brian Friel and Irish Drama*. London-New York: Routledge.

Pine R. 1999. *The Diviner: the Art of Brian Friel*. Dublin: UCD Press.

Pine R. (ed.) 2006. *The Cambridge Companion to Brian Friel*. Cambridge: CUP.

MARIA VACCARELLA

King's College, London

"A Kind of Medical Chaucer":
Testimony, Storytelling and Caregiving
in Ian McEwan's *Atonement*

Ian McEwan's *Atonement* (2001) may be profitably described as a profound meditation on testimony, in connection to the preliminary practice of witnessing and in contrast to its own reverse, perjury. The novel centres on Briony Tallis's lifelong effort to find atonement for the perjury she committed in her youth. This study aims at exploring the significance of bearing witness in *Atonement*, specifically in the form of storytelling and in connection to the pervasive medical context of the novel.

Though issues of medical ethics and figurative uses of illnesses are often at the core of McEwan's texts, there is a particularly significant connection between medicine and narrative in *Atonement*. In Part One, Robbie Turner makes sense of his choice of becoming a medical doctor after his literary studies through a primitive medical humanistic approach:

> For this was the point, surely: he would be a better doctor for having read literature. What deep readings his modified sensibility might make of human suffering, of the self destructive folly of sheer bad luck that drive men toward ill health. Birth, death, and frailty in between. Rise and fall – this was the doctor's business, and it was literature's too (McEwan 2002, 93).[1]

This call for active listening and witnessing, shared by writers and caregivers, is further explored later in the novel. Nonetheless, the character

---

[1] On this point, see also G.S. Rousseau: "In our century nothing has influenced the physician's profile more profoundly than the loss of his or her identity as the last of the humanists. Until recently, physicians in Western European countries received broad, liberal educations, read languages and literatures, studied in the arts, were good musicians and amateur painters; by virtue of their financial privilege and class prominence they interacted with statesmen and high-ranking professionals, and continued in these activities throughout their careers. It was not uncommon for Victorian and Edwardian doctors, for example, to write prolifically throughout their careers: medical memoirs and autobiographies, biographies of other doctors, social analyses of their own times, imaginative literature of all types" (Rousseau 1986, 159).

who undertakes this task is not Robbie, who will never become a doctor, since he dies during the Dunkirk evacuation. It is Briony, who will go into nursing, while nourishing her hope to become a novelist. As literary scholar Dominic Head maintains, "[...] the theme of guilt and atonement is inextricably linked to an investigation of the writer's authority, a process of self-critique conducted through the creation of the writing persona Briony Tallis" (Head 2007, 156).

There is a noteworthy relationship between Briony's expiatory caregiving of WWII soldiers as a trainee nurse and her unburdening recounting of her youthful misdeed in the last book of her career as a novelist, which coincides metafictionally with the first three parts of McEwan's *Atonement*. Briony's complex *Bildung* is to be achieved through a metaphorical journey from the realm of childish recklessness, which shaped her perjury, to a more mature dimension of attentive testimony of her patients' illnesses and of the hidden truth underlying her crime. Narrative is thus reconfigured as a crucial technique for the effective enactment of her growing process, indissolubly linked to her penance. As McEwan states in an interview:

> Part of the intention of *Atonement* was to look at story-telling itself. [...] I wanted to play with the notion of story-telling as a form of self-justification, of how much courage is involved in telling the truth to oneself (Noakes 2002, 19-20).

When we first meet Briony, she is a teenager imbued with literature and striving to find some valuable subject matter in the real world for her own writing. Her moralistic play *The Trials of Arabella* fails to arouse the interest she expected. When she witnesses some scenes of the budding relationship between her sister Cecilia and Robbie Turner, although she cannot fully grasp their meaning, she still finds the events worth exploring and exploiting. Literary critic Brian Finney states that "[s]he ruthlessly subordinates everything the world throws at her to her need to make it serve the demands of her own world of fiction" (Finney 2004, 69). Thus, in her fictional world, Robbie's risqué letter to Cecilia, their lovemaking in the library and her cousin Lola's assault are all convenient elements of a perfect plot for a breathtaking story. Lola's ambiguous attitude towards her assaulter, Paul Marshall,[2] and Mrs Tallis's long-standing aversion to working class Robbie will

---

[2] It is worth remembering here that Briony is under Lola's influence. It is Lola, who defines Robbie a "maniac," when Briony tells her about the contents of his letter to Cecilia. Briony, two years younger than Lola and much more naive, blindly accepts her cousin's "diagnosis" ("A maniac. The word had refinement, and the weight of medical diagnosis", McEwan 2002, 119) and decides not to inquire what Lola thought about the mysterious encounter of Robbie and Cecilia at the fountain "suspecting that the explanation was simple and that it would be better not to expose her ignorance" (*ibidem*). After her assault, Lola claims she could not see the face of her aggressor, but is immediately willing to confirm Briony's accusation of Robbie ("She had little more to do than remain silent behind her cousin's zeal. Lola did not need to lie, to look her supposed attacker in the eye and summon the courage to accuse him, because all that work was done for her, innocently and without

dramatically help to turn Briony's fictional reworking of the events into a legally binding testimony. This pivotal moment in the plot of *Atonement* exemplifies McEwan's preoccupation with "the important structuring and meaning-giving task that narrative in general and fictional storytelling in particular perform in our lives" (Schemberg 2004, 9).

Although nursing was one of the few respectable professional settings for a woman at the beginning of the twentieth century, Briony's vocational choice at the age of eighteen is not as straightforward as it may seem, but is actually entangled in a network of complex personal and social implications. On the whole, it is evident that her caregiving of wounded soldiers meets her need of expiation. However, it must be remembered that the nursing profession allows her to retrace – partially, at least – the ordeal of the two victims of her crime. She will be a nurse like Cecilia – who broke up with her family, who wouldn't believe in Robbie's innocence – and her training, as devised by Florence Nightingale, will be explicitly informed by a militaristic discipline, in parallel with Robbie's enlistment in the army, his only possibility of being released from prison. Cecilia herself is fully aware that, while nursing had been an empowering choice for her, it would represent a more radical rupture in Briony's life, and she writes to Robbie: "I keep thinking of her. To go into nursing, to cut herself off from her background, is a bigger step for her than it was for me. I had my three years at Cambridge at least, and I had an obvious reason to reject my family" (McEwan 2002, 212). What Cecilia – or Briony's fictional reconstruction of her – doesn't understand at this stage is that Briony's sense of guilt is her "obvious reason" to reject a prospective secure future.

On a more general level, nursing provides Briony a new sense of responsibility towards her patients, which helps her come to terms with her own troubled ethical dimension. The rationale of the nursing profession has been often explained through Emmanuel Levinas's ethics of alterity.[3] The primacy of the suffering Other is manifest within the clinical encounter, since the patient as Other is primarily accessed in her/his suffering and, as a consequence, the caregiver's response to her/his call for aid entails an ethical component. In Julia Hallam's formulation, "[n]ursing knowledge (epistemology), and its essence in being-for-the-other (its ontology), means being responsible for the other, being answerable to their pain and vulnerability (its ethics)" (Hallam 2005, 26). As a nurse, Briony will be constantly "exposed" to the face of the suffering Other, while the foundation of her professional deontology will lie in that "bigger

---

guile by the younger girl. Lola was required only to remain silent about the truth, banish it and forget it entirely, and persuade herself not of some contrary tale, but simply of her own uncertainty" *ibidem*, 168). Moreover, there had already been a flirtatious scene between Lola and Paul Marshall, in which the teenage girl "was pleased rather than embarrassed" (*ibidem*, 60-61). Lola and Paul will eventually get married.

[3] For example, see Naef (2006).

step" described by Cecilia, which recalls Levinas's concept of "offering oneself that is a suffering, a goodness despite oneself" (Levinas 1991, 54).

Drawing on Levinas's ethics of the face, Rahel Naef suggests that bearing witness to the suffering Other "constitutes a well articulated and particular way of caring" (Naef 2006, 149), which "needs to be valued, respected, and supported as a fundamental and meaningful nursing practice, a moral way of engaging in the nurse-person relationship" (*ibidem*, 155). The underlying assumption of critical works, which explain the nursing ethics as a form of testimony,[4] is that caregiving is participative to the point that a nurse may be personally affected by what she witnesses. While experiencing the Other's vulnerability, the nurse's own vulnerability is disclosed, just like in trauma accounts "the listener to trauma comes to be a participant and co-owner of the traumatic event" (Laub 1992, 57). Nurses can therefore be included in the broader historical category of the "wounded healers", whose own vulnerability crucially contributes to the healing process.[5]

In his seminal book *The Wounded Storyteller* (1995), medical sociologist Arthur Frank writes that "[b]ecause stories can heal, the wounded healer and the wounded storyteller are not separate, but are different aspects of the same figure" (Frank 1995, XII). He traces an ethical commitment in wounded storytelling as well, according to Soren Kierkegaard's concept of the ethical person as editor of her/his life, someone who assumes responsibility for her/his life in the act of recounting it (*ibidem*). In *Atonement*, Briony is represented as both a wounded healer and a wounded storyteller, since her fascination for fictional writing persists during her nursing training:

> She had never lost that childhood pleasure of seeing pages covered in her own handwriting. It almost didn't matter what she wrote. Since the drawer did not lock, she was careful to disguise her descriptions of Sister Drummond. She changed the names of the patients too. And having changed the names, it became easier to transform the circumstances and invent. She liked to write out what she imagined to be their rambling thoughts. She was under no obligation to the truth, she had promised no one a chronicle. This was the only place she could be free. She built little stories – not very convincing, somewhat overwritten – around the people on the ward. For a while she thought of herself as a kind of medical Chaucer, whose wards thronged with colourful types, coves, topers, old hats, nice dears with a sinister secret to tell (McEwan 2002, 280).

The key sentence in this extract points to Briony's unconcern of truth, while she collects and rewrites her patients' stories in her journals. The reader might fear

---

[4] In addition to the abovementioned article by Naef, see also Liaschenko (1998) and Wynn (2002).

[5] For a historical overview of the wounded healer, see Jackson (2001).

that she has not changed at all; she is still an aspiring novelist with a dangerously lively imagination. The ironic comparison to Geoffrey Chaucer just adds to her disproportionate self-confidence. But that is a simplistic assumption, in the end.

At the age of eighteen, Briony has grasped the seriousness of her crime, but also the irreconcilable divide between fiction and reality. While pondering on the consequences of her perjury, she admits that "[t]he only conceivable solution would be for the past never to have happened" (*ibidem*, 288). At the age of seventy-seven, recently diagnosed with vascular dementia, she can only attempt "a final act of kindness, a stand against oblivion and despair" (*ibidem*, 372), a fictional account of her crime, in which, although she is not forgiven, Robbie and Cecilia enjoy a happy end.

Briony had practiced kindness to its extreme, a kindness which becomes fiction or simply lying, while attending the wounded soldiers from Dunkirk. She had lied to Private Latimer, who had lost half of his face, when she had told him "We'll soon have you fixed" (*ibidem*, 302). And she had lied at length to the French soldier with a mortal head injury, in one of the most touching scenes of the novel. Confronted with this delirious young man, who was dying away from his family in a foreign country and who had mistaken her for his sweetheart, Briony had sustained his raving visions and had declared that she loved him, because "[n]o other reply was possible" (*ibidem*, 309). As Maria Margaronis comments, "[i]t would be hard to argue, in this instance, that telling the truth would have been the moral choice" (Margaronis 2008, 147).

Narrative ways of engaging with patients' suffering revolve around this issue of subjective and unique representability. Starting from his reflections on Levinas's ethics applied to the clinical encounter, Craig Irvine states that:

> A work of literature is not the naked face of a patient's suffering. Rather, it is the representation, the identification, of this face. [...] Literature honors medicine's imperative to clothe the naked. Making the Other an object of reflection, literature mirrors medicine's thematization, its bringing to light – its way of knowing (Irvine 2005, 14).

In her theorization of narrative medicine, Rita Charon explains the centrality of bearing witness in the practice of caregiving in a similar way. The role of the health care professional should be perceived "not as a passive hearer but rather as a skilled partner in building true intersubjectivity with sick people" (Charon 2006, 179). This concept discards the long tradition of paternalistic medicine – and maternal nursing, as well – in favour of a rethinking of the caregiver-patient relationship, based on sincere concordance.

Although the reflection on storytelling is a distinctive feature of McEwan's novels, its intersubjective core is best explored in *Atonement*, which perfectly matches Reynolds and Noakes's formulation of the author's poetics:

By speaking about the pain we cannot take it away. But we can add to what happened. We can change the story by telling a different story. There is, in any case, never any one story. Only many stories. And by telling those stories, one of the things that McEwan's work does is to change the stories that went before (Reynolds and Noakes 2002, 7).

Even if in *Atonement* it is implied that neither devoted caregiving nor heartfelt storytelling can atone for Briony's crime, the novel had to be written, she had to "change the story by telling a different story" and, she states at the end of the book, "[t]he attempt was all" (McEwan 2002, 371). In the end, Briony, as a typical McEwanesque character, reconfigures her writing as a form of exploration, rather than illustration (Ryan 1994, 4). The ultimate legacy of the novel is properly grasped in Dominic Head's words:

> [...] the empathic creativity of complex fiction-making, underpinned by atonement and kindness, and signalled through metafictional device, is what *Atonement* pits against the horrors of the twentieth century (Head 2007, 174).

As a matter of fact, this is what McEwan pitted against the horrors of the twenty-first century, too, in his article on *The Guardian* about the terrorist attacks of 9/11, which had took place a few days after the publication of *Atonement*:

> If the hijackers had been able to imagine themselves into the thoughts and feelings of the passengers, they would have been unable to proceed. It is hard to be cruel once you permit yourself to enter the mind of your victim. Imagining what it is like to be someone other than yourself is at the core of our humanity. It is the essence of compassion, and it is the beginning of morality (McEwan 2001).

Confronted with a painful historical event, which will later spur the creation of his novel *Saturday* (2005), McEwan avowed once again the value of "the empathic creativity of complex fiction-making" (Head 2007, 174) as part of our moral engagement with the Other.

References

Charon R. 2006. *Narrative Medicine: Honoring the Stories of Illness*. Oxford and New York: Oxford University Press.

Finney B. 2004. "Briony's Stand against Oblivion: The Making of Fiction in Ian McEwan's *Atonement*". In *Journal of Modern Literature*, 3, 27, 68-82.

Frank A. 1995. *The Wounded Storyteller. Body, Illness, and Ethics*. Chicago: University of Chicago Press.

Hallam J. 2005. "Ethical Lives in the Early Nineteenth Century: Nursing and a History of Caring". In McGann B., Mortimer S. (eds.) *New Directions in the History of Nursing: International Perspectives*. London: Routledge, 22-39.

Head D.J. 2007. *Ian McEwan*. Manchester: Manchester University Press.

Irvine C.A. 2005. "The Other Side of Silence: Levinas, Medicine, and Literature". In *Literature and Medicine*, 1, 24, 8-18.

Jackson S.W. 2001. "The Wounded Healer". In *Bulletin of the History of Medicine*, 75,1, 1-36.

Laub D. 1992. "Bearing Witness or the Vicissitudes of Listening". In S. Felman, D. Laub (eds.) *Testimony: Crises of Witnessing in Literature, Psychoanalysis, and History*. London and New York: Routledge, 57- 74.

Levinas E. 1991. *Otherwise Than Being or Beyond Essence*. Dordrecht: Kluwer [1974].

Liaschenko J. 1998. "The Shift from the Closed Body to the Open Body. Ramifications for Nursing Testimony". In Edwards S.D. (ed.) *Philosophical Issues in Nursing*. London: MacMillan, 11-30.

Margaronis M. 2008. "The Anxiety of Authenticity: Writing Historical Fiction at the End of the Twentieth Century". In *History Workshop Journal*, 1, 65, 138-160.

McEwan I. 2001. "Only Love and Then Oblivion. Love Was All They Had to Set Against Their Murderers". In *The Guardian*, September 15th 2001, available at http://www.guardian.co.uk/world/2001/sep/15/september11.politicsphilosophyandsociety2 (last accessed August 2011).

McEwan I. 2002. *Atonement*. London: Vintage [2001].

Naef R. 2006. "Bearing Witness: a Moral Way of Engaging in the Nurse-Person Relationship". In *Nursing Philosophy*, 7, 146-156.

Noakes J. 2002. "Interview with Ian McEwan". In Reynolds M., Noakes J. (eds.) *Ian McEwan: The Essential Guide*. London: Vintage, 10-23.

Reynolds M., Noakes J. (eds.) 2002. *Ian McEwan: The Essential Guide*. London: Vintage.

Rousseau G.S. 1986. "Literature and Medicine: Towards a Simultaneity of Theory and Practice". In *Literature and Medicine*, 5, 152-181.

Ryan K. 1994. *Ian McEwan*. Plymouth: Northcote.

Schemberg C. 2004. *Achieving 'At-one-ment'. Storytelling and the Concept of Self in Ian McEwan's "The Child in Time", "Black Dogs", "Enduring Love" and "Atonement"*. Frankfurt am Main: Peter Lang.

Wynn F. 2002. "Nursing and the Concept of Life: Towards an Ethics of Testimony". In *Nursing Philosophy*, 3, 120-132.

MASSIMO VERZELLA

Università Gabriele d'Annunzio, Chieti-Pescara

The Paradoxical Vision:
Samuel Butler's Use of Ambiguity in *Erewhon*

In the short essay "A Book that Influenced Me" (1944) with reference to Samuel Butler's *Erewhon*, E. M. Forster writes: "The frontal full-dress presentation of an opinion often repels me, but if it be insidiously slipped in sidewise I may receive it, and Butler is a master of the oblique" (Forster 2008, 280). Indeed, irony and ambiguity are central to Butler's method in prose fiction and can be seen as the very structuring principles governing his treatment of social constructions of norms and values. In Butler's hands paradox, in particular, becomes a tool for debunking metaphysical master plots and popular orthodoxies while acknowledging the impossibility of equating truth with unidimensional meaning. "We do with truth much as we do with God" – Butler writes in his *Notebooks* – "we create it according to our own requirements and then say that it has created us" (Butler 1985b, 301). These ideas echo Nietzsche's questioning of the assumptions regarding the certainty of knowledge as expressed in the early essay "On Truth and Lying in an Extra-moral Sense" (1873) and flow together into Butler's view of scientific knowledge as tentative and "falsifiable", as Karl Popper, who was himself much influenced by Butler's paradoxical method, would put it.

In the wake of Karl Popper's philosophy of science one might argue that scientific theories can always be tested, that is, like myths, they can never be proved and therefore remain essentially uncertain or hypothetical. In Popper's view, knowledge cannot be derived only from observation, owing to the fact that all observation statements are anchored in sets of assumptions and theoretical concepts that are far from being infallible. As a consequence, we can never prove, once and for all, the truth of our scientific theories. On the subject of Darwinism, the same is true; in a short piece entitled "Darwinism as a Metaphysical Research Programme", Popper writes: "I have come to the conclusion that Darwinism is not a testable scientific theory, but a metaphysical research programme – a possible framework for testable scientific theories" (Popper 2002, 195). Interestingly, in this very piece Popper acknowledges his debt to Samuel Butler's ideas on evolution as expressed in his philosophical works on evolution:

> I have always been extremely interested in the theory of evolution, and very ready to accept evolution as fact. I have also been fascinated by Darwin as well as by Darwinism – though somewhat unimpressed by most of the evolutionary philosophers; with the great one exception, that is, of Samuel Butler (Popper 2002, 194).

Evidence collected from Butler's books on the subject suggests that, in his turn, he would have subscribed to Popper's rationalist epistemology, so much so that as soon as he realised that an inductively based, empirically grounded conceptualization was progressively taking a hold on the masses, leading people into the trap of a new dogma, he put aside his early enthusiasm for Darwinism and turned his conclusions upside down in an essay titled "Darwin among the Machines" (published in *The Press* newspaper on 13 June 1863 in Christchurch, New Zealand). In this early essay, which was to become the thematic nucleus of *Erewhon* (1872), he applies the principle of Darwinian evolution to machines, extending the idea of the survival of the fittest from the biological to the mechanical domain.

The idea of a world taken over by machines derives from a widespread fear about the nature of progress in mid-nineteenth century industrial society. While many contemporary viewers might extol the wonders of the technological advancement, the majority of the intellectuals saw the progress of their age as a threat to the life of the mind and to the creative spirit (Wiener 1986). The resulting conflict of social values – progress *versus* stability, philosophical mechanism *versus* Aristotelianism, random evolution *versus* guided evolution – instilled doubt in the confused mind of Samuel Butler, and may account for his decision to channel his concerns about the epistemic implications of this tension into the dispute between two Erewhonian professors: a technophobe and a technophile.

The former argues that the sensations of both machinery and living beings are chemical and mechanical in their operation; from this follows that, in the near future, machines are not unlikely to develop identity and consciousness, which will cease to be exclusively human prerogatives. In line with Charles Bell (1774-1842) and many other philosophers and medical writers, he refers to the fabric of a vital organism as a mechanical configuration and constructs mechanical models of mind and emotion. Finally, in the wake of T. H. Huxley's philosophical materialism, he blurs the distinctions between men and machines by describing vapour-engines as having beating hearts and living affections. To sum up, man is nothing but a peculiar, highly organized type of machine, while machines, on their part, are endowed with a consciousness which is still at its first stages of development but will soon blossom into a powerful means for further enhancing their autonomy and power. After all, the technophobe repeatedly underlines, "machines are still in their infancy" (Butler 1985a, 219); the difference between the life of a man and that of a machine being one rather of degree than kind.

The equivalence man = machine is also constructed by taking this line of argument a stage further: if on the one hand human and animal bodies are mere automata, on the other hand, it cannot be denied that machines are gradually evolving into instinctive organisms. The same way machines have replaced our muscles, computers are destined to replace our brains.

One last thread in the fabric of the technophobe manifesto is the evocation of the Luddite movement that flourished in England in the early 1800s with the aim of putting up violent resistance to modernization of equipment and work procedures. Luddism was not a uniform movement across all of the textile-producing regions and was easily smashed by the British state whereas the Erewhonian anti-machinist party organized itself long before the civil war and at last prevailed over their political opponents. The latter, who adhered to the machinist party, held ideas that Higgs summarizes in his account of the technophile stance. The second professor contradicts the arguments of the technophobe by representing the machine as a "prosthetic god" and by contending that mechanical supplements cannot but improve upon human anatomy. To the idea that machines can become superhuman he opposes a view of the human body as enhanced by artificial limbs and prostheses at the climax of a deliberate Lamarckian effort (Ketabgian 1997).

What is to be made of this clash of contrasting views on the development of the human-machine symbiosis? In a nutshell, Darwin's arguments seemed to lead to the conclusion that after all man is nothing but a sophisticated machine. It was such a narrow view that Butler could not help holding a contrasting mirror in front of it and making fun of it by implying that machines were gradually developing human traits too. In this he was both echoing Carlyle's sentiments about the dehumanizing effects of industrialization, and putting himself in the satirical tradition of Jonathan Swift, who derided the mechanist mentality in his depiction of the brain as "only a crowd of little animals, but with teeth and claws extremely sharp, and therefore cling together in the contexture we behold, like the picture of Hobbes's *Leviathan*" (Swift 2003, 173).

Nevertheless, Butler's objective cannot be reduced merely to the parodic inversion of Darwinism and philosophical mechanism. In fact, he carries his argument one stage further to show what would happen if this machine made mostly of muscle, bone and vital organs ceased to function properly. In a mechanical world reverencing wealth as a standard of success and material production as the focus of life, even a single variation in the tempo of the production/consumption process heavily affects the performance of the social engine. In so far as they are guilty of slowing down the pace of growth, the sick, the weak and the unfit, as social Darwinians would label them, must be weeded out to make room for the healthy and well functioning ones. This can explain why, in the looking glass world of *Erewhon*, a strong social stigma is attached to health problems whereas good fortune, health and prosperity are copiously rewarded. In this ambiguous world, uncannily mirroring both Butler's England and contemporary reality, if a man "fails bodily" in any way before he is seventy years old he is tried before a jury of his countryman and exposed to public scorn. On the contrary, if he exhibits a tendency to vicious or immoral conduct, committing crimes such as fraud or embezzlement, he is "sentenced" to the rather mild treatments devised by a class of men trained in "soul-craft", the straighteners, who are obeyed as readily as our own doctors and appear as perfect types of the modern psychoanalyst.

Due to this bizarre custom, Erewhonians are obliged to deny their bodily ailments, becoming particularly skilled at concealment such as hiding wrinkles and other signs of ageing. Women even try to conceal their pregnancy as long as possible, as if childbearing was nothing but a vexing disorder of the body, an abnormal state. In the attempt to escape public disgrace, a young lady, Mahaina, goes as far as pretending that her chronic health problems are the result of a mild form of dipsomania, an intermittent pathological craving for alcohol. Needless to say, this euphemism is charged with ironic nuances: the very use of this opaque technical term indicates that when it comes to talk about health problems, everybody appears to be eager to violate the principle of transparency to maintain an undefined distance from the other, and prevent real involvement in discussion. Talking about Mr Nosnibor, the rich merchant who is to host Higgs during his scheduled visit to the metropolis, his language teacher says that he is a delightful man, adding that Nosnibor has recently suffered from an illness whose long and difficult name Higgs fails to grasp, except for the fact that it is "much longer than kleptomania" (Butler 1985a, 91). In both cases obscure language and ambiguity are used strategically to distance the sick person from his illness, which is perceived as an act of treason against the social welfare.

While Mahaina has a very hard time trying to conceal her bodily distresses, Mr. Nosnibor, a rich man who has been assigned the custody of the protagonist, undergoes medical treatment for embezzlement and everybody treats him with sympathy and solicitous concern. Paradoxical as it may be, Erewhonian jurisprudence is quite lenient on moral ailments, whilst other forms of misfortune earn for their sufferers stiff legal penalties rather than sympathy. In a society where success is the measure of honour, failure cannot but be a crime. More, as Francesco Marroni has pointed out, in a society where death signals the end of both material and spiritual life, physical health becomes the most precious commodity (Marroni 2007).

Chapter XI is an account of a number of trials which Higgs hears in an Erewhonian Court of Law. The most important case is that of a man who is accused of "pulmonary consumption". After some proselytising on the importance of the law as an instrument for the protection of people and the welfare of the community, the judge moves on to say that such a dangerous man can expect little sympathy from his fellow countrymen. Already there has been a long criminal history of "aggravated bronchitis" and many other illnesses "of a more or less hateful character" (Butler 1985a, 115), and this grave deficiency in "mechanical" propriety and strength must not go unpunished, if the gears of the social engine are to be kept functioning. He concludes his tirade with the following peroration: "You may say that is your misfortune to be criminal; I answer that it is your crime to be unfortunate" (Butler 1985a, 117).

The whole passage may sound like a piece of antithetical verbiage but at a closer look it addresses a central aporia of mechanistic determinism. Are not these people following the laws of nature when they treat physical illness and misfortune of any kind punitively? (Jeffers 1981) Is it socially rewarding to reach back for the poor and the weak, letting them slow down the race towards economic growth and prosperity? The protagonist's sympathies are with the system: "It seems to me that there is no unfairness in punishing people for their misfortunes, or rewarding them for their sheer good luck; it is the normal condition of human life that this should be done" (Butler 1985a, 120). In a presentation copy of *Erewhon*, Butler wrote "meant seriously" in the margin beside this passage. It is not so much a question of being cynical or ridiculing emerging cultural tendencies; Butler hits here with disturbing honesty on the insight that nature and society do favour the fortunate, the healthy and wealthy, almost with the force of a law (Dyson 1965). This was even more so in Victorian society, and Butler was honest enough to admit in his notebooks that "to love God is to have a good health, good looks, good sense, experience, a kindly nature and a fair balance of cash in hand" (Butler 1985b, 33).

In short, Butler does nothing but reverse the polarity of the analogy between crime and disease, forcing the reader to examine his commonplace assumptions:

> Foreign, indeed, as such ideas are to our own, traces of somewhat similar opinions can be found even in nineteenth-century England. If a person has an abscess, the medical man will say that it contains "peccant" matter, and people say that they have a "bad" arm or finger, or that they are very "bad" all over, when they only mean "diseased" (Butler 1985a, 104).

Far-fetched as this may seem, it is undeniable that descriptions of illness as sin abound in Western culture, starting from the *Iliad* and the *Odyssey* where disease occurs as supernatural punishment. In a recent study on the meaning of illness Marc Augé, Claudine Herzlich and other scholars have convincingly made the case that illness is rarely perceived as a set of symptoms that need curing; on the contrary, it is metaphorically constructed as an unfortunate event that threatens both our individual lives and the welfare of the community. In other words, labelling a state of illness is not a social neutral process, the stigma coming not only from the fact that the sick person is unproductive and thus a burden for the community, but also from the idea that the sick body signifies both a moral and intellectual weakness and a change of state, a shift away from the cultural norm, and finally an affront to the cult of prosperity and affluence. The very language used to express health and illness is not customized to transmit information about physical and organic facts, being rather framed to describe the individual's relationship with the socialized exterior (Herzlich 1988). Susan Sontag arrives at similar conclusions when she argues that myths about tuberculosis and cancer assign to the luckless ill the ultimate responsibility for falling ill, which is interpreted as a psychological event whose course can be reverted through the mobilization of will (Sontag 1991). But if illness is a form of social deviation ignited by a self-destructive attitude, in its turn criminal behaviour can be considered an illness that requires medical treatment and sympathetic condescension instead of condemnation.

After all, Erewhonian absurdities are not so absurd and some of the tendencies at work in this seemingly dystopian world are in fact as much engrained in Victorian England and in our own society. Butler's aim here is to overcome the deadening effects of habit through defamiliarization, a technique that shakes up the familiar and renews our awareness and perception of things. The association between illness and guilt, linguistically realized by discarding fixed lexical collocations in favour of uncanny locutions such as "accused of pulmonary consumption" and "convicted of aggravated bronchitis", conjures up a nightmarish scenario that shocks the reader into a critical stance towards the impact of materialistic values on social cohesion and solidarity.

In the first part of this essay I have provided some background to the technophobe's vision of the living body as physical mechanism. The theory of the survival of the fittest and the Darwinian equations between fortune and virtue issued in a crude, egoistic philistinism and in a sclerotic welfare state, the health of the overall system being maintained at the expense of the unfit. The endless mechanization of industrial capitalism merging with Darwin's theory of evolution also produced an interpretation of illness as a disturbance of the organism's adjustment to its environment, a disturbance, that is, of the individual's ability to function in the world. Nothing but shame and guilt can be attached to the unproductive body, a body which has failed to respond to nature's ways and, as a consequence, must be punished in order to strike fear into those who neglect their own physical well-being and become a threat to public health by fostering a sense of helplessness that could change attitudes towards material progress.

Butler was among those who regarded with consternation the crassly materialistic outlook that was prevalent in the industrial countries even if, on some matters, he was at least as materialistic as the *bourgeoisie* he attacked. His real demand is not that we should redeem ourselves but that we should honestly recognize ourselves for what we are, or rather, for what we have become in the aftermath of the industrial age. His sharpest satire was directed both against the people who retain a dogmatic faith in reason and logic (the Pharisees and the men of science) and who therefore never test their theories, and against the metaphysical master plots (Christian religion, Darwinism, philosophical mechanism) that were numbing human beings into collective insensitivity and bigotry.

References

Butler S. 1985a. *Erewhon*. Harmondsworth: Penguin.

Butler S. 1985b. *The Notebooks of Samuel Butler*. London: Hogarth Press.

Dyson A.E. 1965. *The Crazy Fabric*. London: Macmillan.

Forster E.M. 2008. *The Creator as Critic and Other Writings by E. M. Forster*, ed. Heath J. M.. Toronto: Dundurn Press.

Herzlich C. 1988. "Modern Medicine and the Quest for Meaning: Illness as a Social Signifier". In Augé M., Herzlich C. (eds.) *The Meaning of Illness: Anthropology, History and Sociology*. London: Routledge, 151-175.

Jeffers T. 1981. *Samuel Butler Revalued*. University Park and London: The Pennsylvania State University Press.

Ketabgian T. 1997. "The Human Prosthesis: Workers and Machines in the Victorian Industrial Scene". In *Critical Matrix*, 11, 1, 4-32.

Marroni F. 2007. *Spettri senza nome: modelli epistemici e narrativa vittoriana*. Roma: Carocci.

Popper K. 2002. *Unended Quest: An Intellectual Autobiography*. London: Routledge.

Sontag S. 1991. "*Illness as Metaphor*" and "*Aids and Its Metaphors*". Harmondsworth: Penguin.

Swift J. 2003. "A Discourse Concerning the Mechanical Operation of the Spirit". In Ross A., Woolley D. (eds.) *Major Works*. Oxford: Oxford University Press, 165-181.

Wiener M.J. 1986. *English Culture and the Decline of the Industrial Spirit. 1850-1980*. Cambridge: Cambridge University Press.

Section 2
The Languages of Literature

GIOIELLA BRUNI ROCCIA

Libera Università Maria Ss. Assunta (LUMSA), Roma

"Writing, When Properly Managed, Is But a Different Name for Conversation": *Tristram Shandy* and the Ethics of Reading

At the end of the last century Melvyn New provocatively proposed "to read Sterne *against the grain*", arguing that Sterne's writings could only be understood in relation to their historical and cultural context (New 1997, xxxvii). Indeed, a similar concern is very well reflected in the recently published *Cambridge Companion to Laurence Sterne*, edited by Thomas Keymer (2009) to mark the 250th anniversary year of *Tristram Shandy*. If we generally consider the different scholarly approaches and the lively debates that have surrounded Sterne's masterpiece in the past few decades, we must acknowledge that, in the end, the critical relationship between reader and text has not always been one of reciprocity. Put alternatively, Tristram-Sterne has become our contemporary – as Giorgio Melchiori incisively stated in 1974[1] – while, on the other hand, "we are still learning to be *his* contemporaries".[2] The asymmetric character of this relationship becomes strikingly evident when we consider one of the most frequently quoted passage of Sterne's novel – a passage that intrinsically implies the idea of reciprocity: "Writing, when properly managed (as you may be sure I think mine is) is but a different name for conversation" (Sterne 1997, 88).

In recent years this idea of writing as conversation has become a commonplace of literary criticism, while the opening paragraph of chapter eleventh, volume II of *Tristram Shandy*, has appeared as a recurring quotation not only in Sternean criticism, but also in books of pragmatic stylistics, communication and multimedia studies, hermeneutics and digital culture. *Tristram Shandy* as a forerunner of the modern hypertext: this seems to be the most recent, converging idea from a multi-disciplinary perspective. Thus, the author's explicit proposal for an interactive narrative seems to anticipate

---

[1] See the conclusive statement of Melchiori's "Introduction" to the Italian translation of *Tristram Shandy* (Melchiori 1974, xxxi).

[2] This sentence is borrowed from the often-quoted *incipit* of Richard Ellmann's biography of Joyce (Ellmann 1983, 3).

the concept of a re-writable book, where reading moves towards writing and interferes with it. Yet there is a contrasting point that has been strangely neglected: the role of the author, which tends to disappear in hypertextual writing, but which, instead, constitutes a pervasive presence throughout *The Life and Opinions of Tristram Shandy*, establishing the real coherence of the book.

The self-assertive figure of the critic or *hypercritic*, so effectively parodied in Sterne's novel, comes to mind. This is not to deny the truism that critical practice is always, in a sense, an act of appropriation or self-understanding. Yet we cannot easily overlook New's suggestion for a reading *against the grain*, that is, a reading intended to contrast the connatural tendency to look first at ourselves in the authors we approach, to hear primarily our voice or what confirms our assumptions. In this perspective the reference to "the ethics of reading"[3] is utterly relevant, since it implies such issues as the singularity of the literary work and, therefore, its *otherness* – "not as an absolute quality, but one that is meaningful only in relation to a given context; otherness is always otherness *to* a particular self or situation" (Attridge 2004, 11). Thus, according to Derek Attridge, an ethical dimension is inherent in any act of literary signification or literary response:

> But of course ethics concerns persons and not texts […]; if, however, the literary text is an event of signification (which is to say human signification), the demands it makes – to respect its otherness, to respond to its singularity, to avoid reducing it to the familiar and the utilitarian even while attempting to understand it – may be ethical in a fundamental, nonmetaphorical sense (*ibidem*).

Indeed, with respect to *Tristram Shandy*, the main reason for focusing on the ethical dimension of reading is the proper nature of the novel itself, as is shown by the most inclusive and challenging definition of the novel: "Writing, when properly managed (as you may be sure I think mine is) is but a different name for conversation" (Sterne 1997, 88). Actually Sterne's masterpiece, in its intrinsically metatextual nature, displays various attempts at self-defining, using phrases for naming and qualifying the work, and illustrating the laws of its own composition with diagrams and models and verbal explanations. But "to define – is to distrust", according to Tristram (*ibidem*, 178). Nevertheless, all these attempts to describe the work, to explain what it is about and the way it is constructed, to characterize it from a particular point of view – "this dramatic work", "this rhapsodical work", "this book of books" (*ibidem*, 17, 31, 178) –, all this recurring effort of naming *The Life and Opinions of Tristram Shandy, Gentleman* in the very act of producing it, is essential to the intimate purpose of Sterne's

---

[3] For a full discussion, see Attridge (2004). See also the concise, authoritative study of Ezio Raimondi (2007).

writing. All these tentative definitions, though ironically elusive, contradictory, confounding, contribute to creating quite a subtle interplay of names which reciprocally recall one another throughout Sterne's book, intermixing and moving their object continuously under the reader's eye. Significantly, this self-reflexive attitude pervades the whole work, up to the end of the last volume, where the final inconclusive expression "a COCK and a BULL" (*ibidem*, 543), put in Yorick's mouth when answering a question of Tristram's mother, leads the reader back to the very beginning of the story: "I wish either my father or my mother [...]" (*ibidem*, 5).

Names really affect human existence in the Shandean universe: not so much the Christian name given to a baby, as Walter Shandy thought, as the names by which men understand and perceive reality, since they express and convey opinions, and opinions are responsible for the condition of happiness or unhappiness of men, according to Epictetus. The act of naming is of crucial importance in the general design of *Tristram Shandy*, in so far as it reveals the deceit inherent in any definition, the implicit pretension of any monological and denotative language to fix opinions in a definite form. Finally, any attempt at naming human life and experience proves to be unjust, unless it implies as a constitutive component the implicit reference to another voice, to a different perspective, to *a different name*. And it is precisely this acknowledgment of the intrinsic *otherness* of any human word – of its unavoidable subjectivity and ambiguity – that founds the all-embracing definition of Sterne's masterpiece:

> Writing, when properly managed, (as you may be sure I think mine is) is but *a different name* for conversation: As no one, who knows what he is about in good company, would venture to talk all; — so no author, who understands the just boundaries of decorum and good breeding, would presume to think all: The truest respect which you can pay to the reader's understanding, is to halve this matter amicably, and leave him something to imagine, in his turn, as well as yourself (*ibidem*, 88; italics mine).

This indeed can be considered a meaningful expression of the intrinsically dialogical nature of any human word, of any speech act, whatever form it may assume. The very way in which this definition is worded should be intended not as a synonymic substitution – one name in place of another, one concept in place of another – but as a continuity, as a sort of metonymic relation, as an ideal, hypothetical progression of writing towards conversation. It is this self-conscious dynamism, which brings writing towards reading and reading towards writing in the name of conversation, that reveals the ethical tension inherent in the very act of writing, "when properly managed". And here, encompassed in this effective and open-ended assertion, at the beginning of chapter XI in the second volume of *Tristram Shandy*, all the other tentative, partial, puzzling definitions of the work find their proper place, blending together into a design of unsuspected coherence.[4]

Even from a semiotic perspective – which is not inappropriate in relation to such an acute inquirer of language as Laurence Sterne, in the context of a 'logocentric' century, as the eighteenth century has been recently named – we can observe that this definition is completely different from all the others, implying a wider view of the entire communication process. In fact, it is not concerned with the semantic dimension of the novel, trying to explain *what* the story (or the history) is about; neither is it concerned with the syntactic dimension, describing *how* the work is internally constructed. Here the attention is focused on the pragmatic dimension, that is on the human subjects *who* are involved in the complementary actions of writing and reading, *as if* they were in conversation.

In truth, what appears to be continuously thematized throughout *The Life and Opinions of Tristram Shandy* is the relationship between author and reader. Therefore, the model of conversation is proposed in order to affirm the role of the reader as a true participant in the construction of the story.[5] Or at least, such an intention is programmatically declared in the quoted passage, where the appeal to "the reader's understanding" clearly recalls John Locke's most famous work. In particular, in "The Epistle to the Reader" – the prefatory text to *An Essay Concerning Human Understanding* – writing and reading are described as parallel and interactive processes:

> This, reader, is the entertainment of those, who let loose their own thoughts, and follow them in writing; which thou oughtest not to envy them, since they afford thee an opportunity of the like diversion, if thou wilt make use of thy own thoughts in reading. 'Tis to them, if they are thy own, that I refer myself (Locke 1997, 7-8).

Thus, by closely connecting the pleasure of reading with a genuine critical attitude, Locke paves the way for new conceptual models of literary communication. However, the most influential author in relation to Sterne's idea of conversation is the third earl of Shaftesbury, not only for the innovative character of his philosophical conception, but also for the conversational style

---

[4] Such a reading is based on a *literal* interpretation of the text, assumed as a strategy which is implied by the formal nature of the work itself. In other words, a process of literalization, in the sense intended by Michael McKeon in his *Origins of the English Novel*, is essential to the comprehension of the formal method of Sterne's narrative (see generally McKeon 1987, chap. 8). Evidently, Laurence Sterne was familiar with the traditional methodology of biblical hermeneutics, as is shown also by his sermons. What is most interesting here, however, is the way in which these methods are made relevant to the reading of *Tristram Shandy*. For a stimulating discussion on this issue, see Carol Watts (1996, 31-32).

[5] On the active and 'sympathetic' role of the reader in *Tristram Shandy*, in connection with eighteenth-century philosophical thought, see especially Ruggieri (1995).

of his own writings. Indeed, a striking influence of Shaftesbury is perceivable in the passage quoted from *Tristram Shandy*, most evident on the literal level, but also revealed by the close connection between the key notion of conversation, implying equality and reciprocity, and the ethical category of sympathy. "To halve this matter amicably" is the method proposed by Tristram-Sterne to the perceptive reader, in order to encourage his sympathetic participation. The very wording of this meaningful expression recalls Shaftesbury's *Soliloquy, or Advice to an Author*, since the verb used explicitly denotes the 'division' implied by the Socratic dialogue, which the English philosopher revives as the most appropriate method of knowledge (and self-knowledge) for the modern era (see Shaftesbury 1999a).

According to Shaftesbury, only through dialogue preconceptions and false opinions can be unmask. Through dialogue and conversation the deceitful use of language, the reductive use of names and labels to classify people and human behaviour can be brought to light and corrected. But this form of critique, this ability of discerning the real value of persons and opinions, passing through a multiplicity of different perspectives, must be grounded upon the moral virtue of sympathy. Put another way: in Shaftesbury's view conversation becomes the natural and familiar context in which everyone can freely practise his own faculties of understanding and critical judgement, expressing his own feelings of sympathy, sharing with others the pleasure of benevolent humour and self-irony (see Shaftesbury 1999b).

The relevance of a similar conception to Sterne's novel can hardly be overestimated. "I write to instruct", the narrator declares, addressing "Sir Critick", at the beginning of the second volume of *Tristram Shandy* (Sterne 1997, 70). Bringing together ancient and modern learning, Tristram-Sterne makes dialogue the basic underlying principle of his writing, as well as of his moral instruction. Thus, the level showing the material writing of the story exists precisely on account of the relationship between the narrator and the reader.[6] Far from being a mere adjunctive element, the presence of the reader inside the text is essential to the constitution of a full dialogical dimension, from which Tristram himself derives his truthfulness, his intrinsic moral value. In other words, we might say that Tristram's writing is redeemed from its hobby-horsical tendency, *viz.* from the risk of a narcissistic involution, because of its radical orientation towards an interlocutor. It is precisely this tension towards the *other*, this desire for the other's responsive understanding, in the words of Bakhtin, that turns writing into conversation. Indeed, such a tension underlies the whole narrative. From the opening lines, "I wish either my father or my mother [...]", right up to the ending, the writing of *The Life and Opinions* is carried forward by

---

[6] For an insightful treatment of Sterne's writing strategies, see Iser (1988).

Tristram's quest for self-understanding: and the reader is the figure called upon to answer this fundamental desire.

Because of this particular relationship, all the other persons and events can be recalled. But the reader must learn *how to read* the story, that is, how to behave and interact properly, in order to be admitted into the domesticity of Shandy Hall. The subject matter of the story being narrated, with all its interruptions, digressions, suspensions, constitutes the internal dimension of *The Life and Opinions of Tristram Shandy*. However, on this level too, inside the narrative itself, what is truly thematized is the relationship between the members of the Shandy family, recollected and relived by Tristram through an authentic and intimate conversation.

Finally, the crucial point of the narrator's pedagogical instruction is to teach his interlocutor *to read properly*. This is also the essential condition which enables the reader to pass from an exterior dialogical level, the 'formal' level of the relation with the author, to the inward dimension of a more familiar conversation. If we now return to the passage already quoted from chapter XI, in the second volume of *Tristram Shandy*, we can observe the way in which this educational progress of the reader is developed:

> For my own part, I am eternally paying him compliments of this kind, and do all that lies in my power to keep *his imagination* as busy as my own.
> 'Tis his turn now; – I have given an ample description of Dr. Slop's sad overthrow, and of his sad appearance in the back parlour; – *his imagination* must now go on with it for a while (Sterne 1997, 88; italics mine).

The concept of "imagination" connects this passage to Adam Smith's *Theory of Moral Sentiments*, which appeared in Glasgow at the end of April 1759, while Sterne was completing the first volume of *Tristram Shandy*. Departing from the tradition of 'moral sense' philosophy of Shaftesbury, Hutcheson and Hume, Adam Smith proposes a theory of sympathy in which the act of observing others makes people aware of themselves and the morality of their own behaviour. 'Sympathy' is the term used to denote the feeling of these moral sentiments, which arise from an innate desire to identify with the emotions of others. It operates through a logic of mirroring, in which a spectator imaginatively reconstructs the experience of the person he is observing. Let us quote from the opening page:

> As we have no immediate experience of what other men feel, we can form no idea of the manner in which they are affected, but by conceiving what we ourselves should feel in the like situation. Though our brother is upon the rack, as long as we ourselves are at our ease, our senses will never inform us of what he suffers. They never did, and never can, carry us beyond our own person, and it is *by the imagination only* that we can form any conception of what are his sensations [...]. By the imagination we place ourselves in his

situation, we conceive ourselves enduring all the same torments, we enter as it were into his body, and become in some measure the same person with him [...] (Smith 1976, 9; italics mine).

As spectators of the actions of other people, we can imagine how we would feel in their situation. This is precisely what Tristram-Sterne expects of his reader, inviting him to use his imagination in order to take part in the scene depicted. When the narrator proposes "to halve this matter amicably", actually he is inviting the reader to a sympathetic participation in the events narrated, so as to share the emotions and sentiments of the characters and of the person who tells the story. In short, he wants the reader to identify himself with the characters and situations described:

> Let the reader imagine then, that Dr. Slop has told his tale; – and in what words, and with what aggravations his fancy chooses: – Let him suppose that Obadiah has told his tale also, and with such rueful looks of affected concern, as he thinks will best contrast the two figures as they stand by each other: Let him imagine that my father has stepp'd up stairs to see my mother: – And, *to conclude this work of imagination,* – let him imagine the Doctor wash'd, – rubb'd down, – condoled with, – felicitated, – got into a pair of Obadiah's pumps, stepping forwards towards the door, upon the very point of entering upon action (Sterne 1997, 88; italics mine).

Evidently, the reader is not asked to cooperate in the 'material' construction of the story. He is not expected to interfere in what the story is about, or to suggest the way in which the events and actions should follow one another. All that is perfectly established by the author, as this brilliant piece of self-irony shows. The reader, instead, is required to place himself in the situation of the characters, to enter into their bodies and their minds, in such a way as to feel their sensations, to share their emotions, to participate in their feelings. Even more, in Sterne's words, in order "to conclude this work of imagination" the reader should perform and enact that extraordinary tension towards visualization and auralization, which is inscribed in the written page, with the aim of conveying the sense of a face-to-face relationship. This is the reader's responsibility towards a literary work intended and proposed as conversation. Ultimately, the basic assumption of Sterne's novel is that 'conversation', *cum-versari*, implies the willingness to-stay-in-the-situation-with-the-other, looking at him and feeling with him, and this is the proper meaning of 'sympathy' in the wake of Shaftesbury, Hutcheson, Hume and Adam Smith. And yet the appeal to the reader "to conclude this work of imagination" constitutes the radical challenge, continually renewed, inherent in *any* authentic narrative text. As Viktor Shklovsky authoritatively claimed: "*Tristram Shandy* is the most typical novel of world literature" (Shklovsky 1991, 170).

References

Attridge D. 2004. *J.M. Coetzee & the Ethics of Reading*. Chicago: The University of Chicago Press.

Ellmann R. 1983. *James Joyce*. Oxford, New York: Oxford University Press.

Iser W. 1988. *Laurence Sterne: Tristram Shandy*. Cambridge: Cambridge University Press.

Keymer T. (ed.) 2009. *The Cambridge Companion to Laurence Sterne*. Cambridge: Cambridge University Press.

Locke J. 1997. *An Essay Concerning Human Understanding*. London: Penguin.

McKeon M. 1987. *The Origins of the English Novel: 1600-1740*. Baltimore: Johns Hopkins University Press.

Melchiori G. 1974. "Introduzione". In L. Sterne, *La vita e le opinioni di Tristram Shandy gentiluomo*. Milano: Mondadori, ix-xxxvi.

New M. 1997. "Editor's Introduction". In L. Sterne, *The Life and Opinions of Tristram Shandy, Gentleman*. Harmondsworth: Penguin, xxvii-xli.

Raimondi E. 2007. *Un'etica del lettore*. Bologna: Il Mulino.

Ruggieri F. 1995. "Laurence Sterne: The Machinery of My Work". In F. Ruggieri (ed.) *Oltre il romanzo: da Sterne a Joyce*. Napoli: Edizioni Scientifiche Italiane, 55-72.

Shaftesbury A.A.C. 1999a. *Soliloquy, or Advice to an Author*. In Shaftesbury A.A.C. *Characteristics of Men, Manners, Opinions, Times*. Cambridge: Cambridge University Press, 70-162.

Shaftesbury A.A.C. 1999b. *Sensus Communis. An Essay on the Freedom of Wit and Humour*. In Shaftesbury A.A.C. *Characteristics of Men, Manners, Opinions, Times*. Cambridge: Cambridge University Press, 29-69.

Shklovsky V. 1991. "The Novel as Parody: Sterne's *Tristram Shandy*". In Shklovsky V. *Theory of Prose*. Elmwood Park II: Dalkey Archive Press, 147-170.

Smith A. 1976. *The Theory of Moral Sentiments*. Oxford: Oxford University Press.

Sterne L. 1997. *The Life and Opinions of Tristram Shandy, Gentleman*. Harmondsworth: Penguin.

Watts C. 1996. "The Modernity of Sterne". In Pierce D., de Voogd P. (eds.) *Laurence Sterne in Modernism and Postmodernism*. Amsterdam: Rodopi, 19-38.

SONIA BUTTINELLI

Università Roma Tre

The Art-Work of the Future: from Wagner to Joyce

> Want will [...] teach the tortured Need-lacking spirits [...] the simple, homely need of sheer human, physical hunger and thirst; but [...] in fellowship shall we taste their genuine joys, and grow up in communion to veritable men. In common, too, shall we close the last link in the bond of holy Necessity; and the brother-kiss that seals this bond, will be the *mutual Art-work of the Future*. But in this, also, our great redeemer and well-doer, Necessity's vicegerent in the flesh, – *the Folk*, will no longer be a severed and peculiar class; for in this Art-work we shall all be *one* [...] (Wagner 1993, 77).

The present paper aims at tracing the source of two of the numerous Wagnerian notions emerging from Joyce's early critical writings back to the composer's *Prose Works*, namely the notions of "necessity" and "folk", together with the importance for art to be collective.[1] It will focus on two of the German

---

[1] In the endless Joycean bibliography, amongst the volumes that analyze the deep connection between the Irish writer and music, *Picking up Airs. Hearing the Music in Joyce's Text* (Bauerle 1993), by Ruth Bauerle and *Bronze by Gold. The Music of Joyce* (Knowles 1999), edited by Sebastian Knowles must be mentioned. Other interesting studies on this topic – though mainly restricted to Wagner's dramas and to the prominently melodic aspect of his influence on the author of *Ulysses* – are Zack Bowen's volumes *Musical Allusions in the Works of James Joyce* (Bowen 1974) and *Bloom's Old Sweet Song* (Bowen 1995), essential instruments in that they help to identify the countless musical references scattered throughout the Irish writer's work. A book of seminal importance is *Joyce and Wagner: A Study of Influence*, by Timothy Martin (Martin 1991). It is a huge work on Wagner's influence on Joyce, with some shrewd insights into the Zurich essays and the role they played in the making of Joyce's early works. Amongst the first contribution on Wagner's influence on Joyce are Jacques Aubert's *The Aesthetics of James Joyce* (Aubert 1973), and Franca Ruggieri's *Le Maschere dell'artista. Il giovane Joyce* (Ruggieri 1986), two volumes of the most vital concern in which the authors point out repeatedly the deep connection between the Irish Writer and the German composer.

musician's writings, the ones that fascinated and influenced the young Joyce most deeply: *Art and Revolution* (Wagner 1993, 21-65) and *The Art-work of the Future* (Wagner 1993, 67-213). This choice is partly due to the fact that the first volume of Wagner's *Prose Works*, published in 1982 by Kegan Paul, translated by William Ashton Ellis and containing the two essays about art, has been found in the Irish writer's Triestine library (Ellmann 1977, 132).

My aim is to draw attention to Joyce's careful reading and re-using of the musician's writings. The influence of the composer's thought on the Irish writer's early production is more conspicuous than that of Victorian writers like, amongst the others, Pater and Ruskin, and clearly emerges from a thorough comparison between the Wagnerian essays about art and Joyce's works. For instance, the artist outlined in the early critical writings and in *A Portrait*, the drama maker, owes a lot to the Wagnerian idea of the artist of the future, as well as the idea of an all-embracing art born by the union of all the branches of art and the concepts of "necessity" and "folk".

A comparison between some passages from *Drama and Life* and *The Art-work of the Future* clearly shows the importance of Wagner's influence on the young writer. In the 1900 essay Joyce, soon after having expounded for the first time that theory of the impersonality of the work of art that was going to have such a prominent role in all his works,[2] writes:

---

[2] In *Drama and Life*, talking about Henrik Ibsen, Joyce writes: "Here the artist forgoes his very self and *stands a mediator in awful truth before the veiled face of God*" (Joyce 2000, 26, my emphasis). This passage can be considered as the first occurrence of that theory of the impersonality of the art-work which will appear in the fifth section of *A Portrait of the Artist as a Young Man*, in the extremely famous image of the artist that, "like the *God of creation*, remains within, or behind or beyond or above his handiwork, invisible, refined out of existence, indifferent, paring his fingernails" (Joyce 1992, 233). As Richard Ellmann points out, Joyce had this idea reading a letter of Gustave Flaubert to M.lle Leroyer de Chantepie about *Madame Bovary* (18 March 1857): "[...] *Madame Bovary* n'a rien de vrai. C'est une histoire *totalement inventée*; je n'y ai rien mis ni de mes sentiments ni de mon existence. L'illusion (s'il y en a une) vient au contraire de *l'impersonnalité* de l'œuvre. C'est un de mes principes, qu'il ne faut pas *s'écrire*. L'artiste doit être dans son œuvre comme Dieu dans la création, invisibile et tout-puissant; qu'on le sente partout, mais qu'on ne le voie pas" (Flaubert 1927, 164). "*MadameBovary* has nothing real in it. It is a totally invented story; I have not put any of my feelings or of my existence in it. The illusion (if there is one) emerges, on the contrary, from the impersonality of the work. This is one of my principles: one must not write oneself. The artist must be in his work like God in the creation: invisible and omnipotent, in that he is felt everywhere but never seen" [my translation]. In a letter to George Sand (15-16 December 1866) the French artist writes: the artist "ne pas mettre sa personnalité en scène. *Je crois que le grand Art est scientifique et impersonnel. Il faut, par un effort d'esprit, se trasporter dans les personnages, et non les attirer à soi*" (Flaubert 1929, 257). "The artist must not put his personality on show. I believe great art is scientific and impersonal. It is necessary, with an effort of the spirit, to take oneself into the characters, and not to attract them towards oneself" [my translation]. Cp. also Eco (1994, 27-28) and Melchiori (1994, 19).

If you ask me what occasions drama or what is the necessity for it at all, *I answer Necessity*. It is mere animal instinct applied to the mind. Apart from his world-old desire to get beyond the flaming ramparts, *man has a further longing to become a maker and a moulder. That is the necessity of all art*. Drama is again the least dependent of all arts on its material (Joyce 2000, 26, my emphasis).

Real drama is engendered by "Necessity" and it is based on an unrestrained instinct, so much uncontrollable to be called "animal". Furthermore, it must not be artificially constructed, because it happens by itself, automatically: it is through it that the man par excellence, the true artist, is able to satisfy his "further longing to become a maker and a moulder". The same idea flows like a river also through Wagner's Zurich Writings and clearly emerges in the final part of *The Art-work of the Future*, where the story of Wieland the Smith is related. On his way back home, the fabulous artificer finds his dwelling destroyed and discovers his wife's elopement. Then, as Wagner explains us, he is trapped by a wicked king: "There was a king, *Neiding* (Envy) by name, who had heard much talk of Wieland's skill; he burned to trap the Smith, that thenceforth he might work for him alone" (Wagner 1993, 211).

The sovereign, in order not to let Wieland run away, cuts his legs' tendons off. After having surrendered himself to despair, the prodigious smith sharpens his wits and, driven by want, forges a pair of wings. Afterward, "borne on the work of his own Art" (Wagner 1993, 213), he flies away and kills Neiding:

Then *Want itself* bent down its mighty pinions above the tortured Wieland's breast, and fanned its inspiration about his thoughtful brow. From *Want*, from terrible, all-powerful Want, the fettered artist learnt to mould what no man's mind had yet conceived. *Wieland found it: found how to forge him WINGS.* [...] He fulfilled *the task that utmost Want had set within him* (Wagner 1993, 212-213, my emphasis).

Wieland's heir too, the folk, has to fulfill the task want assigned it, as it clearly emerges from the ending lines of *The Art-work of the Future*: "[...] O sole and glorious Folk! This is it, that thou thyself hast sung. Thou art thyself this Wieland! Weld thou thy wings, and soar on high!" (Wagner 1993, 213).

The notion of "necessity" is deeply connected with the concept of "folk": as a matter of fact, if real drama can only be engendered by want and if the folk is the uncontested author of the art-work of the future, then, the folk must necessarily be driven by what Joyce calls "mere animal instinct". Once again in Wagner's words:

A common and collective need is the only true Need; but only he who feels within him a true Need, has a right to its assuagement; but only the assuagement of a genuine Need is Necessity; and it is *the Folk alone that acts according to Necessity's behests*, and therefore irresistibly, victoriously, and right as none besides (Wagner 1993, 75, my emphasis.).

Thus, according to the composer, the folk must act "with all the necessity of a nature-force" (Wagner 1993, 175). In order to better understand the role assigned by the musician to the folk, a passage from *The Art-work of the Future* seems particularly interesting:

> Who, then, will be the *Artist of the Future?*. [...] Let us say it in one word: the *Folk. That selfsame Folk to whom we owe the only genuine Art-work, still living even in our modern memory, however much distorted by our restorations; to whom alone we owe all Art itself.* [...] *The Folk* must of necessity be the Artist of the future [...].[In] the days which our historians betoken as those of prehistoric myth and fable, – the Folk, in truth, was already the only poet, the only artist (Wagner 1993, 204-207).

The folk is, therefore, the unquestioned artist of the future, the only one capable of moulding the great and universal art-work of the future:

> *Not ye wise men, therefore, are the true inventors, but the Folk; for Want it was, that drove it to invention. All great inventions are the People's deed;* whereas the devisings of the intellect are but the exploitations, the derivatives, nay, the splinterings and disfigurements of the great inventions of the Folk. *Not ye, invented speech, but the Folk;* ye could but spoil its physical beauty, break its force (Wagner 1993, 80, my emphasis, except for the word "speech").

Everything engendered by the wise men's sterile minds is nothing but an everlasting exploitation of the folk's want-driven inventions:

> *Not ye, were the invertors of Religion, but the Folk;* ye could but mutilate its inner meaning, turn [...] its out-breathing truth to lies. *Not ye are the inventors of the State;* [...]. *It is not ye that give the Folk the wherewithal to live, but it gives you; not ye who give the folk to think, but it gives you* (Wagner 1993, 80, my emphasis, except for the words "Religion" and "State").

Just like artistic creation, Religion and State are, as well, the result of the folk's work: intellectuals, far from being the inventors of those fundamental institutions, are responsible for their present deterioration. It is the folk's task to redeem those sages, thus fulfilling "its mission of redemption" (Wagner 1993, 81).

A "rather un-Joycean but highly Wagnerian" notion of folk – as Timothy Martin calls it (Martin 1991, 19) – first appears in the starting pages of Joyce's *Drama and Life*:

> Let us criticize in the manner of free people, as a free race, recking little of ferula and formula. *The Folk is, I believe, able to do so much.* Securus judicat orbis terrarum, is not too high a motto for all human artwork (Joyce 2000, 25, my emphasis).

Thus, in Joyce's opinion, the folk has to assess drama taking no care of all those principles that prevent its full realization. Moreover, although such a statement could seem to be in contradiction with what the Irish writer will state, one year later, in the opening lines of *The Day of the Rabblement*,[3] the difference between his ideas of "folk" and "rabblement" clearly emerges from a careful reading of the two essays. A similar distinction can also be found in *The Art-work of the Future*, where Wagner writes:

> From their lofty pedestal, they [the artists of the present] deem that only their direct antithesis, the raw uncultured masses, can mean for the "the Folk". As they look down upon the people, there rise but fumes of beer and spirits to their nostrils; they fumble for their perfumed handkerchiefs, and ask with civilised exasperation: "What! The *rabble* is in future to replace us in Art-making? [...]" *However, neither you nor this rabble do we understand by the term, the Folk*: only when neither Ye nor It shall exist any longer, can we conceive the presence of the Folk (Wagner 1993, 207-209, my emphasis).

However, Joyce's notion of "folk" also seems to owe something to the Wagnerian concept of "ideal public", that the musician identifies with that of ancient Greece. Indeed, the German composer's admiration for Greek drama is, undoubtedly, one of the Zurich Writings' main *leitmotivs*.[4] In fifth-century Athens art had reached heights never touched before: the relationship between the artist and his public was so immediate that there was no need for isolation, because every single word was fully understood by those whom the work of art referred to. Such an idyllic vision is totally different from the realities in which both Wagner and Joyce happened to live and work, as it is demonstrated, for instance by one of Joyce's most eminent contemporaries, Oscar Wilde, that, in *The Soul of Man under Socialism*, praises Sir Henry Irving – a well-known actor-manager – for having encouraged his public's growth:

> His object was to realize his own perfection as an artist, under certain conditions and certain forms of Art. At first he appealed to the few: now *he has educated the many. He has created in the public both taste and temperament.* The public appreciate his artistic success immensely. I often wonder, however,

---

[3] *"No man, said the Nolan, can be a lover of the true or the good unless he abhors the multitude; and the artist, though he may employ the crowd, is very careful to isolate himself. This radical principle of artistic economy applies specially to a time of crisis, and today when the highest form of art has been just preserved by desperate sacrifices, it is strange to see the artist making terms with the rabblement"* (Joyce 2000, 50).

[4] It is interesting to point out that, amongst the numerous aspects that, for many years, linked Richard Wagner and Friedrich Nietzsche, their love for Greek history and drama, together with their admiration for the philosophy of Arthur Schopenhauer, had a prominent role.

whether the public understand that *the success is entirely due to the fact that he did not accept their standard, but realized his own* (Wilde 1986, 42-43).[5]

Public must not behave as a judge beforehand: it must demonstrate to be equal to that task. Indeed, as Richard Wagner wrote in a letter from Dresden, his intention was *"ennobling the public taste* here and of thereby making its voice one to be considered" (Altmann and Bozman 1927, 115). Furthermore, once again in the musician's opinion, one of Greek drama's most distinguishing features is, undoubtedly, its being collective:

> In common, too, shall we close the last link in the bond of holy Necessity; and the brother-kiss that seals this bond, will be the *mutual Art-work of the Future* [the author's emphasis]. But in this, also, our great redeemer and well doer, Necessity's vicegerent in the flesh, – the *Folk* [the author's emphasis], *will no longer be a severed and peculiar class; for in this Art-work we shall all be one* (Wagner 1993, 77, my emphasis, unless otherwise indicated).

Necessity, folk and the communal character of drama: these three elements, combined together, are, according to the German composer, at the basis of the creation of the genuine art-work of the future. Once again on Wagner's evidence, nothing but the co-operation of the whole community can originate real drama:

> This great United Art-work he cannot picture as depending on the arbitrary purpose of some human unit, but can only conceive it as *the instinctive and associate product of the Manhood of the Future.* […] It is not the lonely spirit, striving by Art for redemption into Nature, that can frame the Art-work of the Future; *only the spirit of Fellowship, fulfilled by Life, can bring this work to pass* (Wagner 1993, 88, my emphasis).

The deep connection between these Wagnerian categories also emerges in the pages of *Drama and Life*, where, after having mentioned the prominent role the folk must hold in the realization of real drama, Joyce points out that

> There are some weighty truths which we cannot overpass, in the relations between drama and the artist. *Drama is essentially a communal art and of widespread domain.* The drama – its fittest vehicle almost presupposes an audience, drawn from all classes. *In an art-loving and art-producing society the drama would naturally take up its position at the head of all artistic institutions* (Joyce 2000, 26, my emphasis).

A necessary condition for the creation of real drama is an identity of views between the artist and his public: what made Greek tragedy fall into disgrace

---

[5] On Richard Ellmann's evidence, a copy of Wilde's essay has been found in Joyce's Triestine library (Ellmann 1977, 132).

was that it soon stopped being collective and adopted the idea of "art for art's sake". In conclusion, both in Joyce and in Wagner's opinion, drama will be able to achieve the place it aims at only when a society will be born in which the *folk*, driven by *want*, will give rise to the *communal* art-work of the future.

References

Altmann W., Bozman M. M. (eds.) 1927. *The Letters of Richard Wagner*. London & Toronto: J.M. Dent & Sons Ltd.

Aubert J. 1973. *The Aesthetics of James Joyce* (rev. ed. 1992). London: The John Hopkins University Press.

Bauerle R. 1993. *Picking up Airs. Hearing the Music in Joyce's Text*. Urbana and Chicago: University of Illinois Press.

Bowen Z. 1974. *Musical Allusions in the Works of James Joyce: Early Poetry through Ulysses*. New York: State University of New York Press.

Bowen Z. 1995. *Bloom's Old Sweet Song. Essay on Joyce and Music*. Gainesville: University Press of Florida.

Eco U. 1994. *Le poetiche di Joyce* (1st Portico ed. in *Opera aperta*, 1962). Milano: Bompiani.

Ellmann R. 1977. *The Consciousness of Joyce*. London: Faber & Faber.

Flaubert G. 1927. *Correspondance. 1854-1861*, vol. IV. Paris: Louis Conard, Libraire-Éditeur.

Flaubert G. 1929. *Correspondance. 1862-1868*, vol. V. Paris: Louis Conard, Libraire-Éditeur.

Joyce J. 1992. *A Portrait of the Artist as a Young Man*, ed. by Deane S. London: Penguin Books.

Joyce J. 2000. *Occasional, Critical and Political Writing*, ed. by Barry K., translated from the Italian by Deane C. Oxford, New York: Oxford University Press.

Knowles S.D.G. (ed.) 1999. *Bronze by Gold. The Music of Joyce*. New York and London: Garland Publishing, Inc.

Martin T. 1991. *Joyce and Wagner: A Study of Influence*. Cambridge (Eng.): Cambridge University Press.

Melchiori G. 1994. *Joyce: il mestiere dello scrittore*. Torino: Einaudi.

Ruggieri F. 1986. *Le maschere dell'artista. Il giovane Joyce*. Roma: Bulzoni.

Wagner R. 1993. *The Art-work of the Future and Other Works*, trans. by Ellis W.A. (reprinted from volume I of R. Wagner's *Prose Works*, published in 1895 by Kegan Paul, Trench, Trübner & Co., Ltd.). Lincoln and London: University of Nebraska Press, 21-65.

Wilde O. 1986. "The Soul of Man Under Socialism". In *De Profundis and Other Writings*, intr. by Pearson H. London: Penguin Books, 17-53.

RICCARDO CAPOFERRO

Sapienza – Università di Roma

Apparition Narratives and the Style of the Fantastic

U sually regarded as the century in which the novel was born, the eighteenth century also saw the formation of a variety of other genres, such as imaginary voyages, apparition narratives, and, later, the Gothic. Like the novel, these genres are characterized by a realistic mode of presentation: both *Gulliver's Travels* and *The Castle of Otranto* contain protestations of truthfulness, claims to historicity, and a circumstantial representation of events. Though including super- or non-natural objects, they generate the illusion that the world presented in the narrative is to a large extent analogous to the real world. On the level of content they are, however, radically different from the novel, since they include descriptions of ghosts, monsters, and inexistent countries. In narratives like *The Castle of Otranto*, objects drawn from empirical reality coexist with non-empirical objects.

Thus, "realism" cannot be associated solely with the novel. True, the novel presented itself as a privileged vehicle of truth, as a fiction that could paradoxically say something relevant on moral life. On the other hand, many other works pretended to portray things as they are: though including descriptions of ghosts and monsters, apparition narratives, imaginary voyages, and the Gothic internalized crucial imperatives of empirical epistemology, which prescribed a faithful representation of reality, and tried to capitalize on the increasing appeal of factual or pseudo-factual narratives.

Put otherwise, the revolution in narrative culture that occurred in early modern England entailed not only the emergence of the novel, but also a deep transformation of romance, which constituted its dialectical opposite, but at the same time shared many of its features. In the eighteenth century, the meaning of "romance" had both historical roots and implications across a variety of genres: it indicated chivalric literature, but also contemporary narratives that did not meet the moral prescriptions of the newborn novelistic aesthetics, such as Gothic fiction and imaginary voyages (on the emergence of the category of romance see Williams 1970). On the formal level, these narratives were, nevertheless, very similar to the novel, so similar that, invoking the authority of Bakhtin, it could be tempting to speak of "novelization" (Bakhtin, 1982, 39) – were it not that they took shape *before* the novel was fully stabilized both as a genre and as an aesthetic category.

If observed from the viewpoint of twentieth-century criticism, most of these narratives could very easily fall under the category of the fantastic. Now, many different theories of the fantastic exist, but there is consensus on the presence of ontological hesitation – as theorized by Tzvetan Todorov – as a crucial device of what in the critical idiom is generally called "the fantastic". For Todorov, the fantastic is based on the oscillation between a natural and a supernatural explanation of seemingly extraordinary events; in some cases, the oscillation is superseded, and the fantastic turns into "the uncanny" or "the marvelous", in some other cases it is unresolved, so that we have the "pure fantastic" (Todorov 1973). The presence of ontological hesitation implies an empirically-oriented sense of reality, a realistic worldview that is contradicted by the eruption of an apparently inexplicable phenomenon. The fantastic is, in other words, based on the use of a mode of presentation that implies a restrictive perspective. Many eighteenth-century apparition narratives are, in fact, characterized by ontological hesitation: being intended to persuade disbelievers, they internalize a skeptical view, constructing an implied reader that, because of his materialism, experiences wonder and disorientation.

Were eighteenth-century writers aware of these innovations? Although an inclusive category that accounted for the fantastic was not coined, the rise of the new genres went along with an intense critical work. For instance, in his second preface to *The Castle of Otranto* (1765), Horace Walpole stated that his work was based on the combination of the ancient and the modern romance: the "probability" typical of the novel was used to make credible the reactions of characters facing exceptional circumstances. Walpole acknowledges the existence of a new mode of presentation able to make the unreal look real, and describes *The Castle of Otranto* as a hybrid formation that combines "credible" and incredible entities, a realistic system of verisimilitude and wild inventions (Walpole 1765). A few years later, Clara Reeve echoed Walpole's view, acknowledging the hybrid quality of the *Castle of Otranto*, based on the coexistence of two genres, of two kinds of fictional worlds, one of which is partly grounded in experience (Reeve 1778).

In this paper I shall build on Walpole's ideas. Focusing in particular on Daniel Defoe's *The Apparition of Mrs. Veal* (1706), I shall argue that both the ancestors of the novel and those of the fantastic are informed by a mode of presentation influenced by modern empiricism. I shall demonstrate how the functions that we generally attribute to the fantastic were originally enabled by the use of a pseudo-scientific style that is akin to the style used by realism. This style took shape within scientific culture, and, not surprisingly, one of the first attempts to codify it can be found in the *History of the Royal Society* by Thomas Sprat (1667).

Sprat famously tried to establish rules for writings to be submitted to the Royal Society and published by its official journal, *The Philosophical Transactions*. For Sprat, the language used by contributors had to be characterized by "mathematical plainness", and had to be similar to the language used by "artisans, countrymen, and merchants" (Sprat 1667). Sprat harshly condemned literary rhetoric, regarding it as the unrestrained manifestation of a writer's emotions, detrimental to a text's objectivity. Works designed to convey truth had to be characterized by a one-to-one correspondence between words and things, and had to avoid stylistic tricks. This ideal, influenced by Bacon's reflection on language, would later by satirized by Swift in *Gulliver's Travels*, but it was immensely successful in both scientific and literary circles. Swift himself based the illusion of realism of *Gulliver's Travels* on the pseudo-scientific style promoted by Sprat.

The use of a style characterized by "mathematical plainness" is, as Ian Watt highlighted in *The Rise of the Novel*, a trademark of *Robinson Crusoe*, which, as has often been noted, was heavily influenced by the new science.[1] Robinson provides a great deal of chronological, geographical, and broadly quantitative information, which serves to specify the characteristics of the island and to certify his commitment to empirical truth. Moreover, he avoids using too many metaphors and tends not to deploy too many adjectives to describe the objects he sees or builds.

The language of *Robinson Crusoe* has been crucial in establishing the text's centrality in the genealogy of modern realism. Although *Robinson Crusoe* also contains romance elements, its points in common with scientific culture, in particular its style, have been enough to characterize it as one of the founding fathers of the new province of writing that was to be further explored by authors such as Fielding and Richardson. And, although the canonization of Defoe is a relatively recent phenomenon, late eighteenth- and early nineteenth-century writers, in particular Walter Scott, praised Defoe's fiction for the realism of its descriptions.[2]

The pseudo-scientific language prescribed by the Royal Society was, however, used by other seventeenth- and eighteenth-century writings that can hardly be described as realistic, such as *The Apparition of Mrs. Veal*. To understand *The Apparition of Mrs. Veal* it is useful to focus briefly on the history and functions of apparition narratives. In late seventeenth-century England, when modern science was on the rise, Anglican theologians tried to speak to skeptics

---

[1] Defoe's use of a pseudo-scientific style was famously highlighted in Watt (1957, 101). On Defoe and science, see Vickers (1996).

[2] See Scott's review of Jane Austen's *Emma* (1815-1816, 188-201).

and disbelievers in the only language they valued, the language of empirical description.[3] Joseph Glanvill, a theologian who was also affiliated to the Royal Society, authored a collection of apparition narratives called *Sadducismus Triumphatus*, published posthumously in 1681, that included a great variety of accounts, all of which purport to be based on first-hand experience. Full of protestations of truth and circumstantial data, these accounts were meant to persuade skeptics of the existence of God. In spite of its ambitions, Glanvill's work was not taken very seriously by subsequent scientists, but it spawned a great variety of apparition narratives that tried to revive its sensationalist appeal: though discarding its didactic and epistemological apparatus, they perpetuated its self-conscious empirical focus. And, in the long run, Glanvill was enormously influential on literary culture, inspiring many authors of supernatural fiction, including Poe and Stevenson.[4]

One of the text published in the wake of *Sadducismus Triumphatus* was *The Apparition of Mrs. Veal* by Defoe, who can be regarded not only as a father of realism, but also as a pioneer of the fantastic. *The Apparition of Mrs. Veal* recounts the extraordinary experience of Mrs. Bargrave, a London woman who used to be friends with one Mrs. Veal. Initially very close, the two lost touch, and many years later Mrs. Veal came to Mrs. Bargrave's house. After discussing various religious topics, Mrs. Veal asked Mrs. Bargrave to write a letter to her brother, "and tell him she would have him give rings to such and such; and that there was a purse of gold in her cabinet, and that she would have two broad pieces given to her cousin Watson" (Defoe 1732, 6). Later, Mrs. Bargrave went to visit Mrs. Veal, found out that she had died, and tried to execute her friend's instructions, demonstrating that the information she had given her was reliable. Furthermore, the clothes Mrs. Veal wore on the day of her visit to Mrs Bargrave's were the same she usually wore.

In the preface, the unknown editor declares that "the whole Matter, as it is here Related and laid down, is what is really True; and what She [one of the editor's sources] her self had in the same Words (as near as may be) from Mrs. Bargraves own mouth, who she knows had no Reason to Invent and publish such a Story, nor any design to forge and tell a Lye" (Defoe 1732, i). Accordingly, the narrative is designed to generate a strong sense of truthfulness. It employs an extremely precise language, rife with details. See, for instance, the following passage:

> you must know Mrs. Veal was a maiden gentlewoman of about thirty years of age, and for some years past had been troubled with fits, which were perceived coming on her by her going off from her discourse very abruptly

---

[3] On this point, see McKeon (1987, 83-87).
[4] On Glanville's reception, see Parsons (1966).

to some impertinence. She was maintained by an only brother, and kept his house in Dover (Defoe 1732, 2).

This mode of presentation is typical of Defoe: it includes numbers ("thirty years of age"), specific information on Mrs Veal's appearance and physical existence ("for some years she had been troubled with fits"), and names of places (we are told that Mrs Veal lives in Dover with her only brother). This style is, needless to say, inseparable from a particular kind of verisimilitude, from a set of ontological assumptions. Characters are apparently caught in moments of their everyday lives, implying not so much the exceptionality as the regularity of their actions. In fact, the conversation between Mrs. Bargrave and Mrs. Veal would not have nothing unusual, were it not, as the narrator initially explains, that the latter is an otherworldly entity.

Thus, the style of *The Apparition of Mrs. Veal* seems perfectly factual: it serves to define plausible conditions, stressing the normality of the events narrated. As in *Robinson Crusoe*, the vocabulary used by Defoe is far from being a literary one: it includes names of objects, places, and actions that belong to the sphere of common experience. At the same time, however, this style also has a distinctly aesthetic function: it enables an intense virtual experience. The detailed rendition of the trivial behavior of Mrs. Veal's ghost in fact renders it even more frightening, since the ghost looks distinctly "real". Mrs. Bargrave hears "a Knocking at the Door; she went out to see who it was there, and this prov'd to be Mrs. *Veal*, her old Friend, who was in a riding habit" (Defoe 1732, 3). In other words, Defoe stages Mrs. Veal's exceptionality by building up an absolutely natural setting; he both conforms to the writing practices of the Royal Society and provides a foil for the apparition. A prosaic language is used to give a ghost flesh and blood, to present its return from the dead in a way that looks truthful and can therefore be appealing for readers who are internalizing the empirical worldview.

The style of apparition narratives is meant to assimilate the unreal to the real, to bridge the gap between what is empirical and what is not. At the same time, however, it provides a backdrop against which the exceptionality of the objects clearly stands out. It bears, in other words, paradoxical implications. It generates a sense of continuity, since it places real and unreal phenomena on the same level, and at the same time a sense of discontinuity, since it constructs a realistic setting whose assumptions are suddenly contradicted. It serves, therefore, both to mediate and to highlight the difference between what is empirical and what is not.

Ascertaining the presence of a pseudo-scientific style in apparition narratives and in similar genres, such as imaginary voyages, can help us complicate our view of the forms and origins of the fantastic. Many attempts to theorize the fantastic have been made in the last 40 years, and only occasionally has the idea of "realism" been regarded as crucial to understand its workings.[5] The fantastic, however, shares the same stylistic and ontological assumptions as realism, and the opposition between the two modes is far from being absolute. Both derive from the rise of modern science and from the emergence of a code that was recognizably empirical, and both convey their inventions through a detailed style. The stylistic and ontological workings of the fantastic presuppose the disenchanted worldview and the concrete language that are associated with modern empiricism; they presuppose the rise and pre-eminence of scientific culture.

Redefining the role and origins of the fantastic in relation to realism can, moreover, stimulate a stronger awareness of aspects of the novel that have for many years been eclipsed by the belief in the cognitive power of realism: for instance the use of providential plots and supernatural elements. Focusing on nineteenth-century novels such as Charlotte Brontë's *Jane Eyre* and George Eliot's *Silas Marner*, characterized by an ambivalent representation of the supernatural, one may easily agree with Borges, who thought that all literature is, in fact, fantastic. In spite of their apparent opposition, the novel and the fantastic can be regarded as two versions of the same thing.

References

Bakhtin M. 1982. *The Dialogic Imagination: Four Essays.* Austin: The University of Texas Press.

Brooke-Rose C. 1981. *A Rhetoric of the Unreal: Studies in Narrative and Structure, Especially of the Fantastic.* Cambridge: Cambridge University Press.

Defoe, D. 1719, *Robinson Crusoe.* London.

Defoe D. 1732. "The Apparition of Mrs. Veal" [1706]. In Drelincourt C., Defoe D. (1732) *The Christian's Defence against the Fears of Death: With Seasonable Directions how to Prepare Ourselves to Die Well.* London.

Glanvill J. 1681. *Sadducismus Triumphatus.* London.

Jackson R. 1981. *Fantasy: The Literature of Subversion.* London: Methuen.

McKeon M. 1987. *The Origins of the English Novel: 1600-1740.* Baltimore: Johns Hopkins University Press.

Parsons C.O. 1966. *Introduction to Joseph Glanvill, "Sadducismus Triumphatus".* Gainesville (Fl.): Scholars' Facsimiles & Reprints.

Reeve C. 1778. Preface to *The Old English Baron.* London.

Scott W. 1815-1816. "*Emma*: a novel". In *Quarterly Review* 14, 188-201.

---

[5] The connections between the fantastic and realism are suggested, but not explored, by Jackson (1981), and Brooke-Rose (1981).

Sprat T. 1667. *History of the Royal Society*. London.

Swift, J. 1726, *Gulliver's Travels*. London.

Todorov T. 1973. *The Fantastic: A Structural Approach to a Literary Genre*. Cleveland: The Press of Case Western Reserve University.

Vickers I. 1966. *Defoe and the New Science*. Cambridge: Cambridge University Press.

Walpole H. 1765. Second preface to *The Castle of Otranto*. London.

Watt I. 1957. *The Rise of the Novel: Studies in Defoe, Richardson, and Fielding*. Berkeley and Los Angeles: University of California Press.

Williams I. (ed.) 1970. *Novel and Romance, 1700-1800: A Documentary Record*. London: Routledge & Kegan Paul.

IVANA DIPIETRO

Università di Catania

Bodies in Change:
Lewis Carroll's *Alice in Wonderland*
and Salman Rushdie's *The Firebird's Nest*

> In 1939 Virginia Woolf observed that whenever readers attempt to capture the meaning of *Alice's Adventures in Wonderland* 'we fail – once more we fail [...] The book breaks in two in our hands.' Woolf's metaphor anticipates Umberto Eco's argument that 'in order to transform a cult object one must be able to break, dislocate, unhinge it so that one can remember only parts of it, irrespective of their original relationship with the whole' (Greenway 2005, 135-136).

In this paper I will address the works of two very well-known writers over a span of more than one hundred years – Lewis Carroll's *Alice in Wonderland*, and Salman Rushdie's *The Firebird's Nest* – in order to trace, by means of a comparative approach, a possible influence of the Victorian author on the contemporary one, while focusing on two important conceptual categories: *body* and *change*.

According to Michel Foucault's well-known theorization,[1] the body is the main instrument through which Power exerts control. It can be defined as a particular type of text, a visible one, on which normative modes of living are inscribed. However, it is also that physical entity *with*[2] organs through which, according to Umberto Galimberti (2005, 292-293), men and women's existence in the world is given. Moreover, quoting Merleau-Ponty:

> an awareness of the body is possible only through its dynamic nature and in the tasks that it does. Its awareness of its spatiality can come into being

---

[1] See Foucault (1977; 1980).

[2] I'm referring here to Deleuze and Guattari's definition of BWO (Body Without Organs) in *Anti-Oedipus* (Deleuze and Guattari 1977).

only through its interaction with a situation, not through its location in a static space. This development of body image and spatiality is central for its comprehension of being 'in-the-world' (101) and provides it perspective and the ability to see, judge and rationalize (Mohanram 1999, 17).

The body, as defined by its relations with the space around it, will be therefore considered in this paper as the privileged place to reflect on the modalities of identity construction.

In one of his seminal essays – *Step Across this Line* – Salman Rushdie not only celebrates migration as a universal condition, but also establishes a close connection between "frontier-crossing" and mutation: "To cross a frontier is to be transformed" (Rushdie 2003, 410). The metaphoric act of overcoming those limits within which people are constructed as passive, docile bodies leads inevitably to change, as Rushdie shows in a significant passage about *Alice in Wonderland*:

> Alice the gates of Wonderland, the key to that miniature world in her grasp, cannot pass through the tiny door beyond which she can glimpse marvellous things until she *has altered herself to fit* into her new world. But the successful *frontierswoman* is also, inevitably, in the business of surpassing. She *changes* the rules of her new-found land: Alice in Wonderland, *shape-shifting* Alice, *terrifies* the local by growing too big to be housed. She argues with Mad Hatters and talks back to Caterpillars, and, in the end, loses her fear of an execution-hungry Queen when she, so to speak, grows up. *You're nothing but a house of cards* – Alice the migrant at last sees through the charade of power, is no longer impressed, calls Wonderland's bluff, and *by unmaking it* finds herself again. She wakes up (*ibidem*, 412, emphasis mine).

Rushdie's personal reading of Wonderland stresses the centrality of Alice's alteration (*has altered herself, frontierswoman, shape-shifting*) as a process of adaptation (*to fit*) which inevitably ends up in a dream of rebellion[3] (*she terrifies the local, by unmaking it*).

Following this interpretation, Carroll's tale can be described as the story of a female character's journey into an unknown, "queer"[4] (Carroll 1998, 17) land, where "out-of-the-way things" (*ibidem*, 13) can happen. Some scholars, among whom Talairach-Vielmas (2007, 49-65), explain this underground world as a representation of the commodity culture in the Victorian era, while they see Alice

---

[3] The "shape-shifting" Alice, quoted above, who "terrifies the local by growing too big" suggests a reading of the fairy tale as a dream of rebellion, or, according to John B. Gordon, a piece of "decadent adult literature rather than children's literature" (Phillips 1971, 128).

[4] This adjective recurs frequently in the text: I have counted six occurrences (on pp. 17, 21, 24, 31, 58).

as a model for feminine education.[5] Starting from these relevant interpretations, a more general idea about Wonderland can be formulated according to which this strange and absurd place represents the opportunity for the character to explore her own location, whereas her *Leib* (living body), according to the husserlian terminology proposed by Umberto Galimberti (2005, 283-284), is the instrument to search for it.

Alice's migrant condition itself, then, partakes precisely of that 'migrant sensibility' described by Rushdie which creates new types of human beings

> who root themselves in ideas rather than places, in memories as much as in material things; people who have been obliged to define themselves [...] by their otherness; people in whose deepest selves strange fusions occur, unprecedented unions between what they were and what they find themselves (Rushdie 1992, 124-125).

Born and brought up in the Victorian upper middle class, Alice begins her unusual journey because of boredom. She is "burning with curiosity" (Carroll 1998, 10) after experiencing a strange encounter with a white rabbit, which she impulsively decides to follow down a rabbit hole, clearly, a frontier between human and animal, between the familiar and the unfamiliar, between what she were and what she discovers she is capable of being.

The "deep, deep" well itself reveals to possess the characteristics of an hybrid space, where certainties are shaken and ambivalence reigns. Here the protagonist's body seems, for example, to be weightless, since, following the cult of the angel-woman of the time, women were ideally conceived of "as saint-like, passive, and 'light'. In the Victorian period, the prevailing focus on female weightlessness bound woman's sexual purity to her lack of corporeality" (Talairach-Vielmas 2007, 36). The subsequent events, however, show an uncommon insistence on bodily presence that defies this explanation. Alice's fluctuation between the two worlds and her loss of gravity bespeaks more a sort of 'nomadic consciousness', which leads her to explore a liberating homelessness: her lightness, in other words, permits her to cross boundaries.

The journey she undertakes resembles more a vacation from the apathy and constrains of ordinary life, although 'home' or the memories about it always accompany her throughout the story, and manifest themselves especially when she feels disoriented by unsettling experiences. She clings, for instance, to her lessons of "good English", geography and mathematics at school, in order to explain and categorize the 'incidents of that unordinary life', but, after they

---

[5] In his seminal study on Victorian fairy tales and sensation novels, the scholar stresses the importance of such literary genres in the process of moulding, shaping or framing the female body's appetites for goods.

prove useless, she tries to adapt to the new situation, consequently showing a will to change.

Alice's voyage is the epitome of dislocation, whose most visible consequence is the character's loss of *an* identity, even of its most evident, obvious certainty: her physical appearance. Her body, as a corporeal entity, undergoes sudden, uncontrollable transformations induced by her greedy appetites,[6] which affect her deeply, as in the episode of the pool of tears, or when she, grown too big, addresses her feet, not perceiving herself as a whole sensing unit.

As a consequence of this distressing and estranging process of adaptation, she has to reconsider her identity, to question it ('Who am I?', 'Who was I?' are frequent questions in the famous episode of the Caterpillar) and this leads her inevitably to solitude: "I'm so very tired of being all alone here" (Carroll 1998, 19). She has become an exile, although not a submissive one: "I know something interesting is sure to happen, she said to herself, whenever I eat or drink anything: so I'll just see what this bottle does. I do hope it'll make me grow large again, for really I'm quite tired of being such a tiny little thing" (*ibidem*, 32). This is the first passage[7] in the tale to voice the protagonist's assertion of agency[8] against the roles imposed upon her, or, according to Nina Auerbach's analysis, to voice her "subversive claim to room" (Talairach-Vielmas 2007, 57).[9]

But Alice is not the only example of subversive body resisting the discursive practices of Power. Throughout the tale there are at least two more examples which deserve mentioning. The first is the Duchess's probably male[10] baby, who howls, snorts and grunts turning itself into a piglet while being in Alice's arms. The comparison with and grotesque transformation into an animal despised in

---

[6] Helena Michie (1987, 12-13) remarkably points out that food is "conspicuously absent [...] in novels and conduct books [...]. Hunger [...], which figures unspeakable desires for sexuality and power, becomes itself silenced by Victorian euphemism".

[7] Further important examples can be found in the Mad Tea Party scene, in the episodes with the Caterpillar and the Queen, or in the final sentence against the cards, a sort of performative act, which undoes Wonderland's bluff, as Rushdie himself (2003, 412) remarks.

[8] It is worth observing that Alice's attempt to change and rebel against the model of female education of the time, seems to be unsuccessful after she remains metaphorically framed in the tiny Rabbit's home, when she regrets having embarked on her journey: "I almost wish I hadn't gone down the rabbit hole" (Carroll 1998, 32). Notwithstanding this brief moment of discomfort, she surprisingly discovers that she cannot renounce the life that has already been disclosed to her: "and *yet* – and *yet* – it's rather curious you know, this sort of life" (*ibidem*, 33; emphasis mine).

[9] On the contrary, Talairach-Vielmas (2007, 57) suggests that "size is no sign of female potency".

[10] Carroll's attitude towards boys is reflected in his letters. One of his notes reads: "Boys are not in my line: I think they are a mistake; girls are less objectionable" (*Letters*, vol. I, 455). In *Sylvie and Bruno Concluded*, he describes a character as a "hideous fat boy [...] with the expression of a prize pig". See note 6 to chapter VI in *Alice in Wonderland* (Carroll 1998, 309-310).

most cultures can be read as an attempt to ironically resist Victorian children's tradition, embodied by Alice's maternal attitude towards the infant.

The second example is the most enigmatic creature of Wonderland, added by Carroll in his 1865 revision: the Cheshire Cat. His peculiarity consists in its meaningful bodiless presence, which withdraws a corporeal entity from power's definitions. The Cheshire Cat appears to be "both inviolable and genial [...] [He is endowed] with an ironic detachment" (Knoepflmacher 1998, 174) which makes him free. Moreover, its gender, defined with a neutral 'it', contributes to its ambiguity and playfulness as a non codified, and therefore destabilizing sign.

The relation real/unreal is another central point in Carroll's work, not to mention Rushdie's. As the latter states:

> Unreality is the only weapon with which reality can be smashed, so that it may subsequently be reconstructed [...]. The power of the playful imagination to change for ever our perceptions of how things are has been demonstrated by everyone from Laurence Sterne, in *Tristam Shandy*, to a certain Monty Python in his *Flying Circus* [...] But there lies [...] a terrible danger which is not faced by the realist artist. This danger is whimsy. [...] Can a work of art grow into anything of value if it has no roots in observable reality? (Rushdie 1992, 122-123).

The questions raised here all concern the value of art against that of politics, and the role of imagination in improving reality. And curiously enough, Rushdie himself suggests that "One answer to such questions is 'Lewis Carroll'" (*ibidem*, 123).

But how does Rushdie appropriate, transform or deform this literary icon? And what will be of little Alice once pulled out of Wonderland and Victorian England?[11] The second part of this paper will try to provide an answer to these questions through the analysis of the contemporary writer's short story, *The Firebird's Nest*, published in *The New Yorker* in 1997, on the occasion of India's fiftieth anniversary of independence.

Showing its author's postmodern awareness, the epigraph to the text reads: "Now I am ready to tell how bodies are changed into different bodies" (Rushdie 2004, 45). Bodies, or, more precisely, the tale about them and their process of transformation are here suggested as the most important elements of focalization, thus preparing the reader for the plethora of corporeal references to come.

The story is constructed around two significant elements: fire and water, symbols respectively of destruction and purification and of (re)birth and maternity. This first dichotomy, which will inform the whole narrative, introduces a second one, most beloved by the author, which revolves around the love affair

---

[11] See Greenway (2005, 136).

between the two main characters no better defined than Mr Maharaj and his American bride, clearly two generic names, the first alluding to India's great past of princes, and the second to the western, capitalistic world. Defined in terms of nationality and gender as a generic male East and a feminine West, the two characters embody respectively eastern perilous government's indolence and western dynamism.

Again, in the same dreamlike atmosphere as Alice's, the story's *incipit* introduces a landscape, threatened by progressive desertification, which literally swallows its men, because of drought, in other words, because of want of change. This plague, used as a symbol to portray the intolerable conditions of people, especially women, is the primary cause of the transgression of old patterns and the need for a new order. In its quality of evident materialized event, the drought gives its 'flesh' to challenge normative modes of living, but, while native men passively accept the situation, women are ready to struggle. Female bodies, therefore, become again, as in *Alice*, a space for resistance against dominant discourses.

In this land of desolation and poverty an estranging element, a limousine, makes its way driving back to his home, Mr Maharaj and his bride, defined as "a child of a big city, a foreigner, no virgin" (Rusdhie 2004, 46). If the first term in the description recalls the image of a female child coming from another world – a 'big city' is itself a symbol for the dichotomy 'centre' vs 'periphery' – the second and third attributes (*a foreigner, no virgin*) define her in terms of her (not) belonging to a community and in terms of her cultural/sexual practices. This woman, who has abandoned her country to pursue what she believes to be true love, shares the same naivety and childish behaviour of the Victorian character, following her own white rabbit – Mr Maharaj – into a disturbing journey through her identity. While in *Alice* the rabbit-hole is the visible boundary between every day life and wonder land, the quarry where the couple's limousine halts represents the limit in front of which the protagonist perceives the passage "into another kind of truth; into fiction" (*ibidem*, 62).

As the text shows, the American bride is conscious of her new postmodern dimension, where the many interweaving narratives about the country she is visiting, about her new family and about herself have the power to disorient her. Absorbed by all of them, she assumes their same fictitious and wordy nature becoming the page on which somebody else is going to write her story. She seems to be condemned to the same passive role experienced by Alice in the episode of the trial, where jurors write (about) her on their block notes:

> As though she had entered a fable, as though she were no more than words crawling along a dry page, or as though she were becoming that page itself, that surface on which her story would be written, and across which there blew a merciless wind turning her body to papyrus, her skin to parchment, her soul to paper (*ibidem*, 47).

The connection, in the similes above, between writing surfaces (*papyrus*, *parchment*, *paper*) and bodily components (*body*, *skin*, and even *soul*) conveys the idea of the female body as a one-dimensional, ephemeral entity whose most significant characteristics are its precariousness and the inevitable fate of silence, as the metaphor about the Indian ritual of *sati* demonstrates: "When the woman finished burning there was nothing there. Not a scrap of flesh, not a bone. She burned as paper burns, flying up to the sky and being blown by the wind" (*ibidem*, 48).

Instead of accepting this humiliating condition, the American bride undertakes a painful process of positioning,[12] whose consequences manifest themselves in a fever attack threatening her life. Inevitably, feeling alone and alien, she, too, begins to think of the most secure place she knows: her home. She consoles herself with her own imaginary homeland and its baudrillardian "reification of the real" (*ibidem*, 52) – a clear reference to western capitalism.[13]

The American Bride's perception of being constructed by others' discourses, either as a reflection of her husband's desires or of people's speculations, leads her to (re)action: "in her mind's eye the story is closing around her, the story in which she is trapped, and in which she must, if she can, find the path of action: preferably the right action, but if not, than the wrong. What cannot be tolerated is inertia" (*ibidem*, 56). Her pregnancy represents the turning point in the story, since it gives her the opportunity to offer her own (counter) narrative: the awareness of her continuously changing shape helps her to realize the need of change as the source of life. Moreover, it seems to participate of the idea of the bakhtinian grotesque, as a means to reverse situations, which finds its perfect bodily image in the pregnant and begetting body: this is at the same time two bodies in one, "the one giving birth and dying, the other conceived, generated and born" (Johnson 2003, 222). The value of this image is also in its power to defy the binaries inscribed on the body, either as *Psyche* or *sôma*, or, in Galimberti's terms, as *Leib* or *Koerper*, showing its original playfulness.

After discovering the illusion and hideous mystery that her husband hides, the American bride decides for agency and transforms metaphorically into waves of water which crash upon Mr Maharaj's destructive fire, literally deleting him.[14]

---

[12] The protagonist, too, runs the risk, as her Victorian predecessor, to remain metaphorically entrapped in her husband's abominable palace which crumbles and stinks.

[13] This is the addressee of an authentic accuse, which echoes Rushdie's belief in the liberating power of dreams: "we dream of other dimensions, of paranoid subtexts, of underworlds, because when we awake the actual holds us in its great thingy grasp and we cannot see beyond the material" (Rushdie 2004, 53).

[14] In Rushdie's fiction is not unusual for a wife to rebel against her husband. Also in *Shame* (1983), Sufya Zinobia, the female protagonist transformed into a monster, kills her husband. See Miura (2000, 101-149).

This violent act, manifesting her fear and anger, has a liberating effect not only on people but also on landscape, where a new balance is restored.

In conclusion, not only a carrollian influence on Rushdie can be traced, as the contemporary writer's essays overtly demonstrate, but it can also be interpreted as a postcolonial conscious (re)appropriation of literary tradition for new purposes.

The little Victorian child seems to have grown up into the American bride of the postcolonial era through a process which has paid attention both to her body's increased awareness and to her developed power to act: Alice resists Wonderland's system and then undoes it by waking up, in other words, by withdrawing herself, whereas the American bride's 'awakening' is far more impressive since it frees atavist fears in an outburst of rage with long range, evident effects. The female figures in both texts are examples of Rushdie's 'frontierswomen', who abandon illusory reality to conquer their own decisional space, through sometimes dismaying and unsettling processes.

In both cases their search would not have been possible without their concrete, physical body. In its new role of sensing subject, the protagonists' corporeal entity experiences a continuous adaptation to what is outside, showing resistance to the fixing gaze of the 'other'. Furthermore, an abnormal, sometimes disturbing presence in the texts gives body visibility as the main site through which location is to be searched, by means of the interaction with the space it inhabits.

The final return home of the two characters, far from being a defeat or a loss, is rich of consequences which the reader is invited to imagine: if Alice will always keep remembrances of this journey to inform her future life, the American bride will nurture the hope of fusion between dichotomies. Their modified attitude contributes to their new awareness of that familiar space called 'home', revealing that the importance of such a journey of self-discovery, in the end, lies not in its 'aim' but in its 'how', as these verses from 'Ithaka' by Constantine P. Cavafy, quoted by Rushdie (2003, 410), beautifully convey:

> Setting out on the voyage to Ithaka
> You must pray that the way be long,
> Full of adventures and experiences.
> [...]
> Be quite old when you anchor at the island,
> Rich with all you have gained on the way,
> Not expecting Ithaka to give you riches.
> [...]
> Wise as you have become, with all your experience,
> You will have understood the meaning of an Ithaca.

References

Carroll L. 1998. *Alice's Adventures in Wonderland*. London: Penguin Books.

Deleuze G., Guattari F. 1977. *Anti-Oedipus*. Trans. Hurley R., Seem M., Lane H.R. New York: Viking Press.

Foucault M. 1977. "Potere-corpo". In Fontana A., Pasquino P. (eds.) *Microfisica del potere. Interventi politici*. Torino: Einaudi, 137-147.

Foucault M. 1980. *Power/Knowledge: Selected Interviews and Other Writings 1972-1977*. Brighton: Harvester Press.

Galimberti U. 2005. *Il corpo. Antropologia, psicoanalisi, fenomenologia*. Milano: Feltrinelli Editore.

Greenway B. (ed.) 2005. *Twice-told Children's Tales: the Influence of Childhood Reading on Writers for Adults*. London: Routledge.

Johnson M. 2003. *Postcolonial Perspectives on Women Writers from Africa, the Caribbean, and the U.S.*. Asmara: Africa World Press.

Knoepflmacher U.C. 1998. *Ventures into Childland: Victorians, Fairy Tales, and Femininity*. USA: University of Chicago Press.

Michie H. 1987. *The Flesh made Word. Female Figures and Women's Body*. Oxford: Oxford University Press.

Miura N. 2000. *Marginal Voice, Marginal Body: The Treatment of the Human Body in the Works of Nakagami Kenji, Leslie Marmon Silko, and Salman Rushdie*. USA: Dissertation.com.

Mohanram R. 1999. *Black Bodies. Women, Colonialism, and Space*. Minneapolis: Minnesota University Press.

Phillips R. (ed.) 1974. *Aspects of Alice*. Harmondsworth: Penguin Books.

Rushdie S. 1992. *Imaginary Homelands. Essays and Criticism 1981-1991*. London: Granta & Penguin.

Rushdie S. 2003. *Step across This Line. Collected Non-Fiction 1992-2002*. London: Vintage.

Rushdie S. 2004. "The Firebird's Nest". In Gordimer N. (ed.) *Telling Tales*. London: Bloomsbury, 45-64.

Talairach-Vielmas L. 2007. *Moulding the Female Body in Victorian Fairy Tales and Sensation Novels*. Aldershot: Ashgate.

CARLOTTA FARESE

Università di Bologna

Unlike Emma. Mary Elizabeth Braddon's
Response to Bovarism in *The Doctor's Wife*

The publication in 1864 of Mary Elizabeth Braddon's *The Doctor's Wife* confirms the importance of the role of the woman reader as a character in 19th century European fiction, and provides significant evidence of the success of *Madame Bovary* in the British context. This paper will provide a brief discussion of the intertextual relationship between the two novels, and on the way in which Braddon, distancing herself from her French model, develops an original and interesting reflection on women's reading.

The Doctor's Wife, published by Braddon after a long list of extraordinary commercial achievements – *Lady Audley's Secret* (1862), *Aurora Floyd, Eleanor's Victory, John Marchmont's Legacy* (1863) – was a turning point in her career and provided an innovative approach to the traditional themes and structures of the sensational novel. By writing what she hoped would be seen as a *realistic* novel, she "attempted to navigate an alternative route to critical success" (Phegley 2004, 135). If compared to her previous books, *The Doctor's Wife* had been conceived from the beginning as a more ambitious literary work and, as Braddon herself admitted, it was directly inspired by Flaubert's masterpiece: "The idea of the Doctor's Wife is founded on *Madame Bovary*, the style of which struck me immensely in spite of its hideous immorality" (quoted in Lee Wolff 1979, 162). And indeed, even if Braddon does not rise to the heights of Flaubert's style, and is not always able to attain the studied impersonality of the French novel's narrator, she "constantly strives for an effect of literariness, not least through her extensive use of allusions to novels, plays, poems, and paintings" (Pykett 1998, IX).

However, despite the explicit desire to move away from sensationalism, a great part of *The Doctor's Wife* can be read as a "metadiscourse" devoted to the debate concerning the potentially dangerous effects of the sensation novel on its readers and, in particular, on women. A major role is played, in this respect, by the autobiographical character of Sigismund Smith, who is described as an author of sensation novels in his own right. Through this fictional male *alter ego* Braddon manages to give examples of the complicated and breathtaking plots that were typical of the sensation fiction and, at the same time, denies the existence of a connection between fictional and actual misdeeds. It could thus be argued that *The Doctor's Wife* provides a meta-literary reflection on and a defence of Braddon's own writing and its possible effects on the public. Braddon's book is in fact a novel in which the discussion of women's reading practices and the dangers connected to appropriate and inappropriate novels is embedded in the narrative plot. The means and the results of such an endeavour are multifaceted, paradoxical, and, to a certain extent, contradictory: in order to vindicate the morality of her own "sensational" writing Braddon chooses a model (*Madame Bovary*) that was considered an almost perfect paradigm of both *realism* and *immorality*.

The protagonist, the beautiful and innocent Isabel Sleaford, is presented from the very beginning as a character addicted to reading who spends most of her days fully absorbed in the imaginary world of fiction. The first time we meet her, she is leaning in a chair, with a book on her lap:

> She was lolling in a basket-chair, with a book on her lap, and her chin resting on the palm of her hand, so absorbed by the interest of – the page before her that she did not even lift her eyes when the two young men went close up to her (Braddon 1998, 23).

As a typically obsessive reader of novels and romances, Isabel finds fulfilment only in the secluded world of literature, where she longs to escape from the dullness of everyday life. Isabel's compulsive reading habits, as had already happened to Emma Bovary, bring along a constant temptation to identify with fictional heroines, and an overwhelming desire to experience romantic emotions at any cost:

> She wanted her life to be like her books; she wanted to be a heroine, – unhappy perhaps, and dying early. She had an especial desire to die early, by consumption, with a hectic flush and an unnatural lustre in her eyes (Braddon 1998, 28).

Totally lacking in critical awareness, Isabel is ironically driven to choose literary texts that are dramatically distant from the frustrating banality of everyday life, and this cannot but heighten her dissatisfaction, projecting her in an illusory universe that becomes increasingly incompatible with "commonplace" reality. As the author herself underlines: "Poor Lizzie's life was altogether vulgar and commonplace, and she could not extract one ray of romance out of it, twist it as she would" (Braddon 1998, 29). Like Emma Bovary, like so many other examples of literary women readers, the protagonist of *The Doctor's Wife* is bound to witness the dramatic clash between the real and the ideal, between an ordinary bourgeois existence and the radiant projections of literary fiction. Braddon's novel shows us also the possible consequences of a life exclusively devoted to the reading of novels. Indeed, if it is true – as the sensation writer Sigismund Smith claims in the book – that "no wise man or woman was ever the worse for reading novels" (Braddon 1998, 30) it is also true that young and innocent girls like Isabel Sleaford, lacking any education and critical awareness, are at risk of loosing themselves (and the distinction between reality and fiction) in the pages of the wrong books: "novels are only dangerous for those poor foolish girls who read nothing else, and think that their lives are to be paraphrases of their favourite books" (*ibidem*).

I would argue that the issue here is not only with *Madame Bovary*: Emma Bovary is only the last and most notorious example of the dangers of female reading. But a large number of such examples were provided not only by other works of fiction, but also by countless moral treatises, pamphlets, and conduct books that through the 18th and 19th century insist in denouncing the devilish temptations and dangers faced by the young woman who is so foolish as to open the pages of a book, and especially of a novel.[1] It is certainly undeniable that one of the favourite arguments of this kind of literature (soon to be reformulated in Victorian terms by John Ruskin's *Sesame and Lilies*, 1865) was the idea that the contact with fiction could make young women unfit to reality (i.e. unfit to their social role) because, becoming aware of the limits and constraints they had to submit to, they could conceive the desire to rebel against them. Popular and sensational fiction of the kind that Isabel loved so much provided indeed a lot of potentially seductive material that contrasted quite sharply with the ideals of composure and passivity imposed on the 19th-century bourgeois woman. Our heroine is no exception as she is certainly waiting for a prince charming to come into her life, but most of all, she longs for some change in the monotony of her dull existence. The following passage should give an idea of the potentially unsettling, or even "revolutionary", implication of such a longing:

> She was so eager to be *something*. Oh, why was not there a revolution, that she might take a knife in her hand and go forth to seek the tyrant in his lodging, and then die; so that people might talk of her, and remember her name when she was dead?[...] Miss Sleaford wanted to be famous. She wanted the drama of her life to begin, and the hero to appear (Braddon 1998, 73).

In fact, it would be difficult to deny that at the root of the condition of the woman reader who is constantly dodging into a pretentious world, lies a revolutionary element: the refusal to suffer the miserable mediocrity of every day life. George Gilbert, the man whom Isabel gets married to, doesn't posses any of the romantic and fascinating qualities usually required by a prince charming.

---

[1] For a book-length analysis of the figure of the woman reader in European 19th-century fiction see Farese (2006).

A simple country doctor, George Gilbert, like Charles Bovary, doesn't share any of his wife's literary interests and, most of all, he is totally incapable of reading with the same passion and devotion. Married life, especially if compared to Isabel's fictional standards, proves to be extremely disappointing and after a week of marriage our heroine seems already puzzled:

> Her books had given her some vague idea of this grand passion [...]. She began to think that the poets and novelists were all in the wrong, and that there were no heroes or heroines upon this commonplace hearth (Braddon 1998, 103).

Her great disappointment can be tolerated only with some more intense reading until the arrival, into her life, of the fascinating aristocratic Robert Landsdell – an extraordinary byronic creature – who finally seems to echo Isabel's romantic expectations: "He was Napoleon the first [...], he was a shadowy and divine creature, amenable to no earthly laws" (Braddon 1998, 139). But soon enough she will discover that falling in love with a real man is incredibly more complicated than loving an ideal character that leaps out from the pages of a book. And indeed, the moment Landsdell asks Isabel to run off with him, the young woman prefers to stay in her unhappy marriage and finds consolation once again in the world of fiction. In a work that is in so many ways similar to *Madame Bovary*, adultery is thus finally avoided, but this is not the only difference. Unlike Emma, Isabel witnesses both her husband and her lover's death, the former being killed by a fever and the latter by her own father. She subsequently inherits all of Landsdell's fortune, dedicating the rest of her life to charity. Landsdell's murder is the only, however significant, concession to the conventions of sensationalism. In fact, Braddon doesn't really allow to her heroine the transgressions which were typical of the genre: by the end of the narration the romantic dreamer is transformed into a noble and generous woman, totally devoted to serving her community:

> Is it strange, then, that the chastening influence of sorrow has transformed a sentimental girl into a good and noble woman – a woman in whom sentiment takes the higher form of universal sympathy and tenderness? (Braddon 1998, 402-403).

One of the extremely peculiar features of Braddon's novel is that, in contrast with the large majority of 19th-century versions of the woman reader, it depicts the *Bildung* of a young woman whose purity and ingenuity remain unaltered despite her passionate and compulsive reading. Although the protagonist spends more time in an imaginary world than in the real, and although she bases her life on a constant and obsessive emulation of her beloved fictional heroines, she never betrays her original innocence that will not allow her to commit adultery and to run away with her lover, as her French counterpart does. If Isabel Sleaford is similar to Emma Bovary because of their communal compensatory and comforting escape in the muffled world of fiction, she is totally "unlike Emma" in her honesty and sincere disinterest for money and for material things. The British version of Emma is less worldly and sensual, she longs for poetry, beauty and for an eventful and emotional life, but her love for precious and glittering objects is presented more as a form of aestheticism. The desperate consumerism that drags Madame Bovary into debts and death is utterly unknown to our naive Isabel who lives her love for Robert Landsdell with devotion and sincerity, without ever thinking of his wealth and, even more surprising, without ever having a sexual intercourse with him. It is in fact Isabel's "often noted avoidance of sensuality in and out of marriage" that "divorces Braddon's novel from the Flaubertian original" (Golden 2003, 113). Isabel naively perceives her love for Landsdell as pure as the love that Dante feels for Beatrice and the whole of their relationship is based on their communal love for literature and their constant sharing of literary ideas and quotations. The shared reading between two lovers – a *cliché* constantly present in nineteenth century fiction on women readers – in *The Doctor's Wife* never assumes any negative connotation, as noticed by Kate Flint: "novel reading remains uncondemned as an activity in itself: what is seen to matter is the cultivation of a self-knowing, responsible attitude towards it" (Flint 1993, 291). If, as we have mentioned, 19th-century culture could not but attribute transgressive connotations to the figure of the woman reader who hides into the potentially dangerous imaginative world of fiction, in our novel the heroine's immaculate behaviour finally confirms the dominant moral codes. In *The Doctor's Wife*, as we have seen, Braddon wanted to distance herself from the sensational genre in order to try a more ambitious and realistic literary endeavour. Flaubert's novel functions as a guide and a model of this attempt, but Braddon had to reject the morally questionable aspects of *Madame Bovary* that had been met with harsh criticism at its first appearance in England. As Robert Lee Wolff underlines:

> adapting Madame Bovary for the middle-class English reader of 1864 presented great opportunities and correspondingly great dangers. Emma Bovary's plight aroused sympathetic vibrations in the heart of every romantic young woman condemned to provincial respectability and deprived of romantic adventure. But Victorian English convention made it impossible to follow Emma's example, to run off with Landsdell, or to have an affair with him. This forced MEB into inconsistencies, as she labored so conscientiously to portray real character (Lee Wolff 1979, 162-163).

However, I would argue that the alleged "inconsistencies" of the novel should not lead us to underrate, or indeed ignore, the most innovative aspects of Braddon's novel, as the contradictions are in fact a direct consequence of her intention to vindicate the formative and educative function of women's reading writing against the grain of both Flaubert's novel and Victorian conventions. Choosing progress over fall, therefore, Braddon not only proposed a domesticated and palatable version of *Madame Bovary* for the British public, but she also managed to create a heroine who could finally contradict the general idea that: "had Emma not fed her parched imagination with novels, she would have become and remained a dutiful, if rather bored, wife"(Gay 1999, 165). Isabel Sleaford's *Bildung* as a woman and as a reader, if seen under this new perspective, represents a quite interesting and provoking answer to the French original, a kind of post-Flaubertian (and to a certain extent anti-Flaubertian) vindication of the act of reading. Though absorbed into books as voraciously and as dangerously as Emma, Isabel remains morally and inwardly upright, and Braddon – trying for once to avoid the usual censure of the lascivious and adulterous woman reader – defends her interest of successful sensation novelist and aims at protecting her most affectionate audience: that of her female readers. She does that by saving her creature from the possible dramatic consequences of adultery, but also by killing – instead of her – her husband and lover. We cannot but wonder, with Kate Flint:

> what are the implications of the fact that two men have to die in *The Doctor's Wife* – the worthy doctor and the rakish Byronic would-be seducer – in order for Isabel, unworthy in many ways, to achieve a far happier fate than that of Emma Bovary who is consumed by her own romantic preoccupations rather than rescued by the narrator for an independent woman's life? (Flint 1993, 292).

Braddon allows Isabel to live, prosper and improve, because, in her perspective, the *rêverie* and the act of reading should not necessarily lead to tragedy and destruction. On the contrary, the British counterpart of the impenitent *liseuse* that Flaubert condemned to suicide, can survive to defy current assumptions about the reading woman and create, precisely through her imaginative acts of reading, the conditions to conquer a different, and better, way of life – a new role in the male-dominated context of Victorian society.

References

Braddon M.E. 1998. *The Doctor's Wife*. Oxford-New York: Oxford University Press.

Farese C. 2006. *Creature dell'illusione, figure di lettrici nella letteratura europea dell'Ottocento*. Lecce: Pensa.

Flint K. 1993. *The Woman Reader 1837-1914*. Oxford: Clarendon Press.

Gay P. 1999. *The Bourgeois Experience. Victoria to Freud*. Volume I. *The Tender Passion*. London-New York: Norton.

Golden C.J. 2003. *Images of the Woman Reader in Victorian British and American Fiction*. Gainesville: University Press of Florida.

Lee Wolff R. 1979. *Sensational Victorian: The Life and Fiction of Mary Elizabeth Braddon*. New York-London: Garland Publishing.

Phegley J. 2004. *Educating the Proper Woman Reader. Victorian Family Literary Magazines and the Cultural Health of the Nation*. Columbus: The Ohio State University Press.

Pykett L. 1998. *Introduction to M.E. Braddon, "The Doctor's Wife"*. Oxford-New York: Oxford University Press.

C. Maria Laudando

Università di Napoli L'Orientale

The Joint Venture of Tim Crouch's Performance Between Visual Art, Theatre and Education

The advertisement on the Net for Tim Crouch's latest play *The Author* (that opened at the Royal Court Jerwood Theatre Upstairs in London on 23rd September 2009, just a few days before the beginning of this Conference), starts with a bold quote further underlined in red characters that reads: "I have the choice to continue. I have the choice to stop",[1] and unfolds with a set of ingratiating instructions for the prospective audience followed by a on-line abrupt summary of the plot, thus:

> Settle back into the warmth of the Jerwood Theatre Upstairs. Relax as the story unfolds. For you. With you. Of you. A story of hope, violence and exploitation. Laugh with the actors, tap your feet to the music, turn to your neighbour. You're here.
> Tim Crouch's new play is about the abuse carried out in the name of the spectator.[2]

The links provided by the Tim Crouch's website give further access both to a note written by the playwright himself on his work and to a broadcast interview with Tim Crouch and the two co-directors, Karl James and Andy Smith, discussing the new play. What comes perspicuously to the fore is a series of issues that are not only strictly related with the challenging perspectives elicited throughout the present Conference, but also material for what I would call Tim Crouch's exploratory theatre: the dilemmas and ambiguities implicated in the question of ethical responsibility in our contemporary 'post-everything' world. It is not accidental that both the authorial presentation and the interview lay emphasis upon the intricate bond of complicity, challenge, and responsibility that unites performers as well as spectators (and also, obviously, authors, directors and sponsors/institutions) in a

---

[1] The quote is taken from the dramatic end of the play where the protagonist faces his responsibility as spectator of disturbing material on the Net (Crouch 2009, 57).

[2] For the quotations from this on-line promotional material see http://www.timcrouchtheatre.co.uk/shows/the-author (last accessed August 2011).

play dealing with the risks of abuse in a globalised society haunted by all sorts of visual manipulation. Here, I limit my quote to the written text:

> *The Author* is a play about what it is to be a spectator and about our responsibilities as spectators. It explores the connection between what we see and what we do. I feel strongly that we have lost a thread of responsibility for what we choose to look at. *The Author* uses only words to show us things and sometimes the things those words show us are disturbing. It is not a play for children but it IS a play for audiences.

In its distinctively simple and straight-forward prose, the note smoothly moves from the detached register of a press release to the insinuations of a collective, more direct involvement of the audience in the themes of abuse and manipulation the play deals with. And, in a parallel way, the crafty oscillation on the part of the 'author' between the use of the plural pronoun ("we", "us") and that of the singular ("I"), that further alternates with the impersonal reference to *The Author* ("it"), points to the ambiguous implication of the 'everyday' author Tim Crouch in the psychological violence committed by the homonymic author in the play.

If the expedient of the meta-narrative frame, the play-within-the play, may seem rather cheap and suspect in an age as ours that has seen the saturation and exhaustion of all sorts of self-reflective gimmick, however, in the case of Tim Crouch it represents the culmination of his ongoing theatrical exploration of the risks of live performance, gradually stripping the audience of any illusion of moral safety or integrity. In fact, there is not even a stage, but only two opposing banks of seats where the four performers, including Crouch doubling himself in the role of an author called Tim, sit among the rest of the audience, whose imagination will soon prove accomplice to the violent and sensational material discussed among the quartet. In fact, the audience is forced to face itself through the interaction with the four performers (respectively impersonating a playwright, two actors and a Royal Court Theatre fan) and the uneasy confession of their disturbing involvement in a hard-hitting play – which also suggests an ambidextrous satirical mirroring of the 'in-yer-face' productions typical of that Jerwood Theatre Upstairs where the dramatic action is set.

In a way, *The Author* both strengthens and forces to the limit the self-referential, ambiguous twists and turns between life and theatre, between manipulation and participation, and between different modes of visual and imaginary experience which are already investigated in Crouch's previous plays. Caridad Svich, herself a promising young playwright, has summed up the experimental and metamorphic vocation of Tim Crouch with the felicitous terms of "theatrical transformations"[3] in her on-line interview with the

---

[3] For the quotations from the interview by Caridad Svich see the website of the *Hunter* on-line theatre review at the following address: http://www.hotreview.org/articles/timcrouchinterv.htm (last accessed August 2011).

British artist after the launch of *An Oak Tree* in New York (autumn 2006). Her introductory notes to this intriguing conversation provide useful insights into the major characteristics of Crouch's work as experimental theatre-maker:

> Encountering his work is like walking into a laboratory: the experiment is already afoot, the rules are changeable, the presentation is lucid, and important questions are asked about the stage, space and time and how we tell stories. [...] What distinguishes Crouch's work for me [...] is its engagement with the durational nature of theater and its unabashed embrace of genuine feeling despite its formalism.

Undoubtedly, one distinctive aspect of Tim Crouch's sustained engagement with the 'essentials' of theatre concerns his intriguing and playful interrogation of the audience's role (or, better, agency) within the 'empty', de-materialised space of theatre in comparison and interplay with different contexts/locations of aesthetic experience and arts consumption – what indeed provides the special visual focus of all his plays.

Thus, in the "Introduction" to *My Arm* the author openly recognises the impact of contemporary visual art on his conception of the play not only at the thematic level but, more relevantly, at the structural one. The passage is worth quoting at some length, insofar it provides a significant key of access to Crouch's laboratory:

> *My Arm* attempts to provoke questions about the qualitative distinctions between viewing theatre and viewing visual art. The visual arts have stolen a march on theatre in their ability to handle progressive forms; the state of modern British art is one of the main engines of the story. While I was developing the play I ran a series of classes looking at the division between the social nature of watching a play and the private, stand-alone nature of looking at a painting. [...] As an actor, I've often worked far too hard to 'host' an audience's journey through a play; something visual art rarely does. Visual art expects its viewers to work hard. *My Arm* attempts to let the audience be by itself for periods of time, and for me as the actor to feel all right about that. In the previews of the show, some audience members have felt mildly affronted that I haven't taken greater care of them. This is not rudeness on my part, but more an attempt [to] give the audience a greater sense of its own authority in relation to what it is seeing (Crouch 2003, 9-10).

To begin with, it is important to take into account that the visual dimension is always explored by Crouch in relationship with its impact on an audience, thus calling into question the subtle divide between provocation and abuse, innovation and sensation. As a theatre-maker he is interested in sharpening the visual focus of his performances, as it were, in response to the repeated challenges that contemporary art has launched to the sister art of drama in the age of digital reproduction, as is impressively evident in the emphasis laid upon the theatrical marks of most contemporary art exhibitions (indeed, their own hybrid definitions in terms of performance, installation, or relational art is, in this respect, telling enough). In a way, Tim Crouch's works seem to reclaim for his dramatic work those "progressive forms" – what amounts to the theatre's intrinsically interactive, performative nature, at one time impermanent and durational – that British visual art has succeeded in appropriating for itself more and more confidently in the last decades (even if, often, in highly controversial terms).

In *My Arm* not only does the plot revolve around an empty gesture (at ten the protagonist put his arm above his head and has never taken it down for the following twenty years) that unexpectedly turns into a coveted specimen of sensational art, but the story is always told in a different way – as advertised in the play's back cover – "through live performance, digital film and the animation of everyday objects supplied by the audience before each performance". Thus, even if the play contemplates visual aids and the storyline openly deals with the contradictions and excesses of modern art, what still prevails in the end is the vindication of the uniqueness of each performance – a uniqueness that is safeguarded every time by the contact with a particular, unpredictable audience that is called to react and reflect on the visual props on the stage that the spectators themselves have supplied. Accordingly, a "Production Note" to be read before each performance makes clear the intimate collaboration that is required:

> This performance is partly about giving ordinary things extraordinary significance. What *My Arm* needs is a supply of everyday objects from you: the stuff in your pockets, in your bags, your wallets; stuff you carry around; photographs [...], lucky charms, key rings, badges, toys. Useful things; things without function. Beautiful things or ugly things. Things no bigger than a shoe. Anything you supply will be treated with care and respect. It will be on stage at all times. No conventional magic will be attempted with it – no hammers and handkerchiefs. You will get it back at the end. But the stuff you supply will create a major part of *My Arm*. Please be ready with possible things when they're requested. Thanks (Crouch 2003, 11).

With this expedience, the spectators' investment in the objects selected at random and destined to work as icons in the story duplicates the process of transformation into a cultural symbol the protagonist's incriminated arm undergoes.

It is useful to recall, in this respect, that Crouch's own formation confirms both his vocation as theatre-maker – rather than merely as playwright – and his constant fascination with the world of contemporary visual art: at the beginning as an actor of performance art installations, and then gradually as actor and co-founder of Public Parts Theatre, and now as teacher, writer and leading member of the "News from Nowhere" company, a company "whose aim is to explore the borders between theatre, education and visual arts through performance, teaching and commissioning" (as recites the company's profile facing the title-page of *My Arm*). Obviously enough, the choice of the name is deliberately inspired to what is considered the masterpiece and the manifesto of William Morris's program of artistic and social renovation, *News from Nowhere*, published in 1890 (Morris 1995). In tune with Morris's dream of abolishing any divisions between art, life, and work, Crouch's company pursues a similar ambitious and ambiguous project to embrace artistic vision and social action – a project both theatrical, educational and institutional ultimately founded upon the power of creativity and imagination in the arts as in the everyday. If Tim Crouch plays the leading role as writer/performer, the other two members of the company, Kark James and a smith (for Andy Smith), work as co-directors, always contributing in decisive way not only, obviously, to the very staging of the plays, but also to Crouch's development of his first ideas about a play through free sessions of discussion and continuous elaboration of the work-in-progress.

It was Andy Smith that suggested the idea of a different, improvised performer every night for the role of the Father, the co-protagonist in Crouch's second play, *An Oak Tree* (2005). In his interview with Caridad Svich, Tim Crouch explains in detail how here the core of conceptual hypnotism prompted by the homonymic Michael Craig-Martin's piece (1973) gradually expanded into a two-handed studio of loss and guilt, involving a provincial Hypnotist who has involuntarily killed a girl in a car accident and the dead girl's Father who has turned the tree next to where she died into his daughter (so reversing once again the notorious transformation, vindicated in the 1973 manifesto of conceptual art, of a glass of water into an oak tree). Andy Smith worked as the inspirational figure as non-actor for the parental role:

> I knew that I wanted an actor who 'wasn't an actor.' An actor who wouldn't fall back on the traditional approach. Andy was not an actor. He knew *My Arm*; he knew the area I was working in. He also knew that he didn't want to take the job... So, at my kitchen table, we talked. We talked about the 'animation' of inanimate objects in *My Arm*. It was Andy, in our far-ranging conversation, who suggested that we could replicate the effects of *My Arm* on a human being – that a different person each performance could play the Father – unknowing of their significance. […] It was simple: I had to write a play that would enable me to guide a second actor through it.

In this play too, the inspiration to a specific form of modern visual art – ambiguously implicated with hypnotism – is translated not only into the engine of the plot, but mirrored in the distinctive language of theatre (the choice of a specific hypnotic soundtrack, a 30-second silence that works as a "black hole", the lights, the tone of voice, and so on) and helps to further investigate into an uneasy entanglement of hypnosis, bereavement and the manipulation of improvisational theatre.

With Crouch's third play *England* (2007) the exploration of the nature of theatre as 'an empty space', according to Peter Brook's seminal study (Brook

1987), is played out in strict relation with contemporary visual culture as inspired by the very circumstances of the play's commission: the Traverse Theatre had asked Tim Crouch to write a play for the Edinburgh Fringe Festival to be performed at the Fruitmarket Gallery. Thus, it was the challenge to write a piece of theatre for an art gallery that first spurred the author to elaborate the idea of transplantation at every level starting from an interrogation of the 'real' space and time of the premiere, as emphasised both in the subtitle (that recites "A Play for Galleries") and in the epigraph from one of the most provocative essays on the aseptic space of modern galleries by Brian O'Doherty (1976): "One has to have died already to be there" (quoted in Crouch 2007, 11). Neatly divided into two acts, the first stages two guides that apparently tour the spectators through an art exhibition, whose description will, accordingly, change with every new setting of the performance. But the focus soon shifts from the real art works displayed in the room to the fictional places and fragments of the storyline created through the magic of words, thus: "Look! Look!" (*ibidem*, 16), "I'm curled up on the sofa. Look" (*ibidem*, 17), "This is Guys Hospital in London. Look. Look [...] Look at the clean lines" (*ibidem*, 29). The audience is continuously invited to look, to imagine the story of a serious heart illness which strains the love relationship between an Englishman/Englishwoman (the character on stage, whose gender is left unspecified, is actually split, 'transplanted' into the two actors that have to negotiate the same script) and a brilliant American art buyer and seller whose origin is Dutch. At times, their obsessive insistence on the act of looking at, on the lines of beauty, on the power exerted by everyday visual props upon one's own imagination seem almost to echo a distinctively Hogarthian accent. In particular, the forceful interrogation not only of the national/international value but also of the cost of art obliquely refers, among many other instances of *Englishness*, to the disruptive modernity of the 18th-century painter's *Analysis of Beauty* (Hogarth 1955) with its array of straight, waving and serpentine lines illustrating Hogarth's own ventures for theatricality, visual education and self-promotion.

The second act takes place in a different room in the gallery (where spectators can sit and resume their position as theatre-goers) and, accordingly, the fictional setting moves to a Muslim country in the East staging the uneasy confrontation between the English patient who has just benefited from a heart transplant and the Interpreter for the widow of the heart donor. Indeed, the stage direction makes clear that the audience in the new setting is called to play the crucial role of the bereft wife: "The wife is us, the audience. When the audience enters the space, it is entering her space. The Interpreter interprets her words and translates what is said to her." (*ibidem*, 44). Written to be performed in art galleries, only apparently does the plot revolve around a heart transplant: what is at stake is the spectators' own involvement with a series of endless acts and places of transplantations, transactions and translations. Throughout the play it is the audience that is ultimately required to reflect upon the translational, transnational dimension of contemporary globalised culture thus facing its risks, its challenges, its unbearable inequities. Indeed "it is a tour to the end of the world", as recites the blurb of the published text.

Even if there is no space here to further illustrate those issues, what *England* shares with the other plays is a lucid and crafty exploration of the inherent performative nature of theatre which can't help coming to terms with both its material and imaginary 'location' into a specific culture, but, nowadays, always more and more implicated in a larger g/local de-territorialised context (as Appadurai, among others, has persuasively demonstrated in 1996), and which can't help running the risk of 'intimacy' with its audience. The risks of the fragile, beautiful, bloody-minded precariousness, inventiveness, and deceptiveness of human beings. The risks of interrogating again and again the boundaries of our human and post-human culture, and our responsibility in any single act of advancing or retreating along those dubious and slippery borderlines. Both in the arts and in the everyday.

Indeed, "We have the choice to continue. We have the choice to stop".

References

Appadurai A. 1996. *Modernity at Large. The Cultural Dimensions of Globalization.* Minneapolis: University of Minneapolis Press.

Brook P. 1987. *The Empty Space* (1st ed. 1968). New York: Atheneum.

Crouch T. 2003. *My Arm.* London: Faber and Faber.

Crouch T. 2005. *An Oak Tree.* London: Oberon Modern Plays.

Crouch T. 2007. *England. A Play for Galleries.* London: Oberon Books.

Crouch T. 2009. *The Author.* London: Oberon Modern Plays.

Hogarth W. 1955. *The Analysis of Beauty* (1st ed. 1753). Ed. by Burke J. Oxford: Clarendon Press.

Morris W. 1995. *News from Nowhere* (1st ed. 1890). Ed. by Kumar K. Cambridge: Cambridge University Press.

O'Doherty B. 1999. *Inside the White Cube: The Ideology of the Gallery Space* (1st ed. 1976). Berkeley and Los Angeles: University of California Press.

Web Sites
(last accessed August 2011)

http://www.timcrouchtheatre.co.uk/

Fabio Luppi

Università Roma Tre

John Keats's First Poems According to Gaston Bachelard's *Poetics of Space* (a Modern Reading for an Old Theme)

John Keats's first long poetical attempts – *Endymion, Sleep and Poetry* and *I stood tip-toe upon a little hill* (Keats 1982) – present a repetition of classical settings directly related by critics to the influence of Spenser's *Fairie Queene* and more in general to the pastoral poems of the Renaissance. D'Avanzo (1967) first noted the occurrence in these poems of a *locus amenus*, a bower or a hidden corner used as the place devoted to the birth of poetry. Dickstein (1971) too asserted that *Endymion* "is partly an endless succession of bowers." These bowers function as a protective place, a sort of house, the family home the poet had never had except in his early infancy. Gaston Bachelard's *The Poetics of Space* helps us to reconsider the settings of these first poems as the evidence of Keats' struggle with his own ghosts, that is, with his lost childhood, and the attempt to recapture it.

In the first book of *Endymion* there are four instances of such places. They are not a proper home, nor literally a room, however their function, borrowing Bachelard's words, is the same as that which a house would have: "all really inhabited space bears the essence of the notion of home" (Bachelard 1994, 5). Moreover the most important feature of these places is the fact that they represent a protection for daydreaming: "If I were asked to name the chief benefit of the house, I should say: the house shelters daydreaming, the house protects the dreamer, the house allows one to dream in peace" (Bachelard 1994, 6). This is the main function of the bowers presented in the poem, where the protagonist, Endymion "[...] seemed/to common lookers-on, like one who dreamed/of idleness in groves Elysian" (*Endymion*, Book I, vv. 175-177). In the second book the poet uses the word 'home' to describe a bucolic setting: "[...] overhead,/hung a lush screen of drooping weeds, and spread / thick as to curtain up some wood-nymph's home" (*Endymion*, Book I, vv. 939-941): the wood is in fact a house.

The fact that Endymion is often alone in these places is particularly significant. In the second book, when he meets Diana for the first time, for instance, he whispers: "Alas [...]/[...] will all this gush of feeling pass/away in solitude? And must they wane, / like melodies upon a sandy plain,/without an echo? Then shall I be left/so sad, so melancholy, so bereft!" (Book II, vv. 680-685). This is a rhetorical question since

> [...] all the spaces of our past moments of solitude, the spaces in which we have suffered from solitude, enjoyed, desired and compromised solitude, remain indelible within us, and precisely because the human being wants them to remain so. He knows instinctively that this space identified with his solitude is creative [...] (Bachelard 1994, 10).

No matter if they represent a humble house or a castle since "a house is considered as space for cheer and intimacy, space that is supposed to condense and defend intimacy" (Bachelard 1994, 48). Therefore we find bowery nooks and palaces (Neptune's palace, or Pan's palace): "the two extreme realities of cottage and manor [...] take into account our need for retreat and expansion, for simplicity and magnificence" (Bachelard 1994, 65). However the real houses for *Endymion* are the most simple natural places because "we must [...] look for centres of simplicity in houses with many rooms. For as Baudelaire said, in a palace, 'there is no place for intimacy'" (Bachelard 1994, 29).

All these places bear common characteristics that induce us to reconsider them in a more specific light. They are bowers hidden in the vegetation, made up of leaves and grass; "this centre of animal life is concealed by the immense volume of vegetable life" (Bachelard 1994, 103). The bower where Endymion is led by his sister Peona is "new made of flowers leaves,/dried carefully on the cooler side of sheaves/when last the sun his Autumn tresses shook,/and the tanned harvester rich armfuls took" (*Endymion*, Book I, vv. 438-441). Again, Keats refers to the sacred wood whose master is Pan with significant words: "O thou, whose mighty palace roof doth hang/from jugged trunks, and overshadoweth/ eternal whispers, glooms, the birth, life, death/of unseen flowers in heavy peacefulness [...]". The wood is compared to a palace of peacefulness.

In other words, these places represent a house, but a very peculiar one. In fact since they are made of vegetable life, we can compare them to nests:

> A nest, like any other image of rest and quiet, is immediately associated with the image of a simple house. When we pass from the image of a nest to the image of a house, and *vice versa*, it can only be in an atmosphere of *simplicity* (Bachelard 1994, 99).

Three times Keats refers to these bowers as nests in *Endymion*'s first book: first Peona leads his brother by boat "[...] into a shady, fresh and ripply cove,/ where *nested* was an arbour, overwove/by many a summer's silent fingering" (*Endymion*, Book I, vv. 430-432). Later on Endymion says: "[...] I will ease my breast/of secret grief, here in this *bowery nest*" (*Endymion*, Book I, vv. 538-539).

And again Endymion describes the place where he met Diana with similar words: "And once, above the edges of our *nest*, / an arch face peeped – an Oread as I guessed" (*Endymion*, Book I, vv. 670-671). A similar reference can be found in *Sleep and Poetry* (v. 8) where the poet wonders whether there is a place "more secret than the *nest* of a nightingale" (Italics mine). In the third book, too, Endymion is described "how happy once again in *grassy nest!*" (*Endymion*, Book III, v. 1032).

A passage in the second Book of *Endymion* deserves a longer quotation. An eagle takes the protagonist to a nook:

> [...] there crossed / towards him a large eagle, 'twixt whose wings, / without one impious word, himself he flings [...] / [...] down he fell / through unknown things, till exhaled asphodel, / and rose, / with spicy fannings interbreathed, / came swelling forth where little caves were wreathed / so thick with leaves and mosses, that they seemed / large honey-combs of green, and freshly teemed / with airs delicious. In the greenest nook / the eagle landed him, and farewell took (*Endymion*, Book II, vv. 657-659 and 662-669).

True, the word nest, is not present in this passage. Yet, the identification of this nook with a nest is evident. The nook represents an angle of a primitive house: "Every corner in a house, every angle in a room, every inch of secluded space in which we like to hide, or withdraw into ourselves, is a symbol of solitude for the imagination; that is to say, it is the germ of a room, or of a house" (Bachelard 1994, 136). This is the place for poetry, since "a bowery nook / will be elysium" (*Sleep and Poetry*, vv. 63-64). The same image is also present in *Endymion* when sleep is compared to a bird; in this passage we find constant occurrences of words related to protection in connection with the bower in which sleep is produced. This place alludes to a safe, comfortable nest since the image of the bird is used as a metonymy:

> O magic sleep! O *comfortable bird*, / That broodest o'er the troubled sea of the mind / Till it is hush'd and smooth! O unconfin'd / Restraint! imprisoned liberty! great key / To golden palaces, strange minstrelsy, / Fountains grotesque, new trees, bespangled caves, / Echoing grottos, full of tumbling waves / And moonlight; aye, to all the mazy world / Of silvery enchantment! – who, upfurled / Beneath *thy drowsy wing* a triple hour, / But renovates and lives? – Thus, in the bower, / Endymion was calm'd to life again. / Opening his eyelids with a healthier brain, / He said: "I feel this thine endearing love / All through my bosom: *thou art as a dove* / Trembling its closed eyes and *sleeked wings* / About me" (*Endymion*, Book I, vv. 453-463; Italics mine).

Incidentally beside the nest Bachelard's *Poetics of Space* describes an analogue image: the shell. The same characteristics found in the nest can be seen in the shell (Bachelard 1994, 105-135). In *Sleep and Poetry* (vv. 119-121) too there is this image: "in the bosom of the leafy world / we rest in silence, like two gems upcurl'd/in the recesses of a pearly shell." In *Endymion* it is related to Venus ("she rose/From out her cradle shell", Book I, v. 627) and Neptune (he is "shell borne", Book III, v. 238; Book III, v. 965).

"The nest, quite as much as the oneiric house, and the oneiric house quite as much as the nest – if we ourselves are at the origin of our dreams – knows nothing of the hostility of the world" (Bachelard 1994, 103). Considering these words we must come to the conclusion that a nest not only represents a house, but it represents the house where one is born, the most protective place one can imagine. The poet who dreams of a nest is abandoned in a childish reverie: "in literature, the nest image is generally childish" (Bachelard 1994, 93). Significantly, recollecting his meetings with Diana, Endymion tells his sister Peona that in these bowers he was able to reach "back to boyhood" (*Endymion*, Book I, v. 881) and again, immediately after, he adds: "when love-lorn hours left me less a child" (*ibidem*, Book I, v. 885). We are faced with images related to boyhood and infancy.

This evidence provides us with an interpretation of these bowers as the safe birthplace where the protagonist is lulled and cradled: considering the occurrences of expressions like "cradling into her care" (*ibidem*, Book I, v. 411), "lulled" (*ibidem*, Book III, v. 1031), "lapped and lulled along the dangerous sky" (*ibidem*, Book I, v. 646), "cradling arms" (*ibidem*, Book III, v. 1017), we can easily conclude that these places are related to "[...] a whole series of images [...] characterise[d] as primal images; images that bring out the primitiveness in us" (Bachelard 1994, 91). And finally this leads up to the real main point of this investigation: "before he is 'cast into the world' [...] man is laid in the cradle of the house. And always, in our daydreams, the house is a large cradle" (Bachelard, 1994, 79. The whole of Keats's first attempts in poetry are a constant obsessed repetition of bowers, descriptions of a familiar house.

Inevitably, there is a tendency to portray Keats as the young romantic who died before his time. Like the images of his Grecian urn, he will always be a "fair youth". "I see a school boy when I think of him,/With face and nose pressed to a sweet-shop window" said William Butler Yeats in *Ego Dominus Tuus*, while Lord Byron defined Keats's first poetical attempts as "piss a bed poetry".[1] A critic of the *Eclectic Review* wrote, quoting from *Sleep and Poetry*, that "Mr. Keats has satirized certain pseudo-poets, who, 'With a *puling infant's* force/sway'd about upon a rocking horse/and thought it Pegasus'. Satire is a two-edged weapon: the lines brought irresistibly to our imagination the author of these poems in the very attitude he describes".[2] This means that the critic, referring to Keats in the same words used by the poet, describes him as a young

---

[1] George Gordon Byron quoted by Marjorie Levinson (1988).
[2] The *Eclectic Review*, quoted by Sidney Colvin (1917).

boy whose versification is poor and immature.[3] Keats himself, at the beginning of his career was not satisfied with his poetical results. He realised his poetry was immature and in the Preface to *Endymion* he claimed, referring to himself: "This youngster should die away."

His awareness of his immature attitude towards poetry is reflected in what he significantly wrote in a most famous letter to his friend John Hamilton Reynolds, where he compared human life to a series of chambers of a house:

> I compare human life to a large Mansion of Many Apartments, two of which I can only describe, the doors of the rest being yet shut upon me – The first we step into we call the infant or thoughtless Chamber, in which we remain as long as we do not think – We remain there a long while, and notwithstanding the doors of the second Chamber remain wide open, showing a bright appearance, we care not to hasten to it; but are at length imperceptibly impelled by the awakening of the thinking principle – within us – we no sooner get into the second Chamber, which I shall call the Chamber of Maiden-Thought, than we become intoxicated with the light and the atmosphere, we see nothing but pleasant wonders, and think of delaying there for ever in delight: However among the effects this breathing is father of is that tremendous one of sharpening one's vision into the heart and nature of Man – of convincing ones nerves that the World is full of Misery and Heartbreak, Pain, Sickness and oppression – whereby This Chamber of Maiden Thought become gradually darken'd and at the same time on all sides of it many doors are set open – but all dark – all leading to dark passages – We see not the balance of good and evil. We are in a Mist (Keats 1958).

Keats significantly uses the metaphor of a house with many rooms (that recalls the passages quoted from the *Poetics of Space*). The Chamber of Maiden-Thought represents exactly Keats's condition while writing *Endymion* and *Sleep and Poetry*: here "we see nothing but pleasant wonders", such as the bowers presented in the poems. Keats was apparently aware of his condition since in the second Preface to *Endymion*, written a few months after its publication – and consequently after the many negative reviews it received – he added, as a sort of justification:

> The imagination of a boy is healthy, and the mature imagination of a man is healthy; but there is a space of life between, in which the soul is in a ferment, the character undecided, the way of life uncertain, the ambition thick-sighted; thence proceeds mawkishness, and all the thousand bitters which those men I speak of must necessarily taste in going over the following pages.

---

[3] The "rocking horse" is the heroic couplet of eighteenth century poets (here Keats quoted from an article by Hazlitt, "On Milton's Versification").

Endymion could even be read as the representation of the protagonist's regressive attitude towards reality. At the end of the poem another place, so different from the sweet bowers of the first books, creates a maternal image. However this time we move in a treacherous and scaring setting: it is a cave. Apparently Keats is understanding how dangerous this regression is and finally describes a terrible truth: "the man has yet to come/who hath not journeyed in this native hell" (*Endymion*, Book IV, vv. 522-523). The bower has been replaced by the cave, that is not a shell of luxuries but a native hell. The poet is not cradled and lulled in a daydream of youth anymore. The answer to this impasse is given by the poet himself in *Sleep and Poetry*, where he wrote, referring to the sweet images of the first books of *Endymion*: "Yes, I must pass them for a nobler life,/where I may find the agonies, the strife/of human hearts" (*Sleep and Poetry*, vv. 123-125).

However Keats was not a second Chatterton, but part of that "visionary company" described by Harold Bloom (1961). After *Endymion*, *Sleep and Poetry* and *I Stood tip-toe upon a little hill*, his art got rid of the childish attitude of the first poetical attempts. With *Hyperion* and *The Fall of Hyperion* it is a different matter: they present strong images of desolate immobility or frenzied anxiety. The cold and still spots described in these poems are completely different from the scenes of sweet luxuries of the first period. In the odes, the nightingale deceives only temporarily the poet's imagination because no bowery nest serves as consolation to reality. The bird singing, though eternal (produced by an immortal bird, the symbol of art) fades away, and sleep finally ends up in the question "do I wake or sleep?" The poet does not describe the place he is in, he even says "I cannot see what flowers are at my feet" (stanza V, v. 1). He cannot describe the place but can only imagine it. The consolation of the cradling bower is gone forever; the nest is but a dream, because the poet lives here "where youth grows pale, and spectre-thin, and dies."

It has been pointed out that all these places are in fact mental spaces representing the poet's imagination and his creative intimacy. This is true: however it does not mean we cannot investigate what they are like, what their function is and what they represent in the poet's mind, because all descriptive passages in Romantic poetry are representations of a state of mind. Wordsworth himself claims that his descriptions are recollections, in a way filtered by the poet's imagination.[4]

Thus this objection calls for a direct answer by Gaston Bachelard:

> All great, simple images reveal a psychic state. The house, even more than the landscape, is a "psychic state", and even when reproduced as it appears from the outside, it bespeaks intimacy (Bachelard 1994, 72).

---

[4] It is through imagination and recollection that Wordsworth can get into the life of things in, for instance, *Lines Composed a Few Miles Above Tintern Abbey* or in *Nutting* (Wordsworth 1994).

In poetry, and in fiction in general, all spaces are in fact fictional, imagined, psychic or at least they convey psychic or metaphorical meanings representing a state of mind; if we attempt to distinguish them from real spaces we would have very few lines left to examine.

References

Bachelard G. 1994. *The Poetics of Space*. Boston: Beacon Press.

Bloom H. 1961. *The Visionary Company, a Reading of English Romantic Poetry.* Ithaca: Cornell University Press.

Colvin S. 1917. *John Keats, His Life and Poetry, His Friends, Critics and After-Fame.* London: Macmillan and Co., Limited, Elibron Classics edition.

D'Avanzo M.L. 1967. *Keats' Metaphors for the Poetic Imagination*. Durham (NC): Duke University Press.

Dickstein M. 1971. *Keats and His Poetry; A Study in Development*. Chicago: University of Chicago Press.

Keats J. 1958. *The Letters of J.K.* (Rollins H.E. ed.). Cambridge (Mass.): Harvard University Press.

Keats J. 1982. *Complete Poems* (Stillinger J. ed.). Cambridge (Mass.): Belknap Press of Harvard University Press.

Levinson M. 1988. *Keats' Life of Allegory*. Oxford: Basil Blackwell.

Wordsworth W. 1994. *The Collected Poems of William Wordsworth* (Till A. ed.). London: Wordsworth Editions.

MARIA DOMENICA MANGIALAVORI

Università Roma Tre

Music, Painting and Memory in Virginia Woolf's
To the Lighthouse

The connections between time and memory along with music and painting has become, in the last decades, a rich field of investigation within the intermedial studies, where some modernist writers are regarded as "intermedial authors", for their ability to transfer their interest in arts into the world of literature.[1] To this extent, *To The Lighthouse* is one the most impressive example as it greatly represents Virginia Woolf's deep interests in the world of music as well as in the "painterly quality" of the narrative. In her literary space, painting and music become both objects of the narration and stylistic devices.

Woolf is aware that the form and the language of the novel should have undergone a process of transformation in order to integrate the new protean reality which was developing at the turn of the century. In this period, words tend to be used "musically" in a new novel which is thus more similar to a musical piece. To this extent, due to the lack of a traditional plot, the three parts of *To the Lighthouse*, thematically and symbolically connected with each other, deal with chronological time in three different ways, and led critics to read the novel as an equivalent of the tripartite musical composition of the sonata form. Moreover, the novel, based on the author's childhood memories, employs memory as a technical device, within the text, through the figure of Mrs Ramsay and Lily's painting, two elements which provide the novel with a sense of circularity, where memory entwines with painting and the musicality of language.

1. "The Window": memory through sounds

In "The Window", memory and music are presented as mainly connected to Mrs Ramsay who, in turn, will become the object of Lily Briscoe's memory,

---

[1] Werner Wolf's *The Musicalization of Fiction* (1999) is a key contribution in the history of musico-literary studies and it is considered the starting point of this analysis.

a painter and close friend of the Ramsays. Time is mostly a matter of duration
and inner feelings, although some indications of chronological time are found
quite late in the text, and specifically when all the guests and the main topic of
the "expedition" have already been introduced, as the characters' private time
is more significant than the objective time. Another reference to *temps* comes in
relation to Lily, when she thinks that she is actually thirty-three years old (Woolf
2002, 38): a considerable detail, since in the third part of the book Lily's age is
mentioned again and the sense of the passage of time and of the distance in
time become deeper and more evident (Woolf 2002, 112).[2]

The transience of life, then, is depicted through several images related to
music. In Chapter III, for instance, Mrs Ramsay is captured by the sound of the
waves rolling against the shore, whose reverberation takes her back in time,
when the same sound "for the most part beat a measured and soothing tattoo to
her thoughts", and predominantly "seemed consolingly to repeat over and over
again [...] the words of some old cradle song" (Woolf 2002, 12).

This demonstrates that music is mainly recalled by metaphors and similes.
In Chapter VII, a musical metaphor is employed in order to describe Mr and
Mrs Ramsay's relationship, compared to the harmony of *"two different notes, one
high, one low, struck together"* (my emphasis). However, that "resonance died"
and later Mrs Ramsay points out that daily things "diminished the entire joy,
the pure joy, of *the two notes sounding together*, and let the sound die on her ear
now with a dismal flatness" (Woolf 2002, 28-29; my emphasis).

Similarly, in Chapter X, Mrs Ramsay is minutely described in the act of
reading a fairy tale to James, able to read and think "quite easily, both at the
same time" (Woolf 2002, 41). While reading, she is also thinking that "the story
of the Fisherman and his Wife was like the bass gently accompanying a tune,
which now and then runs up unexpectedly into the melody" (Woolf 2002, 41), a
statement which seems to explain how, in the whole story, the external actions
are just like a bass accompaniment, a sort of backup support to what is the
real melody, that is the inner thoughts, the inner actions of the mind. As Alex
Aronson highlighted, this scene is "an interesting instance of [the] interplay of
two voices singing in counterpoint": at that very moment, she discovers that
"the two, the narrative and her own thought, complement each other" (Aronson
1980, 55).

During the episode of the party, then, Mrs Ramsay experiences the eerie
feeling of the fleeting moment: at the end of the dinner, although aware of
her power to create a pleasant social environment, she sadly realizes that the
event has already become part of the past. She also remembers her time in

---

[2] This is one of the many indications which provide evidence for the theory which
considers *To the Lighthouse* as written in sonata form. A theme presented here in the first
section will be "recapitulated" in the last part of the novel.

London, and feels like nothing has changed: "Oh, she could remember it as if it were yesterday – [...] but now, she went among them like a ghost; and it fascinated her, as if, while she had changed, [...] had remained there, all these years" (Woolf 2002, 63). Then, as a repeated theme in a long musical piece that returns after a few bars, Mrs Ramsay's memory is presented again as in musical variations and as a sort of explanation and clarification: "Mrs Ramsay thought she could return to that dream land [...] at Marlow twenty years ago" (Woolf 2002, 67). The past triggers a positive sensation in the woman, for she realizes that, in memory she does not feel anxiety, as there is no future to be worried about. Finally, when Mr and Mrs Ramsay retire to the parlour, they clearly feel that their unity and the harmony of the dinner party dissipate, like the sound of the two notes previously mentioned, anticipating the mournful atmosphere of the second section.

2. "Time Passes": "many things had changed since then"

"Time Passes" acts as an interlude in the structure of the novel, positioned between two similar, longer, texts, which depict people who act and think within the house on the Hebrides. It is shorter and emptier: people disappear and only two female figures enter the desolate house, which becomes the centre of the narration, symbol of the ravages of war and destruction as well as the passage of time, all aspects that led Stevie Davies to read the section as a "testament to reality dehumanized" (Davies 1989, 38), where a general sense of devastation dominates.

"Time Passes" gives the novel a different narrative rhythm. However, in the third part, there is a vain attempt to re-establish the life of the opening section, for the events of the central part are so influential that nothing can be as it was before.

The section opens with a brief depiction of how the narrative moves from life to death, from movement to a sort of disturbing immobility and silence, broken by the sole presence of two women and the whistling of the wind. Here two of the characters that will disappear are presented, Andrew and Prue, who are wrapped around darkness as an anticipation of their death. On the contrary, in the same paragraph, Lily is connected to the image of light, as she will be the central character in the third part, trying to finish the painting she started ten years before in that very place and through which she will try to rescue Mrs Ramsay, icon of light and life, from death.

The sense of time elapsing is closely connected to the idea of darkness and perishability, which particularly concern the house, symbol of the whole family. The description of the house as empty and dark is the prelude to Mrs Ramsay's death, that is described swiftly in brackets in a secondary sentence, although it is a crucial event: "[Mr Ramsay stumbling along a passage stretched his arms out one dark morning, but, Mrs Ramsay having died rather suddenly the night before, he stretched his arms out. They remain empty]" (Woolf 2002, 95). Mrs Ramsay died during night time, a detail which contributes to stress the symbolism of a loss which can bring nothing but obscurity and unhappiness.

However, the section encompasses the decade of the war describing the chaos and misery into which the war threw the entire humanity and it portrays the "apocalyptic aspect of silence, linking it to death and war's destruction" (Fisher 1993, 104). Among the chaos, only Mrs McNab partly succeeds in restoring the order. Like Lily Briscoe, she has a vision of the ghost of Mrs Ramsay bent over the flowers with one of her children by her side, taking into life the dead woman even though for few moments.

The episode is enriched with the repetition of fragments of sentences, sometimes with some variations that confer musicality on the language. The narrator points out that "she could see her, as she came up the drive with the washing, stooping over her flowers [...] – she could see her with one of the children by her in that grey cloak". The image is then recalled by dividing and partly changing the same sentence into two parts: "Yes, she could see Mrs Ramsay as she came up the drive with the washing" and later "She could see her now, stooping over the flowers" (Woolf 2002, 101). As a ghost, then, Mrs Ramsay peoples Mrs McNab's and the reader's imagination, the latter helped by the use Woolf does of the brackets which enclose the description of the blurred ghostly woman wandering through the house. She is not real anymore, "she is dead", and she can only be brought to life through Mrs McNab's thoughts, exactly like Lily will do in the final part of the novel.

The last two chapters describe how the house, "alone" and "deserted" for years (Woolf 2002, 102), has now started to be renovated, thanks to Mrs McNab and Mrs Bast, who rescued the house "from the pool of Time". The language, from now on, appears rich in positive expressions: "rescued", "fetched up from oblivion", "restored to sun and air" (Woolf 2002, 103). Words and sounds recalling the lively social life of the past substitute total silence and destruction, and open the path to a new life which, however, will be different from the previous one. Mrs Bast points out that "they'd find it changed" (Woolf 2002, 104), and the sentence is repeated twice, highlighting the changes time have produced on everything, even though the house is still there, as is the lighthouse.

After the cleaning, the house is invigorated and "there rose that half-heard melody, that intermittent music which the ear half catches but lets fall" (Woolf 2002, 105): the life of the house is significantly symbolized by a melody that is ephemeral and difficult to catch fully, like music and life itself. Silence will take possession of the house again. "Then indeed peace had come", the author indicates, although it is a disconcerting peace, unreal and sometimes surreal, perfectly matching the silent sound of the sea.

3. "The Lighthouse": all had changed

"The Lighthouse" seems an attempt to re-establish a harmony that vanished with Mrs Ramsay's death. The connection between memory, music and painting becomes closer, and most of the events of the first part are presented again with a few although significant changes. The two "old" incomplete events, the "expedition" to the lighthouse and Lily's painting, are finally carried out. However, here Woolf focuses on the "act of re-creation", although that past harmony cannot be completely rebuilt because time has left its signs.

The artist is now at the centre of the narration. Lily observes life and tries to recreate, in her art, its numerous, manifold aspects. On a still morning of September in the house in the Hebrides, she is sitting "at her *old* place at the breakfast table, *but alone*" (Woolf 2002, 109; my emphasis), musing upon the profound changes occurred in ten years. The reiteration of some images contrasting with the previous image of the big Ramsay family and their hosts, highlights Lily's unpleasant feeling of emptiness. Moreover, reiterations and refrains related to Mrs Ramsay or to the verses from "The Castaway" by William Cowper, which resound like an echo through the text until the end, add a sense of melancholic musicality.

Then, in an empty space, once full, what Lily can do is nothing but going back in her mind to things and people. Her art is then "an attempt to fill in an empty space" (Ferrer 1990, 54), and her painting is one of the first things she recalls, through an involuntary memory generated by a few ordinary events: "Suddenly she remembered. [...] She had never finished that picture. It had been knocking about in her mind all these years. She would paint that picture now" (Woolf 2002, 110). And painting is the art chosen by Virginia Woolf to convey the meaning of the entire novel. As Daniel Ferrer pointed out, "in Lily Briscoe's action painting, the spasm was organized into a rhythm, a dance" (Ferrer 1990, 55), suggested by the very short sentences and the alternation of painting and pausing:

> [S]he made her first decisive stroke. The brush descended. It flickered brown over the white canvas; it left a running mark. A second time she did it – a third time. And so pausing and so flickering, she attained a dancing rhythmical movement, as if the pauses were one part of the rhythm and she stroke another, and all were related; and so, lightly and swiftly pausing, striking, she scored her canvas with brown running nervous lines which had no sooner settled there then they enclose [...] a space (Woolf 2002, 118).

Through art, Lily finds a way to preserve her experience, to catch a single instant and lift it out of the flow of time (Fisher 1993, 109), succeeding in what Mr and Mrs Ramsay failed. However, it was from that wise woman that she learnt the attitude to capture the moment. While mourning Mrs Ramsay's death and painting on the lawn, Lily reflects that "nothing stays, all changes; but not words, not paint" and later on, she realizes that in catching the succeeding "eternal assign and flowing" (Woolf 2002, 120) her painting will remain forever. By this, the author seems to suggest that art may be the only hope of certainty in a world destined to change.

The events of the first section are here evoked through memory and it is through memory that Lily can achieve her aim of finishing the painting. Though long dead, Mrs Ramsay lives in Lily's consciousness for a few moments and, like Mrs McNab, she has a vision of the woman, calling up the memory of her "from a very distant past" (Ferrer 1990, 48), from where the painting is also recovered:

> The moment at least seemed extraordinarily fertile. She rammed a little hole in the sand and covered it up, by way of burying in the perfection of the moment. It was like a drop of silver in which one dipped and illumined the darkness of the past. [...] and she dipped into the blue paint, she dipped too into the past there. [...] She went on tunnelling her way into her picture, into the past (Woolf 2002, 128).

Lily gets the impression of that woman sitting on the drawing-room step, but she soon realizes that that figure is only a figment of her imagination: the step is empty, the canvas is blurred. But her vision suddenly blooms and she is able to carry out her project and eventually give Mrs Ramsay the opportunity to be remembered in the future.

Among the other few remaining characters, James too is involved in the memory of an important moment of the past. As Mrs Ramsay foresaw – "and she thought, he will remember that all his life" (Woolf 2002, 45) – the negative attitude of his father has indeed affected him since then: "Something, he remembered [...] 'It will rain [...] You wont be able to go to the Lighthouse'" (Woolf 2002, 138). By considering the novel as a three-movement musical piece, this episode can be easily compared to a recapitulated theme which was first introduced in the opening section of the work. "The lighthouse" contains many examples of themes re-presented with a few changes, according to the writer's intent to activate the reader's faculty of memory.

Differently from the first part, the theme of silence, anticipated in the previous section, now pervades the text, as well as a sense of stillness which is not positive but rather unreal, distant and unusual, which suggests a sort of surrealist painting, where things and people stand together on the same canvas, almost random, creating an absurd situation in which nobody either speaks or moves.

While on the boat, looking at the lighthouse, Cam feels that time inexorably flows, making experience of a sensation which rises in the middle of the sea, symbol of the ever-changing, the ever-moving, the constant forward moment of time and the changes it brings.

4. How "tempo" works

In *To the Lighthouse*, memory and time deeply entwine with music and painting. Each of the sections, however, deals with time in a different way, although a fascinating aspect of the novel concerns the examination of "tempo"[3] and the way it contributes to give a certain rhythm to the novel.

In "The Window" and "The Lighthouse" the analytic description of the characters' thoughts causes an extreme slowness, an *adagio* in which every fragment of time is enormously enlarged. In "Time Passes", though, the events follow one another very quickly, thus ten years separate the first *adagio* from the second (Trevi 1997, 31-32). However, if "The Window" can be read as an *adagio*, "The Lighthouse" is more a *lento*, due to the many references to stillness and motionlessness which confer a further degree of slowness to the narration. The middle section, then, answers to the canon of a *prestissimo*, for time passes very quickly, even though the positive and cheerful aspect of the *prestissimo* temporal marking disappears and a sense of sadness emerges.

Considering E. M. Forster's opinion that *To the Lighthouse* is "a novel in sonata form" (in Brown 1963, 64), the three sections could be read as exposition, development and recapitulation. Thus, the first "movement" introduces the characters and the themes whereas in the third section there are repetitions, with some variations, of the original themes. The middle section, in this case, stands for the development, that is a development in themes but also in time. However, "Time Passes" can be also considered an interlude due to its bridge-like feature which connects two different sections, as well as a *staccato*, for the swiftness of the temporal indications.

The relationship between Woolf's novel with music is not only a formal matter if it can be also investigated within the text in connection to the style, so that "abolishing chapter and verse, [she] creates a rhythmic wave-like form and undulating passages as in music" (Davies 1989, 37). Thoughts, words and time, as well as sounds, pauses and silences are basic rhythmic elements that contribute to the rhythm of the novel. Nonetheless, the tripartite structure "finds fulfilment in repetition" and "phrases and images resonate and recombine in unexpected patterns, with the most recent image or word endlessly reorganizing previous ones in the reader's mind" (Fisher 1993, 107). In this way, not only painting and memory, but also music and memory become clearly connected: the painting, the images created by the author, the rhythm of the sentences and

---

[3] "Tempo" is considered as a measurement of time which can associate narrative to music, and thus narrative can be read as a composition inclined to suggest to the reader a specific sensation of quickness or slowness. As far as *To the Lighthouse* concern, each of the three sections has different but unifying features, so that the novel as a whole can be considered a multi-rhythmic, well orchestrated, work.

their repetition throughout the text, activate the mechanism of memory in the reader's mind, so that he or she has the impression of having already seen an image, heard that sound, that rhythm, that silence.

References

Aronson A. 1980. *Music and the Novel: A Study in Twentieth-Century Fiction.* Totowa: Rowman & Littlefield.

Auerbach E. 2000 (I ed. 1956). "Il calzerotto marrone". In *Mimesis. Il realismo nella letteratura occidentale.* Torino: Einaudi.

Brown E.K. 1963. *Rhythm in the Novel.* Toronto: Toronto UP.

Davies S. 1989. *Virginia Woolf. To the Lighthouse.* London: Penguin Book.

Ferrer D. 1990. *Virginia Woolf and the Madness of Language.* New York: Routledge.

Fisher J. 1993. "'Silent as a Grave': Painting, Narrative, and the Reader in *Night and Day* and *To the Lighthouse*", in Gillespie D.F. (ed.) *The Multiple Muses of Virginia Woolf.* London: Missouri UP.

Fusini N. 2002. "Introduzione". In Woolf V. *Al faro.* Milano: Mondadori.

Fusini N. 1998. "Introduzione". In Woolf V. *Romanzi.* Milano: Mondadori, I Meridiani.

Gillespie D.F. (ed.) 1993. *The Multiple Muses of Virginia Woolf,* Columbia-London: University of Missouri Press.

Harper H. 1982. *Between Language and Silence: The Novels of Virginia Woolf.* Baton Rouge: Louisana State UP.

Laurence P.O. 1991. *The Reading of Silence. Virginia Woolf in the English Tradition.* Stanford: Stanford UP.

Moore M. 1984. *The Short Season Between Two Silences.* Boston: George Allen & Unwin.

Trevi E. 1987. *Musica distante.* Mondadori: Milano.

Vlad R.1989. *Capire la musica e le sue forme.* Firenze: Giunti.

Wolf W. 1999. *The Musicalization of Fiction: A Study in the Theory and History of Intermediality.* Amsterdam: Rodopi.

Woolf V. 1988. "Modern Fiction". In McNeillie A. (ed.) *Essays.* London: Hogarth Press.

Woolf V. 2002. *To the Lighthouse* (I ed. 1927). Hertfordshire: Wordsworth Classics.

MARIA GRAZIA NICOLOSI

Università di Catania

Re-membering the Past in Adam Thorpe's War Novels

By way of a slightly paradoxical introduction to the novels that I intend to examine in some detail, I would like to start with a quote from Adam Thorpe's[1] acclaimed experimental first novel *Ulverton* (1992). In the episode set in 1953 the secretary of a famous cartoonist who furtively reads from his diaries, in the entries about World War II disappointingly finds:

> Up to December 1939. Nothing. That is, nothing on myself. I think he must have got his years wrong [...] Up to August 1940. Nothing! [...] Up to end of 1940. Nothing [...] Up to August '41. Nothing (Thorpe 1992, 293, 294, 295).

I propose for a moment to take this character's flippant words rather seriously as an early intimation of Thorpe's later concentrated interest in the implications for novelistic discourse of the sense of "nothingness" bequeathed it by early twentieth-century history.

In the 583-page long unpunctuated stream of consciousness of his dauntingly complex second novel *Still* (1995) Thorpe records the vicissitudes of "Ricky Thornby", a psychically crumbling, second-rate Film Studies teacher and failed film director engaged – on the eve of the new millennium – in the making of a grand "epic war film" on WWI: "[...] a masterpiece with no pictures, no sound and ONCE only, unique screening" (Thorpe 1995, 245).

---

[1] Born in Paris in 1956, Adam Thorpe lived as a boy in Beirut, Calcutta, Cameroon and the south of England due to his father's job for Pan Am. He graduated at Magdalene College, Oxford, in 1979. After a working experience as a farm labourer, he tried a career as mime artist, founding the "Equinox Travelling Theatre" and performing the Mystery Cycle on tour through the English villages in Wiltshire and Berkshire. From 1983 he was Polytechnic lecturer in London while writing poetry. His first full-length collection of verse was *Mornings in the Baltic* (1988), soon followed by *Meeting Montaigne* (1990); later on he published *From the Neanderthal* (1999) and *Nine Lessons from the Dark* (2003). In 1990 he moved to rural Languedoc in France where still lives with his wife and children, by now engaged in a steady writing career as both poet and novelist.

The pseudo-epistolary memoir *Pieces of Light* (1998) casts the identity quest of the once celebrated Shakespearean actor and director "Hugh Arkwright" against the vast backdrop of both World Wars and of British colonialism in Africa on the verge of its dissolution.

The suggestively titled *Nineteen Twenty-One* (2001) maps out the retrospective "trench tour" across the uncanny postwar landscape of ruins at Ypres embarked upon by the would-be novelist "Joseph Monrow", who fails to turn his 'rite' of initiation/memorialisation/atonement into the accomplished "first great war book" it was meant to inspire.

The Rules of Perspective (2005) weaves together, through deceptively neat twin narrative threads, interlaced with enigmatic diary fragments by another 'voice', the last hours, just before Germany's surrender, of "Heinrich Hoffer", the Modern Art Museum's *pro tempore* Director in the small German town of Lohenfelde, and of his 'enemy', the amateurish art enthusiast American private "Neal Parry".

By pushing to extremes the representational uneasiness inherent in historical fiction – correctly related by Carroll to the problematic grafting of historical consciousness onto (fictional) subjects (1982, 147)[2] – Thorpe miraculously manages to turn "nothingness" into the undisclosed potential of "a rich collective counter-memory" (Middleton and Woods 2000, 33). Thorpe's readiness to approach widely divergent ways of thinking about history from an 'eccentric' imaginative perspective enables the writer to produce a fictional space for the readers' encounter with historical representations of the past still to be imagined, in other words, for encounters with a past world *still to come*.

In his well-known study of the nineteenth-century historical novel (1937), György Lukács diagnosed its demise as ensuing from the "end of historicism" (1937, 234) which attended the "end of the former dialectical struggle" of bourgeois ideology (*ibidem*, 232). The post-1848 philosophical turn ushered in a "modernizing trend" (*ibidem*, 9), characterised by a "dehumanized decorative monumentalizing of history" as well as by its "privatization" (*ibidem*, 267). Although cast within a clearly Hegelian historical scheme, in failing to recognise the temporal logic proper to novelistic discourse, as opposed to that of the epic, Lukács reductively viewed the modernist "spatialization of time" as a sort of "historical falsification" (*ibidem*, 9), which thus sanctioned the so-called "end of history" (*ibidem*, 267). Despite its apocalyptic undertones, Lukács's work made no connection between modernism's peculiar translation of historical discourse into intelligible cultural forms through spatialising metaphors and

---

[2] As Ricoeur contends, "[t]he true mimesis of action is to be found in the works of art least concerned with reflecting their epoch [...] The quasi-past of the narrative voice is then entirely different from the past of historical consciousness" (1988, 191).

the historically unprecedented events of WWI that hastened the crisis of the nineteenth-century linear progressive understanding of time and literally displaced real human beings into the alien landscape of 'modern' warfare, uncannily resembling anachronic inner space.

In the face of that inscrutable war-related memory malaise called "shell shock" (Winter 2006, 52-76), the existential motivation to narrate, founded upon the notion of a stable individual and social identity (Brennan 1990, 44-70) built out of shared, fully communicable, "textual memories" (Middleton and Woods 2000, 1-15), suddenly became obsolete. As a guarantee to the authenticity of the experience to be conveyed (Watson 2007, 185-218), the fears and resistances arisen out of the traumas of recent history had to find their way into any discourse laying claim to the truth (Fussell 2000, 36-74).

According to Schachter, damaged self-identity may be understood as *spatially* hollowed out (2000, 9ff.), and the process of "healing by remembrance" (*ibidem*) in terms of a seemingly paradoxical temporal inversion between primary and secondary recollections, no wonder then that postwar historical narratives obsessively reiterated the trope of place. Having to deal with overwhelming chrono-logical disturbances by expressive means flexible enough to trade in positions of vacant, or recently vacated, representational spaces, the writers who resorted to such a spatial troping of memory as *unheimlich* found themselves unable to aestheticise it precisely because the radical crisis in the conceptualisation of time-bound phenomena, such as history, experience, individual and national identity, had disturbed in its wake all formerly available modes of representation.

Literally, or metaphorically, "shell-shocked" into the recognition of the meaninglessness of human suffering and death, faced with the impossible task of restoring the 'original' contents of memory to their proper *place* in the mind by "filling up" its "holes" (Schachter 2000, 65-67), the WWI generation felt that it inhabited an uncanny 'space-time'. In order to survive the cultural, ideological and ethical devastation brought forth by an utterly abject war which had dislocated, in soldiers and civilians alike, any firm sense of national identity (the known paths of one's 'home') to the No Man's Land of trench warfare and postwar ruins, and shattered any sense of historical continuity into the dead-end of personal and collective amnesia, a "chronotope" (Bakhtin 1981, 250) had to be devised for their lost "memory archives" by reinventing new meaningful symbolical and representational sites. The urgent need of a new sense of 'place', of which the literary tradition was hoped could be an important part, demanded an ontological relocation of temporality and a meaningful epistemological readjustment of historical time.

Following Fussell's suggestion (2000, 310-35), my contention is that the cultural and discursive formations originating with WWI have had tremendously far-reaching effects in shaping the literary, artistic and philosophical imagination of postwar intellectuals, infectiously reaching out to later representations, to the extent that the imagery and language originally attached to the WWI experience remarkably lingers on in much contemporary British historical fiction. The list of books published over the last few decades which may support this claim could be endless: suffice to mention Pat Barker's *Regeneration* (1992), about the war poet Siegfried Sassoon's struggle against WWI traumatic memory in search for his true identity, and Sebastian Faulks's *Charlotte Gray* (1999) about WWII, where the alleged paternal sexual abuse distorting the eponymous character's identity turns out to be a false memory stemming from listening to her father's WWI stories.

In Thorpe's war narratives such concerns appear to be most inextricably implicated in the aporias of identity, memory, and the representation of time past. Thorpe attempts to trace back the cultural entanglement of postmodernity with a still unsettled historical balance with a past that is either resisted or apprehended as not really completely past. In order to do so, the writer adopts the distinctly *spatial* figuration first established by WWI narratives as the most compelling tactics to come to terms with that troubled Benjaminian "theatre of memory"; for, as the philosopher poignantly wrote, "[l]anguage shows clearly that memory is not an instrument for exploring the past, but its theatre. It is the medium of past experience, as the ground is the medium in which dead cities lie interred" (Benjamin 1979, 314).

By means of a sophisticated figural method of "emplotment" (Ricoeur 1985, 42-45), which I will briefly rehearse by 'mimicking' Thorpe's own language, the writer pursues some of the most intractable epistemological, ontological, and ethical issues opened up by WWI in the areas where they have yielded especially conflicted pictures of the relation to the past. If one intends to chart what specific relation these questions bear to the "monumentalizing" and "privatization" trends observed by Lukács, one will see that the writer, firstly, deconstructs the 'terminal' status modernism conferred on the national literary tradition by figurally locating it among the 'ruins': "Yet this, camping in the ruins – this was the future – he knew it. This was all that could be looked forward" (Thorpe 2001, 85). Secondly, although situated at textually vanishing points, where the writer's historical imagination is confronted with the "mind's attraction to dissolution" (Thorpe 2005, 90), Thorpe does not eschew the ethical implications the literary work of re-membrance carries as "the desire to do justice to the past" (Ricoeur 1988, 153): "*Why do we live? To remember. And if we die? What happens to our memories then?*" (Thorpe 2005, 90, 208; original emphasis). Finally, Thorpe's narrative intervention is engaged with the problem of temporality without, however, 'playing tricks with time': "I'm not turning the clock back, I'm taking it off the wall and mending it" (Thorpe 1998, 146), as he aims at producing *real* epistemological (or even ontological) effects able to open up the present apprehension of time past.

Through fabulation and the "configurational act of mimesis" (Ricoeur 1985, 70-87), Thorpe provides his readers with the imaginative 'equipment' to embark on a spatial journey back to the 'ruins' – what may be called the "war chronotope" – "as a model of the past [...] a means of representing the distance between present and past as material space" (Middleton and Woods 2000, 64). A textually composite landscape thus resurfaces *at the place* of the "shock", where the past was "blasted out of the continuum of history" (Benjamin 1999, 253). Indeed, Thorpe's texts disrupt or do away altogether with continuity and linear progression in favour of a complex disjunctive patterning which is pertinent, I believe, to see as inspired by the *spatial* understanding of History posited by Benjamin:

> No fact that is a cause is for that very reason historical... The historian who takes this as his point of departure stops telling the sequence of events like the beads of a rosary... he grasps the constellation which his own era has formed with a definite earlier one (Benjamin 1999, 255).

In showing the impossibility to re-present the "absolute epic" time (Bakhtin 1981, 15-16) of un-presentable historical events, Thorpe seems to accept the modernist matrix of Benjamin's insight that "[t]o articulate the past historically does not mean to recognize it 'the way it really was' (Ranke). It means to seize hold of a memory as it flashes up at a moment of danger" (1999, 247). Proust's notion of "involuntary memory", as opposed to willed recollection, is the explicit model – without, however, unproblematically endorsing it in full – through which Thorpe's narrators set about the task of re-membering their conveniently 'forgotten', and therefore unspeakable, past: "I'm talking about calling up, not reading the moment. I'm talking Proust here, I'm talking dunked madeleines, I'm talking Pears soap lathering to my infancy" (Thorpe 1995, 383). Again, it is worth noting how close to this is Benjamin's reading of Proust's (and Bergson's) "*mémoire involontaire*" as a sort of "chronotopic" disorder, alongside Freud's notion of displacement (Benjamin 1999, 157), via a specific reference to the 'modern' aftershock experience:

> The greater the share of the shock factor in particular impressions, the more constantly consciousness has to be alert as a screen against stimuli; the more efficiently it does so, the less do these impressions enter experience (*Erfahrung*), tending to remain in the sphere of a certain hour in one's life (*Erlebnis*). Perhaps the special achievement of shock defence may be seen in its function of assigning to an incident a precise point in time in consciousness at the cost of the integrity of its contents (Benjamin 1999, 159).

The interplay of faulty memory and war experience is no less constitutive of both self-identity and historical consciousness in Thorpe's war novels: "At the end of the path is a hole, into which we tumble. [...] *A hole the size of a man...*" (Thorpe

2001, 147). Contrary to the still widely held belief that "memory returns whole, as a vivid, accurate composition of narrative and image, ready to be slotted back into the hole it left in an otherwise complete tapestry" (Middleton and Woods 2000, 97), Thorpe's narratives are structured *around* memory "holes": "The mind has holes and you fall into them screaming" (Thorpe 1995, 132); "I have to keep all my options covered, there are so many holes in the world" (*ibidem*, 486). Rather than attempting to 'fill' them up, Thorpe's intricately interwoven re-membrances flaunt their gaps as in fact assisting in restoring to the literary and cultural discourses of postmodernity their historical consciousness.

The kind of historicity that this narrative structuration sustains is figured as the act of "tearing a hole" (Thorpe 2001, 19-20) in the fabric of history, a poignant metaphor for the unaccountably selective workings of memory: edging towards the verbal border of unspeakability, 'loss' is made productive of a paradoxically 'excessive' new mode of historical knowledge. Although caught in the contradictions inherent in the belatedness of re-membrance and restricted, in point of principle, by the ambivalent fluctuation between remembering and forgetting, Thorpe's narrating voices recognise that the movement to 'access' the past is enabled precisely by the constraints imposed upon their utterance by the 'unfinished', open temporality characteristic of memory.

According to Ricoeur, by "reducing the extension of time to the distention of the soul" in "the spaces traversed by expectation, attention, and memory" (1985, 21), it is "narrative time" that offers the resource of a "threefold present" as a 'solution' to Augustine's acute awareness of the ontological aporias imbedded in the "lived experience of time" (*ibidem*, 7-12). Augustine's paradoxical temporality is also Postmodernism's, which has been alternately vilified or praised for its deeply felt "presentness of the past" (Hutcheon 1988, 4). In this sense, Thorpe's novels may be regarded as a paradigmatic illustration of how, within postmodernism, the war "chronotope" (Smethurst 2000, 82-84) may be translated into communicable experience and reclaimed to narrativity only by an always already *posthumous* discourse which miraculously reinstates presence, in the face of loss and oblivion, "from the other side of the war" (Thorpe 2001, 29), " through alien air at some God-forsaken hour in some totally God-forsaken place" (Thorpe 1995, 1), wherein time is suspended, "*as if* back from the war" (Thorpe 1998, 158; my emphasis).

In asserting its continuing effect in the present, the memorialisation of the past is thus *almost* turned by Thorpe's bold manipulation of the narrative form into postmodern reversible time: "I would like to have married you, thirty-odd years ago, before you were born" (Thorpe 1995, 31); "Supposing time does not exist at all, or only as a surface made of ice on which we can slip from here to there, so that I might slide backward one day and all this will be a possibility in the future, but not a certainty?" (Thorpe 2005, 38). The formidable cause-effect model, which grounds historical determinism and translates mere possibility into the fatalistic rush towards catastrophe, has been here reversed to digressive infractions which, in expanding to all times and the whole world, gesture towards Augustinian eternity (Ricoeur 1985, 22-26).

In this context, Benjamin's perhaps most puzzling iconic image, his memorable "angel of history", might stand for Thorpe's own allegorical figuration of his tentatively redeeming narrative poetics:

> A Klee painting named "Angelus Novus" shows an angel looking as though he is about to move away from something he is fixedly contemplating. His eyes are staring, his mouth is open, his wings are spread. This is how one pictures the angel of history. His face is turned toward the past. Where we perceive a chain of events, he sees one single catastrophe which keeps piling wreckage upon wreckage and hurls it in front of his feet. The angel would like to stay, awaken the dead, and make whole what has been smashed. But a storm is blowing from Paradise; it has got caught in his wings with such violence that the angel can no longer close them. This storm irresistibly propels him into the future to which is back is turned, while the pile of debris before him grows skyward. This storm is what we call progress (Benjamin 1999, 249).

With remarkable foresight, Benjamin grasped that it was precisely its "posthumous" character which endowed with hesitant Messianic accents the end-of-history rhetorics of his troubled times.

References

Bakhtin M. 1981. *The Dialogic Imagination*. Austin: University of Texas Press.

Barker P. 1992. *Regeneration*. London: Penguin.

Benjamin W. 1979. *One-Way Street and Other Writings*. London: Verso.

Benjamin W. 1999. [1st ed. 1968] *Illuminations* (Arendt H. ed.). London: Pimlico.

Brennan T. 1990. "The National Longing for Form". In Bhabha H. K. *Nation and Narration*. London: Routledge, 44-70.

Carroll D. 1982. *The Subject in Question: The Languages of Theory and the Strategies of Fiction*. Chicago and London: University of Chicago Press.

Faulks S. 1999. *Charlotte Gray*. London: Vintage.

Fussell P. 2000. [1st ed. 1975]. *The Great War and Modern Memory*. New York: Oxford University Press.

Hutcheon L. 1988. *A Poetics of Postmodernism: History, Theory, Fiction*. London and New York: Routledge.

Lukács G. 1981. [1st ed. 1937]. *The Historical Novel*. London: Penguin.

Middleton P., Woods T. 2000. *Literatures of Memory, History, Time and Space in Postwar Writing*. Manchester and New York: Manchester University Press.

Ricoeur P. 1985. *Time and Narrative*. Chicago and London: University of Chicago Press, vol. 1.

Ricoeur P. 1988. *Time and Narrative*. Chicago and London: University of Chicago Press, vol. 3.

Schachter D. 2000. *The Seven Sins of Memory: How the Mind Forgets and Remembers*. Boston: Houghton Mifflin.

Smethurst P. 2000. *The Postmodern Chronotope: Reading Space and Time in Contemporary Fiction*. Amsterdam, Atlanta (Ga.): Rodopi.

Thorpe A. 1992. *Ulverton*. London: Secker & Warburg.

Thorpe A. 1995. *Still*. London: Secker & Warburg.

Thorpe A. 1998. *Pieces of Light*. London: Jonathan Cape.

Thorpe A. 2001. *Nineteen Twenty-One*. London: Jonathan Cape.

Thorpe A. 2005. *The Rules of Perspective*. London: Jonathan Cape.

Watson J.S.K. 2007. *Fighting Different Wars: Experience, Memory, and the First World War in Britain*. Cambridge: Cambridge University Press.

Winter J. 2006. *Remembering War: The Great War and Historical Memory in the 20th Century*. New Haven (Ct.) and London: Yale University Press.

Section 3
Literature and the Media

ROBERTA BORGNA

Università di Udine

Is Life in the 21st Century "A Long Way Down"?
Thematic and Linguistic Issues
from One of Nick Hornby's Latest Novels

Focusing on one of Nick Hornby's latest novels, *A long way down* (2005), this essay explains why, in my opinion, Hornby's work represents a successful attempt at coming to terms with the thorny subject of suicide; I discuss this point via an exploration of thematic, narrative and linguistic issues.

Many writers other than Hornby have tried to deal with this topic, but his sharp and piercing glance at contemporary English society, only seemingly superficial, challenges the agreed-upon conventions and taboos which traditionally regulate discussion over certain unsolved and unsolvable social ills. Despite the laughable tone that usually permeates his pages, he is in fact very convincing when he populates his fictional worlds – mainly urban and chaotic – with controversial, funny but plausible, down-to-earth and up-to-date characters, a thing which allows him to get close to the sensitivity of contemporary readers by inducing processes of unexpected and often denied self-recognition. As he does not pretend to offer philosophical or taumaturgical answers, the readers welcome his novels as short-term antidotes to endure the contradictions, *ambiguities* and *dilemmas* of the brand new Millennium. In this case, more than in any previous one, Hornby reaches his goal thanks to a skilful use of a 'multimedia' writing; the last part of this essay seeks to analyse this in some detail.

In *A long way down* the writer opts for a polyphonic narrative pattern, recalling William Faulkner's *As I lay dying* (1930):[1] on New Year's Eve, four potential suicidals meet on the roof of the Toppers' House.[2] The first character, Martin Sharp, is a former TV host who has lost his career and family and has

---

[1] Moreover, Faulkner's novel and Hornby's, both revolve around the subject of death.

[2] The building might be identified with Archway Tower above the Metro Station in Northern London. The novel is full of actual references to London spots, which are meant to guarantee a level of plausibility, otherwise threatened by the frequent presence of unreliable ingredients.

been sent to jail for sleeping with a 15 year-old girl. Maureen, 51, is an old-fashion Catholic, isolated from the rest of the world because she has committed her whole life to her son, a seriously disabled boy of 19. His inability to speak and to understand what she says has not prevented her from inventing his progressive growth: on his bedroom's walls, posters of actresses and football players are hanging as simulacra of "a whole unlived teenage life" (Hornby 2005, 117). Jess is 18, foolish, impolite and not well-educated. Her desire to die is apparently due to her boyfriend, who left her without an explanation which she thinks she deserves; only later in the story do we come to know that she is the second daughter of a Labour Junior Minister for Education, and that her conflictual relationship with her family and her insolence are due to her sister's unexplained disappearance. The fourth character, JJ, is a failed American musician in his early thirties, who split up with his rock band and his girlfriend almost at the same time. He delivers pizzas as a temporary job, and fears he might have to flip hamburgers for the rest of his life to earn a living. He compares his ambitions for suicide with those of well-known artists, in his words "people who were too sensitive to live" (Hornby 2005, 24). Then he adds: "suicide was invented for people like Virginia Woolf and Nick Drake. And me. Suicide was supposed to be cool" (Hornby 2005, 25), but when he is asked about his reasons, he thinks his depression is too "vague" (Hornby 2005, 113), and therefore he pretends to suffer from an incurable brain cancer, which he describes as CCR (actually the acronym of a not very famous band).

Hornby has been harshly criticized[3] for failing in creating a serious, gloomy and threatening atmosphere at the very beginning of the book, when it might have been more appropriate to try to convey *pathos*, instead of *bathos*, parody and comic elements, in order to make the suicidal intent believable. In my opinion, however, it is not Hornby's concern whether we believe them or not; suicide is obviously a big issue, but somehow the writer succeeds in having it lie underneath the surface, never blaming the characters for their decision, nor questioning the integrity of suicide in general. Moreover, as other issues arise during the novel, suicide might also be interpreted as a macroscopic 'pretext' to see reality from a liminal, therefore enlightening, perspective.

Soon after they meet, the four of them confess the reason why they want(ed) to top themselves, and they promise each other to delay their suicidal attempts until Saint Valentine's Day. A 'gang of suicidals' forms thereafter, and it becomes a group, if not of friends, at least of people aware of their otherness. Martin explains that "even though we had nothing in common beyond that one thing, that one thing was enough to make us feel like there wasn't anything else – no money, or class, or education, or age, or cultural interests" (Hornby

---

[3] See the book's reviews on http://apps.metacritic.com/books/authors/hornbynick/longwaydown (last accessed August 2011)

2005, 44). Although not getting on well, the group survives, because it gives them a strong sense of *belonging*, thus acting positively in the difficult process of healing; however, being part of a 'gang' implies the necessity to admit that they have a problem, and this makes them feel set apart, different, thus *not belonging*. They feel trapped in a limbo, for they do not belong to the world of the living anymore, but they are not dead yet. Their precariousness increases after the meeting with a taxi driver whose wife has died: they first feel shame for their own reasons, which, compared to the man's, appear weak to their eyes all of a sudden; but though they are rationally able to recognize that there are circumstances and problems which somehow could 'legitimate' suicide more than others, nonetheless their impulse to die remains. Moreover, when they come back to the roof on Saint Valentine's day and cannot prevent another man from jumping, the tension reaches its highest peak: watching their own tragedy performed, they suddenly become conscious that they would never have been (nor would they be in the future) able to jump, and so once more cannot provide any definition, nor any location for themselves.

This feeling is metaphorically epitomized by a song, the Cure's "In between days" quoted by JJ, who is the most autobiographical character: he likes music and literature, as much as we know Hornby does. Moreover, JJ represents a projection of Hornby himself when he was younger and he embodies "the fear of never being able to fulfil potential, which was a very big thing in me when I was his age" (Hattenstone 2005),[4] as Hornby claims in an interview; in the same interview he explains that there is a direct connection between Maureen's son and his own, who is affected by autism. This is why he feels very close to this character, and seems to understand her more than any other. Although this does not mean that he accepts one person's reasons and denies another's, his attitude seems to influence the other characters, who become progressively aware of the heavy burden Maureen has been carrying over the last twenty years, and feel compelled to behave kindly towards her; his empathy affects also the reader, so when at the end of the novel she is gifted with a proper happy ending, one does not consider it as an implausible epilogue, but tolerates it as if she deserved some kind of 'reward'. Here Hornby replaces a traditional God with 'Cosmic Tony', a supposed genie made up by JJ, who satisfies her desires; he is based on an ironic deification of the former British Prime Minister Tony Blair.

Maureen is the only character struggling with religious matters, especially with the Catholic dogmatic condemnation of suicide. But the religious bond is not strong enough to prevent her from willing to jump. Nor is it any other: Jess reflects upon bonds in a moment of surprising depth:

---

[4] JJ expresses the very same concept in other words: "the trouble with my generation is that we all think we are [...] geniuses", and that "we have to *be* something" (Hornby 2005, 23).

> Most people have a rope that ties them to someone, and that rope can be short or it can be long. (Be long. Belong. Get it?) You don't know how long, though. It's not your choice. Maureen's rope ties her to Matty and its about six inches long and it's killing her. Martin's rope ties him to his daughters, and, like a stupid dog, he thinks it isn't there. [...] I am tied to Jen, and not to my mum and dad – not to home, which is where the rope should be (Hornby 2005, 142-143).

Jess' theory is highly exemplary of a narrative technique Hornby recurrently employs in his works, "a classic Hornby manoeuvre, the extended, back-to-comparative-basics analogy" (Taylor 2005): it often happens that, trying to explain something, a character tells a little story based on everyday life, which is supposed to support his/her previous statement. Sometimes such a mechanism is accompanied by the typical Hornbian sentence, 'well, not...': soon after s/he has established a comparison, feeling it does not mark out his/her problem clearly, s/he starts 'smoothing' it, in order to convey the actual meaning s/he was aiming at. Most of the times, these stories turn out to be also self-therapies, illuminating moments of growth which, at the same time, allow the reader to get acquainted with the character's viewpoint and way of thinking. Though a peculiar and rather innovative technique, its limit consists in its plausibility: all the characters use it, so it is evidently a Hornbian narrative device, rather than a widespread way of thinking. Maureen's reflections offer a clarifying sample:

> Not having Matty with me was like missing a leg. It felt that strange. But I also enjoyed the lightness of it, so it probably wasn't at all like missing a leg, because I don't suppose people who've had a leg taken off do enjoy the lightness of it very much. And I was going to say that it was much easier to move around without Matty, but it's much harder to move around with only one leg, isn't it? So maybe it would be more truthful to say that being on the plane without Matty was like being without a third leg, because a third leg would feel heavy, I expect, and it would get in the way, and you would be relieved if it was taken off (Hornby 2005, 155).

In the book a central role is given to the media, meant both as artistic media and communication media: in recent years a combination, interaction and even trespass of different artistic media has become a usual, widely used, and even abused practice, to such an extent that Mario Costa claims that nowadays "identity and specificity of media are threatened not only by the effect of migration, but also as a result of hybridization" (Costa 1999, 9, translation mine).

When Jess, who plays the highest attantial role in the story, tells the newspapers that an angel looking like Matt Demon told them not to jump off the roof, she unleashes the media's interest and involvement. She also organizes a meeting on the basement of Starbucks, inviting each character's relatives so as to try to sort their problems out in a kind of improbable group therapy. This last event, which in Jess' mind was supposed to lead to a happy *dénouement*, could easily be inspired by, or either be the inspiration for a television format (with its rules and roles precisely described); it is to be noticed that television and other visual media turn out to be the privileged thematic and situational sources of many of the episodes that fill the book. Furthermore, not only does Hornby derive some patterns from television and cinema, to such an extent that one could easily trace back the root of this practice to his work as a screenplay writer; moreover, the novel seems to be written as a screenplay itself, and attempts have already been made to re-write it as a script.[5] Hornby's books are not new to adaptations, but it would be reductive to assert that this novel was exclusively based on cinematic strategies.

In this novel Hornby is involved in the effort of rethinking the interaction of literature with other media within a literary context in terms of narrative, stylistic, and thematic influences. Additionally, by calling into question the characters' literary tastes, the writer proves that also their interest in and knowledge of literature have been overcome by mainstream TV programmes, or at least are driven by stereotypical, television and off-the-shelf standards. Maureen's reading habits, for instance, are limited to cheap romances; therefore she cannot consider literature as a means of understanding life. Her familiarity with contemporary life is rather based on the *EastEnders*, a very famous, but not particularly committed British TV series, and she thinks her 'mates' could easily be some of its characters. Jess is 'scared' of books: her sister used to read a lot, and in her mind she believes books' contents could have spurred her to disappear. Whenever she hints at literature, her attitude is debunking (see the recurrent *Pride and Prejudice*'s parody). Martin has been a TV host for so long that his public persona has impinged on his private one to such an extent that, though a well-educated man, in his mind TV patterns overcome any possible literary influence, and his literary quotations are only means for showing off the class-conscious and snobbish supremacy he feels. He spent quite a long time "looking up suicide inquests" on the Internet (Hornby 2005, 7), and he states that his attempt failed though "he scored very high on Aaron T. Beck's Suicide Intent Scale" (Hornby 2005, 43), which again was found on a web site. JJ reads almost every book, and he also likes them all: because he did not go to College, he is convinced that literature gives evidence of one's education. Therefore he fills his speeches with quotations (literary and musical), but often does not understand them (or quote them) properly.[6] His literary tastes reflect Hornby's:

---

[5] A group of students from Jena Gymnasium (Germany) published on Internet their attempts to re-write the book as a script (http://toppersjump.wordpress.com/category/screenplays/). Foreseeing its potential success, the actor Johnny Depp bought the rights of Hornby's book, even before it was published.

[6] Shakespearian quotes and allusions would deserve a further study.

I read [...] every book I can get my hands on. I like Faulkner and Dickens
and Vonnegut and Brendan Behan and Dylan Thomas. Early that week [...]
I had finished *Revolutionary Road* by Richard Yates [...]. I was actually going
to jump with a copy [but] I left it at home (Hornby 2005, 22).

JJ's selection is not accidental: Dickens is Hornby's favourite writer ever[7],
while the first writer he quotes, Faulkner, is the literary source for the narrative
frame of the novel. The novel's storytelling technique, instead, is based on
a theatrical representation, in which the characters break the fourth wall
addressing the audience directly, looking for further interaction. This imaginary
stage could equally be a psychoanalyst's couch, or better the comfortable sofa
of a TV show: after the Matt Demon-like angel's made-up revelation, they
take part in several talk shows and give interviews to TV programmes and to
the gutter press. One could also compare the story to accounts written by the
characters themselves, diaries or therapeutic confessions or rather Internet blogs,
where they recollect the ninety days of their adventures (once more a deadline
based on a newspaper article), in order to give evidence of the benefits of their
liaison. The writer intervenes as an editor, for the book is clearly the result
of an *assemblage a posteriori*, rather than the 'neutral' collage of simultaneous
reports. Moreover, the main plot intertwines with the accounts of their personal
experiences to such an extent that digressions can often be found which open
imaginary windows on the characters' past lives and families, thus resembling
literary or Internet hypertexts.

In light of these premises, I would argue that the hybridization Costa refers
to is perfectly exemplified by Hornby's tendency to mingle different elements
together, either genres or media, voices or vernaculars, in order to compel
literature and other artistic media to reflect upon themselves and their forms,
and to borrow discursive strategies from one another. The writer needs them to
become as much effective as they can in dealing realistically and pragmatically
with tough issues such as suicide, especially when such a topic seems to lay
hold of the complex and composite context of urban 21st century London.

The broad use of modern and technological elements finds a parallelism
in the setting, where no room has been left for history and the past: in the
realistically recreated London where the story is set, monuments and historic
buildings have been removed from sight, and everything is in the mainstream,
up-to-the-minute and in fashion; Captain Coffee's Café, a little heritage from the
past, has been replaced by Starbucks, where Jess finds it paradoxically easier to
feel her privacy guaranteed. And even during the most intense moment of the
story, the London Eye encroaches on the characters' sight, becoming the only

---

[7] See Hornby (2004).

element of a horizon which unexpectedly[8] turns into a void: this contemporary and highly criticized emblem of the brand new Millennium, epitomizes a supervisor and somehow recalls an Orwellian 'London Eye is watching you'; but it is also a symbol of fate which keeps going, indifferent to people's troubles and misfortunes, and even to their potential suicidal thoughts; "Is that actually going round?" (Hornby 2005, 257), asks Martin in one of the final statements. And Maureen's answer, though the answer of the most unsophisticated of the four, seems nonetheless the only possible one: "It didn't look as though it was moving, but it must have been" (Hornby 2005, 257). Here Hornby's idea, rather than Maureen's, hints at a restless and relentless destiny, which people cannot do anything but submit to.

In conclusion, what is to Hornby the meaning of the long way down? It is not the quickest jump from the roof to the ground, but the longest way home, through the stairs and back along the streets where normal life is, and where it could be hard – though beautiful, perhaps – to accept its natural course until death, whenever it happens to come and not when we would like it to. The final decision summarized by the seemingly preposterous question "how about we give it another six months?" (Hornby 2005, 25) symbolizes no more the extreme attempt to find a place in the world of the living, though for each isolated character this would still be a challenge; instead, it is a pretext to justify the survival of a group which otherwise would have no other plausible or socially acceptable reason for sharing some further moments of a long way down...on earth.

References

Costa M. 1999. *L'estetica dei media: avanguardie e tecnologia*. Roma: Castelvecchi.

Faulkner W. 1930. *As I Lay Dying*, New York: Jonathan Cape & Harrison Smith.

Hattenstone S. 2005. "Interview with Nick Hornby". In *The Guardian*, April 23ʳᵈ, available at http://www.guardian.co.uk/books/2005/apr/23/fiction. shopping (last accessed August 2011).

Hornby N. 2004. *The Polysyllabic Spree*. San Francisco: Believer Books, McSweeney's.

Hornby N. 2005. *A long way down*. London: Penguin Books.

Taylor D.J. 2005. "About a Boy Who Grew". In *The Independent*, May 6ᵗʰ, available at www.independent.co.uk/arts-entertainment/books/reviews/a-long-way-down-by-nick-hornby-753017.html (last accessed August 2011).

---

[8] Previous descriptions of the sight from the roof were full of London's distinctive monuments and buildings.

ILARIA ODDENINO

Università di Torino

Ern Malley: Contemporary Perspectives
on Australia's Bogus Bard

To describe a poet as a "bogus" leaves very few doubts as to the authenticity of the author in question. In fact, it leaves very few doubts as to whether the author ever existed at all, and in the case of Ern Malley both assumptions can hardly be disputed. He is, under each and every angle, a fake, a phoney, a counterfeit, and therefore it is not surprising that his creation has often been regarded as Australia's biggest literary hoax of all times. Yet, his lack of a physical, corporeal presence has not prevented him from having an extraordinary life of his own, an ever-changing protean existence forever re-moulding itself around different readings and interpretations. What I am going to do in the course of this essay is briefly retrace his story, from the moment he was born, if so it can be said, through the exposition of the hoax and the controversies that followed, to the legacy of the Ern Malley affair in contemporary Australian culture. My main aim is to prove that what may at first seem little more than an amusing anecdote is in fact a serious piece of literary history, to the point that, to follow in Michael Heyward's footsteps, it can be said to represent the "definitive moment in Australia's literary modernism" (Heyward 1993, 293). I would also like to draw your attention to some of the more recent appearances of this mysterious character, who, as in a modern-day *Frankenstein*, has outsmarted and outlived his creators and now enjoys a fairly well-established popularity.

The birth of Ern Malley was accomplished, after a cerebral gestation and an intellectual labour, at the beginning of October 1943, when he sprang, full-grown, like Minerva, from the brains of his progenitors (Ellery 1944, 9). Their names were James McAuley and Harold Stewart, two Sydney-born poets in their late twenties, who, "in the literary frolic of an afternoon" (*ibidem*), decided to assemble random extracts from an equally random collection of books to mimic, or rather, to debunk, what could be loosely labelled 'modernist poetry'. This chance ensemble of texts included a *Concise Oxford Dictionary*, a *Collected Shakespeare*, a *Dictionary of Quotations*, and, of all things, a report on the drainage of breeding-grounds of mosquitoes. From these, the hoaxers haphazardly picked words and phrases which were later woven into what they described as "nonsensical sentences"[1] (Heyward 1993, 173), even though, as we will see, this is utterly objectionable. On top of that, they "misquoted, made false allusions, deliberately perpetrated bad verse and selected awkward rhymes from a Ripman's Rhyming Dictionary" (*ibidem*) and this devilish concoction was held together by a train of free associations and conscious interruptions. They thus put together sixteen poems, and a letter by Ethel, Ern's sister, who, having found her brother's poems after his premature death at the age of twenty-five, thought of submitting them to a more knowledgeable person than herself to find out whether they were of any artistic value. Their designated target, or scapegoat really, was Mr. Max Harris, an Adelaide poet who, from a very young age, had taken upon himself the role of advocate, promoter and deliverer of all those "-isms" which had systematically encountered a stubborn resistance in his country, from dadaism, to surrealism (he indeed thought of himself as a surrealist poet), to what is often referred to as high modernism. The battlefield on which the Ern Malley "war" took place, was an avant-garde art-and-literature journal edited by John Reed and Max Harris himself, *Angry Penguins* (Harris and Reed 1944). It was a plush, flamboyant and somewhat pretentious publication where the thirst for the new was sometimes satiated at the expense of a certain approximation of critical judgement and indiscriminate/elitist support of fellow "rebels", so to speak. However, its significance remains undeniable, as *Angry Penguins* provided the only truly loud and unapologetic response to a cultural environment which in the 1940s was still affected by a good degree of philistinism, and which was still struggling to break free from the grip of a decades-long tradition of realism in literature (with its roots in the Bulletin school of writers) and pastoral landscape in painting (with its roots in the Heidelberg school). When Harris read the poems he thought he had finally encountered the modernist genius his country had so far failed to produce and, in a fit of excitement, he dedicated the Autumn 1944 issue of *Angry Penguins* to his latest discovery.

The publication of the Ern Malley issue did cause a sensation, as Harris had hoped, but for all the wrong reasons. Indeed, only days after its release, the hoax was exposed on the first page of a magazine called *Fact*, where McAuley and Stewart released a joint statement explaining the reasons behind their deeds; this is a brief extract:

> For some years now we have observed with distaste the gradual decay of meaning and craftsmanship in poetry; Mr. Max Harris and other *Angry Penguins* writers represent an Australian outcrop of a literary fashion which has become prominent in England and America. The distinctive feature of the fashion, it seemed to us, was that it rendered its devotees insensible of absurdity and incapable of ordinary discrimination. [...] Their work appeared

---

[1] The article originally appeared on *Fact*, 25 June 1944.

to us to be a collection of garish images without coherent meaning and structure; However, it was possible that we had simply failed to penetrate to the inward substance of these productions. The only way of settling the matter was by experiment. [...] What we wished to find out was: Can those who write, and those who praise so lavishly, this kind of writing tell the real product from consciously and deliberately concocted nonsense? (*ibidem*).

To clarify, what they meant by "humourless nonsense" was what "began with the *Dadaist* movement in France during the last war, which gave birth to the *Surrealist* movement, which was followed in England by the *New Apocalypse* school, whose Australian counterparts are the *Angry Penguins*" (*ibidem*).

It is vital at this point to have a closer look at Malley's work; the following poem is the first one of his collection, and it is also the very first one Harris was presented with:

Durer: Innsbruck 1495.

<blockquote>
I had often, cowled in the slumberous heavy air,

Closed my inanimate lids to find it real,

As I knew it would be, the colourful spires

And painted roofs, the high shows glimpsed at the back,

All reversed in the quiet reflecting waters

Not knowing then that Durer perceived it too.

Now I find that once more I have shrunk

To an interloper, robber of dead men's dream,

I had read in books that art is not easy

But no one warned that the mind repeats

In its ignorance the vision of others. I am still

The black swan of trespass on alien waters. (Malley 1974, 25)
</blockquote>

I suspect this is not what most reader expected after what has been said so far. There are more obscure compositions, and there are ones with verses which are indeed quite phoney, but I believe it is important to stress the fact that if one actually reads the poems, he/she then immediately realises that the answer to the hoaxers' question ("Can those who write, and those who praise so lavishly, this kind of writing tell the real product from consciously and deliberately concocted nonsense?") is much more articulate that a "no, they can't". In fact, the question they pose automatically breaks up into a thousand sub-questions: what is a *real* product in the first place? What makes a *good* poem? Does the technique described by Mc Auley and Stewart automatically exclude the possibility for the poems themselves to be of value? And is it not possible that the hoaxers, by trying to parody such an unconventional, experimental style (with all the freedom that a creative act of this nature entails) might have ended up deceiving themselves and creating an original work of art? This last point was the main argument held by Herbert Read on the following number of *Angry Penguins*, published in December 1944, where a great number of poets, painters, literary critics and intellectuals had their say on the affair. Among the contributors was, for example, the pioneer Melbourne psychiatrist Reg. S. Ellery, who declared:

> The fact that the Ern Malley poems are compounded from an odd assortment of lines and phrases, unacknowledged plagiarism and unrelated ideas, is of little moment. Poetry is, among other things, the art of selection. The conventional poet selects his words from the vocabulary of his native tongue; but there is no reason why an idea or an image should not be set down in selected phrases. Pre-fabricated poetry may indeed become the medium of modernity (Ellery 1944, 9).

Quite visionary indeed. Another meaningful passage, to quote just one more Malley supporter in the same edition, comes from the pen of the art critic Adrian Lawlor, who asked his readers: "Where does what's 'genuine' detach itself from what's 'false' in the *act* of artistic creation?" and then went on saying:

> There is great art and small, certainly, good art and bad art, but there can be no demonstrable distinction (none that I can discover, at least) between "spoof" and "inspiration", when the artwork effectively *speaks* to a *listening* world. There is, then, no fake or false *art*, whatever the degree of goodness or badness in any given work of art whatsoever (Lawlor, 1944, 11).

The issue also featured less enthusiastic positions such as that of the literary critic Dorothy Green, who began her intervention by stressing the fact that because of the public's incapability of discerning the exact object parodied, what came out scarred and discredited from the affair was modern art in general, whereas what deserved to be slaughtered was merely the misunderstanding and the misuse of such respectful conception of art by Australian poetasters of little merit – namely, Mr. Max Harris (Green 1944, 16).

It is clearly impossible to say who was right and who was wrong, but what we do know for a fact is that for the first time poetry was on the first page of all newspapers and magazines (an unprecedented and, until the exposition of the hoax, unforeseeable event) and that it forced Australia to a serious reflection upon the state of its literary world. Not only did the affair become Max Harris's scarlet letter, which he wore, often with pride, until his death in 1995 (Heyward 1993, 268) – it is here worth mentioning that the journal he edited after *Angry Penguins*, which ran from 1951 to 1955, was called *The Ern Malley's Journal*, whose first issue famously opened with the line: "I still believe in Ern Malley" – but in a way it became the country's scarlet letter too, because "by creating a more powerful image of modernist identity than had hitherto existed in Australia and then discrediting it" (*ibidem*, 293) the hoax actually made a certain species of poetry in Australia become untenable for a while.

Sixty years have passed. What happened next? First of all, *The Darkening Ecliptic* (this is the name under which the poems were collected) has known a significant editorial fortune, being published and republished several times after its first appearance in 1944 on *Angry Penguins* up until very recently. Apart from single publications, the poems have been included in anthologies (such as *The Penguin Book of Modern Australian Poetry*), or have featured in thematic journals and magazines, one of them being for instance the Paris magazine *Locus Solus* in 1961, in an edition devoted to collaborative writing; the choice of that particular edition also invites a reflection on how "these unsettling works of the imagination may be seen as early examples of the postmodernist technique of *bricolage*, of knocking something together from whatever materials are close to hand"[1], as John Tranter and Philip Mead have suggested (1991, xxx), thus opening the ground for unexplored and forever evolving critical possibilities. Speaking of new critical perspectives on the Malley affair, if one looks back at it having in mind Roland Barthes' foundational essay of 1968 (Barthes 1977), one cannot help but feel that in more than one way Ern Malley seems to have fulfilled the French philosopher's dream of the "death of the author". "To give a text an Author" Barthes wrote, "is to impose a limit on that text, to furnish it with a final signified, to close the writing. [W]hen the Author has been found, the text is 'explained' – victory to the critic" (*ibidem*, 147). But if criticism abandons the role of passive exegete to the author's intentions, if it stops thinking that "wherever there is a design there must be a designer" (Burke 1992, 23) and that wherever there is appearance of meaning there must be intention (*ibidem*), the myth of the author/God is overthrown, and the attention is finally shifted from the author to the reader; the death of the author actually results in the birth of the reader. This was the main point behind Barthes' "authorcidal" intention, which could easily be applied to the poems I have been discussing. One could continue along these lines and relate, for example, the Ern Malley affair to the theories on authors and authorship of another French philosopher, Michel Foucault, who opened his essay "What is an author" (Foucault 1977) with a quotation from Beckett aimed at showing that the answer to the question "Who is speaking?" could in fact be another question: "What does it matter who is speaking?".

Furthermore, the evolution in the last few decades of the so-called "postcolonial studies" is forcing us to reconsider the very terminology with which we have so far been describing cultural phenomena in postcolonial countries, and therefore the main landmarks I have been using to describe and understand that affair could, or in fact *should* be reconsidered. Why was it so important to find a tradition of modernist poetry in Australia in the 40s, or ascertain the lack thereof? Why this "unreflective use of Eurocentric and imperial discourse to describe and define the energies of a post-colonial culture?" (Ashcroft and Salter 2000, 293) The discourse of Modernism is firmly rooted in the cultural logics of the empire, and the use of "a set of largely uncontested parameters upon a non-European cultural reality, may be seen to be metonymic of the operation of imperial domination", as Aschroft and Salter have pointed out (*ibidem*). In this sense, they explain:

> The use of the category 'modernism' in Australia ensured that cultural production in the first decades of the century which used features of the stylistic innovations prevalent in Europe were seen to 'inherit', 'mimic', 'copy' or 'follow' European cultural fashion. On the contrary, however, the imposition of the term 'modernism' effectively submerged the specific energies of the cultural activities occurring at the time (*ibidem*).

This is just to give you a few examples of how, as the years go by, the affair tirelessly continues to lend itself to different interpretations, which make it as interesting and challenging today as it ever was. However, what has perhaps contributed more than anything else to take this non-existing author into the 21th century is the work of the Australian writer Peter Carey, whose 2003 novel, *My Life as a Fake*, combines a faithful reconstruction of the historical events with the vicissitudes of Bob Mc Corkle, Ern Malley's fictional counterpart (so the fictionalised version of a fictional poet) who takes on the physical, corporeal existence Malley never had. Here he truly becomes a modern-day Frankenstein, a Miltonic hero, created then rejected by he who gave him life, monstrous, at times dis-human, but indisputably a great poet. The latest appearance of the bogus bard, portrayed as a Christ-like figure, is probably little known compared to Carey's novel, and it is a beautiful series of paintings produced in 2004 by the Australian artist Garry Shead.

One of Karl Kraus's famous aphorisms maintained that "a poem is good until one knows who wrote it", a statement which seems here particularly fitting. However, it is perhaps even more fitting to let the (bogus) poet himself conclude, and no verses seem more appropriate than the following ones, taken from his poem *Sybilline*:

It is necessary to understand

that a poet may not exist, that his writings

are the incomplete circle and straight drop

of a question mark

and yet I know I shall be raised up

on the vertical banners of praise. (Malley 1974, 33)

References

Ashcroft B., Salter J. 2000. "Modernism's Empire: Australia and the Cultural Imperialism of Style". In Booth H. J., Rigby N. (eds.) *Modernims and Empire*. Manchester: Manchester University Press, 292-323.

Barthes R. 1977. "The Death of the Author". In *Image-Music-Text. Essays Selected and Translated by Stephen Heath*. Glasgow: Fontana/Collins, 142-148.

Burke S. 1992. *The Death & Return of the Author – Criticism and Subjectivity in Barthes, Foucault and Derrida*. Edinburgh: Edinburgh University Press.

Carey P. 2003. *My Life as a Fake*. London: Faber and Faber.

Ellery Reg. S. 1944. "Ern (Jig Saw) Malley". In *Angry Penguins*, December, 9.

Foucault M. 1977. "What Is an Author?" (translated by Bouchard D.F., Simon S.). In *Language, Counter-Memory, Practice*. Ithaca (NY): Cornell University Press.

Green D. 1944. "The Cloud-Foot Unwary". In *Angry Penguins*, December, 16.

Harris M., Reed J. (eds.) 1944. *Angry Penguins*, December.

Heyward M. 1993. *The Ern Malley Affair*. London: Faber and Faber.

Lawlor A. 1944. "Two Letters". In *Angry Penguins*, December, 11.

Malley E. 1974. *The Darkening Ecliptic/Poems by Ern Malley; Paintings by Sidney Nolan*. London: R. A. McAlpine.

Tranter J., Mead P. (eds.) 1991. *The Penguin Book of Modern Australian Poetry*. Ringwood (Vic.): Penguin Books Australia.

Section 4
Past and New Directions

MARIJA BERGAM

Università di Bari Aldo Moro

Robinson Crusoe's Sea-Change: Caribbean Transformations

The commonly accepted conceptualization of what is – sometimes controversially – defined as "postcolonial literature" usually includes some reference to its *counter-discursivity*. Thus, Helen Tiffin wrote in her famous essay from 1987 that "the rereading and rewriting of European and historical fictional records [were] vital and inescapable tasks" (Tiffin 1987, 18) of the so-called postcolonial works. It is rewarding, and often necessary, to approach from this point of view Caribbean literary production. As is well known, the material conditions and the social environment determined by the plantation economy resulted in a severe loss of the cultural, particularly linguistic, heritage of the majority of West Indian population. The regional literary pioneers, from the beginning of the last century on, had to deal with the paradox of writing in the imperial tongue while self-consciously striving to create local literatures from an ambiguous position: writing both in opposition to, and yet necessarily drawing from, a given colonial literary canon. Furthermore, the Caribbean was the stage of the first colonial encounters, re-enacted and alluded to time and again in major works that constitute part of the dominant literary canon. The first record of these cultural contacts, the one presumably left by Columbus, set the tone for the subsequent representations (fictional and otherwise), the response to which necessitated the creative use of intertextual practices, which would become representative of postcolonial literatures.

Among the most resonant, and possibly most re-written, of the canonical works alluded to above is, of course, Defoe's *Robinson Crusoe* (1719), whose "strange and surprising adventures" on a deserted island in the Caribbean basin have been read as an allegory of colonialist venture, considering both their material effects and Crusoe's relationship with his "man Friday". Critical assessments by notable scholars and artists are numerous and well known, but it is worth recalling Joyce's succinct and insightful appraisal, recorded during a 1912 conference in Trieste (and hence quoted in Italian):

Egli [Robinson Crusoe] è il vero prototipo del colonizzatore britannico come
Venerdì (il fedele selvatico che vi giunge in un giorno infausto) è il simbolo
delle razze assoggettate (Joyce 1979, 159).

This essay sets out to show that, contrary to what might be expected, the
reappearance and re-deployment of the Crusoe figure in two well-known
Caribbean works does not proceed by directly inverting or exclusively denouncing
Crusoe's actions, or his relationship with Friday. On the contrary, the appropriation
and subtle transformations observed in these works can be read as emblematic
of a wider poetics, one that imaginatively employs the dominant metropolitan
discourses and their literary manifestations in order to create something new, yet
not created *ex novo*. In these works, *colonial mimicry* identified by Homi Bhabha
as "the desire for a reformed, recognizable Other" (Bhabha 2004, 122), and clearly
evident in Crusoe's treatment of Friday, is transmuted into "mimicry as design,
both as defense and as lure", as Derek Walcott would have it (Walcott 1997a, 55).
Similarly, the focus on the practice of cannibalism – which Defoe's text contributed
to consolidate – shifts from its status as one of the defining features "of the
discourse of colonialism as it pertained to the native Caribbean" (Hulme 1986, 3)
to a name for a liberating discursive practice whereby the writers from the New
World appropriate and modify European texts for their own purposes.[1] Diverse,
and sometimes diverging, strategies of the usage of a given European language
and its concomitant literary canon are the means by which this is effected.

The first work here presented is a novel by Trinidadian Samuel Selvon,
a sequel to his celebrated *The Lonely Londoners* (1956). *Moses Ascending*, first
published in 1975, is narrated by the eponymous West Indian hero, now long
settled in London. Its subversive intertextuality is apparent at every level:
the title points to Biblical narrative, and more obviously to the earlier, above
mentioned novel, whose protagonist has now ascended the social ladder. The
memoir genre is partially parodied, too, as the autobiographic "opus magnus"
Moses claims to be writing – though unrevealed to the reader – infuses the
text, at times becoming superimposed upon it. In order to appreciate Selvon's
parodical transformation,[2] some background information is called for: at the
beginning of the narration Moses manages to purchase a derelict property in
Shepherd's Bush, finally rising from destitute immigrant anonymity to his "new
station" as landlord (Selvon 1984, 2). Fresh circumstances in life finally permit
him to dedicate all his time to the literary ambitions he has been harbouring, and
which are frustrated when his friend Galahad observes it lacks real substance
and fails to address the burning issues. Moses' subsequent decision to allow the

---

[1] See Huggan (2006).

[2] The term "parody" is employed following Genette's definition in *Palimpsests* (Genette
1997), as a kind of playful semantic transformation of the hypotext.

personal memoirs he is working on to be hybridised, as it were, by including the topical concerns leads him into an ill-conceived attempt at practical "research", which precipitates the plot and, predictably, lands him in trouble.

Of particular interest is Moses' relationship with his factotum Bob, whom he introduces as "my man Friday, a white immigrant [...] from somewhere in the Midlands, who came to seek his fortunes in London" (Selvon 1984, 4). Moses' allusion to *Robinson Crusoe* serves a multiple function: Moses is mindful of showing on all occasions how well-versed in English literature he is, and the Master-Servant relationship he has established with Bob sets off predictable associations; secondly, the irony of the situation is not lost on Moses, whose personal experiences and anecdotes continually expose and reverse the widespread stereotypes and assumptions regarding black immigrants.

> As we became good friends, or rather Master and Servant, I try to convert him from the evils of alcohol, but it was no use. [...] I decided to teach him the Bible when I could make time (Selvon 1984, 5).

Sure enough, the ground where Moses wages his battle is that of the English language, which becomes the true protagonist of Selvon's work. It is here, above all, that the inverted roles of Robinson and Friday appear in all their dramatic force: upon discovering that his man Bob is illiterate, Moses turns his thoughts with consternation "to this poor white man who could not read nor write" (Selvon 1984, 129). Furthermore, throughout the narrative, the spontaneously used phrases and idioms of standard English are shown to operate on ideological and ethnocentric premises. Thus, Moses admonishes his loyal servant and friend: "[Y]ou don't have to bask in your *darkness*" (Selvon 1984, 129; my italics), or "if you are not capable I will send you back to *the Black Country*" (Selvon 1984, 32), referring to Leicestershire; by the same token, he can contemplate how "a black man [...] *though he is as white as the driven snow* – if you will pardon the expression – that it got something, somewhere, sometime, what we do wrong" (Selvon 1984, 30).

It will have become clear by now that Moses' speech is far from the Queen's English he claims for his memoirs. He narrates the events in a peculiar version of Trinidadian dialect, heavily permeated with archaisms and stylistic turns typical of eighteenth century prose he seems to have utterly assimilated, with the addition of inevitable malapropisms and errors.

> I plod dejectedly up the basement steps, weighed down with the double-barrel barrage she had fired at me. My burden was not only her spitefulness and calcumny [*sic*] which Time would heal – I have been sorely pressed by vicissitudes ere this and am an old hand at turning the other cheek – but there was the crushing blow of Bob's treachery (Selvon 1984, 105).

In the episode Moses is referring to, Brenda, his tenant, occasional lover and a zealous BP activist, has given him a heavy blow by characterising the style of his memoirs as a pathetic failure: "you should stick to oral communication and leave the written word to them what knows their business" (Selvon 1984, 105). Brenda has couched her critique in an almost nonsensical pseudo-academic style, but Moses is nevertheless dumbfounded by his failure to shine at the language whose mastery is the cornerstone of his self-respect and pride as a British citizen. Rather than a Monarch of all he surveys[3] and a respectable "scribe", Moses seems exposed as a *mimic man*, a reformed imperial subject characterised by Bhabha as "the effect of a flawed colonial mimesis, in which to be Anglicized is *emphatically* not to be English" (2004, 125). He is revealed to be not so much a Crusoe, as a deluded Friday, whose English is fluent though perpetually broken (as in Defoe). His real standing is finally confirmed when his "tragic flaw" – an unchecked sexual appetite – causes him to fall-out with Bob. The roles are again reversed, and Moses descends physically and socially to the basement, submitting to the will of his old servant/friend, whom he is now only allowed to call "Robert": this English Friday rechristens himself and resumes the position habitually associated with the white man (as Moses fears some will misconstrue it), while the anti-hero is left to ponder the implications and the possible ways out of his impasse.

Although Moses' pretentions are clearly satirized by the author, and his fabled memoirs remain incomplete, his peculiar voice still orchestrates the extraordinary polyphony of the novel, posing a challenge to the vision of a pure, standard, unitary language, just as the preconceptions and ignorance of the wider society are represented through his own prejudices and moral lapses.

Walcott's play *Pantomime* (Walcott 1980), first performed in Port of Spain in 1978, represents more properly a hypotext of Defoe's novel, which figures in the play as a rehearsal of a Christmas pantomime. Harry Trewe, the English owner of a small resort in Tobago, insists on staging the pantomime to entertain his prospective guests. He argues his employee, ex calypsonian Jackson Phillip, into accepting the role of Friday, after which an even better idea springs to his mind: reversing the roles and having Jackson play Crusoe.

> We could work up a good satire, you know, on the master-servant – no offense – relationship. Labor-management, white-black, and so on (Walcott 1980, 109).

The initially reluctant Jackson warms to the role as he gradually identifies some subversive potential in Trewe's idea; conversely, Harry shows little intention of exploiting the possibilities implicit in the improvisation, and insists on keeping it light. He is worried that pursuing the implications of the reversal to their logical end, they might, in his words, "commit Art", and that it might

---

[3] The indirect quotation of Cowper's "Verses Supposed to Be Written by Alexandar Selkirk" (1782) is an ingenious allusion by the author to one of *Robinson*'s best known hypertexts, also cited by Walcott in his *The Figure of Crusoe*.

get offensive; he then changes his mind and orders Jackson to forget about the whole thing, but Jackson protests:

> I think that you cannot believe: one: that I can act, and two: that any black man should play Robinson Crusoe. [...] This is the story... this is history. This moment that we are now acting here is the history of imperialism; it's nothing less than that (Walcott 1980, 125).

The problem seems to be – apart from the fact that Trewe cannot really accept a complete reversal ("white would become black, you know", 127) – a different conception of Robinson's experience, and of acting for that matter. Trewe's Robinson suffers from a kind of *horror vacui*, he decries the loss of his family and despairs of his utter loneliness, though in an earthly paradise; Jackson, on the other hand, insists that "If he is not practical, he is not Robinson Crusoe" (Walcott 1980, 146). So Jackson proposes that the first thing Robinson should do, when cast ashore, is kill a goat. Jackson's conception of Crusoe as "the First True Creole" is similar to Walcott's own, as they both exalt his protestant practicality and his survival skills, but Trewe's reading is not wholly dissimilar from Crusoe as represented in Walcott's poems, the hermit who

> [...] built
> His Eden:
> Goats, corn crop, fort, parasol, garden,
> Bible for Sabbath, all the joys
> But one
> Which sent him howling for a human voice.
> (Walcott 1986, 69)

There is a point at the end of the first act when the two men temporarily resume the roles they are given in "real life", and Jackson assumes not only the demeanour of a servant, but a British accent as well! However, as he himself has previously remarked, it is too late to go back to the way things were before. The interaction between the two is fairly strained, as Harry attempts to explain his urge to stage the pantomime in the first place. Jackson grasps Trewe's position as a desperately lonely castaway and proposes to make of him a brand new man, but before the cathartic resolution, the two are made to stage conflictually their deepest fears and prejudices. One should keep in mind that Walcott characterised the play as a confessional psychodrama, "an entirely human drama between two people and though there are infinite resonances that spring from their conflict, these did not interest me directly" (Gunness 1997, 55).

During the give-and-take between the two arguing whether and how the pantomime should be represented, Jackson kills Trewe's parrot because it kept repeating "Heinegger" whenever Jackson was near him. Caricaturing the obedient savage, and slipping into deep Creole, Jackson comments: "Me na strangle him, bwana. He choke from prejudice" (Walcott 1980, 155). The parrot, of course, is the supreme symbol both of New World exoticism, and more importantly, of colonial mimicry. It is this latter shortcoming that Harry, reacting to the death of the bird, ascribes to West Indians: "You people create nothing. You imitate everything. It's all been done before, you see, Jackson. The parrot. Thinks that's something? Its from *The Seagull*" (Walcott 1980, 156). The charge directed against Jackson is actually an indirect quotation of the critics and writers such as V.S. Naipaul, to whom Walcott replies in his essay "The Caribbean: Culture or Mimicry": "What is called mimicry is the painful, new, laborious uttering that comes out of belief, not out of doubt" (Walcott 1997a, 57). This belief in the possibility of renaming and repossessing the New World is the faith that supposedly characterises Jackson's Crusoe, and Walcott's New World poet. It is the process whereby Friday's descendants "learn to shape from them [as Walcott says of Crusoe's journals], / where nothing was / the language of a race" (Walcott 1986, 94).

Jackson, who contrary to Selvon's Moses seems to have acquired this awareness, is therefore not susceptible to Harry's accusation. He dons different roles and accents, and switches between these as between so many masks, until he forces Harry to drop his English composure and confront the memory of his estranged wife. He then urges Harry to come back to the play, when the latter stutters, playing again Crusoe:

> The self-same moment I could pray;
> And [...] tata tee-tum-tum
> The Albatross fell off, and sank
> Like lead into the sea. (Walcott 1980, 164)

It is telling that it is the ex colonial subject, Jackson, who reminds Harry that this is not Crusoe, but Coleridge's "The Rime of the Ancient Marina" [sic]. It is even more significant that by obstinately pronouncing it as "Marina", he is shown to possess the knowledge of the so-called canon, and to be able to inflect it according to his own tone of voice. Even when he concedes that Harry may be right in correcting him – "Is your language, pardner" (Walcott 1980, 165) – it is done in a form that contradicts the content. It is this self-aware code-switching and irony that distinguish him from Moses. The latter remains a mimic man, whose life-style and speech show his "yearning to be adopted" (Walcott 1998, 27); Jackson does not suffer a similar "crisis of consciousness" (Baugh 1988, 242): he skilfully peels off his masks, and moves between different dialects and registers, though ultimately his true calling seems to be that of the calypsonian, and his language Trinidadian Creole. This, of course, does not mean that West Indians should stick to one form of culture or one dialect only: both Walcott's and Selvon's works, though in their different ways, are the proof of this. The most effective response to the imperial representation of the Other is revealed to be not the outright condemnation of figures like Crusoe, but rather making them a symbol of the "problems organic to West Indian life" (Walcott 1997b, 35), to quote yet again Derek Walcott.

References

Baugh E. 1988. "Friday in Crusoe's City: The Question of Language in Two West Indian Novels of Exile". In Nasta S. (ed.) *Critical Perspectives on Sam Selvon*. Boulder and London: Lynne Rienner Publishers, 240-249.

Bhabha H. 2004. "Of Mimicry and Man". In *The Location of Culture*. London and New York: Routledge, 121-131.

Cowper W. 1782. "Verses Supposed to Be Written by Alexandar Selkirk, During His Solitary Abode in the Island of Juan Fernandez". In Milford H.S. (ed.) (1905) *The Complete Poetical Works of William Cowper*. London: H. Frowde, 311-312, available at http://www.luminarium.org/eightlit/cowper/selkirk.htm (last accessed August 2011)

Defoe D. 1719. *The Life and Adventures of Robinson Crusoe*. (1910). Oxford and London: H. Frowde.

Genette G. 1997. *Palinsesti: letteratura al secondo grado*. Torino: Einaudi.

Gunness C. 1997. "White Man, Black Man". In Hamner R.D. (ed.) *Critical Perspectives on Derek Walcott*. Boulder and London: Lynne Rienner Publishers, 290-291.

Huggan G. 2006. "Cannibal Rights: Intertextuality and Postcolonial Discourse in the Caribbean Region". In Maver I. (ed.) *Critics and Writers Speak: Revisioning Post-colonial Studies*. Lanham (Md): Lexington Books, 56-66.

Hulme P. 1986. *Colonial Encounters: Europe and the Native Caribbean 1492-1797*. London and New York: Methuen.

Joyce J. 1979. "Daniele Defoe". In Corsini G., and Melchiori G. (eds.) *Scritti italiani*. Milano: Mondadori, 142-160.

Selvon S. 1985 . *The Lonely Londoners* [1956]. New York: Longman.

Selvon S. 1984. *Moses Ascending* [1975]. London: Heinemann Educational Books.

Tiffin H. 1987. "Post-colonial Literatures and Counter-discourse". In *Kunapipi*, vol. IX, n. 3, 17-34.

Walcott D. 1980. *Remembrance and Pantomime: Two Plays,*. New York: Farrar, Straus and Giroux.

Walcott D. 1986. *Collected Poems*, New York: Farrar, Straus and Giroux.

Walcott D. 1997a. "The Caribbean: Culture or Mimicry?". In Hamner R.D. (ed.) *Critical Perspectives on Derek Walcott*. Boulder and London: Lynne Rienner Publishers, 51-57.

Walcott D. 1997b. "The Figure of Crusoe". In Hamner R.D. (ed.) *Critical Perspectives on Derek Walcott*. Boulder and London: Lynne Rienner Publishers, 33-40.

Walcott D. 1998. "What the Twilight Says". In *What the Twilight Says. Essays*. London: Faber and Faber, 3-35.

VALENTINA CASTAGNA

Università di Palermo

Reading *The Book of Margery Kempe* in the 21st Century: Gender, Authorship and Performance

1. Introduction

The history of *The Book of Margery Kempe*, written at the beginning of the 15th century by a burgess of Bishop's Lynn (Norfolk), is quite revealing of the way Medieval Studies have entered the 21st century. Its links with the present have become stronger thanks to the critical approach, first of Women's Studies and then of Gender Studies (see Partner 1993; and also Bennett 1993[1]), to the issues of authorship, sexuality and the body, and ultimately of *performance* (Hopenwasser 1999; Bradford 2001; McAvoy 2005).

As Lynn Staley Johnson maintained at the end of the last century, the revision of the literary canon has "allowed texts like *The Book of Margery Kempe* into the classroom, the conference hall and the journal" (1994, xi). Staley Johnson added that although the appreciation of Kempe's work had drastically increased in the '80s and '90s, *The Book of Margery Kempe* "has more still to teach us" (*ibidem*). And, actually, since then criticism has investigated themes which had been formerly overlooked: many scholars have quite recently worked on the representation of sexuality, on the relationship between spirituality and fasting (Del Lungo Camiciotti 2008), and on her travel accounts as a pilgrim (Goodman 2002; Castagna 2007).

In the 15th and 16th centuries, the book had quite good circulation especially in monasteries (where it must have been read by both friars and laywomen; see Parsons 2001). However, after the Anglican schism, the text was lost for five centuries. The manuscript was surprisingly rediscovered, in the 1930s, by William Butler-Bowdon in 1934 and subsequently published by Meech and Allen.

---

[1] We are going to see how also some representatives of Queer Studies have contributed giving new life to Margery Kempe's text. It is the case of Carolyn Dinshaw in the critical field and of Robert Glück in the creative field.

By then, the name of Margery Kempe was well-known through the excerpts of her book that Wynkyn de Word and, later, Henry Pepwell had copied out at the beginning of the 16th century. These were nonetheless the most canonical passages in the book and they only outlined one aspect of Margery's personality: her devoutness. Such readings were mostly misleading, for instance, Pepwell added to his text that the extracts were from the life of a devout anchoress, which Margery was not. The complexity and modernity of *The Book of Margery Kempe* was totally overlooked. It is interesting to see how George Ballard described *The Book* and its authoress in the 18th century. In his volume *Memoirs of Several Ladies of Great Britain: Who Have Been Celebrated for Their Writings or Skill in the Learned Languages, Arts, and Sciences* (1752), he included an entry on Margery Kempe ("Memoirs of Margery Kempe"). Through his surprised remarks about the disappearance of the original text (he was able to trace two copies of de Worde's version) and about the little he knew of her life, the figure of Margery, nonetheless, definitely emerges as one of an "author" (Ballard 1752, 8).

It is then just at the end of the 20th century – especially since the 1990s – thanks to scholars working within the field of Gender Studies, that the book has raised complex and challenging issues and has started to be read as, to put it in Sidonie Smith's terms, "a fascinating work, full of life and energy and travail as it captures the quality of medieval Christian life, the mobile atmosphere of pilgrimages, the pressures of orthodoxy, the smell of the burning stake against which the heretic was pressed in her heresy" (Smith 1987, 60).

The first readings of the book focused on the figure of Margery either as a mystic or as a hysteric, if not as both (Thurston 1936; Cholmeley 1947; Watkin 1953; Knowles 1961; Wood Tuma 1977). Her mystical experience was at the centre of criticism and was seen as non-canonical. As Lynn Staley Johnson, one of her major contemporary critics, has stated, those distinguished scholars were mostly interested in the history of mysticism and in devotional prose (1994, xi). The traditional comparison with the contemporary anchoress Julian of Norwich, seen as canonical mystic-theologian, was based on stereotypes of gender. While Julian was the emblem of placidity, Margery was considered a hysteric, rather a peculiar mystic. However, her eccentric text of mystical writing, because of its constant reference to Margery's experience as a pilgrim, as an "outlaw preacher", as a woman and a wife (especially, to her relationship with her husband, her pilgrimages, and money questions), has now found its place within the canon of English literature as an *ante-litteram* autobiography. In fact, *The Book of Margery Kempe* is now mostly recognized as the first autobiography in English (see Mueller 1984; Smith 1987; Glenn 1992; see also the Penguin *Dictionary of Literary Terms & Literary Theory*, Cuddon 1999).

2. Authorship and literary genres

The Book, then, has been defined as an autobiography, as a spiritual autobiography of a laywoman (Del Lungo Camiciotti 2002), a devotional treatise (the "Proem" itself defines the book as such), an oral life-story (Cross 1992), and also the first novel in English (Staley Johnson 1994). The problem of placing it in a particular literary genre arises, on the one hand, from the textual presence of the scribes and, on the other, from the content of Margery's narrative. Her account abounds with details from daily life and material preoccupations, which made the first modern readers think that Margery's mysticism was not genuine, and perhaps too materialistic, particularly when compared to Julian of Norwich, whose works are more orthodox.

The complexity of this medieval text (and of its female authorial voice) is acknowledged and it throws up issues that are still argued over in contemporary literature, such as that of women's identity, female authorship, and the influence of patriarchal society on the relaying of women's image. David Aers maintained that *The Book of Margery Kempe* is "a precious work for anyone interested in the history of gender, subjectivities, and English culture" (Aers 1988, 73).

Scholars such as Smith, Staley Johnson and Mueller have fairly recently come to show that Margery establishes her literary authority through the use of clear narrative strategies (Castagna 2006). Although the intervention of the scribes to whom she dictates her experience, is, to a certain degree, undeniable,[2] it emerges from the events, especially from Margery's comments on gender roles and her arguments with religious and political authorities, that Margery is aware of the idea of authority, which, above all, she sees in the external Authority of God (i.e. that which legitimates her text, travels, and public-speaking).

The positions of such scholars and their focus on the concept of authorship have at their basis the idea that Margery is not that illiterate creature she says she is, rather an author who follows the narrative conventions of literary genres like the Saints' lives and of those used by other women mystics who recorded their experience before her. Furthermore, Margery is aware of the social conventions that would silence her, but makes use of them – mining the system of oppression from within – by legitimizing herself through her mystical relationship with Christ.

In the analysis of medieval texts, then, the gendered approach has acquired ever greater importance, also in an attempt to rediscover a genealogy of women writers (Smith 1987; Mueller 1984). Smith, in particular, considers Margery as a forerunner of women's autobiographical writing.

---

[2] Lynn Staley Johnson (1991), though, maintains that the figure of the scribe might be a trope, one of Margery's strategies sustaining the principle of authority of her book. She goes as far as to define Margery's book as a "novel".

Thus, in the 1990s it has become clear that the main instrument for interpreting Kempe's narrative was the laying bare of those social mechanisms that determined the subaltern role of women within the family and society itself. This reading has empowered Kempe as an authoress and at the same time has highlighted Kempe's strategies of self-empowerment not only in the private but also in the public domain.

The most recent readings show that Margery actually understood the role of the writings by mystics among both religious and lay people, and made good use of it in legitimizing her act of writing and the inherent attempt to claim her own subjectivity through the text.

3. Sexuality, gender and performance

As mentioned above, a second question which has aroused the interest of Margery Kempe's critics is the interplay of spirituality and sexuality in the text, the way in which Margery tells of her private "dalliance" with Christ. Her language shows the main characteristics of "mystic speech" and she demonstrates her knowledge of mystic texts by mentioning them, and also in the way she describes her divine communication with God, it being like a fire burning her from the inside. The term "dalliance" itself implies a form of 'sexual' intimacy in the conversation.

This is an issue that has triggered different responses at both a critical and a creative level, in terms of rewriting. Eva Figes's dramatization of the Book in *The True Tale of Margery Kempe*, for instance, simply modifies the text by including in its dialogues "sounds of love-making" (1985). By doing so, the writer – who, in the title of her radio play, stresses at the same time the strong relationship between orality and writing and the link to popular culture – emphasizes Margery's preoccupation with desire and pleasure: a hindrance to her holiness, in opposition with her enactment of chastity through the use of the white robe and the ring.

Another interesting work of fiction inspired to *The Book of Margery Kempe* is the provocative 1994 novel by Robert Glück entitled *Margery Kempe*, which supports the idea of Margery's *queerness* (also analysed in Carolyn Dinshaw's 1999 study *Getting Medieval*). Glück specifically draws on Margery's sexual drives and creates a double narrative rich in physical details where he intertwines her love for the young Christ, narrated at the beginning of the *Book*, to his love for a young man.

All these responses together make the debate on *The Book of Margery Kempe* more lively and they highlight the physicality of Margery's language, not only when in mystical conversation with Christ, but also when confronting her adversaries.

In her interesting article "Virgin, Mother, Whore: The Sexual Spirituality of Margery Kempe", published just a few years ago, Liz McAvoy (2005) argues that Judith Butler's critique of the notion of fixed gender identities and her theory of performative gender are suitable to analyse the way Margery Kempe portrays herself. In fact, Butler suggests that gender is constituted by a series of performed acts, "gestures, enactments, generally construed" which are "performative in the sense that the essence or identity that they otherwise purport to express are fabrications manufactured and sustained through corporeal signs and other discursive means" (Butler 1990, 136). Drawing on Butler's positions, McAvoy argues that Margery, like other medieval women, was "able to negotiate with [her] sexualized bodies the restrictive hegemony of gendered identity" (2005, 122). She demonstrates how through the "re-appropriation" of the roles of the virgin, or of the mother, Margery could gain a social position from which to speak and express herself thus recovering "agency in her re/construction of self with which much of her text is occupied" (*ibidem*).

McAvoy, in fact, maintains that if "Margery's gendered body as wife or mother has no specific ontology beyond the acts which help to constitute its 'reality', then contained within these acts is always the potential for re-contextualisation and therefore subversion of their traditional hegemony" (*ibidem*, 124). In other words, Kempe re-appropriates these social roles playing with gender stereotypes based on female sexuality and enacts them in order to be legitimized as an independent woman, speaking for herself, by the system which denies women's agency. It is well known that while, on the one hand, medieval women's bodies were important because they granted the reproductive capacity, on the other, they were feared and demonized because they were considered as a threat of corruption. As a result of this dichotomy, Margery's body is seen by McAvoy as "the site of conflict between opposed ideologies and conflicting desires" (*ibidem*, 126).

4. Conclusions

To conclude, scholars who work within the fields of Gender Studies and Medieval Studies have recovered *The Book of Margery Kempe*, producing a total change of perspective. In fact, there has been a shift from the analysis of Margery, the persona of the narration, to that of Kempe the author of the text. Margery Kempe has entered the 21st century as the deft authoress of her *Book*, who was able to use all the narrative strategies available at that time and common to subgenres like the Saints' lives and devotional treatises. Then, the use of the concept of performance in the analysis of *The Book* has given back Kempe that agency she had been denied by readings based on gender stereotypes.

References

Aers D. 1988. *Community, Gender and Individual Identity. English Writing 1360-1430*. London: Routledge.

Ballard G. 1752. "Memoirs of Margery Kempe". In *Memoirs of Several Ladies of Great Britain: Who Have Been Celebrated for Their Writings or Skill in the Learned Languages Arts and Sciences*. Oxford: printed by W. Jackson for the author, 8.

Bennett J. 1993. "Medievalism and Feminism". In *Speculum* 68, 2, 309-331.

Bradford C. 2001. "Mother, Maiden, Child: Gender as Performance in *The Book of Margery Kempe*". In Devlin-Glass F., McCredden L. (eds.) *Feminist Poetics of the Sacred: Creative Suspicions*. Oxford: Oxford University Press, 165-181.

Butler J. 1990. *Gender Trouble*. London: Routledge.

Castagna V. 2006. "Margery Kempe and Her Becoming Authoress". In *Textus* 19, 2, 323-338.

Castagna V. 2007. "Margery Kempe: una mistica del Quattrocento in pellegrinaggio". In *Fogli di Anglistica* 1, 1-2 n.s., 83-91.

Cholmeley K. 1947. *Margery Kempe. Genius and Mystic*. London: Green & Co.

Cross R.C. 1992. "Oral Life, Written Text: The Genesis of *The Book of Margery Kempe*". In *The Yearbook of English Studies* 22, 226-237.

Cuddon J.A. 1999. *The Dictionary of Literary Terms & Literary Theory*. London: Penguin.

Del Lungo Camiciotti G. (ed.) 2002. *Il libro di Margery Kempe. Autobiografia spirituale di una laica del Quattrocento*. Milano: Àncora.

Del Lungo Camiciotti G. 2008. "Il significato del digiuno nell'esperienza delle mistiche inglesi tardo medievali". In *LC. Rivista Online del Dipartimento di Letterature e Culture Europee* II, 1, Università degli Studi di Palermo, available at http://www.dilce.unipa.it/rivista/documenti/n_01_2008/09_g_dellungo.pdf (last accessed August 2011), 63-75.

Figes E. 1985. *The True Tale of Margery Kempe*. London: BBC Radio 2.

Glenn C. 1992. "Author, Audience, and Autobiography: Rhetorical Technique in *The Book of Margery Kempe*". In *College English* 54, 5, 540-553.

Glück R. 1994. *Margery Kempe*. London: Serpent's Tail.

Goodman A. 2002. *Margery Kempe and Her World*. London & New York: Longman.

Hopenwasser N. 1999. "A Performance Artist and Her Performance Text: Margery Kempe on Tour". In Suydam M. A., Ziegler J. E. (eds.) *Performance and Transformation: New Approaches to Late Medieval Spirituality*. New York: St. Martin's Press, 97-131.

Knowles D. 1961. The English Mystical Tradition. London: Burns and Oates.

McAvoy L. 2005. "Virgin, Mother, Whore: The Sexual Spirituality of Margery Kempe". In Chewning S.M. (ed.) *Intersections of Sexuality and the Divine in Medieval Culture: The Word Made Flesh*. Aldershot: Ashgate, 121-138.

Mueller J.M. 1984. "Autobiography of a New 'Creatur': Female Spirituality, Selfhood, and Authorship in *The Book of Margery Kempe*". In Stanton D. (ed.) *The Female Autograph*. Chicago: The University of Chicago Press, 57-68.

Parsons K. 2001. "The Red Ink Annotator of *The Book of Margery Kempe* and his Lay Audience". In Kerby-Fulton K., Hilmo M. (eds.) *The Medieval Professional Reader at Work: Evidence from Manuscripts of Chaucer, Langland, Kempe and Gower*. Victoria: ELS University of Victoria, 143-158.

Partner N.F. 1993. "Studying Medieval Women. Sex, Gender, Feminism". In *Speculum* 68, 2, 305-308.

Smith S. 1987. "The Book of Margery Kempe: This Creature's Unsealed Life". In *A Poetics of Women's Autobiography*. Bloomington: Indiana University Press, 64-82.

Staley Johnson L. 1991. "The Trope of the Scribe and the Question of Literary Authority in the Works of Julian of Norwich and Margery Kempe". In *Speculum* LXVI, 820-838.

Staley Johnson L. 1994. *Margery Kempe's Dissenting Fictions*. University Park, Pennsylvania: The Pennsylvania State University Press.

Thurston H. 1936. "Margery the Astonishing". In *The Month* 168, 446-456.

Watkin E. I. 1953. "In Defence of Margery Kempe". In *Poets and Mystics*. London: Sheed and Ward 104-134.

Windeatt B. (ed.) 1985. *The Book of Margery Kempe*. Harmondsworth: Penguin.

Wood Tuma G. 1977. *The Fourteenth Century English Mystics: A Comparative Analysis*. Salzburg: Universitat Salzburg.

FRANCA DELLAROSA

Università di Bari Aldo Moro

"Connecting Across Centuries": Memory, Displacement, and Exile in Caryl Phillips' Stage Plays[1]

The quote that appears in the title of this paper, "Connecting Across Centuries", by effectively highlighting a crucial constituent in Caryl Phillips' poetics, points to an issue whose urgency is manifest in the writing experience of this Caribbean-born from African ancestry, British-raised, and presently US-based novelist, playwright, and nonfiction writer. This urgency is also inscribed in the wider process involving a community, and nation, called to come to terms with, or re-assess, their own past, and has to do with the individual, as well as collective, need to elaborate on historical trauma in order to tentatively construct a viable future, given its consequence on the structuring of current plural notions of identity. The full quote, taken from a 1994 interview, assumes one of Phillips' earliest texts – the play *The Shelter*, first performed at the Lyric Studio, Hammersmith, London, on 1st September, 1983 – as somewhat casting the mould for many explorations to come, that would include both fiction and nonfiction writing. In Phillips' words,

> If I were to look at one piece of work of mine which has the beginning of this structural paranoia and schizophrenia, that [i.e. *The Shelter*] would be it. You could say that I've been writing or exploring the way of writing and connecting across centuries for ten years (Schatteman 2009, 20).

My aim in this paper is to probe into the rendering of *structural paranoia and schizophrenia* as symmetric thematic and formal concerns, shaping in particular Phillips's writing for the stage. I shall leave aside the copious and quite as remarkable crop of his fiction, in order to specifically interrogate

---

[1] This paper is the earliest product of a research focus that has developed out of my ongoing work on late eighteenth- and early nineteenth-century literature and theatrical culture engaging with the issues of slavery and abolition, whose most recent outcome is the volume *Slavery on Stage: Representations of Slavery in British Theatre, 1760s-1830s* (Bari: Edizioni dal Sud, 2009). The legacy of the trauma of slavery in contemporary culture and creative writing constitutes the agenda of this novel research line.

his theatre, as Phillips' recent return to the stage invites the critic to do. His adaptation from Simon Schama's historical narrative *Rough Crossings* (2007) arguably, as a reviewer suggested, brought "Phillips' own identity full circle, returning him both to the country and the art-form from which he's been exiled." (Logan 2007) The play was first produced in September 2007 by Headlong Theatre, Birmingham Repertory Theatre, Liverpool Everyman and Playhouse, Lyric Hammersmith and West-Yorkshire Playhouse, in the context of the commemoration of the bicentennial anniversary of the abolition of the transatlantic slave trade, and provides a new dramatic exploration of the black diaspora, that consistently contributes to Phillips' developing historiography, "wherein", as has been argued, "the historical is seen as both synthesised and interacting with the contemporary" (Thomas 2006, 3).

The beginnings, to start with. Phillips's debut as playwright with *Strange Fruit*, first performed at the Crucible Studio in Sheffield in October 1980, while straightforwardly traditional in terms of form, had that novelty of subject and setting that Phillips has recognised as being at the basis of his choice to *write* stage plays, rather than continuing his early career as director. In those years, the playwright recalls, "there wasn't a Black British dramatic tradition [...] I wanted to do plays about black people, but I was stuck [...] [in part, by] the availability of the texts" (Bell 1991, 582).[2] The close, claustrophobic focus of the play is on a lower-class family of West-Indian immigrants, where the petty-bourgeois setting of the terraced house in "one of England's inner city areas" (Phillips 1980, 7) speaks volumes about the attempt at social homologation of first-generation immigrants:

> The main items of furniture are as follows: against the back wall there is a heavy sideboard on top of which sits a brightly crocheted coverlet, a large plastic punchbowl and ladle, a yellow glass vase containing plastic flowers, and a box of paper tissues. D.R. is a cabinet full of crockery that has never been, and never will be used. In the centre of the display is a plate commemorating the Queen's Silver Jubilee (Phillips 1980, 7).

The "dilemma of intergenerational communication" which, admittedly, is the play's main concern (Phillips 2007), is encapsulated, we may say, within the wider *dilemma of intercultural communication*, as brought about by the condition of displacement that the experience of immigration invariably entails, as is powerfully epitomised in the exchange exposing a woman immigrant's utter inability to make sense of her daughter's school report: the esoteric acronyms, resisting interpretation, that make British educational system an opaque,

---

[2] For critical discussion of Phillips's early playwriting, see Stone (1994, 173-179); Thomas (2006, 11-21).

impenetrable object to the eyes of the protagonist's friend, are the figure of what, in the end, turns out to be her own failed attempt at integration.

> [...] *Re-enter Vernice with the report.*
> Mother: Did you get it?
> Vernice: Me have it. The girl just throw it at me and storm out the house.
> Mother: Well open it then. Go ahead.
> Vernice: You open it. [Mother *reluctantly takes it, opens it, and begins to read.*] Well?
> Mother: She's not doing too well.
> Vernice: What?
> Mother: Well. You do know that they've moved her out of the GCE into the CSE stream, which means that her chances of ending up with an HND or even a BSc rather than just an OND are greatly diminished.
> Vernice: Fockin' CSE, GCE, CND, this that and the other is just one seta flickin' initial to me. What the hell the matter with she?
> (Phillips 1980, 12-13)

Conversely, Mother states, "My children are qualified, they have 'O' levels and 'A' levels and have both been to College". These words entail the worn-out single immigrant mother's vindication of her children's entitlement to social integration: "you're telling me I should be happy that they are managing to keep out of trouble [with the police]" (Phillips 1980,10) reads the cue in full. Such a construction is smashed against the irredeemable conflict with her two rebellious sons, whose quest for identity takes opposite political directions, with the race tensions and intolerance of 1970s Britain in the background and the rejection of the CRE, "bloody-Uncle-Tom" model of integration (Phillips 1980, 23)[3], in favour of a form of immature pan-African radicalism in the one son and the painful and flawed retrieval of his Caribbean legacy in the other. The title *Strange Fruit*, whose echo of Billie Holiday's upsetting evocation of racial violence is a breathing shadow in the background, is itself meant to be "evocative of the puzzling situation that many parents unwittingly find themselves in with their children", as Phillips himself has stated in an article he contributed to *The Guardian*, devoted to tracing the tragic genealogy of the American song (Phillips 2007). The play sets the cross-generational conflict in a context where the existential level painfully interacts with the historical and the social predicament of second-generation immigrant youths:

> Alvin: [...] I can't live here, I can't live there. What am I supposed to do? What we supposed to do? Live on a raft in the middle of the Atlantic at a

---

[3] The Commission for Racial Equality (CRE) was a statutory body, established under the Race Relation Act 1976. It had the power to conduct a formal investigation and to issue a non-discrimination notice in appropriate cases. In October 2007, along with the Equal Opportunities Commission and the Disability Rights Commission, it merged into the Equality and Human Rights Commission. See http://www.equalityhumanrights.com (last accessed August 2011).

point equidistant between Africa, the Caribbean and Britain? Is that what you want us to do? Leave us till we sink? Till there's no trace of us? Lost between two waves, yet another black generation is dispossessed (Phillips 1980, 99).

The youthful bitterness surfacing in these words, which permeates the articulation of displacement as an existential as well as historical condition, materialises in the trope of Alvin's self-perception as the recipient of an *unstable* Atlantic multiple identity – which may well amount to no identity, a state of irretrievable loss. Significantly, that same metaphor, in Phillips' mature writing, is reversed into the positive affirmation of one's belonging to the "Atlantic home":

> After thirteen years of compulsive itinerancy, I know my Atlantic 'home' to be triangular in shape with Britain at one apex, the west coast of Africa at another, and the new world of North America (including the Caribbean) forming the third point of the triangle. If one draws a line between these three points, I regard the area of Atlantic Ocean that is described to be a much travelled pond. Across the centuries, countless millions have traversed this water, and unlike myself, these people have not always had the luxury of choice (Phillips 2001a, 304-305).

The interaction of the historical and the existential emerges powerfully in Phillips's third play, the previously mentioned *The Shelter*, to the extent that it constitutes a structural principle, literally *connecting across centuries*. A two-century blank space does indeed gape between Act I and Act II, where Act I is set "sometime toward the end of the eighteenth century", and the second act "in the bar of a pub in Ladbroke Grove, London, sometime in the 1950s" (Phillips 1984, 13, 33). No space indication is preliminarily given in Act I, while detailed directions locate the setting on an island, where the two only characters, a man and a woman, who are identified by their personal pronouns as *her* and *him*, are evidently shipwrecked.

As the author's introduction makes clear, the idea of the play was inspired by a postcard he happened to see in France, which appears in the cover of the print edition of the play, and impressively points to the relationship between the black man and the white woman, which, as Phillips observes, from the master narrative of Othello and Desdemona onwards, "has always provoked the greatest conflict, the most fear, the most loathing" (Phillips 1984, 10). The picture, as described by authorial comment, offers interesting clues for interpretation:

> A white woman's face, probably that of a woman of thirty or thirty-five, who had probably just cried, or who would cry; and curled around her forehead, with just enough pressure to cause a line of folds in the skin above her eyes,

were two black hands; obviously power and strength slept somewhere within them but at this moment they were infinitely gentle, describing with eight fingers that moment where a grip of iron weakens to caress of love (Phillips 1984, 10).

While the gesture seems to convey a balmy, soothing action, as implied in Phillips' words, it may well be that pain, as a condition intrinsic to interracial relationships, be entailed as well – as if the folds created by the black man's hands on the woman's forehead were wounds provoked by a crown of thorns, in a sort of Christ-like posture:[4] which makes sense, in the light of the trans-historical plight that materialises in the play as affecting the lives of the protagonists of both Act I and Act II, that are only seemingly disconnected. In fact, the device of juxtaposing isolated fragments of personal histories distant in time and place results in the highlighting of the very real causal connections between the imagined social interaction experienced by the isolated male and female individuals at the time of transatlantic slavery, and the still entrenched racism of mid-twentieth century British society towards those British subjects – or, as the male character Louis quite inertly remarks, British *objects* (Phillips 1984, 43) – whose *complexion*, to use a word resonating with echoes of the eighteenth-century vocabulary of race, is darker than white.

This interconnectedness of the historical, once again, with the individual, and the individual with the collective, also surfaces within Act I, as conjured up in the black man's indictment of Western ruthless spoliation of Africa, that cannot but entail the summoning of the individual for a responsibility which is collective and historical:

Him: I was born near 200 year ago in a small village in my native Africa.
[*Pause.*]
Her: Your statement lacks any proportion. It is that of a nigger.Him: A village so small that I cannot remember the name of it... and your father came and set fire to the hut of my family, raped my mother and killed my own aged father, but he did not kill me for I was young and strong. He beat me till I bled unconscious on the ground. He chained together my hands and my legs, then he fired an iron rod and branded my skin as easily as a hot knife finds its way through a waxen candle. The smell jolted my person to consciousness (Phillips 1984, 27-28).

The earliest slaving voyages of John Hawkins in the age of Elizabeth are evoked here as setting the scene of a collective, trans-historical tragedy, whose effects would change permanently the individual lives, the economies and the societies of three continents across the Atlantic, as determining the black diaspora.

---

[4] As was suggested to me by Annamaria Sportelli.

A span of twenty-odd years separates Phillips' early dramatic output, with three plays produced between 1980 and 1983,[5] from his mature experimentation, as carried out in the historical fresco of *Rough Crossings*, his recent stage adaptation from Simon Schama's (2007) historical narrative. The play, that opened on 14 September 2007 at the Birmingham Repertory Theatre, and then toured the various theatres in the UK which were involved in the co-production, provides an extremely complex dramatic exploration of a series of connected segments in the transatlantic history of the African slave trade, including the role enslaved Africans played in the American Revolution, the uncertain fortunes of the Abolition movement in late eighteenth-century Britain, and the creation of the Sierra Leone settlement. The drama is focused on the process of emigration from the inhospitable wilderness of Nova Scotia and resettlement in West Africa of a group of former slaves who had served in the British Army during the American War of Independence, and had been promised in return freedom and land. America, Africa and Europe constitute the diverse and intertwined spatial planes of a multi-focal, systemic representation of history, which are shown in a sequence of seemingly disconnected, juxtaposed tableaux. The choice of this rhapsodic structure is not without consequences at the level of the handling of the temporal dimension, which, at times, deliberately flouts historical sequence, to privilege a *re-writing* of history which capture the intelligibility of relations and events into *form*.[6]

The problematic negotiation of historical truth within creative work (whether film, or fiction, or drama) is one aspect in the play that especially invites analysis; its relevance is partly envisaged in Phillips' unsympathetic remarks on Steven Spielberg's film *Amistad*, which may also be read as providing metacomment on his own work: "A healthy history is one that is open to debate and interpretation, to re-evaluation and reinterpretation. A history that is grounded in 'authenticity' is dangerous. [...] An imaginative reconstruction, subject to factual errors, to decisions that had to be made to heighten the drama, to scene-shifting, to acts of invention. This is precisely what should happen in drama" (Phillips 2001b, 84).

This is, in fact, what does happen in *Rough Crossings*. The act of twisting historical contingency into dramatic recreation is a feature Phillips often resorts to; as a way of exemplification, I would cite the encounter between John Clarkson and Granville Sharp while "joyous Blacks appear and begin to celebrate and dance" (Schama 2007, 56) after the Somerset decision, as an

---

[5] Phillips' second play, *Where There is Darkness*, was first produced at the Lyric Theatre, Hammersmith, in February 1982.

[6] Phillips has often commented on the crucial value of his commitment to form. See *A New World Order* (2001b), and a number of interviews, in particular, his exchange with S. Clingman in Schattemann (2009, 107 ff).

especially blatant case, given that in 1772 Thomas Clarkson's younger brother, who was in charge as the agent of the Sierra Leone Company, was eight years old. The play's ambition is evidently to create a sort *stereoscopic*, but also at times knowingly distorting, encounter with past history, both as an act of ultimate *loyalty* to the right and duty of the creative writer to intervene on the imagined world, but also in the light of history's reverberations in the present. As John McLeod has suggested in his very recent critical reading of the play, in dramatizing the historical figures of the black leaders, the uncompromisingly radical Thomas Peters, and the integrationist minister David George, Phillips "involves himself with an exploration of African American leadership across centuries" as "they come to stand (in) for two predominant strands in African American dissidence", deliberately recalling the two great leaders of African American politics of the twentieth century, i.e. Malcolm X and Martin Luther King (McLeod 2009, 197).

Rough Crossings is a complex and problematic text. It engaged with the legacy of the trauma of slavery at a particular historical moment, i.e., in the context of the year-long, nation-wide commemoration of the Bicentennial Anniversary of the passing of the Abolition Bill in March 1807. Cultural historians as well as literary critics have just started assessing the import of this national exercise in re-memorialization of the past, which may turn out to be particularly problematic when experienced from the perspective of the victimizer. Projects such as *1807 Commemorated*, carried out by the Institute for the Public Understanding of the Past at the University of York and the Institute for Historical Research, along with museum partners,[7] have charted the cultural and institutional initiatives in the field. In such a context, a play like *Rough Crossings* has, indeed, something to say. In the author's words,

> People need to understand how this world that they are living in came to look like it does. And Britain, as the most multicultural country in Europe, has a responsibility to explain the faces on its national canvas. That's why *Rough Crossings* is so exciting, that's why the abolition conversation has been useful. They're good tools to open up that debate (qtd. in Logan 2007).

---

[7] See the website http://www.history.ac.uk/1807commemorated/ (last accessed August 2011), where the mission of the project is illustrated: "*1807 Commemorated* engages with the ways in which the bicentenary of the abolition of the slave trade is commemorated in Britain and the public memories which are shaped by it. This remembrance is highly significant as it structures and informs notions of personal, family, regional and national identity. [...] *1807 Commemorated* creates a framework which can be used to comprehend the public memory of the bicentenary, and the design and implementation of strategies for policy-makers and museum practitioners concerned with the representation of traumatic pasts." Aspects of the current debate are dealt with in Kowaleski Wallace (2006), and Oldfield (2007).

References

Bell C.R. 1991. "Worlds Within: An Interview with Caryl Phillips". In *Callaloo* 14, 3, 578-606.

Kowaleski Wallace E. 2006. *The British Slave Trade and Public Memory*. New York: Columbia University Press.

Logan B. 2007. "Crossing Over". In *The Times*, September 15th, Knowledge, p. 17.

MacLeod J. 2009. "British Freedoms: Caryl Phillips's Transatlanticism and the Staging of *Rough Crossings*". In *Atlantic Studies* 6, 2, 191-206.

Oldfield J.R. 2007.*'Chords of Freedom': Commemoration, Ritual and British Transatlantic Slavery*. Manchester-New York: Manchester University Press.

Phillips C. 1980. *Strange Fruit*. Oxford: Amber Lane Press.

Phillips C. 1984. *The Shelter*. Oxford: Amber Lane Press.

Phillips C. 2001a. *The Atlantic Sound*. New York: Vintage.

Phillips C. 2001b. *A New World Order: Essays*. New York: Vintage.

Phillips C. 2007. "Blood at the Root". In *The Guardian*, 18th August Saturday, available at http://www.guardian.co.uk/books/2007/aug/18/jazz. urban/print (last accessed August 2011)

Schama S. 2005. *Rough Crossings: Britain, the Slaves and the American Revolution*. London: BBC Books.

Schama S. 2007. *Rough Crossings. Adapted for the stage by Caryl Phillips*. London: Oberon Books.

Schatteman R. (ed.) 2009. *Conversations with Caryl Phillips*. Jackson: University Press of Mississippi.

Stone J.S. 1994. *Studies in West Indian Literature: Theatre*. London-Basingstoke: Macmillan.

Thomas H. 2006. *Caryl Phillips*. Horndon, Tavistock: Northcote House.

PAOLA D'ERCOLE

Università di Salerno

A Migration of Dreams and Ideas: from Books to Bricks and Mortar

> Not here in our London Ghetto,
> the gates and gabardines of the
> older ghetto of the Eternal city [...]
> its narrow streets have
> no speciality of architecture;
> its dirt is not picturesque.
> (Zangwill 2006, 1)

Certain key characteristics of English literature in the 1880s can be easily recognized in the two halves which constitute this title: the first part *a migration of dreams and ideas* contains in itself the concept of movement which represented the starting point for most of the philanthropists and social writers operating in the last two decades of the XIX century. In order to be convincing in their reports and books, to describe the real conditions of poor, they had to start from the streets, the real home of the residuum. The second part *from books to bricks and mortar* depicts the notion of civilisation which was instead the main goal of those reformers. They were launching the idea, the dream in their books while architects and urban engineers had to transform it into reality, with the common aim to help poor people meet culture. However this final part of the title also evokes the main goal of literature: to be immortal. In this specific case, the aim is reached not only through books but through contemporary buildings – still existing in the 21st century – so that the Past can live again through the Present.

1. Introduction

The relationship between architecture and philanthropy was quite strong and productive above all in the East End of London during the period between 1880 and 1905; Sir Walter Besant's novel *All Sorts and Conditions of Men* (1882) is generally the only one cited for this purpose, as the inspiration for the building of The People's Palace in Mile End. It wasn't indeed the only dream of that period translated into real bricks and mortar. In *London 1900*, Alistair Service, the architectural historian, asserts

> It is a remarkable fact that many of the most original London buildings constructed at the end of the nineteenth century were commissioned by private charities dedicated to improving the lives of the poor working classes. It seems that for social reformers of the time, the rejection of historical styles represented a symbol of their revulsion of any association with a past that had allowed so much suffering and hardship to grow in the midst of its developing civilisation (Service 1979, 173).

This notion of rejecting historical styles is questionable since reality was far more complex and in terms of charitable endeavour, the relationship between people that gave and those that received must be analyzed to understand how all this is reflected in the architectural form. The East End during this period provides an abundance of buildings in which to study this connection, such as in housing, schools, libraries and in particular within the Settlement Movement[1] which – without rejecting historical styles – recreated the past as an idealised medieval world of pre-industrial simplicity. To illustrate some of these complexities, three buildings will be analyzed: The People's Palace in Mile End, George Green's School in Poplar and the Jews' Free School in Spitalfields.

2. The stained slums of empire

The 1870s and the 1880s found England at the height of its prosperity and power – indisputably the greatest and richest nation in the world. The West End's image was one of conspicuous consumption whilst the East End was of potentially dangerous poverty, referred to as the "terror of the great unwashed" (Bulwer-Lytton 1842, xiv),[2] "England's Metropolitan Heathenism" (Mullens 1868, 21), the

---

[1] The Settlement movement was a reformist social movement, beginning in the 1880s and peaking around the 1920s in England and the US, with a goal of getting the rich and poor in society to live more closely together in an interdependent community. Its main object was the establishment of *settlement houses* in poor urban areas (such as Toynbee Hall in East London), in which volunteer middle-class *settlement workers* would live, hoping to share knowledge and culture with, and alleviate the poverty of, their low-income neighbours (Wade 2004).

[2] This rather disparaging term was coined by the Victorian novelist and playwright Edward Bulwer-Lytton. He used it in his 1830 novel *Paul Clifford*: "[…] he is certainly a man who bathes and 'lives cleanly' (two especial charges preferred against him by Messrs. The Great Unwashed) […]".

"City of Dreadful Night" (Thomson 1880).[3] Surveys were undertaken on poverty in order to 'civilise' those people, with the idea of a stable and vigorous community – an idea which occupied the minds of many at this time, an issue which grew in importance in the twentieth century. Social integration both in residential terms and in terms of social intercourse would be of benefit to all and might end hostility between classes. In an East End environment described in terms of "grinding monotony", "dreary", "depressing", "a desert",[4] the masses were regarded as being devoid of culture. Relief of poverty therefore went hand in hand with civilising the masses and providing cultural enrichment and the relationship between giver and recipient, between West and East, becomes central and it is made explicit with certain buildings that contrasting dramatically with the grim surroundings give a sense of 'exposing to good taste', 'impressing of a higher culture'.

3. Palace of delight

The People's Palace in Mile End Road was inspired by the novel *All Sorts and Conditions of Men* by Walter Besant, written in 1882. Here the young heiress Angela, from Newham College, Cambridge, and the well-educated Harry enthuse about creating a cultural, educational and recreational institution:

> What we want here, he said, is a little more of the pleasures and graces of life [...] a theatre and a music-hall in Whitechapel Road that has to serve for two millions of people [...] a Palace of Pleasure. [...] There must be a great college to teach all these accomplishments. Happy Stepney! Glorified Whitechapel! Beautiful Bow! What things await ye in the fortunate future! (Besant 1997, 69-71).

The novel was a huge success and certainly inspired John Barber Beaumont, a Unitarian philanthropist and Sir Edmund Currie, heir to a distillery fortune. Through the Beaumont Trust they set out to create a combined library/museum and concert hall to bring culture to the workingmen of East London, for the intellectual improvement and rational recreation and amusement for people living at the East End of London. It is likely that it was through Currie that E. R. Robson (who had resigned from the London School Board in 1884) was commissioned as architect. Four years after Besant's novel, Robson exhibited his designs for the People's Palace at the Royal Academy and he finally was

---

[3] A long poem by the Scottish poet James "B.V." Thomson, written between 1870 and 1873, and published in the National Reformer in 1874, then in 1880 in a book entitled *The City of Dreadful Night and Other Poems*.

[4] All the quotations are taken from Morrison (1983).

responsible for the design of the Queen's Hall, the south front, the library, the technical schools and the clock tower of The Peoples' Palace.

Did Robson look to the future with a rejection of historical styles?

The Builder gives us some wonderful descriptions of different stages of the design process. On Saturday 29 May 1886, it read: "A grandiose conception, though we question whether it quite suggests the idea of a people's palace; there is rather a taint of aristocracy about it" (No. 2260, p. 772). The design was deemed to be too costly and *The Builder* in June 1886 described the new design as: "somewhat of an Oriental character, though the details are Renaissance in feeling" (No. 2264, p. 914). On Saturday 14 May 1887, less than a year after the laying of the Foundation Stone, Queen Victoria opened the Queen's Hall and also laid the foundation stones of the technical schools. According to the *Times*:

> Its marble statues, painted glass, and gilded balconies give an air of splendour and magnificence which is all the more striking for being met with, in so unlovely a neighbourhood as that of the East End of London (*Times* 1887, 878).

However, the design of 1886 was never built. It quickly became entangled in the complex cultural and electoral politics of the period. An impressive library, swimming baths, winter gardens, gymnasium and technical schools followed, paid for by a number of benefactors. The project, however, lacked a clear role both in terms of philosophy and function and this manifested itself in The People's Palace architectural form as this assessment by Pevsner argues: "An effort to bring civilised entertainment to the East End [...] Grecian gone gaudy [...] A debased version of what Greek Thomson was doing [...] With isolated clock tower in front" (Pevsner 1952, 420-421).

Rational Recreation[5] was seen as leisure time for the working class as designed by the middle class. It was not recognised that although the local people were poor, they had a culture of their own. The East End was not a cultural void in which culture had to be poured. It can be seen as an attempt to substitute the policies of civilization instead of policies of genuine economic reform. But what have the working classes to do with *recreation*? It is assumed that *recreation* means amusement, idle and purposeless and the People's Palace offered recreation to all who wished to fit themselves for its practice and enjoyment: it was however a *recreation* of a kind which demanded skill, patience, discipline, drill, and obedience to law. In few words, the Palace was going to take boys out of the streets, to remove both from boys and girls the temptation to go away and get married. It would fill that lad's mind with thoughts and make those hands deft and crafty. And because the Mile End Road run through the most extensive portion of the most dismal city in the world, the city which had been

---

[5] For the whole issue of *rational recreation*, see the pioneering study of P. Bailey (1978).

suffered to exist without recreation, it had been chosen as the fitting site of the Palace.

Although very popular with the public, a fire in 1931 cast a shadow over the future of the People's Palace which was eventually sold to Queen Mary College and now forms part of its campus. It might be interesting quoting at this point Sir Walter Besant's words in 1884: "I see before us in the immediate future a vast University whose home is in the Mile End Road" (353).

4. Spreaders of enlightenment

As a result of the work of the London School Board, the city had recognisable symbols of enlightenment. Between the 1870 Elementary Education Act and 1895, there were over 400 Board Schools in London. Many of these were in Queen Anne's style designed by E. R. Robson (1835-1917), the first architect of the London School Board. Whilst the Board Schools were of great importance in the raising of standards, the pioneering role of charitable trusts and foundations in education should not be forgotten. Notable examples of this period are George Green's School, in Poplar, for which the 'new polemics' meant an entirely new building and the Jews' Free School, in Spitalfield, to which a major extension was given.

4.1 *George Green's School, 1883*

George Green's School's founder was an important shipbuilder of Blackwall and a prominent local non-conformist philanthropist. He had a major impact on Poplar in the nineteenth century through his work in the Docks and his various benevolent institutions-almshouses, Trinity Chapel, sailors' homes and schools. This School was founded in 1828 and its development was influenced by its relationship with state education. Following the 1870 Education Act, elementary education was now becoming a responsibility of the state and a number of Green's schools were taken over by the School Board of London. The new needs were obviously in Higher or Secondary Education. The Charity Commissioners therefore agreed that the school trustees should establish a *middle class* school giving a wider secondary-type education. Amendments were made to the Foundation to make it 'a ladder to the Universities' and the new school was built in 1883 on East India Dock Road where previously stood 'Monastery House'. The designer John Sulman (1849-1934) was known for Congregational churches and indeed Williamson and Pevsner gave an apt description:

> This design has a Northern European picturesqueness and despite the bold
> High Victorian stripes of brick and stone, (has an) Arts and Crafts feeling in

the asymmetrical fenestration and areas of blank walling. (The East) Tower with the Rhenish roof forms the girls' entrance and screens the north east classroom block. Boys' entrance tower (is) central with a gabled timber lantern. To its east, and rising behind, the galleried Hall (Pevsner 1952, 433).

The classrooms may have been functional, but there is certainly a beauty, a romance, a scholarly feel to the whole. Indeed, the physical appearance of the building has an emotional effect on the beholder. *The Survey of London* comments: "the effect, if lacking in forcefulness, is memorable and individual" (Hobhouse and Porter 1994, 140). George Green's School was clearly meant to have presence, to be somewhat separate from the community, 'to civilise'. In harkening back to a medieval past, it is intriguing to find that the school song, written by a teacher of the school between 1884-1922, declares: "For deeds of honour, bravery And knightly gentleness" while the rousing chorus affirms: "St George for Merry England – St George for Poplar Too!".

It may have pleased that teacher to know that even in the early 21st century the school song was still being sung by George Green students.

4.2 *Jews' Free School, 1883*

The Jews' Free School (JFS; started life in 1732 in Spitalfield as a Talmud Torah (religious school) attached to the Great Synagogue. Eighty-five years later, on 13 April 1817 – eleven years earlier than George Green – a boy's school was opened in Ebenezer Square near Brick Lane, at the heart of a poverty-stricken district with a growing Jewish population. According to Dr Gerry Black in *The History of the Jews' Free School*,

> Between 1880-1900 one third of all London's Jewish children passed through its doors. In 1900 the Jewish Free School was the largest school in Europe with more than 4000 pupils [...] It played a significant part in countering the efforts of missionaries to convert East End Jews to Christianity (Black 1998, 43).

For more than 100 years, most pupils arrived at JFS unable to speak English. The school provided them with a refuge, educated them in both secular and religious studies, anglicised them, and sent them out into the wider community. The ethos of the school however was not straightforward. A large proportion of the pupils would not have been resident in this country for long, including Germans, Dutch, Russians and Poles, yet in order to protect them from Christianity and Socialism the anglicised elite talked of the great majority of children entering the school practically foreigners, and leaving it as potential Englishmen and women. This matter is dealt with in Fishman's *East End 1888*, where he points out that the young schoolmaster Israel Zangwill (the chronicler of Jewish life, who wrote *Children of the Ghetto* among other books) clashed with the authorities over such an ethos. Indeed he handed in his resignation. Apparently his story writing had led to a controversy with the school authority. As a consequence of the ethos, the school was not pretentiously Jewish. By 1883 the numbers of children had reached 2900 and it was decided to rebuild the original Bell Lane section of the school: it stood four storeys high and *The Builder* of 7 July 1883 describes the design at length:

> The quadrangle which forms a central hall, with its cornices, friezes, panels and other architectural features, being carried out in glazed bricks, chiefly cream coloured and with bands of grey, buff and brown, the enriched panels and friezes being of glazed terracotta (No.2109, p. 4).

It must have been a wonderful sight! Another site in Bell Lane was acquired in 1890 and the western part of the school was rebuilt, a wing facing Petticoat Lane. Designed by Robson, it was completed in 1907. Hence there were now three main fronts, all in red brick and terracotta but of differing styles. *The Survey of London* describes them as such:

> The wide four storeyed front to Bell Lane is a well ordered design of early Italian Renaissance derivation [...] which impart[s] a distinctly Bolognese flavour [...] The Strype Street block has a four-storeyed front of light red brick, banded with black brick and combined with white glazed terracotta [...] free Jacobean will serve as a label [...] The lofty four storeyed front of the Middlesex Street block is an eclectic design [...] reflecting the Gothic manner of Alfred Waterhouse (Hobhouse and Porter 1957, 241).

The Board Schools had a clearly recognisable style. Charitable Foundation Schools did not, but they were often buildings with 'presence', making a statement in an elaborate way.

It appeared highly unlikely that the school would continue after 1945. However, after an interval of 13 years, the Jew's Free School re-established itself as JFS secondary school in Camden Town in 1958. The new school was initially classified as a secondary modern, but later became the first school in London to use the word 'comprehensive' in its title. After 43 years in Camden Town, JFS outgrew its site, and it moved to Kenton in September 2002.

5. The spirit of the age

Philanthropic endeavours at this time display incredible energies and passions, a moralising zeal, and a devotion to service and duty. The spirit of the age saw a concentration of minds towards tackling poverty. From the *Rational Recreation* at The People's Palace to the Anglo-Jewish stance at the Jews' Free School protecting itself from Christianising influences, the issue of 'civilising' permeates this study and is reflected in the architecture discussed. Within the notion of social integration, the importance of hierarchy (integral to a feudal past) was deemed necessary. This was expressed in the location and style of buildings as well as actual activities undertaken within the work. The People's Palace had 'an air of splendour and magnificence'; George Green's School was clearly different from anything in the local neighbourhood offering 'a ladder to the Universities' and a possible way out; The Jews' Free School intended to inspire and elevate the lot of impoverished Jews and clearly differentiated itself from the London County Council (LCC) Schools and the Church of England (CofE) Schools. Alistair Service's assertion that social reformers of the period rejected historical styles strikes as too simplistic in the light of the East End experience. Certainly there are examples of this (for example Whitechapel Art Gallery 1901) but architectural styles included elements of eclecticism, cross currents and contradictions. The work of charitable organisations in the East End of London in the late Victorian period did not develop a coherent architectural language. In terms of both social reform and in terms of architectural developments it was a period of complexity. This is not to deny work which incorporated elements of great energy, inventiveness, variety and effectiveness.

References

Bailey P. 1978. *Leisure and Class in Victorian England. Rational Recreation and the Contest for Control, 1830-1885.* London: Routledge and Kegan Paul Ltd.

Besant W. 1884. "The Amusements of the People". In *The Contemporary Review*, vol. 45, 342-353.

Besant W. 1997. *All Sorts and Conditions of Men, An Impossible Story.* Oxford: Oxford University Press.

Black G. 1998. *The History of the Jews' Free School.* London: Tymsder Publishing.

Bulwer-Lytton E. 1842. *Paul Clifford.* Exeter: J. B. Williams.

Fishman W.J. 1988. *East End 1888 – A Year in London Borough among the Labouring Poor.* London: Duckworth & Co Ltd.

Hobhouse H., Porter S. (eds.) 1957. *Survey of London, Vol. XXVII. Spitalfields and Mile End New Town.* London: Athlone Press.

Hobhouse H., Porter S. (eds.) 1994. *Survey of London, Vol. XLIII. Poplar, Blackheath and Isle of Dogs.* London: Athlone Press.

Morrison A. 1983. *Tales of Mean Streets.* Suffolk: The Boydell Press.

Mullens J. 1868. *London and Calcutta, compared in their Heathenism, their Privileges, and their Prospects.* London: James Nisbet & Co.

Pevsner N. 1952. *London 2. The Buildings of England series.* London: Penguin Books.

Service A. 1979. *London 1900*. London: Granada Publishing Ltd.

The Builder. 1883. July 7th Saturday, Vol. XLV, No. 2109.

The Builder. 1886. May 29th Saturday, No. 2260.

The Builder. 1886. June 26th Saturday, No. 2264.

Thomson J. 1880. *The City of Dreadful Night and Other Poems*. London/New York: Reeves and Turner.

Times. 1887. May 14th Saturday, No. 2312.

Wade L.C. 2004. "Settlement Houses". in *Encyclopaedia of Chicago*. Chicago Historical Society, available at. http://www.encyclopedia.chicagohistory. org/pages/1135.html (last accessed August 2011).

Zangwill I. 2006. *Children of the Ghetto. A Study of a Peculiar People*. New York: Elibron Classics.

MARIA LUISA DE RINALDIS

Università del Salento

Walter Pater's Venus and Pre-cinematographic Reproduction of the Human Body

Walter Pater wrote just a few pages on Botticelli (Pater 1893, 53-65), but those pages represent one of his most in-depth and best-written essays. Published in August 1870 in the *Fortnightly Review* as "A Fragment on Sandro Botticelli", republished in *The Renaissance* in 1873, "Sandro Botticelli" has defined and still defines our perception of the Italian painter. If the Birth of Venus provides us, as Pater wrote, with "a more direct inlet into the Greek temper than the works of the Greeks themselves" (Pater, 1893, 62), then on another level Pater's writing introduces and establishes a re-conception of the reproduction or simulacrum as a privileged object in itself. His writing can be seen as filmic, in that it takes its material from the past, in many cases from visual images, works of art, recycled, 'filmed' with a verbal narrative throughout which there is a sense of the hybridism between languages, as is clearly demonstrated in the essay "The School of Giorgione" (1877). In this paper I shall attempt to read the 'character' of Venus with the aim of making explicit the relationship between Paterian writing and late nineteenth-century and early twentieth-century visual culture. In the 19th century we can discover the "archaeology" of cinema in the development of numerous visual technologies and in the invention of such new media as photography (Fiorentino 2007; Crary 1990); we can trace, obviously with hindsight, a pre-cinematographic modality in the animation of images and in the spectacular way of looking at the old that Pater presented. On a methodological level I will be using the most recent approaches in studies of Pater, in particular those that focus on the visual (P. Colaiacomo, V. Caratozzolo, C. Williams).

Pater's essay examines the question of Botticelli's fame: "[...] people have begun to find out the charm of Botticelli's work, and his name, little known in the last century, is quietly becoming important" (Pater 1893, 53). Botticelli had in fact been practically unknown as a painter in England until the mid 19th century. His work had been discussed by Crowe and Cavalcaselle, in 1864, and before that by Rio, commented on by Swinburne and Lagrange, critics whom

Pater knew, but it was only in 1870, thanks to Pater (who was to influence Ruskin's less enthusiastic reaction), that a significant change came about in the perception of Botticelli's art, triggering a veritable decade-long "Botticelli craze", as the programme at the Grosvenor Gallery illustrates (Staley 1996, 66). Thus Pater's cultural choice is significant, reviving interest in a painter of (as he himself states at the end of the essay) secondary importance, while rendering this secondary status a positive force in the appreciation of the artist. Botticelli merits careful consideration precisely because he is part of a group of artists who do not have "about them the stress of a great name and authority. Of this select number Botticelli is one" (Pater 1893, 65). Pater's research begins to play its part here, in re-appropriating, re-positioning, in providing a new reading.

Pater asserts that "In an age when the lives of artists were full of adventure, his life is almost colourless", there is no legend surrounding him (*ibidem*, 54). Botticelli appears devoid of colour, adventure, external traits, and consequently difficult to grasp. But this quality is contrasted with his unique and original sensibility; above all a "poetical painter" (*ibidem*, 55), illustrator of Dante, he is presented as a visionary:

> But the genius of which Botticelli is the type usurps the data before it as the exponent of ideas, moods, visions of its own; in this interest it plays fast and loose with those data, rejecting some and isolating others, and always combining them anew. To him, as to Dante, the scene, the colour, the outward image or gesture, comes with all its incisive and importunate reality; but awakes in him [...] a mood which it awakes in no one else, of which it is the double or repetition, and which it clothes, that all may share it, with visible circumstance (*ibidem*, 57).

Implicit in the term "usurps" is an appropriation, a violent one, of the external form and its remodelling according to an interior vision, as dictated by the concept of style which Pater expounds in his 1888 essay devoted to that topic. He is exploring the process of translating a poetic text into images, aware of the manipulation of data that translation demands when working through different mediums: "the words of a poet, which only feebly present an image to the mind, must be lowered in key when translated into visible form" (*ibidem*, 56). Indeed Pater aims to accustom us to experiencing the image, the "visible circumstance", grasped during a mental operation which selects, rejects, reproduces, and reveals the attempt to connect the surface of the image with an interior exigence, with thought. This sets him apart from Ruskin, whose approach to the image is more objective.

In the essay "Diaphaneité" (1864; Pater 1917, 247-254), Pater discussed the idea of a type of character defined by transparency, for which "the veil of an outer life not simply expressive of the inward becomes thinner and thinner" (*ibidem*, 249). We find this type again, defined exactly by its features of evanescence and by a "colourless, unclassified purity of life" (*ibidem*, 248), in the Paterian interpretation of the figure of Botticelli and of the characters he depicted. They are defined by their indefiniteness, by their formlessness: "So just what Dante scorns as unworthy alike of heaven and hell, Botticelli accepts, that middle world in which men take no side in great conflicts, and decide no great causes, and make great refusals" (Pater 1893, 59). The dematerialization of the human form, its transformation into abstraction, is the initial process within the Paterian image. Botticelli's characters, both sacred and profane, are "in a certain sense like angels, but with a sense of displacement or loss about them – the wistfulness of exiles, conscious of a passion and energy greater than any known issue of them explains" (*ibidem*, 58). Here we have the idea of form as defective with respect to its content and identity. But how does the image take form? The exiling of content brings about an indecipherability which transforms into the possibility of accessing meaning on exclusively individualistic, subjective terms. Pater's reading of Botticelli's Madonnas, as Paul Tucker reveals, shows how Pater interprets Botticelli by deconstructing Christian iconography (Tucker 2002). They do not conform to any recognized canon of beauty; in them there seems to be something "mean or abject even, for the abstract lines of the face have little nobleness, and their colour is wan". They do not belong, they too are "neither for Jehovah nor for His enemies". In the reading of the *Madonna del Magnificat* the emphasis falls on elements that create a dialectic within the image, making it into a negative: the white light is "cast up hard and cheerless from below" and the main tonality is that of "trouble" brought by the proximity of the "mysterious child, whose gaze is always far from her […]". And when she is transcribing the words of the Magnificat "[…] the pen almost drops from her hand, and the high cold words have no meaning for her […]", because her children are "those others, among whom, in her rude home, the intolerable honour came to her, with that look of wistful inquiry on their irregular faces which you see in startled animals […]" (Pater 1893, 60-61).

The image, as I said, becomes dialectical, a polarity opens within it, it is read on the basis of a no longer univocal relationship with the surface of the representation. The figure of Venus is in itself an image of 'otherness', a "complementary" one with respect to that of the sacred female subject (Tucker 2002, 125). The first image that Pater offers is focused on the context in which the figure is placed, a frame with no contents:

> What is strangest is that he carries this sentiment into classical subjects, its most complete expression being a picture in the *Uffizii*, of Venus rising from the sea, in which the grotesque emblems of the middle age, and a landscape full of its peculiar feeling, and even its strange draperies, powdered all over in the Gothic manner with a quaint conceit of daisies, frame a figure that reminds you of the faultless nude studies of Ingres (Pater 1893, 61).

Or rather what the frame contains, that Venus who rises from the water, briefly referred to, is defined and shaped by the details that surround the figure. But the textualisation of the painting presented by Pater will never render that body, and the figure herself will be, as Pater says of the particular design of the painting, "incongruous with the subject". Indeed there is incongruity in Botticelli's painting: "the colour is cadaverous or at least cold", scarcely appropriate for representing this luminous classic goddess (*ibidem*, 61). The gap separating the Renaissance painting from the Greek world is that which always separates subject from object, expressing no more than an effort, a desire to grasp it. Pater verbalizes the image of Venus thus:

> The light is indeed cold - mere sunless dawn; but a later painter would have cloyed you with sunshine; and you can see the better for that quietness in the morning air each long promontory, as it slopes down to the water's edge. Men go forth to their labours until the evening; but she is awake before them, and you might think that the sorrow in her face was at the thought of the whole long day of love yet to come. An emblematical figure of the wind blows hard across the grey water, moving forward the dainty-lipped shell on which she sails, the sea "showing his teeth", as it moves, in thin lines of foam, and sucking in, one by one, the falling roses, each severe in outline, plucked off short at the stalk, but embrowned a little, as Botticelli's flowers always are (*ibidem*, 62-63).

The bodily nature of the figure is still missing; we have the cold, surrounding light, which helps us focus on the scene encompassing it. But we have only a few references to Venus: she wakes before the others and has an expression of sorrow on her face which is attributed to the anticipation of the coming day. The image is fixed between two temporal infinites, a past and future time, suspended between forces which go through it and destabilize it. There is no longer a focus, a stability in the figure but rather instability, which is openness to difference, otherness, while a sense of movement is provided by the wind and emphasized by the movement of the sea and the falling roses. The image of the Goddess of pleasure, which loses material solidity in Pater's reading, is characterized by pathos, emotional intensity, which is suspended energy, potential transformation. Contradicting Winckelmann's vision of the past, of noble serenity and quiet grandeur, Pater mobilizes the figure, opening it up to a dialectic of opposing forces, revealing the Dionysian nature of the image, that content which, we can say with Kracauer, inadvertently pushes through the surface and guarantees "unmediated access to the fundamental substance of the state of things" (Kracauer 1995, 75).

The mobilization of past images is a distinctive element of the research carried out, a few decades later, by Aby Warburg (1866-1929), a History of Art scholar and founder of the discipline of Iconology. In the essay "Botticelli's *The Birth of Venus* and *Spring*" (1893) he writes:

The female figure who welcomes Venus [...] shows a remarkable affinity with the Horae as described by Poliziano, including the fluttering accessory forms. She stands at the water's edge, turned to face leftward in strict profile, and holds out to Venus the wind-blown mantle that she grasps in her outstretched right hand above and in her left hand below. [...] Her gown, embroidered all over with cornflowers, clings to her body, clearly revealing the outlines of her legs. A fold curves gently downward to the right from the back of her left knee, fanning out in smaller folds below. Her narrow sleeves, puffed at the shoulders, are worn over a white undergarment of soft material. Most of her fair hair wafts back from her temples in long waves, but some has been made into a stiff braid that ends in a bunch of loose hair (Warburg 1999, 102).

Again here we do not find the features of the figure but her accessories, which define the substance (Michaud 1998, 68). By focusing on her clothes, the drapery, on everything that gives a sense of movement, Warburg shows how the Renaissance artist tries to artificially reproduce the illusion of movement. Indeed the Renaissance artists looked to the classical world for an aesthetic of movement which combines instances of self control and pathos, experienced as loss of self (Warburg's notion of *Pathosformel*) (Michaud 2002; Careri 2002). Of this movement in the bodies we find an example in the theme of the nymph, dangerous personification of paganism, which undoubtedly recalls Pater's interpretation of the Mona Lisa. At the same time Warburg interweaves the pictorial and narrative image, enlarging the image, opening it up within its literary and cultural background and context, so that the work is not a closed entity but a juxtaposition of elements in tension with one another.

If Warburg's method differs from that of Pater in the textual and instrumental apparatus surrounding the image, it does, however, share the emphasis on the Dionysian aspect of art and on the movement and animation of the figures, which seem to be endowed with a force of their own. And if Warburg's is already a History of Art at the time of mechanical reproduction, which uses, as in *Mnemosyne*, superimposition, we can retrace in Pater's writing a narrative mode strongly directed towards the photographic and cinematographic visual. Photography can reveal aspects of the original subject which are imperceptible to the human eye, collect images which escape natural vision, as studies by Muybridge on creating fixed images of horses galloping have shown. Photography deals with contingency, absolute detail. It portrays rarity, immobilizes a scene at its decisive moment, and makes use of superimposition, off-centre frames, distortion of perspective (Benjamin 2000; Barthes 2000): "[...] what it produces in me is the very opposite of hebetude; something more like an internal agitation, an excitement, a certain labor too, the pressure of the unspeakable which wants to be spoken", Barthes writes (2000, 19). That accident which "pricks" is the *punctum*, the thing that makes the person/object phantasmally come out of the photo, creating a blind field. This is the experience Pater provides for his readers-spectators, performing as they do an interior movement. His writing works with the dis-narrative modality of photography, since the images offer partial, unfocused, superficial visions which release unconscious meaning. The reading of Venus is constructed pre-cinematographically, using the principles of superimposition, which is first of all internal to the image itself, polar, dialectical and related to the sacred figures that precede it and with those that Pater later brings to bear on it:

> The same figure [...] appears again as Judith, returning home across the hill country [...]; as *Justice*, sitting on a throne [...]; and again as *Veritas*, in the allegorical picture of *Calumnia*, where one may note in passing the suggestiveness of an accident which identifies the image of Truth with the person of Venus (Pater 1893, 64).

Indeed in this final part of the essay we can perceive an acceleration in the movement, or, we could say, the creation of movement in the image is more overt, and Venus becomes "metamorphic energy in its purest form, incarnating, in no less intensity than the Mona Lisa [...] 'the fancy of a perpetual life'" (Colaiacomo 1996, 238, my own translation). The accelerated motion causes loss of definition, recalling the accelerated vision of someone looking out of a train window while the train is moving, an experience which modified vision in the 19th century. Linking an image to another – montage –, Deleuze tells us, produces a direct presentation of time, which is not the freezing of movement, but the promotion of abnormal movement, in that it detracts from the focal point. The cinematographic image creates an autonomous world made of fragments and disproportions; it does not reproduce reality, it fakes it. If the aberration of movement in modern cinematographic images releases time from all its connections, and reveals it as "infinite", the representation of Venus through the emphasis on sorrow accentuates the sense of confinement and thus projects a desire to escape to an imaginary world and transcend time. If the power of falsehood which photography and the cinema incarnate is "inseparable from an idea of multiplicity" where "'I is another' has replaced I=I" (Deleuze 2006, 151, my own translation), the image of Venus provides us with a reading of a work of art at the time of mechanical reproduction starting from the loss of authority, of the uniqueness of the thing. Venus is a multiple image, open, kinetic. It sends back an idea of self as a flux, unstable and flexible, a series of mobile identities connecting with one another. Ungraspable, without individual features, it reflects nineteenth-century anxieties about the relationship between the individual and the masses, and projects visions of subjectivity which are already postmodern, contemporary. A phantasmal and ambiguous image, no longer tied to an invariable form, but one which self-defines and self-modifies, it foresees the society of the spectacle where a life/ representation inversion takes place: the spectacle being "a concrete inversion of life", "the autonomous movement of the non-living" (Debord 1994, par. 2).

References

Barthes R. 2000 [1980]. *Camera lucida*. London: Vintage.

Benjamin W. 2000 [1936]. *L'opera d'arte nell'epoca della sua riproducibilità tecnica*. Torino: Einaudi.

Colaiacomo P. 1996. "Walter Pater e i Greci". In Bizzotto E., Marucci F. (eds.) *Walter Pater (1839-1894). Le forme della modernità / The Forms of Modernity*. Bologna: Cisalpino, 227-243.

Careri G. 2002. "*Pathosformeln*. Aby Warburg e l'intensificazione delle immagini". In Bertozzi M. (ed.) *Aby Warburg e le metamorfosi degli antichi dei*. Ferrara: Franco Cosimo Panini, 50-61.

Crary J. 1990. *Techniques of the Observer. On Vision and Modernity in the Nineteenth Century*. Cambridge (Mass.), London: MIT Press.

Debord G. 1994 [1967]. *Society of the Spectacle*. London: Zone Books.

Deleuze G. 2006 [1985]. *L'immagine-tempo. Cinema 2*. Milano: Ubulibri.

Fiorentino G. 2007. *L'Ottocento fatto immagine*. Palermo: Sellerio.

Kracauer S. 1995 [1963]. "The Mass Ornament". In Kracauer S. *The Mass Ornament: Weimer Essays* (English trans. Levin T. Y.). Cambridge (Mass.): Harvard University Press, 75-88.

Michaud P.A. 1998. *Aby Warburg et l'image en mouvement*. Paris: Macula.

Michaud P.A. 2002. "*Zwischenreich. Mnemosyne*, o l'espressività senza soggetto". In Bertozzi M. (ed.) *Aby Warburg e le metamorfosi degli antichi dei*. Ferrara: Franco Cosimo Panini, 173-182.

Pater W. 1893 [1873]. "Sandro Botticelli" [first publ. 1870] In *The Renaissance. Studies in Art and Poetry*. London and New York: Macmillan, 53-65.

Pater W. 1917 [1895]. "Diaphaneité" [first publ. 1864] In *Miscellaneous Studies*. London: Macmillan, 247-254.

Staley A. 1996. "Art is Upon the Town! The Grosvenor Gallery Winter Exhibitions". In Casteras S. P., Denney C. (eds.) *The Grosvenor Gallery. A Palace of Art in Victorian England*. New Haven and London: Yale University Press, 59-74.

Tucker P. 2002. "'Reanimate Greek': Pater and Ruskin on Botticelli". In Brake L., Higgins L., Williams C. (eds.) *Walter Pater: Transparencies of Desire*. Greensboro, University of North Carolina: ELT Press, 119-132.

Warburg A. 1999. "Sandro Botticelli's *Birth of Venus* and *Spring*". In Warburg *The Renewal of Pagan Antiquity*. Los Angeles: Getty Research Institute, 89-156.

SAURO FABI

Università di Macerata

"*How* is Poetry Going?": Bottlenecks and New Paths for a Seemingly Marginal Art

"How is poetry going in America? There is none in England: the muse has gone, like the swallows in winter" (Zytaruk and Boulton 2002, 393). D.H. Lawrence wrote these lines in 1915, in a letter to US literary critic Harriet Monroe, fearing the First World War's annihilating effects on poetry. Ironically, less than 15 years later, in 1928, in his controversial essay "Is Verse a Dying Technique?" Edmund Wilson claimed that the Modernists (and the Romantics), rather than the war, were to be blamed for narrowing poetry's role in society and culture.

1. The death of poetry

The main point of Wilson's essay centres around the difference between the Classical idea of poetry and the Romantic & Modernist one. For the Romans and the Greeks, according to Wilson, the idea of poetry was mainly based on the formal features of a work, so that virtually anything written in verse, meter and rhyme was viewed as a poem, from treatises on medicine or farming to imaginative and fictional literature. Western poetry remained identified with verse for centuries. Then, at the beginning of the Nineteenth century, the Romantics tried to redefine poetry. In his *Biographia Literaria*, Coleridge firmly denied that any excellent work in meter could be properly called a poem and famously claimed that "a poem is that species of composition which is opposed to works of science by proposing for its immediate object pleasure, not truth", thus "a poem of any length neither can be, nor ought to be, all poetry". Some fifty years later, Matthew Arnold went one step further stating that the main characteristics of poetry were "moral profundity" and "natural magic" so that *true poetry* was in fact "very rare and very precious". Finally, the Modernists managed to turn poetry into something even more rare and quintessential, a "superior amusement" (in T.S. Eliot's words): a distillate concentrated in small evocative fragments that didn't require verse, meter or rhyme.

In other words, the transition was from a mostly connotative definition of poetry to a completely denotative one, the former based on the shared knowledge of the main technical, formal and structural features of the poetic text, the latter fully dependent on some superior, almost transcendental characteristics whose presence could be detected only by "true" poets, learned scholars or, more generally, by what Bourdieu would define as the dominant agents of artistic consecration belonging to the field of literary production (1996, 305). According to Wilson, one of the chief consequences of this dramatic change has been the progressive alienation of poetry from the reading public and the consequent narrowing of poetry's role in society.

Wilson's essay set off a debate that is still ongoing. An ever increasing number of critics, scholars and poets have drawn attention to the widening gap between poetry and mass audience. Amongst the most recent contributions, Joseph Epstein's "Who Killed Poetry" (1988) stands out as one of the most influential. Epstein takes up exactly where Wilson left, but while for Wilson poetry was agonizing, Epstein, writing in the late Eighties, officially declares its death, or, more precisely, its murder. The killers, once again, are the Romantics and the Modernists, who have elevated poetry to a quasi-religious art and turned the poet into "a kind of priest" (*ibidem*, 13), blessed with the gift of inspiration, endowed with exclusive visions and superior insight, and bound to write highly subjective and often difficult poems. Consequently, today's poetry has become an increasingly exclusive literary form that seems to "flourish in a vacuum" (*ibidem*, 14), virtually isolated from the mass audience. The vacuum is the closed world revolving around the universities, with their apparatus of writing-programs, scholarly critics, specialized journals, and poetry prizes. Protected by this soft shell, poetry has increasingly turned into an art for a culturally selected elite: those happy few, who, as Epstein points out, "are rarely happier than when they are even fewer" (*ibidem*, 13). On the same wavelength, Dana Gioia's influential "Can Poetry Matter?" (1991) blames the mushrooming academic creative-writing programs for giving rise to a glut of questionably talented poets who "exist" only within the universities and their publishing outlets, with the result of relegating poetry, *de facto*, to subcultural status.

More recently, in his article "Notes Toward an Investigation of the Marginality of Poetry and the Sympathetic Imagination" (1995), Neil Covey has backed Epstein's and Gioia's arguments with the addition of a sociological and ideological perspective. According to Covey, today's poets have inherited the Modernists' successful attempt at restating the artist's "aura" in an age that witnessed the early rise of mass-culture, and now poets seem unable to restore the severed link between poetry and mass audience. Actually, there is a lot of "popular poetry" going on (typical examples are pop songs and rap lyrics), but it is generally not granted the status of poetry. Even if a poetic consecration is accorded, "popular" artists are generally removed from the context to which they once belonged and placed in the more elevate realm of full fledged poetry (so Bob Dylan is no longer a mere author of pop/folk songs, but rather a poet who brings poetry into music). The problem is one of attitude and ideology, and as long as poetry will be perceived as the last stronghold of high culture against *vis-à-vis* a supposedly deceived mass culture, it will remain trapped as the genre of what Raymond Williams termed "the dissident middle-class", "doomed" to address a restricted and ever-diminishing audience.

Not surprisingly, the consecrated poets' response to this kind of claims has been typically dismissive, mainly on the grounds that poets are not deliberately elitist, but have been pushed into marginality by the ignorance and narrow-mindedness of the mass-media that have virtually hidden the very existence of poetry from the mass-audience. Thus, it would be up to mass-culture and mass-media (rather than the poets) to take the first step. Put in these terms, the issue would lead to a bottleneck. Nonetheless, there are (and there have been) poets who seem willing to take the first step and, interestingly enough, they often belong to the cultural and artistic area that is generally less associated with mass-culture: the avant-garde.

2. Some new paths

In Britain, one of the first poets who tried to bridge the gap between poetry and mass-audience was Edwin Morgan. Since the very beginning of his literary activity, Morgan has always been looking for a kind of poetry that might be able to "speak out on man and society" (Morgan 1996, 28), undoing what he defined as "the modernist attempt to separate poetry from society" (1974, 13). In order to achieve this ambitious goal, during the sixties Morgan joined the international concrete poetry movement, whose declared aim was to bring poetry closer to society by relying on the creative use of graphic art, advertising, and mass media techniques. The result – greatly influenced by Russian Constructivism[1] – was a new kind of poetry foregrounding the visual (concrete) shape of letters and their structural placement on the page rather than the content or meaning of language. Its key-features were, essentially, the use of reduced language (in order to maximise the communicative impact on a wide audience) and the relevance of the formal structure, which had to be simple – even playful at times – clear, rational, self-evident and strictly functional to the organization of the "verbo-visual" material.

One of Morgan's first experiments along this line was his *Siesta of a Hungarian Snake* (1968; Morgan 1990). The "body" of the poem is essentially a

---

[1] For a more in-depth analysis of the relationship between concrete poetry and Russian Constructivism, see Fabi (2009).

verbo-visual rendering of its title. It shows the shape of a snake stretched out on the ground and visually thicker in the middle (presumably sleeping off its meal). The sequence of Ss and Zs carries out the rest of the ludic metaphor, being at the same time both a frequent letter combination in Hungarian language and a traditional means of indicating sleep in comics.

At that time, a recurring critique to this kind of poems was that they would fail to become popular because they were too "light" to be recognized as poetry by a wide audience, and too lacking in what is usually defined as "poetical depth". In response to this type of criticism, Morgan tried to combine the formal characteristics of "traditional" concrete poetry with a more substantial semantic content. The result of this process were the so-called "emergent poems", of which one of the most frequently anthologized is *Message Clear*.

The poem consists of a series of rearrangements of the letters which form the last line. The sentence ("I am the resurrection and the life") is a quotation from the Gospel of St. John and contains within itself all of the letters which make up the whole poem. Each letter retains its original positioning. Line after line, some letters are erased. The remaining letters seem to emerge, visually, from the bottom line, as if the whole poem were already implicitly contained within this line. The poem can be read in a conventional way as a reflection on the identity of an agonizing prophet, but it's once again the structure of the text which conveys its communicative potential. The same structure, which in this case can be considered as a compositional method, is to be found in every emergent poem, regardless of the content of the last line. In *Manifesto* the sentence from which the poem emerges is written in transliterated Russian and the whole poem is a sort of English paraphrase (almost an extended translation) of this sentence ("proletarians in every land are one").

According to some critics, these texts would be more at home in puzzle magazines than in poetry books. Yet, the communicative force of these poems lies precisely in this sort of ambivalence. By *constructing* his poems as word plays and imposing very strict formal and structural limits on his own creativity, Morgan intends to "desacralize" the very concepts of "poem" and "author" and to achieve a sort of obliteration of the author in favour of a more direct and fully engaged relationship with the audience, who is presented with a text whose compositional rules are self-evident and easily imitable.

During the Seventies, Morgan's poetic interests leaned towards less radically experimental forms, but the influence of concrete poetry can still be detected in many of the most stimulating literary trends of the last decades among which is the so-called "altered books" movement. The first and most influential "altered book" is Tom Phillips' work in progress: *A Humument*.

Phillips took an obscure late Victorian novel – *A Human Document*, by W. H. Mallock – and began treating the pages with acrylic and ink, isolating the words that interested him while erasing the others or painting them over. The materiality and the typographical layout of the original book is still there, but has been treated by Phillips so that the form, structure and content of the original text have changed and Mallock's prose has been transformed into a series of verbo-visual poems, virtually linked together by a new plot. As in the case of Morgan's "emergent poems", the text is governed by a strict, self-imposed rule, namely that no words outside the original novel are to be added: the unselected words are eliminated and the remaining ones are joined together by graphical "rivers" connecting the types.

This peculiar technique is well illustrated on page 222 where the main character is struggling to overcome an existential crisis. The graphical frame inside the page is populated by thick, sharp, geometrical red stripes crossing the background of a dark sky: a visual scenery that interacts with the evocative words framed in the upper left corner ("this/night/wounds/time"). As we read on, the narrating voice goes on questioning his own intellect and identity ("I am/I am/what?...") and finally seems to find a way out of his own crisis. This process is enhanced by the dark skies gradually becoming lighter, as if night turned into daylight, though the red cuts still persist, suggesting that the narrator's efforts to regain his lost harmony might still prove inadequate.

A Humument is a celebration of the cultural and literary afterlife of seemingly dead works and, at the same time, a reflection on the relationships between verbality and visuality, prose and poetry, text and its material support, old and new, author and reader. Due to the peculiar structure of the work, the reader is free to chose and read the book in a traditional way, from cover to cover, or play with it, opening it at random and scrolling through a few pages before jumping elsewhere. Technically, it is an avant-garde work, but through the years it has gained an exceptional popularity, generating an impressive "altered book" movement whose works are now quite widespread, both in print form and on the Net.

One of the most peculiar characteristics of works such as *A Humument* is the symbiotic nature of the intertextual relation between text and undertext. The latter, being still materially present under or through the alterations, can only be experienced by way of the new text which, in its turn, would not exist without the original, partially hidden text. Thus the two texts, despite their radically different nature, materially coexist in an intrinsic, symbiotic connection: a dual relation which is not unlike the one that links the code of a computer program to its graphical interface. This is particularly the case with one of the most recent forms of computer poetry, which can be termed as "cyberpoetry" or "ergodic poetry".

According to Espen Aarseth – author of the influential *Cybertext: Perspectives on Ergodic Literature* (1997) – "in ergodic literature, non-trivial effort is required to allow the reader to traverse the text". The effort required of the reader is not an effort of interpretation (as with the ambiguous open works typical of the

Modernist literary tradition), but rather an effort of intervention in the physical structure of the text. So the ergodic text reader, as in the case of concrete poetry or altered books, becomes an active player of a game, and is relatively free to manipulate "the topological structure of the textual machinery". A basic example of this kind of texts is Jennifer Ley and Jason Nelson's 2005 *We have Incense and Prayersticks*, whose textual structure is similar to that of gamebooks. As with Oulipo's "tree literature", the reader is invited to participate in the story by making choices that affect the course of the narrative, which branches down various paths. Here the graphical interface, organized in a hierarchical tree structure, encourages the users to construct their own poem out of an existing one, by clicking on the check-boxes placed at the beginning of each verse. Users can unfold the whole poem or select their own path navigating through a set of predefined choices.

A more adventurous example of ergodic text is Daniel Benmergui's *Today I Die*, released in May 2009, where the relationship between poetic text and ludic play becomes tighter, as does the interaction between verbality and graphics. The scene opens underwater, with the body of a dead woman floating in the dark with a rock tied around her waist. A handwritten poem floats above her: "dead world/full of shades/today I die." Through point-and-click experimentation, players can re-write the story and change reality by discovering and swapping new words into the poem. The verbal *material* is deeply bound up with the game dynamics and altering words in the poem changes the behaviours of game characters. Likewise, the interaction with characters produces new (contextual) words that can be manipulated to alter the poem and eventually provide different endings to the "story". *Today I Die* is actually a game (and an acclaimed one) but its creative and structurally integrated use of words effectively presents the user with an unusually challenging kind of "playable poetry".

3. Back to the future

In all these texts, one can discern a common attempt to bridge the gap between poetry and mass-culture and/or mass audience. Interestingly enough though, the authors of these texts are reluctant to be identified as poets: authors of ergodic texts tend to consider themselves videogame makers, Tom Phillips once clearly defined himself as a "non-poet", and the concretists have always achieved more success and recognition as advertisement makers than as poets. On the other hand, the "field of poetic consecration" seems to pay little attention to these kinds of texts.

As with pop-music lyrics, poetry scholars and critics generally have a hard time granting these texts the status of poetry, arguably because of the apparent lack of depth, insight and inspiration that ought to be found in "true" poetry.

Here, we seem to have come full circle back to Wilson's essay, and maybe his claim for a less ideological and more technical definition of poetry might still prove relevant today. In fact, it seems likely that a critical and cultural approach to poetry and poeticity based less on concepts like "profundity" or "insight" and more on formal features (such as the primacy of the signifier, the dominance of what Jakobson calls the "poetic function" of language, and so on) would allow more room for texts like the ones just discussed. I don't expect of poetry to embark on a sort of culturally imperialist war for the immediate annexation of new kinds of textualities and I'm perfectly aware that such texts as the ones here considered deserve fresh and specific methodological and theoretical tools. Nonetheless, the development of such tools would probably prove useful to expand the current scope of poetry studies as to give adequate attention to phenomena that are typically perceived as outside of the field of poetry, or even in opposition to it, for purely ideological reasons. Such an "expansion" won't clearly solve all the bottlenecks of poetry, but it would probably contribute to reducing its marginalization, whilst relieving critics and scholars from the burden of judging what is and what is not poetry, whether good or otherwise.

References

Aarseth E.J. 1997. *Cybertext: Perspectives on Ergodic Literature*. Baltimore: The John Hopkins University Press.

Benmergui D. 2009. *Today I Die*, available at http://www.ludomancy.com/games/today.php?lang=en (last accessed August 2011).

Bourdieu P. 1996. *The Rules of Art: Genesis and Structure of the Literary Field*. Stanford: Stanford University Press.

Covey N. 1995. "Notes Toward an Investigation of the Marginality of Poetry and the Sympathetic Imagination". In *South Atlantic Review*, 60, 2, 137-151.

Epstein J. 1988. "Who Killed Poetry?". In *Commentary*, 86, 2, 13-20.

Fabi S. 2009. "The Popular Avant-garde: The Role of Russian Constructivism in Finlay's and Morgan's Concrete Poetry". In Cavone T.V., Corti C., Trulli M. (eds.) *Forms of Migratio/Migration of Forms*. Bari: Progedit, 203-216.

Gioia D. 1991. "Can Poetry Matter?". In *The Atlantic Monthly*, 267, 5, 94-106.

Ley J., Nelson J. 2005. *We Have Incense and Prayersticks*, available at http://www.secrettechnology.com/resident/ley.htm (last accessed August 2011).

Morgan E. 1974. "A Glimpse of Petavius" (1963). In Morgan E., *Essays*, Manchester: Carcanet, 5-30.

Morgan E. 1990. *Collected Poems*. Manchester: Carcanet.

Morgan E. 1996. "Sovpoems" (1961). In Morgan E., *Collected Translations*, Manchester: Carcanet, 27-31.

Phillips T. 2005. *A Humument: A Treated Victorian Novel*, London: Thames and Hudson.

Wilson E. 1928. "Is Verse a Dying Technique?". In Dabney L.M. (ed.) *Edmund Wilson: Literary Essays and Reviews of the 1930s & 40s*, New York: Library of America, 19-34.

Zytaruk G.J., Boulton J.T. (eds.) 2002. *The Letters of D.H. Lawrence, 1913-16*, Volume II, Cambridge: Cambridge University Press.

GIAN PIETRO LEONARDI

Sapienza – Università di Roma

Gay and After: Notes Towards a Definition of the Post-Gay Novel[1]

> Straight is the line of duty;
> Curved is the line of beauty;
> Follow the straight line, thou shalt see
> The curved line ever follow thee.
> (William McCall)

The post-gay novel stages and brings to its extreme consequences the unresolved conflict between the will to give voice to underrepresented sexual minorities and their necessity to socialize and interact in larger contexts. At the same time, it discloses the dynamics and the complexities of the emergence of a new culture and the attempt to affirm its position and place in a dominant ideology. My aim today is to show how and to what extent the appearance of this sub-genre within queer-themed fiction written in English at the beginning of the new century challenged both the assumptions of gay texts and expectations of straight readers. By adopting Raymond Williams' concepts of the emergent, the dominant, and the residual in literature, I will try to assess the place the post-gay text occupies in contemporary literary landscape. In the end, I will briefly turn to Alan Hollinghurst's *The Line of Beauty* to see if and how the paradigm applies to a novel which has unanimously been hailed as the perfect example of the post-gay novel, but nevertheless won the 2004 Man Booker Prize and was a major literary success in terms of book sales and overall recognition.

I am aware that by dealing with such a controversial notion I lay myself open to criticism. I want to stress, therefore, that my conceptualization of the 'post-gay' here does not intend to diminish the fact that many gay people

---

[1] I wish to express my gratitude and sincere thanks to Professors Rosy Colombo and Donatella Izzo, for their generous encouragement and support. I am also indebted to Francesco Gnerre for many stimulating discussions on the topic of this paper.

still suffer abuse despite living generally in a more tolerant society. My paper, however, does not intend to present a theoretical manifesto of an abstract 'post-gay literature', nor outline the guidelines of a new literary canon. I have talked about 'gay texts' as opposed to a 'gay literature', which implies a coherent and comprehensive, but at least on paper unalterable, list of books whose principal aim is to embody and reinforce the aesthetic and ethical values of those who advocate it. On the other hand, the repressive face of the canon, which lies behind every declaration of intent, sheds lights on the aporias and paradoxes of the winnowing process of choice and evaluation. 'Gay texts', instead, in their inconsistency and multiplicity, provide a narrative space for queer subjectivity, both inside and outside the canon, but they also present the reader some semantic and ideological issues. Is the gay signature the trademark of these texts, or rather the plot? Or the presence of overtly gay characters? Does gay sensibility or vision affect their writing in any way? Gay texts, be they written by male or female authors, by straight or queer people, tend to defy heteronormative and hegemonic fictions, presenting a world and a story that encode the gay subject, but also show there's someone willing to decode it.[2] Another major issue to be considered here is the debate on the rebirth of the author figure,[3] or the person who has "produced the text as we have constructed it" (Nehamas 2002, 100), whose funeral was celebrated prematurely by many poststructuralist critics. The notion of the implied gay reader has also changed in the last decade. The computerization of large sections of the population has also affected the way gay people, and particularly gay young adults, perceive themselves and interact with others as sexual beings. If once they turned to the literary world as a source of self-identification, and the coming out novel is the prototype of such a quest which has no comparison in straight lives, now they turn to the Internet and to virtual communities. This split between theory and practice, between lived experience and political community, has further displaced the role of literature as an identity construction or promotional means.

Finally and significantly, I want to call attention to a more sociological aspect of the issue. In *Marxism and Literature*, Raymond Williams theorizes culture in terms of what he defines the dominant, the emergent, and the residual. By 'emergent', which is the point I want to focus on here, Williams means that "that new meanings and values, new practices, new significances and experiences, are continually being created" (Williams 1977, 123). He further develops the concept by recognising that:

> a new class is always a source of emergent cultural practice, but while it is
> still, as a class, relatively subordinate, this is always likely to be uneven and

---

[2] For more on this topic, see Faderman (1995).
[3] For more on this topic, see Benedetti (2005).

is certain to be incomplete. For new practice is not, of course, an isolated process. To the degree that it emerges, and especially to the degree that it is oppositional rather than alternative, the process of attempted incorporation significantly begins (Williams 1977, 124).

Williams' 'epochal analysis', thereby, proposes to study the relations of the competitive forces and ideologies that shape and structure a hegemonic mainstream, which is, after all, continuously under threat by the forces that it seeks to dominate. Since it cannot allow to leave residual practices and experience at the margins or outside itself, it tends to assimilate and domesticate the oppositional values offered by an emergent culture. The process of emerging, as a matter of fact, is presented as an act of recognition, legitimacy or, in the last analysis, as a form of consent. The emergence of a post-gay culture, therefore, configures itself as a coalescence process between two forces, the first relying on the reinterpretation of inherited literary forms and models, the other on the identification of a specific vocabulary and grammar which can overthrow the old order.

Started in the United States in the 90s around a bunch of magazines, though the term was coined in 1994 by the British journalist and author Paul Burston, the debate on the post-gay sexuality soon won the attention of those writers who felt the 'gay writer' tag too sticky and limiting.[4] In his introduction to *The Penguin Book of Gay Short Stories*, David Leavitt makes this point clear:

> many people ask me if I consider myself a 'gay writer'. My answer is that the question is irrelevant; as long as the culture I live in considers me a gay writer – and it considers every writer who tackles gay subject matter a gay writer – I'm stuck with the label. My sexual identity will subsume all other aspects of my identity – I might be a 'gay Jewish writer', never a 'Jewish gay writer' – no matter how loudly I protest (Leavitt 1994, xviii).

As a consequence of this presumption and in reaction to the trend, a number of gay writers sought to encompass a wider range of experience, to envisage new forms of self-representation, and above all to move out from the realm of victimhood. This new tendency had already been anticipated in an influential essay written by Edmund White in 1991, "Out of the Closet, on to the Bookshelf". In his disquisition, White recognizes that, at the time he is writing, gay literature has already entered the age of maturity and is ready to besiege the literary establishment. While some writers still insist on the singularity of the gay experience, White argues that others represent a larger context in which gay men interact fluidly and without distinction with peers and straight relatives and friends. As a confirmation of this new attitude he quotes Armistead Maupin:

---

[4] A series of interviews to some of these authors were collected in Gnerre and Leonardi (2007).

my innovation was simply to incorporate gay characters naturally into a larger world which is what David Leavitt does and Michael Cunningham does. I've never made any bones about being gay and I don't mind being called a gay writer, but I know I reach a large heterosexual audience as well[5] (White 1994, 279).

Eleven years later, White returned to the topic acknowledging that by the end of the 70s and throughout the 80s, gay writers aimed principally at representing "the full range of the gay typology, as anthological as that of any society"[6] (White 2004, 19), but

this moment in gay writing is now coming to an end and is spawning [...] something one could call post-gay writing, in which one or two characters might be gay but in which they are inserted into a more general society (White 2004, 19).

This conception was further developed in 2005 by David Leavitt who, admits that the season of gay self-segregation and discretion is now over:

when I started writing, a gay novel, at least, was fairly easy to define. In it the hero or heroine's homosexuality stood by necessity at the dramatic center of the plot. More than that, such a novel presumed that any gay person's homosexuality stood at the center of the plot; that in the paper-rock-scissors game of identity, gay was always the rock (Leavitt 2005).

Leavitt, auspicating for a restoration of "the alphabetical and promiscuous flow of literature", argues that:

more and more, gay fiction is giving way to post-gay fiction: novels and stories whose authors, rather than making a character's homosexuality the fulcrum on which the plot turns, either take it for granted, look at it as part of something larger or ignore it altogether (Leavitt 2005).

From what has been said so far, the 'post-gay novel' represents an urban reality which is not populated exclusively by gays and aimed at the preservation and conservation of gay singularity. Homosexuality is not longer the core of the narration, as much of the gay literature of the past decades seemed only interested in, but, nonetheless, it is not relegated it to the domain of the forbidden or unspeakable. The characters *happen* to be gay, their sexual identity is either taken for granted or seen as part of a narrative project rather than as a means of struggle. In foreswearing the one-dimensionality of the character, the myth of the purity and essentiality of identity is put into question. And yet, post-gay,

---

[5] The essay was originally published in the *New York Time Magazine* in 1991.

[6] A version of the essay was presented at the University of Michigan on April 16, 2002 and published in the issue of *Michigan Quarterly Review* in summer 2002.

like other post-realities, does not claim nor mean that the old architecture has been completely abjured or swept away.[7] Like the term 'queer', post-gay is not to be intended here as a simple and chronological evolution of the word gay. It does not mean either 'not gay', 'anti-gay' or 'ex gay', but a critique of gay politics and gay culture intended exclusively for gay people. It is a reaction against the fetishization of gay stereotypes and cultural separatism. In the late post-gay modernity the end of the identity politics is an unquestioned fact, sexual and gender bias seems to be overcome. The subject, and its fictionalized alter ego, is free to identify or disidentify him or herself according to features not strictly connected to gender and sexual issues. Accordingly, even straight people and characters can be defined post-gay.

Alan Hollinghurst's *The Line of Beauty* tells the story of the coming out into society of a young gay post-graduate Oxford student, who's about to undertake a PhD at UCL on the style of Henry James. In the summer of 1983, Nick Guest sneaks into the house and life of the Feddens, introduced by Toby, a fellow university student with whom he has had a crush. In fact, he is still a virgin, both sexually and socially, in a time of innocence, "the last summer of its kind there was ever to be" (Hollinghurst 1988, 3), namely the last summer before AIDS. But this is also the crucial and delicate transition period between a residual capitalistic society and the emergence of a neoliberist vision of the world. As the story proceeds, however, Nick loses his virginity in a semi-private garden to a black man who works in the local government and he gains access to the public and political world, through Gerald Fedden's election as Conservative MP for Barwick. Four years later, at the end of the novel, Nick is a different man: the world he's been living in is collapsing under his feet, AIDS has made its appearance in his life as an uninvited guest, and Gerard's political ambitions come to an abrupt end following a financial and sexual scandal. The book resolves in Nick's final and unappealable expulsion from this Garden of Eden of Thatcherite Britain. This coming out is not be considered solely in terms of sexuality, but as a revisitation and recollocation of the long-standing tradition of apprenticeship. It is more social than political. Indeed, more than as a conventional character of a coming-out novel, Nick Guest is presented as a revisited subject of a classical *Bildung*. He mildly oscillates, as a matter of fact, between the ideal of self-determination and the desire and demand of socialization. His homosexuality, rather than introducing him to the London gay scene, offers him an illusionary chance to feast with the gods. Yet, he is not a natural part of the society in which the Feddens adroitly move, and his sexuality is tolerated only as long as it is kept hidden. In the end, Nick is redeemed by his passion and devotion for Henry James and for his style. Throughout the novel, moreover, he acts as a Jamesian reflector, a voyeuristic spectator who looks the

---

[7] For more on this topic, see D'Erasmo (2008).

scene with a cold and detached, almost surgical, shrewdness. And it is in this aesthetic context that he performs his definitive coming out. To its credit, *The Line of Beauty* spans through the social and political geography of Thatcher's Britain of the Eighties, rather than being merely an unapologetic defense of gay hedonism and rampant debauchery. The novel curves like William Hogarth's ogee, a shape consisting of a concave arc flowing into a convex one, and which the title alludes to. Accordingly, Nick fluidly flows through the opportunities life seems to offer him, rather than clinging to the mask of sexual identity.

References

Benedetti C. 2005. *The Empty Cage: Inquiry into the Mysterious Disappearance of the Author*. Ithaca (NY): Cornell UP.

D'Erasmo S. 2008. "The End of Sexual Identity". In *The Boston Review*, available at http://www.bostonreview.net/BR33.5/derasmo.php (last accessed August 2011).

Faderman L. 1995. "What is Lesbian Literature? Forming a Historical Canon". In Haggerty G.E., Zimmerman B. (eds.) *Professions of Desire: Lesbian and Gay Studies in Literature*. New York: Modern Language Association of America, 49-59.

Gnerre F., Leonardi G.P. (eds.) 2007. *Noi e gli altri. Riflessioni sullo scrivere gay*. Milano: Il dito e la luna.

Hollinghurst A. 1988. *The Swimming Pool Library*. London: Vintage.

Leavitt D. 1994. "Introduction". In Leavitt D., Mitchell M. (eds.) *The Penguin Book of Gay Short Stories*. New York: Viking, xiii-xx.

Leavitt D. 2005. "Out of the Closet and Off the Shelf". In *The New York Times*, available at http://www.nytimes.com/2005/07/17/books/review/17LEAVITT.html (last accessed August 2011).

Nehamas A. 2002. "Writer, Text, Work, Author". In Irwin W. (ed.) *The Death and Resurrection of the Author?*. Westport: Greenwood Press, 95-116.

White E. 1994. "Out of the Closet, on to the Bookshelf". In Bergman D. (ed.) *The Burning Library. Writings on Art, Politics and Sexuality, 1969-1993*. London: Picador, 275-283.

White E. 2004. "Writing Gay". In White E. *Arts and Letters*. San Francisco: Cleis Press, 3-20.

Williams R. 1977. *Marxism and Literature*. Oxford: Oxford University Press.

VALENTINA PONTOLILLO D'ELIA

Università di Milano

"A Madman Shakes a Dead Geranium": T.S. Eliot Updated for Our Times?

It is unclear and, of course, it is still a matter worth debating, whether today the works of T.S. Eliot should be considered upscale or, the other way round, out-of-fashion – if not six feet under.

T.S. Eliot's reputation has been in decline for more than a generation, mainly due to the fact that his beliefs are out of favour. He is still considered a disturbing and challenging author whose writings provide a remarkable variety of conceivable readings – all the more, after the public appearance of the volume entitled *The Inventions of the March Hare. Poems 1909-1917*, containing the poet's early poetic production. The amazing display of four-letter words in this collection of Eliot's *juvenilia* reveals, as perceived by to accredited scholars, the crude and malign personality of a poet who, willingly, basks in the aesthetic of ugliness. Is this champion of amorality – as he has been considered – the same author of *The Four Quartets* and of a bulk of well-known conservative writings? This essay intends to show that Eliot's early poems are not inconsistent with his remaining production, suggesting that what is missing in recent scholarship is a coherent presentation of the poet's early works.

Let us begin with a brief overview on Eliot's reception: it could be useful, especially by keeping in mind Frank Kermode's statement that criticism is the medium in which past work survives.

Today, confirmed Elioteans, amateurs as well as young graduate students know perfectly well that the best criticism on Eliot was written between the 30's and the 40's (Thormählen 1994). In that period – and up to the 60's – Eliot had an exceptional, established reputation both as a poet and as a critic. But after three decades of excellent standing and success, crowned by winning the Nobel Prize for Literature in 1948 and the honorary degree he received here in Rome in 1958 (Gordon 1998), Eliot fell from favour. He was accused of *élitism* and intolerance and the result was a sort of outspoken hatred that affected the poet and his works for more than 30 years. In the mid-90's, several academics complained about an alarming disinterest in Eliot (Thormählen 1994). Actually, the amount of criticism written on the leading man of Modernism was, at that point, still amazing. Unfortunately, for the most part, it was pure bashing criticism.[1] A general tone of vexation arises from the books and articles published between the early 90's and 2000's and Eliot's works (poetry, social and literary criticism) were rejected on the grounds of political correctness. As Craig Raine has recently observed, even critics who declared themselves strongly sympathetic to the poet, demonstrated a striking determination to convict the poet of racism and genderism (Raine 2006, 153-154). A convinced Eliot supporter like Christopher Ricks, for instance, assumes that the poet deserves the accuses of anti-Semitism, but he inconstantly extends a certain patient licence towards his verses. He's not sure, in the end, whether his beloved poet is a racist or not (Ricks 1988).

Such a strong aversion towards the author of *The Waste Land* was most probably the consequence of the eternal game of trends and fashions affecting even the most detached academic minds. Yet, along with the serious, practical difficulties in "obtaining access and permission to quote from his work" (Thormählen 1994, 216), this operated obviously in a detrimental way to the circulation of new critical perspectives on the American writer.

The publication of *Inventions of the March Hare* in 1996, as well as that which followed afterwards, invigorated the stale cliché of Eliot as a reactionary poet. *Inventions of the March Hare* contains about 39 hitherto unpublished poems plus many variants of well-known verses. The original manuscript was started in 1909, and it contained all of Eliot's work of that time, up to 1917. The poet himself deprecated it: he dismissed his early verses by stating that "the unpublished poems in the notebook were not worth publishing" (Ricks 1996, xii). In spite of this, the manuscript – disappeared for a while and finally re-discovered in 1968 – was published several years after the poet's death, thanks to his widow's zeal. A lively literary debate obviously sprung from the publication of this volume.

Scholars simply could not cope with verses such as those of a ballad provokingly entitled, for instance, *The Triumph of Bullshit*. Scabrous allusions to sex, to the body, to homosexuality gained the collection "the wrong amount of attention" (Ricks 1996, xvi). In short, *Inventions of the March Hare* became a new riddle for literary criticism: enraged critics disapproved of explicit usage of bad words and reproached Eliot for dragging up the shallowness and depravity of men and women in his numerous so-called 'urban poems'. Any attempt to map out a coherent account of Eliot's poetic development, from that moment on, proved to be, to say the least, daunting. From a purely literary point of view,

---

[1] The most interesting examples are the widely discussed in Julius 1995 and Carey 1992. The early 90s were a bracing moment at which a great deal of works on Eliot appeared. Among those mentioned – unpleasant and misleading readings – it can be useful to remember also Michael Hastings's fiction-play *Tom & Viv*. The play, in Lyndall Gordon's words, was "inaccurate" and it finally "undermined Eliot's reputation with the wider public". See Gordon (1998, 695).

Inventions of the March Hare appeared, in fact, to be inexplicably inconsistent with the remaining part of Eliot's *oeuvre*. The point is that critics, but for a few exceptions[2], failed to do justice to the complex experience offered by Eliot's 'new' verses and they also failed to see that, besides the unmistakable presence of several stylistic anticipations of his later work (Vendler 1996), *Inventions of the March Hare* shows a close relation with the American poet's masterpieces in its non-standard language as well as in its themes; among them the lack of communication between man and woman, the sense of despair, and so on.

In recent years, young scholars – tired of a long-lasting tradition of critical readings rooted in banality, have changed things around. Indifferent to the shifting winds of Eliot's misfortunes, as a matter of fact, a few critics decided not to dwell on prejudice (Raine 1996). In 2003, for instance, Prof. Loretta Johnson gave voice to a new generation of Eliot scholars, calling for a more objective approach to his poems (Johnson 2003). Johnson sustains that Eliot's *juvenilia* – still strikingly under-edited – deserve proper attention, and she sticks to the conviction that even his so called 'bawdy poems' are related to the author's lifelong interests: philosophy, metaphysical poetry, the classics and, as David Chinitz demonstrated convincingly, also jazz and popular ballads (1999/2000, 332). Johnson's effort was courageous: she provokingly put her finger at critics and at readers, accusing them of being prudish, while also recognizing a continuity between young Eliot's politically incorrect lines and his later production. A common principle, she claims, is to be found between the 'obscene' *Ballade pour la grosse Lulu* (July 1911) and, say, *A Cooking Egg*, dated 1919. Eliot's *Ballad* alludes to François Villon's *La Ballade de la Grosse Margot* (Taylor 2001, 139-147) – both for the title and for the profession of the two protagonists. *A Cooking Egg* – which has an epigraph from Villon's *Testament* – shares the Ballad's disillusioned tone and its low life subject matter, a kind of bogus erudition and a constant reference to down-to-earth elements: well-known trademarks in Eliot's works.

Two years later, in 2005, another American critic – Ashley Marshall – followed in Johnson's steps, attempting to give Eliot's prose works a new assessment (Marshall 2005). Admitting that over the course of his career, Eliot's criteria for literary judgement changed in a radical way, Marshall also acknowledges also that the poet's contradicting 'behaviour' can be of service in reconstructing a sense of cohesion for his work. In other words, a conflict-ridden position – a steadfast conflict-ridden position – represents a sort of looking-glass for a new evaluation of the American author's prose work and poetry. According to Marshall, sudden shifts in his approach to literature, or in the way he treats the poetic subject, do not invalidate the quality of the poet's work: earlier focus on certain issues indeed can be enriched or expanded by the comparison with

---

[2] See for example Gioia (1997) and Brooker Spears (1998).

new ideas. If not in his prose works, continuity and consistency are evident in his poetry, in technical dexterity, the use of ambiguity, the cold detachment and in the irony the poet exhibits even in his first drafts. In his inquiry, Marshall implicitly gets rid of reductive readings proposed by the scholars through the years, refusing at the same time to consider Eliot as an eccentric, divided personality: the authoritative poet, the strong academic personality *versus* the semi-Nazi misogynist, and again, the poet-critic who championed "poetry as poetry" *versus* the writer whose art serves ends beyond itself. In spite of this, the *motif* of Eliot's "eccentricity" (Bogen 1999) is not easily eradicated: the usual chronological fashion adopted in the interpretation of his writings in order to highlight possible progressive stages of his poetical development, has been superseded by a more up to date partition into topics. Thus we have critical inquiries on 'Eliot the Impersonal Poet', or 'Eliot the Personal Poet', 'The Social Critic', 'The Religious Poet' or 'The Philosopher', and so on, reiterating the idea that the American poet's *oeuvre* can be analyzed only if digested in small bits.

Needless to say, *Inventions of the March Hare* triggered other phenomena. Besides adding a new facet to the poet's supposed unpredictable personality – say 'Eliot the Bawdy Poet' – , his supporters welcomed his *juvenilia* as poems perfectly fitting our amoral times (Romer 1998) or launched themselves in wild flights of speculations concerning the possibility of retooling T.S. Eliot for the 21st century (Clausen 1998).

If the 21st century really needs a poet "able to speak to our [...] times" (Romer 1998, 22) either our times are helpless in dealing with poetry in general either T.S. Eliot's works – even his masterpieces – are not to be included in the contemporary literary canon because, perhaps, *The Waste Land* today is nothing more than a standard text carelessly studied at school. Both options are quite troublesome and depressing. Moreover, does Eliot really need to be up-dated for our times?

Making super-human efforts and standing at the antipodes from Eliot's refusal of what he properly called "the lemon squeezer school of criticism" (Eliot 1956, 112), some critics have gone even further, trying hard to introduce Eliot to the variegated academic trends of the last ten years. If the turn towards globalism has been one the most forceful movements in literary studies, this experience has expressed itself in the academy in a variety of ways: post-colonialism has superseded comparative literature programs; diasporic studies has further advanced the post-colonial inquiry; again, we talk about transatlantic studies, eco-criticism and gender studies and so on. What better way to give these new trends authority than by using T.S. Eliot's name? What better way to make Eliot relevant to these contemporary schools than proving the writer's works and his influence reached such places as Iceland, Israel or India? According to Hilene Flanzbaum, who ventured her guess at the beginning of 2009, Eliot's works can be even analyzed in terms of 'globalism' (Flanzbaum 2009). Obviously, as

Eliot recognized, "each generation brings to the contemplation of art its own categories of appreciation makes its own demand upon art, and has its own uses for art" (Eliot 1956,104). Anyway, up-dated, retooled, Eliot is thus introduced to the 21st century: and if the poet who invented our contemporary ears, sensibility and mind is now reconciled to the contemporary schools of criticism, he does not represent a real provocation any longer.

In conclusion – and this is a view I would like to launch in order to see what it becomes: today the weaknesses of Eliot criticism represent general deficiencies in modern Anglo-American criticism. As a matter of fact, there is nothing more clichéd than the desire for a fresh start and laconic labelling or strong apologies are not a great help to the ongoing scholarship.

References

Bogen D. 1999. "Literary Detritus". In *American Book Review*, May-June, 31.

Brooker Spears J. 1998. "Review of Inventions of the March Hare". In *South Atlantic Review* 63, 1, 98-102.

Carey J. 1992. *The Intellectuals and the Masses: Pride and Prejudice among the Literary Intelligentsia 1880-1939*. London: Faber and Faber.

Chinitz D. 1999/2000."T.S. Eliot's Blue Verses and Their Sources in the Folk Tradition". In *Journal of Modern Literature*, Winter, 23, 2, 332.

Clausen C. 1998. "Young Possum". In *The American Scholar*, 67, 1, 181-184.

Eliot T.S. 1956. "The Frontiers of Criticism". In T. S. Eliot *On Poetry and Poets*. London: Faber and Faber, 103-118.

Flanzbaum H. 2009. "The International Eliot". In *English Literature in Translation, 1880-1920*, 52, 4, 494-497.

Gioia D. 1997. "Eliot Uncovered – Review of *Inventions of the March Hare*". In *The Washington Times*, March 16th; available at http://www.danagioia.net/essays/eeliot.htm (last accessed August 2011).

Gordon L. 1998. *T.S. Eliot – An Imperfect Life*. London: Vintage.

Johnson L. 2003. "T.S. Eliot's Bawdy Verse: Lulu, Bolo and More Ties". In *Journal of Modern Literature* Fall, 27, 1/2, 14-25.

Julius A. 1995. *T.S. Eliot, Anti-Semitism, and Literary Form*. Cambridge: Cambridge University Press.

Marshall A. 2005."T.S. Eliot and the Limit of Criticism". In *The Modern Language Review*, July, 100, 3, 609-620.

Raine C. 1996. "T.S. Eliot is Innocent". In *The Observer*, September 8th, Review Section, 1.

Raine C. 2006. *T.S. Eliot*. Oxford: Oxford University Press.

Ricks C. 1988. *T.S. Eliot and Prejudice*. London: Faber and Faber.

Ricks C. (ed.) 1996. *The Inventions of the March Hare. Poems 1909-1917 by T.S. Eliot*. London: Faber and Faber.

Romer S. 1998. "The Hand of Laforgue's Shadow". In *The Times Literary Supplement*, 4957, 20-22.

Taylor J.H.M. 2001. *The Poetry of François Villon: Text and Context*. Cambridge: Cambridge University Press.

Thormählen M. (ed.) 1994. *T.S. Eliot at the Turn of the Century*. Lund: Lund University Press.

Vendler H. 1996. "Writhing, and Crawling and Leaping and Darting and Flattering and Stretching". In *London Review of Books*, 21, 8-9.

MARIANNA PUGLIESE

Università Roma Tre

Antigone in Liz Lochhead's *Thebans*:
the Structure, the Character and the Language

It used to be said that women had nothing to do with Greek plays that in fact were created by men for men. Yet, much of the contemporary rewriting of myth and of the recent staging of Greek drama has been dominated by female writers, as Marina Carr, Anne Carson and Liz Lochhead.

Acknowledged as one of Scotland's most significant dramatists, Liz Lochhead is considered the most popular woman writer on the contemporary Scottish literary panorama. And, in line with the revisionist stance of modern and postmodern literature, so frequently involved in rewriting the tradition, all her production is concerned with interpreting myth in a broad sense: her demythologising approach to reality initiate the prolific reworking of classical masterpieces, which start with *Tartuffe* (1986) and go on with *Dracula* (1989), *Medea* (2000), *Misery Guts* (2002) and *Thebans* (2004).

Antigone is one of the most explored myths in western literature, and Steiner's *Antigones*, providing us with unequalled exempla – here passed on for mere reasons of space – has examined the far-reaching legacy of this great classical myth.

The following paper will discuss how, within *Thebans*, Liz Lochhead manipulates the classical myth of Antigone in accordance with the developments of the Scottish political culture and, at the same time, to explore the new potentialities of theatre in Scots. Her main concern is to follow Graham McLaren's suggestion and extend the range of the Scots idiom, as well as contribute to the reborn Scottish theatre tradition.

In rewriting old works, stories and myths, Liz Lochhead encourages her audience to rethink the entire notion of representation and particularly the notion of representing women. Through a persistent metatextuality and thus through emphasis on representation itself, her plays increase the audience's attention on the ways in which meaning is produced and controlled. Her drama, in fact, indicates that no representation is ever a mimetic reflection of the real, but is always the product of choices and contexts ideologically determined and influenced.[1]

Lochhead's works suggest that through their representations, each subject, women included risks to be appropriated and controlled as an object. Therefore, in order to free women from such a constricted and impotent role, she uses historical and literary material to expose how history has long served the patriarchal order and its power.

She takes distance from the majority of earlier revisions written by male authors and manages to present clichés and stereotypes which need to be modified from within. In *Mythologies* Roland Barthes had already suggested that the best way to tackle myths is by elaborating them in a new, creative way and thus by inventing other stories out of the existing material (Barthes 1972, 135). In a similar perspective, if we consider myth as a system of power, in as much as it can impress on people's mind and determine their thoughts and behaviour, Judith Butler's theory according to which systems of power can only be subverted from within (Butler 1990, 270-282) might be a further help in understanding both the link between repetition and subversion in feminist rewriting, and the reasons why so many contemporary women writers have turned their attention to the genre of adaptation.

Moreover, following Deleuze's concept that repetition always involves a potential for difference (Deleuze 2001), retelling old stories can often determine cultural change. Manipulating the myth, in fact, which is generally an alternative storytelling, can be potentially subversive and tackling.

In her Introduction to Thebans Liz Lochhead says:

> There is not a single word in *Thebans* that isn't merely my response to, my version of, something in the texts, in one of the umpteen different translations I read. (I like unspeakable old Victorian ones with lots and lots of footnotes on the Greek, myself). [...] because I am not a translator but an adaptor I was free to use whatever versions of the myths seemed to fit our purposes, including Euripides un-hanged Jokasta, so there's nothing pure or Sophoclean about this particular telling of the tale, which links *Oedipus* to *Antigone* with bits of *The Phoenician Women* and fragments of *Seven against Thebes* (Lochhead 2004, Intro).

The link between past and present is certainly not at all accidental and the nexus between reinterpretation and the power of reinterpreting is deeply connected to the problem of identity and self-consciousness. Representation and performance are indeed thematically emphasised through the foreground of the play's narrative construction and through a superb use of language. *Thebans*

---

[1] Metatextuality hence acts as one of the several alienation devices evident in all her production, which aim at encouraging scepticism and any passive acceptance of reality as unique, fixed and unchangeable.

is in fact the result of an outstanding blending through which Liz Lochhead reduced five different tragedies in one single play. "We wanted to make it very much the story of one cursed family. And of the powerless suffering citizens under its rule" (Lochhead 2004, Intro), she declared.

The *Antigone* is in fact included as a branch of the Oedipus plays and presented as part of a Theban trilogy which actually never existed. The decision to mix the plays together gives resonance to the description of the myth and to the author's interaction with the mythical story-line. The effect is a stress on the narrative – especially in the Oedipus and Jokasta sequences – while little space is left for exploration of the subtleties of the poetry or for reflection on the moral and spiritual issues of responsibility and fate. In so doing, the play follows the recent tendency to select and adapt Greek material in a manner which emphasises narrative of the myths rather than their rewriting through the conventions and poetry of Greek drama.

Concerning her resolution to merge different plays into a single one, the author states:

> Please be assured that I haven't taken leave of my senses – I do know that *Oedipus The King, Oedipus at Colonus* and *Antigone*, the so called *Theban* trilogy, are by Sophocles, that *Seven against Thebes* is by Aeschylus and *The Phoenician Women* is by Euripides. [...] The conflation, and redirection, into a single play came about for the specific theatrical task in hand (*ibidem*).

The production was in fact widely publicised as Lochhead's following step after her successful adaptation of Euripides' *Medea*. In 2000, in fact, one of Scotland's leading theatre companies[2] won Lottery Funding to produce modern versions of Greek tragedies for a contemporary Scottish audience. The intent was to

> create lasting work that would impact on Scottish culture. [...] and so create plays that would transform great and ancient classical works into pieces that would speak not only directly to a Scottish audience but also of universal modern experience (G. McLaren in Lochhead 2000, Intro).

If truth be told, in Scotland there is no great tradition of the Classics, and with the so called Greek Project Graham McLaren wanted to create plays that would directly speak to the Scottish audience and impact on contemporary Scottish culture. The average Scot, even the average well-informed Scot, has often very little idea that there is any significant theatre produced in Scotland at all.

The National Theatre of Scotland, set up in 2004 and launched in 2006, ought therefore to be the best place where to fulfil the task and become the leading art form through which people living in Scotland better express and understand their lives. Of all the art forms, in fact, theatre is traditionally considered the

---

[2] Theatre Babel, founded in 1994 and directed by Graham McLaren.

one most closely associated with the ideas of nation and nationhood: it is in fact the public arena where people who live in the same place and usually speak the same language, can share experience and redefine identities.

Ancient drama rewritings – or translations as they have been largely defined – would therefore aim at wide spreading the main elements of the myths among Scots and, at the same time, contribute to creating a new drama tradition for Scotland as well as boosting a national political awareness. According to John Corbett: "In times when the process of national refashioning is at its most urgent", translations from other languages reveal to be particularly useful, as they "help fashion and refashion the self-image of Scotland" (Corbett 1999, 7), that is, form its own culture in relation to the culture of others.

Since Scottish identity has always been a matter of difference rather than of self-determination, the intent of enhancing national and cultural identity through confronting with the past and with the rest of the world has made the newly formed National Theatre of Scotland the best place to accomplish such premises and look for growth and improvement.

According to modern sociolinguistics, attitudes to languages and language varieties commonly reflect social and political processes at work (Downes 1984), and in a similar perspective Liz Lochhead's use of language – and of Scots in particular – can be seen as a response to the need for national political changes. The resurgence of the linguistic potential of Scots, which for many centuries had been dismissed and forgotten, moves along with the theatre renaissance that the Scottish scene has been undergoing since the 1970s. Being drama, in fact, a speech-based genre, it sets to be the finest means to explore and demonstrate the vitality of vernacular, and since language is the first expression of a nation's history and culture, the claim for Scots certainly becomes the major claim for Scottish identity.

Dialect translations in Scotland are indeed solutions to have people accept as natural the representation of foreign plays in such a range of non-standard medium. The dialect texts would in fact prove performable and theatrically effective to the Scottish spectators, and as a result be authentic and authoritative for their target audience.

Like *Medea*, *Thebans* is entirely based on the opposition between standard English and Scots-English. In *Thebans*, though, Lochhead's use of Scots is not too experimental, (as it used to be in *Tartuffe*, for instance) as she relies more on accent than on strong dialect expression. And, since style and registers switching are common in Scots dialects, her characters all incorporate stylistic shifts between accents and more or less standard options according to their social status, so that their linguistic behaviour changes with their class position. In Lowland Scotland, in fact, correlations between style, status and language, range from the use of a more prestigious standard English to "local, non-standard varieties, in which the choice of Scottish elements (and Scottish phonology and phonetics) [becomes] maximal" (Aitken 1984, 527).

Liz Lochhead's characters are generally differentiated by their varying commands of the standard and vernacular forms at their disposal and in such ways they modify their language habits according to the identities they want to convey. Such socio-linguistic hierarchy is however visibly conservative: the grammar and vocabulary of the lower classes are indeed less eloquent and refined than the ones adopted by the ruling ones. For instance, in the guard's recounting of the burial of Polyniekes and in the part Antigone had in it, Scots idiom takes over, vividly revealing all the effectiveness of ordinary language.

In employing Scots, it can be assumed that Liz Lochhead's main concern has been to look at Scotland through Scottish eyes: continuing a process started with the adaptation of Molière's *Tartuffe* and sustained with Euripides' *Medea*, she goes on giving importance and dignity to the sounds and rhythms of urban Scots as a cultural resistance to the dominance of English and to the Received Pronunciation in British theatre.

The iambic trimeter is abandoned and rhythm is adopted as a more natural and musical way to convey meaning: namely, it replaces punctuation as a means of establishing sense. Throughout the text, the sound and musicality of each word is physically celebrated: "Thebans born of the race that sprung up fighting/sprouting armed/awake/and angry/from the soil/when Cadmus killed the serpent/sowed the serpent's teeth" (Lochhead 2004, 54).

Some language is extremely naturalistic in order to shape the play with real thoughts and feelings and thus remind the audience that these mythic archetypes are nothing more than normal human beings. Sentences are in fact short and often disjointed, words are repeated to stress meaning and emphasize tragic irony. Some other language, instead, is poetic, rhythmic: and rhythm is nothing but pure poetry, written to be spoken loud.

In such a framework, Scots expressions can achieve higher resonance and hence surpass meaning alone, in as much as vernacular itself, being creative and effective in its striking solutions, intensifies the pathos. The combination and the opposition of Scots and English is thus exploited as more effective than Standard English alone: a bi-polar continuum throughout the text certainly adds an extra dimension to such a feeling of the spoken word. "I'm interested in voice", the author says, "whether it's in drama, whether it's in poetry, or whether it's in fiction" (Todd 1995).

Liz Lochhead extends oral forms towards the written registers of literature and often reduces the line extension, achieving in this way a more pungent and hard-hitting effect without ever losing the sense of the original. Her language, though poetic, is much more crude than we might expect of the play and, yet, it never mislays the grand political implications contained by the source.

Antigone is in fact shaped as a likely political figure – even though at times she is represented as a one dimensional figure, in love with death. Antigone is the equal of man, in both resolution and braveness. She dares to be the equal of man in as much as she challenges Kreon's will and enters the public life of the city making a political choice forbidden to her as a woman. All Athenian women, regardless of their socio-economic class, were in fact marginal members of the πόλις, since they had no role in its public and political life. Unfortunately, this is particularly true in Scotland, where women still suffer from the restrictions of a fundamentally patriarchal society, and are undergoing social and political changes at a very slow pace.

To Antigone, instead, nothing is impossible and this is additionally emphasised in the text through the use of italics in highlighting the word "impossible": "don't let the dead hear you say *impossible* and/hate you/it's *imperative*/I won't stop while I have/breath in me/or last scrap of strength to follow this through/until the end/danger and death are not dishonour"(Lochhead 2004, 62).

Being a woman, and a woman writer, which is as deep-felt as being connected to Scotland and its divided destiny, is described as a phenomenon upon which hegemonic features are linked to patriarchal and gender attributes, with no place for the subordinated and marginalized group of women. And as a consequence of such an hegemonic subordination, female Scottish writers have experienced a double exclusion – from the English and from the male-dominated Scottish discourse – that is both cultural and gender marginalization.

In a community that still in the 20th century is homophobic and racist,[3] the play indeed addresses a community that is in some way marginalized and, in so doing, perfectly fulfills the general intentions of the National Theatre of Scotland – and of Theatre Babel's project – since, dealing with a wide range of social and political issues like racism, sectarianism and the plight of asylum seekers, it is socially committed and politically engaged.

Finally, in spite of representing strong woman roles, like Antigone and Jokasta, *Thebans* fundamentally remains a play about human soul beyond gender. Black humour and cynical observations throughout the text actually serve to expose contemporary burning themes like politics, mother love and dysfunctional families. Stitching together plays by Sophocles and Euripides to tell the tragic story of the House of Laius, *Thebans* deals with fratricide, a living burial and, ultimately, civil war.

Without ever giving answers, but only presenting a reality that disturbs, Liz Lochhead poses questions and invites her audience to actively empathize with the *hi-story* told and the disconcerting characters presented.

---

[3] In this regard, it should be remembered that after the September 11 terrorist attacks there was a huge increase in racially motivated attacks in Glasgow (*Evening News*, March 3rd, 2003), and that Edinburgh, for instance, in 2003 has not formally given sanctuary to any asylum seeker (*The Scotsman*, March 1st, 2003).

It is hard to think of a time in human history when these plays wouldn't seem to be prescient and contemporary, but in our apocalyptic days as, in a great city at the heart of the most powerful empire in the world, towers were razed to the ground, as a new plague spread, as the people of Iraq waited for the overwhelming might of the enemy to be unleashed upon them, as the Palestinians saw that the Israelis would concede nothing to stop the fighting, as a ruler found himself locked into a scenario where he couldn't lose face, as we all waited for a war to begin which we were powerless to stop, it was hard not to feel that the Euripides who wrote Jokasta's great plea to her sons to step back from the brink was, uncannily, writing about and just for us, here, now (Lochhead 2004, Intro).

Liz Lochhead said that she was just starting working on *Thebans* when September 11 happened and since then, things do not seem to have changed that much.

References

Aitken A.J. 1984. *Scots and English in Scotland*. In Trudgill P. (ed.) *Language in the British Isles*. Cambridge: Cambridge University Press.

Barthes R. 1972. *Mythologies* (translated by Lavers A.). London: Jonathan Cape Ltd.

Butler J. 1990. *Performative Acts and Gender Constitution: An Essay in Phenomenology and Feminist Theory*. In Case S.-E. (eds.) *Performing Feminism: Feminist Critical Theory and Theatre*. Baltimore and London: The John Hopkins UP.

Corbett J. 1999. *Written in the Language of the Scottish Nation. A History of Literary Translation into Scots*. Clavendon: Multilingual Matters Ltd.

Deleuze G. 2001. *Difference and Repetition*. London and New York: Continuum:

Downes W. 1984. *Language and Society*. London: Fontana.

Lochhead L. 1986. *Tartuffe. A Translation into Scots from the Original by Molière*. Edinburgh: Polygon.

Lochhead L. 1989. *Mary Queen of Scots got her Head chopped off & Dracula*. London: Penguin.

Lochhead L. 2000. *Medea after Euripides*. London: Nick Hern Books.

Lochhead L. 2002, *Misery Guts,Aafter Molière*. London: Nick Hern Books.

Lochhead L. 2004. *Thebans, After Sophocles and Euripides*. London: Nick Hern Books.

Todd E.B. 1995. *Liz Lochhead*. In *Verse*, 8.3 and 9.1 (Winter/Spring 1991). Republished in Crawford R. *et al.* (eds.) *Talking Verse*. St. Andrews: Verse, 83-95.

ANNAMARIA SPORTELLI

Università di Bari Aldo Moro

"I Am Often Asked Whether there Can Be a Long Imagist or Vorticist Poem": Evolution or Involution of Epic in Modernist Poetics

There is a connection underlying the theoretical reflection of some schools of thought following each other at a distance – be it temporal, geographical or conceptual – in the course of the Twentieth century. This link unites various phases of study anything but unitary and homogeneous due to the specificity of each, where each is solicited by the same interrogation of the literary form which seems to contain all the others, the form of the long poem. Its resistance to the attribution of genre has made it the locus of negotiation for other genres. Its features, primary and secondary, were of use to avant-garde experimentation on literary form and its oscillations, in Tynjanov, for example. Derrida, in *De la grammatologie* (1967), decreed its end, identifying it with the "linearity" which is neither loss nor absence but the removal of multidimensional symbolic thought – and, with its end, he decreed also the end of the "book". New Historicism, on the other hand, with its attention to the materiality of the poetic form, laid new emphasis on Vico and his description of the origin of language as poetry which, emerged from "silent times" (Vico 1990), spreads into song in the "language to infinity" evoked by Foucault (1977) against the phantom of death. As will be seen, all borrow from the long poem the material to exemplify their theory, whilst at times it is the practice of that type of poetic writing which legitimizes their theoretical discourse.

In his essay on avant-garde and tradition, written in 1929, Tynjanov highlighted the insufficiency of any static definition for the identification of genre and also of the long poem, taken as its exemplification. He pointed out that all the revolutionary substance of Pushkin's "long poem", *Ruslàn and Ljudmilla* resided in the fact that it was a *"non-long poem"*, which criticism had perceived as a deviation from the system while it was "in fact a shift of the system" (Tynjanov 1968, 24, my translation). I feel that there is nothing casual about the fact that, exemplifying the phenomenon of oscillation and shift, Tynjanov should choose the long poem. Amongst its features, not fundamental but secondary, yet nevertheless necessary to make what is a "non-long poem" a long poem – i.e. the features necessary for the conservation of genre – he singles out extension:

> The notion of extension is substantially a notion based on the energy spent
> [...] we define "large form" that for whose construction we spend most
> energy. The calculation on large form is different from that we make on small
> form insofar as every detail, each stylistic tactic, depending on the extension
> of the construction, has a different function, possesses a different force and,
> on it, there leans a greater weight (Tynjanov 1968, 25, my translation).

Extension, therefore, is the perception and memory of the genre; on its
breadth the construction can shift with unlimited width. Due to this, not the
straight line of the evolution of the genre, but the broken line of its shift makes
every form deform itself, every work "eccentric", where construction does
not resolve itself in the material, does not correspond to it, but is connected
eccentrically to, and emerges from it. That which changes and is important
for the individuality of the genre is the principle of construction which makes
continually renewed use of its constitutive factors and materials. In short, it
is the secondary traits, those vague phenomena – multiform, fluctuating and
difficult to categorize – which act on the quintessential secondary factor, i.e.
extension, that as mentioned above conserves the memory of the 'genre' and
into which, dialectically, the deviations and errors, the transgression and the
difference insert themselves. Now, what Tynjanov seems to object to is that
which we could define "the primacy of the pure", insofar as the form in its
specific effectiveness, as energy that is, does not exist without material, or rather
without a certain quality by which it is considered 'noble' or 'degraded'.

Derrida's position in regard to the long poem, in truth the epic, has been
mentioned directly above. Nor is it irrelevant here that for the 'broken' line of
Tynjanov, which is vital for the survival of the form in a new form, Derrida
substitutes the minor shocks which little by little destroy the linear model, or
rather the model of the epic, not to reconstruct it in an alternative form, but
to deconstruct it into a "mythogram". Such a process of deconstruction aligns
its symbols in that multidimensionality "in which sense is not subject to
successiveness, to the order of logical time or the irreversible temporality of
sound" (Derrida 1967, 99). Derrida writes:

> The disquiet of philosophy, of science and of literature has been perceivable
> for more than a century. Their revolutions must be interpreted as shocks
> which little by little are destroying the linear model. By this we intend the
> *epic* model. That which is meditated on today cannot be written according
> to the line or the book, unless one imitates the action of teaching modern
> mathematics with an abacus (Derrida 1967, 102, my translation).

The 'archaic quality' of the epic as well as its incompatibility with the
modern, due to the disappearance in the modern age of the notion of poetry
as social encyclopaedia, find their origins in the removal of all that resisted
linearization.

The impossibility of the epic is one and the same with the affirmation of the long poem as the poetic aporia and historical form of the crisis in the Romantic age. Its incompleteness, or rather its statute as the Unfinished, testify to the poets' lack of faith in a form of writing unable to comprehend the universality to which they aspired, and to which the project of the *magnum opus* stood as witness. At the same time, in writing in *perpetual song*, they recuperated in part features that contradicted linearity, such as the possibility of internal transaction. By transaction is intended a biunivocal relation that rejects any closure: for example, Milton will be read as a precursor of the Romantics but also as a reader of himself where, for instance, he defines more than once *Paradise Lost*, first as "adventurous song", in book I (l. 13), then as "sacred song", in the third book (l. 28), "tragic song", in the sixth (l. 25) and "heroic song", in the ninth. And the Romantics will be read as readers of themselves and exegetes of Milton. In such a context, the long poem is a form capable of absorbing the differences as transactions rather than negations or incoherence. So that what Derrida defined as "the law of the law of literary genre" (Derrida 1980, 4), that is to say the law of contamination and impurity, temporarily closes the circle on questions of differences of theory and poetics.

Such fluidity and formal indefiniteness in Foucault animates the play of language which "to stop this death which would stop it" has only one power, "that of giving birth to its own image in a play of mirrors that has no limits" (Foucault 1977, 54). In the depths of the mirror one catches a glimpse of another language:

> And when, as a stranger among the Phaeacians, [Ulysses] hears in another's voice the tale, already a thousand years old, of his own history, it is as if he were listening to his own death: he covers his face and cries, in the gesture of a woman to whom the dead body of the hero is brought after a battle. Against this speech which announces his death and which arises from deep within the new *Odyssey* as from an older time, Ulysses must sing the song of his identity, and tell of his misfortunes to escape the fate presented to him by a language before language (Foucault 1977, 54).

Linearity is defeated by the murmur that takes up again, narrates itself and doubles itself without end according to "an uncanny process of amplification and thickening, in which our language is today lodged and hidden",[1] re-emerging in a fecund simultaneity in which poetry, as Shelley theorizes, finding

---

[1] The passage reads: "[…] from the day that man began to speak toward death and against it, in order to grasp and imprison it, something is born, a murmuring which repeats, recounts, and redoubles itself endlessly, which has undergone an uncanny process of amplification and thickening in which language itself is today lodged and hidden" (Foucault 1977, 55).

inspiration only in itself, becomes an infinite echo: "all high poetry is infinite; it is the first acorn which contained all oaks potentially" (Shelley 1972, 48).

Despite the fact that twentieth-century theoretical reflection, as seen, has reawakened interest at various levels in extended form, Poe's anathema against the long poem seems to have inscribed itself silently into the theoretical and terminological consciousness of critical practice. It would be worthwhile mentioning that when Poe decreed its end – "I hold that a long poem does not exist, I maintain that the phrase 'a long poem' is simply a flat contradiction in terms" (Poe 1969, 415) – he was referring in fact to epic works *par excellence*, such as the *Iliad* and *Paradise Lost*. The same term, *long poem*, was later used by A.C. Bradley in 1905 to describe Romantic long poems, a title which includes the ballad and pastoral, the "internalized romance", as Harold Bloom defined *The Prelude*, the fragments of *Christabel*, *Endymion* and no less *Alastor*, *Don Juan* and *Lamia* (Bradley 1965). However, Poe's veto on this form can be traced back to the European Romanticism from which Poe derived it, from the poetics of Coleridge in his principles of the systematization of criticism where he had theorised about the myth of lyrical brevity along with the impossibility of extended form, in Chapter XIV of his *Biographia Literaria*.[2] Yet it is precisely in the context of high Romanticism that one finds a discrepancy with regard to the subject (which reveals itself to be no more than a sign of a generational difference, or its confirmation) that is to say, a hiatus between Coleridge's rejection of the long poem and the variegated championing of the form on the part of the more radical wing of English Romanticism (Shelley, Keats and Byron). To the latter one must assimilate Blake in an approach which revisit concepts such as unity, extension, energy, intensity, contradiction and aporia.[3]

The other element to emerge from these correlations is that Poe's refutation of the theory of extended poetic form came to found his well-known narratological theory of the short story, due to the inverse symmetry by which they are related. The dialectics between poetry and prose underlies Poe's theorising, and was to influence later nineteenth-century literary movements (such as the Symbolists) and explored by both Thomas Stearns Eliot (1965) and Benedetto Croce (1950). It is worth remembering that Frank Kermode, with whom I had the occasion to discuss the subject, retains intact his abjuration of the long poem, as expressed in 1957 in his fundamental *Romantic Image*, in the chapter dedicated to Arthur Symons. Indeed, he suggested to me that I should return to Dryden to find a less

---

[2] "In short, whatever specific import we attach to the word, poetry, there will be found involved in it, as a necessary consequence, that a poem of any length neither can be, or ought to be, all poetry" (Coleridge 1983, II, 15).

[3] See for instance Keats's letter to B. Bailey (8 October 1817): "Besides a long Poem is a test of Invention which I take to be the Polar Star of Poetry [...] The same invention seems indeed of late years to have been forgotten as a Poetical excellence" (Keats 1958, I). See also Blake's essays "On Homer's Poetry" and "On Virgil", both written in 1820 (Blake 1893).

than lukewarm advocate of the form,[4] making reference to the *Preface to Sylvae* in which Dryden, discussing *Paradise Lost*, pointed to the existence, within the still admirable work, of flat passages, stylistic slumps amongst the sublime poetic apices which contributed to making the poem an imperfect poetic epic, uncertain both in its structuring and its final outcome.

To return to the 1957 text, it should be said that Kermode individuates in *The Symbolist Movement in Literature* (1899) by Symons the crucial work "out of which the important poets of the early twentieth century learnt the elements of French Symbolist poetic" (Kermode 1986, 107), as they assimilated from it "many of the varieties of modern obscurity" (*ibidem*, 116). This obscurity is a feature shared by modern criticism as well, still engaged in and debating the issues brought to light by symbolist aesthetics. Amongst these, he points up "the problem of the possibility of long poems [...] derived directly from Poe" (*ibidem*, 116), noting how Symons relates with agonized awareness to this particular question, which remains latent but fundamental for a poetics that rejects almost all the conditions which might be necessary for the survival of the long poem. Hence, extension can form an element of risk insofar as it provides the occasion for the surpassing of the point of perfection, which would lead to the irremediable destruction of the work; moreover, it can constitute fecund *humus* to the onset of "*cette maladie du style, qui arrive à détruire une oeuvre, primitivement belle*", as Kermode suggests (*ibidem*, 116) quoting from Balzac's *Le chef-d'oeuvre inconnu*, dated 1832. His interrogation involves also Ezra Pound and the writing of his *Cantos* which, begun in 1915, in 1969 reached a point of non-conclusion, taking fifty years to unfold, gather, and dissipate itself. At the time when he started working on the *Cantos*, there is evidence of his meditation on the form of the long poem, in terms of a possible answer to the question which he had been asking himself for some time and which others had asked of him: can an Imagist long poem exist?

> I am often asked whether can be a long imagistic or vorticist poem. The Japanese, who evolved the hokku, evolved also the Noh plays. In the best 'Noh' the whole play may consist of one image. I mean it is gathered about one image. its unity consists in one image, enforced by movements and music. I see nothing against a long vorticist poem (Pound 1970, 94).

His reply may be described as alternation of poetic systole and diastole. Whosoever has conceived the most contracted form, the most elliptical verbal image, will be in a position to create the form which from that image unfolds itself, from that point of energy generates itself, accompanied by movement and

---

[4] "Your list seems to contain the principle enemies of long poems. Others take a more moderate view, like Dryden, who thought long poems 'needed flats among their elevation'. Pound, I think, said something similar" (personal letter, April 24, 1999).

music. Kermode concedes that precisely with the aid of music the form of the long poem could be possible:

> With the aid of music (a fugue has structure but not discursive meaning) a long poem might be possible, whereas if it has to resort to continuous narrative or doctrine it becomes at best a series of short poems tediously bound together by prose (Kermode 1986, 118).

Kermode's words confirm that hybridization – of forms, genres and arts – constitutes a vital structuring principle of the long poem, regardless of its historical occurrences. As a karstic river, indifferent to purity, it collects what it happens to find on its course: echoes, fragments, as well as models from past poetry and structural devices from other arts, like music, which may provide the means to escape the materiality of the word.

References

Blake W. 1927. "On Homer's Poetry", "On Virgil" (c. 1820). In Blake W. *The Poems and Prophecies* (Plowman M. ed.). London-Toronto: J. M. Dent; New York: E. P. Dutton, 285-286.

Bradley A.C. 1965. "The Long Poem in the Age of Wordsworth" (1905). In *Oxford Lectures on Poetry*, with an Introduction by Ridley M.R. London: Macmillan.

Coleridge S.T. 1983. *Biographia Literaria* (1817), 2 Vols. In Engell J., Jackson Bate W. (eds.) *The Collected Works of Samuel Taylor Coleridge*, Vol. 7. Princeton: Princeton University Press.

Croce B. 1950. *Letture di poeti*. Bari: Laterza.

Derrida J. 1967. *De la grammatologie*. Paris: Les Editions de Minuit.

Derrida J. 1980. "The Law of Genre" (tr. Ronell A.). In *Critical Inquiry* 7 (Autumn), 55-81.

Eliot T.S. 1965. "From Poe to Valéry" (1949). In *To Criticize the Critics*. London: Faber & Faber, 27-42.

Foucault M. 1977. "Language to Infinity". [Tr. from "Le langage à l'infini" (1963), in *Tel Quel*, 15, 44-53]. In *Language, Counter-memory, Practice: Selected Essays and Interviews by Michel Foucault*. Ithaca-New York: Cornell University Press, 53-67.

Keats J. (Rollins H.E. ed.) 1958.*The Letters of John Keats, 1814-1821*, 2 Vols. Cambridge (Mass.): Harvard University Press.

Kermode F. 1986. *Romantic Image* (1957). London: ARK.

Poe E.A. 1969. "The Poetic Principle" (1850). In Mabbot T. O. *The Collected Works of E. A. Poe*, Vol. I. Cambridge (Mass.): Belknap Press of Harvard University Press.

Pound E. 1970. "Vorticism" (1914). In *Gaudier-Brzeska. A Memoir*. New York: New Directions.

Shelley P.B. 1972. *A Defence of Poetry* (1821). In Brett-Smith H.F.B. (ed.) *Peacock's Four Ages of Poetry, Shelley's Defence of Poetry, Browning's Essay on Shelley*. Oxford: Blackwell.

Tynjanov J. 1968. *Avanguardia e tradizione*. Introduzione di Sklovskij V. Bari: Dedalo Libri.

Vico G. 1990. *Principi di una scienza nuova intorno alla natura delle nazioni* (1725). In Battistini A. (ed.) *Opere*. Milano: Mondadori.

Part 2
CULTURAL STUDIES

Introduction

Underlying the many interests which have shaped the discussion in the 24th AIA conference culture sessions is a theorizing drive which is clearly visible in the 29 essays included in this second half of the volume. Each text, each cultural phenomenon – and in one case, an entire literary tradition in English – is brought to our attention in a way that illustrates a facet of the collective research being carried out in Italy on the complex world of English-speaking cultures.

We have chosen to open with the section on "Cultural Translation: New Theories and Practices", which includes four essays that ideally conflate the analytical tools of linguistic and cultural studies by positing translation as an act of transformation and transmission of a culture travelling across languages, genres and boundaries. The papers examine the various techniques and strategies enacted by translators who aim at fulfilling educational and political purposes by construing different types of readers, as in the case of DIANA BIANCHI's discussion of the 'Scottification' of classic English children's literature ("Taking on Little Miss Muffet: the 'Scottification' of Classic English Children's Literature"). ALESSANDRA RIZZO ("Cultural Translation and Migration: the Literary Cases of Jhumpa Lahiri and Leila Aboulela") explores instead translated identities and identities-in-translation within a multicultural Anglo-American context to explain the relation between migrancy, translation and culture; to this end, she sets forth a comparative analysis of the similar role played by cultural translation both in the novel *The Translator* (1999) by the Sudanese writer Leila Aboulela and in the collection of short stories, *The Interpreter of Maladies* (1999), by Jhumpa Lahiri, an author of Bengali Indian descent. Translation is also perceived as a complex act of metaphorical and intercultural migrancy across places, histories and languages, where self and other interact and constantly redefine themselves, as for example in IVONNE DEFANT's analysis of the Scottish writer Anne Donovan's novel *Being Emily* which is a 'translation' or re-writing of Emily Brontë's life and *Wuthering Heights* ("Translating Selfhood: *Being Emily* by Anne Donovan"). Finally, the idea that translation is heavily affected by different child cultures is examined by ROWENA

Coles ("How Does a Child Become a *Bambino*? Creating Child Constructions in Translation") through a comparative analysis of Sylvia Plath's *The It-doesn't-matter Suit* and its Italian translation *Il vestito color zafferano* by Bianca Pizzorno.

If we have decided to apply the title "Community and Nation: Hybrid Identities, Reinvented Traditions" to two different sections it is because we thought it was important to provide a common frame to the variety of responses generated by the challenging intercrossing of key notions in the field apparent in that overall title. Carla Locatelli ("English in Filippino Hands: Language, Literature, Culture") discusses the crucial issue of canon formation by rethinking the notions of nation, literature and national literature from a non-Eurocentric perspective. Drawing on the works of two major contemporary critics (G.H. Abad and C. Antoja Hidalgo) Locatelli demonstrates that Philippine Literature in English is firmly tied to the colonial enterprise, and might be viewed as a literature in translation. Furthermore, she highlights the strength of a definition of the *canon* as a social and cultural construct. Elisabetta Zurru ("The Moricjhāpi Massacre: *Re*-constructing Silenced Knowledge") takes into account in her paper the importance of giving alternative views of History in postcolonial fiction, in order to give voice to the people and the events which have been silenced or removed from official accounts furnished by (post)colonial regimes. Zurru focuses on Amitav Ghosh's *The Hungry Tide* (2004), a novel about the massacre of the refugees in Morichjhāpi island in 1978 by the Bengali government. She shows the fictional and narrative strategies through which Ghosh discloses the hidden truth behind the official narrations of this important historical event. In the first of two essays on contemporary Australian culture, Francesca Di Blasio ("We meet/Between the furnace and the flying/In the mouth of cohabitation: Australian Indigenous Culture in the 21st Century") shows how, in novels by female authors such as Liza Bellear and Patricia Sykes, among others, the theme of "a devastated millennial tradition" is emerging, where "aboriginal myths are related to the substance of the earth" and "the land is conceptualized as the result of the bodies of ancestral beings leaving their marks upon it in their continuous wanderings". In her highly theoretical essay, Katherine E. Russo ("When Was Modernism?: Towards an Interstitial Cartography of Australia's Modernity") explores instead the way in which two contemporary Australian poets, Lionel Fogarty and Kim Scott, in, respectively, *Miniung Woolah Binnung* and *Benang*, in dealing with exclusively Australian themes such as child removal and linguistic genocide, both explore an image of the past and re-assess its meaning while also re-appropriating modernist forms.

By bringing to bear on Pasolini's *Petrolio* a transnational/multinational perspective, Marina De Chiara ("Postcolonial Journeys for Tristram: Pier Paolo Pasolini's *Petrolio*") uncovers a complex journey through the Italian culture and society of the 1970s. She focuses on Pasolini's depiction of the character of the novel (named Tristam after L. Sterne's hero) as evoking Edward Said's postcolonial discomfort and argues that the old colonial practices have taken up new shapes which still repeat cultural and economic subalternization. In her paper, NICOLETTA BRAZZELLI ("Departures and Desertions in Abdulrazak Gurnah") raises a number of interesting issues by using the works of Abdulrazak Gurnah, a contemporary writer whose novels focus on the experience of those migrants who after the diaspora are fated to face cultural and racial prejudices in Great Britain. In particular, Brazzelli discusses Gurnah's latest novel, *Desertion* (2005), in which cultural and identity boundaries are overcome in order to redefine contemporary identity as a hybrid and multicultural entity. SABINA D'ALESSANDRO ("The Battle of Images in Ahdaf Soueif's *Mezzaterra*") examines Ahdaf Soueif's collection of essays *Mezzaterra*, where the strategies used by Western media to represent the Middle Eastern conflict are subtly analysed and subverted. In particular, Soueif shows that these representations are constantly defined by a number of colonial decontextualised stereotypes, which assert the difference between the Western Subject *vs.* the Oriental 'Other'. In this way, she unveils the political implications of such representations, which strengthen cultural and racial stereotypes. TANIA ZULLI ("Resurrecting Ayesha's Ghost: the New Challenges of Rider Haggard's Fiction") analyses the relationship between literary and cultural studies which emerge in R.L. Stevenson's and H. Rider Haggard's novels once we conceive them as 'contextualized' entities in their connection with the new epistemic modes of the time and their ideologically oriented approach. She suggests, in a postcolonial perspective, that the colonial and imperial past still influences the life of contemporary Britain.

The two essays included in the section titled "Travelling Concepts, Transforming Bodies" set the human body within a temporal frames that spans from the Renaissance to the challenges of the cyborg age. FRANCESCA GUIDOTTI's "A.C. Clarke's *A Meeting with Medusa*: the Cyborg Challenge to This World and the Next" traces in contemporary culture the evolution of the hybrid, enigmatic figure of the cyborg (cybernetic organism), a living creature whose organic body is modified by the incorporation of inorganic parts. In this story, she assigns a seminal role to Arthur C. Clarke's novel, *A Meeting with Medusa* (1971), in which the author created a more complex and ideologically contradictory cyborg, which in turn paved the way to a more euphoric post-modern version of the theme. In her paper "Body Language: Early Modern Medicine and the Female Body" IOLANDA PLESCIA addresses the debate surrounding the Caesarean section as a new *techne*, thus shedding light on rhetorical constructions and narrations of the female body in early modern scientific and literary texts, with particular reference to Posthumus Leonatus' "extraordinary birth" in Shakespeare's *Cymbeline*.

"Postcolonial London" opens with ADRIANO ELIA ("Catching up with the New Millennium: Hanif Kureishi's *Something to Tell You*"), who takes his cue from Hanif Kureishi's latest novel to review some of the most topical socio-political issues raised in post-7/7 fiction, related to the growth of radical Islam in the UK. ENZA

MARIA ESTER GENDUSA ("Deconstruction and Re-writing of Englishness and the European Cultural Identity in Bernardine Evaristo's Narrative") focuses instead on Bernardine Evaristo's narrative production in terms of genre (hystoriographic fiction), stylistic experimentation (verse-novel) and inspiring motifs. Finally, SIMONA CORSO ("The World Suddenly Feels Bipolar: Martin Amis after 9/11") uses Martin Amis' collection of essays and stories, *The Second Plane* (2008), to address a number of uncomfortable questions about our existence in a supposedly "bipolar world" – and about literature's right to prey upon collective tragedy.

SILVIA ANTOSA, in the first essay included in the "Representations of Antinormative Sexual Identities" section, "Queer Sexualities, Queer Spaces: Gender and Performance in Sarah Waters' *Tipping the Velvet*", presents a very interesting and sophisticated paper which discusses – from a performative perspective – the way in which sexual heteronormativity (and the heteronormative spaces it produces) is challenged by queer identities. NADIA SANTORO's contribution, "Herland and/or Queerland: Some Suggestions for Reading Virginia Woolf's *Orlando*", offers a reading of *Orlando* which intersects queer theory (especially following Judith Butler's suggestions) and sexual difference theory, by developing ideas elaborated by Italian feminism. FRANCESCA MAIOLI's paper, "Nomadic Subjects on Canvas: from Essentialism to Hybridity in Jenny Saville's Paintings", analyses Saville's production showing that, starting from a traditional essentialist feminism, her work develops into a challenging notion of the body as the site for an identity project based on hybridity, transition and transformation.

Addressed in the section "New Challenges for Drama Studies and Cultural Theory" one finds questions relating to the 'spectrality' of Shakespeare and late Renaissance drama, cross-cultural topics, and intermediality. MAURIZIO CALBI ("Performing in the Desert: Spectrality in Kristian Levring's *The King Is Alive*") focuses on two experimental movies, K. Levring's *The King is Alive* and M. Figgis's *Hotel*, and shows how in these movies the 're-mediation' of seventeenth-century literary materials works towards an alternative aesthetic, but in radically opposed ways: the 'desertification' of the experience in one case; the baroque cannibalization in the other. MARIACONCETTA COSTANTINI ("From Scottish Thane to Metal Revenant: Cross-Media Transpositions of *Macbeth*") discusses the effects of Shakespearean 'hauntology' in recent heavy metal adaptations of *Macbeth*. Albums like *Thane to the Throne* or *A Tragedy in Steel*, she argues, invite us to reflect on the cultural implications of Shakespeare's uncanny metamorphoses within an intersemiotic globalized culture. Drawing on the analysis of the various ways in which hyper-environments construe the presence of an interactive participant in multimodal communication, ARIANNA MAIORANI ("The Stage as a Multimodal Text: a Proposal for a New Perspective") investigates the stage as a multimodal interactive text. ARIANNA MARMO ("A Room of One's Own: Ophelia's Darkroom in Almereyda's *Hamlet 2000*") examines instead Almereyda's *Hamlet 2000*, a postmodern remake of the tragedy located in the 'rotten' city of New York, where Hamlet is an aspiring filmmaker and Ophelia is a photographer. She suggests that in this film Ophelia is portrayed like her photos: divided between 'what is not here' and 'what has actually been'.

The field included in "Visual and Media Studies" attracted a plurality of interests and approaches. SERENA GUARRACINO ("William Kentridge's Opera Stagings: Trans-coding the Western Musical Canon") offers a reading of opera stagings by visual artist William Kentridge, in order to show how the South African video-maker has trans-coded the Western musical language into contemporary visual arts – thus trans-coding the ambivalent place of music at the core of Western Orientalist imagery in a postcolonial narrative of hegemony and subalternity. MARIA CRISTINA CONSIGLIO ("Wiseguys Don't Work on Mother's Day: Italian-Americans on the Screen") explores instead the relationship between the stereotype of Italian-Americans and the language used in some movies, starting from the hypothesis that the Italian-American language, as it has been represented on the screen, can be seen as a sort of anti-language connected with crime and not merely as a neutral sociolect. IRENE RANZATO ("Manipulating the Classics: Film Dubbing as an Extreme Form of Rewriting"), drawing examples from three well-known films – Joseph Mankiewicz's *Suddenly Last Summer*, Ang Lee's adaptation of Jane Austen's *Sense and Sensibility*, and Baz Luhrmann's (and Tonino Accolla's) adaptation of *Romeo and Juliet* – demonstrates how rewriting through dubbing in Italy has never stood in awe of the classics, and has always privileged the target audience's presumed 'horizon of expectations'. EMANUELE MONEGATO ("Photographing 7/7 Dilemmas: *The Day After* by Johannes Hepp and *People's Cinema*") analyses German photographer Johannes Hepp's "London July 07. 2005 England", starting from the consideration that a division could be drawn between visual representations produced while the terrorist attack takes place and in its immediate aftermath, and/or representations produced when the initial emotional reaction has been revised and elaborated. Finally, C. BRUNA MANCINI ("Internet in a Cup, or a Cup of Internet: the Coffee-house Goes Online") suggests a continuity between the role coffee shops had in London in the early eighteenth-century and today's Internet cafés. Particular attention is devoted, in the essay, to the experience of Starbucks and its aim to turn "Ordinary into Extraordinary".

Richard Ambrosini
(Università Roma Tre)

Alessandra Contenti
(Università Roma Tre)

Daniela Corona
(Università di Palermo)

Section 1
Cultural Translation: New Theories and Practices

DIANA BIANCHI

Università di Perugia

Taking on Little Miss Muffet: the 'Scottification' of Classic English Children's Literature

1. Introduction

In her study about the use of Scots language in 19th century fiction Emma Letley reports of how James Henderson, editor of *Young Folks*, warned R. L. Stevenson against using broad Scots in his forthcoming novel *Kidnapped*, fearing that this would put off the young readers of the magazine on which the novel was going to be serialised (Letley 1988, 274). Obviously Stevenson ignored Henderson's advice and went ahead with his project regardless, going against what was at the time the widespread 'rule' of using English and avoiding 'dialect' forms in children's literature (*ibidem*, 261). His rebellion however did not attract any followers since *Kidnapped* remained for a long time the only novel for young readers with a substantial use of dialect (*ibidem*, 263).

Scots continued to be censored both within children's literature and educational contexts and it is only recently, on the wave of a renaissance of Scottish language and literature, that this state of things has changed. Institutions are now promoting the language, including it in the curriculum of Scottish schools while a variety of projects have started with the aim of improving literacy in Scots among young people.[1] Amongst the agencies and individuals engaged in such initiatives, a very active role has been played by the small publishing house Itchy Coo, founded in 2001 by Scottish writers James Robertson and Matthew Fitt and supported by the Scottish Arts Council. Created with the specific purpose of providing materials of different kinds in Scots, from factual to fictional, Itchy Coo has published, in addition to original texts for different age groups, a number of translations into Scots of classics of English children's literature. The latter are particularly interesting, both in

---

[1] See the Scottish Government's recent document about the study of the Scots language, available on line at http://www.scotland.gov.uk/News/Releases/2009/01/27102433 (last accessed August 2011).

terms of their nature and function. They are obviously not typical translations which are generally produced to fulfil a need for communication from a source language that the recipient cannot understand. It is not even clear whether they can be defined as "intralingual translations" as one may be tempted to do[2] following Jacobson's classic grid (2004). Translating from dialect, (or into dialect we may add), has not been contemplated within traditional translation theory as Munday has recently pointed out (2009, 6). Perhaps, given the troubled history between English and Scots, we may consider them as a case of 'cultural translation', a term that has been increasingly used in recent years to account for types of translation originating in a context of asymmetrical cultural and political power, typically in postcolonial contexts (Bollettieri Bosinelli and Di Giovanni, 2009, 26-38). More importantly, such a definition allows us to connect this production to recent Scottish literature which has been characterised by a strong impulse to question and engage with past representations of Scotland and their relationship with the dominant English culture. In particular we ask whether these texts for children have contributed to such a debate, since translation is dialogic by definition and invites cultural confrontation. In the following analysis we have tried to clarify these issues by focusing on what may be considered the two key texts of this corpus of translations, the Scots versions of *The Twits* by Roald Dahl (1980) and *Winnie the Pooh*, by A. A. Milne (1926-2004). As we will see the analysis of the adaptations and changes made by the translators will enable us to conclude that such texts also engage with the history of the relationship between England and Scotland, questioning stereotypical concepts of Englishness and Scottishness and inviting the potential readers to confront such issues.

2. Dual readership and children's literature in dialect

Before starting our analysis, it is important to make some general observations about the readership of these texts and children's literature in dialect. From the publisher's website statements it is clear that, while targeting a young audience, adults are addressed as well, albeit in a less direct way and with a 'tongue-in cheek' attitude, as for example when the books are described in Scots as: "braw books for bairns o aw ages", i.e. "beautiful books for children of all ages" (http://www.itchy-coo.com/). This reference to a dual readership could be regarded as superfluous. Children's literature is by definition a type of literature where adults are substantially involved, not only as the obvious

---

[2] Scots is considered by some as a dialect of English (see Jones 2002) so these translations could be seen as taking place within two varieties – one standard and one not – of the same language.

producers and controllers of the texts but sometimes even as textual constructs within the books themselves, when there are allusions and ideas clearly directed to expert readers (Wall 1991). In the case of texts for children written in a non-standard language, the presence of an adult appears almost inevitable. In fact, far from being simpler – as is sometimes imagined – literature written in dialect is a sophisticated exercise that challenges literary conventions, with implications that are more likely to be understood and appreciated by experienced or older readers. This means that children's literature written in dialect intensifies its dual readership as it is very likely that a child will require the help of an adult to decode the graphic symbols and match the writing with the sounds of oral Scots.

3. English-Scots translations as a case of "cultural reversal"

The dual readership of these texts written in dialect becomes particularly important when we consider it in the light of the English-Scots translations. As we have previously discussed, it is their cultural rather the linguistic aspect that comes to the fore pointing towards the history of the relationship between the two nations, something that adult readers are more likely to be aware of rather than children. In particular, it is worth noting that within British culture the relationship between English and Scots has often been articulated in translational terms, for example through the representation of Scots as an 'incomprehensible language', an 'alien idiom' that had to be decoded and 'translated', particularly in comedic contexts (Bianchi 2008, 46-47). This transformation of Scots into a 'foreign language' has been symbolically represented by William MacIlvanney in *Docherty* where a pupil is forced by the schoolmaster to repeat in English what he has just said in Scots:

'[...] what's wrong with your face, Docherty?'
'Skint ma nose, sur.'
'How?'
'Ah fell an' bumped me heid in the sheuch, sur.'
'I beg your pardon?'
In the pause Conn understands the nature of the choice, tremblingly, compulsively, makes it.
'Ah fell and bumped ma heid in the sheuch, sur.'
The blow is instant. His ear seems to enlarge, is muffed in numbness...
'That, Docherty, is impertinence. You will translate, please,
into the mother-tongue.'[...]
'I bumped my head sir.' (MacIlvanney, quoted in Craig 1999, 77).

Given this past history it is clear then that these English-Scots translations effectively reverse the direction of translation activity between the two languages, positioning English as the 'foreign language' that needs to be decoded and translated. Borrowing the critical terms used by Michael Cronin in his discussion of English-Irish translations (1996, 185-188) we would like to define these English-Scots translations as "an act of cultural reversal" (*ibidem*, 186), aimed at redressing a past where Scotland was the 'Other' and Scots the exotic language that was at best the object of ridicule and at worst banned within 'civilised society'. In the same way we wonder whether these translations could be seen as "an act of imagination and appropriation" (Rosenstock, quoted in Cronin 1996, 188) and have a "liberatory potential" (*ibidem*) and, if so, how this liberation has been articulated within the translated texts.

4. The Twits in Scots

Published in 2006 as *The Eejits* and translated by Matthew Fitt, *The Twits* by Roald Dahl was apparently chosen because of its suitability to be translated into Scots (Lumsden 2006). The story of Mr and Mrs Twit, described as two revolting people who are dirty, ugly, cruel to animals and children adapts well to a language full of concrete and down-to-earth words, grotesque imagery, and, as Fitt says, a tradition of "verbal attack" (*ibidem*). The images are rendered more vivid through a range of strategies, going from localization to the exploitation of Scots words for sound effects. The register is rendered more familiar as slang words are sometimes chosen instead of more bland alternatives. So, for example, colloquial terms such as "coupon" and "cludgie" (toilet) (TT, p. 1)[3] are chosen to translate "face" and "bathroom" (ST, p. 9). Cultural references such as the name of dishes "beef-stew" and "ice cream" (ST, p. 12) are adapted into typical Scottish dishes such as "potted-heid" and "cream crowdie" (TT, p. 4). The phonological properties of Scots are exploited to create rhythms and rhymes where there were none in the original, as in "[...] but the hairy man cannot do that" (ST, p. 11) rendered as "[...] but the hairy-bairdie mannie cannae" (TT, p. 3). The overall effect is that of heightening the comic quality of the text and ultimately its general appeal. The translation also changes the relationship between narrator and narratee, replacing many impersonal constructions with personal ones, which has the effect of reducing the distance between narrator and reader obtaining a more intimate register. See for example in "*What* a lot of hairy-faced men **there are**[4] around nowadays" (ST, p. 9), rendered as "*Whit* a clossach o hairy-bairdie men **ye see** gaun aboot nooadays" (TT, p. 1) or "But **in**

---

[3] We will use the abbreviations TT (Target Text) and ST (Source Text) followed by the page number of the editions we used for our analysis.

[4] Here and in other extracts the words in bold indicate my emphasis.

truth he was neither of these things" (ST, p. 10) rendered as "But **tae tell ye the truth** he wis nane o thae things" (TT, p. 2).

5. Winnie-the-Pooh in Scots

The Scots version of *Winnie the Pooh*, translated by James Robertson, appeared in 2008 and attracted a certain degree of attention in both English and Scots newspapers. Unlike *The Twits*, *Winnie-the-Pooh* was perceived more of a challenge by the translator, particularly as it was seen as "quintessentially southern English" (Robertson, quoted in Wade, 2009). This translation shows a number of inspired changes, for example the character of the fearful and timid Piglet rendered as Wee Grumphie (pig in Scots) which also exploits the onomatopoeic characteristics of the word. However, the adaptations are much fewer than in *The Eejits* and the text tends to remain quite close to the original syntactically and lexically. This was perhaps due to the different translator or, alternatively, the higher status of the text as a classic of children's literature may have determined a more respectful strategy. An area where the translation presents a higher degree of adaptation, is, perhaps understandably, that of the interjections which, being culture specific, have to be adapted. The rendering of these maintains the 'stereotypical' quality of the original and turns its 'Englishness' into clichéd Scots interjections, sometimes even heightening the stereotypical aspects. So "Oh" and "Ah" are turned into the well-known Scottish "Och" and "Ach"; while the slightly odd "Oh help *and* bother" (ST, p. 24) is rendered as the string "Och, jings, crivvens and help ma boab" (TT, p. 25) which intensify the stereotypical quality of this representation of Scottishness, distancing the story from the reader. A similar effect is obtained through a revealing change that appears at the very beginning of the narration: the Scots version of *Winnie the Pooh* starts with a deictic shift where the proximal " Here is Edward Bear" (ST, p. 1) of the English version is replaced by a distal pronoun "Yon's Edward Bear" (TT, p. 1) (That is Edward Bear), projecting the story that follows away from the reader.

6. Distancing Englishness, embracing Scottishness

Interestingly, this distancing strategy can be found in two other texts that also have strong connotations of Englishness: the well-known nursery rhymes: *Little Miss Muffet* and *Humpty Dumpty*. These were published in 2003 in the form of retellings in Scots in *King o the Midden*, a collection of original poems presented as an "hilarious collection of weird, revolting and downright daft poems" in Scots intended to capture "life in Scotland as it is today" (Fitt and

Robertson 2003, cover blurb). In these two versions, by Glasgow storyteller Margaret Tollick, the invisible, omniscient speaker of the originals is replaced by a mocking, surly voice, that comments and criticises, disrupting the crystallized images and the fairy tale quality of the traditional poems. The centre-stage position of the speaker in both *Little Miss Muffet* and *Humpty Dumpty*[5] shifts through the use of the deictic "yon" and "there" and it is the voice of the margin that we are listening to, aggressive and sarcastic:

Little Miss Muffet

See yon Miss Muffet
That sat on a tuffet
Feart o an ettercap?
Weel, Andra an me,
We baith agree
She seems a richt wee sap!

Humpty Dumpty

Humpty Dumpty sat on a waw.
Of coorse he should niver hae been **there** at aw!
If he'd heeded his mither,
cam doon when she wanted,
He widnae hae gotten his heid sae sair dunted (Tollick 2003, 9).

As a conclusive remark to this analysis it is clear that while both texts are remarkable translations and very enjoyable, they construe a different relationship with their readership. The translation of Roald Dahl's novel invites the reader to get closer to the story, to laugh with the narrator at the grotesque and vicious pranks that the Twits play on each other. At the same time it is a laughter with a long echo, that reaches into the past when Scottish people were represented as dirty and uncivilized people or the Highlanders described as ogres, child-eating savages.[6] *The Eejits* embraces these old stereotypes and in so doing it exorcises them. On the contrary, the translation of Milne's classic (2008) seems to invite its readership to look at the story from a distance, to critically

---

[5] Here are the original poems: "Little Miss Muffet, sat on a tuffet, eating her curd and whey, along came a spider, and sat down beside her, and frightened Miss Muffet away" and "Humpty Dumpty sat on a wall, Humpty Dumpty had a great fall, all the king's horses and all the king's men, could not put Humpty together again".

[6] See for example the very negative descriptions of Glasgow inhabitants in Edwin Muir's *Scottish Journey* (1979). The myth that Highlanders ate children was apparently widespread in the 18th century, and particularly associated with the fear caused by the Jacobite rebellions of 1745 and 1746 (see, for example, the reference in Chapter XVII of Harriet Martineau's work *The Billow and the Rock*, 1847).

enjoy the adventures of the characters in the imaginary land of One Hundred Acre, as fictional as certain concepts of Englishness and Scottishness.

7. Conclusion

This paper has focused on the analysis of recent translations from English into Scots of classic texts of English children's literature with the aim of getting insights into their nature and function. As we have seen, far from being 'innocent', i.e. detached from life and history, as children's literature is often perceived, these hybrid texts go beyond their intended objective of improving the readership's mastery of Scots. Their educational function obviously goes further and connects with the wider debate that has been going on in Scottish culture about definitions and representations of Scottishness. Through their strategies of appropriation or estrangement they engage with such notions and function as a critique of stereotypical representations of identity. Herein resides their "liberatory potential".

References

Bianchi D. 2008. "Translating Tough Talk. The Dubbing of Glaswegian Speaking Characters into Italian". In Helin I. (ed.) *Dialect for all Seasons*. Münster: Nodus Publikationen, 45-54.

Bollettieri Bosinelli R.M., Di Giovanni E. (eds.) 2009. *Oltre l'Occidente*. Milano: Bompiani.

Craig C. 1999. *The Modern Scottish Novel*. Edinburgh: Edinburgh University Press.

Cronin M. 1996. *Translating Ireland*. Cork: Cork University Press.

Dahl R. 1980. *The Twits*. London: Puffin Books.

Dhal R. 2006. *The Eejits* (tr. by Matthew Fitt). Edinburgh: Itchy Coo.

Fitt M., Robertson J. (eds.) 2003. *King o the Midden*. Edinburgh: Itchy Coo.

Jacobson R. 2004 (originally published in 1959). "On Linguistic Aspects of Translation". In Venuti L. (ed.) *The Translation Studies Reader*. London (NY): Routledge, 138-143.

Jones C. 2002. *The English Language in Scotland*. East Linton: Tuckwell Press.

Letley E. 1988. *From Galt to Douglas Brown. Nineteenth-Century Fiction and Scots Language*. Edinburgh: Scottish Academic Press.

Lumsden R. 2006. "Roddy Lumsden Interviews Matthew Fitt". September 15th, available at http://www.booksfromscotland.com/News/Roddy-Lumsdens-Blog/150906-Matthew-Fitt (last accessed August 2011).

Martineau H. 1847. *The Billow and the Rock*. Available at http://www.archive.org/details/H_Martineau_The_Billow_and_the_Rock (last accessed August 2011).

Milne A.A. 1926-2004. *Winnie-the-Pooh*. London: Egmont.

Milne A.A. 2008. *Winnie-the-Pooh in Scots* (tr. by Robertson J.). Edinburgh: Itchy Coo.

Muir E. 1979 (originally published in 1935). *Scottish Journey*. Edinburgh and London: Mainstream Publishing.

Munday J. (ed.) 2009. *The Routledge Companion to Translation Studies*. London (NY): Routledge.

Tollick M. 2003. "Humpty Dumpty" and "Little Miss Muffet". In Fitt M., Robertson J. (eds.) *King o the Midden*. Edinburgh: Itchy Coo.

Wade M. 2009. "James Robertson: Why I Made Pooh Bear a Scot", *Times Online*, March 27th, available at http://entertainment.timesonline.co.uk/tol/arts_and_entertainment/books/children/article5986628.ece (last accessed August 2011).

Wall B. 1991. *The Narrator's Voice. The Dilemma of Children's Fiction*. Basingstoke: Macmillan.

ALESSANDRA RIZZO

Università di Palermo

Cultural Translation and Migration:
the Literary Cases of Jhumpa Lahiri and Leila Aboulela

1. Introduction

Homi Bhabha comments that if "the act of cultural translation [...] denies the essentialism of a prior given originary culture, then we see that all forms of culture are continually in a process of hybridity" (1990, 211). According to Bhabha, hybridity represents itself "the 'third space' which enables other positions to emerge" (*ibidem*). This thought may be used to describe the mechanism of cultural translation (its non-textual and non-linguistic function) as an instrument that gives voice to hybrid subjects in adopted places. Hybridity itself reflects the image of immigrant people, those who epitomize the postcolonial, "postmodern, post-industrial condition, a sort of epiphenomenon and heightened version of the consequences of postmodernity" (Kràl 2009, 2).

By also borrowing Jhumpa Lahiri's idea according to which all literature involving travel is a form of translation and all immigrant characters are "translators in so far as they must make sense of the foreign to survive" (2002, 119), this paper, which consists of a theoretical and practical section, will focus upon the role of immigrant women writers as cultural translators of their native roots. It is against the scenario of such insights into the concept of cultural translation that a reading of Leila Aboulela's *The Translator* (1999) and Jhumpa Lahiri's short-story collection, *Interpreter of Maladies* (1999), will present the two authors as constantly engaged in the translation of their culture into their literary discourse. Whereas Aboulela does not permit any form of assimilation into the host culture, imposing her own in the foreign country, Lahiri finds a compromise between native and non-native cultural roots. In their works, Aboulela, an Egyptian-Sudanese writer, and Lahiri, an American author of Bengali Indian origins, play with the linguistic concept of translating and interpreting and make use of cultural translation as a form of auto-translation. Essential to each work are the Muslim and the Indian immigrant experiences that function differently in multicultural and cosmopolitan Britain and America, both seen as the sites of a conflicting and problematic relationship between practices of resistance and assimilation.

2. Theoretical section

Boris Buden, in a very recent article, defines *cultural translation* as a "postmodern concept" (2006) and suggests that one possible comprehension of such a phrase might be given "in service of both contradictory paradigms of postmodern theory and postmodern political visions: multiculturalism and deconstruction" (*ibidem*). In his opinion, "multiculturalism challenges the very idea of universality, for it sees every universal concept as culturally relative", which implies that "there is no universal culture, but a plurality of different cultures", whereas deconstruction "challenges [...] the idea that every identity has an origin in some sort of a pregiven essence" (*ibidem*). In these terms, translation acquires a social and political role, transcending its purely linguistic function and becoming significant within a cultural and political framework. Translation is thus transformed into a process of negotiation between two cultures, a concept that substitutes John Catford's idea of translation as a linguistic act of transaction from one language into another.

Language and culture were already seen as constitutive and fundamental elements both in literature and translation before 1990. Since 1999, translation has represented a vital component in immigrant and postcolonial writing, where it favours the creative potentialities of cultures in terms of difference. The need to think about cultures in terms of difference is central to Bhabha's metaphorical use of cultural translation, which represents the process and condition of the immigrant experience itself. Migration produces hybridism, for it is "the act of living on border-lines" (Bhabha 1994, 226). The Indian critic Harish Trivedi contrasts the extremely widespread use of cultural translation by remarking that it must not be confused with the application of the translation of languages and cultures (Trivedi 2005). This would be an abuse, falsifying what real translation actually means, and would produce mono-lingual and mono-cultural universes (*ibidem*). In short, cultural translation is not that technique which might be used to effectively subjugate one source language and culture at the hands of another target language and culture: which is to say, to find "target items which may in some way be considered to be culturally 'equivalent' to the ST items they are translating" (quoted in Shuttleworth and Cowie 1997, 35). On the contrary, the metaphorical use of cultural translation is simply the product of human migration, which finds its best expression within the contexts of postcolonialism and postmodernism and which fulfils various roles in immigrant writing.

Ruvani Ranasinha, Maria Rosa Bollettieri Bosinelli and Elena Di Giovanni have recently discussed cultural translation as the instrument through which marginalised or unheard identities attempt to express their culture and language in alien and indifferent worlds. As Bollettieri and Di Giovanni remark in the introductory essay to their volume, cultural translation is "an operation which goes through the linguistic transposition" (Di Giovanni and Bollettieri Bosinelli 2009, 30; my translation) but which, as Eva Hung states, tries to maintain "cultural specificity" (*ibidem*). If Hung underlines that cultural translation strengthens the identity of the Other in a host country, Lahiri describes translation as a form of immigrant writing through which immigrant writers inscribe their culture within the global literary system and criteria of the target culture (Lahiri 2002). Ranasinha's work also demonstrates how cultural translation concerns particularly a mechanism giving voice to "cultural difference and the experiences of diversity that have been endured" (2007, 5).

In short, cultural translation, to use Iain Chambers's words, can be described as "a continual fabulation, an invention" (1994, 25), a re-negotiation in which "cultures and languages are not mixed, they do not blend, but are accommodated in different capacities" (Kràl 2009, 136).

3. Practical section

Leila Aboulela was born in Khartoum in 1964. In Britain, where she began her postgraduate studies and felt free to express her religious faith, she attempted to affirm the basic tenets of her Islam by making the Muslim faith familiar to the target reader through her literary writing. She lives between Abu Dhabi and Aberdeen.

Her novel *The Translator* involves a strategic mechanism of translation both in a linguistic and metaphorical sense. In a linguistic sense, Sammar, the protagonist, must translate from Arabic into English, as she works as a translator in the Department of an academic Middle-Eastern expert, Rae Isles. She also translates within the English language, as she tries to find a "kind of English appropriate for depicting the multiple cultures" (Cooper 2006, 323) which she has to cope with in Scotland. Sammar is required to translate form Arabic into English, as Rae needs a translator to read the Orient. The Arabic words she translates are not assimilated within the Orientalist discourse, so that her cultural translations demonstrate how an African woman can reinforce the validity of her Islam in a foreign country. *The Translator* is thus a literary work which testifies to the possibility of making cultural translation a tool for domesticating the host country.

The narrative passages in which the use of cultural translation clearly emerges pertain to both Sammar's attempt to be part of British society (by transferring her Islam to Britain) and her need to convert Rae to Islam. Sammar's only possibility of survival is effectively to make a translation "between her worlds in Africa and in Britain, her English and her Arabic, her Muslim sensibility in a Christian world" (*ibidem*, 326). Sammar seeks a way "to familiarize and domesticate the buildings, the buses and the citizens into the concrete daily realities of her life in her new country" (*ibidem*). She wants to believe Britain has become her home:

> Outside, Sammar stepped into a hallucination in which the world had swung around. Home had come here. [...] She saw the sky cloudless with too many stars, imagined the night warm, warmer than indoors. She smelled dust and heard the barking of stray dogs among the street's rubble and pot-holes. A bicycle bell tinkled, frog croaked, the *muezzin* coughed into the microphone and began the *azan* for the *Isha* prayer. But this was Scotland (Aboulela 1999, 19).

In this process of cultural translation, where Sammar exploits the language of the five senses, she transposes the warm days in Khartoum to Scotland. Before leaving Aberdeen to go back to Khartoum, when Rae reveals to Sammar his unwillingness to convert to Islam, she misinterprets his words and her English gets lost. In Khartoum her ability to translate and speak English again is acquired when Rae converts to Islam and asks her to marry him. Sammar will be once again a competent user of the English language, something she will never stop adapting to her requirements as a postcolonial immigrant woman. Sammar also behaves as a cultural translator when she tries to transfer Eastern food to English culture: "[...] *Habbahan*. Without it, the soup would not taste right, would not be complete. At last, she found the *habbahan*. It existed, it had a name: whole green cardamom" (*ibidem*, 86). The strangeness of Sammar's soup becomes familiar in the host country, as the ingredients are "purchased in a Scottish supermarket" (Cooper 2006, 340) and have English names, which implies that "the cultural dislocation of living in a foreign place" (*ibidem*) is naturalised and Rae and Sammar can communicate serenely.

If cultural translation is essentially a practice of resistance in Aboulela's novel, in Lahiri's narrative production, cultural translation becomes an indispensable procedure that immigrant subjects adopt in order to survive in geographical interstices. The writer herself declares that her description of India is a "translation of India" (Lahiri 2002, 117), which is based upon her "parents' impressions" (*ibidem*) and her own sensations registered during her trips back home. Lahiri's Bengali Indian origins exist within her American adoptive customs, something that emphasises her "condition of being caught between two worlds" (Tan 2007, 230). She lives in America (Brooklyn), though she was born in London in 1967 and raised in Kingston, Rhode Island, where her father moved to work as a librarian at the University of Rhode Island.

A brief short survey of characters, plots and events in "When Mr. Pirzada Came to Dine", "Interpreter of Maladies" and "The Third and Final Continent" can give an idea of the author's use of cultural translation. In "When Mr. Pirzada Came to Dine", Lahiri translates the life of the Pakistani Pirzada living a certain period of his life in America, away from his home country. Here Hindus and Muslims share the American soil, the history of Pakistan becomes popular within American culture and, paradoxically, national identities have to deal with their own cultural problems within the confines of foreign spatial and geographical territories:

> In the Autumn of 1971 a man used to come to our house [...]. His name was Mr. Pirzada, and he came from Dacca, now the capital of Bangladesh, but then a part of Pakistan. That year Pakistan was engaged in civil war. [...] Mr. Pirzada, meanwhile, was in America for the year, for he had been awarded a grant from the government of Pakistan to study the foliage of New England (Lahiri 1999, 23).

In "The Third and Final Continent" Mala and her husband make the choice to spend the rest of their life in America, where they try to collect the "pieces of the old culture in the simplest things like traditional Indian spices such as bay leaves and cloves" (Tan 2007, 234). Here America is not represented as a place of dispossession and isolation. Mala's husband emphasises:

> We are American citizens now, so that we can collect social security when it is time. Though we visit Calcutta every few years, and bring back more drawstring pajamas and Dajeeling tea, we have decided to grow old here. [...] Mala no longer drapes the end of her sari over her head (Lahiri 1999, 197).

Lahiri's characters are expert users of cultural translation, a mechanism which allows them to retain their native roots, i.e. talking in Bengali, eating Asian food and travelling back to India.

In the short story, "Interpreter of Maladies", Mr. Kapasi, the Das family's Indian tourist guide, also works as an interpreter. He is obsessed by the Indian-American Mrs. Das. His imagination tells him that he "would explain things to her, things about India, and she would explain things to him about America" (*ibidem*, 59). His imaginary thought would make him an interpreter of cultures, "an interpreter between nations" (*ibidem*). Mr. Kapasi's perspective stresses the difference between native Indians and second-generation Indian immigrant subjects: "The family looked Indian but dressed as foreigners did. [...] Mr. Das squeezed hands like an American" (*ibidem*, 43-44). The communication difficulties between Mr. Kapasi and the Das family highlight the impossibility of connecting diverse generations belonging to culturally different contexts: native Asians compared with Americanized families of Asian Indian origins.

The Translator is an impressive portrayal of cross-cultural encounters with the implications of living in Western countries with non-Western beliefs. Aboulela's Islam and her female characters, Muslim African active women, have a strong identitary position in the West. In *The Translator* cultural translation questions and de-familiarises "British life, and the surprising reversal of power positions between the main characters, where the female Arab-African convinces and converts the white male academic" (Steiner 2008). According to Lahiri, cultural translation is, on the contrary, a strategic expedient that reinforces the immigrant subject's bilingual and bicultural identity in the foreign setting. Cultural translation is creation, invention and also preservation; translation, in general, is not a "response to [her] parents' cultural nostalgia" but "an attempt to forge [her] amalgamated domain" (Lahiri 2002, 118).

References

Aboulela L. 1999. *The Translator*. Edinburgh: Polygon.

Bhabha H.K. 1990. "The Third Space: Interview with Homi K. Bhabha". In Rutherford J. (ed.) *Identity: Community, Culture, Difference*. London: Lawrence & Wishart, 207-221.

Bhabha H.K. 1994. *The Location of Culture*. London: Routledge.

Buden B. 2006. "Cultural Translation: Why It Is Important and Where to Start with It", June, available at http://translate.eipcp.net/transversal/0606/buden/en#redir (last accessed August 2011).

Chambers I. 1994. *Migrancy, Culture, Identity*. London: Routledge.

Cooper B. 2006. "Look Who's Talking? Multiple Worlds, Migration and Translation in Leila Aboulela's *The Translator*". In Polezzi L. (ed.) *The Translator*. Manchester: St. Jerome, 323-344.

Di Giovanni E., Bollettieri Bosinelli R.M. 2009. "L'Altrove della traduzione". In Bollettieri Bosinelli R.M. and Di Giovanni E. (eds.) *Oltre l'Occidente. Traduzione e alterità culturale*. Milano: Bompiani, 12-52.

Kràl F. 2009. *Critical Identities in Contemporary Anglophone Diasporic Literature*. New York: Palgrave Macmillan.

Lahiri J. 1999. *Interpreter of Maladies*. London: Flamingo.

Lahiri J. 2002. "Intimate Alienation: Immigrant Fiction and Translation". In Nair R. B. (ed.) *Translation, Text and Theory: The Paradigm of India*. New Delhi: Sage, 113-120.

Ranasinha R. 2007. *South-Asian Writers in Twentieth-Century Britain: Culture in Translation*. Oxford: Oxford University Press.

Shuttleworth M., Cowie M. 1997. *Dictionary of Translation Studies*. Manchester: St. Jerome.

Steiner T. 2008. "Strategic Nostalgia, Islam and Cultural Translation in Leila Aboulela's *The Translator* and *Coloured Lights*", available at http://www.highbeam.com/doc/1G1-194279515.html (last accessed August 2011).

Tan K.A. 2007. "'Caught between Worlds': The Clash of Cultures and of Generations in the Work of Monica Ali, Jhumpa Lahiri and Zadie Smith". In Stilz G. (ed.) *Territorial Terrors Contested Spaces in Colonial and Postcolonial Writing*. Würzburg: Königshausen & Neumann, 227-238.

Trivedi H. 2005. "Translating Culture vs. Cultural Translation", available at http://iwp.uiowa.edu/91st/vol4_n1/pdfs/trivedi.pdf (last accessed August 2011). Trad. it. Giambalvo M. 2006. In Romeo M. (eds.) *Colonialismo e post(-) colonialismi. Traduzione e contesti culturali a confronto*, *Annali della Facoltà di Economia*. Palermo: Università degli Studi di Palermo, 125-142).

IVONNE DEFANT

Università di Trento

Translating Selfhood: *Being Emily* by Anne Donovan

Anne Donovan's *Being Emily* is a contemporary Scottish novel published in 2008 that investigates how personal identity is interwoven with a deep notion of cultural identity which is constructed not against but through cultural difference. In the novel, cultural difference is explored both in a temporal and spatial dimension. In terms of time, Anne Donovan recurs to evocations of the world created by Emily Brontë – the Emily of the title is Emily Brontë indeed – which function not as mere intertextual threads but they rather establish an encounter between the protagonist and narrator of the story, Fiona O'Connell, and her cultural past. In terms of space, Anne Donovan sets the novel in the multicultural city of twentieth-century Glasgow where Fiona, a Catholic girl belonging to the working class, increasingly learns how to mesh with other cultures. Fiona's friendship with Jaswinder, her classmate and free-thinking Sikh, may be read against some intertextual elements with the story of Catherine and Heathcliff in *Wuthering Heights*. However, as the narrative goes on, intertextual hints are questioned and their meaning is challenged. By the end of the novel echoes of *Wuthering Heights* become more and more suffused and dissipate into the urban space of Glasgow where the story is set in a span of time just before and after the political devolution in Scotland in the late nineteen nineties.

This novel calls forth challenges, ambiguities and directions; in fact Anne Donovan first draws on intertextual traces and then, rather than carrying on in that direction, she interprets intertextual allusions in relation to questions of translation and identity. The link between translation and identity is implied in the notion of cultural translation. The metaphor of cultural translation has been used by Homi Bhabha (1994) to show the alteration of colonizing discourses and to explain cultural identity through the notion of migration that captures the disjoined character of the present and the performative nature of identities. Migrant identities live on borderzones, in a hybrid space that Bhabha calls third space. The third space represents for this theorist of postcolonialism a space of translation because like a translation it bears traces of former meanings that are yet continuously in a process of becoming new. Anne Donovan draws attention to this aspect of translation as transformation, which is at the same time for Bhabha a resistance to translation, but she seems to endorse Harish Trivedi's concept of cultural translation which is based on the overriding of Bhabha's monolingualism and the inclusion of the interlingual aspect of translation, thus asserting a polylingual intervention which is the precondition for the supplementing of cultures and the preservation of difference not just within but between them (Trivedi 2005, 255). Donovan's challenge clusters around her tendency to maintain the border between the fields of Cultural and Translation Studies supple, following the line of thought of Harish Trivedi. Her novel engages with ideas of interpenetration, overlapping and negotiation that are the result of a construction of self as shifting in the cultural values of class, gender, and tradition. This shifting is moulded into a third space where both identities and enunciations lose their univocality in their relationship to the other. Interestingly, the disruption of the homogeneity of self is made possible by the use of language. The bilingual ground of the text – there is a continuous code-switching between vernacular Glaswegian and English – re-presents the cultural experience as a permanent condition of 'estrangement'. As a matter of fact, the process of cultural translation is subsumed into the space of language itself. As language is not a receptacle of culture but it coexists with it, the transformation of the protagonist's self occurs simultaneously in language; in so doing, the dynamics of cultural translation are opened to yet another realm of translation: self translation, which involves Fiona's construction of self between native Glaswegian and adopted English.

The space of linguistic encounter invented by Anne Donovan is a transcultural site which is constructed through a provisional language, a language that is in a constant process of transformation. If, according to Cairns Craig (1996, 12), the colour of vowels has caused Scottish people "to be recognised as incomplete within the British context", it is through the very use and experimentation of the colour of vowels that Scotland has constructed its own sense of identity. In this novel, I see translation as a telling tool to explore the role of difference as a multiple discursive space in the interplay between a local and a foreign dimension that is embedded in the Scottish culture and that reasserts national identity not only as Scottish distinctiveness but also in relationship to transnational contacts and a revision of the cultural past. Through cultural/self translation, which rules out binary oppositions, it is possible to investigate how Anne Donovan revisions the traditional account of Scotland as parochial and introverted and undermines the binary logic that has caused a cultural overdetermination whereby English/ness has been assured the position of dominance (Bell 2004). In the increasing reality of the break-up of Britain, the historical interstices that in traditional readings of Scotland have been simplified can be read as intermediary spaces that open out the sense of being Scottish.

A structuring aspect of the novel is represented by the fluidity of languages, indeed. The protagonist continuously switches from Glaswegian to English and backwards as if she were bilingual. Glaswegian is commonly regarded as a Scots dialect, but, as Donovan transforms and translates it from an oral into a written idiom, even creating her own forms of spelling, she tends to use it as a language to affirm its value. When I asked Anne Donovan about her perception of Glaswegian, she told me that she would probably say that Glaswegian is a dialect but she uses it in her novel as if it were a language.[1] The protagonist's continuous and creative code-switching implies deeper concerns related to the construction of identity whereby the protagonist's self occupies a boundary that is at once inside and outside culture/language.

The linguistic deterritorialization, which is adopted by the writer to cross-fertilize the cultural background of the female protagonist, destabilises the polarities between the foreign and the same. In *Being Emily* the author suggests a translatability whereby the foreign and the same coexist in a nation where history has caused the dynamic notion of migration – the union of 1707 has displaced the Scottish sense of home – to accompany the static concept of 'home' – a metaphor for the traditional model of the nation-state. As a reflection of this complex cultural condition, Glaswegian does not erupt here and there in the interstices of the text, but there is a continuum of language that suggests on the one hand an attenuation of the distance between sameness and otherness, on the other it still maintains the gap between them, creating the effect of a language that is both unique and plural. Like Scots, Glaswegian is both different from English and similar to it.

With its instability, language breaks into the text and establishes an ongoing act of transformation. At the beginning, when Fiona is a twelve-year-old girl, Glaswegian is more dominant than standard English. As the writer herself told me, Scottish people do not have a standard language. The Scottish language changes a lot depending on the circumstances, who and where the speaker is and with whom he/she speaks. It usually happens that children who speak a broad Scottish language use a less broad language when they grow up. They are discouraged by adults from speaking it since, notwithstanding the ratification of the Charter for Minority Languages for Scots in 2001, according to Donovan and Niven (2004, 263) Scots is still regarded as a devalued language. However, children, who do not have such strong metalinguistic awareness as adults, stay much together and they usually maintain solidarity by maintaining a private language that they consider as their mother tongue. Moreover, Glaswegian stands also for a solidarity among working class members, as Caroline Macafee (1983, 22) states. This condition is well portrayed in *Being Emily* as well: the child

---

[1] My interview with Anne Donovan took place in the café in the Festival Theatre in Edinburgh on August 6th 2009.

Fiona belongs to a working class family, and at the beginning language plays for her an important role of class cohesion and is perceived as an extension of the domestic space. We can observe that it is mostly at home and with her family that Fiona speaks Glaswegian, which is for her an intimate language, close to the ear. The prevalence of Glaswegian in the first chapters suggests a tight-knit family, which partly reminds us of the Brontës'. Fiona's early life in thrall to the world of Emily Brontë is narrated in a broad Glaswegian voice full of ironic twists which betray the author's cultural self-consciousness and allow her a critical distance necessary to problematise the link between the past and the present. A humorous touch in the portrayal of the child Fiona can be savoured at the very beginning of the novel:

> Ah was at the sink in the kitchen, washin the dishes wi *Spirit of Haworth* propped up behind the taps, practisin bein Emily Brontë. Ah'd read that she baked the family's bread and learned German at the same time, book in fronty her. Since then ah'd developed a new interest in housework, so long as you could dae it while you were readin. Up till then ah thought if you were gonnae be a poet you had tae float aboot in a dwam or lie on a couch all day (Donovan 2008, 2).

The use of Glaswegian is indeed metonymic of Fiona's cultural experience. The child Fiona, enamoured of the myth of Emily Brontë, ignores the real meaning of art, which is not based on an act of mere reproduction, but on one of transformation. When later on Fiona's life starts spiraling out of the house and taking other directions she understands that both art and translation share a common feature in their transformative thrust. Then even language spirals in other directions and becomes more inconsistent. As the narrative goes on, words in Glaswegian dwindle. The *ah* that is continuously used in the first chapters of the book becomes at a certain point *I* when Fiona makes friends with Jaswinder, her Sikh classmate. As Fiona's tongue becomes more public the protagonist does not drop the letter *g* in the ending *ing* but she maintains it following the rule of standard English orthography. By the end of the novel, Fiona, who is much less together with her family and who has become an artist working part-time as a teacher, tends to be inhabited by both English and Glaswegian and to make herself at home in both languages. When Fiona's cocooned childhood is over, the writer establishes the resistance of linguistic difference wittingly in order to destabilise the monoglossic hierarchy and thus allow cultural overlapping and negotiation and create a space of translation that permits the inhabitation of other cultural spaces. As I will try to explain, according to Cronin (2006, 55) translation is not understood as "a substitutive, metaphorical process of wholesale replacement of one language or culture by another [...] but [...] rather a metonymical process of contiguity and connection".

There is also a dimension of gender to the linguistic and cultural hybridization of Fiona's self. Donovan suggests a link between the construction of gender and nation, which calls into question a postcolonial perception of nation as constructed instead of essential (Christianson and Lumsden 2000, 2). Anne Donovan cuts across a revision of the traditional image of feminized Scotland in literature that is centred upon the equation between the peripheralisation of nation and that of gender. Gender corroborates the role of translation in the construction of Fiona's identity. While many post-colonial writers invoke the idea of cultural translation through the loss of their mother tongue and separation from their mother country, Anne Donovan recurs to the loss of Fiona's mother to allow language to change. At the same time, Donovan rereads Emily Brontë's world and invents a new world for Fiona, which is not a mere copy of the original. The loss of her mother, who suddenly dies in childbirth when Fiona is still an adolescent, goes beyond a mere intertextual element with Emily Brontë's world. This tragedy, which causes Fiona's family and self to fall apart, drives the female protagonist to move into alterity so that her loss can be integrated and transformed. Central to this idea of transformation is the concept of creation that is embodied by art. In the course of time Fiona's interest in Emily Brontë's world is transmuted into another form of art: visual art through which Fiona gives artistic value to everyday objects. Art is used by the writer as a device to represent the idea of transformation that is inherent also in the process of cultural translation whereby a transformed language enables the invention of new selves. Interestingly, the possibility for new positions to emerge is created by the exilic condition of the protagonist in a double sense: because of her Scottishness and because of her gender.

At the end of the novel the cultural values of gender, class and even race are relocated and Fiona has become a woman, guided by the spirit inside herself, the one her mother "had helped tae shape and form" (Donovan 2008, 303). In the last pages of the book, where Fiona gets married to Jaswinder and is expecting a baby – her condition of pregnancy gestures towards the overlapping of racial features in the child she is bearing – Fiona's art, now free of her past obsessions – broken dolls and dead babies – embodies transformation as the possibility of creating an afterlife, a survival and at the same time a transformation of the original, where difference is not covered up but is engaged with. The biblical figures of Mary and Jesus in her painting are translated into the context of contemporary Scotland through a language that preserves foreignness:

> Mary, in blue jeans and a white tee shirt, is hanging out the washing in her back court. I know she'd of had dark skin and eyes but this madonna has a *peelywally* west of Scotland complexion and eyes that hover between blue and green. Jesus is dark-skinned, lighter than Jas but no much; he's haunding her the pegs and they're smiling at each other (Donovan 2008, 311).

Unlike the beginning, now the vernacular has been diluted; source and target contexts coincide because language has been transformed according to the needs of the source culture. We can notice that the substitution of *ah* by the pronoun *I* refers to a subject who is not essential but can be transformed because her position has changed. As Fiona's life enters a wider dimension, the writer recurs to a language which is more understandable but still maintains the metonymic gap – see the unglossed word *peelywally*, which means pale in Glaswegian – that inscribes the difference of the protagonist's culture into the text and reminds us of its uniqueness. Paradoxically, here translation is conceived as translatability because of the linguistic untranslatability. As Bill Ashcroft (2009, 175) writes "the strategies of transformation [of English], by opening up a metonymic gap, are a refusal to translate".

The performative or translational act requires also a disavowal of the notions of time and space as essential. Colonial evocations are implicitly alluded to at the very beginning of the novel where the location of Emily Brontë as a canonical writer of the English master narrative is counterpointed against the peripheralisation of Fiona, a Scottish, Catholic, working-class young girl, who becomes so obsessed with the myth of Emily Brontë that she wants to imitate her. Once cultural binarisms have been superseded, Fiona understands that in order to have an artistic identity she does not need to think herself in the mindspace of Emily Brontë. She abandons writing for art and begins to construct both her personal and artistic identity on her own experiences. Even the notion of space is changed. Many times Anne Donovan uses the word *hame*, which in Glaswegian means home, but if at the beginning *hame* stands for Fiona's family, later on *hame* acquires a new semantic meaning: *hame* identifies Glasgow, a city, which Fiona finds different from London, visited by her to hold an exhibition of her art. The smallness of Glasgow conjures up metaphorically the cosiness of home and is meanwhile juxtaposed with the vibrancy of its multicultural aspect. Once again, Donovan suggests the coexistence of cultural specificity and multiplicity and privileges intercultural relations inside cultural globalization. Home becomes for Fiona first a place of disorientation – she wants to go away from a collapsed family – and then relocation – Jaswinder is able to buy back Fiona's old house that was sold when her mother died and her father became an alcoholic. Anne Donovan's notion of home, which at the end of the story has erased the binary opposition between the private and the public, the past and the present, is understood as location rather than place, whereby the subject is eventually able to see simultaneously from outside in and inside out and where even Scottish history is *reconvened*.

At the same time, Donovan's preoccupation with the significance of home opens depths of meaning of an intertextual element with *Wuthering Heights*. Wuthering Heights, the solid Victorian house of Catherine's childhood, is in contrast with the *fluid home* of Fiona's journey into being. Wuthering Heights is indeed the house of trauma that echoes Catherine's narcissistic desire never to be parted from sameness, so precluding any possibility of growing up in the social arena. Because Catherine cannot renounce her house in nature, she is doomed to roam on the moors, desperately begging to enter the house of fiction without accepting any compromise with the house of culture.

In place of Catherine's self-containment, Donovan creates a character who lives in translation. Through cultural/self translation Fiona draws attention to the possibility of interlinguistic and intercultural spaces that express a sense of the new in the narrative landscape of contemporary Scotland.

References

Ashcroft B. 2009. *Caliban's Voice. The Transformation of English in Post-Colonial Literatures*. London, New York: Routledge.

Bell E. 2004. *Questioning Scotland. Literature, Nationalism, Postmodernism*. Basingstoke: Palgrave Macmillan.

Bhabha H. 1994. *The Location of Culture*. London: Routledge.

Christianson A., Lumsden A. (eds.) 2000. *Contemporary Scottish Women Writers*. Edinburgh: Edinburgh University Press.

Craig C. 1996. *Out of History. Narrative Paradigms in Scottish and English Culture*. Edinburgh: Polygon.

Cronin M. 2006. *Translation and Identity*. London, New York: Routledge.

Donovan A. 2008. *Being Emily*. Edinburgh: Canongate.

Donovan A., Niven L. 2003 "The Scots Language in Education". In Bryce T.G.K. and Humes W.M. (eds.) *Scottish Education. Second Edition: Post-Devolution*. Edinburgh: Edinburgh University Press, 262-271.

Macafee C. 1983. *Glasgow. Varieties of English Around the World*. Amsterdam: John Benjamins Publishing Company.

Trivedi H. 2005 "Translating Culture vs. Cultural Translation". In St-Pierre P. and Kar P.C. (eds.) *Translation, Reflections, Refractions, Transformations*. Delhi: Pencraft International, 251-260.

Rowena Coles
Università di Urbino Carlo Bo

How Does a Child Become a *Bambino*?
Creating Child Constructions in Translation

The paper examines how the translation from English to Italian of a children's story has been conditioned by the different child cultures behind the two languages, aiming in particular at showing how Themes and Thematic progression are affected in translation by such differences. The story examined is *The It-doesn't-matter Suit* by Sylvia Plath (1996) and its translation/adaptation *Max e il vestito color zafferano* by Bianca Pitzorno (1996). When such stories are translated, a target-oriented strategy is also usually adopted. As Oittinen (2006, 35), writer and translator of children's stories, has noted: "children's literature – originals and translations – [...] is literature produced and intended for children and it is literature read by children", suggesting (*ibidem*, 41) that "translators of children's literature should reach out to the children of their own culture". We may thus presume that whereas Plath, when writing *The It-doesn't-matter Suit*, reaches out to a British child in a British culture, Pitzorno, in translating and adapting the same text into Italian, reaches out to an Italian child living in an Italian culture.

The question of defining a national culture is problematic. Yet, although Orwell (1957, 65) stated "national characteristics are not easy to pin down" he also commented: "Nevertheless, nothing is causeless, and even the fact that Englishmen have bad teeth can tell one something about the realities of English life". With regard to cultural differences, Katan (1999, 221) states that:

> [...] cultures vary in their orientation towards expressive or instrumental communication, very much in line with their HCC or LCC orientation.[1] The orientation is towards feelings or facts, the person or the issue. Expressive cultures are happy wearing their heart on their sleeves [...], whereas instrumental cultures believe more in self-control.

---

[1] The concept of HCC (High Context Communication) and LCC (Low Context Communication) was first introduced by Edward Hall (Hall and Hall 1989). He suggests that contexting is a fundamental aspect of culture and that members of a culture will have a shared bias, either towards communication through the text or the context.

Cultures of High Context Communication orientation (HCC), such as the Japanese culture, tend to rely on context, relationships, feelings, circumstances and indirectness in their communication, whereas a Low Context Communication orientation (LCC), such as Swiss-German and German tend to rely on text, facts, directness, consistency and substance. England and Italy tend to hover in the middle of the cline towards the two extremes of culture, with Italy tending more towards a HCC and England towards a LCC.

Katan (*ibidem*, 61) also claims that: "to be a member of a culture, one will need to share beliefs at every level of culture" and follows this statement with a sample set of beliefs congruent with being British and one congruent with being Italian. I have referred to these sets in order to propose a set of values congruent with being a British child and another congruent with being an Italian child (Table 1).

	British child	Italian child
1	Develop independence	Continue dependence
2	Responsible for own actions	Protected by family, especially *la mamma*
3	Dress practically	Dress well, aesthetic sense, *fare bella figura*
4	Respect of individual and privacy	Respect for roles and family hierarchy
5	Facts, directness, substance (LOW Context Culture)	Relationships, indirectness, feelings (HIGH Context Culture)

Table 1. Proposed values congruent with being a British or Italian child.

We must now clarify what is meant by Theme and Thematic Progression (TP). Halliday's (1994, 36) definition of theme is adopted: "The theme is a function of the CLAUSE AS A MESSAGE. It is what the message is concerned with: the point of departure for what the speaker is going to say". Themes are speaker/writer choices and depend on how the speaker/writer wants to present his/her information to the listener/reader. In the following example taken from the story in hand, we see that in the original Plath has chosen the theme *he*[2] (the protagonist Max Nix) and is going to tell the reader about this protagonist, whilst in the translation Pitzorno is going to tell the Italian child about the theme *l'abbigliamento usuale di Max* i.e. Max's clothing.

---

[2] Themes are marked in italics.

He had a green sweater [...]
L'abbigliamento usuale di Max consisteva in un maglione verde [...]

A writer's choice of theme obviously has great weight in the development of a text, as Wang (2007, 167) states: "The initial place has an enormous importance in a clause. Whatever is chosen to be in the first place will influence a reader's interpretation of everything that comes next". Fries (1981, 3) also underlines the element of choice in themes: "They are choices of meanings: what notion will I use as point of departure in the information in this unit?". If, then, the theme is a linguistic element dependent not on language code but on writer choice, then any change in theme in *Max e il vestito color zafferano* will be a choice (optional shift) rather than a constriction (obligatory shift).

Thematic Progression goes beyond sentence level in that it refers to how theme-rheme combinations develop in a text and the patterning is produced Martin's (1992, 489) definition of thematic development pinpoints how thematic choice leads to the structuring of a text as message: "Method of development [...] establishes an angle on field. [...] [it] is the lens through which a field is constructed [...]". Daneš (1974, 114) provides us with an interesting metaphor when he states: "Thematic progression might be viewed as the skeleton of the plot". He identifies three basic types of thematic progression which will now be briefly described.

1. *Simple linear TP1* (or TP with linear thematization of rhemes) where the theme of one clause is selected from within the rheme of the preceding clause

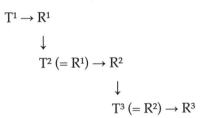

$$T^1 \rightarrow R^1$$
$$\downarrow$$
$$T^2 (= R^1) \rightarrow R^2$$
$$\downarrow$$
$$T^3 (= R^2) \rightarrow R^3$$

2. *TP with continuous, constant theme* where the same theme (but not fully identical wording) appears in a series of utterances, to which different rhemes are linked

$$T^1 \rightarrow R^1$$
$$\downarrow$$
$$T^1 \rightarrow R^2$$
$$\downarrow$$
$$T^1 \rightarrow R^3$$

3. *TP with derived themes*, where the particular utterance themes (T¹T²T³) are
derived from a "hypertheme" [T]

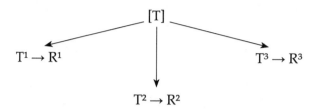

We will now move on to examine how the differences in themes and in
thematic progression between the original story and its translation can be
linked to differences in the culture in which the child reader is brought up.
A brief selection of examples follows starting from the title of the story – the
'theme' *par excellence*. The original title *The It-doesn't-matter Suit* indicates that
Plath is going to tell a story about a suit that is extremely practical, appealing
to the British values at points 3 and 5 of Table 1. The translated title is *Max e il
vestito color zafferano*. Pitzorno is going to tell her Italian child readers a story
about someone called Max and his relationship with a colourful suit, appealing
to the Italian values at points 3 and 5 of the Table 1.

The first part of the back cover reveals similar differences in the information
packaging.

> *Max Nix* lives with his six brothers and Mama and Papa Nix in a small
> village called Winkelburg. *Max* likes where he lives and *he's* happy – except
> for one thing: *Max* longs for a suit. Not just an ordinary work-a-day suit, but
> a suit for doing everything.

The English version's first four themes are constant – the protagonist Max –
and so the British child reader understands that the story is going to tell him or
her about Max (appealing to a LCC). The translation's first theme is the feeling
of *grande desiderio* and so the Italian child reader understands that the story is
going to tell him/her about a wish (appealing to a HCC):

> *Il più grande desiderio di Max Nulli* è quello di indossare un bell'abito a
> giacca, proprio come suo padre e i suoi fratelli. E quando a casa Nulli arriva
> un pacco che contiene un pelosissimo e giallissimo completo, Max se ne
> innamora subito.[3]

---

[3] The difference in the rhematic elements are also revealing. The 'British' Max *longs for
a suit for doing everything* – a very practical approach appealing to a LCC, whilst the 'Italian'
Max *falls in love with the suit straight away* – an emotional reaction.

The beginning of the story presents Max Nix to the child reader: "*Max Nix was seven years old, and the youngest of seven brothers*". If we examine the underlying kernel sentences: "*Max Nix was seven years old. Max Nix was the youngest of seven brothers*", we can see that Max Nix is the constant theme. The author is going to tell the British child reader about Max independently of anyone else (see Table 1, point 1). The translation introduces the protagonist thus: "*Max Nulli aveva sette anni e sei fratelli, tutti più grandi di lui*". Here the underlying kernel sentences show two themes: (1) Max and (2) his brothers: "*Max Nulli* aveva sette anni. *Max Nulli* aveva sei fratelli. *I sei fratelli* erano tutti più grandi di lui". Pitzorno is going to tell the Italian child reader not only about Max but also about his brothers, appealing to Italian culture which holds family hierarchy as an important value.

The original text proceeds, after the presentation of the brothers, as follows: "*Max's whole name* was Maximilian, but because *he* was only seven *he* did not need such a big name. So *everybody* called him just Max".

Thematic progression:

$$T^1 \text{ (Max)} \rightarrow R^1/R^2/R^3$$
$$T^2 \text{ (Everybody)} \rightarrow R^4$$

The original develops in a TP2 with constant, continuous theme *Max* except for the last sentence where the theme changes (*everybody*). The translation offers:

Il suo nome per intero, ad essere esatti, era Massimiliano. Ma siccome *(egli)* aveva soltanto sette anni, *tutti* pensavano che non avesse bisogno di un nome tanto lungo, e così *(tutti)* lo chiamavano semplicemente Max.

Thematic progression:

$$T^1 \text{ (Max)} \rightarrow R^1/R^2$$
$$T^2 \text{ (tutti)} \rightarrow R^3/R^4$$

Here the thematic choice is balanced evenly between *Max* and *tutti*. This seems to reflect a difference between the two cultures regarding the upbringing of children, who are encouraged to become independent earlier in Britain than in Italy (see Table 1, point 1). In the English version, the young child seems to be the protagonist of his own destiny (*he did not need* […]) whilst in the Italian version, the adults decide what he needs or doesn't need (*tutti pensavano* […]).

The next passage carries on from the previous example with the presentation of Max's wish.

Max liked where he lived.
Max was happy, except for one thing.
More than anything else in the world Max Nix wanted a suit of his own.

He had a green sweater and green wool socks and a green felt hunting hat
with a turkey feather in it.
He even had a fine pair of leather knickers with carved bone buttons.
But *everyone* knows a sweater and a pair of knickers are not the same thing
as a suit – a made-to-order suit with long trousers and a jacket to match.

Thematic progression:

$$T^1 \text{ (Max)} \rightarrow R^1/R^2$$
$$T^2 \text{ (More than anything)} \rightarrow R^3$$
$$T^1 \text{ (Max)} \rightarrow R^4/R^5$$
$$T^3 \text{ (but everyone)} \rightarrow R^6$$

The translation offers:

Max era felice di vivere a Sgranalocchi.
Max sarebbe stato felice in assoluto, se non fosse stato per un piccolo
particolare.
La cosa che il nostro amico desiderava più di ogni altra al mondo era
possedere un vestito intero, come i grandi, un completo con giacca e
pantaloni lunghi.
L'abbigliamento usuale di Max consisteva in un maglione verde, calze verdi
di lana, un cappello di feltro verde con una piuma di tacchino, un paio di
braghette di pelle con i bottoni d'osso lavorato.
Ma non mi verrete a dire che un maglione e un paio di braghette sono la stessa
cosa di un vestito da grandi, un vestito fatto su misura con giacca e
pantaloni assortiti.

Thematic progression:

T^1 (Max) $\rightarrow R^1/R^2$
$\downarrow$
$\quad T^2$ (La cosa [...]) $\rightarrow R^3$
$\quad\quad \downarrow$
$\quad\quad T^3$ (L'abbigliamento) $\rightarrow R^4$
$\quad\quad\quad \downarrow$
$\quad\quad\quad T^4$ (un maglione [...]) $\rightarrow R^4$

Once again, the original shows a mainly TP2 progression, where the
constant, continuous theme (x 4) is Max. No theme involves clothing. In the
Italian version, the themes are divided between Max (x 2) and clothes (x 3),
showing the high value given to dress (point 3, Table 1). The Italian version
has a basic linear TP1 development. This could be interpreted as a type of
mediation that Pitzorno offers her Italian child readers, guiding them through

the text step-by-step (point 1, Table 1). The last theme in the original version is factual (multiple theme with textual *but* and topical *everybody*), whilst in the Italian version the last multiple theme has a strong interpersonal element (*non mi verrete a dire*), an element which is a direct appeal to the Italian child's feelings[4] (point 5, Table 1).

In the last example we can see how, in the original, themes regarding personal responsibility for actions are replaced in the Italian version by themes which introduce a magical element which substitutes such responsibility.

> *Papa Nix* untied the knot in the red string.
> *Mama Nix* unwrapped the brown paper.
> *Inside the brown paper* was a grey cardboard box.
> *Paul* lifted the lid off the box.
> *Inside the grey box* was a lot of white tissue paper.
> *Emil and Otto and Walter and Hugo and Johann and Max* all helped to pull
> away some of the tissue paper.

There are two hyperthemes: (1) the Nix family (2) parts of the parcel. They are developed in a sort of 'double' TP3. Intertwined between these two hyperthemes is a TP1 progression which directly links the family actions to the discovery of the parcel contents. Such a Thematic Progression textually underlines the explicit human responsibility of each of the family members, even of the smallest child Max, in the discovery of what the parcel contains (point 1, Table 1).

The Italian text reads:

> *Il signor Nulli* sciolse il nodo che stringeva lo spago rosso.
> *La signora Nulli* svolse la carta marrone.
> *Apparve* una scatola di cartone, verde.
> *Paolo* sollevò il coperchio della scatola verde.
> *Apparvero* fogli e fogli di carta velina bianca avvolti attorno a qualcosa.
> *Emilio e Otto, Walter e Ugo*, avrebbero dato chissà cosa per essere autorizzati
> a togliere almeno uno di quei fogli di carta velina.

In the translation there are also two hyperthemes: (1) older members of the Nix family (2) the act of appearing. In the Italian version, only the parents and eldest son unwrap the parcel. The youngest two children do not appear as themes and so have no part at all in the unwrapping. The different thematic choice between the original and the translation reflects a different attitude towards child participation. The British child reader sees that the family members all participate equally in the unwrapping, each taking responsibility for a part of the 'discovery' of the parcel contents (points 1, 2, 4, Table 1). The

---

[4] Note that in T² there is a similar interpersonal element in the use of "nostro amico" when referring to Max.

Italian version shows the importance of hierarchy in the family and points to the dependence of smaller children on parents and elder siblings.

The second hypertheme in the translation ("appearing") tells of an action carried out by the inanimate objects in the package. No link is made between the members of the family and the effect of their action, as in the original. This produces an event that is 'magical', apparently unconnected to the family's actions, contrasting with the original text which lays its foundation of thematic choice on a place ("inside"). The original presents the British child with a solid physical reality which is the consequence of a person's action (LCC) whilst the translation presents the Italian child with elements of magic which remove the actors' responsibility (HCC).

The present study has examined a specific aspect of language – thematic structure – in order to investigate how the child protagonist in a children's story is presented to a child of a different culture. Themes are author and translator choices and it has been shown, through a brief selection of examples, that themes and their development often differ in translation. Such differences seem to reflect an effort by the translator to make the protagonist of the story accessible to the Italian child reader by adapting the point of departure of the message (i.e. the theme) in order to fit the child's cultural values, which differ to those of the child reader of the original text. Thus subtle cultural differences regarding attitudes, feelings, ways of living, emotions, reactions etc. which are linked to the core values of a particular culture have been identified both in Plath's and Pitzorno's thematic choices.

Brake *et al.* (1995, 34-39), developing the well-known Iceberg Theory[5], state: "The most powerful elements of culture are those that lie beneath the surface of everyday interaction". The child Max Nix is not only translated into Max Nulli at the level of his name, but his whole being is constructed on a system of congruent beliefs and values with which the Italian child reader can identify. Thus the whole translation process leads to Plath's *boy* becoming Pitzorno's *bambino*.

References

Brake T., Walker D.M., Walker T. 1995. *Doing Business Internationally: The Guide to Cross-Cultural Success*. Burr Ridge (Il.): Irwin.

---

[5] The difference between more visible and physical objects of culture and less visible underlying values and strategies was pointed out by Hall in his Iceberg Theory in the 1950s, particularly in *The Silent Language* (1990) that claimed that the most important part of culture is completely hidden, and what can be seen is "just the tip of the iceberg".

Daneŝ F. (ed.) 1974. *Papers on Functional Sentence Perspective*. The Hague: Mouton.

Fries P.H. 1981. "On the Status of Theme in English: Arguments from Discourse". In *Forum Linguisticum*, 6, 1, 1-38.

Hall E.T., Hall M.R. 1989. *Understanding Cultural Differences*. Yarmouth (Ma.): Intercultural Press.

Hall E.T. 1990 (original edition 1952). *The Silent Language*. New York: Doubleday.

Halliday M.A.K. 1994 (original edition 1985). *An Introduction to Functional Grammar*. London: Arnold.

Katan D. 1999. *Translating Cultures*. Manchester: St. Jerome Publishing.

Martin J.R. 1992. *English Text: System and Structure*. Amsterdam: Benjamins.

Oittinen R. 2006. "No Innocent Act: On the Ethics of Translating for Children". In Van Collie J. and Verschueren W.P. (eds.) *Children's Literature in Translation*. Manchester: St. Jerome Publishing, 35-45.

Orwell G. 1957. *Inside the Whale and Other Stories*. Harmondsworth: Penguin.

Plath S. 1996. *The It-doesn't-matter Suit*. London: Faber and Faber.

Plath S. 1996. (transl. Pitzorno B.). *Max e il vestito color zafferano*. Milano: Mondadori.

Wang L. 2007. "Theme and Rheme in the Thematic Organization of Text: Implications for Teaching Academic Writing". In *Asia EFL Journal* 9, 1, 164-176.

Section 2
Community and Nation:
Hybrid Identities, Reinvented Traditions (I)

CARLA LOCATELLI

Università di Trento

"English in Filippino Hands": Language, Literature, Culture

> When the mind loses a name, it loses a perception.
> The name is essential to its continence
> Or it wounds itself in the thing it does not respect.
> O the thing whispers ex cathedra its theme.
> G.H. Abad (2004) *The Pope Expels Certain Saints*

1. Some introductory cultural remarks

Filipino literature in English articulates with great complexity some of the epistemological issues that are central to neo-colonial (not post-colonial) studies. I totally agree with Epifanio San Juan who insists on this difference: post-colonial vs. neo-colonial in Filipino culture,[1] and, in Italy, with Francesca Di Blasio (2005; 2006) whose resistance to the hasty adoption of the term post-colonial denounces the fact that 'post(?)-colonial' could mask neo-colonialism.

I will list some of the epistemological issues enunciated in contemporary Filipino literature, and will relate them to Filipino literary productions, with special reference to three contemporary writers: Cristina Pantoja Hidalgo, Jose Dalisay and Gémino H. Abad.

What I would like to underscore from the start is the asymmetry of the Eurocentric and Anglo-American gazes looking at Filipino history and culture, as opposed to the deep knowledge of Anglo-American and European traditions and institutions by Filipino intellectuals. Their sophisticated information becomes evident to any reader from the very first encounter with the literary production in the Philippines, and with any of their critical contributions to the

---

[1] "Filipino writers cannot escape the vocation of resistance against neocolonial (*not* postcolonial) forces gravitating around the World Bank-IMF, guarantors of transnational hegemony" (San Juan 1994, 123).

theoretical discussions characterizing the Twentieth Century, both in the Euro-American world and in the Philippines.

The diasporic experience of Filipinos in the world has produced an incredible awareness and knowledge of other cultures in the country. San Juan talks about the "metamorphosis of the *migratory sensibility*" which is in itself a significant indication of Filipino social consciousness. Dalisay's novel *Killing Time in a Warm Place* is quoted by San Juan precisely as a cogent example of a "new style of tracking the metamorphosis" (San Juan 1994, 128; Italics added).

Furthermore, we must remember that the Philippines's cultural complexity is expressed in many other languages spoken in the Philippines besides English: in Tagalog-Filipino, Sugbuanon, Hiligaynon, Iloko, *etc.* So, we will have to account for the importance and use of English, and of literary English, for nearly all the living writers in the country. It is not something that should be taken for granted, as an indisputable mark of globalization. It is rather the bilingualism or multilingualism typical of the educated classes that can enrich and transform the cognitive datum of an imported/imposed *lingua franca*.

Given the limited space we can take here, but in order to give a much deserved and sufficiently complex outline of Philippine history, I will just mention both the centuries long Spanish domination, started in 1543 (which named the country in honor of the Spanish king Philip II, after Magellan's landing in 1521), and the beginning of the US domination at the end of the Spanish American war, in 1898. The Treaty of Paris allowed Americans to "buy" the Philippines from Spain for 20 million dollars. This Treaty indicates that both the US and Spain ignored the establishment of a Philippine Republic in the previous year (1898), set up under the leadership of Emilio Aguinaldo, a revolutionary patriot who managed to find a national convergence in the Act of the Declaration of Independence.

The Philippines became US territory after the Treaty of Paris, and in 1935 a ten-year transitional government was deemed necessary as the grounding for full Philippine sovereignty. Thus, "The Commonwealth of the Philippines" became the political designation of the Philippines from 1935 to 1946. US rule lasted till 1946, when the Treaty of Manila recognized Philippine independence.

One of the positive aspects of US rule was the fact that, by 1930, the mortality rate in the country was drastically reduced, and slavery was suppressed. This might explain the fascination of many Filipinos with the US.

In this regard, Pantoja Hidalgo indicates:

> Practically every Filipino dreams of going there, and a great many actually do, for every conceivable reason: to add more titles to their names, to visit cousins three times removed, to find out once and for all if they can make it anywhere having made it there, etc. (2006, 100).

Tellingly, however, she also titles a chapter in her book-length essay on Filipino women writers "The American Nightmare".

During US rule, a comprehensive educational system was set up, and it provided for the teaching of English as the country's *lingua franca*, while some 170 linguistic groups were still active in the 7107 islands which make up the Philippine Archipelago.

The homogenizing effect of English would need further discussion (as "the American nightmare" would), but for now let us bear in mind that generations of Filipinos grew up with a prescribed 'common' language, i.e., the language of the ruling and educated class. Therefore, generations of Twentieth Century writers started writing in English (yet, most did it, and do it, also in their local languages).[2]

Regarding the state of the use of English in the country, Abad forcefully stated in 2008: "indeed the trend among our young writers today is toward bilingualism", and in the very same book he suggests: *"English in Filipino hands, under the pressure of his own milieu and sensibility, becomes not English but Filipino"*. This is the quotation in my title, because I believe that linguistic transformation, hybridization, contamination is central to the epistemological, cognitive and political self-identification and self-definition of the Filipinos. Significantly, Abad talks about the formation of what he defines in the title of one of his collections of essays: *Our Scene So Fair* (and not just "so far") (Abad 2008). Tongue in check at its best, if you ask me!

F.T.R. Tupas, the editor of a study on the politics of language in the Philippines in the light of globalization, indicates from the start the multiple linguistic affiliations that characterize Philippine life. He precisely points to:

> the complexity of my multilingual identity as a student from Aklan who speaks Aklanon as my "home" language, Ilonggo as my "regional" language, Filipino as my "national" language, and English as my "international" language (2007, ix).

We shall see later, with some textual reference, how writers relate to this cultural datum.

2. Some epistemological issues relating to Philippine neo-colonialism

The scanty notes I have provided on Philippine history and Anglo-linguistic hegemony should help us understand some of the crucial literary and cultural issues constantly inscribed into the Filipino cultural production. I would like to list some which appear to me as most relevant. They regard primarily:

(1) *The establishment of a national language* (more or less hegemonic and basically enforced). We have already discussed it, at least to some extent.

---

[2] On the issue of the pervasiveness of English, see Jenkins (2007).

(2) *The production of poetry, novels, plays in a language that speaks the subject, as colonized*, instead of expressing his/her access to writing (some Filipino critics see this as an occurrence in the sentimentalized output produced at home and abroad under American rule).

(3) *The editorial and media construction, and market dissemination of cultural products.*

(4) *Cultural self-understanding and self-representation.*

(5) *The development of specific hermeneutical protocols*, linked to globalization and, therefore, potentially subjected to its imperatives, both economical and critical (the trends of New Criticism, Marxist criticism, Post-Structuralism, Deconstruction, etc. which are typically Anglo-American).

I propose to address these issues (by no means fully exhaustive of the cultural Philippine complexity), albeit schematically, because of our space constraints.

(1) As regards Point One, something has been said already about the enforced establishment of a national language. I will just add here Rodolfo Dato's observation in his *Filippino Poetry* (as early as 1924) since he talks about: "our native bards warbling in borrowed language" (Dato 1924, 5). In recent times he has found an echo in Nick Joaquin:

> The difference between our prewar writing [before World War II, which hit the Philippines in 1941] and our modern writing is that, in the former, the English language is imposing its style on the Filipino writer and shaping him, while in our modern writing it is the Filipino writer who is imposing his style on the English language and reshaping it (2000, 11).

Last but not least, I would like to recall the ironical Pygmalion-like situation imposed on natives, as described by Dalisay:

> I was practicing her English pronunciation [...] I don't think she liked it very much, having to say words like "perfect" and "favor" and "fifty-five". I told her that in this world – he was speaking in English now, enunciating every word – "inn thisss worlddd, you can't get very far without Eeenglishhhh. Eeenglishhhh is what makes us Filipeenos world-class". "World-class *what*?" (2008, 55; Italics added).

Basically the question remains: where does personal improvement come from?

(2) As regards my Second Point, i.e., the problem of speaking/being spoken as a colonized subject, I would like to quote the poet Abad because of the intra-psychic and intercultural scenario he manages to delineate while asking "whence does one speak?":

Speaking is fraught with other speech.
Through all our fathers, Spain
And America had invented our souls
And wrought our land and history.

[...]

In speech take no meaning
from elsewhere,
be more thorough than passion.

Whence does one come
when he speaks, his eyes lighting up?
Before speech all words are dead,
their legends blind.
No one comes from language,
The truth is what words dream.
(Abad, 2004, *The Light in One's Blood*, 117-118)

Is the location of speakers, who are actually moving (within, against, and through neo-colonialism) visible? They are what I would call metamorphic subjects (as 'we' are), i.e., 'they' are not set once and for all, nor fixed by some unchallengeable power.

How much are we honoring the mobile difference within culture, class, subjectivity, community (a term I prefer to "ethnicity" because it seems more accommodating of diversity), etc.?

The visibility of subjective internal differences is one of the central themes in Pantoja Hidalgo's *A Book of Dreams* (2001), an experimental novel where *heteroglossia* is brought in to remind the English speaking reader of the polyphony of Filipino's voices. She often develops a self-questioning sub-theme while focusing on subjective and interpersonal relations. Here is an example from the novel:

These elegant, androgynous, arrogant-looking young men puzzle Ruben. He wonders where they come from, what lives they live when they leave the dance floor. He wonders what hunger, what depths of loneliness impels women – middle aged women – to seek their company. He wonders whether his wife, for instance, has ever considered it, has ever sought them in secret. Would it surprise him if she had? Would it wound him? (2001, 59).

The *difference within* (simultaneously regarding gender, sexual representation, class and age) is here the object of understanding self and other, of recognizing the visible and invisible differences that phenomenologically characterize human experience, and the meanings developing it, and developed by it.

In the novel, the mix of a diurnal and a nocturnal logic (the logic of dreams) is achieved by the palimpsestic quality of the narrative, where multiple quotations from many literary traditions reveal the complexity of a Filipino self-representation. The cognitive challenge of the novel can be epitomized in the *radical* question: "Are the dreams the answers? Or are they the questions?" (Pantoja Hidalgo 2001, 141).

(3) The issue of subjective internal differences coming to visibility is denied by clichés, and therefore it is strongly linked to the issue of editorial and media constructions of marketable ethnic literary products. The homogenizing-global perspective enhanced by the use of English can certainly make Philippine literature in English more widely spread (and as a reader I am grateful for it!), but one has to wonder at what cost.

While addressing the Third Point I have previously outlined, i.e., the media construction and market dissemination of culture, I would like to remember one of San Juan's virulent essays addressing "The Dialectics of Praxis and Contradiction in Philippine Writing". He describes the danger of producing an imitative art, based on imported cultural models, an art which seems viable because it guarantees cultural and marketable recognition:

> Throughout the period of American colonialism (1900-1946), we encounter the Filipino petty bourgeoisie and illustrado class [the intelligentsia] collaborating with the colonial power. [...] Eventually, this policy of stultification bore fruit of such wide diversity, ranging from Zoilo Galang's fraudulent sentimentalism to the self-indulgent, vapid dilettanteism of Jose Garcia Villa and his cult (San Juan 1984, 72-3).

San Juan explains:

> Villa then tried to sublimate his alienation in art-forms belatedly derived from the parallel American movement of the Lost Generation (Gertrude Stein, Anderson, Cummings), rejecting the conventional premises of the Genteel Tradition and commercialized art, in favor of abstract experiments and expressionist/nihilist devices of estrangement (1984, 76).

There is some critical dissent regarding San Juan's evaluation of Villa's work, but it is important to remember with him how the act of conforming to a recognizable model, one that has established its marketability, enhances the construction and dissemination of certain local products.

At any rate, it seems very interesting to note that in 1979 Joseph A. Galdon was stating that: "The novel in English in the Philippines is less than sixty years old and the total number of published novels is less than one hundred" (1979, v). Thirty years later, these figures are drastically modified by an unforeseeable and extraordinary increase in creative production, one that more and more presents the complexity of Filipino subjectivity and literature to the English speaking world.

So long as Filipinos can have a free access to writing, without compromising their voice, the world will enjoy the specificity of a cultural production bearing all the signs of the history lived and the one people are living.

In relation to the valorization of literature that goes along with marketability, I would like to remember a significant point made by Galdon that regards the Euro-American obsession with canon definition (and "anxiety of influence"). Indeed, any canon, ultimately, does not accommodate certain literary productions. He writes:

The Philippine novel in English has been neglected in recent years because (mortal sin of criticism) it has *not been accepted on its own terms*, but has been asked to be something that it could not be (1979, 2; Italics added).[3]

An increasingly strong critique of canon definition comes to the Eurocentric and Anglo-American critical world by non 'westernized' countries. As underscored in the quote above, canon fascination is often a way of regulating literary productions, at the cost of ignoring literatures that should be understood "in their own terms".

Furthermore, Filipinos are extremely aware of the fact that consumeristic literary myths, such as "the dazzle of downtown Manhattan's myriad lights, [*and*] the thrill of meeting the Hollywood icons up close and personal" produce an "anecdotal evidence [*which*] is almost completely contradicted by the literary evidence" (Pantoja Hidalgo 2006, 107-108). This statement should be read as ultimately restoring to literature the responsibility of commitment, of dedication, even of obligation, to be 'truth-seeking', and confers to literature the responsibility of being the voice of a periphery that challenges the center(s).

There is no room here to discuss at length how the dominant aesthetics of Filipino literature is today rooted in a procedural opportunity of realism, convoked as necessary to respect 'the order of things', but simultaneously invoked as the constant transformation of form. This connection of 'form' and 'content' seems to me the distinctive feature of the dominant national aesthetics today in the Philippines. In the words of Abad, here is a synthesis of such a complex cultural semiosis in progress:

When the mind loses a name, it loses a perception.
The name is essential to its continence
Or it wounds itself in the thing it does not respect.
O the thing whispers ex cathedra its theme.
(Abad, 2004, *The Pope Expels Certain Saints*, 9)

"Continence" is the key-word which indicates that signification is a process, rather than a stultified meaning inscribed in a name.

---

[3] This is the hallmark feature of all minorities aspiring to self-representation.

Also Dalisay's novel *Soledad's Sister* is an astounding example of *literature engagée*. Stylistically, its pervasive use of irony, with its subtle spectrum of variations, seems to partake of the postmodern imperatives of derisive dexterity and nimbleness, but ultimately it is a brilliant example of how Philippine literature can challenge the centrality of stereotypes.

Sometimes the Philippine literary challenge takes the form of grim humor (as in Dalysay's novel where the narrative starts with the embarrassing presence of an unclaimed body landing at the airport as cargo); sometimes it ridicules protocols of allusions (both stylistic and cultural); sometimes it laughs at the "one and only" hegemonic perspective on things. All of these are forms of decentering an unquestionable absolute, which is definitely challenged, and if not destroyed, fizzled out.

Soledad's Sister even challenges the supremacy of the proper name to identify a person. The postmodern notion of the iterability of the signifier, which makes names work in the absence of things, becomes the base for a displacing move which makes the semantics of the proper name an open existential issue:

> On a cloud-curtained evening, one Saturday in August, a corpse arrived in a zinc casket in a wooden crate at Ninoy Aquino International Airport. [...] The cargo manifest put the dead woman's name down as "Cabahug, Aurora V." (Dalisay 2008, 2).

So is Aurora Soledad's sister (as apparently alluded to in the title of the novel)? Yes, it is, but Aurora is not the one in the casket. Only towards the end of the novel do we learn that the presumed Aurora is Soledad, and Soledad's sister is Aurora, in spite of the identification conveyed in the opening lines of the novel.

Indeed: "what's in a name"?

The hurried reassurance for a "well round character" is gently derided in articulating the main theme of the story: the worth and meaning of a human being. In short, we could say that the 'moral of the fable' is that a human being exists only if one understands and cares to understand his/her life.

Soledad is a perfectly invisible character, one who becomes visible only if you stay with the story; only if you care to know her story.

As the plot develops you literally get to know her, by way of the negative: who she is not, rather than who she is; what she is not, rather than what she appears to be. Knowing her is something to be achieved, with care and attention to the individual universality of her being.

So she is always in danger of being 'lost', and the meaning and risk of loss is explored in detail throughout the novel, in relation to her, to her sister, to her community, to her country. She is lost in her relations because they are not socially visible and valuable. Soledad can be lost physically (even her corpse can be lost in multiple occasions), and she is lost socially and psychologically (to some extent, when she could not imagine the price of her social transgression).

Ultimately, all the characters in the novel are always in danger of being *desaparecidos*. Soledad's sister observes:

> "Where are they now. Where's everyone?" The unexpected, perhaps unintended directness of his questions struck her in her ribs. Where, indeed, was everyone but gone, no starker reminder of which existed than the woman in the box that was her blood and bone. [...] She felt a sudden need to run out to the van and touch the crate, to reconnect with Soledad in some tangible and physical way (Dalisay 2008, 136-137).

The iterability of the signifier is so ambivalent, that sometimes the name "wounds itself in the thing it does not respect" (Abad 2004, 9), so that it become imperative "to reconnect [...] in some tangible and physical way".

(4) As regards cultural self-understanding and self-representation (my Fourth Point), we must notice some of the recurrent features of the personal and cultural dilemmas surfacing in Philippine literature: self-expression vs. survival; contemporary values vs. traditional values; valorization of the individual vs. valorization of the collective.

The variety of phenomenological definitions of human experience is both unavoidable and enriching. After all, it is worth remembering that in his *The Order of Things* (1973) Foucault writes: "Man is only a recent invention, a figure not yet two centuries old, a new wrinkle in our knowledge [...] he will disappear again as soon as that knowledge has discovered a new form" (1973, xxiii). We do not know yet *how* new forms of knowledge will produce new subjects, but the responsibility of developing certain ways of knowing rests on our desires and ethical choices.

Furthermore, the "invention of man" to which Foucault refers is also something we learn culturally, but our cultural presuppositions are also what makes us blind, in a different way, in every different culture. Learning how Filipinos and post(?)-colonial subjects define themselves as humans and as agents, can only enrich the possibilities of a new knowledge, social, political, and even ontological.

Another point I would like to make is to remember that there is no cultural simultaneity in the development of what is considered human, and therefore globalization must not establish itself as the destiny imposed to all by hegemonic cultures (a destiny because everybody should 'progress' according to their established priorities).

Pantoja Hidalgo writes about her own awareness of the limitations of a certain knowledge production, and her desire for a transformation of knowledge which would accommodate the mobile complexity of so called "expatriates", and also give visibility to silenced subjects (women in this case):

When I began reading Edward Said et al. – it troubled me that those writers
whose essays had given me so much pleasure were all from the west (and
that most of them were men). I was afraid I might have fallen into the trap
of regarding other peoples as my "other", defining them as my antitheses.
And it seemed to me profoundly ironic that I, an oriental, should be guilty
of "orientalism". When critics like Petronilo Daroy, Isagani Cruz, and
Alfredo Salanga wrote of my essays as being very "Filipino", despite my
being what they called an "expatriate writer", I was extremely relieved
(Pantoja Hidalgo 2006, 7).

What I find very interesting in this critical report is the non-essentialist
complexity of a critical inquiry of location, regarding authorship, authority,
rooting and belonging.

Cultural self-understanding as well as the power-dynamics of cultural
recognition and valorization interact in ways that symbolically determine the
specificity of socio-cultural communities. In relation to Filippino culture and
self-recognition Abad wrote:

> In our cultivation of a poetic terrain that had been subtly transformed by
> more than three centuries of Spanish rule, and tilled again in our fascination
> with "democratic vistas" in the English language, the poetic course was as
> always a long and creative struggle with both the poet's medium and the
> poet's subject. English had to be naturalized, as it were, and become Filipino
> – nothing short of *a* national language. [...] At first, indeed, we wrote *in*
> English, and freely borrowed and adopted, and then, we wrought *from*
> English, and forged ourselves and our own "scene so fair" where we worked
> out our own destiny (Abad 2008, 14).

The transformation from a passive and borrowed "wrote" to a "wrought"
("we wrote *in* English [...] we wrought *from* English") indicates the work of self-
expression, which is unavoidable for both individuals and cultures. Furthermore,
the homophonic texture (wrote/wrought) can only emphasize the overlapping of
post(?)-colonial cultures and colonizing cultures; the overlapping of being ruled
by a language which is – at the same time – the language of self-representation.

(5) As regards my Fifth Point, I should mention the development of specific
hermeneutical protocols in the Philippines, which is recognized by various critics
as having been strongly influenced by an Anglo-American tradition. San Juan's
Hegemony and Strategies of Transgression (1995) highlights the movement from
New Criticism and Deconstruction to what he calls "a Poetics of Redemption"
performed at the margins of the market empire:

> the struggle is chiefly for bread, land, shelter – for the integral and organic
> conditions of possibility for rational communicative actions free from the
> violence of capital [...] I envisage the transition from Western "hegemony"

to the transformative and oppositional practices of all those "others" inhabiting margins, pariah zones, quarantines, detention and deportation centers, internal colonies in North America and in Europe (San Juan 1995, 8).

With all due respect for an organic Gramscian intellectual of his prominence, I would like to change slightly San Juan's phrasing regarding "oppositional" practices, and suggest the alternative of "resisting" practices. Actually, this critical alertness is what I have perceived in the Philippines, where internal complex protocols of self-understanding national culture are resisting the outside pressure towards the effacement of its specificity.

Finally, and to conclude, let me quote yet again, another one of Abad's poems:

> Our eyes must claim their right
> to our landscape and its names.
> What cataract of other minds
> has flooded their sight?
> We must even fall from our own sky
> to find our earth again.
> (Abad 2004, 119)

I think this invitation applies today to Europeans as well: when will we "find our earth"?

And when will we understand that the sky we have presupposed as "ours" is not just our own, but is everybody's sky?

References

Abad G.H. 2004. *In Ordinary Time. Poems, Parables, Poetics, 1973-2003*. Quezon City, Diliman: The University of the Philippines Press.

Abad G.H. 2008. *Our Scene so Fair. Filipino Poetry in English, 1905-1955*. Quezon City, Diliman: The University of the Philippines Press.

Dalisay J. 2008. *Soledad's Sister*. Pasig City: Anvil Publishing.

Dato R. 1924. *Filippino Poetry*. Manila: J.S. Agustin and Sons.

Di Blasio F. 2005. *The Pelican and the Wintamarra Tree: voci della letteratura aborigena australiana*. Trento: Editrice Università degli Studi di Trento, Collana Labirinti.

Di Blasio F. 2006. "'Post-Colonial – NOT!': Defining Aboriginality in Contemporary/Post(?)-Colonial Australia". In Palusci O. (ed.) *Postcolonial Studies: Changing Perceptions*. Trento: Editrice Università degli Studi di Trento, Collana Labirinti, 175-287.

Foucault M. 1973. *The Order of Things*. New York: Vintage.

Galdon J.A. (ed.) 1979. *The Philippine Novel in English*. Quezon City: Ateneo de Manila University Press.

Jenkins J. 2007. *English as a Lingua Franca: Attitude and Identity*. Oxford: Oxford University Press.

Joaquin N. 2000. "Tomorrow and Letters". In *Philippine Graphic*, July 17th, 11.

Pantoja Hidalgo C. 2001. *A Book of Dreams. A Novel*. Quezon City, Diliman: The University of the Philippines Press.

Pantoja Hidalgo C. 2006. *Over a Cup of Ginger Tea. Conversations on the Literary Narratives of Filipino Women*. Manila: The University of the Philippine Press.

San Juan E. 1984. *Toward a People's Literature*. Quezon City, Diliman: The University of the Philippines Press.

San Juan E. 1994. *From the Masses to the Masses. Third World Literature and Revolution*. Minneapolis: University of Minnesota MEP Publications.

San Juan E. 1995. *Hegemony and Strategies of Transgression. Essays in Cultural Studies and Comparative Literature*. New York: State University of New York Press.

Tupas F.T.R. (ed.) 2007. *(Re)Making Society. The Politics of Language, Discourse, and Identity in the Philippines*. Quezon City, Diliman: The University of the Philippines Press.

ELISABETTA ZURRU

Università di Genova

The Morichjhāpi Massacre:
Re-constructing Silenced Knowledge

1. Introduction

Since 'official' *History* has often overlooked the violence that colonized peoples experienced both during colonialism and during the regimes following it, an important issue in postcolonial literature is to re-read *History* and to present alternative versions of it, in an attempt to unveil the hidden truth, and re-construct the readers' knowledge of those events which have been silenced or altered by colonial and *post*colonial regimes. This result is often obtained through the narration of individual *h*istories, which run alongside the official account of historical events and interact with it.

The present paper deals with an example of this kind of writing, where fictional narration is interwoven with the 're-narration' of historical facts about which very little is known. In particular, the paper will focus on Amitav Ghosh's *The Hungry Tide* (2004), a novel that revolves around the massacre of the refugees who had settled on Morichjhāpi island in 1979, operated by the Bengali government. It could be argued that *The Hungry Tide* does not, in fact, represent an example of postcolonial writing, since it focuses on a massacre which has been brought about by the Bengali government and not by the British colonizers. In other words, the massacre was not *technically* caused by the colonizers, but by the local government. However, *a*) it would be difficult to deny that the socio-political instability of the Indian subcontinent in 1947 was the result of centuries of British colonization on the one hand and of their subsequent departure on the other, and *b*) not only is postcolonial writing interested in unveiling the colonizers' actions but it also aims at describing the consequences of colonization, first and foremost the violence of the local regimes which took the power after the colonizers' departure. Furthermore, it is not untypical of Ghosh to describe in his works the violence of colonial regimes *and* of postcolonial regimes, a theme he has explored not only in *The Hungry Tide*, but also in *The Circle of Reason* (Mondal 2007, 17).

Therefore, the paper will investigate, through stylistic means (Douthwaite 2000; Conrad and Biber 1999; Leech and Short 2007; Short 1996), the writing strategies the author employs in this novel to re-present this forgotten tragic event.

2. The silenced tide of the Morichjhāpi massacre

2.1 *Socio-historical background*

The massacre referred to in *The Hungry Tide* took place in the area of the Sundarbans, the mangrove forest which stretches along the mouth of the Ganges delta.

The reasons leading to this event have their roots in the long history of communal and caste conflict in the Indo-Bengali area (Mallick 1999, 104). At Indian independence (1947), the Province of Bengal was split into two parts. Almost all of the Hindu landlords fled to West Bengal, which was part of India. East Bengal became part of the Muslim state of Pakistan instead. This meant that communal turmoil was directed against the Hindu Untouchables who had remained in East Bengal. When these outcast people started fleeing to India they did not obtain the same treatment their upper class counterparts had received. On the basis that there was no place in West Bengal for them, they were resettled in other states, where the refugees "often spent many years in prison camp conditions" (Mallick 1999, 105). However, the left wing opposition suggested that they should be resettled in their native Bengal and one of the places mentioned was the West Bengali area of the Sundarbans. Therefore, when the left-dominated opposition came to power, almost 15,000 families started the journey back to West Bengal. Those who survived the trip settled on the island of Morichjhāpi, where they started to build their own community.

However, the new government policy regarding refugees had changed in the meanwhile, so that it refused to tolerate such an action and declared the occupation of the island illegal. The violation of the Forest Acts was pled, since the Sundarbans were part of the Government Reserve Forest and the habitat of the last Royal Bengal tigers. Furthermore, "the West Bengal government started on January 26, 1979, an economic blockade of the settlement [...]. The community was tear-gassed, huts were razed, and fisheries and tube wells were destroyed, in an attempt to deprive refugees of food and water" (Mallick 1999, 107).

2.2 *The 'fictional' representation of the massacre: The Hungry Tide*

The novels by Amitav Ghosh exhibit a close relationship with the historical events they recount, which often constitute, as in the case of *The Hungry Tide*, the backbone of the novels themselves. Indeed, many of Ghosh's works "seek to deconstruct, or at least to put into question, the value of distinguishing between 'fact' and 'fiction'" (Mondal 2007, 19). In other words, Ghosh's novels show a deep-rooted interest in the reconsideration of those 'facts' which are usually considered the territory of official historiography, in the belief that the explanations the latter provides are not necessarily more truthful than those offered by narrative fiction.

Taking this premise into account, it is not surprising that, in *The Hungry Tide*, the narration of the events leading to the massacre and of the massacre itself is supplied with precise dates and historical details, besides having been brought back to life through intense narrative and linguistic strategies.

Indeed, as far as the organization of the narration is concerned, the telling of the massacre does not constitute the main thread of the narration, the "first narrative" in Genette's terms (1980, 48), but it is presented through an heterodiegetic analepsis (*ibidem*), or flashback, which constitutes the "second narrative" of the novel. In fact, the events have been recorded in a diary by the schoolmaster Nirmal, a diary which has been found many years after the massacre. The events in Morichjhāpi and the means selected to recount them appear to share the same destiny: they had been lost but have now be found – and can be unveiled.

2.3 *Text 1 – Nirmal's manifesto*

Two extracts from this diary will be subjected to stylistic analysis. Before turning to the close reading of the two excerpts some information about their co-text should be provided.

As the (hi)story contained in the diary unfolds, readers are informed that Nirmal has witnessed the events leading to the massacre and has left the island only a few hours before it actually occurred. He had been visiting Morichjhāpi regularly since the refugees' struggle started in order to help Kusum, a girl he had known since she was a child. The only evidence of his involvement in the issue is a diary he writes the day before the tragedy.

On its first page he states (Ghosh 2004, 58):

TEXT 1
[1] I am afraid because I know that after the storm passes, the events that have preceded its coming will be forgotten. [2] No one knows better than I how skilful the tide country is in silting over its past.
[3] There is nothing I can do to stop what lies ahead. [4] But I was once a writer; [5] perhaps I can make at least that what happened here leaves some trace, some hold upon the memory of the world.

The focalizer in Text 1 is clearly Nirmal, who is writing in the first person. [1] and [2] are characterized by highly metaphorical language. In [1] the events

Nirmal is witnessing are compared to a "storm". However, in the first clause of [1], it is the "passing" of the storm Nirmal is referring to, rather than its coming. On the other hand, the "coming" of the storm is referred to in the second clause of [1]. Such an inversion allows two interpretations. The first one concerns Nirmal's awareness about the reduced span of time which separates this moment from the attack, so that the passing of the storm appears to be as near as its coming (it should be pointed out that Nirmal starts writing the day before the attack *precisely* because he knows the attack is about to take place). The second one regards the implied suggestion that, in the events he is about to describe, some kind of 'inversion' in the natural order of things is taking place, just as the "coming" and "passing" of the storm have been inverted in the sentence – this second interpretation being supported by Kusum's words in Text 2, as we shall see shortly.

[2] exhibits another instantiation of metaphorical language, since the cancellation of history is assigned here to the "tide country", which becomes a "skilful" entity covering up the "past".

Some considerations can be drawn. First of all, since an inanimate entity cannot perform any action, least of all that of covering up its past traces, the "tide country" is anthropomorphised and represents a metaphor for those governing the country itself. Secondly, the lexemes "tide" and "silting (over)" reinforce each other in the creation of the image of the sand flowing, depositing and covering what lies beneath. Thirdly, the lexeme "past" bears end-focus and not only does it occupy sentence final position, but also paragraph final position – the lexeme is highly foregrounded (Douthwaite 2000). Furthermore, at the semantic level, the lexeme "past" in [2] represents an extension of "the events that have preceded" in [1]. Therefore, it is not only the situation in Morichjhāpi which is likely to be overshadowed, but the past as a whole appears to be at risk in the "tide country" – note also that the adjective "skilful" in [2] suggests expertise and repetitiveness (one needs to practise and repeat an activity before s/he can master it).

The sense of despair and helplessness depicted in the previous two sentences reaches its climax in [3]. The lexeme "nothing", signalling the absence of any possible action, functions as notional subject (Arts and Arts 1982) of the sentence, its meaning being further underlined by the combination of the two verbs "stop" and "lies ahead". Indeed, in Hallidyan terms (Halliday and Matthiessen 2004), the previous verb ("stop") expresses a Material process, (whose action is in actual fact denied by the deployment of the notional subject "nothing"), while the latter ("lies ahead") expresses an Existential process, the role Existent being covered by "what" (*viz.* the forthcoming massacre), whose occurrence, as already anticipated by the denial of the process of doing expressed by the material process, cannot be prevented.

The deployment of the conjunction "But" is sentence initial position in [4], however, appears to disconfirm what has been just claimed in [3]. A Relational processes (*ibidem*) is expressed here ("But I *was* once a writer"). The Relational process is expressed in the past tense, the tense being reinforced through the deployment of the adverb "once". The Attribute which is assigned to the Carrier, ("I"), is that of having been "a writer". Therefore, the sentence appears to suggest that his skills as a writer, even if representing a *past* Attribute, could represent a weapon to counteract the *present* impossibility of action expressed in [3]. This possibility is re-proposed in [5], through the deployment of the adverbials "perhaps" and "at least", conveying the attitudinal stance (Conrad and Biber 1999) of the narrator. Indeed, even if these adverbials convey uncertainty about the final result, they still express the fact that there exists a chance something could be done. It is also interesting to note that the writer of the diary delineates a stark contrast between his possible intervention, which is, indeed, presented as a mere possibility ("perhaps", "at least"), and the certainty of what is about to happen on the island. Indeed, what should be described with a future tense, for it has not taken place yet, is described as a past action ("what happened here"), namely as an event which has already happened. In other words, that on Morichjhāpi a massacre will be committed is beyond doubt; that Nirmal can do something about it cannot be taken for granted instead. If what he *will be able* to do is not certain, what he *wants* to do is much less. The result he wants to achieve is to "leave some trace" of what happened on the island, and graphology helps to clarify Nirmal's intent very clearly. Indeed, the noun phrase (NP) "some trace" is paraphrased in the subsequent NP "some hold upon the memory of the world". This strategy brings about a number of effects. First of all, the maxim of Quantity (Grice 1975) is flouted, since more information is provided than is required, the paraphrase constituting an unnecessary repetition in actual fact. Secondly, the insertion of the comma between the two NPs turns the second NP into a clause, by virtue of been included between the comma and the full stop. Therefore, the second NP is foregrounded by having being upshifted to the level of clause. Thirdly, the NP "the memory of the world" is placed in sentence final position, and it is therefore made psychologically salient. All these strategies contribute to make the 'final destination' Nirmal's words want to reach crystal clear.

This brief *manifesto* clearly expresses the need of this schoolmaster, who was once a writer, to leave a testimony of the Morichjhāpi massacre through his diary – and it seems to mirror one of the aims another writer has achieved with a novel entitled *The Hungry Tide*.

2.4 *Text 2 – Kusum's narration*

Text 2 represents the moment in the narration when the two main issues of the novel, the re-telling of silenced history and the ecological interrogatives concerning the balance between humans, animals and plants in the Sundarbans, clash with each other (Ghosh 2004, 216-217):

TEXT 2

[1] "Saar" [2] she said, wiping her face, "[3] the worst part was not the hunger or thirst. [4] It was to sit here, helpless, and listen to the policemen making their announcement, hearing them say that our lives, our existence, were worth less than dirt or dust. '[5] This island has to be saved for its trees, it has to be saved for its animals, it is a part of a reserve forest, it belongs to a project to save the tigers, which is paid for by people from all over the world'. [...] [6] Who are these people, I wondered, who love animals so much that they are willing to kill us for them? [7] Do they know what is being done in their name? [8] Where do they live, these people? [9] Do they have children, do they have mothers, fathers? [10] As I thought of these things, it seemed to me that this whole world had become a place of animals, and our fault, our crime, was just that we were human beings, trying to live as human beings always have, from the water and the soil [...]".

Even if a detailed stylistic reading of this passage cannot be provided here for reasons of space, some general considerations can be made.

Text 2 is part of a conversation between Nirmal and Kusum, where the latter tells the schoolmaster about the long-lasting blockade the refugees had to endure. In particular, in the excerpt above, Kusum's words are reported in the diary by Nirmal using Direct Speech (DS) – which is unsurprising, since particularly important conversational moments are usually reported using DS and with little narrative intervention (Short 1996, 299). The refugees' helplessness is referred to in [3] and [4] first and foremost at the semantic level, since the refugees constitute the referent for a whole array of negatively value-loaded lexemes: "hunger", "thirst", "helpless", "worth less than dirt or dust". [5], on the other hand, is a case of speech presentation embedded inside speech presentation (*ibidem*), since it expresses the policemen's words, which are reported by Kusum, whose words are in turn being reported by Nirmal. [5] represents a compound sentence constituted by five paratactic clauses: four main clauses and a final relative clause. Each clause offers one 'explanation' of the blockade: the trees, the animals, the reserve forest, the tigers and, most important of all, (note that the fifth clause is foregrounded, hence highlighted, because it is a) the last clause in the sentence, thus it is perceptually salient, and b) an example of internal deviation (*ibidem*), since it is the only relative clause in a sentence where the norm is a sequence of paratactic main clauses), the money paid by the people supporting the project to save the last Royal Bengal tigers. In [6]-[9] a sequence of rhetorical questions is built by Kusum, which brilliantly pinpoint several issues regarding the main themes treated in the novel: the way the international scene can affect a local situation, the way one group can exploit the action of another group to its own end (in this case, the aims of the 'foreigners' are manipulated by the Bengali government), the issue of the natural equilibrium of the environment as well as the issue of ecological demands, and perplexities and questions about the right to freedom and a home. The latter points are reinforced in [10] where not only is an inversion in the natural order of things (see 2.3 above) described, with animals treated as human beings and human beings as animals, but also a clear-cut distinction between these two categories is traced: animals, as a metaphor for 'creatures with no respect for human life', are opposed to human beings, whose only wish is to survive by fishing and planting the soil. Humanity – Kusum's words seem to suggest – is the only crime.

3. Conclusions

In spite of hunger and disease the refugees refused to give up their struggle. Therefore, "the State Government ordered the forcible evacuation of the refugees, which took place from May 14 to May 16, 1979" (Mallick 1999, 110).

Nirmal's last words were written in his diary a few hours before the attack began. Therefore, the end of the story is not told 'firsthand'. Nevertheless, readers are informed that the truth about what really happened is unknown. It has been said that some women, among whom was Kusum, were abused and killed. Their corpses were "thrown into the rivers, so they would be washed away by the tides. Dozens of settlers were killed that day. The sea claimed them all" (Ghosh 2004, 231).

It has been estimated that at least 17,000 people died in Morichjhāpi before and during the massacre (Mallick 1999, 114).

The events in Morichjhāpi were covered up by the government of the time while they were still taking place. There were attempts to silence the press and the people responsible for the tragedy were not brought to trial. Furthermore, the ecological issues related to the preservation of the ecosystem of the island were soon forgotten, when the government allowed its supporters to settle in Morichjhāpi and make use of the facilities built by the evicted people (Mallick 1999, 112).

In this paper, the linguistic and narrative strategies deployed by the author to offer such a vivid reconstruction of what happened during the Morichjhāpi massacre have been revealed through a necessarily brief stylistic analysis. By referring to the events in Morichjhāpi and by providing the readers with such a touching yet neat account, Ghosh has presented an alternative version of a silenced episode, that had been cast out of History. The inclusion of this (hi)story in the work of such a renowned author could not but help restore a correct memory of what occurred.

References

Conrad S., Biber D. 1999. "Adverbial Marking of Stance in Speech and Writing". In Hunston S., Thompson G. (eds.) *Evaluation in Text. Authorial Stance and the Construction of Discourse*. Oxford: Oxford UP 56-73.

Douthwaite J. 2000. *Towards a Linguistic Theory of Foregrounding*. Alessandria: Edizioni dell'Orso.

Genette G. 1980. *Narrative Discourse*. Ithaca: Cornell UP.

Ghosh A. 2004. *The Hungry Tide*. New York: Harper Collins.

Grice H.P. 1975. "Logic and Conversation". In Cole P., Morgan J. (eds.) *Syntax and Semantics 3: Speech Acts*. New York: Academic, 41-58.

Halliday M.A.K., Matthiessen C.M.I. M. 2004. *An Introduction to Functional Grammar*. London: Arnold.

Leech J., Short M. 2007 [1st ed. 1981]. *Style in Fiction: A Linguistic Introduction to English Fictional Prose*. London: Longman.

Mallick R. 1999. "Refugee Resettlement in Forest Reserves: West Bengal Policy Reversal and the Morichjhāpi Massacre". In *The Journal of Asian Studies* 58, 1, 104-125.

Mondal A. 2007. *Amitav Ghosh*. Manchester: Manchester UP.

Short M. 1996. *Exploring the Language of Poems, Plays and Prose*. London: Longman.

FRANCESCA DI BLASIO

Università di Trento

"We meet/Between the furnace and the flying/ In the mouth of cohabitation": Australian Indigenous Culture in the 21st Century

Australia's Indigenous culture is a vivid and ever-growing phenomenon that finds artistic expression in a variety of forms, i.e. in written, visual, and performative texts. It also relies on a millennial cultural tradition, devastated by the traumatic event of the English invasion of the Australian continent in the Eighteenth century, and nevertheless still surviving in the hybrid forms of contemporary artistic production that often gesture towards a mythical past.

Aboriginal Australian myths posit a strong and special connection between the body and the land, in the sense that the human being is perceived as "ontologically" coming from the land, and as made of the very same substance. Symmetrically, the land is conceptualised as literally the result of the bodies of the ancestral beings who, in their continuous wanderings, left their marks and their vitality in/on it. The traditional oral literature of Aboriginal people corresponds to the mythical, philosophical and poetic narration of this perception of reality and its modern (written) versions are meant to re-actualise, and to re-enact the process of creation of the land and of the human body, as they were posited in the "Dreamtime".

My paper focuses on the relation between this cultural background and a selection of Australian contemporary written texts. In particular, it is concerned with the works of two contemporary Australian women writers, Patricia Sykes and Lisa Bellear, who, from different angles, respectively the point of view of a white and of an Aboriginal voice, come to terms with the trauma of the invasion and its post traumatic effects, and meet, as my title goes, "between the furnace and the flying/in the mouth of cohabitation". These narratives of dispossession and reorientation thematise experiences of border-crossing, through significantly hybrid forms of writing which try to recover an identity suspended between past and present. They interrogate the style of the dominant (domineering) white establishment. They also voice challenges and changes for the future, since they invite discussion of seminal issues, such as: the need to preserve cultures that are under the threat of disappearance; the meaning of "minor" literature and culture (in the Deleuzean sense of the term); the confrontation with forms of "otherness"; the preservation or transformation of individual cultures in multicultural societies; social and cultural hybridisation.

1. "To dream a bird is to decide its future": memory of different pasts and desire for the future in Patricia Sykes' Modewarre

Patricia Sykes is a living Australian poet of the state of Victoria who has earned international reputation with two collections of poems that have been awarded various Australian prizes: *Wire Dancing* (1999) and *Modewarre. Home Ground* (2004). Despite its narrative non-linearity, *Modewarre* can be considered an epic poem in three parts: "House of the Bird"; "House of Water"; "House of Detention". It is based on the symbolical totemic figure of the musk duck, "modewarre" in the Indigenous Wathaurong version of the word. The idea of the totem is central in the Indigenous traditional *Weltanschauung*, since it recalls the ancestral beings who created the world, or better a given part of it (a cliff, a desert, a gulf, a hill, and so on) and everything in it, including human beings (a given group, or tribe corresponding to the inhabitants of that particular part of the world). In this cosmogony there is a sort of physical affiliation between the totem and its creations: they share an "identity of substance" originating from their common relation with the land. As I have explained above, this is the main cosmogonic principle in most Aboriginal myths and the pattern at the basis of traditional Indigenous literature, which is seen as a form of re-actualisation of the primordial creative event, and a celebration of the continuity of life. These epistemic premises are among the most diverging and distancing cultural elements between the culture of Indigenous people and white Australians. Not surprisingly, they account for their opposite consideration of the land: the land is something to possess for the latter, but it is something to belong to for the former. In *Modewarre*, Sykes puts into a dialogic dimension these different perceptions, in a way that is not simplistic and that doesn't overlook the difficulties and the pain stemming from this conflict. She manages to propose a multifaceted look on the past and on the future. My analysis of the first part of the poem will hopefully demonstrate that it is centred on the recognition of a cultural specificity which nevertheless has to confront a changing epistemic context. Sykes outlines a progressive path to be taken in order to avoid the loss of identity, a path in which adaptation may lead to preservation.

In the opening section of part one, "House of the Bird", and in the first poem entitled *Modewarre – ways you might approach it* (Sykes 2004, 3), maps are the symbol of a confrontation with an alien perception of reality, as testified by the subtitle:

1 difficulties with maps
1 Because the syllables
2 On the page are not
3 The land beneath the name

4 Because a childhood memory
5 Of place is not the same lake
6 Upon which the duck floats

[...]

12 Because of the woman

13 With the head of a bird
14 Who placed her ancient skull
15 In a cold stare against my own

16 The implacable kiss –
17 A silence inhuman
18 In its lack

19 Her visible intent
20 To be a disturbance
21 In the blood

22 As a pulse which meanders
23 Among the maps
24 Which do not exist
(Sykes 2004, 3)

The land (l. 3) which used to be "whole" is described as being now parcelled and labelled in a series of arbitrary signs (ll. 1-2). At the same time, the ancient pre-colonial past free of maps (ll. 23-24), is personified by "the woman/ with the head of a bird" (ll. 12-13) who calls for attention, although her presence is characterised by silence and lack (ll.17-18), i.e. by the signs of dispossession which are the consequence of the invasion.

However, acts of identity may begin from memories of the past, through the recovery of ancient words, now written, rather than told:

2 acts of identity
1 Because this is a place of death
2 It is necessary to resort to books
3 Skin of the plant on which ink

4 Mimics the intrinsic knowledge
5 Of worms who being earthed
6 Have their heads deep into it

7 Doubly advantaged by there-ness
8 And un-need for meanings
(*ibidem*, 4)

The act of writing is here presented through a series of metaphors which link it to an extremely physical dimension that aims at encompassing the "arbitrariness" of words (presented in the first part). What is at stake now is the ancient ability of literally (re-)creating worlds through words: the pages are the skin of plants (ll. 2-3); the ink on them acts as worms that are "earthed" (l. 5), i.e. made of, and belonging to the earth, the uncompromising substance which is the origin of everything. Finally, the picture of a colonial and a pre-colonial past are fused in the following lines:

3   ancestral
1   Three roads meeting in the one bird:
2   Modewarre (the indigenous)
3   Biziura lobata (the colonial)
4   Musk duck (the common)

5   Between them everything ancestral
6   Their one lung the breath
7   Below water and above it

8   *"and so I am of the junction*
9   *And so my tongue rises to be born"*
(*ibidem*, 6)

This last segment corresponds to the theorisation of an hybrid identity that is able to express itself through words (l. 9) belonging to different traditions, times, spaces and circumstances. This concept is expressed in three different ways, proper to three different contexts (i.e., "the indigenous-the colonial-the common"). The identity that bears the memory of the knowledge of the "three roads" has to be an amphibious one (ll. 6-7), i.e. one that is able to breathe outside and inside water, like the totemic bird. This is the condition for having a future: "*so my tongue rises to be born*". The sense of this progression is thematised in the poem that follows, meaningfully entitled *Song of walking*:

1   *Having come so far, having gone –*
2   This way and none other
3   The ever hidden duck
4   Who had planned to be a silence
5   It is known her voice added weight
6   To creator and beginning
7   That were she touched air water land
8   Whoever follows has to make a choice
(*ibidem*, 12)

Past and present here merge in the expectation of the future. What was meant to remain secret by tradition (ll. 3-4), can be narrated in the hybridised context of the contemporary world. In this sense, narration is the silence of the totemic bird, whose voice had created the world in the original myths (ll. 6-7), but it is also an agent of re-creation, through the material realities of artistic creativity (l. 8). This gives a special meaning to the last, metapoetical segment analysed here, the fourth of the *"Brid"*[1], *eight darknesses* sequence, centred on the artistic production of Nyangangu, an existing woman carver of Arnhem Land:

1   Nyangangu, you carve
2   Like peeling back the skin
3   Inside the brid the next live
4   Brid, there, where you are,
5   Bred of earth, breeding sky
6   Working the uplift, wingbeat
7   As if sculpting a refusal
8   To die of white history
(*ibidem*, 25)

The idea of a stratified identity conveyed by the image of the peeling back of the skin in order to find "the next [...] brid" represents a special form of cultural hybridisation (ll. 2-3). At the same time though, the very process of carving that stratified identity *towards* the core of the wood symbolically represents a backward process towards the past "as if sculpting a refusal/To die of white history". There is a movement from the "youth" of the tree back to its earthly state, when the brid, and the wood it is made of, and the tree which provided the wood *were all* earth. And yet it is vitally important to fix a moment of being of the brid in an intermediate, historicised stage, and to do so by means of the artistic process, i.e. metaphorically in a curve of the wood itself, in the line of a wing. This is the task and challenge of contemporary Aboriginal literature: to re-create an identity stemming from a far away past, but embodying a desiring attitude toward the future.

2. "For the future I release this silenced voice":[2]
   Lisa Bellear's poetry

The following pages will examine a few poems by Lisa Bellear (1961-2006), an Indigenous Australian poet, activist, academic, broadcaster, and photographer. She is the author of *Dreaming in Urban Areas*, a collection

---

[1] Brid is the name given to her bird carving by Nyangangu, a Yolgnu, an artist of Northeast Arnhem Land and the protagonist of the sequence *Eight darknesses*.

[2] The line is taken from an unpublished poem that has been chosen for the tribute leaflet on the occasion of Bellear's funeral, and that can, as such, be considered her testament, a will of future sharing and hope (©Lisa Bellear, *A Significant Life*, unpublished).

published in 1996 from which most of the poems under consideration are taken. Despite her untimely death at 45, Bellear is one of the strongest and most significant voices of the Australian contemporary cultural scene. As Michael Brennan (2009) puts it:

> Bellear's work is a harrowing and a reckoning. Intensity and integrity form a powerful circuit here, as she takes to task the history and current realities and repercussions of Australia's invasion. Her poetry is able to move between sharply lucid portrayals of poverty and dispossession, community and hope, charting the struggle for survival and change. She gives voice to deep-seated frustration and rage, making the unspeakable in Australian history, past and present, speak with clarity, compassion and a righteous anger. All the while, her work expresses a sense of joy in community, strength of commitment and the will to see and effect change. Despite the deep reaches of pain evoked in her work, there is still optimism and the complexity of a survivor's humour. Throughout, there is a startling honesty, which lends every poem a striking clarity of vision and statement.

Bellear, a "stolen child" of the Noonuccal people of Minjerribah (Stradbroke Island, Queensland), gives voice, through her poetical production, to the sufferings and recovery of her people, and offers an outlook on the contemporary Aboriginal condition in Australia as deeply anchored in the past. In fact, the pre-colonial past occupies a very special place in Bellear's poetry, and is rarely evoked as something that has ceased to be. On the contrary, as in *Chops 'n' things* (Bellear 1996, 8), a poem dedicated to the Indigenous playwright and performer Eva Johnson, the evocation of the pre-colonial past is mostly set in terms of an aspiration for the future, a desiring rush towards something which has not really passed, but that is yet to come. This is evident in the opening line of the poem ("I can't wait to", l. 1) and in the progressive sequence of the lighting of a fire to be watched as it burns "down to the embers" (ll. 4-5):

1 I can't wait to curl around
2 A lemon scented tree
3 Light a fire and
4 Watch it burn down to
5 The embers as the sun
6 Floats away, far away
(Bellear 1996, 8)

Polysemy is poetry's privilege and, in fact, what we have here is a complex parallel between an extinguished fire and a disappearing sun (ll. 5-6), two metaphors of death, contradicted in the following stanza by the image of the ancestors who appear precisely *in* the extinguishing fire (ll. 10-14). Their "yarning and laughing" (l. 8) is vivid and lively, joyful and a bit sardonic, and the progressive form of the present tense confirms the sense of something which is happening "right now" and continuing into the future:

1 Our ancestors are
2 Yarning and laughing
3 At this Koori woman
4 And through the
5 Flames, the embers
6 And the burnt chops
7 And the charcoaled
8 Potatoes wrapped in foil
9 They're saying, tidda girl
10 You're ok,
11 Keep on dreaming
12 Keep on believing
(*ibidem*, 8)

The last two lines confirm the sense of a legacy, a desire for continuity and openness towards the future: "Keep on dreaming/Keep on believing" (ll. 17-18); "dreaming" recreates the special connection with the past that this verb is able to convey when taken in its proper Aboriginal English meaning, as I have said above. The concept of "Dreamtime" or "Dreaming" gives the most intense significance to the correlation and dialectical relationship between past and present, or, even better epistemologically speaking, future. The recollection of the past in traditional Indigenous culture is the form of memory that is best capable of giving shape to one's own identity and future; as such it is an antidote against disappearance and oblivion.

The ending of another poem, *Woman of the Dreaming* (*ibidem*, 11), literally thematises the movement to and fro between past and present (ll. 25-29), and the preservation of identity deriving from this movement widens to involve not only individual consciousness, but also the collective awareness (ll. 29-31) of a cultural specificity:

25 Woman of the dreaming
26 Find your soul,
27 And peace and love and
28 Eternal fire and spirit will
29 Connect with our ancestors
30 And our land
31 Will begin to smile, again.
(*ibidem*, 11)

What Brennan, in his assessment of Bellear's artistic achievement, calls "the complexity of a survivor's humour" can clearly be found in *Souled out* (*ibidem*, 43), a poem characterised by a sharp sense of irony against the representations of "true Aboriginality" by white people. The pun in the title (between "soul" and "sold") anticipates the theme of the poem: i.e. the most recent economic exploitation by white Australians of the image of the traditional Aborigines and of their ways of life. White people pervert aspects of Aboriginal culture (spirituality, l. 10, respect for the Elders, l. 15, Dreamtime, l. 17) into a series of commercialised clichés, whereby these terms take on the hue of "fake" and "falsity":

1   Only $200 – Ladies!
2   Gents and you could
3   Become an Aborigine
4   For two whole days!
5   Hey lady, what's sar matter
6   Haven't you seen
7   One before?
8   Come and experience
9   The lifestyles and
10 Mystical spirituality
11 That is quintessential
12 To the life and existence
13 Of a Traditional Aborigine
14 We'll also have a real
15 Properly initiated Elder
16 Who will empower you
17 With Dreamtime secrets
18 From an ancient culture
19 And for an extra fifty bucks
20 We'll throw in some
21 Real live witchetty grubs
22 And eat them, just like
23 The Natives did all those
24 Dreamtimes ago.
(*ibidem*, 43)

In this poem the point of view on the traditional Indigenous past is firmly held by an alien gaze that is utterly unable to read it properly. The dialectic between past and present, which is at the core of Aboriginal contemporary culture and literature is obliterated by white coarse slogans. This results in a sarcastic attack on the part of the Aboriginal poet against the totally misleading representation of the past on the part of greedy whites. The focus on the ancient traditions of Indigenous culture – and the recovery of a sense of identity stemming from it –, give way to a political and polemical attack against the dispossessor, highlighting the difficulty of preserving both identity and culture after the trauma of the invasion, this being the challenge Indigenous culture of Australia has to face for the next millennium.

References

Bellear L. 1996. *Dreaming in Urban Areas*, St. Lucia Qld.: University of Queensland Press.

Bhabha H. 1994. *The Location of Culture*. London & New York: Routledge.

Brennan M. 2009. *Lisa Bellear*. January, available at http://www.poetryinternational. org/piw_cms/cms/cms_module/index.php?obj_id=679 (last accessed August 2011).

Briskman L. 2003. *The Black Grapevine. Aboriginal Activism and the Stolen Generation*. Sidney: The Federation Press.

Brock P. (ed.) 1989. *Women, Rites & Sites: Aboriginal Women's Cultural Knowledge*. Sydney & Boston: Allen & Unwin.

Corona D., Castagna V., D'Alessandro S. (eds.) 2007. *Narratività storica e riscrittura*. Palermo: Annali della Facoltà di Lettere e Filosofia di Palermo.

Di Blasio F. 2005. *The Pelican and the Wintamarra Tree: voci della letteratura aborigena australiana*. Trento: Editrice Università degli Studi di Trento, Collana Labirinti.

Di Blasio F., Tamisari F. (eds.) 2007. *La sfida dell'arte indigena australiana. Tradizione, innovazione e contemporaneità*. Milano: Jacabook.

Hamilton P. 2006. "Sale of the Century? Memory and Historical Consciousness in Australia". In Hodgkin K., Radstone S. (eds.) *Memory, History, Nation: Contested Pasts*. New Brunswick & London: Transaction, 136-152.

Heiss A. 2003. *Dhuuluu-Yala To Talk Straight*. Canberra: Aboriginal Studies Press.

Minh-ha T.T. 1989. *Woman, Native, Other. Writing Postcoloniality and Feminism*. Bloomington: Indiana University Press.

Noonuccal Oodgeroo (K. Walker) 1965. *We Are Going* (1964). New York: The Citadel Press.

Reichl S. 2002. *Cultures in the Contact Zone. Ethnic Semiosis in Black British Literature*. Trier: WVT.

Said E. 1978. *Orientalism. Western Conceptions of the Orient*. New York: Pantheon Books.

Said E. 1993. *Culture and Imperialism*. New York: Knopf.

Simonsen K.M., Stougaard-Nielsen J. (eds.) 2008. *World Literatures World Cultures. History, Theory, Analysis*. Aarhus: Aarhus University Press.

Spivak G.C. 1988. *In Other Worlds: Essays in Cultural Politics*. New York & London: Routledge.

Spivak G.C. 1999. *A Critique of Postcolonial Reason: Toward a History of the Vanishing Present*. Cambridge (Mass.) & London: Harvard University Press.

Sykes P. 2004. *Modewarre. Home Ground*. Melbourne: Spinifex.

Young R.J.C. 2005. *Colonial Desire: Hybridity in Theory, Culture and Race*. London & New York: Routledge.

KATHERINE E. RUSSO

Università di Napoli L'Orientale

"When Was Modernism?": Towards an Interstitial Cartography of Australia's Modernity

Modernist writers struggled, in Ezra Pound's words, to "make it new" (1925). The term Modernism derives from the latin *modo* which means current, yet the term modern is frequently used in literary criticism to refer to the avant-garde, radical, progressive or even revolutionary connotations of the literary works of the period between the 1890s and the 1930s (Childs 2008; Cianci 1991). As Raymond Williams notes in the lecture "When Was Modernism?" (1987), the term modern has shifted from meaning 'now' to 'just now' as it was named and valued after the event at a time when the ideas of artistic worth and function appeared to be under threat. Thus, definitions of Modernism often fail to recognize the historicity of their own designation,

> 'Modernism' is confined to this highly selective field and denied to everything else in an act of pure ideology, whose first, unconscious irony is that, absurdly, it stops history dead. Modernism being the terminus, everything afterwards is counted out of development. It is *after,* stuck in the post [...] If we are to break out of the non-historical fixity of post-modernism, we must search out and counterpose an alternative tradition taken from the neglected works left in the wide margin of the century (Williams 1987, 35).

Following Williams's line of thought, recent studies have moved towards a constellated conceptualisation of Modernism: modernist literary criticism has changed as neglected works from the Empire are placed at the centre of Modernism's narrative (Brooker and Thacker 2005; Mercer 2005). It is now, perhaps both impossible and undesirable to speak of a single Modernism, and the practice of referring to Modernisms is widespread (Nicholls 1995).

Yet, the question of when Modernism started and ended, and whether we can regard it as a time-bound movement, remains unresolved in current literary criticism (Cianci 1991). Definitions of Modernism still seem to imply a precise limitation to the period between the 1890s-1930s, yet also a direct relation with late modernity. Modernism is often alternatively described as a celebratory response or reaction to late European and Anglo-American modernity and modernisation (Childs 2008, 18). Hence, the invariant periodization of Modernism may be due to the persistent use of a non-differential, Western, perspective on time and modernity. As Homi Bhabha argues, the racist discourse of modernity often underlies Modernist criticism as it based on the discriminatory temporality of the synchronous (1994, 344). Modernism's "sharing of equality is genuinely intended, but only so long as we start from a historically congruent space; the recognition is genuinely felt, but on terms that do not represent the historical genealogies [...] that constitute the partial cultures of the minority" (Bhabha 1996, 56). While works which are geographically remote but temporally synchronous may enter the Modernist canon, Modernisms which fall outside 'white' temporal frameworks of modernity continue to be represented as belated, as "what is after, stuck in the post" (Williams 1987, 35). Following the latter line of thought, this paper suggests that while Australian Modernist writers, such as Patrick White and Kenneth Slessor, have entered the Modernist canon as they write from the synchronous space of white modernity, Indigenous Australian writers question previous white definitions of Modernism and modernity and have therefore been excluded from the Australian modernist canon.

Pushing Williams's and Bhabha's arguments further, it may be contended that studies of Modernism commoditize a selective conceptualisation of time and modernity for contemporary readers. The reification of a specific conceptualization of time lies at the basis of what may be termed Modernism's "possessive investment" in white modernity, a story that remains largely invisible in the persistent severing discourses of development of histories of literature (Lipsitz, 1998). White modernity continues to be the unmarked norm of Modernism's historicity (i.e. of what counts as part of its history), which includes or excludes literary works according to shifting definitions of modernity and pre- or post-modernity (Chambers 1997). The insertion of previously excluded Australian modernist works interestingly shows a set of linked dimensions with Ruth Frankenberg's definition of the social organization and construction of 'whiteness',

> 'Whiteness' refers to a set of cultural practices that are usually unmarked and unnamed. [...] I have found most useful those analyses that view race as a socially constructed rather than inherently meaningful category, one linked to relations of power and processes of struggle, and one whose meaning changes over time (1993, 1-11).

Australian modernist writers have been notoriously slow to make a major impact, and were attacked by literary critics and journals of the time (Mcnamara *et al.* 2006). The representation of the complex life of the city, of industry and technology, and of war, responded to the impulses of a different life from that of the imaginary pioneer myth set in the bush and the outback. Correspondingly, Australian critics have often expressed a certain anxiety about the belatedness of Australian Modernism, as Vincent Buckley's reveals in his revaluation of the centrality of Australian Modernism in *Essays in Poetry, Mainly Australian*, "we are still not quite modern, as other literatures understand modernity. Yet we are on our way to being mature" (1969, 25). However, during the 1950-1960s, critics, such as Buckley and H. P. Heseltine rewrote the history of Australian literature to show that the Australian modernist poet and novelist, Kenneth Slessor and Patrick White, were to be considered Australia's literary "modernity and maturity" (Carter 2000, 275).

Conversely, the distancing and objectifying effect of Australian academic critique with its denial of its own temporal and historical contingency still disallows the possibility of Indigenous writing entering the space of the Australian modernist canon, labelling it as a 'contemporary', hence time-lagged, form of social protest. However, Stephen Muecke has recently suggested that "Indigenous modernity is quite different from European modernisation processes since it developed its own forms, later including modernist and postmodernist aesthetics" (2004, 5). Therefore, the main goal of studies of Indigenous Australian Modernism should not be the mere extension of the definition of Modernism to the Antipodes, but the investigation of how Modernism has been traversed, nourished, and contested by Indigenous Australian writers.

The employment of modernist forms for a different purpose underlies the fundamental contribution of Indigenous Australian writers to Modernism forcing "*us* to question previous definitions of the term itself" (Gikandi 1992, 254; my Italics). Already during the 1980s, the Australian critic, Mudrooroo, claimed that a new generation of Indigenous poets and writers had left a strong narrative preference for social realism behind to traverse old territories in new ways. Mudrooroo criticized the realist tradition of Indigenous literature and asserted that the poetry of Lionel Fogarty marked a pivotal shift in the history of Indigenous literature as its style and form was the most suitable to the Indigenous field of creation, the 'Dreaming' (Mudrooroo 1992; 1997). The strategic essentialism of Mudrooroo's definition pointed to Lionel Fogarty's employment of the English language as he was "shifting the complex meanings away from the familiar reality" signifying "a different reality structure" hidden within the English language (*ibidem* 1997, 83-84). According to Mudrooroo, Fogarty had broken free from received modes of representation, such as realism, only to resist the colonizing structures of the English language and disclose what Mudroroo defines as "an essential quintessence of Aboriginality" (1986, 49). Yet, the Australian critic also drew an overlooked, but significant, comparison between Fogarty and James Joyce, "As in *Finnegans Wake* by James Joyce, Lionel is using the alien English language in ways it has not been used before" (*ibidem* 1986, 49). In retrospect, Mudrooroo's controversial redefinition of Fogarty's poetry as the most authentic Aboriginal mode of representation shows many similarities with modernist critiques. According to Mudrooroo, he was

[...] the poet whose genius born from the struggle gave birth to a new style, or system of poetry drawing from a myriad of influences to forge an essential quintessence of Aboriginality. Here was no ersatz Bourgeois black in white face, but an Aboriginal man, a guerrilla poet using the language of the invader in an effort to smash open its shell and spill it over for poetic expression (*ibidem* 1986, 49).

Mudrooroo's key remarks on the "genius" and "newness" of Fogarty's style, but also on language as a surface that must be smashed open to reveal true poetic expression, anticipate a definition of Fogarty's poetry as modernist. Although Mudrooroo's Indigenous identity has since been disputed, his critical work has been well known among critics of Indigenous literature for at least three decades and has inspired many Indigenous writers. However, his groundbreaking, although rather oblique, modernist definition of Fogarty's poetry has been scarcely acknowledged. Arguably, the failure to recognize Fogarty's poetry as modernist may be due to his radical decolonization of Modernism: Fogarty's modernist poetry is not derivative but transformative, it is "iterative and interrogative" as its belatedness rewrites modernism and instates "a differential history that will not return to the power of the Same" (Bhabha 1994, 339).

Vers libre and symbolism are deployed by Fogarty for a strategic alliance of the aesthetic, the political and the spiritual and, most interestingly, an Indigenous appropriation of the modernist belief in the 'power of the word'. Words are chosen with precision for their intensity, the English language transcended in Indigenous spiritual symbols. Fogarty seeks to rise above the prison-house of Australian colonialism, and more specifically to escape the reality of the Cherbourg Aboriginal Reserve in Queensland where he grew up, the colonial education system, the harsh history of Australian eugenics, through his "spiritual and political understanding" (Fogarty 1995, ix). As Fogarty himself already revealed in the poem "Tired of Writing" (1982), *vers libre* is adopted to allow 'Indigenous thought patterns' to flow as, "in fine line/Our true times/ Are never true". The poem is a reflection on poetry as a necessary tool to solve the immediate issue of communicating in English Indigenous concepts:

> Carrying targets of beauty and living
> first tongue, painless are my words.
> We foresee sterile crippled shadows
> healing are answers.
> Midnight whitened muscles that
> frosted a country's autumn.
> My mind in time
> is what rhymes
> [...]
> Sometimes me write bad

just to be glad.
Little we read
dead seeds may be reeds of lifefullness.
So I wrote,
But will you remote, note
Space took pace
Rat race what a play, ace
Just in fine line
Our true times
Are never true
[...]
I see words beyond any acceptable meaning
And this is how I express my dreaming.
(Fogarty 1995, 109)

Hence, Fogarty's allusiveness is much more than wilful opacity for he develops a modernist strategy of linguistic displacement, shifting the sign from one meaning to another, only to express his "dreaming". The modernist proposition on language, its consideration of everyday language as clichéd, one-dimensional, abstract; and its efforts to revitalize perception through poetic language, its dislocation of meaning, are strategically adopted by Fogarty to disrupt linguistic expectations and allow the English language to "[carry] targets of beauty and living first tongue" as "dead seeds may be reeds of lifefullness" (*ibidem* 1995, 109).

According to Mudrooroo's essentialist interpretation, Fogarty's poetry may appear meaningless if "we fail to understand that we are confronted by groups of feeling-images rooted deep within the Aboriginal psyche and experience" (Mudrooroo 1986, 53). As Sabina Hopfer further suggests in an article (2002, 57) written in collaboration with Fogarty, the formal techniques of imagism are wielded by Fogarty in an effort to create a new language which may reflect an Indigenous symbolic reality. Fogarty's manuscripts combine image and word. The words are composed around painted signs and symbols and they form a structural entity with designs that signify the spiritual dimension of the Dreaming.

Already in 1995, Fogarty voiced his desire to publish his drawings in the introduction to the collection of poetry, *Munaldjali, Mutuerjaraera*: "What I want to achieve in my writing one day is to put Aboriginal designs of art inside the lettering to bring a broader understanding to the meaning of the text [...]" (1995, ix). Yet, the combined publication of his designs and poems was achieved only in 2002 when the literary journal, *Southerly*, published a series of poems and designs that were later republished in the poetry collection, *Minyung Woolah Binnung* (2004). Significantly, a close reading of the poem "Embassy" (2002; 2004) reveals a conscious rewriting of Modernism as Fogarty clearly refers to T. S. Eliot's *Waste Land* (1922):

I ravelling in another lands people
sparkling thoughts struck minds
Cringe psychology humour didn't
made me trendy trendy poems.
Raucous sense front faces
constantly came displayed.
Crossover filming symbolism hit
those Abo's childrens signs
[...]
I ravelling in your white land was too fast too slow
and massed to closed states
Motto till drops drink side ways
[...]
Waste howls around a hellish man
Waste land
surrounded a british man...
This place as the levels to spring
forward outer the hidden thing
Our mind are done in
Our spirits are done in
But the power to be over the possible
Will find the power of the pen
Is the safety to be out of
the blood and dives respects
being the oneness.
(2002, 69; my Italics)

The poem was inspired by the establishment of the Indigenous Embassy erected in a tent outside the Parliament House in Canberra in 1972. This famous historical episode was the apex of the Indigenous movement for Land Rights. It was covered by broadcast media and is quite well known by the general Australian public. Yet, the gap between the mediatic representation of this historical episode and Fogarty's rewriting of the episode as a symbol of the possibility of interrupting the white image of Modernism and modernity is evident. Fogarty's poem addresses the denial of what has often been left unsaid in the retrospective construction of Australia's Modernism, the impossibility of facing that "difficult borderline, the interstitial experience between what we take to be the image of the past and what is in fact involved in the passing of time and the passage of meaning" (Bhabha 1996, 60). White modernity – the devastating creation of a White waste land – is interrogated by the tragic experience of Indigenous displacement but also by the diffused strength of Indigenous spirituality.

In the last lines of the poem, Fogarty gestures towards the Indigenous interconnection between place and spirituality, but this is kept secret, unrepresented, as a "hidden thing" (Fogarty 2002, 69). As Mudrooroo insists, Indigenous Australian writers often echo the traditional secret/sacred prescriptions of their ancestors inscribing a camouflaged or 'hidden' metatext in their writing. Yet, the hidden Indigeneity or 'maban reality' of Fogarty's poetry can be uncovered by a retroactive reading that discloses the hidden metatext only to the initiated reader (Mudrooroo 1997, 80). In Fogarty's poems, most of the messages are purposefully hidden in "levels to spring forward" (Fogarty 2002, 69) to the initiated reader while they are withheld from the intruding perceptions and readings of those readers who cannot participate in the shared, communal Indigenous knowledge of his poetry. The lack of recognition of cultural difference on behalf of the reader renders the terms of Fogarty's modernist expression incommensurate. However, I believe that the strength and power of Fogarty's poems may lie in their challenging invitation to enter a committed intercultural reading. Fogarty's poems have been recently included in a collection of poetry edited by the poet John Kinsella with Rod Mengham, *Vanishing Points: New Modernist Poems* (2004). It may be interesting to further discuss why the inclusion of Fogarty's poetry in Modernism has been acknowledged only by a fellow poet since Mudrooroo's article was published already in 1986. Arguably, Australian critics may have not been ready for Fogarty's complete "appropriation" of the privileged centrality of white Modernism (Ashcroft *et al.* 1988, 51).

References

Ashcroft B., Griffiths G., Tiffin H. (eds.) 1998. *Key Concepts in Post-Colonial Studies*. London: Routledge.

Bhabha H.K. 1994. "'Race', Time and the Revision of Modernity". In *The Location of Culture*. London and New York: Routledge, 338-367.

Bhabha H.K. 1996. "Culture's In-between". In Hall S., du Gay P. (eds.) *Questions of Cultural Identity*. London, Thousand Oaks and New Delhi: Sage Publications, 53-60.

Brooker P., Thacker A. (eds.) 2005. *Geographies of Modernism: Literatures, Cultures, Spaces*. London and New York: Routledge.

Buckley V. 1969 [1st ed. 1957]. *Essays in Poetry, Mainly Australian*. New York: Books for Libraries Press.

Carter D. 2000. "Critics, Writers, Intellectuals: Australian Literature and Its Criticism". In Webby E. (ed.) *The Cambridge Companion to Australian Literature*. Cambridge: Cambridge University Press, 258-293.

Chambers R. 1997. "The Unexamined". In Hill M. (ed.) *Whiteness: A Critical Reader*. London and New York: New York University Press, 187-203.

Childs P. 2008. *Modernism*. London and New York: Routledge.

Cianci G. (ed.) 1991. *Modernismo/modernismi. Dall'avanguardia storica agli anni trenta e oltre*. Milano: Principato.

Fogarty L. 1995. "Tired of Writing" In *New and Selected Poems. Murranldjali, Muturrijavalra*. Melbourne: Hyland House, 109. First published 1982 in *Yoogum, Yoogum*. Ringwood (Vic.): Penguin Books.

Fogarty L. 2002. "Embassy". In *Southerly*, 62.2, 65-69.

Fogarty L. 2004. *Minyung Woolah Binnung, What Saying Says: Poems and Drawings by Lionel Fogarty*. Southport (Qld.): Keeaira Press.

Frankenberg R. 1993. *White Women, Race Matters: The Social Construction of Whiteness*. London: Routledge.

Gikandi S. 1992. *Writing in Limbo: Modernism and Caribbean Literature*. New York: Cornell University Press.

Hopfer S.P. 2002. "Re-reading Lionel Fogarty: An Attempt to Feel Into Texts Speaking of Decolonisation". In *Southerly*, 62, 2, 45-64.

Lipsitz G. 1998. *The Possessive Investment in Whiteness: How White People Profit from Identity Politics*. Philadelphia: Temple University Press.

McNamara A.E., Stephen A., Goad P. (eds.) 2006. *Modernism & Australia: Documents on Art, Design and Architecture 1917-1967*. Melbourne: The Miegunyah Press.

Mengham R., Kinsella J. (eds.) 2004. *Vanishing Points: New Modernist Poems*. Cambridge: Salt.

Mercer K. (ed.) 2005. *Cosmopolitan Modernisms*. Cambridge and London: MIT Press.

Muecke S. 2004. *Ancient and Modern: Time, Culture and Modernity*. Sydney: University of New South Wales Press.

Mudrooroo [Johnson C.]. 1986. "Guerrilla Poetry: Lionel Fogarty's Response to Language Genocide". In *Westerly* 3, 47-55.

Mudrooroo [Johnson C.]. 1992. "A Literature of Aboriginality". In *Ulitarra*, 1, 28-33.

Mudrooroo [Johnson C.]. 1997. *The Indigenous Literature of Australia: Milli Milli Wangka*. Melbourne: Hyland House.

Nicholls P. 1995. *Modernisms: A Literary Guide*. New York: Palgrave Macmillan.

Williams R. 1987. "When Was Modernism?". In Pinkney T. (ed.) 1989. *The Politics of Modernism: Against the New Conformists*. London and New York: Verso, 31-35.

Section 3
Community and Nation: Hybrid Identities,
Reinvented Traditions (II)

MARINA DE CHIARA

Università di Napoli L'Orientale

Postcolonial Journeys for Tristram:
Pier Paolo Pasolini's *Petrolio*

In his novel *Petrolio*, published posthumously in 1992, Pasolini describes Italy during the years when terrorism was at its height, when publisher Giangiacomo Feltrinelli died, apparently torn apart while placing his own 'terrorist' explosive device – but, most likely, murdered by fascists, or better, by CIA, in March 1972.

Pasolini chooses the Israeli-Palestinian conflict as a metaphorical touchstone for Italy, and he writes that, in those years, the country somehow had an "eastern appearance, almost Palestinian, in its events, things, bodies, in the various ways of life, in the air" (2005, 246).[1] This 'Palestinian' appearance suddenly projects Italian history on an international scene. Indeed, according to Pasolini as well as to Edward Said – the famous Palestinian scholar, author of *Orientalism* (1978), who died in 2003 in the United States where he had lived in exile – the Israeli-Palestinian question is part of a much wider and more complex conflict between the West and the East, between the West and Islam, where the West corresponds to the capitalist power of multinational companies, which has recently become a synonym for 'globalization'.

Whereas, according to Pasolini, Palestine still represents the East, the Arab East, Israel, on the contrary, represents the West, it is a symbol of industrialization and industrial cosmopolitism (Pasolini 2005, 170). In this context, the term cosmopolitism – widely proclaimed by the ideology and literature of European Enlightenment, as in the case of 18th century travel literature, for instance – does not evoke spaces of enlightened freedom and emancipation; it rather stands, in Pasolini's view, for the death of the very idea of nation, due to the loss of cultural identity and the new multinational capitalism's levelling pressures.

---

[1] I will offer here a rough translation into English of the quotations taken from the 2005 Mondadori edition of *Petrolio*.

Petrolio is a sort of testament for Pasolini.[2] It is an unfinished novel, in fact the author was still working on it when he was killed in November 1975. But it is a very untypical novel, featuring only few narrative passages, and using the language of essays, newspaper articles, reviews, private letters, and poetry: stories, fragments, notes, all come one after the other, with characters and situations in an unstable balance between a worldly and a mythical dimension, a realistic and a dream state, between licentious, Boccaccio-style tales and psychoanalysis, between political-philosophical meditation and moral fairytale. Holding these parts together is, somehow, Carlo's schizoid self, Carlo being a sort of *alter ego* of the author, who splits in Carlo I and Carlo II: the former is an educated bourgeois, vaguely left winger and perfectly integrated within the system, while the latter is, in a sense, an awful, hidden and evil double, who soon turns into a woman, like the legendary Tiresias.

Going through incestuous sex, homosexual embraces and orgies, State murders, police roundups, student revolts, current scandalous events, incursions both in the lowest and filthiest peripheral meanders of Italian cities and in the inaccessible mansions of upper class indecency, the key point of the novel is always an investigation of the role of the intellectual and his relation to the Power. According to Pasolini, power is a symptom of a never-appeased fascism Italy still has to face.

The title, *Petrolio*, offers a sudden opening into the Enrico Mattei affair, who was ENI President at the time and died in 1962 in an air crash on which light has never been fully shed.[3] Pasolini looked into the affair for a long time and he found out documents and papers that impeached many political sectors evidently involved with the financial world, with CIA and mafia. In the novel, politics and finance reveal to be strictly linked by oil policies, financial investments, American multinational companies' pressures on agreements with Arab countries. These political and economic events were sucking lifeblood out of an unlimited reservoir: the so-called Third World. Indeed, financial and political decisions, together with the community and intervention politics to be applied in the Third World, were traced in the name of oil.

Pasolini outlines the Italian situation in the '60s and '70s as an ongoing colonial situation, where the American tentacular meddling into the Italian

---

[2] In a letter to Alberto Moravia, Pasolini talks about a "testimony of the little knowledge he has acquired" (2005, 581). I'd rather suggest that *Petrolio* truly represents Pasolini's final poetic summation of his intense socio-political awareness.

[3] Enrico Mattei was succeeded by Eugenio Cefis as ENI President, and later Montedison President; parts of Cefis' speeches celebrating the power of multinational companies, the decline of national economies, and the new horizons of financial capital, are fully reported in *Petrolio*. An excellent account of the political implications of Mattei's oil strategies, both at a national and an international level, from the Fifties through the Sixties, is Nico Perrone's *Enrico Mattei* (Perrone 2001).

cultural and economic politics has claimed its victims (Mattei, Feltrinelli, and other State and CIA murders) in favour of what the poet calls a "neo-capitalist hell" (Pasolini 2005, 637).

Petrolio persistently evokes mythical journeys to the East and initiation journeys, where Pasolini's intense reasoning on his own fascination with the Orient emerges; it is the Arab Orient, so imbued with exoticism, astonishment, sensuality and guilt. But what also emerges is Pasolini's reading of the colonial dimension as the inescapable background on which the European concept of Islam is delineated. It is indeed quite a surprise to find many consonances between Pasolini and the ideas expressed by Edward Said, in both *Orientalism* (1978) and *Culture and Imperialism* (1993). It is not just the interest they shared in Antonio Gramsci's thought, it is rather the similar way in which, for both of them, the questions of Islam and of the Israeli-Palestinian conflict seem to be part of a broader colonial question.

Yet, we can also draw a direct correspondence between Pasolini's novel and one of the cornerstones of eighteenths-century travel literature, namely Laurence Sterne's *A Sentimental Journey Through France and Italy*, published in 1768. In *Petrolio*, in fact, in a section called "Gli Argonauti", the journey to the East is presented as a "series of 'visions' drawing on the Myth of the initiation journey"; within these 'visions', the so-called 'cultured tales' are presented, the first of which is entitled "Acquisto di uno schiavo". It is a very illuminating tale on the links connecting Orientalism to the colonial and imperial spirit of modern Europe, the same 'enlightened' Europe which, instead, created shadow zones in the rest of the world in order to operate undisturbed despite the humanistic and cosmopolitan belief always proclaimed. In Pasolini's story, the spirit of Orientalism – caught in the sense that Said proposes in his magisterial *Orientalism* – appears in its indissoluble and close relationship to the real essence of modern European culture: that is, the colonial and imperial dimension opposing, for centuries, the North of the world to the many 'Souths' of the world.[4]

In the tale, the 'hero' is a British journalist whose name is Tristram, like the well-known literary character created by Sterne in his masterpiece *Tristram Shandy*. Yet, Tristram reappears – though under the name of Yorick, but once again hiding the author himself – also in Sterne's famous *Sentimental Journey*, where the main character recounts, in a very peculiar way, his experiences and emotions while making his *Grand Tour* through France:[5] the result is a parody

---

[4] On the question of the subaltern 'Souths' of the world, see the essays collected in Chambers (2006).

[5] As Giuseppe Sertoli aptly remarks in his very exhaustive "Introduction" to the 1983 Mondadori edition of *A Sentimental Journey*, Yorick literally repeats Tristram's journey, to maintain Sterne's original intention to relate, with *Tristram Shandy*, Tristram's *grand tour*, enacting a literary parody of that very successful and well known genre called *travel literature* (XI-XII).

of the 18ᵗʰ century trend that depicted travelling as a way to gain 'experiences' and, above all, a way to develop one's own feelings, finally reaching a very much desired full maturity of the self.[6] During his sentimental journey, the scepticism of Sterne's traveller, who initially does not believe in communication and real encounter between peoples having different customs and languages, eventually turns into a celebration of solidarity and a democratic sense of the human nature that all men actually share, in every country, language and culture, despite their apparent differences. According to Sterne, 'sentimental' is the way we feel, thanks to curiosity and a warm-hearted solidarity, when we are close to someone who seems to be alien, different, far-away from us – due to our prejudices. This 'sentimental' disposition is the only way we can overcome misunderstandings and distances between different worlds, in Sterne's view. On the other hand, Pasolini describes his Tristram as a typical anti-colonial and anti-authoritarian neoliberal, but "within the broader frame of the euro-centrism that constitutes his real, deep and impossible to eradicate, racial prejudice" (Pasolini 2005, 173).

Tristram wants to personally verify the existence of a slave market in the area of Sudan, South of the Sahara. There, in the attempt to find the money for their pilgrimage to Mecca, the poorest Muslims sell their labour-power in plantations and yards while crossing the deserts of the Sudanese area; but after working and travelling for years, once they get to Gedda, on the other shore of the Red Sea, they are captured and chained like slaves. Tristram sets out to buy a (female) slave. The Middle East and the area of Sudan are unknown places to him who has left behind "a well-known place, or better, THE place *par excellence*: England, Europe (Western civilization)" (*ibidem*, 174).

The slave trader keeps men and women piled in the filthy and small rooms of a shabby hotel. Tristram can choose among the girls who start to undress while laughing, or rather, mocking that white man they see as 'other' from their negritude, just like he sees them as other: "there was no chance of meeting in such otherness" (*ibidem*, 175). After seeing both girls and young boys, he chooses no one: "risking to have no experience at all, neither a private (sadistic) one nor a social one (knowing a different world that people were beginning to call Third World)" (*ibidem*, 177). While on his way out of the hotel, Tristram notices a beautiful little girl, aged twelve or thirteen years, wearing her poor dress, and he suddenly chooses her as his slave. He takes her to a house with garden he rented in a European and posh area, on the other side of Khartoum.

---

[6] Sterne's *Tristram* and his *Journey* cannot be easily summarized, made as they are of all the innumerable voices they transcribe, together with "intervals, pauses, silences, interior monologues, gestures, attitudes" (Mazzacurati 2006, 50). On the 'polyphonic', 'digressive' and 'intertwined' structure of Tristram's autobiography and Yorick's journey – so evidently at work in Pasolini's *Petrolio*, which undoubtedly re-enacts Sterne's idea of 'writing' as 'conversation' – see Laudando (1995) and Mazzacurati (2006).

Once there, he performs his most sadistic sexual fantasies on the little girl who passively accepts both maltreatment and kindness from her jailer; for Giana, the little slave, "the idea of being a slave was deeply rooted in her consciousness" (*ibidem*, 178). Before leaving, after some days, Tristram frees his little slave and consigns her to a convent mission where a Dutch friar welcomes her together with a lot of other children who had also been left to him. Tristram then flies to Cairo and gets to Alexandria by train; in a bookshop, he buys an anthology of Karl Marx's *Capital*, since he had never read it neither in Cambridge nor in London:

> The fact that he was an 'initiate' belonging to the most unbiased cultural élite in his country allowed him to read nothing but newspapers and magazines. As a matter of fact, after Cambridge, he had read no books at all, apart from some stupid essays on Ejzenstejn and Hitchcock: he knew nothing about the history of religions, linguistics, and so forth, and about anthropology he had only read something by Lévi-Strauss when his theories were trendy. As for Fanon (who was equally trendy), he only knew his name. He thus imagined that behind the mystery of Giana and her traders there was a 'magic world', but, for pure ignorance, he instinctively downgraded it to a negative and all in all insignificant fact (*ibidem*, 181).

Disappointed by his encounter with the Third World, Tristram knew he had failed in integrating his culture with Giana's, just like Giana had failed in integrating hers with Tristram's. There was no democratic relationship between their cultures that remained strangers to each other. Yet, something unexpected happens when the ship carrying Tristram back to England briefly stops in Naples: there, among some children in their underwear, playing in little gardens and bathing in dirty pools, like twenty years before, "he noticed a street urchin, 'una scugnizza', dark and ragged", undoubtedly looking like Giana: "She could almost be her sister. She belonged to the same 'culture'" (*ibidem*, 182). The plebeian little boys in Naples reminded Tristram of those he had seen in a dormitory in Khartoum. Their substance was different from the dominant culture that could "integrate popular culture and make it its own, that is obliging it to degenerate, to stay at the lowest levels of consciousness the way it had stayed at the lowest levels of society for centuries" (*ibidem*, 183). Just then, Tristram almost fainted and fell down on the dirty grass of the small gardens in Forcella: and it was right there that he had a revelation: "He was suddenly converted to Marxism" (*ibidem*, 183).

Unlike Sterne's main character in *Sentimental Journey*, who engages with his journey in Europe at a time when the enormous intellectual contribution that Said defined *Orientalism* was not consolidated yet, Pasolini's Tristram features all the characteristics of a modern European traveller, fully imbued as he is with 'Orientalist knowledge'. As Said explains, modern Orientalist knowledge originated from a modern imperial context, since it is deeply linked to the wide empires in the East attained by Great Britain and France, from Napoleon's invasion of Egypt in 1798 on. However, ever since the 17th century, the acquisition of overseas colonies had strongly influenced European knowledge and literary imagination; this new horizon will be later explored by creating new literary genres. Just consider the 17th century huge literary production of travel novels that turned into the 'bourgeois' form of travel literature in the 18th century, based on the European *Grand Tour* trend.[7]

Like one of the European explorers who, a few centuries ago, used to push towards far territories and cultures in order to 'elevate' their spirit – but actually re-confirming their self and prejudices – Pasolini's Tristram is presented as the Sternean impartial – 'ironic' – observer sent to a place for which he feels absolutely nothing. The theme of the detachment between the traveller and the place he visits is also present in the work of Said who, struck by the deeply irreconcilable relation between Orientalist scholars and their object of inquiry, noted that many experts on Islam, both in Europe and the United States, spend their life studying the subject but they never manage to love, or simply admire, its religion and culture (1995, 345).[8]

Despite his being liberal and educated, Pasolini's Tristram shows a 'natural' inclination to enslave the other; in fact, whereas the little Sudanese girl, Giana, tries to satisfy his sexual fancies, he writes articles that do not grasp anything of the other culture, and he is perfectly aware of that. The deep lack of understanding and distance between the two worlds, the East and the West, is then the effect of a predatory, racist and colonial mode the West (and here Tristram, the English journalist) adopts to approach the East. This is the reason why Orientalism is, ultimately, a discourse of power emerged in a colonial context, a discourse that dehumanizes the other in order to do with him/her what you would not think of doing with a 'human being' due to ethical hesitations. The fact that Tristram is so rooted in his consciousness enables him to rape the little girl with no damage for his dignity.

---

[7] Said's *Culture and Imperialism* gives a memorable account of the way in which the European literature of colonial and imperial times – with a particular focus on the English case – was a part of the dominant colonial ideology.

[8] Like Pasolini, Said has unceasingly insisted that even if the decolonization process had been accomplished by the '60s, old colonialist practices were replaced by new modes and forms: it is the concept of imperialism, to which Said dedicated *Culture and Imperialism* in 1993, meant to be the continuation of *Orientalism*, and where he remarked that the complicity between imperialism and culture entails that many Islam specialists are consulted by, or admittedly work for, governmental authorities (the USA, for instance) whose specific purposes and interests in the Islamic world simply come down to economic exploitation, rule, and aggression, rather than caring knowledge and study. Pasolini reported that very complicity in his sharp newspaper articles, later collected in *Scritti corsari* (1975), where he attacks Italian intellectuals for their subservience to fascism.

In the final revelation, where the little Sudanese slave appears again in the skin and poverty of the Neapolitan street urchin, a common fate is traced, the fate of the misfortunes shared by all the Souths of the world.[9] Pasolini, like Gramsci, fantasizes on the recovery of the social equity proposed by Marxism as the only chance to stop conflicts between worlds that are so close and yet so far. But maybe, for Pasolini, this was already a shattered dream leaving nothing else but ashes, just like the ashes of Gramsci he celebrated in his famous poem in 1957.[10]

References

Chambers I. (ed.) 2006. *Esercizi di potere. Gramsci, Said e il postcoloniale*. Roma: Meltemi.

Laudando M.C. 1995. *Parody, Paratext, Palimpsest. A Study of Intertextual Strategies in the Writings of Laurence Sterne*. Napoli: Dip. di Studi Letterari e Linguistici dell'Occidente, IUO.

Mazzacurati G. 2006. *Il fantasma di Yorick. Laurence Sterne e il romanzo sentimentale*. Napoli: Liguori.

Pasolini P.P. 2000. *Scritti corsari*. Milano: Garzanti.

Pasolini P.P. 2005. *Petrolio*. Milano: Mondadori.

Perrone N. 2001. *Enrico Mattei*. Bologna: Il Mulino.

Said E. 1993. *Culture and Imperialism*. New York: Alfred Knopf.

Said E. 1995 *Orientalism*. London: Penguin Books [1st ed. 1978, New York: Pantheon Books].

Sertoli G. (ed.) 1983. *Sterne. Viaggio sentimentale*. Milano: Mondadori.

---

[9] The so-called 'southern question' Gramsci wrote about, is actually re-proposed on a planetary scale, although offering new terminologies, like the term 'globalization' that Said defines as the new transnational order (the order of multinational companies), where colonialism appears again as a form of subservience of the South of the world to the North of the world (1995, 351).

[10] In consigning *Petrolio* to his publisher Einaudi in 1975, Pasolini writes that it is "something poetic like *Le Ceneri di Gramsci*, even though in prose" (2005, 637). It is, indeed, Pasolini's last tribute to Gramsci, before that night between the 1st and the 2nd of November 1975, when he was murdered for not giving up his honest political dreams.

NICOLETTA BRAZZELLI

Università di Milano

Departures and Desertions in Abdulrazak Gurnah

1. The diasporic discourse

Abdulrazak Gurnah, an outstanding novelist and a literary critic, was born in Zanzibar in 1948 within an Islamic background, and migrated to Great Britain in 1968, where he now teaches English and Postcolonial Literature at the University of Kent.[1] Gurnah's arrival coincided with Enoch Powell's notoriously xenophobic speech "Rivers of Blood", focusing on the imminent perils of opening up Britain's frontiers to the peoples who had been subjects under colonial rule. To some extent, Gurnah's novels seem to reflect the writer's own experience within that context of racial tension, because they portray uprooted, alienated and unwanted individuals; the stories he narrates are set within the broad historical network of the empire, but they also include the representation of postcolonial Zanzibar in which feudal élites, after achieving national independence (1963), were replaced by more radical Black revolutionaries (King 2005).

From the publication of his first novel, *Memory of Departure* (1987), through *Paradise* (1994), *Admiring Silence* (1996) and *By the Sea* (2001), to *Desertion* (2005), on which my paper will focus, Gurnah explores the theme of the migrant's displacement, estrangement and dispossession (Whyte 2004), as his characters move – voluntarily or not – from Zanzibar to England:[2] cut off from their roots, their land, their past, they embody the 'category' of exile and cultural difference theorized, according to different perspectives, by Homi Bhabha (1994), Edward Said (2000) and Paul Gilroy (2003). Gurnah's personal contribution to the

---

[1] On Abdulrazak Gurnah, see the bio-bibliographical profile in http://www.contemporarywriters.com/authors/?p=auth46 (last accessed August 2011).

[2] Gurnah is also the author of essays on African literatures such as Gurnah (2000), of critical articles such as Gurnah (2002) and of autobiographical pieces such as Gurnah (2004). He edited volumes such as Gurnah (1993) and Gurnah (2007).

contemporary literary scene is structured in his novels through the themes of racial violence, the legacy of slavery, and the cultural definition of the British black subject, together with the migrant's search for a home: these issues are incorporated in many-layered narratives of encounters and marriages, thus employing the domestic novel's traditional matter (Blake *et al.* 2001, 51). His stories of migration and exile are part of the grand-scale demographic movement produced by British imperialism (Segal 1995, 21-24). In his essay "Writing and Place" Gurnah remarks:

> I know I came to writing in England, in estrangement, and I realise now that it is this condition of being from one place and living in another that has been my subject over the years, not as a unique experience which I have undergone, but as one of the stories of our times (Gurnah 2004, 59).

And yet Gurnah's fiction shows that the modern migrants also belong to a multi-faceted past, that predates the intrusion of Western powers. On the Eastern coast of Africa, before the British and the Germans, Arab rulers and Indian traders operated on a large scale. Gurnah's stories of cultural encounters hint at the social instability and multiple overlapping identities that are the main characteristics of East African coastal societies. Heterogeneity and hybridity are inscribed into the postcolonial experience, establishing a relation of historical continuity between colonialism and nationalism, and between nationalism and its significant other, the diasporic movements (Radhakrishnan 1996, 119-132).

In a sense, belonging to a well defined national entity is less important as the arena for subject formation than small-scale yet often global familial networks. Dislocation often occurs through migration from one nation to another, but it is the alienation from home in a geographically and socially more restricted perspective that causes anxiety and a sense of loss (Abiola and Gikandi 2004, 1, 441).[3] An exploration of the psychological and emotional aspects of diaspora, as well as of the role of the familial webs, is provided in *Desertion* through the character of Rashid, who left Zanzibar, his native country, to be educated in England. Rashid is the narrator of Gurnah's novel: his role is to weave together stories of failed hopes and disappointments, cruelty and betrayal, though the reader becomes aware of his existence only in the second part of the novel.[4]

Desertion is divided into three parts, set in different times and places; the first section occurs at the end of the 19th century, in a colonial town along the East African coast, when a nearly dead European is found on the beach by a

---

[3] "I don't feel British. But I have lived here long enough to understand how things operate here. I never forget how I look" said Gurnah in an interview. See V. Nair, "In Conversation with Abdulrazak Gurnah", May 2005, available at http://archive.deccanherald.com/Deccanherald/may152005/articl14802005513.asp (last accessed August 2011).

[4] On *Desertion*, see the reviews published in 2005 on *The Nation*, *The Observer*, *The Independent*, *The Guardian* and *Wasafiri*.

local character: this event gives rise to the most fateful development of the plot. The second part focuses on the ambitions and frustrations of Rashid, his brother Amin and his sister Farida, during the tumultuous years heading towards the independence of Zanzibar, while the third takes place in England during the post-independence period: Rashid settles down to a conventional academic life and only now he is able to face his own demons and return to Zanzibar. It is Rashid who, on his difficult route towards a new identity, puts together the fragments of remote and different familiar stories, shaped by departures, arrivals, tragic love affairs. *Desertion*, in a sense, mainly recollects two ill-fated love affairs, at first seemingly very different but eventually strongly connected to each other.

2. Fragments of stories

In 1899, in a bright morning, Martin Pearce, a British orientalist and traveller, appears half starved and wounded in an unnamed Muslim town between Bagamoyo and Mombasa, abandoned by his Somali guides. Hassanali, an Indian shopkeeper, brings him home and nurses him back to strength with the help of his wife Malika and his sister Rehana. The British colonial officer, Frederick Turner, breaks in and takes Pearce with him, accusing the Indian family of having robbed their guest. However, Pearce's return to Hassanali's house to thank his hosts leads to a love affair between Pearce and the beautiful Rehana, who years before had been deserted by her husband: the Englishman is enraptured by Rehana's gorgeous eyes and tragic aura. The relationship causes a scandal that forces them to move to Mombasa, where they openly live together; but, when Rehana is pregnant with his child, Pearce abandons her to return to England.

Pearce and Rehana's relationship is "unimaginable" precisely because it runs against the social codes that conduct behaviour on both sides in colonial encounters:

> This was 1899, not the age of Pocahontas when a romantic fling with a savage princess could be described as an adventure. The imperial world observed some rigidity about sexual proprieties. The empire had become an extension of British civic respectability (Gurnah 2005, 116-117).

Much less radical is Amin and Jamila's relationship in the 1950s, but they, too, challenge the social norms and expectations: indeed, Rashid's older brother Amin embarks on a similarly difficult liaison with Jamila, a fascinating divorced woman; it is later revealed that Jamila is Rehana's grandaughter, and this is why Amin's parents force him to end the affair. Within the Zanzibari Muslim community, they bow to a rigid moral code.

Another love affair, not tragic but very complicated all the same, is narrated at the end of the novel: at a conference in Cardiff, Rashid delivers a paper on "race and sexuality in settler writing in Kenya" and there he meets Barbara Turner, whose grandfather is Frederick Turner: they discuss about doomed love affairs during the British empire, and, after a short time, she decides to go to Zanzibar with Rashid, to find Jamila, because "everything is scattered, dispersed to the farthest corners of the world. No one can find anyone" (Gurnah 2005, 261).

Throughout the narrative frame, Rashid reflects on the weaving of the different stories his narration encompasses and on the manifold possibilities he faces: there are events he should have known, while others were hidden to him; therefore, he puts at the centre of his work as a narrator a meditation on the imaginative reconstruction of the past and on the re-interpretation of geography as a means of self-identification:

> I could not begin without imagining how Rehana and Martin might have come together, and all I had of that were a few scraps of gossip and scandal. I decided that the Englishman's first appearance was were I would start (Gurnah 2005, 120).

The narrative voice provides a continuous but always changing pattern:

> There is, as you can see, an I in this story, but it is not a story about me. It is one about all of us, about Farida and Amin and our parents, and about Jamila. It is about how one story contains many and how they belong not to us but are part of the random currents of our time, and about how stories capture us and entangle us for all time (Gurnah 2005, 120).

The question of "entanglements" runs through *Desertion*: the stories of empire and migration are able to unsettle previous understandings, cannot be controlled, because they overlap each other in an inexplicable way (Nasta 2004, 352-363). On the one hand, entangled stories include the representations of previous sequences of events; on the other, they make up the 'reality' in which these events occur. In this sense, the writer constantly tries to surprise his reader; his work is full of secret histories emerging 'miraculously', like genies from a magic bottle. At the same time, many references to writing and to the forms of narration are incorporated in Gurnah's novel: in the memoir composed by Rashid many other narrations are included, such as Amin's letters and notebooks, read and interpreted by Rashid himself, who puts them together with other fictional perspectives, as well as with a scholarly attention to historical facts.

Not only private events shape the development of *Desertion*. Gurnah explores the imperial takeover of Zanzibar by the British: Martin Pearce speaks Arabic, he wants to understand native culture and history and he does not regard empire as a favour done to its subjects; he seems disgusted with the colonial enterprise. In fact, he exclaims: "I think that in time we'll come to be ashamed of the things we have done" (Gurnah 2005, 85), denying the idea of a British ethical responsibility towards the colonized, which by contrast is strongly asserted by Frederick Turner, a colonial administrator who loves to quote Romantic poets and thinks that the British empire is different from the other empires, because it is 'moral'. He remembers that Shelley in his sonnet "Ozymandias" (1818) suggested that on their road towards greatness the British should remain true to their tradition of liberty and not be tempted into despotic hubris.

The third representative of the British empire in the novel is Burton, a Kurtz-like Conradian character who joins the natives "in their drumming and dancing": he seems sure of the future disappearance of African populations, who will be replaced by the settlers. In this case, the historical figure of the traveller and writer Richard Burton is called to mind. The conversations and feelings of the three Englishmen conveying three different perspectives on the imperial adventure highlight the process of othering that, as Simon Gikandi (1996) has shown, has been an essential element in the historical construction of English identities.

3. Love, identity, memories

The fatal relationship between Pearce and Rehana is described in few lines, because the narrative voice declares himself unable to represent the strangeness of the event:

> I don't know how it would have happened. The unlikeliness of it defeats me. Yet I know it did happen, that Martin and Rehana became lovers. Imagination fails me and that fills me with sorrow (Gurnah 2005, 110).

Due to this device, the rhythmical pattern of the narration is broken. Improbable stories of that kind exist on the threshold between scholarship and fiction, between history and fantasy. Rashid's performance at the conference illustrates this point, because, as a scholar, Rashid suggests that the story of Rehana and Pearce is indeed almost impossible to believe, as he stated upon first hearing it. It is too rare an instance of interracial love to be the basis of historical research. Rashid's own story brings it into the academic forum, but places it at the margins of history, as it were. It is anecdotal evidence, and speaks to the imagination rather than to experience. *Desertion* conveys the passionate and transgressive love story between the Englishman and the African woman not only as an alternative version of the past, it also employs it as a source of narrative 'entanglement'.

In fact, within the narrative frame, Rehana and Pearce's story becomes both an example and a precedent for the younger couple, Amin and Jamila; it entangles them in its implications and similarities and it offers consolation as well as it gives a sense of fatefulness to the more recent pattern of events. In his turn Rashid, after the breakup of his marriage to Grace, identifies himself with the sorrows of other lovers belonging to his lineage: he feels that failure is the common lot of all generations. The act of writing is a failure itself. It is not narratives *per se* that capture and entangle individuals but physical meetings and chance encounters.

Zanzibar is at the core of the novel: once the centre of spice and slave trade (Sheriff and Ferguson 1991; Gilbert 2005), the sun-baked tropical island is at the same time a place of separation, but also a land of spatial relationships and historical links; a tropical Eden, a territory of the *Arabian Nights*, as well as the site where the dirty work of the empire was carried out, Zanzibar is constructed as a kind of crossroads of human destinies. The ocean, with its rhythm, dominates the landscape, and shapes the narration, together with the balmy and moist air and the light breeze; but also the echoing noises, the dust, the ruined walls, the interiors, where secret passions develop and vanish, shape the scenery.

As for V.S. Naipaul's Trinidad in *A Way in the World* (1994), the imperial net connects the whole world to Britain, in the complexity of individual and collective experiences: single stories achieve a meaning in the larger frame in which diaspora movements, changes of identity and culture reshape the life of single characters and their perception of the world. Forbidden love affairs and cultural collisions reverberate generation after generation and across continents, from the heyday of the empire to the aftermath of decolonization. Thus, Gurnah's fiction crosses the borders of time and space.

Miscegenation – a negative colonial accident – is one of the main issues explored in *Desertion* (Wright 1997, 84): the whole novel seems to trace the consequences of an affair between an African woman and an Englishman, the danger of interracial relationships and, at the same time, their inevitability. Despite the ideology of the empire based on racial purity, sometimes individuals are willing to step outside the cultural constraints of family and religion and pursue their desires: unfortunately this does not translate into romantic happiness or social improvements. Gurnah implies that the attitudes of families and communities hardly change over the course of the years.

Desertion also represents migration and exile as related to a 'home' that is not conceived on a national scale. "A stranger in the middle of nowhere" (Gurnah 2005, 222), at a certain point Rashid is sure that his journey is over, and that he is going to live in England forever. After the end of his relationship with Grace, he begins an affair with Barbara Turner, finding a new sense of belonging to the former colonial nation. The family, not the home country, is the arena where a sense of belonging can be re-created, though the family may be global and transcultural; in this sense, Gurnah presents a transcultural and global re-imagination of the family and of love relationships (Falk 2007, 60-63).

The desertion in the title of the novel emphasizes loss, abandonment and disgrace: every story implies a desertion, because men abandon women, Pearce abandons Rehana, Amin abandons Jamila; young people abandon their country, as Rashid had done, leaving Zanzibar exactly when it needed his help: Rashid's feelings about Zanzibar are clearly revealed when he reflects: "It was time to go home, in a manner of speaking, to visit and to put my fears at rest and to beg perdon for my neglect" (Gurnah 2005, 261). Moreover, the English are forced to desert the territories of the empire (surprisingly enough, Gurnah argues this happened too early): a sense of failure pervades the whole novel.

The double journey of leaving and then returning to the home country after its independence, and then leaving again, with a homelessness perceived as a betrayal, recalls Naipaul's narratives of displacement, as well as the multiple points of view, the different gazes on history, despite the presence of only one narrator. The master narrative is questioned, the postcolonial perspective investigated: the two discourses are placed in dialogue with one another. The double relations of past and present that the novel creates – an implausible past presented as fact within the fictional frame, and metafictionally through a web of intertextual links – points to the social function of imagination. Memory is seen as a refuge from the unsettling diasporic experience; it is an essential part of the discourse of (hyphenated) identity, and for the migrant author the act of writing stories becomes a form of therapy; thanks to his literary efforts, he is able to tie up loose threads and give them a coherent, although unstable and problematic order on the page.

References

Abiola I.F., Gikandi S. (eds.) 2004. *The Cambridge History of African and Caribbean Literature.* 2 vols. Cambridge: Cambridge University Press.

Bhabha H. 1994. *The Location of Culture.* London: Routledge.

Blake A., Gandhi L., Thomas S. 2001. *England through Colonial Eyes in Twentieth Century Fiction.* Basingstroke (Hampshire), New York: Palgrave.

Falk E. 2007. *Subject and History in Selected Works by Abdulrazak Gurnah, Yvonne Vera, and David Dabydeen.* Karlstad: Karlstad University Studies.

Gikandi S. 1996. *Maps of Englishness: Writing Identity in the Culture of Colonialism.* New York: Columbia University Press.

Gilbert E. 2005. *Dhows and the Colonial Economy of Zanzibar, 1860-1970.* Athens: Ohio University Press.

Gilroy P. 1993. *The Black Atlantic: Modernity and Double Consciousness*. Cambridge (Mass.): Harvard University Press.

Gurnah A. 1987. *Memory of Departure*. New York: Grove.

Gurnah A. (ed.) 1993. *Essays in African Literature: A Re-evaluation*. London: Heinemann.

Gurnah A. 1994. *Paradise*. London: Hamilton.

Gurnah A. 1996. *Admiring Silence*. London: Penguin.

Gurnah A. 2000. "Settler Writing in Kenya: 'Nomenclature is an Uncertain Science in these Wild Parts'". In Booth H.J., Rigby N. (eds.) *Modernism and Empire*. Manchester: Manchester University Press, 275-291.

Gurnah A. 2001. *By the Sea*. London: Bloomsbury.

Gurnah A. 2002. "An Idea of the Past". In *Moving Worlds*, 2, 6-17.

Gurnah A. 2004. "Writing and Place". In *Wasafiri*, 42, 58-60.

Gurnah A. 2005. *Desertion*. London: Bloomsbury.

Gurnah A. (ed.) 2007. *The Cambridge Companion to Salman Rushdie*. Cambridge: Cambridge University Press.

King B. 2005. "Abdulrazak Gurnah and Hanif Kureishi: Failed Revolutions". In Acheson J., Ross S.C.E. (eds.) *The Contemporary British Novel*. Edinburgh: Edinburgh University Press, 85-94.

Naipaul V.S. 1994. *A Way in the World*. London: Vintage.

Nasta S. (ed.) 2004. *Writing across Worlds: Contemporary Writers Talk*. New York: Routledge.

Radhakrishnan R. 1996. *Diasporic Mediations Between Home and Location*. Minneapolis, London: University of Minnesota Press.

Said E. 2000. "Reflexions on Exile". In *Reflexions on Exile and Other Essays*. Cambridge (Mass.): Harvard University Press, 173-187.

Segal R. 1995. *The Black Diaspora*. London: Faber and Faber.

Sheriff A., Ferguson E. (eds.) 1991. *Zanzibar Under Colonial Rule*. London: James Currey.

Whyte P. 2004. "Heritage as Nightmare: the Novels of Abdulrazak Gurnah". In *Commonwealth Essays and Studies* 27, 1, 11-18.

Wright D. (ed.) 1997. *Contemporary African Fiction*. Bayreuth: Bayreuth African Studies Series.

SABINA D'ALESSANDRO

Università di Palermo

"The Battle of Images" in Ahdaf Soueif's *Mezzaterra*

Within the postcolonial debate on the Western politics of representation this paper will consider the ways in which the Egyptian writer Ahdaf Soueif[1] (who lives in London) challenges, on a critical as well as on a narrative level, the Western representative mechanisms that make use of stereotypes which contribute to the construction of an inferior otherness (Fanon 1967) according to asymmetrical identitarian paradigms as emphasised by Said. In her collection of essays, *Mezzaterra*[2], Soueif takes a critical position in the vein of Edward Said. As she herself points out: "I have hoped to add my voice to that of Edward Said" (Soueif 2004, 10), whose highly influential book *Orientalism* (Said 1978) has drastically changed the way Western representations of the East have been analysed, theorized and problematised since its publication in 1978.

Focusing on the Middle Eastern conflict during the years of Bush's administration Soueif aims not only at demystifying stereotyped representations but also at unveiling the political and economical powers, which are the driving

---

[1] Ahdaf Soueif, the daughter of an intellectual Muslim family, was born in Cairo in 1950 and studied English Literature at Egyptian and British universities. Since 1981 she has been dividing her time between London and Cairo, crossing national boundaries and occupying multiple locations. She is one of a number of Arab authors who moved to Europe in the second half of the twentieth century and who from their adopted homes attempt to describe their encounters with cultural otherness. Consequently, she is inevitably caught in the net of power relations that govern interactions between East and West.

[2] The term "mezzaterra", as Soueif explains in her preface to the homonymous collection of essays, refers to "common ground", to a "theoretically constructed" territory, where different cultures can combine their knowledge and ideas, rather than clash in the name of cultural dominion. It is to this "mezzaterra" that the author alludes in projectual terms, whilst referring to processes of productive symbiosis that in other ages marked the countries on both sides of the Mediterranean ("A few Westerners inhabited it too: Lucy Duff Gordon was one, Wilfred Scawen Blunt another") (Soueif 2004, 6). Furthermore, for the purposes of Soueif's critical discourse, it is important to stress the author's utilisation of the Italian term "mezzaterra", which stemmed (as explained by Soueif herself in an interview, see D'Alessandro 2007) from the fact that, in Italy, she noticed forms of Mediterranean "synthesis" between Europe and the Middle-East.

force behind such conflict: "In doing this I have hoped to help in demythologising the representation of Muslims and Arabs and to place the current conflicts in the arena where they belong: politics and economics" (Soueif 2004, 10). In *Mezzaterra* Soueif writes: "Looking at my essays now I find that they are mainly concerned with the problem of representation" (Soueif 2004, 4). She expresses concern about the fact that in nearly every book, newspaper or magazine article, film, TV or radio programme that "claimed to be about the part of the world that I came from I could never recognise myself or anyone I knew. I was constantly coming face to face with distortions of my reality" (Soueif 2004, 2).

With a view to denounce the use of decontextualised stereotypes she analyses examples of monolithic images taken from Western media in order to demonstrate how dominant representations of Arabs, Muslims and particularly, Palestines are defined by a homogenizing otherness removed from its historical context, that is ethnically and racially determined. They, even if they come from various social contexts, are not differentiated according to ethnicity, race, class and gender. Although Soueif was referring specifically to the situation in 2004 this misrepresentation is still a topical issue today. She puts forward the argument that this degrading mechanism of representation doesn't only tend to hide the powerful forces that control the political battlefield but ends up revitalising the old dichotomic opposition between Westerners/Orientals – we/you, so that "The old language of colonialism surfaces once again" (Soueif 2004, 14). Soueif emphasises the cultural and ideological revitalisation of these images and the consequent political implications that these rhetorical devices involve.

She refers to Jean Genet's concept of the "mask" of the image thereby alluding to the fact that an image can be deceptive, that it can lie, hide the truth and therefore be used to manipulate reality in a way that suits the aims of its creator. Referring to the ongoing conflict she sustains that "by promoting a picture of the Arab world that is essentially passive, primitive and hopeless, a picture that hardly ever depicts Arabs as agents of action (except for terrorists and suicide bombers), the media validates the politician's dreams of domination" (Soueif 2004, 18). Therefore such representations perpetuate and reinforce stereotypes which according to Soueif "have a pedigree", in order to legitimize interventions and to justify them ideologically (Soueif 2004, 164). Hence, images of Arabs, Muslims and Palestinians can be used for sinister ends, reinvoking, reinforcing and perpetuating stereotypical representations that have roots stretching back into the colonial past.

As Elio Di Piazza points out, "such structuring devices "have been adopted in the colonial period in [...] literature with a view to legitimise the Empire and to provide ideological justification" (Di Piazza *et al.* 2005, 5). According to Soueif it is exactly the presence of this colonial past that has made it so easy for the West to construct a powerful but untrue picture of the Islamic, Arab and Palestinian worlds. She argues that when the West identified the USSR as "the enemy", the image of the "Evil Empire" had to be constructed from scratch as preconceived ideas did not exist in the West. However, when it came to representing the Islam, it was easy for the idealogues and propagandists of the West to revive old colonialist and orientalist ideas of the Islam as a fundamentally fanatical, violent ideology that is strongly opposed to modernity and therefore poses a threat to Western ideology.

> If the New World Order was a mechanism to control the Arab and the Muslim worlds then I felt that the media of the West was complicit in it; for they always represented those worlds in terms that excused or even invited the imposition of control (Soueif 2004, 3).

In the "Political Essays" section in *Mezzaterra* written between 2000 and 2004, Soueif takes an inquisitive look at the destructive influence of the neocolonial[3] politics of the US (and its allies Israel and the Arab dictatorships). "Under the Gun: A Palestinian Journey", the first of the articles that are collected in *Mezzaterra* was written in 2000 when the Guardian offered Soueif the opportunity to go to Palestine. What motivated her was the discrepancy between the news coverage by the BBC and the CNN on the one hand and al-Jazeera on the other, which were so different as if the political events had been happening on two different planets. In this article, like in "The Waiting Game", Soueif explores various towns, different communities as well as individual points of views in order to open a kaleidoscopic window that gives the reader a vivid impression of how the occupation and its ramification has been affecting every aspect of people's lives. Her aim is to present a more balanced picture than mainstream news coverage. Thus, when collecting information for her articles she does not shy away from meetings with her opponents. She portrays Jewish Palestinian-Rights campaigners that whole-heartedly believe in their campaign as well as Palestinians that are trying to make quick money selling off their compatriots' property.

Soueif is much concerned with the effect of the American foreign policy on the Arab world. She thinks that neither the US nor the British government (with few exceptions) accepts that there is a linkage between their politics, the events of September 11 and what is happening in Palestine. At the time of writing she analysed examples taken from Western Media arguing that on TV we are presented with "the battle of the images", with George W. Bush on the one hand and Osama bin Laden on the other. Bush is usually reassuringly surrounded

---

[3] "Neocolonialism" is a term coined in 1961, four years after Ghana had won its independence. In 1965 the Ghanaian leader, Kwame Nkrumah, elaborated it in theoretical terms in his book Neo-colonialism: The Last Stage of Imperialism (Nkrumah 1965). Nkrumah suggests "[…] neocolonialism represented the American stage of colonialism, that is an empire without colonies" (Young 2001, 46).

by American senators, ministers and army commanders, all ready to assist him in his plight and also by objects such as the American flag that has become an instantly recognisable symbol of power. Whereas the media has turned Bush into a kind of megastar that is fighting for freedom and democracy, "At the end you expect a curtain call" (Soueif 2004, 73) as Soueif puts it, bin Laden is portrayed as his counterpart. Always alone without a network of supporters, characterised by his beard and turban, he sits close-up in the frame. Instead of a flag his symbol of power is the machine gun propped up against the wall. Occasionally shots of bin Laden are linked to turbaned fighters scrambling along steep mountain paths. Soueif argues that the American media are responsible for creating the circumstances for the appearance of the Taliban, who act as a proof of the "backwardness" of Islam. The message seems obvious: "[...] a backward fanatical oppressive Islam confronting a liberal inclusive democratic West" (Soueif 2004, 73-74).

As Soueif's argument shows the media play a fundamental and active role in the construction of cultural stereotypes. This is particularly evident in America where according to Soueif "The American people are the prisoners of their media" (Soueif 2004, 79). Through media exposure bin Laden's turban has become a symbol of terrorism just like his machine gun. As a consequence, prejudices and mass hysteria develop as Soueif shows citing the examples of three Arabs that were arrested in Birmingham just for wearing turbans or a number of Sikhs that were beaten up for exactly the same reason. According to Derek Gregory "the colonial present" is not only produced by politics and economics "It is also set in motion through mundane cultural forms and cultural practices that mark other people as irredeemably 'other' and that license the unleashing of exemplary violence against them" (Gregory 2004, 16). However, that seems to be exactly what the British and American media are doing when reporting on matters to do with Arabs, Islam and Palestine, presenting Arabs and Muslims as if "[...] they were one-celled creatures" (Soueif 2004, 10) with identical points of view.

Soueif cites the example of three pictures showing some Palestinians dancing in the streets after they had heard the news of the attack on America. Although correspondents of Arab news channels stressed that these were isolated incidents and in spite of the numerous condolences from Palestinians and Palestinian organisations received by the US Consul-General in Jerusalem, the images of dancing Palestinians were singled out for publication and repeatedly appeared in the American media. Soueif's concern recalls Gregory's point of view:

> Even those Muslims who disagreed with bin Laden and condemned what happened on September 11 are incarcerated with the terrorists in a monolithic super-organic 'culture' that serves only to reinforce 'hostility, distrust and hatred of the West' and to 'fuel fanaticism' (Gregory 2004, 22).

Soueif draws our attention to the fact that much of the information on Arabs, Muslims and Palestine derives from the Middle East Media Research Institute (MEMRI), co-founded by Meyrav Wurmser whose husband, David Wurmser, is the head of Middle East Studies at Richard Perle's American Enterprise Institute and the director of the Center for Middle East Policy at the Hudson Institute.

> According to the *Guardian*, MEMRI is connected with Israeli army intelligence and feeds the media and politicians with highly selective quotations from extreme Arab publications (Soueif 2004, 128).

When discussing the political situation in Iraq, British and American politicians are often resorting to rhetorical devices that stress the difference between "us" on one side and "them" on the other. Soueif observes that British and American heads of State are constantly on the TV screen discussing what "we" should do about the Middle East thereby not only creating a clear divide between "us" and "them" but also implying that "we" are in a superior position that enables "us" to solve "their" problems for "their" benefit. As Gregory argues

> For what else is the war on terror other than the violent return of the colonial past, with its split geographies of 'us' and 'them', 'civilization' and 'barbarism', 'Good' and 'Evil'? (Gregory 2004, 11).

Soueif stresses that America's political myth of freedom and democracy inevitably leads to a hatred for the supposingly "uncivilised", "non-democratic" part of the world. Rather than trying to overcome this hatred by re-assessing their own political systems, values and beliefs they have opted for a "civilising" mission, which has had disastrous effects on the Arab world. While visiting refugee camps Soueif highlights the daily individual problems that the occupied have to deal with: the breaking up of families, the loss of family members and friends, the inconvenience of checkpoints and curfews, the disrespect shown by Israeli soldiers. It does not come as a surprise that the forty thousand people that live under curfew define themselves as "[...] mice in a trap" (Soueif 2004, 35). The writer argues that one of the tasks of the occupation is to push people into more and more primitive living conditions by strangling the city with curfews, closures and threatened demolitions. These conditions are the breeding ground for resentment, anger and consequently violence as the "[...] monster barrier of steel and concrete" (Soueif 2004, 139) separates farmers from their land and refugees from their homes.

Soueif draws attention to the fact that hundreds of images depicting atrocities committed by American Army soldiers in Iraq had not been published at the time when her article "This torture started from the top" appeared in the *Guardian* in May 2004. These images, described by Young as "Nature Morte" (Young 2001, ix), show naked men, being tortured in a similar way to the victims of Nazi concentration camps (Soueif 2004). Said himself, in his article "Zionism from the Standpoint of Its Victims", emphasises "[...] the Zionist set out systematically either to reduce the Palestinians to a nonexistent population or to strip down those who remained to the status of a silent coolie class" (Said 1997, 18). Soueif's concern is to unveil the Western traditional mechanism of representation with a view to show how it destroys individual humanity and dignity.[4] Outraged by the flippant comment of the BBC1's newscaster on the 29th of April 2004 (10 p.m.) who referred to these images as "'merely mementoes'" (Soueif 2004, 164), Soueif argues that they form part of a long tradition, they have a "pedigree" (Soueif 2004, 164). However, she suggests that the Americans have pushed this discourse further. What she refers to as the "[...] pornography of occupation" (Soueif 2004, 164) is cruder and more sinister than that of old Europe. What particularly disturbed the Arab world were the images of American women soldiers ridiculing naked Arab men, thereby adding sexual humiliation to physical pain. One of these images depicts: "[...] a young woman in military uniform [who] points at their penises, does a thumbs-up and laughs" (Soueif 2004, 163). Soueif points out that these images have their origins in the postcards that the French sent home from their travels in Algeria or Morocco in the first half of the twentieth century. Typical postcards would depict erotic images of prostitutes with bared breasts showing off their thighs, over captions like "'*Le Harem Arabe*' or '*Fille Mauresque*'" (Soueif 2004, 164). But here these images reveal a striking inversion: of the female Western viewer, whose gaze, defined by Rey Chow "[...] the primary agency of violence" (Chow 1994, 126), brings the representation of the other into being.[5]

The pictures showing Muslim men being humiliated by American women testify the unbalanced relationship of gender and race. Gregory, quoting the novelist John Wideman, puts forward the idea that "It is this asymmetry that marks this as a colonial gesture of extraordinary contemporary resonance" (Gregory 2004, 21).

Since the seventies, post-colonialism and its feminist components have been tackling a number of questions posed on various levels by Eurocentric thinking and its representative models on the critical and literary plane. Although dealing with a number of different social and political issues, Soueif's essays in *Mezzaterra* share the common aim of demystifying and de-alienating Arab/Muslim cultures by presenting an alternative point of view on current affairs from the perspective of a woman who has an insight into both Arab/

---

[4] See also Thompson (1988).

[5] Also the Orientalist paintings produced in Britain in the nineteenth century played a powerful ideological role, just as the images that we see in the media today. As Linda Nochlin, in her article *The Imaginary Orient*, argues: "Pictorial Orientalism, apparently, was taken by most art historians concerned with this genre to be innocent of any taint of imperialist ideology and to constitute an innocent and colourful representation of an exotic reality [...]" (Nochlin 1989, xix). See also Thornton (1994) and Peltre (1998).

Muslim and Western world. As Gareth Griffiths underlines, in her article "The Myth of Authenticity", "It is only through such counter-narratives that alter/native views can be put" (Griffiths 1994, 239). Thus, Soueif's alternative writing tends to interrupt the linearity of the flux of Western discriminating cultural representation, by sparking off a polyphony of previously ignored or neglected voices of local people that emerge from the shadows of the "periphery" and re-write their own languages, stories and cultures, whilst critically re-examining the stereotyping Western mechanism of the media that endures in the present.

References

Chow R. 1994. "Where Have All the Natives Gone". In Bammer A. (ed.) *Displacements: Cultural Identities in Question*. Bloomington: Indiana University Press, 125-151.

D'Alessandro S. 2007 "Ahdaf Soueif". In Corona D., Castagna V., D'Alessandro S. (eds.) *Narrativa storica e riscrittura. Saggi e interviste*. Palermo: Annali della Facoltà di Lettere e Filosofia, Collana Studi e Ricerche, Università degli Sudi di Palermo, n. 50.

Di Piazza E., Corona D., Romeo M. (eds.). 2005. *Maschere dell'impero*. Pisa: Edizioni ETS.

Fanon F. 1967. *I dannati della terra*. Torino: Giulio Einaudi Editore.

Gregory D. 2004. *The Colonial Present*. USA, UK: Blackwell Publishing.

Griffiths G. 1994. "The Myth of Authenticity". In Ashcroft W., Griffiths G., Tiffin H. (eds.) *The Post-colonial Studies Reader*. London: Routledge, 237-241.

McClintock A., Mufti A., Shohat E. (eds.). 1997. *Dangerous Liaisons*. Minneapolis, London: University of Minnesota Press.

Nkrumah K. 1965. *Neo-colonialism: The Last Stage of Imperialism*. London: Heinemann.

Nochlin L. 1989. *The Politics of Vision*. Colorado, Oxford: Westview Press.

Peltre C. 1998. *Orientalism in Art*. New York, London: Abbeville Press.

Said E.W. 1978. *Orientalism*. New York: Pantheon Books.

Said E.W. 1997. "Zionism from the Standpoint of Its Victims". In McClintock A., Mufti A., Shohat E. (eds.) *Dangerous Liaisons*. Minneapolis, London: University of Minnesota Press.

Soueif A. 2004. *Mezzaterra*. London: Bloomsbury.

Thompson J. 1988. *The East. Imagined, Experienced, Remembered*. Dublin: National Gallery of Ireland.

Thornton L. 1994. *Women as Portrayed in Orientalist Painting*. Paris: ACR Edition.

Young R. 2001. *Postcolonialism*. USA, UK: Blackwell Publishing.

TANIA ZULLI

Università Roma Tre

Resurrecting Ayesha's Ghost:
the New Challenges of Rider Haggard's Fiction

In *Culture and Anarchy* (1869), Matthew Arnold declared that culture spoke "through all the voices of human experience, [...] art, science, poetry, philosophy, history, as well as religion" (Arnold 1965, 93); he coalesced life and culture creating an evenly balance between them, and introduced an idea of the latter as the product of many different aspects of everyday life. Equally, man could not be conceived as isolated, but he was part of a totality he intrinsically depended on in the creation of a culture, because "[p]erfection, as culture conceives it, is not possible while the individual remains isolated: the individual is obliged [...] to carry others along with him in his march towards perfection" (*ibidem*).[1] The numerous axiological horizons of nineteenth-century society engendered a symbolic field that characterized every aspect of life; today, this field has become the theoretical foundation of some contemporary cultural discourses.

Postcolonial literature is a case in point in the exploration of the link between current theories and their past heredities. Concepts such as multiculturalism, hybridity, interracial encounters have a legacy that can be traced back to nineteenth-century socio-cultural representations. This legacy, if aptly explored, generates a number of complex relations that make us re-think of the present under the constructive, multifaceted light of the past. In a lecture given at the London School of Economics a few years ago, Paul Gilroy affirms that: "[...] for Britain, developing durable and habitable multiculture depends upon working through the legacies of departed empire" (Gilroy 2006, 27). Working through the legacies of empire implies taking into account the presence of both its cultural and literary environment, as well as their hermeneutical value. In my paper, I

---

[1] The quotation by Matthew Arnold is related to a general nineteenth-century holistic view of man as a being that can be fully comprehended only if observed in its single parts. Specifically, the holistic view of man as the product of a creative combination started with Ruskin in *The Seven Lamps of Architecture* and *Fors Clavigera*, passed through Arnold's philosophy and was fully accomplished at the end of the century by Forster's 'only connect', that envisaged the retrieval of all the values of life.

will deal with new challenging stimuli that can be found in colonial fiction by privileging a contrastive, sometimes destabilizing reading; in the background, the relationship between colonial culture and literature will be considered. This twofold approach will envisage a synchronic perspective, considering the intermingling of literary texts and culture at large in the late nineteenth century, and a diachronic one, which will take into account the relationship between past and present, and the heredity left by past colonial concepts to modern postcolonial, neocolonialist and anti-colonialist perspectives.

Literary texts have been largely defined as the place where social transformations, theoretical interactions, cultural voices, artistic representations, philosophical and religious expressions can be found. All literary texts finally disclose a political and social resonance, while both society and culture appear productively organized in the realms of fiction. Such considerations are endorsed by recent criticism, and they are crucial in the case of colonial culture, as the reading of colonial novels 'in context' provides an invaluable help in mapping out the internal dynamics of colonialism itself.

At the same time, understanding modern multicultural societies and their own complications implies harking back to their historical antecedents, that are easily traceable in the imperial past:

> [...] the political conflicts which characterize multicultural societies can take on a very different aspect if they are understood to exist firmly in a context supplied by imperial and colonial history. Though that history remains marginal and largely unacknowledged, surfacing only in the service of nostalgia and melancholia, it represents a store of unlikely connections and complex interpretative resources. The imperial and colonial past continues to shape political life in the overdeveloped-but-no-longer-imperial countries (Gilroy 2004, 2).

The colonial past of a country is often the reading key of its postcolonial present; moreover, present postcolonial ideologies are constantly influenced by their imperial antecedents through a double process of attraction and aversion. In literature, such dichotomic attitude is present in the fictional and non-fictional production of many South African authors. Among late nineteenth-century writers, Henry Rider Haggard emerges as a complicated case; his concern for contemporary politics, his direct interest in the colonies, and his genuine attention to human relationships between colonizers and colonized put him in a position which exceeds that of the mere writer of adventure stories. Moreover, the hermeneutical deviations produced by his connection to imperialism acquire additional meanings if analyzed under a modern critical approach. By reading Haggard's novels under a contemporary – postcolonial – light, one can detect a strong and complex link between current theories on immigration, otherness, and hybridism and earlier discourses on race and ethnicity.

Rider Haggard was a writer of adventure narratives; he also wrote books on the role of the Salvation army in the colonies, books on agriculture, notes on the costumes and traditions of African populations, but he is mainly remembered for his adventure novels, among which *King Solomon's Mines* and *She* were the most successful. Haggard's personality was very convoluted, as his biographers have differently emphasized; this individual complexity is at the core of his multifarious, variously arranged, sometimes only apparently contradicting interpretation of imperialism. Despite some crystal-clear colonialist attitudes, Haggard's fiction reveals an openness towards racial blending and understanding of the brutality of colonial rule, together with a romantic nostalgia for an uncontaminated African past. Gerald Monsman affirms that Haggard's fiction "reflects an agenda of imperial dissent, suggests an idealistic belief in the value of Anglo-African cultural rapport, and anticipates innovative anthropological and cultural principles" (Monsman 2006, 1). Also, Lindy Stiebel comments that "Haggard as romance writer [was] more conscious of the 'misery and despair' that Imperialism brought to its subjects. Within his fictions, beneath the cover of narrative convention and fictional characters, some contradictory part of Haggard is free to show more humanity and humility, more fears and pessimism as to the outcome of the imperial project than the public, imperialist Haggard could allow" (Stiebel 2001, 31-32).

Haggard's "contradictory imperialist impulses" (*ibidem*, xi) are scattered throughout his whole production; they are present, for instance, in his novel *King Solomon's Mines* (1885), where a group of British adventurers set out for a journey into the heart of Africa searching for King Solomon's treasure. Allan Quatermain, Captain John Good and Sir Henry Curtis introduce themselves to the native population of the Kukuanas as Gods coming "from the biggest star that shines at night", and claim their superiority by showing European objects of common use unknown to the savage people ("the magic tube that speaks", a gun, false teeth, a glass eye, etc); also, Allan Quatermain calls his servant Umbopa "dog and slave" (Haggard 1998, 115).[2] However, elsewhere in the novel, Quatermain affirms that he doesn't like the word *nigger* and prefers to use the word *native* (Haggard 1998, 9); similarly, Captain Good establishes a strong relationship with a native girl, Foulata, who will die with the hope of a second life to be lived with her love; Umbopa's real identity is not that of a servant, but that of a noble Zulu aristocrat, whose friendship with the white adventurers is definitely out of the boundaries of a colonizer-colonized

---

[2] The passage runs as follows: "Ye may perhaps doubt our power to avenge". I went on, heedless of this by-play. "Stay, I will show you. Here, *thou dog and slave* (addressing Umbopa in a *savage* tone), give me the magic tube that speaks; and I tipped a wink towards my express rifle. Umbopa rose to the occasion, and with something as nearly resembling a grin as I have ever seen on his dignified face he handed me the gun" (Haggard 1998, 115; my Italics).

relationship (D. Butts in Haggard 1998, xiv). His white friends are "brothers" he would be glad to have in his reign, showing thus that white men are welcome in native lands and hinting at the idea of interracial mixing as something not necessarily disturbing.

This idea is further supported by a group of brave female protagonists who populate Haggard's most famous adventure romances; their notion of interracial relationships and ethnic communion is mostly driven by passionate, romantic love. It is the case of Foulata in *King Solomon's Mines*, whose last words before dying draw the picture of a future union with her white lover among the stars:

> "Say to my lord, Bougwan, that – I love him, and that I am glad to die because I know that he cannot cumber his life with such as me, for the sun cannot mate with the darkness, nor the white with the black. Say that at times I have felt as though there were a bird in my bosom, which would one day fly hence and sing elsewhere. Even now, though I cannot lift my hand, and my brain grows cold, I do not feel as though my heart were dying; it is so full of love that could live a thousand years, and yet be young. Say that if I live again, mayhap I shall see him in the stars, and that – I will search them all, though perchance I should there *still be black* and he would – *still be white*" (Haggard 1998, 281; my Italics).[3]

It is also the case of Ustane, the beautiful native girl in *She*, whose devotion to her beloved Leo leads her to a terrible punishment, and eventually to death. The sheer division between European white superior populations and black subjects is often contradicted by Haggard; as in this straightforward declaration: "I cannot believe that the Almighty, who made both white and black, gave to one race the right or mission of exterminating, or even of robbing or maltreating, the other and calling the process the advance of civilization" (Pocock 1993, 95). On the other hand, the vision of the Imperial enterprise is quite clear, as he shows through the words of Ayesha, the heroine of the already mentioned novel *She*. Ayesha's authority incarnates the real essence of the Imperial system; the heartless killing of her subjects being a way to confirm her superiority. When asked about it, she answers thus: "Thou hast seen how in the heavens the little clouds blow this way and that without a cause, yet behind them is the great wind sweeping on its path whither it listeth. So it is with me [...]. My moods and changes are the little clouds, and fitfully these seem to turn; but behind them ever blows the great wind of my purpose" (Haggard 1991, 176). That is, the great wind of the Imperial machine moves the little clouds of colonizers

---

[3] This union will not, however, take place, and the two lovers will remain forever separated. What is important though, is the potential of interracial love, which aims at eternal life ("[my heart] is so full of love that could live a thousand years, and yet be young"); the same concept will be fully developed as Ayesha's driving force in *She*.

committed in different missions, and every single operation, be it peaceful or cruel, aims at a final design.

Needless to say, *She* (1887) is one of Haggard's most famous adventure novels; it was written in less than two months, between February and March 1886, and published in volume format in 1887. Its alluring title contains all the essence of a story centered on a fascinating female figure, that of Ayesha, the beautiful white queen of a savage African population, who has the gift of eternal life and beauty, though she governs her reign through sheer terror. The character of She-Who-Must-Be-Obeyed[4] is many-sided; she contains past and present, life and death, history and religion, and embodies the late Victorian world picture fully, with its social and political transitions, a sense of the precariousness of human existence, as well as the idea of nature's perpetual life renewal. Moreover, issues of gender and race revolve around Ayesha's figurative authority, making her one of Haggard's most impressive heroines.[5]

More than lingering on more examples of Haggard's praise and/or contempt of Imperialism, it is essential to underline the capacity of his fiction to *problematize* the imperial experience. The fact that the works of an author who has always been regarded as a supporter of imperial ideologies may contain anti-colonial thoughts, should let one think of the intrinsic potential of colonial fiction itself (or at least of some colonial narratives). Ayesha's eternal existence, achieved through many successive incarnations, echoes the immortality of colonial (and colonialist) writing, ready to be continuously re-interpreted. Resurrecting the ghost of Ayesha is a way to let Haggard's narratives come alive and be rendered according to different critical instruments; the few examples taken from his novels are only a suggestion to prove that there is enough material to be analyzed in order to give birth to new challenging discourses. Ayesha's immortality, "the ontologically absurd idea of eternal time originating from a distant past and extending into an inscrutable future" (Di Piazza 2009, 215) is a metaphor of the endurance of colonial theories which, sinking their roots in a remote past, scatter the seeds of a not so inscrutable future.

The key concept for such a kind of study seems to be that of *cultural ambivalence* that recalls the idea of intercultural reading, interracial exchange, ideological duality. Rider Haggard epitomizes this conceptual model, both in his persona and in his fiction, as Ian Fletcher argued in an essay on the South

---

[4] The Queen's name comes from one of Haggard's childhood memories, that of a "disreputable rag doll of particular hideous aspect, with boot-button eyes, hair of black wool and a sinister leer upon its painted face" (Haggard 1976, 28).

[5] Despite the evident praise of the imperial experience the novel contains a few examples which run in an opposite direction, fostering a different vision of the colonial world. For instance, Haggard's attitude towards the native populations is expressed in Horace Holly's respect for the Amahaggers' marriage customs which reflects the author's own interest in examining people of different races as part of a common humanity.

African writer: a more naïve author than Conrad and Kipling, Haggard deals with their same topics, while "[his] novels and romances reflect his wavering moods. Sometimes he is sceptical about the European virtues and highly pessimistic about progress, enlightenment and civilization. At others, he exalts the white man, and particularly the English gentleman" (Fletcher 1971, 136).[6] This makes Haggard's works very interesting in the perspective of modern studies on interracial conflicts, and discloses fertile areas of investigation, making his fiction instrumental for the analysis of racial issues both in the nineteenth century and today.

References

Arnold M. 1965. *Culture and Anarchy: An Essay in Social and Political Criticism*. In Super R.H. (ed.) *Matthew Arnold, Complete Prose Works*, 2 vols. Ann Arbor: University of Michigan Press.

Chrisman L. 2003. *Postcolonial Contraventions, Cultural Readings of Race, Imperialism, and Transnationalism*. Manchester: Manchester University Press.

Di Piazza E. 2009. "Haggard and Kronos, a Letter from Beyond the Grave". In Costantini M., Marroni F., Soccio E. (eds.) *Letter(s). Functions and Forms of Letter-Writing in Victorian Art and Literature*. Roma: Aracne, 2009, 213-222.

Fletcher I. 1971. "Can Haggard Ride Again?". In *The Listener*, July 29th.

Gilroy P. 2004. *After Empire*. London: Routledge.

Gilroy P. 2006. "Multiculture in Times of War: An Inaugural Lecture Given at the London School of Economics". In *Critical Quarterly*, 48, 4, 27-45.

Haggard H.R. 1991. *She* (introduced by Karlin D.). Oxford: Oxford University Press.

Haggard H.R. 1998. *King Solomon's Mines* (introduced by Butts D.). Oxford: Oxford University Press.

Haggard L.R. 1976. *The Cloak that I Left*. Bungay, Suffolk: Boydell Press.

Monsman G. 2006. *Rider Haggard on the Imperial Frontier*. Greensboro: ELT Press.

Pocock T. 1993. *Rider Haggard and the Lost Empire*. London: Weidenfeld and Nicolson.

Stiebel L. 2001. *Imagining Africa: Landscape in H. Rider Haggard's African Romances*. Westport (Ct.): Greenwood Press.

---

[6] Also Laura Chrisman defines Haggard "acutely ambivalent about the process of capitalist modernization both in the UK and in South Africa" (Chrisman 2003, 40).

Section 4
Travelling Concepts, Transforming Bodies

FRANCESCA GUIDOTTI

Università di Bergamo

A.C. Clarke's *A Meeting with Medusa*: the Cyborg Challenge to This World and the Next

1. The cyborg paradigms

Contemporary culture is haunted by the hybrid, enigmatic figure of the cyborg: a living creature whose organic body is modified by the incorporation of inorganic parts. Grounded in scientific discourses, the fine arts and the media, ever since its first appearance the cyborg has proved to be a very effective symbol for present and future challenges.

The term "cyborg", a contraction of 'cybernetic organism', was coined in 1960 by Manfred Clynes and Nathan Kline, two doctors of the Rockland State Hospital of New York who came to suggest that human beings could survive in harsh environments through technological ameliorations (Clynes and Kline 1961). Needless to say, the doctors were chiefly thinking of future astronauts and envisioning new frontiers for space flight (Henry 1966).

The cyborg, however, is not just an offspring of cold war techno-culture; even if unnamed, it had long been in existence as a literary invention, a narrative theme related to science fiction. According to most scholars cyborgs make their first appearance at the end of the nineteenth century as the alien invaders of H.G. Wells' *War of the Worlds*, whose atrophied organic bodies are somehow indistinguishable from the complex machines they operate (Wells 1898).

Between the twenties and the thirties several science fiction stories published in the pulps develop this idea. The cyborg is presented as a technological variant of the so called BEM ('bug-eyed-monsters'): a 'canned brain' endowed with superior scientific knowledge and often hostile to humanity (Guidotti 2003, 71-73).

It was in the fifties however that the theme gained importance. In his short stories, published under the pseudonym "Cordwainer Smith", the American writer Linebarger[1] portrays a gallery of post-human beings burdened with a

---

[1] P.M.A. Linebarger was also an East Asia scholar and an expert in psychological warfare.

fragile and troublesome identity, always on the verge of collapse (Smith 1993). Neither men nor machines, these cyborgs can work wonders; nonetheless, they often suffer for what they have lost and live their lot in loneliness.

In what is usually regarded as the classical – and still popular – characterization of the cyborg, hybridity often comes to the detriment of human identity and dignity, and technology steals more than it gives. Situated in the continuum between the two poles of the technological freak and the bionic superman, these creatures are paradigmatic of a humanism ideologically more concerned with than fascinated by the consequences of their metamorphosis. Such cyborgs are equally exposed to emulation and to parody,[2] and Postmodern writers were to take advantage of both these possibilities.

If most cyberpunk characters register the shift from a strong to a weak subjectivity, as well as from grand narratives to fragments (Guidotti 2003, 157-187), contemporary cybernetic organisms can also be seen as metaphors for exploring a techno-culture where former categories have collapsed and, as a consequence, individual perceptions need to be redefined. Donna J. Haraway, among others, claims that to contemporary mankind the only hope comes from a conscious acceptance of contamination and hybridization, as well as from the democratic potential of the technological landscape:

> The machine is not an *it* to be animated, worshipped, and dominated. The machine is us, our processes, an aspect of our embodiment (Haraway 1991, 180).

This quick excursus through science fiction and cultural history was intended not only to introduce the work I'm going to discuss, but to show its interplay with the different versions of the theme. The lengthy short story *A Meeting with Medusa*, written in 1971 by Arthur C. Clarke,[3] features a complex and ideologically contradictory cyborg, at the same time doomed by his fate and ready to take advantage of it in order to accomplish extraordinary deeds. Although the story has often been studied in terms of a gloomy humanism,[4] I believe it also paved the way to a more optimistic Postmodern approach to the theme, an approach which was soon to spread both within science fiction and without.

This interpretation is also consistent with Clarke's works and perspective. The British science fiction writer, who was also a scientist, an inventor, a futurist and, among other things, a supporter of secular Humanism, always held to an

---

[2] An overt parody can be found in Borges and Bioy Casares (1967).

[3] This was the last short story Clarke ever wrote, before concentrating entirely on novels. It won a Playboy editorial award and a Nebula award.

[4] According to Zikovich (2001, 11) the story brings "into focus [...] the slow but steady transformation of Falcon, who is gradually and by no means painlessly alienating himself from his human origin in order to get used to his new status of cyborg".

optimistic view of science and progress (McAleer 1992). In his fiction he often imagines that, centuries ahead, humanity might be able to outgrow its present limitations and fully develop its potential, thus giving rise to a Utopian society, both technologically advanced and ecologically sustainable. Several of Clarke's works[5] develop the idea of a 'transcendence trough evolution', a transformation which eventually can make future men not only happier but also, in a way, closer to gods.

This happens, for instance, in the novel *2001: A Space Odyssey* which, like the screenplay of the movie, was written in collaboration with director Stanley Kubrick[6] and which is relevant for the issue under discussion since, as Clarke once wrote, *A Meeting with Medusa* should be considered as a further development of the same theme.[7]

In the novel *2001: A Space Odyssey* the transition to a higher order of evolution takes place through contact with mysterious alien monoliths. In the end astronaut David Bowman, transformed into an immortal Star Child who can easily live and travel in space, saves a humanity on the verge of world war 3 by destroying all thermonuclear weapons.

To some extent, in the short story *A Meeting with Medusa* the main character undergoes a similar transformation. And this may well lead us to tracing new meanings which coexist, or possibly conflict, with the classical paradigm.

2. *A Meeting with Medusa*

The story is reported by an omniscient narrator, who mostly shares the point of view of the protagonist, Howard Falcon. It opens with the chronicle of an air crash, occurred to the giant dirigible *Queen Elizabeth IV* during its maiden voyage. Commander Falcon is badly injured and, in order to save his life, surgeons transform him into a cyborg.[8]

---

[5] See the short story *The Sentinel* (1948) and the novels *Childhood's End* (1953), *2001: A Space Odyssey* (1968), *Imperial Earth* (1975).

[6] The novel was written simultaneously with the screenplay of the movie even if the former, which follows early drafts of the latter, is far less enigmatic and more explicit. Both were partly based on previous short stories by Clarke, mainly *The Sentinel*, written in 1948 for a BBC competition and first published in 1951 under the title *Sentinel of Eternity*.

[7] Clarke (1985, 252): "I had been thinking about Jupiter for a long time; witness the final sequence of the movie *2001: A Space Odyssey*. And in some ways the sequel *2010: Odyssey Two* is also a sequel to this story; I had room there to develop in more detail some of the concepts I had first worked out in 'Medusa'". In Kubrick's movie, the mission is to Jupiter, not to Saturn, because the special effect supervisor found it difficult to reproduce Saturn's rings. In the novel's sequel Clarke also replaced Saturn with Jupiter.

[8] Readers learn that Falcon is a cyborg only at the end, even if there are several previous clues.

Seven years later Falcon convinces his old friend Webster, head of Long-Range Planning, to send him on a space mission to the still unexplored Jupiter, where he can make the most of his newly acquired extraordinary physical resistance and promptness of reaction. Once there, Falcon has an unexpected encounter with a gigantic alien creature, which he calls "medusa" and from which eventually he flees when it draws too near.

In the last chapter the cyborg is back to Earth. Webster welcomes him as a hero but is soon shocked by the coldness and detachment of his friend, as well as by his lack of identification with mankind:

> *Men*, thought Webster. He said 'men'. He's never done that before. And when did I last hear him use the word 'we'? He's changing, slipping away from us (Clarke 1985, 309).

In the end, switching to free indirect speech, the narrator discloses that Falcon intends to become a mediator between the ephemeral organic human race, to whom the past belongs, and the immortal metal lords of time to come:

> Some day the real masters of space would be machines, not men – and he was neither. Already conscious of his destiny, he took a sombre pride in his unique loneliness – the first immortal midway between two orders of creation.
> He would, after all, be an ambassador; between the old and the new – between the creatures of carbon and the creatures of metal who must one day supersede them.
> Both would have need of him in the troubled centuries that lay ahead (*ibidem*, 310).

The last chapter of the story is very interesting because it sets up two diverging interpretations of the cyborg's evolution: Webster's pessimistic musing and Falcon's optimistic élan. Neither is more comprehensive or trustworthy, but the reader is led to interpret the cyborg's proud claims about his future achievement in the light of Webster's concern for his supposed degeneration.

And yet, if we choose to focus on the gradual development of the cyborg's point of view rather than on Webster's final assessment, Falcon's human and post-human trajectories can be read as a progressive shift to relativism and self-determination, away from the bondage of predetermined cultural rules. Only after getting over conventionalism and anthropocentrism will Falcon be able to redefine his own individuality in order to establish an authentic contact with the radically other.

The story deals with space flight and alien encounter, but also with the interpretation of reality and identity. As the pilot and commander of the largest ship ever built by man, Falcon initially relies on his senses and on technology, which seem at once to guarantee both a safe flight and an intensely emotional experience.

Needless to say, this is only a passing illusion and the topos of catastrophic maiden voyages is soon enacted.[9] In a moment the tragedy takes place as the dirigible is hit by the camera platform supposed to record its inaugural flight. The fallibility of both sensory and technological systems is now apparent, as effectively shown by the lack of media coverage for the space disaster.

Paradoxically enough, the experience of limits, tested in the air crash, is stretched farther after a successful space mission.[10] In this case fallibility has nothing to do with the technical aspects of the flight; instead, Falcon becomes aware of being fallible whenever his convictions about reality and identity are challenged.

The encounter with the aliens is crucial in this respect. The recurrent image of medusa in the short story has often been interpreted as a symbol of Falcon's fear of losing his original human identity (Zikovich 2001), along the Freudian paradigm of castration (Damiani 2001, Garber and Vickers 2003). This may be true, since in Clarke's tale the medusa is first associated to the doomed dirigible *Queen Elizabeth*, which reminds Falcon of "a squadron of large but harmless jellyfish, pulsing their mindless way above a shallow tropical reef" (Clarke 1985, 255). However the Jovian medusa is also something more.

On their first meeting, Falcon is unable to recognize the shape of the unknown living form and describes it as a "pallid forest" or "a single enormous tree – like one of the giant multi-trunked banyans of the East" (*ibidem*, 286). Only after one second, closer encounter does he realize that:

> It did not resemble a tree at all, but a jellyfish – a medusa, such as might be met trailing its tentacles as it drifted along the warm eddies of the Gulf Stream (*ibidem*, 297).

This creature is an enigma that neither Falcon nor the terrestrial scientists at Ground Control can decipher. It unexpectedly resists the attack of predator Jovian mantas and prevails on them by means of a mysterious weapon, similar to a radio aerial. Now the question is whether the medusa possesses some kind of intelligence. Exobiologist Dr. Brenner, who used to provide full explanations based on his own terrestrial frame of knowledge, now admits there is no safe ground for a pronouncement.

Nevertheless, as a precaution, the scientist urges Falcon to act according to the Prime Directive, i.e. to follow the instructions devised for encounters with intelligent creatures. Obedience to these rules, never before applied, involves

---

[9] The air crash recalls the tragic lot of many dirigibles, among which the *Italia* (1928) and the *Hindenburg* (1937). Unlike the *Queen Elizabeth*, however, the Hindenburg disaster was described as the "first media event" because of its live radio broadcast. See Toland (1972).

[10] The space ship is named *Kon-Tiki* after the raft used by the Norwegian explorer Thor Heyerdahl in his 1947 successful expedition from Peru to Polynesia in order to demonstrate that pre-Columbian settlers might have followed that route.

immobility and inactivity, as the exobiologist repeatedly warns: "don't alarm it" (*ibidem*, 303), "keep your distance", "make no attempt to approach, or even to communicate, until 'they' have had plenty of time to study you" (*ibidem*, 302).

Needless to say, the Prime Directive is once more grounded on man's limited experience. Its compilers wanted to avoid repeating the mistakes of so many terrestrial conquerors and colonizers, who had brought about acts of violence and usurpation by claiming that they held the right to a dominant position in the natural order:

> Man had – it was hoped – profited from his mistakes on earth. Not only moral considerations, but also his own self-interest demanded that he should not repeat them among the planets. It could be disastrous to treat a superior intelligence as the American settlers had treated the Indians, or as almost everyone had treated the Africans... (*ibidem*, 302).

Despite good intentions, results are disappointing. The Prime Directive presupposes not only equality, but also homogeneity between the two participants in the act of making contact, which of course is not the case; the rule, moreover, suggests that both should be treated as human while, ironically enough, in this specific occurrence neither can be considered as such. Furthermore the Directive defines the duration of the required inactivity in deliberately vague terms ("plenty of time"), so that the decision is ultimately left to the "man" – or rather to the cyborg – "on the spot" (*ibidem*, 302): he is the one who is supposed to be able to judge with a clear mind, even under the pressure of extraordinary events.[11]

Falcon is conscious of the intrinsic flaws of the rule not much in its formulation, but rather in its basic assumptions. The Prime Directive, with its lack of unbiased objectivity, epitomizes the fallibility of human thought, especially when it must mediate between two divergent positions each of which, taken individually, is excessive to the point of being ludicrous:

> Falcon [...] recalled a TV discussion he had once seen between a space lawyer and an astronaut. After the full implication of the Prime directive had been carefully spelled out, the incredulous spacer had exclaimed: 'Then if there was no alternative, I must sit still and let myself be eaten?' The lawyer had not even cracked a smile when he answered: 'That's an *excellent* summing up' (*ibidem*, 305).

In the end Falcon instinctively opts for retreating and escaping the embrace of the medusa's tentacles, which he takes as markers of an aggressive attitude. However, in the long minutes between the ignition and the takeoff, things

---

[11] Clarke (1985, 302): "Exactly what was meant by 'plenty of time', no one had ever been able to decide. It was left to the discretion of the man on the spot".

change unexpectedly: the medusa is now gently patting the balloon, as if it were just trying to be friendly (*ibidem*, 306-307).

Having come to the final phase of his space mission, the cyborg is ready to take stock. In his mind there has always been room for doubt, and he is perfectly aware that whatever interpretation of and reaction to the alien's behaviour may be mistaken. Falcon also knows that, even if he had decided to interact, he wouldn't have been able to find the right words, simply because all words are necessarily intended for and conceived by men.

> Maybe he should try to talk to it over the radio. Which should it be: 'Pretty pussy'? 'Down, Fido'? Or 'Take me to your leader'? (*ibidem*, 307).

In the end Falcon is prepared for a radical change. The meeting with the alien has urged him towards a self-determination which, by the way, is consistent with some recent libertarian interpretations of the medusa symbolism (Garber and Vickers 2003). Aware of the impossibility of establishing contact through man-made rules, Falcon sets out to resume his mission[12] in a different form; in other words he reshapes his identity in order to get rid of all former restraints and acquire a new status. This means not only giving up anthropomorphism, but also reconsidering all dualisms dictated by culture.

The last lines portray a self who, reborn from his ashes, stretches into the future. Falcon now refuses any identification with the past[13] and with a man-made vision of this world and the next. He embraces the broad notion of relativism, exempt from any indulgence in a misconceived right to domination.

As a consequence, the cyborg is content to take up a marginal position in the cosmic design: instead of aspiring to supreme power, he chooses to be an intermediary between the current and the future masters of space. This also means deconstructing the myth of an essential identity on behalf of a performative identification of the self; in other words, by explaining *what he will do*, Falcon can also tell us *who he is*. He has finally found the way to make the most of his hybridism, without any more fear or regret.

To me, this cyborg is ultimately a metaphor for what human minds can do, even without the need of a post-human body. Rather than a reminder of a wretched fate, his loneliness is a point of departure and an invitation to follow.

---

[12] When he is leaving Jupiter for the Earth, Falcon murmurs: "Some other time" (Clarke 1985, 308).

[13] Falcon had previously made an artful use of memory in order to convince Webster, who was reluctant to entrust him with the mission to Jove. By suggesting the equation "Jupiter is to Earth as Earth is to India" (*ibidem*, 264-265) the protagonist had reminded his friend of their flight on India, taken ten years before; this had restored Webster's confidence not only in the expertise of Falcon as a flyer but also, and mostly, in his human identity and motivations.

References

Borges J.L., Bioy Casares A. 1967. *Crónicas de Bustos Domecq*. Buenos Aires: Losada.

Clarke A.C. 1948. "The Sentinel." In Clarke A.C. *The Sentinel*. London: HarperCollins, 147-161.

Clarke A.C. 1953. *Childhood's End*. New York: Del Rey.

Clarke A.C. 1968. *2001: A Space Odyssey*. New York: New American Library.

Clarke A.C. 1976 (1 ed. 1975). *Imperial Earth*. New York: Harcourt.

Clarke A.C. 1985. "A Meeting with Medusa". In Clarke A.C. *The Sentinel*. London: HarperCollins, 251-310.

Clynes M., Kline N. 1961. *Drugs, Space, and Cybernetics: Evolution to Cyborgs*. In Flaherty B.E. *Psychophisiological Aspects of Space Flight*. New York: Columbia UP, 345-371.

Damiani S. 2001. *Medusa. La fascinazione irriducibile dell'altro*. Bergamo: Sestante.

Garber M., Vickers N.J. 2003. *The Medusa Reader*. New York: Routledge.

Guidotti F. 2003. *Cyborg e dintorni: le formule della fantascienza*. Bergamo: Sestante.

Haraway D.J. 1991. *A Cyborg Manifesto: Science, Technology, and Socialist-Feminism in the Late Twentieth Century*. In Haraway D.J. *Simians, Cyborgs and Women. The Reinvention of Nature*. New York: Routledge, 149-181.

Henry J.P. 1966. *Biomedical Aspects of Space Flight*. New York: Holt.

McAleer N. 1992. *Arthur C. Clarke – The Authorized Biography*. Chicago: Contemporary Books.

Smith C. 1993. *The Rediscovery of Man: The Complete Science Fiction of Cordwainer Smith*. Mann J.A. (ed.) Framingham (Ma.): NESFA Press.

Toland J. 1972. *The Great Dirigibles, Their Triumphs and Disasters*. New York: Dover.

Wells H.G. 1898. *War of the Worlds*. London: Heinemann.

Zikovich Z. 2001. "The Motif of First Contact in Arthur C. Clarke's *A Meeting with Medusa*". In *New York Review of Science Fiction*, vol. 13 (7), n. 1, 8-13, 10-17.

Iolanda Plescia

Università Roma Tre

Body Language:
Early Modern Medicine and the Female Body

The title of the 2009 AIA conference invites reflection on the "dilemmas, ambiguities and directions" posed by the twenty-first century that has just begun. Many have wondered what exactly we might call our present age: a post-post-modernism, perhaps, as Malcom Bradbury somewhat unenthusiastically suggested in a 1995 article in which he argued that postmodernism was over, and had in fact been over for some time, having ended in or about November 1989.

Bradbury concluded that article by stating that "Increasingly, too, we will have to start concerning ourselves with the question not just of what we are 'post', but what we are 'pre'" (Bradbury 1995, 774). 'Interdisciplinarity' is one key concept that has been continually evoked in recent debates as a possible blueprint for future scholarship efforts, as an indispensable methodological and hermeneutical approach, well suited to the complexities and quandaries of our present time.[1] Bradbury's call to look at our age not only as an ending of sorts, but as the early stages of something new, may perhaps also justify a closer look at another 'early' moment in cultural history, one in which interdisciplinarity was, in a sense, the operative word.

Such an approach was in fact a widespread outlook at the very beginnings of modernity, in the early modern age, though it may sometimes be seen as an apparently effortless and at times downright naive process whereby the Renaissance intellectual purported himself to be an expert in many fields, a gigantic figure able to stand astride what we now call 'the two cultures'. However, the ability to resort to different domains of knowledge during crucial early modern scientific debates responded to a deep-rooted yearning for "unity of knowledge" (Klein 1990, 11), a synthesis of myth, history and technological progress, which reflects a conviction that answers to the fundamental questions must be sought not only in evidence and hard fact, but also in reference to belief systems and symbolic relations. The similarity of this position to so many

---

[1] See, among others, Klein (1990).

current efforts towards achieving 'holistic', 'whole' knowledge that applies to body, soul and mind is remarkable – a reaction, perhaps, to that very experience of fragmentation that has defined our culture for most of the twentieth century.[2]

The human body and its early modern conceptualizations have offered an ideal testing ground for the study of Renaissance cultural paradigms; since it "has become a point of intersection between various fields because it has always been a powerful metaphor for the understanding and exploration not only of political change, but also of social issues" (Fortunati *et al*. 2003, vii) the body may be considered as the ideal 'text' for an experiment in interdisciplinary reading. The aim of this brief paper is to outline a specific case study that deals with the female body as it is conceptualized at the intersection between medical and literary discourse: while the rich and ever-expanding theoretical debate on the body cannot be accounted for here in any detail, a close scrutiny of this particular case, to begin with, may offer some insight into the tangle of issues relating both to myth and science through which the 'early modern' female body is understood.[3]

The case in point here is the pregnant body of Posthumus's mother in Shakespeare's *Cymbeline*. One of Shakespeare's absent mothers, she appears briefly along with her husband and two other sons, in a vision that visits Posthumus Leonatus in act 5, scene 4 of the play. Both parents and children are long dead, and have entered Posthumus's dreams to tell him the story of his birth: it is here that his mother reveals a detail which, I have argued elsewhere, will prove to be of great import to the construction of the hero's identity as the embodiment of the best British and Roman values.[4] Like another Shakespearean hero entrusted with the task of ushering in a new order to save a troubled land,

---

[2] One current wide-ranging interdisciplinary effort is the Socrates/ETNP Acume 2 program, "Interfacing Sciences, Literature and Humanities", coordinated by Vita Fortunati, which brings together scholars from a variety of fields and European countries. This paper itself draws on material from my ongoing research project on the female body and the theory of humours within the "Theories of Bodies and Life in Renaissance Culture" Acume 2 subproject, coordinated by Maria Del Sapio.

[3] At least two important contributions relating to the early modern period must be mentioned, David A. Hillman and Carla Mazzio's edited collection of essays *The Body in Parts* (1997) and Gail Kern Paster's *The Body Embarrassed* (1993).

[4] The argument I present here is based in part on a longer article in which I explored the allusion to Caesarean childbirth in *Cymbeline*, relating it to the 'Romanness' of the play ("'From me was Posthumus ript': *Cymbeline* and the Extraordinary Birth", in Del Sapio Garbero *et al*. 2010, 135-147). Much of the material on the early modern debate surrounding Caesarean delivery that is presented here is also accounted for in that essay, though my argument here is mostly indebted to Filippini (1995), and Blumenfeld-Kosinski (1990). On the much debated vision scene, see Nosworthy's Introduction to the Arden edition (2004, xxxiii-xxxvii), which argues in favour of the scene's authenticity.

Macduff, Posthumus is, in a sense, "of no woman born",[5] since he is effectively delivered *after* his mother's death in childbirth, through a Caesarean section:

> *Moth.* Lucina lent me not her aid,
> but took me in my throes,
> That from me was Posthumus ript,
> Came crying 'mongst his foes,
> A thing of pity! (5.4.43-47)

The word that defines the surgical incision in both *Macbeth* and *Cymbeline* is "rip", which recalls the Latin *eripio* (though the actual etymology seems to be entirely different), and conjures up an image so violent as to evoke another word often associated with women's bodies, that is, 'rape'. Such an intrusion into the pregnant woman's body is designed to facilitate birth regardless of the "woman's part" in it (to borrow Posthumus's expression in his well-known tirade against all womankind, 2.4.172); it also fosters the equivocation that allows Macduff to boast that he is "of no woman born". Janet Adelman has brilliantly argued that both cases represent a male "fantasy of exemption from the woman's part" (Adelman 1992, 139, 143):[6] because of their miraculous, surgical birth, which symbolically erases the woman's role (her exertion, and thus her power) in childbirth, these men possess the heroic qualities and pure, unadulterated lineage that will enable them to bring about, or help re-establish, political and social peace in their lands. Such men are made of the stuff of the classical gods, as they share the same kind of birth with Aesculapius (extracted from his dying mother's womb by Phoebus), Bacchus (saved by Jove, who rips him out of his mother's womb and sews him into his own thigh to bring the pregnancy to term, in what may be seen as quite a 'sci-fi' turn), and Adonis (born with Lucina's help after his mother Myrrha had been turned into a tree).

As is often the case with Shakespeare, it is impossible to say whether the rather cryptic allusions in *Cymbeline* may unquestionably be linked to an interest in contemporary science as well as the mythical foundation mentioned above, but it may be seen at least as an extremely interesting coincidence that in an early modern Europe obsessed with the study of anatomy, the pregnant body had suddenly found itself at the centre of a web of implications involving medical science, the moral and theological sphere, and also the broader scene of popular culture, when a debate arose over the feasibility of Caesarean sections on living women. C-sections had been theorized and at times practised on pregnant women's corpses since antiquity, in order to make a desperate attempt

---

[5] *Macbeth*, 5.8.31.

[6] See also Adelman (1992, 130-164 and 193-238) for a broad discussion of this argument. Maria Del Sapio Garbero (2005) has also recently dealt with the parthenogenetic theme: see pp. 148-152, as well as her discussion of *Cymbeline*, in particular pp. 204-210.

at saving the foetus, or – with the advent of Christianity – at least manage to keep the child alive long enough for it to be baptized. However, a heated dispute arose in the late sixteenth century over the advisability of performing Caesarean sections on living women when François Rousset published his *Traitté nouveau de l'hystérotomotokie ou enfantement caesarien* (1581). For the first time, a medical writer was advising surgeons to cut into women's bodies to attempt to save both mother and child, and to do so boldly and swiftly if need be: "[Rousset] encourages surgeons [...] not to waste time through cowardly reflections but to go ahead with a Caesarean as quickly as possible" (Blumenfeld-Kosinski 1990, 42). Another 'modern' choice was Rousset's decision to write his book in a vernacular language, French, to benefit those who could not read Latin, the official language of the scientific community (though the *Traitté* was soon translated into Latin).

It is Rousset's book that introduced the term 'Caesarean' (which was then translated into various European languages), the product of an interesting case of "creative etymology" (Blumenfeld-Kosinski 1990, 143-153) that bears witness to the early modern scientist's simultaneous involvement with different epistemological paradigms that are equally explored, and at times craftily exploited. Rousset combined the Latin etymology from 'caedere' ('to cut'), with a reference to an obscure passage in Pliny the Elder's *Natural History*, which vaguely mentioned the birth of the one of the Caesars, whose identity is disputed. While Rousset "went back to Pliny's possible identification of the 'first of the Caesars' as Scipio Africanus" (Blumenfeld-Kosinski 1990, 153) he effectively reinforced the mythical story of Julius Caesar's miraculous birth, which was well rooted in popular consciousness (though it seems to have no actual historical base), thus claiming a noble, almost god-like role for the surgeon. The doctor's 'new science' is therefore legitimized by the legendary name bestowed upon the procedure, in a characteristically early modern interfacing of different epistemological paradigms; it is precisely the use of myth that enables the factual credibility of the doctor's knowledge to be taken seriously, at a time when surgeons were seeking to establish their art as an autonomous discipline.[7]

The male doctor thus gains admittance into the confinement room, a space traditionally ruled by the midwife and her female helpers, and is encouraged to cut open the womb – conceptualized by Simon Forman, for instance, as "a world of ytself" (quoted in Paster 1993, 178). That the novelty was perceived as radical is testified by the fact that not all members of the scientific community were ready to accept such an inversion of natural childbirth: Jacques Marchant, a surgeon in Paris, characterized this attempt to surgically penetrate the womb as an unacceptable practice from a moral point of view, even venturing so far as to

---

[7] See also Filippini (1995, 28-30).

suggest a new name for the procedure, "Tarquinian section" (Filippini 1995, 30). Significantly, he substitutes the name of Caesar with that of another legendary historical figure, Tarquin the Proud, whose sexual assault on Lucretia was believed to have spurred the Romans to rebellion, leading to the establishment of the republic.

What I find extremely interesting here is that the early modern debate on the advisability of operating on pregnant women is rhetorically organized around the same 'ripping' vs. 'raping' imagery that recurs in *Cymbeline*: the ripping of the mother's womb that will allow Posthumus to become a hero of untainted virtue, the potential rape of Imogen, whose chaste womb represents Britain itself. It is very clear from the narrative of Posthumus's birth that Lucina, the midwife, has abandoned her traditional place in the birthroom: a newly found scientific knowledge is urging on, and the *sage femme*'s skill is no longer needed. However, the emerging scientific culture is not yet completely autonomous in its methodology, and cleverly makes its case by exploiting mythical stories and etymological inventions. The complex issue of naming, of imposing a definition that will in some way define and shape perception of 'the thing' – for lack of a better word – lies at the very centre of this early modern medical debate.[8]

To conclude by bringing this reflection closer to the present, I would like to mention, though only briefly, a more recent representation of the pregnant body which may be re-read in the light of this intersection between mythical and scientific discourse, Marina Warner's depiction of Dulé's birth by C-section in her novel *Indigo* (published in 1992):[9] problematizing myth – or rather, the process of myth-making –, Warner rewrites the story of the miraculous birth of a hero who is once again called upon to free his people.[10] Dulé is extracted from his dead mother's womb – a young African woman whose body is washed upon the shore of the island of Liamuiga, a victim, along with many others, of a fatal journey on a slave ship – not by a male doctor but by Sycorax (herself a re-written figure from Shakespeare's *Tempest*), who possesses the knowledge of a midwife, a witch, and a surgeon of sorts:

> She reached the body, below, curled up like a child […]. When she unfolded the young woman inside the green leaves in which she was wrapped, she could feel the shape of the infant inside as she had seen in her waking dream, so she took the oyster knife and she cut through the wall of the

---

[8] On the relationship between rhetoric and early modern science, see Cummins and Burchell (2007), and Spiller (2004).

[9] See, in Italy, Daniela Corona's recent monograph on Warner (2001), as well as Del Sapio Garbero (2009) on Warner and Shakespeare.

[10] Another instance of preoccupation with a (highly disturbing) mix of mythology and technology is to be found, for example, in Angela Carter's *The Passion of New Eve* (1977), in which a male body is surgically transformed into a woman capable of giving birth, a new Tiresias in the postmodern Waste Land.

young woman's abdomen. When she put her hands through the rent to take the baby, she clenched her teeth and felt it slip warm and greasy between her hands (Warner 1993, 84).

The special circumstances of Dulé's delivery do shape the islanders' perception of the baby – "there were some among the people of Liamuiga who [...] saw the baby Dulé as not only strange, but holy" (Warner 1993, 87) – but it is Sycorax's image that will be affected the most. By re-instating a midwife in the position of the doctor, Warner perceptively shifts the focus from the issue of the legendary delivery to the position of the woman who takes it upon herself to give life not through her own body, but through her skill. Her husband will seize the opportunity – "he had only been waiting for an excuse" – to leave her and remarry, since "[Dulé's] delivery *set Sycorax apart*; her husband proclaimed her magical powers *marked her out* an official wisewoman" (Warner 1993, 86, my italics). It is not surprising, then, that in this postmodern novel the hero is doomed to fail and will be taken as a prisoner after an attempt to rebel against a violent colonization.

Surely today the methodological 'fuzziness' that has been described with regard to this particular case in early modern medicine might be considered somewhat disturbing – disciplinarian distinctions have served their purpose, and the current debate on interdisciplinarity has shown that, far from removing boundaries altogether, such an approach calls for perhaps an even higher degree of awareness of subject specificities, as well as the willingness to pool knowledge and collaborate. The apparent ease with which different modes of knowledge are explored and linked together by early modern scientists, however, is by no means naive: rather, it is the product of a profound appreciation of the rhetorical effectiveness and symbolical impact of mythical narration as an alternative and influential way of tackling the issue of who we are and what our bodies mean to us. One of the challenges of our own age just might be to find a way to reconcile what postmodernism has made us aware of with a very persistent need, nevertheless, to *connect*.

References

Adelman J. 1992. *Suffocating Mothers. Fantasies of Maternal Origin in Shakespeare's Plays, "Hamlet" to "The Tempest"*. London and New York: Routledge.
Blumenfeld-Kosinski R. 1990. *Not of Woman Born. Representations of Caesarean Birth in Medieval and Renaissance Culture*. Ithaca: Cornell University Press.
Bradbury M. 1995. "What Was Post-modernism? The Arts in and After the Cold War". In *International Affairs*, 71, 4, 763-774.

Cummins J., Burchell D. (eds.) 2007. *Science, Literature and Rhetoric in Early Modern England*. Aldershot: Ashgate.

Corona D. 2001. *C'era due volte…: la narrativa realistica di Marina Warner*. Palermo: Flaccovio editore.

Del Sapio Garbero M. 2005. *Il bene ritrovato. Le figlie di Shakespeare dal "King Lear" ai "Romances"*. Roma: Bulzoni.

Del Sapio Garbero M. 2009. "Le mutazioni di Ariel: Shakespeare e Marina Warner". In D'Amico M. and Corso S. (eds.) *Postcolonial Shakespeare*. Roma: Edizioni di Storia e Letteratura, 99-120.

Del Sapio Garbero M., Isenberg N., Pennacchia M. (eds.) 2010. *Questioning Bodies in Shakespeare's Rome*. Goettingen: V&R Unipress.

Filippini N.M. 1995. *La nascita straordinaria. Tra madre e figlio: la rivoluzione del parto cesareo*. Milano: FrancoAngeli.

Fortunati V., Lamarra A., Federici E. (eds.) 2003. *The Controversial Women's Body. Images and Representations in Literature and Art*. Bologna: Bononia University Press.

Hillman D.A., Mazzio C. (eds.) 1997. *The Body in Parts. Fantasies of Corporeality in Early Modern Europe*. New York: Routledge.

Klein J.Th. 1990. *Interdisciplinarity: History, Theory, and Practice*. Detroit: Wayne State University Press.

Paster G.K. 1993. *The Body Embarrassed: Drama and the Disciplines of Shame in Early Modern England*. Ithaca: Cornell University Press.

Shakespeare W. 2004. "Cymbeline". In *The Arden Shakespeare* (Nosworthy J.M. ed.). London: Thomson Learning.

Spiller E. 2004. *Science, Reading, and Renaissance Literature: The Art of Making Knowledge, 1580-1670*. Cambridge: Cambridge University Press.

Warner M. 1993. *Indigo*. London: Vintage.

Section 5
Postcolonial London

ADRIANO ELIA

Università Roma Tre

Catching up with the New Millennium:
Hanif Kureishi's *Something to Tell You*

Hanif Kureishi's latest novel *Something to Tell You* (2008) is the semi-autobiographical account of Jamal Khan, a middle-aged psychoanalyst of Pakistani origin who tells us his own story from his teenage years in 1970s London to the present day, evoking memories of his adolescent life through a series of historical flashbacks. Jamal has indeed something to tell us, a secret influencing the flow of events in the plot.

Most reviews have considered *Something to Tell You* as an honest and entertaining account and description of London over the last decades since the mid-1970s, when Jamal was a college student.[1] It is quite a wide-ranging novel, and among the main themes introduced by the author we find, in random order, sex, drugs, rock'n'roll, race, identity, class, love, politics, philosophy, psychoanalysis, Islamic fundamentalism, the fear of ageing, loss, regret, middle-age desire, the sense of guilt, pop culture, bohemian intellectuals, celebrity culture, most of which have always been topical issues in Kureishi's work. The story is set in London, a place of possibility and transformation whose ethnic map at the beginning of the new millennium has become more complex than ever: "[on the Uxbridge Road] the shops were Caribbean, Polish, Kashmiri, Somali. Along from the police station was the mosque [...] Behind it was the football ground" (Kureishi 2008, 14).

Considering *Something to Tell You*, I would like to make two main points. My starting assumption is that contemporary novels like this one may be

---

[1] See Mars-Jones (2008): "*Something To Tell You* is a return to the territory of his first and still best-loved novel, *The Buddha of Suburbia*, but it also includes a perverse riff on the work that made his name, *My Beautiful Laundrette*". Regarding the genesis of the novel, see O'Connell (2008): "The novel took Kureishi a long time to write ('five, six, seven years'). 'I wanted it to be like 'Buddha' only modern', he explains". See also Tay (2008): "Just as *Buddha* is a kaleidoscope of 1990s suburban life, *Something to Tell You* is a chronicle of London in the new century". The novel has been defined by Kureishi himself as a 'criticism of the notion of limitless pleasure', a sort of reassessment of the sexual revolution. See Donadio (2008).

regarded not only as 'just' works of fiction, but also as inspired socio-historical documents observing and commenting on today's society, and even predicting what could happen in the future. Moving on from this, I will make a reflection on some social and political changes that have occurred in Britain from 1980s Thatcherite London up until the present day.

Fiction may often have a strong appeal in offering reliable descriptions of 'real' life. Without going back to Dickens or to the 'condition of England' novels, we could mention plenty of works of fiction that have acutely described contemporary social and political issues, sometimes even accurately foreseeing what would happen in the future. For several different reasons, novels such as Fyodor Dostoyevsky's *The Possessed* (1870-72), George Orwell's *1984* (1949), or Graham Greene's *The Quiet American* (1955), are endowed with a prophetic strength and a depth of insight on social issues which at times was alien even to historical and sociological speculation. With regard to Kureishi's work, the prophetic short story 'My Son the Fanatic', first published in 1994, and the novel *The Black Album*, which appeared a year later, predicted the rise of Muslim fundamentalism in the United Kingdom and the recent emergence of a brand new political actor, the 'home-grown terrorist', a terrorist of Arab origin but born and bred in Britain, and willing to kill his fellow compatriots in the name of radical Islam.

Following this trend, *Something to Tell You* intertwines facts with fiction and offers significant clues to the socio-cultural evolution of London since the 1970s, through the 7/7 London bombings up until today. It abounds with references to contemporary Britain, such as the following passage describing the London bombings:

> Four explosives, hidden in plastic food containers in backpacks, had been set off by suicide bombers in central London, three on the tube and one on a bus in Tavistock Square. The number of dead and injured was yet to be counted. [...] My patients referred to the events as 'our 9/11' [...] Police cars and ambulances rushed about; the sound of the sirens was abysmal. All day and night police helicopters thrashed above the damaged metropolis (Kureishi 2008, 471, 472, 473-474).

There is even a mention of the killing of Brazilian electrician Jean Charles de Menezes, who was mistaken for one of the suspects who attempted to perpetrate a further bombing attack on 21 July 2005, two weeks after the London bombings, and was shot dead by the Metropolitan Police on a tube train at Stockwell station: "an innocent man was pursued through a tube station and shot – was it six, seven or eight times? – in the head at point-blank range, by our defenders".[2]

---

[2] Kureishi (2008, 474). So far, no one has been convicted for the killing. For an up-to-date account of the De Menezes case see http://en.wikipedia.org/wiki/Jean_Charles_de_Menezes (last accessed August 2011)

We might assume that the above quotations are part of a newspaper article or of a news report. Instead, it is the opening of the fourth and final part of *Something to Tell You*. This is just one single example, but throughout the novel there is an insistent and overt mention of protagonists of British social life over recent decades as diverse as Tony Blair, whom most characters in the book despise, former foreign secretary Robin Cook, and also rockstars such as Mick Jagger, the Rolling Stones, David Bowie, and many others.

To make my second point, in *Something to Tell You* the reappearance of some other characters – this time fictional and not real – is crucial. Kureishi readers are familiar with them, and they offer us meaningful evidence of the socio-political evolution that has occurred in Britain since the 1980s. By considering what they have done since their first emergence in Kureishi's earlier work, we might understand some social changes that in the meantime have happened in Britain.

Among these characters, we find Karim Amir, the protagonist of *The Buddha of Suburbia* who, together with his friend Charlie Hero, makes a cameo appearance at a party. Now Karim is a film celebrity (not unlike Naveen Andrews, the actor who played Karim in the four-hour BBC film adaptation of *The Buddha*, who is now one of the protagonists of the celebrated serial *Lost*); Charlie is also still a famous rockstar. In my opinion, the most interesting character reappearing in this novel is Omar, the gay British-Asian protagonist of the film *My Beautiful Laundrette* (1985). In the 1980s he was an emblem of Thatcherite entrepreneurism (while at the same time oddly disrupting sexual taboos through his gay love affair with Johnny, the National Front militant played by Daniel Day-Lewis). Twenty-five years later, Omar has become a millionaire by selling his laundrette business and becoming a media tycoon producing TV programmes "for, by and about minorities" (Kureishi 2008, 243). In *Something to Tell You*, this over-integrated media entrepreneur has been made a Labour Peer (Lord Ali of Lewisham) by Tony Blair, whose war in Iraq he had supported.

Therefore, in a contradictory way, Ali has made a fortune producing TV programmes for minorities. He knew that minorities were going to become more and more fashionable, which in Britain has indeed been the case since the 1980s, and is in fact what had happened to him:

> The 'Pakis' had always been considered socially awkward, badly dressed, weirdly religious, and repressed. But being gay, Omar Ali was smart enough to know how hip and fashionable minorities – or any outsiders – could become, with the right marketing, as they made their way up the social hierarchy (Kureishi 2008, 243).

At the same time, though, Omar Ali felt so integrated in British society to the point of explicitly supporting the war in Iraq in order to provide all

Muslims with the liberalism and freedom that he enjoys in Britain. This clearly emerges during a conversation between Lord Omar and Jamal's best friend, the successful theatre director Henry Richardson, where the former speaks out his own views on the war in Iraq:

> 'As a gay Muslim I believe other Muslims must have the opportunity to enjoy the liberalism we do. I won't be hypocritical –'
> Henry interrupted. 'So you urged Blair to kick the shit out of as many innocent Iraqis as he could?'
> Look, these Iraqis, they have no science, no literature, no decent institutions and only one book. Can you imagine relying on just that? [...] We must give them things, even if it means killing a lot of them. Nothing worthwhile was ever done without a few deaths (Kureishi 2008, 245).

To confirm the overlapping of fiction and reality in *Something to Tell You*, it must be stressed that this Lord Omar Ali, described by Kureishi as "a plump Asian in a Prada suit with a lot to smile about" (Kureishi 2008, 242), displays some similarities with a real person, Waheed Alli, a gay multi-millionaire media entrepreneur and politician.

Waheed Alli was the co-founder of *Planet 24*, a TV production company responsible for groundbreaking and hugely popular television programmes such as *Big Breakfast* and *Survivor*. Like Omar, Waheed Alli was made a Labour Peer by Tony Blair, and is one of very few gay Muslim politicians in the world.[3] Now, if we consider the life of Waheed Alli and of his alleged fictional counterpart Lord Omar, we are led to a number of considerations.

First of all, we become aware of a paradox of Margaret Thatcher's legacy. On the one hand, the 1980s was a period of strong institutionalised racial abuse: with the *1981 Immigration Act* Thatcher even abolished the *ius soli*, so that it was no longer sufficient to be born on British soil to become a British citizen, and this was definitely a discriminatory measure. On the other hand, though, it was thanks to Thatcher's de-regulation and competition that, despite being 'immigrants', people like Lord Omar Ali or, similarly, Waheed Alli, could become multimillionaires. This also confirms the fact that, when it comes to money, racism does not get in the way, and that money has no colour. These characters have done so well in economic terms, and this gave them the chance even to be awarded official titles that just a couple of decades earlier they would never think they would manage to obtain. Lord Omar, like Waheed Alli, became a *Life Peer* in the House of Lords. With a controversial decision, Salman Rushdie was also awarded a knighthood in June 2007, and in December of the same

---

[3] Mars-Jones (2008). In political terms Waheed Alli is considered Asian, but in fact both of his parents are from the Caribbean. For further information see http://en.wikipedia.org/wiki/Waheed_Alli (last accessed August 2011).

year Kureishi himself was appointed *Commander of the Order of the British Empire* (CBE) for services to Literature and Drama. It is ironic that Kureishi, who only some three decades earlier had experienced strong racial discrimination, has eventually been granted a place in the prestigious order of British chivalry, an icon of the power of the former British Empire. We must recognise, though, that today this title possibly has a lesser value and prestige than before: on the same day Kureishi was awarded it, the Australian popstar Kylie Minogue was also granted a similar honour, the OBE (*Officer of the British Empire*) for 'services to Music'. With all due respect to Kylie Minogue, this is a sign of the times: Kureishi himself reminds us that it was Blair who had started to give awards to popular art.[4]

Secondly, we notice a continuity between Margaret Thatcher's policies and those developed by Tony Blair and Gordon Brown. After the collapse of Marxism and Communism, which can be dated around 1989 with the opening of the Berlin Wall, we still live under the Thatcherite spell of competition, consumerism (seen as a degeneration of capitalism), values which were re-elaborated and endorsed by Tony Blair.

Thirdly, and most importantly, at the beginning of the new millennium we must be aware of a number of brand-new and peculiar socio-political phenomena showing us the changing face of racism and revealing significant differences with 1980s Britain. We notice, for example, the emergence of a new post-7/7 political actor, the 'home-grown terrorist', as well as of 'Islamophobia', that sense of mistrust towards Muslims, which, as Kureishi notes in *Something to Tell You*, can also be experienced in linguistic terms, with the occurrence of new insults against Muslims based on religion rather than on the colour of the skin. In the novel there are some examples of this latest verbal abuse, and after the 7/7 bombings there was a clear emergence of an Islamophobic perception that had been previously alien to the British psyche:

> 'Muslim' – or 'Mussie' – was a new insult, along with 'ham-head' and 'allahAllah-bomb'. In our youth it had been Paki, wog, curry-face, but religion had not been part of it. [...]
> I [Jamal] was aware of others' eyes on me as I entered tube trains wearing a backpack. Opening it to take out my book was invariably entertaining. Dark-skinned people were searched at random [...]

---

[4] See Donadio (2008). "To many, Kureishi's C.B.E. is a sign of needed change. His accolade, along with Salman Rushdie's being knighted in June, indicates that these writers 'aren't voices from elsewhere, these are voices from here, these are our voices', says Hannah Rothschild, a friend of both writers and a documentary filmmaker. 'There's no divide anymore. They are us, we are them'. [...] 'It was Blair, really, who started giving awards to trash', he said, half-joking. 'Rubbish entertainers, people from the arts. Before that writers didn't get anything, really'. Then again, he added, 'If it's good enough for Kylie Minogue, it's good enough for Hanif Kureishi, isn't it?'".

"I've [Ajita] been walking about the city in the burqa. [...] There has been some curiosity and many hostile looks, as though people wonder whether I'm carrying a bomb. A man even said, 'Your bomb looks big in that'" [...]
"I [Jamal] walked for a while, looking at the city, aware of every person with a bag; every trip on the tube a potential death. Will it be now? Will he be a bomber? Will I be killed?".[5]

The institutional reaction against radical Islam culminated in the establishment of a strong policy of security, with the use of CCTV cameras virtually everywhere. This phenomenon has been aptly defined by Paul Gilroy as 'securitocracy', that is, the "elevation of security over the other functions of government" that has transformed London into a sort of CCTV metropolis (Gilroy 2006, 31). In the novel, Kureishi makes explicit reference to this new scenario:

with the development of CCTV – encouraged by a blind home secretary – everyone now watched everyone else, as though the whole country were under suspicion (Kureishi 2008, 374).

To conclude, with *Something to Tell You* Kureishi has proved once again to be an inspired chronicler and observer of politics and society, capturing the *zeitgeist* and comparing the contemporary age with the period when he grew up. This novel is a striking example of post-7/7 fiction on modern Britain, bridging the divide between the humanities and the social sciences. Using his characteristically fluid, witty and outspoken style, Kureishi manages to be at the same time a writer, a historian, a sociologist and a comedian. *Something to Tell You* raises a number of questions that at the beginning of the new millennium should be given attention, i.e., is multiculturalism dead and buried after the July 7 2005 London bombings? Is there any connection between Blair's foreign policy and the rise of radical Islam in Britain? Is security (or, in its most extreme version, to use Gilroy's formula, 'securitocracy'), really the solution to the rise of radical Islam, or could it make things even worse? Is Islamophobia, this recent phenomenon involving mistrust and hatred against Muslims, justified after 9/11 and the 7/7 bombings, or is it just a new kind of racism directed this time towards Muslims?

Ultimately, there are no easy answers to such essential questions, and I think we all, as European citizens, should reflect deeply on these issues that we experience in our lives on a daily basis.

---

[5] Kureishi (2008, 482, 474, 481, 493). The characters involved are indicated in brackets: Ajita is Jamal's former girlfriend. See also Ascherson (2008).

References

Ascherson N. 2008. "In a London of Infinite Possibilities". In *The New York Review of Books*, vol. 55, no. 17, November 6th.

Donadio R. 2008. "My Beautiful London". In *New York Times*, August 8th, available at http://www.nytimes.com/2008/08/10/magazine/10kureishi-t.html (last accessed August 2011).

Gilroy P. 2006. "Multiculture in Times of War – An Inaugural Lecture Given at the London School of Economics". In *Critical Quarterly*, vol. 48, no. 4, 27-45.

Kureishi H. 2008. *Something to Tell You*. London: Faber and Faber.

Mars-Jones A. 2008. "True Tales from the Couch". In *The Observer*, February 24th Sunday, available at http://www.guardian.co.uk/books/2008/feb/24/fiction.hanifkureishi (last accessed August 2011).

O'Connell J. 2008. "Sex and Books: London's Most Erotic Writers". In *Time Out*, February, available at http://www.timeout.com/london/books/features/4312/7.html (last accessed August 2011).

Tay J. 2008. "Love and Lust in London". In *The Star*, April 27th Sunday, available at http://thestar.com.my/lifestyle/story.asp?file=/2008/4/27/lifebookshelf/20632091&sec=lifebookshelf (last accessed August 2011).

ENZA MARIA ESTER GENDUSA

Università di Palermo

Deconstruction and Re-writing of Englishness and the European Cultural Identity in Bernardine Evaristo's Narrative

If analysed through a theoretical grid whose critical paradigms originate within an analytical area where British cultural studies, gender and postcolonial studies interweave, Bernardine Evaristo's fiction shows peculiar narrative strategies – in terms of genre, stylistic experimentation (novels-in-verse and a novel-with-verse) and inspiring motifs – which allow her (from the specific perspective of an Anglo-Nigerian London-born woman writer of mixed origins) to intervene within traditionally hegemonic representational circuits – be they British or European – so contributing to re-write/re-right the notion of English national identity and to re-examine European history from new non-exclusionary perspectives.

A versatile author, Evaristo is now critically acclaimed as one of the most original women writers within the contemporary black British literary landscape (Niven 2004). And these two phrases – "woman writer" and "black British" – implicitly suggest the critical paradigms along which the present analysis will develop. Indeed, Evaristo's narrative production is pervaded by its author's engagement with questions related to national as well as European identity politics and by her sensitiveness to the inextricability of the gender-race nexus.

Together with a process of historical excavation, the thematic innovations characterizing her novels aim to deconstruct and recast the symbolic assumptions on which Englishness – in the context of ancient and new notions of 'fortress' Europe – is constructed. Indeed, they reveal themselves as a way to interrupt the transmission of the persistent gender-biased and racist cultural models informing the representations of the national character as elaborated within official discursive practices.

Her 1997 *Lara* is centred around the representation of a complex metropolitan hybrid female identity, which proves the fruit of several ethnic belongings. Being of black Nigerian and white English parentage, in the London of the 1960s, Lara, the eponymous protagonist of the novel, falls victim to an essentialized dominant discourse which, on the basis of her skin colour, questions her right to lay claim to British citizenship. Specular to this discourse are social practices that condemn her to continually defer any cultural belonging to the British society. In addition, Evaristo makes visible that Lara is also exposed to inferiorizing gender power relations at play within the Nigerian community itself, where a patriarchal asset confines her to a subaltern subject position with respect to both her Nigerian father and to Josh, her Nigerian boyfriend.

Trapped within the impossibility of straightforward self-identification, Lara feels she has to reconstruct her family history so as to attain a personal sense of self. She thus sets out on a journey into those London areas mostly peopled by immigrants of African or Afro-Caribbean descent and, eventually, she starts travelling both on the physical level – criss-crossing the European, African and American continent – and, on the imaginative one, across her ancestors' generations. These multiple displacements make it possible for Lara to retrace the fabric of her family's multicultural heritage and to inscribe herself in the deriving network of belongings that she herself establishes. On a wider level, Lara's re-appropriation of her family past also generates for London itself the possibility to recuperate its symbolic bonds with its colonial past and to engage dialogically with it. The ensuing image of London constructs itself not only through its conflictual internal reconfigurations – mainly due to the progressive arrival of (im)migrants from England's ex-colonies (such as Lara's father) – but also in relation to Lara's multiple decentrings and, via Lara, to her ancestors' life stories.

Being interspersed with first-person narrations by some of the figures peopling Lara's family history, the articulation of the narrative fabric acts as an attempt to subvert Western master narratives – by giving a voice to minor historical actors – and to challenge the canonical logocentric literary matrix by interrupting and fragmenting its traditional flux. Moreover, the deliberate choice of writing a verse-novel allows her to break the fixity of Western traditional literary genres whose boundaries thus undergo a productive cross-fertilization. Their permeability is to be seen as the stylistic underpinning of Lara's overcoming of a divided self as she refuses the white/black dichotomy initially informing her subject position.

At the end of the novel, in reaction to an inferiorizing gender-race nexus of power relations, Lara's identity negotiations enable her to proclaim a renewed sense of belonging to England: as a mixed-race subject and as a young woman. The novel thus shapes a new definition of Englishness which comes to be extended to a female citizen who proves the fruit of several cultural interconnections and diasporic inscriptions. It is this mode of (trans)national belonging that Lara, after reconciling her plural cultural connections, consciously appropriates when laying claim to her right of citizenship in what she assertively calls "*my* island – the 'Great' Tippexed out of it – tiny amid massive floating continents" (Evaristo 1997, 140; my emphasis). Indeed *Lara* delineates a transnational mode of citizenship that – by querying traditional interrelated inscriptions of race and gender – constructs itself, in line with Black feminist politics, on the elaboration of new historicized and inclusive identity paradigms of the metropolitan female selfhood, which necessarily alter the coercive equilibrium of the nation-state.

The question of national identity also pervades *The Emperor's Babe* (2001), where it is transplanted in Roman Britannia. Preceded by a phase of historical research that Evaristo carried out personally in Italy and inspired by Peter Fryer's *Staying Power* (a groundbreaking text documenting the presence of black people in the British Isles since the Roman period and, so, well before the arrival of *SS Windrush* in 1948), the novel becomes the occasion to scrutinize British as well as classical European history and to question the axiom of a supposed racially 'pure' British past. Faithful to Oscar Wilde's aphorism prefacing the novel itself – "The only duty we owe to history is to rewrite it" –, *The Emperor's Babe* "throws into sharp relief", as Louise Bernard (2009, 125) suggests, "the idea of heritage as a peculiar kind of industry".

The novel is centred around the life experience of Zuleika, a London-born young woman of Sudanese origin. Forcefully married to Felix, a much older Roman senator, when she is only eleven, she ends up having a short – albeit intense – love affair with Roman Emperor Septimius Severus (who is of African origin himself), which will ultimately determine her death.

Evaristo's deliberate emphasis on Severus's being a Libyan-born emperor and her unconventional depiction of the ethnic differentiation characterizing Roman Londinium unveil the misuses inherent in the process of transmission of official history. The novel thus participates in the imaginative deconstruction of a Manichean symbolic economy which, in turn, has proved instrumental to the cultural practices of colonialism.

Configured as an outpost of the Roman empire or, more precisely, as a "less than dazzling little colonia" (Evaristo 2002, 15), Evaristo's Britannia is epitomized by a decentred Londinium whose ethnic and linguistic blending inevitably recall the cosmopolitanism of today's London. The deriving superimposition results in an effective imaginative cross-fertilization whereby, on the one hand, Roman Londinium is re-actualized through visions of contemporary London and through Evaristo's deliberate linguistic anachronisms mixing different as well as temporally distant languages – namely Latin, Italian and contemporary everyday English. On the other hand, the positive projections of Evaristo's Roman city may hint at the productive transnational potential of the contemporary metropolis.

Against this backdrop Evaristo's generic formula of the novel-in-verse is chosen to defy the rigidity of the Western logocentric canon and acts as the stylistic fabric of a narrative which becomes the site of a symbolic revision of British history. Seen in this light, Zuleika's status as a free black woman (rather than a slave) further contributes to denaturalize those folk images of black people reproduced by imperial discursive practices, while alerting attention to History as a "representational construct" (Ermath 1992, 56).

However, Evaristo's imaginative re-construction of London, deliberately aimed at redressing forms of national amnesia and History's erosions, is not conducted in simplistic terms. Although elsewhere she refers to Zuleika as a "victorious" woman (Niven 2004, 282), able to make the most of her short life, the novel clearly problematizes issues of national belonging and policies of gender identity. In fact although Zuleika is and feels a Roman citizen – as she herself asserts when saying: "Yet I was Roman too./ Civis Romana sum" (Evaristo 2002, 54) –, her right of laying claim to citizenship is openly questioned by her sister-in-law who symbolically ostracizes her because of her ethnic origins. Indeed she will not hesitate to say: "A real Roman is born and bred,/ I don't care what anyone says,/ and that goes for the emperor too,/ jumped-up *Leeebyan*. Felix will never/ take you to Rome, Little Miss *Nooobia*" (Evaristo 2002, 53). In addition, Zuleika's relationship to the Roman empire recalls women's problematic terms of inclusion within the modern nation-state: forced into a loveless marriage at a very young age, she partakes of the imperial richness not as a woman *per se* but as the wife of a Roman senator, whose self-realisation is confined within the stifling boundaries of domesticity.

Her transgression to this rigid system of gender roles, that is her affair with the Emperor, will be violently punished. If Felix's relationships with his mistresses are socially accepted as a reflection of his power, Zuleika's breach of the conjugal bond is condemned within the patriarchal structures of power at play in Roman Londinium, as soon as the Emperor's death leaves her defenceless towards such a gender-biased system.

In *Soul Tourists* (2005) the deconstruction of 'race' as a discrete and homogenous elaboration is extended to the whole of Europe and embraces multiple time levels. The novel enables Evaristo to unveil and subvert those discursive dynamics which have obscured the symbolic figurations of ethnic Otherness through deliberate omissions of historical facts.

Centred on the voyage across Europe and as far as the Middle East of two black Britons, Stanley Williams and Jessie O'Donnell, the novel is intended to imaginatively recuperate lost voices that reveal the Africanist presence in the European past, a presence deliberately silenced within the official practices of History-making. Along the voyage, Stanley – who shares with his now dead and beloved mother the uncanny power to perceive immaterial entities – meets, among others, Lucy Negro (William Shakespeare's Dark Lady), the Black Nun (Queen Marie-Therese's daughter born following the Queen's presumed relation with a black man), Mary Seacole, Alexander Pushkin and, ultimately, Queen Charlotte Sofia.

However tenuous their links with the European past may be, as they are ghostly figures speaking from a marginal historical space, their voicing – albeit a fictional rendering – is nevertheless instrumental to Evaristo's delineation of a "usable past for Black Britons of today" (King 2002, 147). Their presence works as a sort of guarantee for Stanley's right to belong, a motif pervading the narrative from its very start. Deeply rooted in the material circumstances of 1980s England, the initial sections of the novel portray Stanley's identity negotiations and his own interrogation of a preconceived idea of national character, handed down over him and consequently filtered by his Jamaican father. In this respect, it is important to underline Evaristo's subtlety in casting light onto the different sense of social positioning experienced in London by black immigrants, on the one hand, and by their children, on the other, due to the changes in race relations policies. However, if it is true that London enabled Stanley to follow a trajectory "from grammar school boy to university graduate, to City analyst" (Evaristo 2005, 19), this social climbing has not dissolved his feeling of inadequacy, as his following reflections on a white waitress's attitude reveal: "When we ordered the full monty, she all but stomped out in to the kitchen. 'It's because we are black,' [Stanley] muttered" (Evaristo 2005, 43).

Nevertheless, social (and racial) uneasiness is not the only dominant feeling throughout the novel. Indeed, faithful to the changes occurred in the British socio-cultural scene since the 1950s, Evaristo's narrative succeeds in undoing reductive perceptions of the so-called "second generation immigrants" and in registering their increasing self-awareness as social actors, as Jessie's reply to Stanley within the abovementioned scene testifies to: "You can decide that or you can decide she is a sad cow and would be that way with anybody. The choice is yours, Mr Paranoid Williams" (Evaristo 2005, 43).

It is not a case, then, that towards the end of the novel, Stanley's self-consciousness seems to have undergone a considerable development, as he wonders:

> Was he, Stanley, really an outsider? Maybe one did not have to blend in or
> be accepted to belong. You belonged because you made the decision to and
> if you truly believed it, no one could knock it out of you (Evaristo 2005, 189).

On the stylistic level, unlike *Lara* and *The Emperor's Babe*, *Soul Tourists* is not a novel-in-verse, but rather an atypical and mostly original novel-with-verse whose prose is interspersed with poetry as well as with a vast array of textual forms, such as a coroner's report and budgets, not to mention the road signs introducing each single chapter. Such a composite narrative fabric results in what has been defined as "postmodern experimentation in narrating versions of historical fiction in the form available to poets" (Bernard 2009, 125). Thus, in Evaristo's work History – with the upper case "H" – comes to be re-written through a historiographical excavation which nourishes itself from a mixture of textual forms revealing everyday aspects of personal micro-histories, once excluded from official representational circuits.

What is important to underline is that, in her contestation of English and European hegemonic historiography, Evaristo does not seem to pursue a reversed epistemological truth with respect to the dominant one, but, on the contrary, she offers an itinerary where the internal heterogeneity of social groups may assume a normative value, so as to eschew any temptation to romanticize ethnic difference or any potential ethnocentric reversal.

This is apparent in her latest novel (her first one entirely in prose), *Blonde Roots* (2008), where Evaristo offers a reversal of the history of slavery – with white English people who are slaves to black people – as an attempt to overcome traditional identity polarities. In the novel the history of slavery is mainly told through the perspective and the experiences of Doris, a young English woman whose life spans the three points of a reversed slave trade: the Cabbage Coast in England, Londolo (the capital of the United Kingdom of Great Ambossa on the Aphrikan coast) and the West Japanese Islands near Amarika.

The novel seems to suggest that the crisis of hegemonic discourses is now extreme as Evaristo reverses stereotypical perspectives and replaces them through alternative figurations, able to subvert the traditional black/white polarities and to question totalizing narratives. Suffice it to say that, in the novel, partly structured as a sort of long memoir, it is Doris, a white woman, that feels the need to retrace the roots of her family background in order to counterbalance the omissions of History and its hegemonic discourses. Indeed in the initial book of the novel, Doris assertively states: "I am proud to declare that I come from a long line of cabbage farmers" (Evaristo 2008, 7).

Probably less vivid than *The Emperor's Babe* as far as the depiction of a historical Black London is concerned (Wajid 2008), *Blonde Roots*, productively blends facts and fiction. In the mixture, the past – especially the brutal realities of the slave trade – are rendered through the use of contemporary English so as to suggest that its historical effects are still at play in the present era.

In conclusion, Evaristo's production contests a homogenous and discrete vision of English national identity as well as of the European cultural imaginary. Simultaneously, she puts into perspective the mono-cultural view on which such vision rests and, consequently, she imaginatively recuperates the microcosms of a European interracial past which the official archive has purposely obscured. In turn, with their 'multi-ethnic-accented' mode of citizenship, her characters become vehicles through which the marginal counterparts of the British/European hegemonic identity models are voiced and given visibility. In this sense, as Dave Gunning contends (2009, 165), "Evaristo is able to [...] assert a vision of history tuned to the political requirements of her age".

Finally, the oppositional nature of the identity configurations introduced by Evaristo can be fully appreciated only if we examine them through the lenses of the inextricable gender-race hermeneutic nexus. In this sense, Evaristo's novels can be seen as part of a specific change occurring within British cultural practices as highlighted by Lola Young (2005, 13), who refers to "a process of becoming embedded in British culture whilst re-constructing and re-defining what 'British' means".

Stretched to its extremes in *Blonde Roots* and implemented through Evaristo's recourse to historiographic imagination, this shift, far from engendering further severances, significantly results in the imaginative re-creation of historical connections which inevitably imply the political act of shaping inclusive notions of identity and of socio-cultural positioning, as Evaristo herself seems to suggest in a recent interview: "I have thus far interrogated African history within a European/Western context, and also the past with the present, never one to the exclusion of the other. My preoccupations are in my DNA" (Collins 2008, 1203).

References

Bernard L. 2009. "Bernardine Evaristo." In Arana V. (ed.) *Dictionary of Literary Biography*, vol. 347. Detroit: Gale, 119-127.

Collins M. 2008. "'My Preoccupations are in my DNA'. An Interview with Bernardine Evaristo". In *Callaloo*, 31, 4, 1199-1203.

Ermath E. 1992. *Sequel to History: Postmodernism and the Crisis of Representational Time*. Princeton: Princeton UP.

Evaristo B. 1997. *Lara*. Turnbridge Wells: Angela Royal.

Evaristo B. 2002 [1st ed. 2001]. *The Emperor's Babe*. London: Penguin.

Evaristo B. 2005. *Soul Tourists*. London: Penguin.

Evaristo B. 2008. *Blonde Roots*. London: Hamish Hamilton.

Fryer P. 1984. *Staying Power*. London: Pluto.

Gunning D. 2005. "Cosmopolitanism and Marginalisation in Bernardine Evaristo's *The Emperor's Babe*". In Sesay K. (ed.) *Write Black Write British*. Hertford: Hansib, 165-178.

King B. 2002. "Review of Bernardine Evaristo's *The Emperor's Babe*". In *World Literature Today*, 76, 1, 147.

Niven A. 2004. "Bernardine Evaristo with Alastair Niven". In Nasta S. (ed.) *Writing Across Worlds*. London: Routledge.

Wajid S. 2008. "Londolo Calling". In *The New Statesman*, August 4th, 51-53.

Young L. 2005. "Foreword". In Sesay K. (ed.) *Write Black Write British*. Hertford: Hansib, 13-14.

SIMONA CORSO

Università Roma Tre

"The World Suddenly Feels Bipolar": Martin Amis after 9/11

> Your whole letter is full of mistakes from one end to the other.
> I see you have taken your ideas of Turkey from that worthy author Dumont, who has writ with equal ignorance and confidence. 'Tis a particular pleasure to me here to read the voyages to the Levant, which are generally so far removed from truth and so full of absurdities I am very well diverted with them. They never fail to give you an account of the women, which 'tis certain they never saw, and talking very wisely of the genius of men, into whose company they are never admitted, and very often describe mosques which they dare not peep into.
> Lady Mary Wortley Montague, *The Turkish Embassy Letters* (Letter XXXVIII, 17 June 1717)

"The twenty-first century began by naming a date" writes Susan Neiman in her inspiring history of evil in modern thought (Neiman 2002, XI), and the text that I have chosen to reflect on the new challenges raised by the new century revolves around that date. It is Martin Amis' recent, controversial book *The Second Plane*, which was first published in Britain and the United States in 2008, and has more recently appeared in Italian translation. It is a collection of essays, editorials, review articles and two short stories, all inspired by the terrorist attacks on the World Trade Centre. The title, as Amis points out in the first chapter, emphasizes the importance of the advent of the second plane, described as "the defining moment" (Amis 2008, 3). The second plane clarified the nature of the disaster that had occurred only moments earlier – the impact of the first plane, making clear to New Yorkers and to the world that they were witnessing the most terrible and most spectacular terrorist attack in human history.

The fourteen pieces of Amis' book are arranged in chronological order: "an acknowledgement – Amis writes – of the obvious truth that our understanding of September 11 is incremental and can never hope to be intact and entire" (*ibidem*, IX). The first piece is an article that appeared in *The Guardian* only one week after the attacks; the final one was published by *The Times* on the 11th of September 2007, on the occasion of the tragedy's sixth anniversary. One might expect that with the passing of time resignation would replace Amis' initial outrage, that the fury of the immediate *post eventum* would be followed by a more lucid analysis, 'incremented' by the thousands of pages that have been written by historians, journalists, political analysts, and experts of terrorism over eight long years. But the opposite is true: Amis' rhetorical vehemence grows, his discourse becomes more and more radical. As one reviewer points out, in a book that presents itself as a pamphlet against fanaticism, wrath and fear end up radicalizing Amis himself (Tayler 2008).

The Second Plane confronts us with important issues, which have dominated public debate in recent years: the supposedly 'bipolar' nature of the contemporary world – secular West versus religious Orient –; the potentially destructive force of religion; the writer's responsibility towards history and his or her role in the interpretation of current affairs; the age-old philosophical question whether the death of real people may become the subject matter of art, literature, or, more recently, cinema. In other words, *The Second Plane* throws us back into heated debates which have divided the world in recent years and offers us an example – with its vocabulary, its logic or pseudo-logic – of the rhetoric used by the West's self-proclaimed advocates, including Amis.

"The world – writes Amis – suddenly feels bipolar. All over again the West confronts an irrationalist, agonistic, theocratic/ideocratic system which is essentially and unappeasably opposed to its existence. The old enemy was a superpower; the new isn't even a state" (Amis 2008, 8-9). Amis immediately draws our attention to one of the inevitable consequences of 9/11: like any other catastrophe, the New York terrorist attacks have brought their victims together in search for identity. What prevails is not the search for culprits – this can be left to the legal authorities – but the need for an enemy: a demand that is psychological as well as political. As one might expect, Amis chooses the most rhetorically effective strategy: he speaks of 'enemy' and, to suggest the scope of the new enemy, he evokes America's enemy *par excellence*, the Soviet Union. There is, however, an important difference: while the old enemy was easy to locate – and therefore perhaps easier to fight – the new enemy of the West is everywhere and nowhere. It is, of course, Islamic fundamentalism, the topic of Amis' most ambitious essay – but also, probably, his weakest: "Terror and Boredom: The

Dependent Mind".[1] When Amis describes Islamic fundamentalism as a fatal combination of irrationality, religious bigotry, and – one suspects – sexual frustration, the zeal of the editorialist prevails over the demands of detailed analysis. Amis' analysis is full of pathos, reductive, and probably defined by the constraints of the genre that he has chosen: a long newspaper article rather than an in-depth and systematic study. But this is not what disturbs us. For the lay reader (but perhaps not for the scholar of radical Islam) Amis contempt for "horrorism" is quite understandable even if his analysis lacks accuracy. What disturbs us – and what has disturbed many reviewers – is Amis' tacit assumption that the boundaries between Islam and Islamic fundamentalism are blurred and that one can easily turn into the other. On one of the first pages of "Terror and Boredom" we read: "Naturally we respect Muhammad. But we do not respect Muhammad Atta" (*ibidem*, 79). (Muhammad Atta, it is worth recalling, was one of the pilots who hijacked American 11, the first plane to hit the World Trade Center). This seemingly innocent and casual association, which links the Prophet to a criminal mass-murderer who shares his name, is a perfect example of Amis' style of argumentation. While does Amis feel the need to stress that "not respecting" Muhammad Atta does not mean "non respecting" Muhammad? Is there a similarity between the respect for Muhammad and the respect for Atta? A few lines later, Amis explains that Islamic fundamentalism (which he calls "Islamism", and therefore treats as distinct from Islam but also as its degenerate form) is a crisis of reason, an extreme form of "dependence of the mind". But then he adds: "Islam follows you everywhere, into the kitchen, into the bedroom, into the bathroom, and beyond death into eternity. Islam means 'submission' – the surrender of independence of mind" (*ibidem*, 79). Once again, the reader is encouraged not to draw a straight line between Islam and radical Islamism. In fact, Amis calls extremism an evil that is intrinsic to all religions

---

[1] Even Amis' title is misleading. His reference to boredom and terror immediately evokes Hannah Arendt's influential definition of modern evil (1963): the supposed *banality* of terrible crimes that are committed by ordinary people, who consider themselves mere executives, bound by a chain of command and whose seeming unawareness has caused unprecedented catastrophe. Arendt's reflections on the banality of evil (the 'modern', bureaucratized evil of totalitarian societies) is explored by Susan Neiman, who argues very convincingly that the 9/11 terrorist attacks ought to be understood as the manifestation of a different kind of evil, "a form of evil so old-fashioned that its reappearance is part of our shock. [...] It was awesomely intentional. The foresight involved was massive. The murderers focused their end precisely in view, and they went to every imaginable length to achieve it – from the exact planning required for years of coordination to the preparation of their own certain deaths" (Neiman 2002, 283). The attacks on the World Trade Centre are a crime carried out with the outmost intentionality, amplified by the terrorists' mastery of technology. These terrorists, writes Neiman, do not have much in common with 'banal' criminals like Eichmann – loathsome rather than merely fearsome figures – but rather resemble the Sadean villains, who inspire fear in its purest form.

but then adds: "All religions have their terrorists: Christian, Jewish, Hindu, even Buddhist. But we are not hearing from those religions. We are hearing from Islam" (*ibidem*, 49). Many other examples could be mentioned. If fundamentalism is the enemy, Amis seems to say, Islam is its negligent father, guilty because unable to contain the violence of his children. Amis' latent Islamophobia has been noted by many reviewers, but it is not an isolated phenomenon, as recent debate has shown. Some years ago, a polemical exchange between Amis and Terry Eagleton triggered a heated discussion among writers and intellectuals – from Ian MacEwan to Ronan Bennett, from Germaine Greer to Christopher Hitchens – which revealed that the wave of Islamophobia has not spared the intellectual élite. One of the prominent victims of Islamic fundamentalism – it has become clear – is moderate Islam itself. Observers of contemporary London – multicultural, multiethnic, multi-religious – agree that *the colour bar* is rapidly turning into a *religion bar* and that lasting peace is impossible without true tolerance between religions, as Barack Obama has forcefully stressed in his Cairo speech.

"Religion is a sensitive ground [...] Here we walk on eggshell" writes Amis in "Terror and Boredom" (*ibidem*, 49) and adds rather bluntly: "Today, in the West, there are no good excuses for religious belief – unless we think that ignorance, reaction and sentimentality are good excuses" (*ibidem*). One of the main claims of Amis' book is that "religious belief is without reason and without dignity, and its record is near-universally dreadful" (*ibidem*, 14). And yet, when we read the numerous reviews of *The Second Plane*, we find that almost all reviewers resent Amis' simplistic and off-hand treatment of Islam, but that very few object to his dismissal of religion as such. Most reviews, in other words, seem to take for granted what Amis presents as his basic assumption: "the opposite of religious belief is [...] independence of mind – that's all" (*ibidem*, 77-78). Amis' claim goes right to the heart of what has been presented by some as a 'clash of civilizations'. According to many commentators, especially in Europe, the only possible Western response to religious fanaticism is secularism. In the United States, 9/11 has caused much fervor among Christian communities – the most noticeable and perhaps worst manifestation of this fervor being George W. Bush's crusade against the 'axis of evil'. Europe, by contrast, has responded with a wave of radical atheism, promoted by public figures such as Christopher Hitchens, Richard Dawkins and Sam Harris, whose influence is also felt in the United States. This is the context in which Amis states his views about religion: atheism is the only true response to fundamentalism. The slogan – suggested by Amis and many other European intellectuals – seems, however, to cause more problems than it solves. The dichotomy of secular West and religious East does not seem much different from the notorious distinction between forces of good and axis of evil drawn by President Bush after the terrorist attacks and used to rush his country – and the Western world – into a 'global war' of revenge.

Having declared that "today, in the West, there are no good excuses for religious belief – unless we think that ignorance, reaction and sentimentality are good excuses", Amis adds: "This is of course not so in the East, where almost every living citizen in many huge and populous countries is intimately defined by religious belief. [...] All religions, unsurprisingly, have their terrorists: Christian, Jewish, Hindu, even Buddhist. But we are not hearing from those religions. We are hearing from Islam" (*ibidem,* 49). With remarkable succinctness, Amis condenses into a single paragraph some of the most trite and aggravating clichés of the 'clash of civilizations' debate:

- the difference between West and East can be reduced to a single point:
- with or without religion;
- all religion is a form of ignorance;
- cultures shaped by religious practice are more ignorant than societies
- where atheism prevails;
- ignorance leads to violence;
- religious societies are intrinsically violent: the more religious they are, the
- more violent they become.

Rod Parsley, a well-known American television preacher, used to declare in his speeches that America was founded to destroy the false religion of the Antichrist (Banerjee and Luo, 2008); Amis opts for the secular version and distinguishes between Western enlightenment and Oriental ignorance. The difference between the two seems slight.

And yet, Amis' fierce and, I would say, naive, attack on religion – his *j'accuse*, directed not only against Islam but against religion *tout court* – has been of little interest to his reviewers. Should this lead us to the conclusion that Amis' equation – intellectual freedom equals atheism – is little more than a cultural cliché in recent debates about morality? Or should we assume that in post-enlightenment Europe religion has become a taboo? Presumably our struggle against religious fanatics will not become any easier if we define religion a "system of thought without reason or dignity, defined by its universally revolting history". Nor is this attitude going to help us in the dialogue between cultures – also because Amis' extremist stance excludes from this dialogue a vast number of possible interlocutors – and not necessarily the worst. In *Koba the Dread*, a study of Soviet terror, Amis wrote that "Stalin's war against religion was part of the war against human nature". Sameer Rahim – one of the few reviewers who express bewilderment at Amis' militant atheism – comments that it is a shame that the author seems to have forgotten his own remark (Rahim 2008).

The Second Plane is also the manifesto of a committed writer, a way in which the writer claims his right to have a say on the great political and cultural issues of his time. In the course of the fierce debate generated by Amis's statements on the 'clash of civilization', Terry Eagleton confessed that: "I have no idea why we should listen to novelists on these matters any more than we should listen to window cleaners" (quoted in Adams 2008). Eagleton's statement is deliberately provocative; and yet, on the day after the attacks, many writers asked themselves the same question and wondered what exactly their task was: whether they had the right or even the duty to speak, or whether they simply had to keep cleaning the windows, so to speak – that is to continue to write their novels, plays and poems. The great number of literary texts inspired by September 11, a corpus that some critical studies are starting to map, shows that writers could not refrain from dealing with the catastrophe, if nothing else to help the community absorb the trauma (see, among others, Keniston and Follansbee Quinn 2008; Versluys 2009). After all, this is what literature – realistic, lyrical, or fantastical – has always done: embrace History with its stories. In the aftermath of Auschwitz, Adorno famously wished that poetry would stop, since what had occurred was beyond representation. This warning was ignored from the start, also because, as Susan Neiman remarks, silence is just an aesthetic choice of a different nature (Neiman 2002, 262). In *The Second Plane* Amis comments at great length on the writer's role in the face of historical catastrophes. Not surprisingly for a writer who has never been intimidated by great historical evils – from gulags to Nazism to nuclear weapons – his proposal is not only that a writer should speak his mind but that he should do so with all the means at his disposal. The idea of collecting texts of different genres – editorials, book reviews, essays, short stories – in one book devoted to a great historical theme is eloquent in this respect.

The Second Plane is an author's and intellectual's panoramic vision of the times we live in, or rather, of a particular moment in the history of Western culture. It would be interesting to analyze how Amis' treatment of his topic changes according to the constraints of different literary genres: to ask ourselves if the novelist thinks about Al Qaeda in the same way as the journalist writing for *The Times*. But for reasons of time, let me only mention one discrepancy that struck me when I was reading the book. The protagonist of "The Last Days of Muhammad Atta" seems to have more in common with Camus' bored criminals (or with the sexually repressed males in many of Amis' novels) than with the radical Islamists described in "Terror and Boredom". Neither the short story nor the essay are among Amis' best work, but the difference between them suggests that even a political writer like Amis knows that the novel, as Milan Kundera once put it, has its own reasons, which a writer must respect even when they clash with his.

To conclude, just one last remark on one of the final sentences of Amis' "Author's Note": "If September 11 had to happen, then I am not at all sorry that it happened in my lifetime. That day and what followed from it: this is a narrative of misery and pain, and also of desperate fascination" (Amis 2008, IX).

If we bear in mind the 3,200 who died in New York on the 11th of September 2001, and the thousands of men, women and children who were killed in wars that were prompted by the terrorist attacks, Martin Amis' remark will send shivers down our spines. We may choose to ignore it as yet another irresponsible remark by a writer who has chosen provocation as his main register, but, alas, it reflects a condition that is well known to all of us: the narcissism of the writer and the intellectual. As members of Amis' own club, let us be wary, and make sure that narcissism does not turn into vampirism.

References

Adams T. 2008. "Amis' War on Terror by Other Means". *The Observer*, January 13rd.

Amis M. 2008. *The Second Plane. September 11:2001-2007*. London: Jonathan Cape.

Arendt H. 1963. *Eichmann in Jerusalem*. London: Viking.

Banerjee N., Luo M. 2008. "McCain Cuts Ties to Pastors Whose Talks Drew Fire". *New York Times*, May 23rd.

Keniston A., Follansbee Quinn J. (eds.) 2008. *Literature After 9/11*. New York and London: Routledge.

Neiman S. 2002. *Evil in Modern Thought. An Alternative History of Philosophy*. Princeton and Oxford: Princeton University Press.

Rahim S. 2008. "Review: *The Second Plane* by Martin Amis", February 2nd, available at http://www.telegraph.co.uk./culture/books/fictionreviews/3670883/ Review-The-Second-Plane-by-Martin-Amis.html (last accessed August 2011).

Tayler C. 2008. "Beware the Nut-rissole Artists". *The Guardian*, January 26th.

Versluys K. 2009. *Out of the Blue: September 11 and the Novel*. New York and Chichester: Columbia University Press.

Section 6
Representations of Antinormative Sexual Identities

SILVIA ANTOSA

Università di Palermo

Queer Sexualities, Queer Spaces:
Gender and Performance in Sarah Waters' *Tipping the Velvet*

My paper focuses on the role performed by space in the formation of sexual identities and, conversely, on the influence of sexuality on the constitution of places and spaces. I will discuss how sexualities can be spatialized and spaces sexualised, and I will examine a novel by the British contemporary writer Sarah Waters, who significantly constructs the queer sexuality of her characters by redefining the space they inhabit.

Sexuality cannot be properly investigated without an understanding of the spaces through which it is constituted. The very expression 'sexual orientation' testifies to the complex interaction between sexuality and space. It refers to sexuality as being 'oriented' toward its object of desire. In Sara Ahmed's words: "If orientation is a matter of how we reside in space, then sexual orientation might also be a matter of residence, of how we inhabit spaces, and who or what we inhabit spaces with" (Ahmed 2006, 543).[1] By focusing on the concept of sexual orientation, we can theorize a particular connection between sexual identities and space. The starting points are the assumptions of postmodern geographers (Bell and Valentine 1995; Ingram *et al.* 1997; Brown 2000; Browne 2006, 885-893; Browne *et al.* 2007) who have recently redefined space as an area that can be occupied both on a real and a cognitive level. Space is thus not only a geographical context where events take place, but rather a network of actions and interpersonal relations. Moreover, it is an entity whose borders can be defined through embodied social practices and power relations of integration and exclusion. It is through these practices that the norms regulating spaces are acted out. Social practices thus codify spaces and trace their ideological

---

[1] The idea of orientation applied to sexuality is central to defining its connection with space for two main reasons: it highlights the spatialized construction of sexuality and foregrounds its relational and social nature. Some critics have pointed out the difference between the words 'sexuality' and 'sexual orientation', by stating that the latter focuses more on the relation between desire and its object than on the idea of autonomy of fluidity, which is, instead, well-conveyed by the former (see Offord and Cantrell 1999, 218).

and cultural borders. In this way, they spatially reproduce within these borders a social order founded on gender differences, which are structured on a hierarchical level (McDowell 1999; Antosa 2007). As a consequence, public and visible spaces vividly represent dominant, patriarchal and heterosexual identities, which have their virtual location in the ideological centre of the Western cultural world. According to Adrienne Rich, this world is founded on a "compulsory heterosexuality" (Rich 1993, 203-223), which has turned it into a 'heteronormative'[2] institution. Therefore, antinormative identities have to be segregated out of the patriarchal and heteronormative realm.

From this point on, I will define these antinormative identities as queer. Queer is not just a synonym for lesbian and gay, but refers to a system of thought that questions the supposedly stable relationship between sex, gender, sexual desire and sexual practice, on which the heteronormative system is founded.[3] 'Queer'[4] disrupts the stability of heterosexuality and foregrounds alternative expressions of sexuality which go beyond the binary gender system, including transgender people, cross-dressers, drags and so on.

Gender differences and gender roles can thus be organised on a spatial level. If we focus on the private/public dichotomy, we find out that it has historically been used as a means of oppression on the basis of gender. According to Nancy Duncan, "The private/public dichotomy [...] is frequently employed to construct, control, discipline, confine, exclude, and suppress gender and sexual difference preserving traditional patriarchal and heterosexist power structures" (Duncan 1996, 127). Like gender, sexuality has also been regulated by the separation between private and public. In particular, public places, epitomised by the street, are commonly perceived as being asexual. However, this notion is founded on "the naturalization of heterosexual norms" (Duncan 1996, 137). In other words, sexuality performed by heterosexuals in public places is seen as a universalized act and is assumed to be 'normal'. For this reason, the heterosexing of places is an almost invisible process. As the geographer Gill Valentine brilliantly emphasized, "[...] repetitive performances of hegemonic asymmetrical gender identities and heterosexual desires congeal over time to produce the appearance that the street is normally a heterosexual space" (Valentine 1996, 150).

---

[2] The term 'heteronormativity' refers to "the set of norms that make heterosexuality seem natural or right and that organize homosexuality as its binary opposite" (Corber and Valocchi 2003, 4).

[3] According to Judith Butler: "The institution of a compulsory and naturalised heterosexuality [...] regulates gender as a binary relation in which the masculine term is differentiated from a feminine term [...] through the practises of heterosexual desire. The act of differentiating the two oppositional moments of the binary results in [...] the respective internal coherence of sex, gender, and desire" (Butler 1990, 22-23).

[4] The root of the word 'queer' is from the Greek for cross, oblique, adverse (Cleto 2002, 5).

In the wake of queer theorist Judith Butler, who highlighted the constructed and discursive strategies through which gender roles have been naturalized in the course of time, it could be argued that "the heterosexing of space is a performative act naturalized through repetition and regulation" (Valentine 1996, 146). As a consequence, heterosexual performances are taken for granted not only in public but also in private spaces such as the home. How private, however? Since they are denied visibility in public places, homosexuals and queers are either relegated to marginalized and bounded spaces (such as ghettos and bars), or to the domestic environment.[5] But even the home, which symbolises the private sphere, is too often an alienating site for queer people. It is no accident that the sense of concealment and silencing of homosexuals in history has been defined by the spatial metaphor of the 'closet'. The closet is typically a small, dark, bounded space within the domestic environment. It can be referred to the ubiquitous lives led by queer people, who are close at hand, but are, at the same time, invisible and silenced (Brown 2000, 6-9). In *Epistemology of the Closet* (1990), Eve Sedgwick Kosofsky pointed out that "the closet [has been] the defining structure of gay oppression this century" (*ibidem*, 71). The dynamic action of 'coming out of the closet' is another important spatial and existential metaphor, which involves breaking the laws of silence and concealment, both on the private/individual level as well as on the public/social one. In other words, those who come out and freely perform their own identity both in private and in public spaces, "cut into and disrupt the 'normality' of heterosexual space by performing their desires in a way that produces another space" (Valentine 1996, 148).

In coming out and claiming space in public, queers create another space of representation and visibility. Moreover, in breaking down the private/public dichotomy, they also break through the taken-for-granted heterosexuality of public places by re-inscribing them as queer sites (Valentine 1996, 154). In short, they publicly display the artificial, performative nature of heterosexualised spaces and the inefficiency of the private/public dichotomy. Adapting Judith Butler's well-known expression "subversive bodily acts" (1990, 79), Bell and Valentine talk about *"subversive spatial acts"* in order to connect the apparent performativity of all gendered identities to highlight the construction of space as gendered, sexed and sexualised (Bell and Valentine 1995, 19, emphasis in the text). Queer space establishes a new spatial category, where identity boundaries and gender roles are no longer rigidly defined in terms of a dichotomy, but open out to a sort of constant flux. Spaces are thus continuously reshaped by the relations between the different sexual identities which 'inhabit' them. As

---

[5] This process of physical and psychological marginalization has led homosexuals and queers to create counter-spaces dominated by what some critics define as 'homonormativity'. On this topic see also Ahmed (2006, 543-574) and Myslik (1996, 156-169).

a consequence, the above-mentioned divisions between inside and outside, centre and margins, visible and invisible are undermined and blurred.[6]

The disruptive action caused by queer identities in altering the normative existential and spatial rules is at the core of a number of contemporary literary texts. I will deal with one British writer in particular, who constructs the queer sexuality of her characters by redefining the space they inhabit: Sarah Waters. Born in Wales in 1966, Waters took her PhD in English Studies with a dissertation on gay and lesbian historical fiction from 1870 onward. Since the publication of her first novel, *Tipping the Velvet* in 1998, she was acclaimed as one of the most promising writers on the English literary scene. Sarah Waters' first three novels (*Tipping the Velvet*, 1998; *Affinity*, 1999; and *Fingersmith*, 2002) are neo-Victorian fictions.[7] They feature lesbian heroines, who literally transgress (in the etymological sense of 'crossing, stepping over') the rigid Victorian normative spaces and reinscribe them in performing their own gender and sexual identity. Waters 'puts on stage' the unspoken and the unwritten of Victorian fiction, by introducing queer sexualities into heteronormative spaces, such as the home and the street, which epitomise the private and the public spheres. Significantly, each novel revolves around one specific place: the theatre or music hall in *Tipping the Velvet*, the women's prison in *Affinity* and the private madhouse in *Fingersmith*. These closeted institutions represent a deviation from the norm and become a sort of 'other' space, a narrative 'elsewhere' in which antinormative identities used to be confined because of their threatening potentiality. Waters' protagonists manage to open up and transform these negatively charged places through their performance of gender.

Tipping the Velvet is a case in point. It is a narrative that foregrounds the fluid and performative nature of identity through its vivid representation of London. The urban spaces of the Victorian city play a central role in the characterization of the protagonist. Moreover, they bring to the fore the way in which the heroine challenges the supposed naturalness of gender and sexual roles, by foregrounding the notion of identity as performance. Set in Victorian England in the 1890s, it tells the story of a young girl's coming of age. In particular, the novel deals with her psychological and sentimental growth as she discovers and affirms her social and sexual identity. The protagonist, named Nancy Astley, experiences a number of turning points in her life. Each of them corresponds to a different urban setting. At the beginning of the novel,

---

[6] Critics have recently turned away from an approach in which they investigate GLBT (Gay/Lesbian/Transgender and Bisexual) spaces and communities, in order to explore the performance of sexual identities and examine their impact on and relation with surrounding space (Bell and Valentine 1995, 8-9).

[7] In her novels, Waters subtly challenges the conventions of the main Victorian literary genres, such as gothic fiction, the sensation novel and the novel of sentimental education. For an analysis of Waters' rewriting strategies, see Costantini (2006, 17-39).

Nancy lives in Whitstable, Kent, and frequently goes to the local theatre, where she falls in love with a 'masher', or male impersonator, Kitty Butler. Nancy follows her to London, and becomes first her dresser and later her performing partner under the name of Nan King. Following her disappointment in love, Nancy leaves her job and wanders the streets of a suburban area of London. She cross-dresses in stage clothes as a man for safety reasons, and freely goes about the streets, a masculine realm that was not allowed to women (Melchiorre 2009, 191-192). Cross-dressing enables her to cross the geographical and social boundaries usually assigned to women. She soon becomes a 'rent boy', (or gay girl[8]) a prostitute dressed up as a man, and then the kept woman of a wealthy widow named Diana Lethaby. Nancy stays with her for more than one year as Neville, once again in men's clothes. In this period she gets to know the homosexual underworld of the late Victorian aristocracy. After that, Nancy finds herself on the streets again, wandering and begging. Eventually, she meets Florence, a dedicated socialist and charity worker, and starts a relationship with her while joining the socialist cause.

In this novel, the stage plays a central role in the sexual growth of the protagonist. Nancy is a theatre spectator, but soon after becomes a gender performer first on the music hall stage (as a male impersonator[9]) and then in her real life. Music hall shows put on stage alternative views of well-defined social roles and pointed out the hidden fears concerning gender performances (Bailey 1998, 8-9, 11). As Stefania Ciocia underlines, "the novel's action gradually moves from the theatre as such, where performers and audience are neatly differentiated, occupying well-marked and separate places, to the boundless stage of the square and the city streets, where the gap between actors and spectators is erased by a universal and subversive participation to the show" (Ciocia 2005). In eliminating the gap between the space of the audience and the space of the performers, Nancy also erases the distance between the music hall and the city. She thus transforms the urban sites of London into a sort of huge stage. Throughout the narrative, the theatrical space evolves from the enclosed locations of the West End playhouses to the improvised, open-air shows in the streets. Similarly, Nancy erases the ideological and social 'gap' between gender and sexual differences, in moving from a binary gender view to the boundless space of the performativity of identity.

Furthermore, Nancy's different performances correspond to different levels of self-awareness of her sexuality, going from a private, 'closeted' lesbian

---

[8] In the nineteenth century, the expression "gay girls" referred to prostitutes.

[9] Male impersonators usually mocked the figure of the "swell", a young gentleman who was taken as a symbol of a misogynist, masculine society. To improve their performances, Nancy and Kitty are asked to wander around London to watch male behaviour. In observing without being seen, they assume the role of *voyeur*, thus parodically appropriating a traditional masculine role.

relationship to a public commitment. Her involvement with Kitty Butler, her first lover, is a private affair. The interlude with Diana Lethaby is a semi-private relationship known to a private circle, mainly made up of homosexuals. Only the love story with Florence becomes a public act. This transition from a private, closeted view of one's own sexuality to an overt, public one is also narratively constructed on a larger spatial scale. Once again, the urban spaces of London play a crucial role in the character's acquisition of self-awareness and public visibility.

As a matter of fact, Nancy moves from Whitstable to the theatres of the West End, from the dangerous slums of the East End to the centre of London, Victoria Park. She moves from the margins to the centre of the city both on a spatial and on a personal level. This transition is parallel to her sexual growth, which leads her to subvert the heteronormativity of urban places and to remould them. The centre she reaches at the end of the novel is no longer the public space denied to women and queers, but a queer site where she feels free to perform her own sexuality. This public visibility is underlined in the last but one paragraph of the novel, where Nancy declares her love to Florence: "I turned back to [Florence], took her hand in mine, crushed the daisy between our fingers and – *careless of whether anybody watched or not* – I leaned and kissed her" (Waters 1999, 472; my Italics). At the end of her journey, Nancy manages to disrupt the assumed 'naturalness' of heterosexual space by freely performing her own gender and sexual identity in a public context. And this time she does not need to cross-dress or to perform a gender role: what she puts on the stage of her life is nothing else but herself.

References

Ahmed S. 2006. "Orientations. Toward a Queer Phenomenology". In *GLQ: A Journal of Lesbian and Gay Studies*, 12, 4, 543-574.

Antosa S. (ed.) 2007. *Omosapiens 2. Spazi e identità queer*. Roma: Carocci.

Bailey P. 1998. *Popular Culture and Performance in the Victorian City*. Cambridge: Cambridge University Press.

Bell D., Valentine G. (eds.) 1995. *Mapping Desire. Geographies of Sexualities*. London and New York: Routledge.

Brown M. 2000. *Closet Space: Geographies of Metaphor from the Body to the Globe*. London-New York: Routledge.

Browne K. 2006. "Challenging Queer Geographies". In *Antipode*, 38, 885-93.

Browne K., Brown G., Lim J. (eds.) 2007. *Geographies of Sexualities: Theory, Practice, Politics*. Ashgate: London.

Butler J. 1990. *Gender Trouble. Feminism and the Subversion of Identity*. London and New York: Routledge.

Ciocia S. 2005. "Journeying Against the Current": a Carnivalesque Theatrical Apprenticeship in Sarah Waters' *Tipping the Velvet*". In *Literary London Journal*, 3, 1, available at http://www.literarylondon.org/london-journal/march2005/Ciocia.html (last accessed August 2011).

Cleto F. 2002. "Introduction: Queering the Camp". In Cleto F. (ed.) *Camp: Queer Aesthetics and the Performing Subject: A Reader*. Ann Arbor: University of Michigan Press, 1-42.

Corber R.J., Valocchi S. 2003. "Introduction". In *Queer Studies: An Interdisciplinary Reader*. Oxford: Blackwell.

Costantini M. 2006. "'Faux-Victorian Melodrama' in the New Millennium: The Case of Sarah Waters". *Critical Survey*, 18, 1, 17-39.

Duncan N. (ed.) 1996. *BodySpace: Destabilizing Geographies of Gender and Sexuality*. London and New York: Routledge.

Ingram G.B., Boutilhette A.M., Retter Y. (eds.) 1997. *Queers in Space: Communities/Public Places/Sites of Resistance*. Seattle: Bay Press.

McDowell L. 1999. *Gender, Identity & Place: Understanding Feminist Geographies*. Cambridge: Polity Press.

Melchiorre S.M. 2009. "Londra in *Tipping the Velvet* di Sarah Waters". In Bini B., Viviani V. (eds.) *Le forme del testo e l'immaginario della metropoli. Atti del seminario 29-31 ottobre 2007*. Viterbo: Sette Città, 187-196.

Myslik W.D. 1996. "Renegotiating the Social/Sexual Identities of Places: Gay Communities as Safe Havens or Sites of Resistance?". In Duncan N. (ed.) *BodySpace: Destabilizing Geographies of Gender and Sexuality*. London and New York: Routledge, 156-169.

Offord B., Cantrell L. 1999. "Unfixed in a Fixated World: Identity, Sexuality, Race and Culture". In Jackson P.A., Sullivan G. (eds.) *Multicultural Queer: Australian Narratives*. Harrington Park Press: Binghamtom, 207-220.

Rich A. 1993. "Compulsory Heterosexuality and Lesbian Existence" (1980). In *Poetry and Prose*. New York: Norton, 203-223.

Sedgwick Kosofsky E. 1990. *Epistemology of the Closet*. Berkeley: University of California Press.

Valentine G. 1996. "(Re)negotiating the 'Heterosexual Street': Lesbian Productions of Space". In Duncan N. (ed.) *BodySpace: Destabilizing Geographies of Gender and Sexuality*. London and New York: Routledge, 145-154.

Waters S. 1998. *Tipping the Velvet*. London: Virago.

Waters S. 1999. *Affinity*. London: Virago.

Waters S. 2002. *Fingersmith*. London: Virago.

NADIA SANTORO

Università della Calabria

Herland and/or Queerland:
Some Suggestions for Reading Virginia Woolf's *Orlando*

In the well-known and often quoted overture of *A Room of One's Own*, Virginia Woolf mildly mocks any pretence of coming to a conclusion concerning the true nature of woman and fiction. On the contrary, her rambling dissertation, as its later and more outspoken companion-piece *Three Guineas*, becomes a space for problematizing the ideologically saturated character of words like "nature", "sex", "objectivity".

Written only a year before, *Orlando* aims, in similar fashion, at putting to question the discursive *a priori* that structure our knowledge, showing in her "truthful, but fantastic" (Woolf 1972, 112) narrative the story of a desire that tackles reality without shrinking to its arbitrary criteria. The aim of this essay is to show how the novel deconstructs binary oppositions and questions, in its depiction of sexual difference, both the dream of complementarity embodied in the androgynous myth and the unbounded gender manufacturability advocated by some readings of the novel.

1. Toward a recognition of difference

A cursory glance at the critical reception of *Orlando* from the late Sixties of the twentieth century until today shows a substantially unanimous reading of the novel. Briefly, the text would fictionalize the androgynous ideal Woolf will advocate only a year later in *The Room of One's Own*. But how to reconcile in the text the claiming of a sexual difference, as a "partial perspective", an epistemological optics able to grasp "the singing of the real world" and the problematization of conventional gender roles, as confining scripts both for men and women?

Woolf actually redeployed the androgynous imaginary to flesh out her critique of love as oneness and fusion that can be traced back at least as far as Plato's *Symposium*. Unlike some scholars' attempt to connect androgyny to another archetype, namely the double, Liliana Rampello reads it not as an other representation of self-doubling, but, rather, of a "re-doubling", through which Woolf attempts to narrate "the different quality of women's and men's experience of the world in its uniqueness and entirety" (Rampello 2005, 54; my translation).

We come across the first representation of love in the early chapters of the novel. Here we meet Orlando, attempting to face the erotic assaults by one of the many cross-dressers who people the novel, the Archduchess/Archduchy Harriet Griselda. The double-nature of Love reminds the myth Aristophanes tells in the *Symposium* and its underlying "somatophobia". In her rereading of Socrates' dialogue, Luce Irigaray highlights how not only is love the theme of Diotima's dissertation, but it is also the principal device used to convey a reasoning aloof from any dichotomous way of thinking. As the learning process Diotima portrays as "never fulfilled, always becoming", Eros is "always in movement" (Irigaray 1993, 21), in transit among different and contradictory states of being, sensible and intelligible, mortal and immortal, immanent and transcendent. This nomadic quality of desire is what drives Orlando in her endless quest for "Life! A lover" not "Life! A Husband!" (Woolf 1993, 167).

What marks Orlando in her embodiment as a woman is precisely her will to preserve the "daimonic, mediumistic function of love" (Irigaray 1993, 28). According to Irigaray, the fecundity of love, prior to any procreation, is what allows the reciprocal engendering and transformation of the lovers, where corporeality is the shifting threshold unto mutual transcendence. In her recent reading of *Symposium*, Luisa Muraro points up precisely the dimension of exchange, endless becoming in the "asymmetrical and imbalanced" couple (2002, 41) represented by Poverty, the woman who knows the dependent and relational character of the self and Invention. This latter, re-translated as "Passage", concerns the porous quality of "there-being", the fertile exchange between words and bodies mediated through writing Woolf wrote about in *A Room of One's Own*. In the essay as well as in *Orlando*, as Liliana Rampello suggests, androgyny could in fact be recast as the capacity to accede to the "embodied universal" (Rampello 2005, 163) by men and women, as they both partake of a larger reality than the one dictated by the oppressive and potentially excluding shackles of identity.

In the second half of the novel, we encounter Love as "sensible transcendental" (Irigaray 1993, 30), as a space of growing and becoming without a preconceived goal in view and without reducing the other to a means for an end. The enclosure of Orlando's lovers, in the real or metaphoric rooms of his desire and sonnets is sets against Orlando's quest, as a woman, of a *jouissance* shattering the strict binary divisions of "compulsory heterosexuality" (Rich 1994).

By marrying Marmaduke Bonthrop Shelmerdine, a sea-captain with colonial fantasies, Orlando paradoxically manages to get rid of her Victorian "appealing womanhood" (Woolf 1993, 169). What she learns through her unconventional *ménage* is the non-coincidence between symbolic independence and material interdependence dodging cleverly the disciplining gazes of the "spirit of the age" *(Woolf 1993, 183-184)*. If in her relationship with Marmaduke, Orlando puts into question androgyny, as material and symbolic symmetry between the sexes, two images are used by Woolf to mark her scepticism toward a hypothetical androgynous marriage. Following the Mozartian sparkling intermezzo in the 18th-century London, among petty courtier-intellectuals and cross-dressed *flânerie*, Orlando's traumatic awakening in the garish and bigot 19th-century, is marked by the appearance of two grotesque androgynous combinations.

The first one, noticed by Orlando during a carriage walk, calls to mind one of those Memory's associative plays, so frequent in the novel. But, the playful "redressing" between self and inner time worked out by that "capricious seamstress" is replaced by the firm will of the ideological message, crafted as a seamless extension of "reality" (Woolf 1993, 160).

If the "syntax" of realism is the object of a persistent parody by invalidating its tidy symmetries, in this passage Woolf aims at uncovering the appropriative quality of the dominant symbolic order, its will to reshape the world through the diorama, the panopticon-like transparency. Beside the "androgynous" assimilation of the many others subjected to Empire, the two sides of institutionalized femininity are metonymically conjured up through the "widow's weeds and the bridal veils" (Woolf 1993, 160) supported by the union between Man and Woman. The categorical imperative to match-making, subliminally inscribed here and in another passage, where poor Orlando sees wedding rings spawning in every nook of the city, fuels Woolf's irony, who reread the "normality" of heterosexual coupling as deviance and sexual aberration (Woolf 1993, 166-167).

As Wanda Tommasi suggests, Orlando's "proximity to neuter" (Tommasi 1987, 87) can be read as a means to disrupt the eternal gesture of "objectification of the female", "the game of bringing back every alterity to the Same, philosophy has always carried out" (*ibidem*, 91-92; my translation). The "neuter", ruled out from philosophical speculation, governed by the principle of non-contradiction, reminds both the "residue", the interval (in-betweeness) between the sexes, engulfed by the "the monstrosity of the universal subject simultaneously male and neuter" (Cavarero 1987, 46), and a modality of thinking that "(it) refuses to choose in as much as those two possibilities do not exhaust the entire reality, they do not account for all the possibilities of experience" (Tommasi 1987, 89; my translation). "Maleness" and "Femaleness" can thus act as embodied locations able to challenge power devices and the exclusionary frames underlying identity politics. Androgyny reread by Rampello as "transcendence", namely the "undoing" of sex as gender, a refusal of a corporeality crystallized as a static cultural token, ties to a vision of sexual difference as a place of "a creative agency" (Muraro 1995; my translation). The practices of re-signification advocated by Judith Butler, as well as the inscription of sexual difference in the symbolic pursued by Diotima community, aim to restore the sexed experience from the alienating performance, culturally and socially sanctioned, in order to reshape it as a place of collective renegotiation, of mutual recognition that "resists models of assimilation" (Butler 2004, 4).

2. Performance and/or performativity

Gender as performance, as socially and culturally codified "masquerade" permeates *Orlando*. Masculinity and Femininity could be seen as the main characters of a tragicomic masque, apparently specular doubles of a "regulatory fiction" (Butler 1990, 24) staged for purposes of order and social control. The materiality of sex, as discursive concretion mystifying its power-effect, circumscribes Orlando's lives both as a man and as a woman.

In this regard, the widening of perspective offered by *Orlando*, as far as identity and sexuality are concerned, allows the reader to think about how bodies are, at the same time, materialized and made abject if they contradict the "heterosexual matrix" (Butler 1990) that reduce the dual nature of human beings to the polarization of sexual desire. Upon her return home, Orlando experiences the norm's violence, that – on failing to pigeonhole her – orders her to live under a regime of compulsory invisibility (Woolf 1993, 119-120).

Cross-dressing, as well as androgyny acquire different meanings according to the subject, man or woman, who employ these acts of "corporeal stylizations" (Butler 1990, 139) to enlarge the scope of "what is real" (Butler 2004), to transfer the creative bricolage of gender crafting to a re-crafting of the fixity of reality. If the reading of Orlando's sex-changes as "dress-change" highlights the undermining of any clear-cut distinction between "outward appearance" and "true sex" (Bowlby 1988, 51), on the other hand, it posits problematically the easy interchangeability of sexed selves as costumes. Although playing with gender hold a significant role in the text, as it does in everyday-life, this reading dismisses how, as Butler has argued in *Bodies that Matter*, this self same "playing" can achieve public recognition or, on the contrary, threatens the subjects with unreality.

But, on the other hand, the complex corporeal semantics analyzed by De Lauretis in *Soggetti eccentrici* (1999) and the intense narrative of transgender lives in *Undoing Gender* (2004) by Butler show how the assumed dispossession of the body by the social is offset by the never-ended process of bodily translation. According to Butler, the ek-static nature of self signals both our "undoing" by social norms not of our making but it is also the condition for a re-negotiation of the same norms on a collective basis (Butler 2004). Ironically undercutting both the search for a "true" femininity that would lay concealed behind the oppressive façade of patriarchal culture and the one-sided inscription of body by the symbolic, the novel shows how "in gaining materiality the body becomes a perturbing guest in the social" (Sandra 1986 in Bono and Kemp 1991, 179).

The store of pleasures and bodily images Orlando repeatedly refers to, in order to recall the memory of her corporeal self intertwines with the "implanted memory" she "acquires" on getting to London. The "sacred responsibilities of Womanhood" (Woolf 1993, 113), object of an early mild irony by Orlando, become thus the mental framework, "the schema" projected onto the body, through which the docile feminine subject comes to being. In a extremely comic passage Orlando's body become the stage of shameful, incontrollable desires, taking shape moreover through scrawls that as in *A Room of One's Own*, seem to convey "the submerged truth to the top" (Woolf 2000, 33). But, neither does the "truth" refers to the insipid setting of love-romance, parodied later, nor to the disclosing of an uncorrupted and unrepressed sexuality, unmediated by literary and cultural conventions. Instead, it is the discursive investment of the body, not as an origin, but a "naturalized effect" of a specific "device of sexuality" (Foucault 1978), disciplining sex and its bodily sensations (Woolf 1993, 167).

In the novel the inquiry into the feminine as a (male) place of compulsive metaphoricity and the ironic overturning of those discursive strategies used to police the boundaries between the sexes and their dreaded con-fusion, intertwine with the problematization of a univocal "truth", of inarguable criteria patterning sexed corporeality.

In several passages of the novel, Orlando pursues a tactics of "productive undecidability" (Butler 2004, 142) in order to question the need to conform to the norm she sees about her and risks engulfing her. The biographer's disquisition about the mystery of her "real" sex surveys, in a contradictory way, all the possible options embodied by Orlando's sex-change: but, cornered in the classical dichotomy of social gender versus biological body, he abandons in the end, the criterion of truth/falseness.

Issues of history and representation not only are problematized by at once using and subverting the tropes used in the "staging" of the past, but also by weaving together personal and cultural memories with the narrative present, past times and varied setting. Moreover, the refusal of "sequence as the royal road to *con*sequence" (Dinshaw *et al.* 2007) is pursued by Woolf by what can be called a "queering of time".

If queer politics challenges the totalizing pretences of identity categories to fully describe the subjects, forging new and problematized links among gender, sex and sexuality undermining any teleological, normalizing narrative, by the same token, re-crossing time through a queer lens is a tactics to revise the social scripts most people live through for the sake of "normalcy". In *Orlando*, time is the anamorphic optic through which exploring the contingency of taken for granted frames of reference. But, also, the possible place wherein shattering the reassuring daily mediocrity and the objectifying mark of power, by investing time with the unbalancing force and intensity of desire.

Orlando's multidirectional desire for happiness, escaping from any predestined *telos*, unties the "complicity" between social and symbolic order by refusing both petrified sexual roles and the compulsive synchronization of her inner time to the stages of a typical biography's time line.

The happy end of a typical romance novel, through which the biographer tries, unsuccessfully, to fill up the "dead-time" of thought, of Orlando's uneventful life is refused by her looking for happiness in the excess and gratuity of reading and writing.

Privileging these "unproductive moments" (Lonzi, quoted in Boccia 2002, 67) is a tactics against the confining of female desire in the strict binaries of "domestic" romances (narrative) technologies that describe while prescribing how a woman life should be. Getting carried away by her shifting train of thought, Orlando tries to keep alive her desire for change among simulacra of humanity governed by the logic of the Same. "Profiting from (her) difference" (Lonzi 1991, 41), she is free to feed her nomadic self beyond the freezing of the past in a presumed "pre-edipic utopia" (Fusini 1998, 1354) locating her perpetual becoming in the "conditional present" (Braidotti 1994) to destabilize the sedentary quality of identities as well as of the words that should describe them. During the phantasmagorical pageant of (her)-selves, the desire for an autonomous subjectivity propels her active re-mapping of her disjointed slices of memories and the re-opening up of the archive of the past outside the "drive of the proper(ty)" (Sargisson 1996, 122).

Opening up the house could mean thus both the critically re-opening of the national archive, but also through the analogy with Orlando's multi-chambered self, underlines the bond among the multiple rooms of Woolf's writing and the identities moulded in/by them. The room as a shell, the covering of our secret selves or, also, the palimpsest being inscribed with Orlando's identity passages, is a central image in "Profession for Women". Here, as in *Orlando*, it is the token of a shared space beyond the grammar of individual rights towards the exceeding of a future, not contemplated by any vision of static future harmony (see Woolf 1966-1967, 288-289).

References

Boccia M.L. 2002. *La differenza politica. Donne e cittadinanza*. Milano: Il Saggiatore.
Bowlby R. 1988. *Virginia Woolf: Feminist Destinations*. Oxford: Blackwell.
Braidotti R. 1994. *Nomadic Subjects: Embodiment and Sexual Difference in Contemporary Feminist Theory*. New York: Columbia University Press.
Butler J. 1990. *Gender Trouble. Feminism and the Subversion of Identity*. New York and London: Routledge.

Butler J. 2004. *Undoing Gender*. New York and London: Routledge.

Cavarero A. 1987. "Per una teoria della differenza sessuale". In Diotima (ed.) *Il pensiero della differenza sessuale*. Milano: La Tartaruga, 43-79.

De Lauretis T. 1999. *Soggetti eccentrici*. Milano: Feltrinelli.

Dinshaw C., Edelman L., Ferguson R.A. *et al.* 2007. "Theorizing Queer Temporalities. A Roundtable Discussion". In *GLQ: A Journal of Lesbian and Gay Studies*, 13 (2-3), 177-195.

Foucault M. 1978. *La volontà di sapere* (trans. Pasquino P., Procacci G.). Milano: Feltrinelli (orig. ed. 1976, *La volonté de savoir*, Paris: Gallimard).

Fusini N. 1998. "Commento e note a *Orlando*". In Fusini N. (ed.) *Virginia Woolf. Romanzi*. Milano: Mondadori, 1341-1368.

Irigaray L. 1993. *An Ethics of Sexual Difference* (trans. Burke C., Gill C.G.). New York: Cornell University Press (orig. ed. 1984, *Une ethique de la différence sexuelle*, Paris: Minuit).

Lonzi C. 1991 "Let's Spit on Hegel" (trans. Newman V.). In Bono P., Kemp S. (eds.) *Italian Feminist Thought: A Reader*. Oxford: Blackwell, 40-59 (orig. ed. 1974, *Sputiamo su Hegel. La donna clitoridea e la donna vaginale*, Milano: Scritti di Rivolta Femminile).

Muraro L. 1995. "Oltre l'uguaglianza". In Diotima (ed.) *Oltre l'uguaglianza. Le radici femminili dell'autorità*, Napoli: Liguori, 105-132.

Muraro L. 2002. "La maestra di Socrate e mia". In Diotima (ed.) *Approfittare dell'assenza. Punti di avvistamento sulla tradizione*. Napoli: Liguori, 27-44.

Rampello L. 2005. *Il canto del mondo reale. Virginia Woolf. La vita nella scrittura*, Milano: Il Saggiatore.

Rich A. 1994. *Blood, Bread, and Poetry: Selected Prose, 1979-1985*. New York: W.W. Norton & Company.

Sandra 1986. "Suggestions from Irigaray". In Bono P., Kemp S. (eds.) 1991. *Italian Feminist Though: A Reader*. Oxford: Blackwell, 177-180.

Sargisson L. 1996. *Contemporary Feminist Utopianism*. London: Routledge.

Tommasi W. 1987. "La tentazione del neutro". In Diotima (ed.) *Il pensiero della differenza sessuale*. Milano: La Tartaruga, 80-103.

Woolf V. 1966-1967. "Professions for Women". In Woolf V. *Collected Essays*, Woolf L. (ed.), vol. II, London: Chatto and Windus, 284-289.

Woolf V. 1972. *"A Writer's Diary": Being Extracts from the Diary of Virginia Woolf*, L. Woolf (ed.) London: Hogarth Press.

Woolf V. 1993. *Orlando: A Biography*. Lyons B., Gilbert S.M. (eds.) Harmondsworth: Penguin.

Woolf V. 2000. *A Room of One's Own*. Harmondsworth: Penguin.

Francesca Maioli

Università di Milano

Nomadic Subjects on Canvas:
from Essentialism to Hybridity in Jenny Saville's Paintings

Jenny Saville's paintings represent huge and fleshy female bodies which can be described as the embodiment of materiality both in terms of *materia* (matter) and *mater* (mother),[1] and the quintessence of everything that our culture labels as 'ugly'. Their attitude, however, is deeply ambiguous. These weighty bodies talk about canons of beauty and cultural conditioning, and at the same time they visualize the inner dimension of femininity to discuss its lived experience and, at a later stage, the instability of its meaning in a world where fluidity and hybridity are increasingly relevant. In this paper I am going to focus on hybridity in the paintings of Jenny Saville, showing that she started painting huge female bodies under the influence of the French feminists of the Seventies and Eighties and, just like many women artists and writers, she widely used the female or feminist *topoi* connected to the representation of the female body as hybrid and monstrous. However, she has been using these *topoi* in a way that is quite different from most representations of the monstrous female body, as I am going to discuss by comparing her bodies to those a few well-known women writers using the same images. Besides, while she first used the stereotypes of the female body as a hybrid entity especially in terms of animal features, over the last years, and following a non linear and winding path, she has developed a more personal view of the body, identity and hybridity. This has lead her towards a different kind of feminism, one in which newer notions of identity

---

[1] The classical association of femininity with materiality has been discussed by several thinkers, but never in relation to Saville's gargantuan women. See for example Nead 1992. She notices that woman "is both *mater* (mother) and *materia* (matter), biologically determined and potentially wayward. Now, if art is defined as the conversion of matter into form, imagine how much greater the triumph for art if it is the *female* body that is thus transformed – pure nature transmuted, through the forms of art, into pure culture. The female nude, the, is not simply one subject among others, one form among many, it is *the* subject, *the* form" (*ibidem*, 18). From a different theoretical perspective, Judith Butler explains the etymology of matter-*mater*-matrix with generation and production of meaning (see Butler 1993, 31).

and hybridity have replaced the quite traditional feminist essentialism that underlies her earliest works, and sexually hybrid bodies have taken the place of the animal-like women portrayed in her earliest paintings.

The bodies portrayed in Jenny Saville's paintings often display an exaggeration of specific female attributes pointing to an equation of femininity with a definite, supposedly disgusting, animal quality. In most cases, they are representations of women whose fat and flabbiness suggest lack of control, and this is connected to a specific unruliness of matter itself that can be considered animal-like. Generally, it is to be noticed, they are also characterised by their enormous size, one that allowed Sarah Kent to define Saville's women as 'mountainous', a term that recalls the protagonists of much feminist fiction, such as for example Dog Woman in Jeanette Winterson's *Sexing the Cherry*, Fevvers in Angela Carter's *Nights at the Circus*, and Ruth in *The Life and Loves of a She-Devil* by Fay Weldon. The protagonist of the latter is a woman who is compared to a mountain and keeps getting bigger and bigger as her husband falls in love with her petite rival, Mary Fisher, whose features are in a sense summarised in a painting by Jenny Saville: *Branded* (1992). This shows a fat woman with a few words written on her skin: *supportive, petite, precious, decorative, delicate* and *irrational*. These are all terms that could be used to describe Mary Fisher, and in a sense both Ruth and Mary Fisher are represented in this painting: the former is very similar to the woman in the painting, while the latter is in a sense recalled by the words inscribed on the woman's body. However, Saville's character does not identify herself with either of them. As most of Saville's women, she shows a very ambiguous attitude, one that suggests defiance rather than a desire, or even an attempt, to fulfil the unrealistic ideal embodied by Mary Fisher. The woman's hand gripping a roll of fat can be interpreted both as a synecdoche for a woman who looks at herself through the mirror in self-disgust and one whose self-exhibited nakedness is an attempt to defy cultural standards. A key element in Saville is precisely the fact that she is speaking directly to women in order for every woman to interpret her paintings as an expression of her own anguish or chance of empowerment.[2]

Besides, the focus of this painting is on the woman's breasts and stomach, while the head is smaller than these distinctively feminine elements. The insistence on those specific sexual markers owes much to a feminist essentialism that is typical of Saville's earlier works: the gripping of the roll of fat can be a way to denounce cultural conditionings or an empowering statement in feminist terms. In this sense, the stereotypes artificially written on the woman's skin clash with her nature and ultimately her power, which rests in the ability

---

[2] Meagher (2003) reports the enthusiasm many fat women express when seeing a painting by Saville, which is clearly very different a reaction from that men or anorexics could have: she writes that the British painter received a lot of letters from enthusiastic fat women thanking her for presenting their condition as one of desirability.

to generate life from her belly, something that those very men who inscribed a set of meanings onto her flesh are unable to do. While in this work femininity as a biological fact is an empowering element, Jenny Saville's production evolves towards the notion of biology as a discourse, and of the body as a written entity where *sex*, rather than gender, is the primary kind of cultural inscription.

Women such as this one, or such as those represented in *Strategy* (1993-1994) or *Plan* (1993), can be compared also to another character: Winterson's Dog Woman. Just like them, she is a very uncommon figure with a defying attitude who openly describes herself in terms of "caves in my face" that "are home enough for fleas" (Winterson 1989, 24). She adds that she once outweighed an elephant and, on another occasion, the parson didn't let her enter church because "the gargoyles must remain on the outside" (*ibidem*, 14). Gargoyles and their complex burden of Christian and heathen symbolism have definitely something in common with Saville's grotesque women and their combination of natural and cultural elements.

If these characters have much in common with animals because of their size and because their exceeding fat suggests a particular unruliness of the body, other bodies point very explicitly to a similarity between female bodies and flesh in terms of animals slaughtered to be eaten. Examples of this can be found for instance in *Fulcrum* (1998-99) and *Host* (2000). The latter presents the most explicitly animal character in Saville's production: a headless body with multiple breasts. It is in all likelihood the body of an animal, and more specifically that of a pig. Such an unusual subject within Saville's production, and the breasts, however, immediately recall a naked woman. The emphasis is on transformation and ambiguity, which is heightened when looking at the table where the body is resting: in its shiny whiteness, it looks more like a surgical table than a piece of furniture to be found in a slaughterhouse. What puzzles the viewer is above all the awareness that Saville essentially paints human and specifically female bodies, so the observer cannot figure out the choice of this single subject. The confusion is partially overcome when we are informed that the painting was inspired by Marie Darrieussecq's novel *Pig Tales* (*Truismes*),[3] in which a woman becomes so fat that she finally turns into a pig. The novel criticises the treatment of women in Western society by showing how a specific plumpness is associated to sexual attraction and to a rediscovery of sexual impulses. However, as the plot unravels, it is clear that, while men are free to follow their animal impulses and instincts, in a woman this is perceived as a definite animal-like quality which ends up turning

---

[3] See Paparoni (2006, 90). Unfortunately the English title is unable to maintain the double meaning that is implicit in both French and Italian and suggestive of an animal quality that is also defined by an excessive sexual activity.

the woman into an object of disgust and, ultimately, into an outcast.[4] The woman, turned into a pig, can only be free after killing her mother, who is responsible for her primary social education.[5] Significantly, while the lascivious woman is turned into a pig, the men appearing in the novel are as rich and powerful as they are vicious, and this emphasizes the idea that patriarchy is the unchanging institutionalisation of a double standard.[6]

While this painting reflects a quite traditional feminist view aimed at denouncing the condition of women in modern society, in the same period Jenny Saville also starts depicting new and more radical subjects. The seeds of her transition towards newer theories of identity, however, can be found in one of her earliest works, *Plan*, which is the painting that connects Saville's earlier interest in French feminism with her more recent 'nomadic' turn, achieved by following a non linear, 'nomadic' path.

The title of the painting is rather ambiguous, just like most of Saville's titles: the word 'plan' suggests the idea of a project (both the figure's forthcoming surgery and the construction of identity in general as a project) as well as a topographical drawing (the body as a map of inscriptions, ambiguities *etc.*). The traces on the woman's body – a series of circles drawn around the softest parts of her figure – recall both geography, because the circular lines evoke those indicating mountains on a map, and surgery, as they are similar to the lines that surgeons draw on the patient's body before a liposuction. The former reading is clearly a reference to explorations, mapping and colonization, a set of practices that in the past were often represented in terms of male violation of a virgin land described as a beautiful woman.[7] This woman laid in front of us is like an open land, and her very position invites the viewer to explore her. Surgery, on the other hand, raises a complex web of issues concerning power and control.

---

[4] On the negative association of food and fat with female sexuality see Bordo (1993) and Michie (1987).

[5] Clearly, the author refers to the notion of gender as something socially specific and the traditional feminist assumption that "one is not born a woman but becomes one", and mothers are the ones who have to pass on femininity to their daughters.

[6] As Paparoni points out, besides, the connection between pigs and women is all the more significant since pigs are the quintessential impure creatures. This association between pigs and women would confirm the reading of women as impure creatures in need of control in a traditional religious sense (2006, 90-91). Besides, he adds that the reference to surgery recalls experiments of organ transplants form animals to humans. And it is to be noticed that animals, and specifically pigs, are very common in contemporary art. Tobin Siebers even states that "Animal flesh is central to the new art. This is because the symbolism linking animal flesh to human destiny is primordial: our treatment of animals, spanning from the days of animal sacrifice to those of the modern factory farm, takes its justification from the ritual belief that animal bodies may be manipulated to change human bodies. Animal sacrifice would be of no importance, however, if it did not summon the spectre of human sacrifice" (2000, 236-237).

[7] On this, see for example Kolodny (1975) and Rose (1993).

The viewer is stimulated to ask who has control over this body and whether it is really her own decision to undergo a surgical operation or if there is a web of cultural conditionings forcing her to do it. Is surgery, one may wonder, a source of empowerment or submission?[8] Her being presented as an invitingly open landscape strengthens this ambiguity: perhaps it is the woman herself that is inviting the viewer to explore her. As the woman in *Branded* or in other of Saville's paintings, this figure is rather destabilising since it is staring at the observer, in an inviting look that sums up all the issues of activity-passivity and ugliness-sensuousness that complicate Saville's paintings. Her look is a defiant one, saying both 'I'm not here to be watched' (possibly because the woman is waiting for surgery to become more desirable and thus more pleasurable to be looked at) and 'I'm here to be watched even though I'm not perfect'. It is to be noticed, besides, that the traces on her body are all circle-shaped except for a single straight line above the woman's genitalia,[9] as if to underline that specific region of her body. The woman's pubis is at the forefront and is rather big in comparison to her head, which is smaller and half out of the canvas. This is clearly a reference to the already discussed importance of sex and gender, and more specifically of a sexed reading of the body, since both sex and gender are the first inscriptions to be found on the flesh, and the body is never really 'naked', unfiltered. This painting, then, through the reference to surgery and to a sexed reading of the body, initiates a discourse that Saville will pursue in her later works: the question of identity as a project, and one that necessarily concerns the body. The notion of the body as a vessel for cultural meanings leads Saville to more radical notions of the body and sexual identity since, just like gender, sex is conceived in terms of a cultural inscription rather than a mere biological issue. In this sense, surgery is the chance to change one's body via medical procedures to help the outer surface look more like the inner perception of oneself. The body, then, is something that is not natural. It is part of the subject's project of identity, something that prevails even over biology. Saville's initial essentialism, in short, turns into a very postmodern view of biology as a discourse normalising the body, which is an unstable and 'malleable'[10] or 'plastic' entity.[11]

Not surprisingly, Saville's specific interest over the last years seems to be residing in portraying bodies in transit or in transition: bodies undergoing a

---

[8] And it must also be noticed that surgery is linked to the individual's affluence, and therefore it may be a free choice only for those who can afford it.

[9] Which is, at a closer look, part of a wider circle that appears to be a straight line just as it happens in geographical drawings.

[10] Lichtman (2004) explains that the malleable body is a body "in progress that provides a site where parts may be added or deleted at any time, arranged and re-arranged in any sequence".

[11] See Bordo (1993, 245-276).

transformation after violence or surgery, to invite viewers to meditate on the causes and effects of surgery, and on the transformative power of the body in relation to self and social identity. The British painter's idea of the body in transition centres on a specific notion of the wound: "I like bodies in a state of transformation, whether through injury or surgery. Even as a child, if I was on the school playground and I saw a girl fall and skin her knee, I would look at it and be fascinated" (Schwabsky 2005, 107) The wound stands for several different things: it is the tangible sign of violence or surgery, with their burden of transformation and change, the marker of a suffering leading to atonement,[12] an artificial sign over flesh in general as a reminder of the essentially artificial nature of the body and of the identity that it tries either to promote or to conceal. The body is never neutral, unfiltered, and the wound is the point where a less prejudiced reading of the body can begin, since it suggests than the skin functions as a garment to hide something else, something deeper, and indicates the point where self and social identity, psychic dimension and social conditionings may converge and confront each other, the blank space for a different reading of the body. It is the place where hybridity begins or, more specifically, where inside and outside communicate and open up a way for transformation. The wound, in its combination of naturalness and artificiality, self and other, suffering and empowerment, stands for both a key point in reading postmodern bodies and a symbol of representation as a collage of diverging instances.

This is apparent in Saville's recent interest in transsexual bodies, which represents her move on from a former feminist essentialism to the most recent gender theories, where the body is read not only as the site of individuality and belonging, but also as the unstable signifier to convey the construction of an articulated sense of self identity. Her bodies are entities in transition, nomadic bodies, bodies that represent contradiction and the point where diverging issues converge and balance, before they finally implode to create and re-create something new. These bodies and the identity they express recall Braidotti's nomadic bodies:

> The nomad [...] is a figuration for the kind of subject who has relinquished all idea, desire, or nostalgia for fixity. This figuration expresses the desire for an identity made of transitions, successive shifts, and coordinated changes, without and against an essential unity (Braidotti 1994, 22).

Saville's later paintings about transsexuals, in this sense, raise several questions about identity – not simply sexual identity – as a construction and a project, a matter of choice rather than a simple question of 'nature' or 'biology'. Unlike the sexually hybrid bodies described by Angela Carter in *The Passion of New Eve* or by Winterson in *Sexing the Cherry* and *The Passion*, these are bodies

---

[12] See Paparoni (2006).

in perpetual transition. These characters were not born hybrid as in Winterson's novel, nor were they forced to undergo a surgical operation as Evelyn/Eve in Carter's work. Hybridity is a condition they desire, and identity their project.

Paintings like *Passage* (2004-2005) or *Matrix* (1999), for example, represent transsexuals in their hybrid nudity before they find a stable identity through surgery. It is to be noticed that both titles are very significant: *Passage* clearly refers to the idea of change and transition, as well as passing through different stages and sufferings to grasp a definite sense of identity, while *Matrix* goes back to the discourse on matter-mother which I referred to at the beginning of this paper. Significantly, the word 'matrix' comes from the same root as *'mater'* (mother), 'matter', and 'material', and indicates the mould which, in the Aristotelian-thomistic notion of conception, stands for the male element opposed to the female one which symbolises the raw matter for creation.[13] The painting shows a naked transsexual with female genitalia and breasts, a male head in the upper left corner of the canvas and a definitely masculine tattoo on the figure's right arm. The painting, both in itself and in its title, recalls Courbet's *The Origin of the World*, since both the figure and the noun 'matrix' seem to agglomerate matter, mould and mother all in one. The hybrid quality of the figure seems to be hinting at the fact that one's identity is a matter of creation, that anyone can be the mater (creator) of his /her very self (the matter), a very postmodern statement that is, however, complicated by the afore mentioned issue of surgery as both a matter of self-definition and a modification of the body according to stereotypes that the subject has unconsciously internalised.[14] On the other hand, there is a clear reference to art and representation, since hybridity stands also for the assemblage of different elements that the artistic project necessarily requires. Hybridity, in this painting, is not only the combination of two sexes: it also the combination of past and present,[15] and a hint to the androgynous nature of art (the combination of female generation and male creativity) as well as to painting as the assemblage of different fragments and instances. Besides, art has traditionally been endowed with a regulatory aim, which is not different from the normativity that is inherent in the medical, and specifically surgical, project. If art wishes to create the perfect form, aesthetic surgery was born as a way to normalise deformed bodies, and sex changes are ways to stabilise a body (and an identity) that is seen as unstable, chaotic, and destabilising.

However, Saville chooses to depict bodies at the exact moment of transition, in their chaotic state, as she rejects any attempt to stability and underlines the

---

[13] On this, see for example "Mothers, Monsters and Machines", in Braidotti (1994, 75-94).

[14] Even transsexuals, who wish to change their bodies according to their inner self perception of themselves, are not untouched by stereotypes and dominant conventions, and tend to perform a femininity that is deeply indebted to conventional images.

[15] In this case, the past and present of this figure in transition towards a new life, but in general past and present is referred to quoting authors and styles from the past.

transitory nature of identity and, ultimately, of life. Her paintings deny the existence of a separation between mind and body, and present the body as the hinge where self and social identity converge, where identity as a project can be reflected if we live towards transition. Saville, then, after an initial attraction for French feminism and its essentialist implications, comes to a very different notion of identity, sex and gender. In the beginning her work was influenced by French feminism, but her wish to explore the inner implications of femininity and to challenge the in-out separation and the setting of margins which is implicit in art, leads her to a territory that is new, and more radical than the essentialism influencing many feminist artists of the Seventies and Eighties.

Her bodies deconstruct borders and margins, merge inside and outside and, in proposing themselves as projections of inner states, they represent the transition and fluidity that necessarily belong to our inner life as an essential component of identity, which is never fixed and stable and necessarily connects body and mind. In this sense, she operates a total deconstruction of borders that implicates deconstructing sexes and genders. Her bodies are nomadic bodies in that transition and instability are their essential qualities. Saville's bodies manage to reach "that postmodern realm of gender nirvana, brilliantly theorized by Judith Butler as a zone of shifting sexual identities and the rejection of essential difference between male and female" (Nochlin 2000, 96). Jenny Saville, in short, proposes merging sexes and genders, art forms and styles, to promote hybridity as the only viable way to obliterate stereotypes – the stereotypes she began her career from – and gain a full subjectivity as a human being and an artist.

References

Bordo S. 1993. *Unbearable Weight. Feminism, Western Culture and the Body.* Berkeley: University of California Press.

Braidotti R. 1994. *Nomadic Subjects: Embodiment and Sexual Difference in Contemporary Feminist Theory.* New York: Columbia University Press.

Braidotti R. 2003. *In metamorfosi. Verso una teoria materialista del divenire.* Milano: Feltrinelli.

Butler J. 1993. *Bodies that Matter: On the Discursive Limits of Sex,* London: Routledge.

Carter A. 1977. *The Passion of New Eve.* London: Virago Press.

Carter A. 1984. *Nights at the Circus.* London: Vintage.

Darrieussecq M. 1998. *Truismes.* Paris: Gallimard.

Kolodny A. 1975. *The Lay of the Land: Metaphor as Experience and History in American Life and Letters.* Chapel Hill: The University of North Carolina Press.

Lichtman L. 2004. *MEME: Replicating a Body and Technology*, unpublished thesis, Victoria University, Melbourne.

Meagher M. 2003. "Jenny Saville and a Feminist Aesthetics of Disgust". In *Hypatia: A Journal of Feminist Philosophy*, 18.4 (Fall), 23-41.

Michie H. 1987. *The Flesh Made Word*. New York: Oxford University Press.

Nead L. 1992. *The Female Nude: Art, Obscenity and Sexuality*. London, New York: Routledge.

Nochlin L. 2000. "Floating in Gender Nirvana". In *Art-in-America-1939*, 88.3 (March), 94-97.

Paparoni D. 2006. "Jenny Saville and the Origin of the Wound". In AA.VV. *Damien Hirst, David Salle, Jenny Saville: The Bilotti Chapel*. Milano: Electa, 85-98.

Rose G. 1993. *Feminism and Geography: The Limits of Geographical Knowledge*. Cambridge: Polity Press.

Schwabsky B. 2005. "Jenny Saville: Unapologetic". In Eccher D. (ed.) *Jenny Saville*. Milano: Electa, 86-111.

Siebers T. (ed.) 2000. *The Body Aesthetic: From Fine Art to Body Modification*. Ann Arbor: The University of Michigan Press.

Weldon F. 1983. *The Life and Loves of a She-Devil*. London: Hodder & Stoughton.

Winterson J. 1988. *The Passion*. London: Vintage.

Winterson J. 1989. *Sexing the Cherry*. London: Vintage.

Section 7
New Challenges for Drama Studies and Cultural Theory

MAURIZIO CALBI

Università di Salerno

Performing in the Desert:
Spectrality in Kristian Levring's *The King Is Alive*

This article provides a 'thick description' of Kristian Levring's certified Dogme film *The King Is Alive* (2000, issued in DVD format in 2002), and shows some of the ways in which *King Lear* circulates as a stripped-down 'unaccomodated thing' in the film. It also offers some more general theoretical remarks about adapting Shakespeare at the beginning of the new millennium, mostly through the lenses of recent performance theory and deconstruction.

The film is about a group of white tourists (all American except for a French woman, Catherine) who are marooned in an abandoned mining town in the Namibian desert while on their way to the airport on a coach driven by Moses (Vusi Kunene), a black man. It is only twenty-five minutes or so into the film that *King Lear* emerges as one of the intertexts, perhaps *the* primary intertext, in the form of a fragmented, half-remembered script which will affect all the characters of the film as they endeavour to come to terms with the dreadful experience of 'dis-location' and 'dis-adjustement' in the desert. The Shakespearean text appears in an almost casual way, as Henry (David Bradley), a former theatre-actor whose current job is that of reading inane Hollywood scripts, starts observing his fellow travellers engaged in various senseless activities to while away the time. He 'anatomises' them from a distance, on a raised stage-like platform he shares with Kanana (Peter Khubeke), the 'local' who has been there since the German colonisers left, and who provides some kind of authoritative voice-over commentary throughout the film. Henry's main target is Ashley (Brion James), the businessman who has been the most vociferous about his need to catch the plane back home because of his many appointments. He watches him performing some improvised dance steps, and this prompts his cynical outburst. He speaks of "some fantastic striptease act of basic human needs", and further comments as follows: "Is man no more than this? [*Laughs*] It's good old *Lear* again... Perfect".

This "striptease act" under conditions of 'de-racination' will eventually involve all the characters. It will not spare Henry—Henry, as we will find out later, is trying to come to terms with his relationship with his estranged daughter by speaking into a mini-recorder. *King Lear* itself undergoes this "striptease". The text itself becomes as "poor, bare, forked" (also in the sense of ambiguous) as the "animal" to which "unaccomodated man", a man without the paraphernalia of custom, is likened in Shakespeare's play (3.4.104-6).[1] It turns into a half-remembered script reconstructed from memory, a script materially made of rolls precariously stuck together with a plaster. It is worth quoting extensively the dialogue between Henry, who is writing down lines from *Lear* as he remembers them, and the French woman Catherine (Romane Bohringer), who has come to his hut to borrow a book:

> *Henry*: Do you know why it is called a role [...]? In the theatre [...], a long time ago, when things were written by hand [...], in order to avoid having to write the whole play out several times, each player was given his own roll [*hands the roll over to Catherine*]. *Catherine: Space Killers. Henry*: No, no, you're reading the wrong side. *Catherine*: Did you write this, Henry? *Henry*: No, I'm paid to read that stuff [...] Turn it over. *Catherine* [*reading from the script*] "I cannot heave my heart into my mouth. I love your majesty". *Henry*: That's Cordelia. *Catherine*: *C'est Othello? Henry*: No, it's *Lear*. *Catherine*: Are you writing *King Lear* by hand? *Henry*: As much as I can remember of it, or I think I can remember [...]. Just imagine we could put on *King Lear* here in this god-forsaken place, with all these lost souls. *Catherine*: They couldn't learn this [...]. *Henry*: Actually I was thinking that you could play Cordelia. *Catherine* [*hands the roll back*]: I'll take one of your books [*Leaves*].[2]

The roll's *recto* is thus a worthless movie script, and arguably symptomatises Henry 'selling out' to Hollywood, as shown by his curt reply to Catherine's ironic question about whether he wrote the script: "I'm paid to read that stuff"; the roll's *verso*, instead, inscribes a text which is supposed to be a repository of Western (or, more specifically, European) values, and re-marks Henry's newly acquired oppositional stand toward the 'industry', his being *versus*, his being against. His writing / re-writing of the script, as well as his subsequent role as a director of the play, thus make him akin to a Dogme film director who has taken the DOGME95 "Vow of Chastity", a director who willingly operates under a system of constraints and makes a virtue out of "unaccommodating" filmmaking – shooting on location, with no imported sound or external props, and so on – in order "to force the truth out of [his] characters and setting" (Dogme rule number 10) (see Cartelli and Rowe 2007, 146).

---

[1] All references to *King Lear* are to the Arden edition of the play, ed. Kenneth Muir, and are inserted parenthetically in the text.

[2] The book she picks us is William Faulkner's *As I Lay Dying*, a book which appears in Jean-Luc Godard's *À bout de souffle*.

Amy Scott-Douglass argues that "Levring's film attempts to reclaim Shakespeare *for* Europe, *from* Hollywood" (2003, 260). Crucial to her argument is the interpretation of the two Cordelias – Catherine, the self-styled quasi-intellectual French woman, and Gina (Jennifer Jason Leigh), the sexually charged 'dumb' American blonde – as allegories of, respectively, European and American Cinema. She clarifies as follows:

> The conflict between these two Cordelias can be read as a characteristic Dogmatic critique of both American and European cinema: the first Cordelia, representative of the French New Wave, has the correct approach to art and a natural affinity for Shakespeare; however she ultimately shirks her responsibility and rejects the role she's been offered, at which point the second techno-pop American Cordelia hungrily jumps at the chance to play the role, but, just like Hollywood […], she lacks the intelligence or substance to deliver a quality performance (*ibidem*, 260).[3]

Yet, I want to argue, the film does not bear out Scott-Douglass's reading of the distinction between the two Cordelias as clear-cut opposition. Even if Catherine does not recognise the specific Shakespearean play at stake during her dialogue with Henry ("*C'est Othello?*"), it is true that she shows "a natural affinity for Shakespeare" when she reads the lines: "I cannot heave my heart into my mouth" (1.1.90-1). Or, at least, her delivery can be contrasted with Gina's own reading or mis-reading of the lines during rehearsal – Gina says: "I cannot leave […] I cannot have," and cannot bring herself to pronounce the word "heave".[4] Yet Catherine does not simply refuse to play the part of Cordelia. She says *nothing* to Henry's offer, picks up William Faulkner's book, and leaves the room. In other words, she refuses to play the part of Cordelia but she does so in a Cordelia-like way. She undermines the position of Henry qua Hollywood script-reader-turned-*auteur* just as he is about to establish his authority as theatre director over his fellow travellers. And because Henry will soon take on the role of Lear, and deeply identify with it, after the first Lear (Ashley) falls ill, this refusal deflates in advance Lear's patriarchal attributes as well as his senile 'love game' ("Which of you shall we say doth love us most?") (1.1.50). In short, Catherine is some kind of 'active' Cordelia who doesn't take kindly the rejection she brings upon herself. Later on in the film, Catherine speaks to Gina in French, a language the latter likes but does not understand at all; she pretends to tell a fairy-tale but in fact abuses both Gina and Henry. I will leave out most of the verbal abuse directed at Gina. I only want to point out that the insults hurled at Henry have do to with his 'mad' project of staging a play in the middle of the desert. She calls him "an old retard"

---

[3] It is worth pointing out that Jennifer Jason Leigh played Caroline/Cordelia in the 1997 cinematic version of Jane Smiley's *A Thousand Acres*, a rewriting of *King Lear*.

[4] Interestingly, the Cordelia-like figure in Godard's *King Lear* (1987) also gets it wrong: "I cannot *have* my heart into my mouth" (my emphasis).

and "an old dick-head", and also reinterprets his offer of a role to her as a form of sexual advance. (In her opinion, he was turned down by the "French chick", and so he moved on to the "Yankee bitch"). It must be said that there is hardly anything in the film that suggests this. However, this allegation brings to the surface the 'dark side' of Lear as a character embodied by Henry, what perhaps remains in the 'unconscious' of the text: in Lacanian terms, behind the Symbolic function of the Father/King there emerges his uncanny shadowy double, a Father/King who *enjoys too much* the possession of his own daughters, a *Père-Jouissance* who resembles the Father of the primal horde in Freud's *Totem and Taboo*.[5] I want to add that if Catherine does not play Cordelia 'officially' during rehearsals, she nonetheless plays the role in other liminal locations, as when Henry discovers her half-naked reciting lines from the play "O dear father, / It is thy own *welfare* that I *care* about" (4.4.24).[6] However, in this case life – the fictive life of the filmic characters – does not imitate art. There is no change in the relationship between Catherine and Henry after this scene. In fact, it seems that the more Catherine explores the role of Cordelia by herself, the more jealous she becomes of Gina, her replacement. On the one hand, Catherine's jealousy – a jealousy which first emerges *before* the rehearsals start[7] – produces self-abjection: we often see her with dishevelled hair and a smeared face, adopting a pose which brings to mind Tom-O-Bedlam's in the original play, as she watches the rehearsals from enclosed narrow spaces. On the other hand, jealousy causes her to shift from a Cordelia or Cordelia-like subject position to the position of Goneril: she eventually poisons Gina (just as Goneril poisons her sister Regan) by having her eat carrots from a dented toxic can (cans containing carrots, left by the Germans, are the survivors' sole food).

As to Gina, the film shows the growth of her intimate relationship with Henry, who willingly acts as her surrogate father. In one scene, for instance, we see them discussing the progress (or lack of progress) of the play, in isolation from the rest of the group, and it is in this context that Charles's stand-offish and arrogant attitude towards the play becomes an issue. Following this conversation, Gina gets Charles (David Calder) to play the part of Gloucester by accepting to 'perform' sex with him. Paradoxically, it is in order to extend to the fictive world of the play her Cordelia-like filial affection toward Henry that she 'sacrifices' herself sexually

[5] I am borrowing from Slavoj Žižek's reinterpretation of Freud and Lacan. To Žižek, the *Père-Jouissance*, the Father-who-enjoys too-much, is "an excessively *present* father [...] who [...] cannot be reduced to the bearer of a symbolic function" (1991, 158).

[6] My emphasis. This is of course Henry's script, his partial rewriting of the play, which shows a daughter's affection toward her father even more than in the 'original' text. In the conflated text of *King Lear* we have "O dear father, / It is thy business that I go about" (4.4.24).

[7] Catherine's jealousy toward Gina emerges for the first time on their first night in the desert. After having one drink too many, they both flirt with Henry, the "serious guy", and they both insist he joins the dance party.

to Charles. It is a gift to Henry, a gift which Henry, unlike other characters who vociferously draw attention to it, including Charles's son Paul (Chris Walker), seems to be unaware of, or complacently ignores. Gina's demeaning 'immolation' exposes, in more senses than one, the 'masochism' of Cordelia's "Love, and be silent" (1.1.61) in the original play.

Gina thus spends the night with Charles, who does not seem to realise how disgusting this sexual experience is for her. It can be argued that Charles, even before entering the play to be Gloucester, has been playing Gloucester all along, in that he continually scolds his "legitimate" son Paul/Edgar, and frustrates all his attempts to relate to him, to "get to know him" – a re-vision *and* inversion of the original. Moreover, in the love-making scene Charles can be seen as the "lusty" Gloucester who admits that "there was good sport at the making" (1.1.22) of his son, in that he exults in his masculine prowess: "I am in good shape, don't you think?". Wrongly assuming that Gina has enjoyed sex, he declares that he has been waiting for this – for love – all his life, which is a kind of Gloucester-like blindness. When Gina, on the point of death, tells him how much she despises him, he hangs himself. When we see him hanging from the ceiling we cannot fail to recall Cordelia, or perhaps, more literally, in Lear's words from the original text, the "poor fool" who's "hang'd" (5.3.304).

As Charles contentedly sleeps, Gina starts reciting the lines from the play in which Cordelia reproaches her sisters' unkindness towards their father, whom they should respect not simply as their father, but also because he is elderly: "Had you not been their father, these white flakes/Did challenge pity of them. Was this a face / To be oppos'd against the warring winds?"(4.7.30-32). As Gina pronounces the words "white hair" (which in the film replace "white flakes"), the camera moves away from her to offer a close-up of *Charles's* white hair, which not only suggests, as the original play does by doubling the plot, that Gloucester is a double of Lear, but that he is his uncanny reverse side, and thus not entirely separable from him. In other words the Lacanian cruel and obscene *Père-Jouissance* emerges once again, and so much so that Gina seems to be unable to carry on with her lines. She keeps on offering variations on the line "Was this a face?": "Is this a face? [...] This is a face [...]. Was this a face ? [...] Was this a face to [...]?". After "Is this a face?", she throws away the script. These lines begin to speak *of* her; they begin to speak *her*; they begin to speak her incredulity toward the fact her "face" could prompt men to debase her. They also perhaps echo *Doctor Faustus*, when Faustus addresses Helen: "Was this the face that launched a thousand ships?" (Scene 12, 81).[8]

---

[8] The reference is to the New Mermaids edition of *Doctor Faustus* (Marlowe 1968), which is based on the A text of the play, with an "Appendix" with scenes from the B text. Of course this is also the line that is chosen by almost all the would-be actors in *Shakespeare in Love*, and its insertion here can be seen as yet another criticism of Hollywood's movie industry.

Taking the cue from Amy Scott Douglass's reading, I have argued that not only is there more than one Cordelia but that each Cordelia is and is *not* Cordelia, as when, for instance, Catherine embraces the plot function of Goneril, or when Gina speaks Cordelia's lines but 'functions' as Edgar, degraded by his father. It should be clear that if each Cordelia also embodies other character functions, then one cannot neatly line them up on each side of the divide as representatives of the opposition European versus American cinema. This not just a critique of Scott Douglass's interpretation. It is to make a more general point about the multifarious and complex ways in which Shakespeare *appears* – and I want this word to encapsulate its connotation of spectrality to the full – in the film.

As Cartelli and Rowe observe, at the outset the film evokes the "generic conventions of 'survival-narrative' films" (2007, 146). This is certainly the case up to the point when Jack (Miles Anderson), an Indiana Jones kind of character, leaves to find help, after giving instructions to his fellow travellers about how to survive in the desert. (Although he sounds so convincing as an explorer, his dead body will be discovered – and this is the irony – not far away from the ghost mining town by Ray [Bruce Davison], who has wandered off in the desert reciting Kent's lines). After an impromptu dance party on the first night, and a period during which the marooned tourists scrupulously follow Jack's instructions and / or while away the time, the "survival narrative" is replaced by some kind of 'survival kit' called *King Lear*. Indeed, from the moment Henry mentions the play and up to its very last few minutes, the film coincides with the performance of *Lear* it includes, a performance, as argued earlier, which is far from being confined to the rehearsal space. Yet, to adapt a theoretical point W.B. Worthen makes in his analysis of Baz Luhrmann's *Romeo+Juliet*, this is not a performance *of* the original text, an unproblematic re-presentation of a fixed and stable entity which somehow pre-exists – and authorizes – the act of performance. It is, instead, "an iteration that necessarily invokes and displaces a textual 'origin'" (1998, 1104). It is not even a performance *of* Henry's re-writing of the text from memory, even if this re-writing already indicates a history of textual revision, transmission and adaptation, and thus the instability of what the performance is supposed to be a performance *of*.[9] That there is no simple univocal correlation between the characters of the film and characters of the play they interpret bears witness to this. I have provided some examples of the lack of a one-to-one correspondence in relation to Catherine, Gina and Charles. Example could multiply. Another interesting example is Ray, who plays Kent during rehearsals but is also forced to take on the role of Albany – the

---

[9] Referring to the Q1 (1608), Q2 (1619) and F (1623) texts of *King Lear* as "stages of revision" in relation to Henry's reconstruction of the text from memory, Mark Thornton Burnett argues that the film "establishes *King Lear* not only as a Shakespearean text that can be adapted but as a body of work for which there is a legitimate precedent for ghostly reinvention [...]. [It] lends itself to desert(ed) appropriation because [...] the text has already been incarnated and reincarnated in spectral versions of itself" (2007, 116-117).

ways in which his wife Liz 'performs' Goneril with Moses/Edmund continually arouses Ray's sexual jealousy. As Mark Thornton Burnett argues, the film "invites and frustrates efforts to fit and classify according to a Shakespearean paradigm" (2007, 118). Cartelli and Rowe make a similar point. They underline that "[t]he characters 'acting' in Levring's film don't all play one Shakespearean role, nor do they ever play all of the role they variously quote, cite, or impersonate" (2007, 158-159).

I now want to give Worthen's theoretical point about performance *not* being a performance *of* a (pre-existing) text a more Derridean inflection, and argue that the *Lear* performance in the desert is a (re-)iteration that retrospectively *produces* the 'original' as a ghostly *indeterminate* thing.[10] I want to suggest that the stripping down of *King Lear* in the desert, a stripping down which parallels the "fantastic" metaphorical – and sometimes literal – striptease of the characters, *does* reveal what Lear on the heath calls the "thing itself" (3.4.104). But this is not a "thing-in-itself", some kind of essential core of meanings which can be simply transposed through performance. It is a spectral "Thing" which inhabits without residing. It inflects the positions of the characters without ever being present as such. (By definition performance puts presence under erasure; it is simultaneously repetition *and* first time). It inflects and affects in a traumatic way, and there is indeed no character in the film who does not find himself/herself in a position of 'dis-adjustment'. It induces the characters to embark on the exploration of roles they didn't know they could play, or play to that extent, and this should be taken both literally and metaphorically. Liz (Janet McTeer), for instance, clearly resents her husband before *King Lear* enters the scene, but it is only by playing Goneril to Edmund during rehearsals and outside rehearsals that she discovers the destructive potential of sexual jealousy. (She willingly accepts to be part of Henry's 'mad' project, so that she gets to play, in her own words, "the real bitch"). But it must be added that this is not a unilateral process. The "Thing", that is, does not pre-determine the position of the characters. As the characters play roles in such a way as to 'fit' their predicament and contingent needs, the play-"Thing" takes on meanings it didn't know it had. (This is the case with the continuous uncanny emergence of King Lear/Gloucester as *Father-Jouissance*).

It is perhaps in the penultimate scene of the film that this spectral "Thing" – the spectro-textuality of *Lear* – makes itself felt most forcefully.[11] We see all

---

[10] I'm referring to Derrida's work on spectrality and, more specifically, to his remarks on the – spectral – "'Thing' Shakespeare", a "Thing" which lends itself to infinite permutations and yet remains irreducible to them (1994, 22). On textuality as "spectro-textuality", see also Calbi (2008, 39-40).

[11] This is in tune with what Cartelli and Rowe argue. They assert that in this scene characters "begin to [...] 'claim' lines or passages associated with their own emerging subject-positions in the film, so that the play begins to *speak – haltingly, in bits and pieces – through them*" (2007, 159; my emphasis).

the remaining characters in a stupefied and yet hieratic pose gathered around a bonfire as they speak lines from *Lear*, mostly from the fifth act. They all look spellbound, but most notably so is Henry / Lear, with his blood-curdling "Howl, howl, howl!" speech. It is worth citing the lines in full:[12]

> *Amanda / the Fool*: This cold night will turn us all to fools and madmen (3.4.77).
> *Liz / Goneril*: By the laws of wars thou needst not answer / An unknown adversary; thou art not vanquish'd, / But cozen'd and beguiled (5.3.151-3).
> *Moses / Edmund*: As you have charged me, I am guilty / And I have done much more (5.3.161-2).
> *Paul / Edgar*: Let's exchange charity (5.3. 165).
> *Moses / Edmund*: 'Tis true. / The wheel has come full circle (5.3. 172-3).
> *Henry / Lear*: Howl, howl, howl, howl! O! you are men of stones: / Had I your tongues and eyes, I'd use them so / That heaven's vault should crack. She's gone for ever. / I know when one is dead, and when one lives; / She's dead as earth (5.3.256).
> *Ray / Kent*: Is this the promised end? (5.3. 262)

The scene shows that the characters tentatively begin to learn to live with ghosts, with their own ghosts *and* the ghost of others, as well as with the 'ghost' of Shakespeare. I'm saying *tentatively* because there is no final solution to the 'disadjustment' we have encountered again and again in the film. For a start, the lines do not form a coherent whole. This is not a dialogue, or at least not entirely. More significantly, the scene starts with the Fool's lines from 3.4 of the conflated text and ends with Kent's poignant rhetorical question, which is a radical undermining of any sense of adequate closure. They are sitting in a circle, and one of the lines – Edmund's – refers to "the wheel" which "is come full circle", which suggests a going back to the beginning and a sense of endless repetition and crisis, a going round in circles with no exit – one can easily imagine the characters carrying on delivering fragments from the play for an indefinite period. (Arguably, the cinematographic version of Peter Brook's *Lear* looms large in this scene). Yet some of the characters speak to one another; or, to be more precise, they address each other through a highly mediated ghostly speech. This is the case, for instance, with Edmund/Moses's "As you have charged me, I'm guilty. And I've done much more", to which Edgar/Paul replies: "Let's exchange charity", which is a way of coming to terms with the hostility they have previously felt toward one another. But Lear's "Howl, howl, howl!" speech interrupts and frustrates any incipient sense of community as the merging of selves through the reciprocal exchange of lines. Perhaps the relation among characters at the end of the film can be described, by referring to Emmanuel Levinas's conception of ethics, as a "relation without relation", a relation which maintains the distance of infinite

---

[12] I'm transcribing the lines as they are spoken in the film. They roughly correspond to the lines in the conflated edition of the play, to which I'm referring in brackets.

separation "without this distance destroying the relation and without this relation destroying the distance" (1969, 41).

It is worth mentioning briefly, by way of conclusion, the spiritual dimension of this scene. It has little to do with forms of spiritual awakening on the part of the characters, if by this one means the discovery of the self's innermost truth as 'contained' in a Shakespearean text. The figure of the circle, which is almost obsessively foregrounded in the penultimate scene, cannot fail to recall the 'linear' journey the tourists undertake at the beginning of the film, a journey which leads them 500 miles off the expected destination. The DVD segmentation of the film into chapters is instructive here., as the first chapter is entitled "Straight line to Nowhere". It is not by chance that the name of the black driver who *fails* to lead them to the expected destination is Moses. This is not to argue that the straight line which leads nowhere is replaced, at the end of the film, by a circle which leads somewhere. It is to suggest that the spiritual dimension, if there is any, has to do with what Derrida calls a "desert-like messianism (without content and without identifiable messiah)" (1994, 28). To Derrida, this messianism "has a curious taste, a taste of death" (*ibidem*, 169). It inscribes some kind of "awaiting without horizon of the wait, awaiting what one does not expect yet or any longer" (*ibidem*, 65). This is relevant to the film. It is precisely because the tourists are beyond any horizon of expectation, because they do no longer *count* on being rescued, that salvation (in all senses) comes. It comes in the form of two truckloads of African people. The tourists look at them with utter incredulity. The African people, two in particular, look back with utter surprise and compassion – ghosts exchanging looks with ghosts.[13] We do not know what happens to the tourists after this final performance. As the African people approach, we have a quick succession of flashbacks, which allows us to have a glimpse of the tourists' former selves while on the coach to this "nowhere". But this performance in the desert makes it clear that their former selves are *more* unsubstantial than the shadows–the theatrical shadows – they have become in the ghost mining town. What remains is Kanana's voice announcing their departure: "They're not here, now they're gone". We are then offered one last panoramic shot of the ghost mining town – the stage of this performance. The tourists are gone but the memory of the performance of *Lear* seems to haunt this location. It bears witness to the fact that the King is alive. The King maybe "a thing of nothing", a spectral "unaccomodated" thing, but this "Thing" re-presents itself in many unexpected guises and survives in the most unpredictable of contexts.

---

[13] In this scene African people are saving white people. This can also be read as an inversion and displacement of the colonialist narrative whereby white people save the 'natives' from themselves; or, more specifically, as a questioning of the colonial *modus operandi* the survival-narrative film does not fail to inscribe.

References

Calbi M. 2008. "Ghosts, Burgers and Drive-Throughs: Billy Morrisette's *Scotland, PA* Adapts *Macbeth*". In *Anglistica*, 12, 1, 39-57 (special issue *The Phantom in the Opera*, De Filippis S. and del Villano B. eds.), available at http://www.anglistica.unior.it/content/phantom-opera (last accessed August 2011).

Cartelli T., Rowe K. 2007. *New Wave Shakespeare on Screen*. Cambridge: Polity Press.

Derrida J. 1994 [1993]. *Specters of Marx. The State of the Debt, the Work of Mourning, and the New International* (trans. Kamuf P.). New York and London: Routledge.

Lévinas E. 1969. *Totality and Infinity* (1961) (trans. Lingis A.). Pittsburgh: Duquesne University Press.

Marlowe C. 1968. *Dr Faustus* (Gill R. ed.). London: Ernest Benn.

Scott-Douglass A. 2003. "Dogme Shakespeare 95: European Cinema, Anti-Hollywood Sentiment, and the Bard". In Burt R. and Boose L.E. (eds.) *Shakespeare the Movie, II: Popularizing the Plays on Film, TV, Video, and DVD*. London and New York, Routledge, 252-264.

Shakespeare W. 1972. *King Lear* (Muir K. ed.). London: Methuen.

Thornton Burnett M. 2007. *Filming Shakespeare in the Global Marketplace*. Houndsmill: Palgrave Macmillan.

Worthen W.B. 1998. "Drama, Performativity, Performance". In *PMLA*, 113, 5, 1093-107.

Žižek S. 1991. *Looking Awry. An Introduction to Jacques Lacan Through Popular Culture*. London and Cambridge (Mass.): MIT Press.

MARIACONCETTA COSTANTINI

Università Gabriele d'Annunzio, Chieti-Pescara

From Scottish Thane to Metal Revenant:
Cross-Media Transpositions of *Macbeth*

Cross-media exchanges are an essential part of our postmodern experience. At the beginning of the twenty-first century we are used to dealing with multimodal and inter-semiotic forms of expression, whose meaning and identity emerge from the interstitial spaces across boundaries. As Jameson suggested (1983, 112), postmodernism is characterized by "the effacement [...] of some key boundaries or separations, most notably the erosion of the older distinction between high culture and so-called mass or popular culture".

Mass mediation has undoubtedly contributed to blurring distinctions. In a world of global communication, most traditions have been deprived of their specificity. The very term "popular" underwent a relevant transformation at the end of the twentieth century, since it lost its class-cultural (i.e. working-class) flavour to become a "highly problematic", "more inclusive" signifier (Hall 1981, 238).

Another key factor of change is the logic of late consumer capitalism. Forms of art and cultural practices are increasingly affected by consumer demands, as shown by the close interaction between artistic experimentation and the media, commodity production and the manipulation of aesthetic standards. The very creativity of youth cultures tends to be controlled by the media industry, which promotes rapid changes in taste, commercializes styles, and makes efforts to re-commodify even the challenges to consumer imperatives.

Within this protean system, the approach to literature has significantly changed. No longer perceived as 'whole' autonomous works, literary texts have been 'cannibalized' by a cultural dynamic based on the dissemination and multiplication of signs. The many transpositions of novels into films and other visual media, the semi-literary status assigned to non-canonical genres, the commodification of classics fostered by cultural revivals, prove the extent to which the old elitist notion of literature has been questioned. Most evident in the case of theatre texts, whose inter-semiotic nature favours "transfers to different media" (Dente and Soncini 2008, 9), this process of assimilation has promoted practices that are largely influential within popular culture and, for this very reason, demand to be assessed.

My paper explores some peculiarities and contradictions of a specific cultural process: the appropriation of the Shakespearean canon by heavy metal bands. More precisely, I will lay the focus on the metal reshaping of one play: *Macbeth*. A source of inspiration for highbrow artists, who have used it to perform trans-media experiments, *Macbeth* has also fed the imagination of youth subcultures. A growing interest in the play has been lately shown by heavy metal bands, who have reworked its gothic elements into provocative music. This phenomenon invites scrutiny, since its poses questions about the permeability of genres, the aporias of popular culture, and the anxieties of a historical conjunction in which literary *revenants* speak in strangely familiar tones.

The idea of spectrality is, indeed, crucial to defining our relations with the Bard. As Garber argues (1987, 176), Shakespeare is first of all a ghostly authorial figure that confronts us with the problem of retroactive canonization, "an imposed, undecidable, but self-chosen attribution of paternity". His dramatic works, moreover, feature a number of spectral apparitions that appeal to the postmodern taste for the uncanny. On a theoretical plane, finally, Shakespeare's authoritative writing adds flesh to the Derridian notion of hauntology, since its constant dissemination into new forms poses the problem of our 'debt' to the past.

In *Spectres of Marx*, Derrida (1991, 115) argues that haunting and inheritance are inextricably linked to each other: heirs are faced with the responsibility of receiving and adapting a legacy marked by ambiguity; and the "debt [that] remains at work" in the process of transmission raises challenging questions. "How will the debt be settled? What interest is due?" (Castricano 2000, 15). Such questions inevitably face descendants who must cope with the idea that "[t]he future can only be for ghosts" (Derrida 1991, 45). Derrida's view of hauntology applies well to literary masterpieces, which move throughout the centuries like spectres. Infinitely 'translated' and adapted, they acquire ever new meanings and, by escaping the logic of confinement, convey an idea of 'disjointed' time that makes us rethink our relation with history.

These effects are enhanced by the cross-media and subcultural circulation of texts, which raises further issues. How destabilizing is the reshaping of the literary canon into non-literary artefacts? What is lost and what is gained in the process of trans-mediation? The topicality of these issues comes to the fore if we consider the 'encounter' between *Macbeth* and heavy metal. The hybrid products resulting from this encounter are doubly spectral. Apart from reviving the horrors of a gothic past to highlight *contemporary* horrors, metal hybrids alter the canonized image of Shakespeare, since they ventriloquize his voice while taking upsettingly innovative forms.

The contemporary predilection for *Macbeth* is hardly surprising. Since the 1960s, the postmodern interest in this play has taken various forms – from musicals to Tanztheater performances, from classical to rock music versions (Scarlini 2001, 62-81; Burt 2007, 379-381). Metal musicians, more specifically, have shown an increasing relish for *Macbeth*, as attested by the recent release of concept albums entirely or partly based on it. In 2000, the Colorado band Jag Panzer transposed the play into a metal album, *Thane to the Throne*. A similar choice was made in 2001 by Shakespeare in Hell, a band from New Orleans.[1] While sweeping the States, the metal craze for the Bard spread elsewhere. In 2003 a German band, Rebellion, released an album in English, *A Tragedy in Steel*, also based on *Macbeth*. In comparison with Jag Panzer, Rebellion carried its experiment a step forward; it inserted passages recited by a narrator and other voices. Such performance elements have been lately emphasized by other bands, such as the Portland-based Metal Shakespeare Company.

Although Shakespeare had 'nourished' metal imagination before,[2] the year 2000 inaugurated a new phase of ransacking and incorporation. The albums released by Jag Panzer and Rebellion, in particular, bear evidence of a mania that calls for attention. Both bands transposed *Macbeth* into a neo-power (or neo-prog) musical style which is, by definition, characterized by a pastiche of forms and models.[3] From a visual perspective, they created hybrid cover pictures by merging traditional, modern and fantasy elements together. A similar effect was achieved at a musical level. Both bands combined old with new musical styles, even though the experiment conducted by Jag Panzer is more extreme (its interludes draw inspiration from a variety of musical traditions, including old Celtic tunes, classical fugues and Spanish melodies).

What the two bands preserved of the original is its quintessential gothicism. A play so deeply concerned with taboo, rife with ghosts and violators of the natural order (Garber 1987, 90-91), could not but captivate metal subculture. Accused of revelling in horrors by their detractors, metal bands have always had a penchant for monstrosity and the macabre. The ghastly images of their covers, the scary make-up and clothes worn at concerts, their devices of aural distortion, and their subversive lyrics, are all forms through which they express an enduring fascination with the dark side of life. As noticed by scholars, however, this collective phenomenon cannot be easily dismissed in terms of youth degeneracy. Precisely because it questions the rules of decent behaviour,

---

[1] Shakespeare in Hell released a 'dual' concept album, *Hecate*. Mainly based on *Macbeth* and *Hamlet*, this album is less interesting than other transpositions, since it consists of verbatim quotations from the plays.

[2] It suffices to remember a classic by Iron Maiden, "The Evil That Men Do" (1988), based on a quotation from *Julius Caesar* (III.2).

[3] The "neo-power" or "neo-prog" phase of heavy metal is marked by a nostalgic return to the music of the past, a passion for pseudo-Tolkienian fantasies, and unwonted combinations with opera and the musical. Although it started in the mid-1990s, this style is still largely influential nowadays (Signorelli 2000, 14-16).

metal creates a counter-discourse that exposes the flaws of the hegemonic system. A rebellious means to express adolescent alienation (Arnett 1996, 17-18), it is also a vehicle for popular emotions imbued with 'political' meanings: namely, a "dissatisfaction with dominant identities and institutions" and "an intense yearning for reconciliation with something more credible" (Walser 1993, xvii).

These emotions account for the metal revival of *Macbeth*. In addition to embodying apocalyptic millennium fears, the revisited play addresses the insecurities of the Bush administration period, in which individuals felt impotent in the face of powerful forces (i.e. terrorism, state-controlled media, capitalistic greed).[4] By reaching into the past, metal bands carry out a search for greater authenticity, a search for the 'natural' freed from the trappings of conventional culture and the artificiality of contemporary life.

Their identification with the Scottish thane is favoured by the latter's condition of vulnerability. An agent but also a victim of anomie, Macbeth is cheated by malign apparitions that articulate his inmost desires and, after yielding to temptation, meets a tragic destiny. Both Jag Panzer and Rebellion emphasize the protagonist's condition of powerlessness and, instead of exalting the final restoration of order, voice a nostalgia for the code of heroism to which he sticks. Less tyrannical than his Shakespearean archetype, the metal Macbeth is 'humanized' as a valorous albeit fallible thane, while his spectral opponents (the witches, the apparitions, and the ghost of Banquo) ruthlessly pave the way to his fall.

Another character that undergoes revision is Lady Macbeth, whose role is drastically reduced. Her loss of stature is well in line with the prevailing gender views of heavy metal. With few exceptions, the genre provides "a spectacle of male potency for a male audience", while women have to identify with masculine constructions of power (Walser 1993, xvi, 108-136). Decidedly male-centred is Jag Panzer's adaptation of Lady Macbeth, who is described as a mere accomplice of her husband. Her subordination is aurally confirmed by the ventriloquizing voice of a male singer, who interprets the very few lines she is assigned. At a visual level, moreover, Lady Macbeth displays two stereotypical female qualities: beauty and fragility. Her slender image in the album cover contrasts with the muscle-bound figure of Macbeth, portrayed in the act of murdering Duncan.

This shift in empowerment is less marked in Rebellion's album. Even though it subscribes to a male notion of heroism, the German band preserves more elements of the play, including the act of persuasion performed by the Lady. The greater visibility conceded to women is also evident in the role played by the witches, whose tempting sentences are repeatedly sung in chorus (the band

---

[4] In Walser's opinion (1993, 161-162), heavy metal flourishes at critical times. His analysis of metal popularity under Reagan's presidency sustains the argument that the new rise of the genre after 2000 has similar 'political' meanings.

recruited women singers to interpret female roles). On the contrary, Jag Panzer replaces the weird sisters' voices with musical interludes or indirectly refers to their presence through other characters. The gender stereotypes exalted by the American band are confirmed by the cover illustration of *Thane to the Throne*, in which the sisters are visibly represented as androgynous beings.

Silenced, 'unsexed' and hyper-connoted as *supernatural*, the witches exercise their power over Macbeth without challenging the superiority of *human* male values. This superiority is obsessively remarked by sound effects. The raucous voices of the singers, their shouts accompanied by loud guitar solos, convey a sense of masculine strength that is heroically connoted.

Jag Panzer emphasizes Macbeth's self-assurance in the whole album. The first lyric, "Thane of Cawdor", opens with the protagonist's proud utterance:

> I am mighty. Death follows in my wake
> None will stand against my sword.

Enhanced by the overdriven voices of the singers, Macbeth's ambition becomes the track's overwhelming emotion. He stands as a potent criminal hero, who displays few traces of the indecision he is attributed in the play.

In *A Tragedy in Steel*, Rebellion adopts similar strategies. The track "Disdaining Fortune" depicts Macbeth as a valiant masculine warrior, who fearlessly confronts the traitors on the battlefield:

> Brothers look down in the valley
> The traitors are strong their numbers are great
> Here we are we won't surrender
> Fight for glory or meet our fate.

Highlighted by metal sounds and powerful voices, his heroism is also attributed to his "defiance of death" in "Die with Harness on Your Back":

> I've been drunken with horror
> Death can't frighten me
> I've long forgotten
> What the feeling of fear might be.

But what is the ultimate meaning of Macbeth's resurgence as metal hero? An answer can be found by examining his relations with male antagonists. The first enemy he encounters is the ghost of his murdered friend Banquo. In the play, Banquo is deceived by Macbeth, who addresses him gently while plotting his murder. In both metal albums, instead, Macbeth complains of being the ghost's victim.

Let us start with Jag Panzer. In "Treachery's Stain", Macbeth accuses Banquo of betrayal, while the chorus justifies his murder with a familiar biblical allusion (Galatians 6: 7-9):

> Banquo, how can thee betray me?
> Banquo, now I must slay thee.
> Reap what you sow, sow what you reap.

Another track, "Spectres of the Past", lays stress on the guilt-ridden murderer, who addresses the phantom in entreating suffering tones:

> He haunts my night. He haunts my day
> Leave my mind, my friend; leave my guilt, I pray.

On its part, Rebellion highlights Macbeth's feelings of "brotherhood"[5] for Banquo and attaches malign connotations to the ghost. Insistently associated with betrayal, Banquo is depicted as the real violator of a bond of friendship, while the victim he haunts is somehow redeemed by suffering.

In a similar way, the battles in which Macbeth engages against his former friends increase his status. In both albums, their fights are presented as *duels* between warriors who, despite their mutual hatred, share communal values like courage and honour. Most interesting, in this regard, is Macbeth's struggle against Macduff. In a track by Rebellion titled "Revenge", their contest is turned into a *dialogic* duel *at a distance* that blurs the boundaries between guilt and innocence. Mutual revenge is also highlighted by Jag Panzer, who represents the final contest between the protagonist and Macduff as an agon between characters endorsing similar values.

Equally noteworthy is the fact that neither album closes with the 'political' figure of Malcolm. This lack shows that what appeals to metal subculture is only the passionate nature of Macbeth and his fellow warriors. Instead of the diplomacy of the lawful heir to the throne, metal bands are drawn to the strength and courage of the Scottish thanes, which they exalt against the limits of their own society.

Vulgar and ideologically confused though it seems, metal music participates in the rock tradition of rebellion and yearning for more authentic values. Its shocking language and icons are proud responses to the deceptions of a global-scale system of control, which is rejected to pursue alternative forms of belonging. In comparison with most youth subcultures, metal is not only resistant to political and economic imperatives.[6] It also feeds on other styles and practices, and subverts their cultural significance through incorporation.

---

[5] "Banquo and I we silently ride/Brothers in arms side by side" ("The Prophecy"); "Banquo my friend soon you'll be dead" ("The Dead Arise").

[6] Metal subculture has survived many censoring campaigns. With a few exceptions (Brown 2007), it also seems to enjoy a significant freedom from the pressures of market laws.

Such mechanisms are evident in Jag Panzer's and Rebellion's adaptations of *Macbeth*. Accentuated by loudness and sound distortion,[7] the idea of *power* on which the play pivots is connotatively altered by the two bands, who lay stress on its ambiguous, politically incorrect meanings. Their noisy celebration of a pre-democratic age, their defiant praise of masculine potency, their lament for the hero's vulnerability in the face of superhuman forces, are all strategies of cross-media transposition of the Renaissance play into musical products that convey strong anti-establishment messages.

Deprived of its highbrow status, the Shakespearean discourse on power is thus appropriated by a postmodern subculture which, in its roaring language, challenges the logic, order, conventional decency and authority of the dominant system. Against them, which give rise to ever new monsters, the two bands resurrect the revenants of the Bard and his fictional creatures. Their aggressive refashioning of the canon is a late form of validation of Derrida's dictum. If "the future can only be for ghosts", why shouldn't *Macbeth* feed the metal hunger for spooky disobedience?

References

Arnett J.J. 1996. *Metal Heads. Heavy Metal Music and Adolescent Alienation*. Boulder (Co.): Westview Press.

Brown A. 2007. "Rethinking the Subcultural Commodity. The Case of Heavy Metal T-Shirt Culture(s)". In Hodkinson P., Deicke W. (eds.) *Youth Cultures. Scenes, Subcultures and Tribes*. New York: Routledge, 63-78.

Burt R. (ed.) 2007. *Shakespeares After Shakespeare. An Encyclopedia of the Bard in Mass Media and Popular Culture*, vol. 1. Westport (Ct), London: Greenwood Press.

Castricano J. 2000. "Cryptomimesis. The Gothic and Jacques Derrida's Ghost Writing". In *Gothic Studies*, 2, 1, 8-22.

Dente C., Soncini S. (eds.) 2008. *Crossing Time and Space. Shakespeare Translations in Present-Day Europe*. Pisa: Edizioni Plus-Pisa University Press.

Derrida J. 1991. *Spectres of Marx: The State of the Debt, the Work of Mourning, and the New International*. New York: Routledge.

Garber M. 1987. *Shakespeare's Ghost Writers. Literature as Uncanny Causality*. New York, London: Methuen.

---

[7] Van Leeuwen (1999, 25) explains that the loudness of hard rock music is meant to strengthen the double bonds between musicians and audience, between public and private space.

Hall S. 1981. "Notes on Deconstructing 'The Popular'". In Samuel R. (ed.) *People's History and Socialist Theory*. London, Boston, Henley: Routledge and Kegan Paul, 227-240.

Jag Panzer. 2000. *Thane to the Throne*. Century Media Records.

Jameson F. 1983. "Postmodernism and Consumer Society". In Hal F. (ed.) *The Anti-Aesthetic. Essays on Postmodern Culture*. Port Townsend (Wa.): Bay Press, 111-125.

Rebellion. 2003. *A Tragedy in Steel*. Drakkar Records.

Scarlini L. (ed.) 2001. *Shakespeare & Shakespeare. Trascrizioni, adattamenti, tradimenti 1965-2000*. Venezia: Marsilio.

Shakespeare in Hell. 2001. *Hecate*. Self-released.

Signorelli L. 2000. *Heavy Metal. I classici*. Firenze, Milano: Giunti.

Van Leeuwen T. 1999. *Speech, Music, Sound*. Basingstoke, London: Palgrave Macmillan.

Walser R. 1993. *Running with the Devil. Power, Gender, and Madness in Heavy Metal Music*. Hanover (NH): Wesleyan University Press.

ARIANNA MAIORANI

Loughborough University, UK

The Stage as a Multimodal Text:
a Proposal for a New Perspective

1. Introduction

Recent research on Internet communication and computer generated environments has revealed a new way of considering the role of space in representational communicative acts (Maiorani 2009a; 2009b). Actually, all communicative acts can be considered as 'representational' in that all events, occurrences, states, etc. have to be encoded and 'represented' in a message in order to be communicated. Multimodality as an analytical method is concerned with the way these representations construe and convey ideology through the use of different semiotic systems.

The specific semiotic condition of Internet communication requires that all communicators assess their presence on line by the very act of construing and representing their identity: this can be made through the creation of a personal web page or of a simple profile to which an e-mail address is attached, or through the creation of more complex representations like avatars in action/interaction based communicative environments and on line worlds like Second Life and Massive Multiplayer Online Role-Playing Games (MMORPG).

Interaction on line takes place not only *through* multimodal representations of meanings, but also *within* representational structures that actually allow semiotic processes to take place. Representational structures, in multimodal analysis, are those *choices* that all semiotic modes offer in order to represent the different relations between the items that are part of our world (in terms of systemic functional linguistics, all *Participants*, including people) and the processes in which they are involved (Kress and van Leeuwen 2006, 42). These structures are necessarily realised in space and time; however, while the time dimension impacts on the development of communication, the space dimension determines the nature itself of representational structures and plays an essential role in the meaning-making practices of communication, especially after the advent of the Internet and the unfolding of new aspects of space as a semiotic rather than a physical dimension.

This research in progress uses the functional framework of multimodal analysis derived from Halliday's Functional Grammar to study space as a semiotic affordance in communicative contexts that involve representation. It is part of a wider research that investigates how the notion of space as a semiotic dimension has developed since the advent of the Internet, and how this has influenced our way to perceive and elaborate messages of all kinds. Focus will be on on testing the applicability of the functional framework of analysis to the stage as a multimodal text that interacts with the verbal text of a play. The research, in this respect, is at an early stage and it therefore deals with the theoretical basis on which multimodal systemic functional analysis of stage sets can be developed. The assumption underlying it is that a stage set, as well as a film set or a game hyper-context, are comparable semiotic affordances that actively contribute to the meanings being made and to the way they are perceived by the public through interaction.

2. Space as a semiotic dimension: the example of hyper-environments

Like a stage or a film set, the sets in which Massive Multiplayer Online Role-Playing Games (hereafter MMORPG) take place are semiotic multimodal contexts designed to enable the activities of the games to take place. Each game, like a play, is based on a pre-existent script and locations are designed precisely to allow players' avatars to enact, like characters, that script and develop their own multimodal narratives. Similarly, a stage play is also based on a pre-existing script but it is the stage arrangement that locates characters in a semiotic dimension where they are enabled to enact the verbal text through a multimodal representation designed by the stage director. Like the script of a MMORPG, the verbal text of a play becomes multimodal when enacted in and environment constructed on stage as a locative Circumstance. In this perspective, it can be argued that it is the different ways of locating characters in relation to specific sets that differentiate the different versions of a play.

Players of a MMORPG construe their digital identities as avatars through a quite structured process. An online game avatar has to be a socially active element within the game and has to communicate with other avatars forming the game on line community. In other words, an avatar must be enabled to play a role. From a systemic functional perspective, as multimodal texts, avatars have to serve three basic communicative functions: representing any kind of experience in the game, establishing interpersonal relationships and being perceptible in a coherent form. These are the same three communicative functions that a character has to serve in order to exist as such both in a play script and on stage. These functions are fulfilled through the realisation of three basic types of meanings, which are realised in all sorts of communicative acts: Experiential (those meanings that account for the representation of any kind of world experience), Interpersonal (those meanings that account for the establishment and development of relationships), and Textual (the enabling meanings that make a text cohere and be perceived as a whole). Each type of meaning is realised by and can be studied through specific structures.

In a multimodal message, meaning is made through the interplay of several semiotic codes. Multimodal systemic functional analysis studies the discourses construed by multimodal messages: it applies the basics of Halliday's Functional Grammar[1] model to all semiotic systems, studying the semiotic interplay between different codes from a functional, unifying perspective.

As shown in Fig. 1, the functional analysis of the process of creation of an avatar highlights a specific textual quality of on line role-playing games: the existence of two levels of multimodal textual creation. The figure takes as an example *The Matrix* film trilogy and its transposition into a MMORPG. It shows how meanings are transmediated from the three semiotic variables construing the Context of Situation in which the original text (the films) develops to the Hyper-Context of Potential Situation which is made available for the game players to develop their own game narratives through the use of avatars.

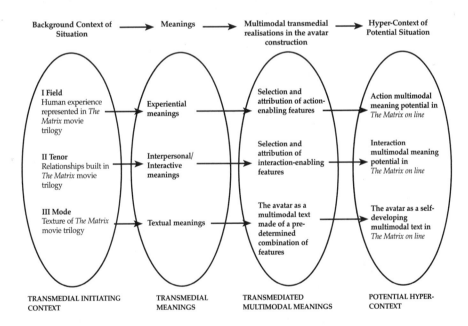

Fig. 1. From text to avatar to Hyper-Context: transmediation of meanings.

---

[1] Halliday's Functional Grammar has been developed for more than thirty years; the most updated version of its model is published in the third edition of *Introduction to Functional Grammar* (2004).

Exactly like a stage script, the Background Context of Situation of a MMORPG provides the guidelines which determine a closed number of combinations of features among which the player will have to choose in order to create a game identity. The physical characteristics of the avatar, as multimodal Textual meanings, will realise it as a text, thus fulfilling the Textual metafunction; the avatar's skills, determined by the choice of physical features as potential multimodal Experiential meanings will allow it to perform specific ranges of actions (or Processes) in the game environment, thus fulfilling the Experiential metafunction; the ability to form alliances with other avatars as potential multimodal Interpersonal meanings, also determined by the choice of physical features and attributes, will allow (or not allow) the avatar to establish social relationships within the game social community.

3. Stage space and meaning transmediation: the three functional dimensions

An important difference must however be taken into consideration when discussing this parallel between MMORPG environments and theatre plays: the avatar as *represented Participant* in an online game and the player as *interactive Participant* inherently overlap, while characters on stage are independent identities. While in MMORPG players are *interactive* and *represented Participants* at the same time, a play, as well as a film, does not allow this overlapping and maintains a clear distinction between two different kinds of *interactive Participants*: the audience and the stage or film director, who do not overlap semiotically with any of the characters on stage. The way the space on stage is experienced by the audience of a play is therefore different from the way a player experiences the hyper-space of an online game: as both interactive and represented Participants, game players are at the same time *within* and *outside* the semiotic space of the game locative Circumstance while the audience of a play, even when addressed directly, is semiotically construed as being external to it. It is the stage director, and not the audience, who mediates the interplay between the characters of a play and the locative Circumstance that will be set on stage.

The director of a play construes a representation of characters that only exist as verbal text until they are inserted in his or her own interpretation of their appropriate set and with what he or she considers to be their appropriate physical appearance. In this perspective, the director has to operate a transmediation of the meanings that construe characters in the script to the multimodal meanings that will construe the characters acting in the semiotic space of the stage set. In order to do so, the director has to provide a functional template for characters played by actors/avatars, characters who may have been originally created by the play's author but who, in order to leave the written page, need to be transmediated into a semiotic space that enables representation in front of an external audience.

Fig. 2 shows a schematic representation of the process through which this transmediation is operated: the functional template for characters will be provided by the director with three functional dimensions that will enable the multimodal representation of the script in the form of a stage performance. These three dimensions will develop in space not as a physical but as a semiotic dimension itself. The interplay between the characters and the semiotic space that enables them to exist will realise a specific version of the play. Exactly as it happens with MMORPG, starting from a Background Context of Situation (the play script), the director will provide a functional dimension enabling representation for all three kinds of meanings: a Textual dimension in the form of a set or locative Circumstance that, like a hyper-environment, will be used as an affordance enabling the performance of the verbal text; an Interaction dimension that will enable interaction between characters as represented Participants within a specific locative Circumstance, and between the characters and the audience as interactive Participant who will perceive action as being represented in that specific location; and an Action dimension, allowing the performance of actions in the provided location.

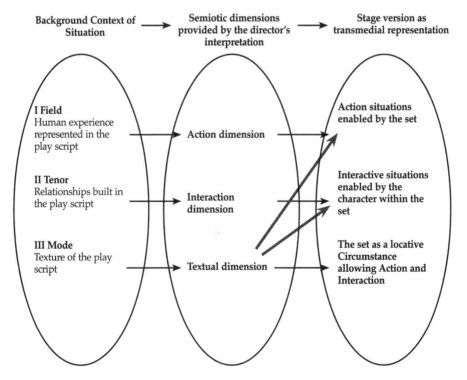

Fig. 2. Transmediation of meanings operated by the director of a stage play.

One of the major problems when studying stage representations and theatre literature in the past is that we know very little about stage conventions that occurred in some major playwrights' times. About the Elizabethan theatre, for example, Dessen (1984, 8-9) says in his seminal work on modern attempts at interpretation:

> A particular disturbing feature of any study of staging and stage practice is that, quite simply, we have no way of knowing how much we do not know. […] when one turns to the stage practice and theatrical conventions of the past, especially in the plays of Shakespeare (which seem to speak to us readily across the wide gap of time), the historian or director or critic or editor can never be sure when we are talking the same language, when we are sharing the same assumptions.

By analysing stage direction through the grid provided by Fig. 2 we would be able to consider all kinds of theatre performances from a homogeneous perspective that is semiotically oriented rather than being concerned with historical reconstruction or reception. This kind of study can tell us how a specific play can work as a performance in relation to the typology of stage available, whose space is considered in its meaning-making value rather than in its physical aspect. The results would help to understand the possible 'agreement' that could be established between text performance and the public in terms of semiotic elaboration of the representation.

Interestingly, also Dessen seems to make a parallel between stage and film sets (1984, 10-11) in terms of space and representation:

> To audiences today, cinema may represent the epitome of realism, yet if we can , for a moment, examine our own assumptions, what is 'real' about sitting in a darkened auditorium, watching figures larger than life (especially in 'close-ups') projected onto a flat screen […] Granted, the camera can provide far more detail for the viewer of cinema or television than could be presented on the Elizabethan stage, but complex events (a long journey, the flight of an arrow) still require selectivity in presentation that enlists our conventional responses, while in any medium exposition of essential information without some form of narrative shorthand proves very cumbersome.

It is precisely by agreeing to and interacting with a specific semiotic dimension proposed by the director that the audience of a play experiences the specific representation of a play.

4. An example of analysis

As a point of departure, this method of analysis will be applied to the Elizabethan stage in relation to a film version of it. The choice is due precisely to the many uncertainties and gaps that still exist in the study of the actual practice of theatre staging in this period, and also to the fascination it has always had on contemporary theatre and on films that try to re-interpret it or to reconstruct it.

Elizabethan theatres were specifically thought to enable a specific kind of theatre in a specific time and for a specific society. The analysis proposed here is at its first stage of development and it is based on the basic permanent structure of stage at that time, which may allow the study of the interplay between performance space as a semiotic dimension and a great number of plays created in that period. The Textual dimension provided for representation by the Elizabethan stage seems to be based on a functional structure that is strictly related to the verbal text and the extent to which this involves or does not involve the audience as interactive Participant. In this perspective, the stage as a locative Circumstance seems to complement the verbal text in terms of 'positioning', construing in interplay with it different degrees of relevance and prominence of characters and actions. This kind of study may make up, at least in part, for the lack of precise information about many aspects of the actual stage practice in this period, as underlined by Bradley (1992, 6) in his research on the process of text staging:

> It is curious that the finest players in Europe, performing at court before the most sophisticated and learned audience England has ever known, left no independent body of theory. They looked over their shoulders at the principles of classical decorum and of the unities of time, place, and action, but for the most part they did otherwise. They spoke of Acts, but they wrote in Scenes. From this innocent habit has descended a long line of scholarly misconception of their working principles.

Interpersonally, the basic structure of the Elizabethan stage appears to be comprised of two well distinguished levels which realise the Interaction dimension: the *gallery*, or 'upper stage', and the *proscenium*, or main stage. The interesting aspect of the *gallery* is that, it seems to be able to serve several functions in relation to the verbal text:

- It may have marked, by differentiating characters and dramatic passages in terms of positioning and prominence, different levels of importance of the characters in a play as well as of the action that took place as the play's plot developed.
- It may have facilitated the development of the rhetorical structure of the play's verbal text by enabling two levels of performance through which action and interaction could be realised and perceived.
- It may have often marked specific moments in the play where the audience was addressed directly and more directly involved in the characters' personal reflections and judgements. In other words, it might have been a good spot for the performance of the Elizabethan *asides*, whose tradition dates back to the classical theatre the Elizabethan playwrights drew upon.
- It seems to divide the stage into two categories of visually textual display theorised by Kress and van Leeuwen (2006, 186 ff.): the 'ideal' area, the upper

part of space where, in visual representation, action and interaction related to supernatural dimensions and ideal environments would conventionally take place; and the 'real' area, where action and interaction related to the 'here and now' of the representation would conventionally take place.

Experientially, the action dimension would be therefore provided with specific portions of stage whose use might have determined, at the same time, the dramatic relevance and typology of each single episode with respect to the whole play.

The *proscenium* was to be perceived three-dimensionally and very much outstretched towards the public, while the *gallery* was to be perspectively perceived more as a bi-dimensional space, almost a visual link, or a multimodal 'bridge', between the multimodal text of the stage performance and the verbal text of the written play script.

Interestingly, this multi-dimensional quality of the semiotic space of the Elizabethan space seems to be very cleverly captured in a filmic transposition of a play based on Shakespeare's *Hamlet, Rosencrantz and Guildenstern are dead* (1966, 1967) by Tom Stoppard. The film, released in 1990, is also directed by Stoppard and highlights a further aspect of the stage as multimodal text complementing the verbal text.

Analysis in the multimodal systemic functional perspective has been performed on various film narrative sequences:[2] one in particular seems to be very useful to show how the method of analysis proposed here works. The sequence in question (1:26:54 to 1:28:22) is the one where Rosencrantz and Guildenstern watch as spectators the audience (the King and Queen) of the puppets' dumb show in Hamlet (where the king and Queen themselves are represented). The play within the play is therefore mirrored once again for the film audience. The analysis of this particular sequence shows that Stoppard provides his film characters with the same structure and functional dimensions of the Elizabethan stage:

- The puppets perform the 'play within the play' in what could be considered a *gallery;* interpersonally they 'speak' both to the King and Queen who are watching them and to Rosencrantz and Guildenstern, as well as to the film audience. The puppets enact in the 'ideal' area of the semiotic space the truth that Hamlet thinks to know after his encounter with his father's ghost and that is not yet revealed in the 'real world'.

---

[2] The term "narrative sequence" is used here as in Maiorani (2011): "by narrative sequence is meant here a coherent micro-episode of the movie script which is realised multimodally in the movie as a specific, distinguishable and narratively relevant sequence. This choice takes into consideration both the point of view of a playwright who structures the plot according to specific and coherent episodes whose progression determines the texture of the script, and the director's point of view, who actually construes their version of the script as a macro-narrative sequence composed by a series of textured narrative sequences".

- The action performed by the puppets in the *gallery* has to do with something that in the play, as well as in the film, cannot yet be proved to be real, a supernatural apparition. However, this dumb show, like an *aside,* provides the audience with an insight into the plot.
- The King and Queen are represented as being on stage on the *proscene,* in the 'real world' of the ongoing play, while the film protagonists, Rosencrantz and Guildenstern, are represented as being the audience. From this position, the Queen and King trigger again the main action (that which develops in the 'here and now' of the film plot) when the dumb show is interrupted. While Rosencrantz and Guildenstern look at them as spectators, the King and Queen are represented as wearing masks, as if the two protagonists, being themselves characters, could not escape their nature and their semiotic dimension by getting outside the ongoing play. When they become involved again in the main action triggered by the sovereigns, thus becoming part of the main stage, the King and Queen do not wear masks anymore.

The whole sequence representation holds on to this multi-dimensional structure, which can be reconstructed and studied through a multimodal functional analysis. Interestingly, at the end of this filmic narrative sequence, when the representation turns to the 'here and now' of the play, Rosencrantz and Guildenstern perform one of their *asides* while getting to the *gallery* provided by the film set. The same thing does Hamlet while emphatically commenting on the outcome of the players' representation.

5. Conclusions

In another interesting sequence of the film (0:12:44 to 0:20:23), the two protagonists meet the company of actors and puppeteers on their way to Elsinore; their leader, who looks very much like Shakespeare himself, immediately addresses them as "an audience", and turns the large carriage where he is travelling with the rest of the company into a rudimental Elizabethan stage that deploys before them. At the beginning of the story, Rosencrantz and Guildenstern find themselves on their way Elsinore and with no memory of their past or of why and how they started their journey; when they first meet the comedians, it is as if Stoppard was trying to remind them that they are nothing more than characters created for the semiotic space of a stage and that they cannot be anything else nor function outside that space. When later, in the filmic narrative sequence analysed above, they become spectators of the audience of the puppet show, Stoppard plays on the border between the characters' dimension in the film and the character's dimension as elements of a play themselves. In the film as well as in the stage play, Rosencrantz and Guildenstern are trapped in their own essence of stage characters by the very nature of stage as a semiotic dimension that is 'apart' from the outside world of the audience. Even as an audience they cannot but watch the very play they belong to and which is thought and realised for the specific structure of the Elizabethan stage.

What this analysis also reveals is that Stoppard seems to test his Elizabethan characters against the semiotic dimension of the film set space, and that he seems to realise the fact that the semiotic dimension of stage is of a specific kind and that if a play and its characters are written for a specific stage as a semiotic affordance they will only work in interplay with that, and that alone. The analysis performed on various narrative sequences of the film confirms that whenever Rosencrantz and Guildenstern move away from the main stage or the gallery reconstructed in the film locations they are lost and without a clue. These results also highlight the fact that while a film, as a multimodal text, develops in different functional dimensions, the stage play develops in functional dimensions whose structure always acknowledges the presence of a public and is therefore always realised in a locative Circumstance which can not enclose the action and interaction in its entirety. The semiotic space of the stage is always *apart from* and *aware of* the semiotic space of the audience. If applied to other typologies of stage structure, this kind of analysis may reveal interesting patterns both in the way a single play has been staged in different historical periods and in the way stage conventions have evolved in time according to the development of theatre literature and technical affordances.

References

Bradley D. 1992. *From Text to Performance in the Elizabethan Theatre. Preparing the Play for the Stage.* Cambridge-New York: Cambridge University Press.

Dessen A.C. 1984, *Elizabethan Stage Conventions and Modern Interpreters.* Cambridge-New York: Cambridge University Press.

Halliday M.A.K. 2004. *An Introduction to Functional Grammar*, 3rd edition. London: Arnold.

Kress G. and van Leeuwen T. 2006. *Reading Images. The Grammar of Visual Design*, 2nd edition. London and New York: Palgrave.

Maiorani A. 2009a. "Developing the Metafunctional Framework to Analyse the Multimodal Hypertextual Identity Construction: *The Lord of the Rings* from Page to MMORPG". In Ventola E., Moya Guijarro A.J. (eds.), *The World Told and the World Shown.* London: Palgrave, 220-241.

Maiorani A. 2009b. *The Matrix Phenomenon. A Linguistic and Multimodal Analysis.* Saarbrücken: VDM Verlag Dr Müller.

Maiorani A. 2011. "Reading Movies as Interactive Messages: A Proposal for a New Method of Analysis". In *Semiotica* 187, 167-188.

ARIANNA MARMO

Università Roma Tre

A Room of One's Own:
Ophelia's Darkroom in Almereyda's *Hamlet 2000*

*H*amlet is one of the best-known and most performed texts in the western culture, not only on stage but also on screen. Its modernity allows directors to play with the play creating original renditions and different interpretations. In the last years many transpositions of *Hamlet* have been performed on screen, contributing to increase Shakespeare's popularity and cultural influence. As Douglas Lanier pointed out (2002, 162), "one overarching aim of recent Shakespeare films has been to definitively establish the screen image [...] as the principal vehicle for sustaining Shakespeare's cultural authority in a post theatrical, post literary age".

Seen from this perspective, Almereyda's *Hamlet 2000* shows how a contemporary adaptation can fully exploit its power to enhance Shakespearean poetry, "keeping all spoken dialogue as written by Shakespeare but set within and energized by a contemporary context" (Almereyda 2000, ix). As the title highlights, this *Hamlet* is a post-modern, challenging remake of the tragedy located in the 'rotten' city of New York, where Elsinore is transformed into the Denmark Corporation, Claudius his chief executive officer, Hamlet an aspiring filmmaker, and Ophelia a photographer. In a huge and claustrophobic space such as New York, Ophelia and Hamlet struggle to find a room where their identity and artistic creativity can survive. While Hamlet, who is always engaged to cut and paste sketches of his own daily living and past like in a video diary, promotes nostalgia by exploiting the editing technique, Ophelia instead takes refuge in her apartment's dark room, a place connected with her art, femininity and death.

This paper mainly focuses on the representation of Ophelia as a contemporary young photographer whose point of view helps to emphasize the contrast between to be and to seem, or in Almereyda's perspective, to blow out of proportion the gap between a real, genuine world, and a fake, fairy-like one. As showing the relevance of the heroine's artistic activity, I will also take into consideration the girl's defence of her private space (as a metaphor for chastity and self-fulfilment) against the spying network surrounding her.

Ophelia's mental breakdown and her suicide assume, then, some interesting connotations, since they represent her failure to resist both her fatherly authority and the 'mousetrap' created by the society she lives in.

The first low-angle shots filmed from the rear-window of Claudius's limousine show New York with its neon-lit buildings, and screens. Since the beginning, the city appears as "a complex character in the film [...] with its contradictions of beauty and squalor" (Mitchell 2000). With its constant presence all over the 106-minute-long film the Big Apple is the leading feature: the camera, in fact, never breaks free from Manhattan's hold until Hamlet's ride to Ophelia's funeral, and the characters are never exposed to a real landscape until they arrive at the girl's grave (Crow 2003, 190).[1] This is more than casual irony: Almereyda seems to consider Ophelia as the turnover element who represents nature in contrast to the fake human constructions. In motivating his decision to shoot in New York, the director affirms that this is "another way to touch the core of Hamlet's anguish, to recognize the frailty of spiritual values in a material world, and to get a whiff of something rotten in Denmark on the threshold of our self-congratulatory new century" (Almereyda, 2000, xi). Manhattan represents the linchpin of globalized capitalism, a place where the inter-be status expressed by the Buddist Monk Thich Nhat Hanh's video clip (Guntner 2007, 127)[2] is only predicted but not realized, since every human interaction is sifted by technological devices such as answer machines, wires, closed-circuit cameras, and screens. As Mark Thornton Burnett remarked (2003, 49), the city seems the "ideal breeding ground for psychotic neuroses" as we will see in the Guggenheim Museum where Ophelia gets mad. Both she and Hamlet are the fallen protagonists who fight to resist the alienation the society imposed on them, but without obtaining any positive fulfilment. In such a surrounding the two lovers try to create a private space of their own to escape from reality: Hamlet finds shelter in his projection booth, Ophelia in her photographic darkroom.

Almereyda satisfies the 21st century voyeuristic pleasure by playing with open and closed spaces: Polonius lives in a glasshouse with transparent overhead walkways; Hamlet dwells at the Elsinore Hotel, a skyscraper full of closed-circuit cameras, and glass windows. Ophelia, instead, lives in a rundown building full of thrift shop paintings and Polaroid photos where she set up a darkroom. This Ophelia seems to be a fairy tale character: represented as a watery, flower-dressed teenager, she symbolises the uncontaminated, authentic and uncorrupted world in contrast with the infected, rank one with whom Hamlet copes. Like his uncle and his mother, Hamlet goes around New York in

---

[1] See also Cartmell (2004, 209-215).
[2] See also Rowe (2003, 37-55), and Burt (2003, 265-303).

a Limousine, while Ophelia escapes the conventional urban means of transport by riding a bicycle, and searching for a contact with a real, open-air landscape.

Ophelia's artistic attitude (she sketches a drawing of a waterfall on a paper she will give to Hamlet in the first scene of the film; she takes picture, and she gets mad in the Guggenheim Museum) finds expression in a space of her own, where she can reconcile herself with her intimacy, femininity and her memories: the darkroom. In here the girl can develop her photos: unlike Hamlet, Ophelia refuses digitalised technologies; she prefers to reproduce reality, and not transform it (Worthen, 2006, 293). By taking pictures with both a 35 mm camera and a Polaroid instant camera instead of using digital goods, Ophelia produces nostalgia of *the* past on the audience, and at the same time she experiences melancholy of *her own* past. What emerges from Almereyda's view of Ophelia is that she likes photography because she needs to frame reality, to gather and capture her experiences and her beloved. Through the pictures she can express her point of view of the world, and most importantly she can give her own interpretation of it. If photography is, according to Susan Sontag (1978, 9), a predatory act and the conquest of a space, by taking pictures Ophelia also takes possession of the world surrounding her. Through this act of appropriation of the other as a photographic subject she takes her small revenge on those who attempt to control and manage her life. Photography is the only true independence she possesses, it is her only voice. When she takes photos she is not the subject of someone else, but she chooses her 'subject' and frames it.

It is remarkable that the darkroom also creates a specifically modern association with water (Jones 2003, 116) as the tragic symbol of the missing maternal womb, and it connected with Ophelia's death. Almereyda gives an idea of her suicidal thoughts by showing her end as a recurrent flashforward (Hodgdon 2006, 108). In this adaptation, Ophelia is very often represented as a watery figure: since the beginning, she is filmed while walking along the border of the fountain where she will drown herself like a tightrope walker. The same scenery is repeated when she is in Claudius's indoor swimming pool. This reiterated clue reinforces the perception of Ophelia's imbalance, frailty and shakiness, as well as her proximity to drowning. While standing in front of the pool she fancies jumping into the water. The camera, located in the pool, shoots her from below the water level, standing and gazing into it. Besides her, due to the watery effect of the pool rim, we can see three crosses which foresee her death. The last high-angle shot framing Ophelia, whose function is to look down on the subject who is inevitably swallowed up by the setting, shows her body lying on the water surface surrounded by Hamlet's letters. This shot is briefly anticipated by the news reported by Gertrude's voice-over about the girl's death. It is outstanding that Gertrude's lyrical description of Ophelia's drowning is here reduced to just two words: "drowned, drowned" (Almereyda 2000, 104), pronounced where the queen is in the frame. By cutting her lines,

Almereyda attributes the dramatic core of the scene to the visual power rather than to the poetical language. In fact, using only 40% of the play lines he challenges the primacy of poetic description (Jackson 2007, 27):[3] Shakespearean language, according to him, is "lavish enough", and this is the reason why he wanted "images to keep pace with words, or outstrip them" (Almereyda 2000, vii). As a result of this contraction the visual elements create an overwhelming alternative reality to Shakespearean poetry without damaging the original power of the text.

As we have seen, in this adaptation the images seem to take over the language: the director plays with frames, colours, and points of view as well as Shakespeare plays with words. The result is the uncertainty of what is real and present, what is past, recorded or actually lived, and what is anticipated in the future. We do not exactly know what happens between Hamlet and Ophelia, for instance. We can just see them kissing and use our imagination according to what Almereyda hints. The director never openly shows the two lovers' sexual relationship, but he alludes to it in Hamlet's video recording. In this short footage where Ophelia appears for the first time, her pale face and white shirt matches with the sheets of the bed where she lies on. But from this scene to the sequence filmed in the Guggenheim Museum, Ophelia will only wear red clothes which recall the safety light of her darkroom. The persistent use of this colour could be interpreted as Almereyda's allusion to Ophelia's sexual engagement and her violated chastity. Every jacket and skirt she wears, indeed, is stamped with red flowers – probably roses in honour of this "rose of May", as Laertes used to call her – which supposedly are the other subliminal messages implying Ophelia's defloration. Even her spiral-design box containing Hamlet's love letters is red. This apparently insignificant detail is very relevant, though: it suggests not only a tribute to Hitchcock's *Vertigo*[4], but it also anticipates the Guggenheim Museum's spiral outline that will appear shortly after as the ideal location for filming Ophelia's madness.

The red clothes the girl wears also create an association with Grimm Brothers' heroine, Little Red Riding Hood. Almereyda reinforces the linkage with this fairy tale in the scene of Polonius's lesson about chastity: his admonitions such as "Think yourself a baby", "Be something scanter of your maiden presence", and "Do not believe his vows, for they are brokers" (Shakespeare 2006, 198-200) echo Little Red Riding Hood's mother's speech about protecting her daughter from the danger of the wolf's seduction. In his psychoanalytic study of this fairy tales, Bruno Bettelheim (1976, 173) pointed out that "Little Red Riding Hood's danger

---

[3] See also Hindle (2007, 198).

[4] I refer to the playbill of the film. Furthermore, in this film Judy Barton (Kim Novak) attempts to drown herself like Ophelia, but she is saved by John Ferguson (James Stewart). On the connection between Hitchcock's *Vertigo* and *Hamlet* see Vest (1989, 1-9).

is her budding sexuality, for which she is not yet emotionally mature enough". The same idea could be expressed about Ophelia. As she is tempted by Hamlet's affection so Little Red Riding Hood is tempted by the wolf "to look for flowers [...] and to go deeper and deeper into the wood" (Bettelheim 1976, 171). Ophelia's hand hovering the diorama's glass fronted box featuring a view of a gravel road that disappears into a dim forest glade during Polonius' lesson about chastity, creates a strong association between the heroine and the little girl in the Grimm Brothers' fairy tale. To emphasize Ophelia's childlike condition, Almereyda makes Polonius give her some birthday balloons; and again, after ordering her not to "give words or talk with the Lord Hamlet" (Shakespeare, 2006, 201), Polonius grabs her foot and ties her unlaced sneaker, as to submit her to his authority.

Although these elements induce to think that Almereyda's treatment of Ophelia focuses exclusively on her childlike state, some other aspects show instead the director's concern about presenting her as a rebel girl, as far as the character itself allows. According to Barbara Hodgdon (2006, 107), Almereyda's Ophelia is "doubly subjected to the vision of others – within the narrative, to her father, her brother, and Hamlet, as well as by cinematic techniques of *mise-en-scène*, framing and editing". However, I suggest that her mostly silent performance and her fleeting appearance on screen are charged with the visual support of her body language, which shows us a girl fighting for her independence. Since the first shot, in fact, she physically shows disobedience to the fatherly authority: after Claudius's conference, Polonius and Laertes try to keep her far from Hamlet, but she sneaks away to find her lover, and he bravely kisses her lips just in front of them. One more example is when Polonius orders her to refuse Hamlet's attentions: like a contemporary teenager who rejects parental reproaches but who unwillingly has to obey, Ophelia replies by sighing and rolling her eyes.

Besides the fact that she lives alone like an adult and can develop her photos in a place where she fulfils her artistic expression and possibly her sexual ripeness, Almereyda's Ophelia is a heroine who tries her best to fight for her freedom, and to escape male figures who attempt to manipulate her. Even when her father bugs her with a wiretap to spy on Hamlet's mad conduct she tries to react to it. She realizes that those wires surrounding her body symbolize the artificial net she has been trapped in. However, only when Hamlet finds out the trick and insults her for lying she understands she is "the more deceived" (Shakespeare, 2006, 290). Her deceit does not exclusively depend on Hamlet's contradictory profession of love, but also on her subdued condition. I guess these two deceits are the most poignant reasons for her disillusionment and her progressive fall into madness.

As I have anticipated above, the "mad scene" is set in the Guggenheim Museum, whose whirling architecture fits the heroine's puzzled perception of reality. Once there, Ophelia shouts one head's off instead of singing bawdy ballads as written by Shakespeare. This is another relevant textual omission which has been powerfully replaced by a much more impressive visual and auditory action. Her screams echoes all over the building and embarrasses Gertrude who is having a party on the level below. This means that Ophelia is not just a "document in madness" (Shakespeare, 2006, 388), but a document in rebellion: the scream is her last attempt to give voice to her subjection, and even though Claudius tries to shut her up covering her mouth, she struggles to escape the bodyguards' grip, "moving her body like liquid within the space" (Hodgdon 2006, 109). After being dragged down the ramp, exhausted, Ophelia meets Laertes: differing from Shakespeare's text, she does not scatter real flowers, but Polaroid representing flowers. Since she gets rid of her photos, as she previously did when she burned down and dropped Hamlet's Polaroid in the bathroom sink after the "nunnery scene", she explicitly denies her own art. As a sign of her annihilation, she rejects the photographs, whose function is promoting nostalgia, in the very moment in which she offers Laertes a snapshot depicting rosemary "for remembrance", asking him to be remembered.

Photography, this bizarre medium that produces madness, according to Roland Barthes (Barthes 1982), is Ophelia's *memento mori:* she strews pictures as they were real flowers on her own grave. This art that constituted her form of emancipation and symbolized her ability of creation and of re-producing reality cannot reunify her divided self or fill her vacuum (Laing 1990, 195). She can only reject any other form of simulacra, since she realizes she is unable to distinguish between reality and appearance. And not by chance she gets mad in the Solomon Guggenheim Museum planned by Frank Lloyd Wright, one of the promoters of the organic architecture. Aiming at celebrating a symbiotic harmony between the human and natural world, this building seems to represent another simulacrum that overcomes Ophelia. Her last, extreme refusal of fake imitations of nature and all the icons surrounding her – the diorama representing the wood, the stamped flowers on her clothes, the Polaroid photos standing for true rosemary and rue, and the artificial waterfall where she drowns herself – fits Almereyda's tragic vision of 21st century epitomized by the Big 'rotten' Apple.

References

Almereyda M. 2000. *William Shakespeare's* Hamlet: *A Screenplay Adaptation.* London: Faber &Faber.

Barthes R. 1982. *Camera lucida* (transl. by Howard R.). London: Jonathan Cape.

Bettelheim B. 1976. *The Uses of Enchantment: The Meaning and Importance of Fairy Tales.* London: Penguin.

Burnett M.T. 2003. "To Hear and See the Matter: Communicating Technology in Michael Almereyda's Hamlet 2000". In *Cinema Journal*, 42, 3 (Spring), 48-69.

Burt R. 2003. "Shakespeare and Asia in Postdiasporic Cinemas: Spin-offs and Citations of the Plays from Bollywood to Hollywood". In Burt R., Boose L.E. (eds.) *Shakespeare, the Movie II*. London and New York: Routledge, 265-303.

Cartmell D. 2004. "Hamlet in 2000: Michael Almereyda's City Comedy". In Mehl D., Stock A., Zwierlein A.J. (eds.) *Plotting Early Modern London*. London: Ashgate, 209-215.

Crow S. 2003. *At the Shakespeare Cineplex*. Athens: Ohio University Press.

Guntner J.L. 2007. "Hamlet, Macbeth and King Lear on Film". In Jackson R. (ed.) *The Cambridge Companion to Shakespeare on Film*. Cambridge: Cambridge University Press, 120-140.

Hindle M. 2007. *Studying Shakespeare on Film*. London: Palgrave Macmillan.

Hodgdon B. 2006. "Spectacular Bodies: Acting + Cinema + Shakespeare". In Henderson D.E. (ed.) *A Concise Companion to Shakespeare on Screen*. Malden and Oxford: Blackwell, 96-111.

Jackson R. 2007. "From Play-script to Screenplay". In Jackson R. (ed.) *The Cambridge Companion to Shakespeare on Film*. Cambridge: Cambridge University Press, 15-34.

Jones M. 2003. *Shakespeare's Culture in Modern Performance*. New York: Palgrave Macmillan.

Laing R.D. 1990. *The Divided Self*. London: Penguin Books.

Lanier D.M. 2002. "Shakescorp *Noir*". In *Shakespeare Quarterly*, 53, 2 (Summer), 157-180.

Mitchell E. 2000. "A Simpler Melancholy". In *New York Times on line*, May 12th, available at http://www.nytimes.com/2000/05/12/movies/film-review-a-simpler-melancholy.html?src=pm (last accessed August 2011).

Rowe K. 2003. "*Remember Me*: Technologies of Memory in Michael Almereyda's *Hamlet*". In Burt R., Boose L.E. (eds.) *Shakespeare, the Movie II*. London and New York: Routledge, 37-55.

Shakespeare W. 2006. *Hamlet*. London: The Arden Shakespeare.

Sontag S. 1978. *On Photography*. London: Penguin Books.

Vest J. 1989. "Reflections of Ophelia (and of *Hamlet*) in Alfred Hitchcock's *Vertigo*". In *The Journal of the Midwest Modern Language Association*, 22, 1 (Spring), 1-9.

Worthen W.B. 2006. "Fond Records: Remembering Theatre in the Digital Age". In Holland P. (ed.) *Shakespeare, Memory and Performance*. Cambridge: Cambridge University Press, 281-304.

Section 8
Visual and Media Studies

SERENA GUARRACINO

Università di Napoli L'Orientale

William Kentridge's Opera Stagings:
Trans-coding the Western Musical Canon

This essay offers a reading of William Kentridge's work on Western opera, to explore the ways the South African artist and video-maker has trans-coded the Western musical canon into contemporary visual arts. My contention is that the disruptive effect of his experimentations does not remain confined to the formal contamination of the aural with the visual, the performative with the technological; on the contrary, Kentridge's may be termed an actual 'appropriation' of opera from the point of view – or, we may say with Adriana Cavarero, "point of hearing" (2005, 121) – of postcoloniality, where opera can be shaped as a space of resistance for the postcolonial artist.

Opera has been traditionally identified with the voice of colonial Europe, as Edward Said famously argued in his analysis of Verdi's *Aida* (1993, 111-131); yet, recent studies have also explored opera's potential for disrupting Western hegemonic discourses. These studies have especially focused on gender representation, given the centrality of women characters on the operatic stage (see Clément 1989; Locke 1995; McClary 1997). Kentridge's trans-codification of opera, in particular of Mozart's 1791 *Magic Flute*, moves in the same direction: here women's voices are embedded into a visual frame that shapes them as alternative spaces of utterance where the artist's critique to the Western colonial enterprise is articulated. Through these women other, less familiar voices come to be heard, voices that interrupt the narrative of Western Enlightenment (of which the *Magic Flute* partakes) to expose the stories silenced by European history.

Kentridge has acquired world-wide renown as director of short films, including a series titled "Drawings for Projection" produced between 1989 and 1999. These films are made out of the drawing and redrawing of the same few charcoal sketches: the trace of the pencil, drawn and then erased but never completely removed, materializes the workings of memory and forgetting, a theme directly connected, in his early films, to the heritage of apartheid (see Alemani 2006, 8-15). More recently, the artist has staged and directed both theatrical pieces and operas, from Monteverdi's *Il ritorno di Ulisse in Patria* to the *Magic Flute*.[1] His effort can be placed in the context of a new interest in so-called 'concept' opera staging, which avoids traditional settings to explore the potential of operatic music and plots when transcoded into a different set of references articulated around a single visual theme – a 'concept'. Among the directors engaging in this practice Graham Vick, who has reinterpreted Violetta from Verdi's *Traviata* as a Lady Diana *ante litteram*, was both acclaimed and criticized for its perversion of Verdi's masterpiece; while Peter Sellars, one of Edward Said's favourite opera directors, has staged Mozart's three Italian operas (*Le nozze di Figaro, Don Giovanni,* and *Così fan tutte*) as a harsh commentary on contemporary gender politics.[2]

These stagings question the supposed separation of classical music from contemporary issues; indeed, they show that a trans-codification of opera through a displacement of its traditional references may create a space where the representation of today's power relations may be elaborated and deconstructed. These efforts are in tune with what Said has notoriously termed the transgressive power of music:

> [T]he transgressive element in music is its nomadic ability to attach itself to, and become a part of, social formations, to vary its articulations and rhetoric depending on the occasion as well as the audience, plus the power and the gender situations in which it takes place (Said 1991, 70).

As opera audiences change – and thin down remarkably – operatic productions need to bring the genre closer to contemporary issues, divesting it of the elitist aura that has been one of its main characteristics until the end of the twentieth century.

One of the main features of concept opera stagings is to elaborate on the interplay among the multiple codes at work in operatic performance – the musical, instrumental and vocal, the visual, the strictly performative, which are played in counterpoint with one another. As characters move along known musical lines in an environment completely foreign to what audiences have been used to, a number of fractures and fissures emerge in the apparently homogeneous pattern of operatic representation to perform what Lawrence Kramer, borrowing from Jacques Derrida, calls opera's *différance* (2000, 202).

Kentridge's work on *The Magic Flute* includes not only the 2005 staging of the opera, which opened in Brussels and toured theatres until 2007, but also preparatory drawings, aqua-tint, dry-point and projections. It also features

---

[1] Kentridge's work on Monteverdi's opera is beyond the scope of this essay; an exhaustive survey of the staging and related works can be found in Pasini (2008).

[2] Vick's *Traviata* was staged at the Arena di Verona in 2004; while Sellars' Mozartian operas have been staged around the world since 1989, before being published on DVD in 2005.

two installations, *Preparing the Flute* (2005) and *Black Box/Chambre Noire* (2006), consisting in a model theatre where animations from the *Flute* are integrated in a choreography of computer-operated wooden puppets on the soundtrack of themes from the opera, reworked and integrated with original music. In all these works, which constitute an ongoing dialogue with Mozart's opera, the artist interprets the *Flute* in the light of the his experience as a white South African: opera thus becomes a vehicle for his discontent against the white Western culture at the roots of colonial violence (including, but not limited to, apartheid), a culture which nonetheless he cannot discard altogether.[3]

The visual theme that dominates Kentridge's concept is represented by white-on-black animations created through the negative image of drawings in black charcoal on white paper. The visual effect of these animations recalls blackboard drawings, but it is actually based on the use of the camera, to which the graphic element of the negative image is linked. This dialogue between light and darkness is central to Mozart's opera, which sees the mage Sarastro and his Temple of the Sun clashing against the Queen of the Night. The aural language of the opera is thus trans-coded by Kentridge into a visual element, shaping the overall setting of the opera. As the artist writes in his notes on the production, "the metaphor and image of the camera point outwards to decisions about staging and costume. We would have to move from the eighteenth century to the nineteenth century" (2007, 64). It follows that Mozart's Masonic opera, which extols Enlightenment ideals of human reason and education for the creation of an ideal society, is suddenly displaced to an unspecified location in the African continent during the golden age of European empires.[4]

The camera joins the blackboard as the two main visual references in Kentridge's concept, both linked to the theme of power relations and colonial history. The camera was a pivotal instrument of imperial power, used to appropriate the 'virgin lands' and all they included, from landscape to humans and animals. On the other hand, the blackboard is the teacher's instrument and characterizes Sarastro, magician and mentor, who voices the Enlightenment ideals the composer embedded in his opera. Yet, as Kentridge writes, "post-Enlightenment thinking has made us wary of philosopher autocrats. The enforced imparting of their wisdom has had unintended but calamitous consequences throughout history, [...] all through the colonial era, and into our own centuries" (2007, 58). Moved forward in colonial times, Sarastro cannot remain the trustworthy, illuminated sage Mozart portrayed through a diatonic, simple and 'manly' style, in stark contrast with the highly embellished, minor-mode characterized Queen of the Night.

---

[3] All the artworks related to Kentridge's work on Mozart's *Magic Flute* are included in Law-Viljoen (2007).

[4] For the relationship between Mozart's opera and Enlightenment values see Subotnik (1991).

Traditional gender and power relations are put into question by Kentridge's point of hearing, which transcodes Mozart's set of values in a more troubled and contested system. Sarastro's teachings become an Althusserian apparatus, the place where power and knowledge are interdependently created: on a stage that often turns into a giant blackboard, Sarastro teaches to his all-male congregation to "beware of women" (Schikaneder 1956, 27). As Kentridge writes,

> the Priests are [...] not so much eighteenth-century Masons as members of an exclusive society, a kind of Royal Geographic Society. The Queen of the Night and the Three Ladies are not exactly suffragettes, but certainly they feel their exclusion from the society in which the events of the opera play out (2007, 64).

At the end of the opera, one woman will eventually be allowed in Sarastro's congregation: Pamina, the Queen of the Night's daughter. Yet, in order to prepare her for the task, Sarastro takes her away from her mother, to preserve his only female pupil from what he believes (and makes the audience believe) is her mother's negative influence. Throughout the opera, Sarastro shapes the other characters's stories: even the event that triggers the whole plot, the Queen of the Night's plan to have Prince Tamino rescue Pamina from captivity, actually serves Sarastro's end of having the two fall in love with each other, and allow Pamina, duly tamed and married to Tamino, enter the "hallowed halls" of his Temple of the Sun.

As recent studies on opera and gender have shown, the marginal position of women in operatic imaginary grants them an agency that threatens the power of the white male leader (see Locke 1995, 65). In Kentridge's interpretation, both Pamina and the Queen of the Night, the daughter and the mother, function as privileged access points to an alternative interpretation of Mozart's opera, where the female voice, contrasting Sarastro's deeply male bass as well as prince Tamino's heroic tenor, becomes a marginal yet privileged space of utterance. It is an utterance that can find expression both in the extraordinary vocal flights boasted by the Queen of the Night and in Pamina's more subdued lyricism, and even in her silence.

This dynamics is particularly evident in Kentridge's rendition of scene 12, act 2 of the opera. Pamina has just escaped rape and blackmail by the Moor Monostatos thanks to Sarastro's intervention; to explain why he is not punishing the offender, Sarastro sings the powerful aria "In diesen heil'gen Hallen", "in these hallowed halls", where he praises the virtues of patience and forgiveness – a subject quite resonant of South African post-apartheid themes. Yet, as Sarastro sings "within these hallowed walls, / Where human loves the human, / No traitor can lurk, / Because one forgives the enemy" (Schikaneder 1956, 39), Robert Schumann's film *Rhinoceros Hunting in German East Africa* (1910-11) reels in the background, showing two early 20th century hunters chasing and killing a twin-horned African White rhino and posing for the camera with its carcass.

Pamina, following Mozart's score, stays silent throughout the whole aria, Sarastro's hand firmly on her shoulder. Kentridge comments: "how long and how firmly should this hand be on her shoulder? The shift from the hand being reassuring to its being predatory is a matter of a second, or the slightest resistance from Pamina's shoulder" (2007, 76). The reel with the rhino hunt makes the potential violence in this scene resonant: Pamina's silence is also the rhino's, as it is ruthlessly killed by European colonizers animated by the same humanist principles Sarastro is voicing in his aria.

The scene also recurs in *Black box/Chambre noire*, which explores, outside the strictures of opera plot and theatre devices, the research the artist conducted, while working on the *Magic Flute*, on German colonialism in Africa. In particular, his researches focused on the massacre of the Herero people in what today is Namibia by the German army led by general von Trotha between 1904 and 1907, one of the first examples of systematic ethnic cleansing by a European power and to some scholars a pioneer of the Holocaust (see Stratton 2008, 68 ff.). In the version of the aforementioned scene between Pamina and Sarastro as transcoded into the installation format of *Black Box*, the characters are not there anymore, but Sarastro's voice remains as soundtrack for the rhino hunt: it is not difficult, at this point, to identify these hunters with Sarastro himself, thus shedding a chilling light on his proclamation of Enlightenment ideals of human brotherhood. If in Sarastro's world "the human loves the human" (Schikaneder 1956, 39), the violence over the helpless body of the rhino reminds the audience of the crude fact that, in Mozart's own time and for some centuries afterwards, some human beings (including women) were considered less than human, with the consequence that violence could be exerted on them with little or no moral consequence.

Yet, Kentridge's questioning of the superiority of European reason as developed during the Enlightenment era does not reinstate its binary dialectic by simply substituting one term for another (the female for the male, the subaltern for the hegemonic). The Queen of the Night is not an unquestionably positive force, as in Graham Vick's 2005 staging of the *Flute* (which was inspired by Ketridge's). Kentridge does not endorse the Queen's quest for revenge any more than he supports Sarastro's hegemonic worldview: retribution is just another form of violence, whose resonance for post-apartheid South Africa, and the African postcolonies in general, is too broad and complex to be analyzed here.[5] As backdrop for the Queen's revenge aria, where she voices all her rage for having been excluded by male hegemony (and deprived of her own daughter),

---

[5] The experiment of the Truth and Reconciliation Commission was based on the rejection of the feasibility of retribution practices in the South African context; this position has been clearly spelled out by TRC Chairman Archbishop Desmond Tutu in the title of his memoir on the work of the Commission, *No Future Without Forgiveness* (1999).

Kentridge creates a starry sky where satellites spin out of their orbit at the sound of her extraordinary vocal flights – in the end creating a cage around the Queen herself. The Queen, this hot-blooded woman whose project entails the annihilation of light altogether, has to be transcoded again, out of the opera if not out of music, to embody a different form of resistance.

In *Black Box/Chambre Noire* the starry sky recurs, but at its centre, instead of the Queen, the audience finds the wooden cut-out figurine of a Herero woman moving across the miniature stage of the installation, while the stars flow out of another animation, the names of the Herero people murdered by the Germans. This *Totenlist* appear on screen while the voice of Vevangua Muuondjo sings to the tune from the lament from the march of Sarastro's priests (Schikaneder 1956, 74). Kentridge thus does not eschew Sarastro's ethics of forgiveness; yet, he divests it of the authority of the white male master, which has been tainted by colonial violence. Kentridge's transcoding of Mozart's *Flute*, on the other hand, voices the need to rearticulate painful histories such as the Herero massacre – but also as the overall loss of confidence of the Western episteme (embodied by Sarastro himself). In this way, he deconstructs opera as founding narrative of Western identity to contaminate it with other, previously silenced voices from Europe's colonial past.

References

Alemani C. 2006. *William Kentridge. Black Box*. Milano: Electa.

Cavarero A. 2005. *For More than One Voice:Toward a Philosophy of Vocal Expression*. Stanford (Ca.): Stanford University Press.

Clément C. 1989. *Opera, or the Undoing of Women*. London: Virago.

Kentridge W. 2007. "Notes Towards an Opera". In Law-Viljoen B. (ed.) *Flute*. Johannesburg: David Krut Publishing, 42-77.

Kramer L. 2000. "Opera. Two or Three Things I Know About Her". In Smart M.A. (ed.) *Siren Songs. Representations of Gender and Sexuality in Opera*. Princeton and Oxford: Princeton University Press.

Law-Viljoen B. (ed.) 2007. *Flute*. Johannesburg: David Krut Publishing.

Locke R.P. 1995. "What Are These Women Doing in Opera?". In Blackmer C., Smith P.J. (eds.) *En Travesti, Women, Gender Subversion, Opera*. New York: Columbia University Press, 59-98.

McClary S. 1997. "Structures of Identity and Difference in Bizet's *Carmen*". In Dellamora R., Fischlin D. (eds.) *The Work of Opera. Genre, Nationhood, and Sexual Difference*. New York: Columbia University Press, 115-129.

Pasini F. 2008. *William Kentridge. (Repeat) From the Beginning / Da Capo*. Milano: Charta.

Said E.W. 1991. *Musical Elaborations*. London: Vintage.

Said E.W. 1993. "The Empire at Work: Verdi's *Aida*". In *Culture and Imperialism*. London & New York: Vintage, 111-131.

Schikaneder J.E. 1956. *The Magic Flute: an Opera in Two Acts. English Version, after the Libretto of Schikaneder and Giesecke by W.H. Auden and Chester Kallman*. London: Random House.

Stratton J. 2008. *Jewish Identity in Western Pop Culture: The Holocaust and Trauma through Modernity*. Basingstoke: Palgrave Macmillan.

Subotnik R.R. 1991. "Whose *Magic Flute*? Intimations of Reality at the Gates of the Enlightenment". In *19th-Century Music*, 15, 2, 132-150.

Tutu D. 1999. *No Future Without Forgiveness*. London: Rider.

MARIA CRISTINA CONSIGLIO

Università di Bari Aldo Moro

"Wiseguys Don't Work on Mother's Day": Italian-Americans on the Screen

1. Language and representation

In a culturalist perspective ethnicity is seen in terms of representation; it is a cultural creation centred on the sharing of norms, values, beliefs, cultural symbols, practices, and language. Being films fictional narratives, they do not represent reality as it really is; rather they show an imaginary and culturally connoted reality, which tends to be a construction or re-presentation of people and events (Bignell 2002, 179). Thus, Italian-Americans (IAs) are quite always stereotyped as *dagos* (immigrants), *palookas* (prizefighters), *Romeos* (Latin lover), and *Wise Guys* (mobsters) (Bondanella 2004).

Born at the end of the 19th century as a consequence of the mass arrival in the States of poor, mostly illiterate, southern Italians, the stereotype of the gangster of Italian ancestry is so persistent in the American culture (Bondanella 2006, 911) that there is an ongoing struggle of Italian-American (IA) groups against the HBO show *The Sopranos* accused of portraying most of the ethnic group as mobsters, thus contributing to spread the negative stereotype of IAs as profane criminals. It can be hypothesized that, being language the focus of identification, the peculiar mix of southern Italian dialects and colloquial English characterizing the IA speech has played a major role in the formation and maintenance of the gangster stereotype.

IAs, like other immigrant communities, are bilingual and they can choose which language to use according to contextual factors like the setting, the interlocutor, the topic. But bilingual individuals cannot keep the two languages completely apart and, consciously or unconsciously, shift from one linguistic code to the other during the same conversation, a phenomenon known as *code-switching* (Meyer-Scotton 1993, 4). Given the close connection between language and culture, code-switching cannot be considered as a mere linguistic phenomenon:

> The 'we' language, that is spoken at home, the mother tongue, is endowed with many positive affective variables such as intimacy and solidarity [...].

The 'they' language, in contrast, [...] is linked with the outside world of power and money (Zentella 1990, 81).

Thus, the passage from a *we-code* to a *they-code* or vice versa is linked to the speaker's position in the world; by using a given language s/he is asserting her/his adhesion to the behavioural, social and cultural norms of one of the two communities s/he belongs to (Campagna 2001, 265).

In order to ascertain how and to what extent language has contributed to rooting the IA gangster stereotype[1], a comparison between the gangsters represented by the IA film director Francis Ford Coppola in *The Godfather* trilogy and those represented by the English film director Mike Newell in the movie *Donnie Brasco* is here proposed.

2. The insider's gaze

The Godfather, based on the homonymous novel by Mario Puzo (1969), was adapted for the screen by Puzo himself together with Coppola and released in 1972. It is set in 1946 and tells the story of the New York Mafia boss don Vito Corleone and his four children in their struggle with the so-called Five Families for the control of the territory. Part II, released in 1974, is partly based on the novel and partly originally written by Coppola. It functions as both a sequel and a prequel to Part I; the first narrative tells the story of Michael Corleone who succeeds his father as the head of the Mafia family, the second narrative shows, in long flashbacks, don Vito's story from the experience of immigration, which involves issues of integration and opportunities, to his beginnings as a mobster. Part III, released in 1990, was written by Coppola who based his plot on the headlines of the period and his characters on real people. It is set between the USA and Italy in 1979 and shows the dangerous connections between the Mafia, the political world, and the Roman Catholic Church.[2]

Coppola's characters fit the stereotype of the IA gangster but are not mere types, they are psychologically and emotively complex. It seems as if the IA Coppola, working from within the stereotype, wants to change the perception of the IA by the mainstream society and creates the epic of the immigrant who is compelled to face a new and alien reality he cannot understand and

---

[1] Films showing criminal Italian immigrants have been produced since the Silent Era (see for example *The Black Hand* released in 1906), but the definitive connection between IAs and gangster movies was established by *Little Caesar* (1930) and *Scarface* (1932), both fictional biographies of Al Capone (Bondanella 2004, 181).

[2] Information on the genesis of *The Godfather* trilogy can be found in Bondanella (2004, 235-271).

fights (not only metaphorically) to conquer his portion of the American Dream (Bondanella 2006, 927). It is not a case that Part I starts with a close-up of the Italian immigrant Amerigo Bonasera (*nomen omen*) who says: "I believe in America. America has made my fortune".

In a recent interview published on the online edition of *The Scotsman* (Applebaum 2009), Coppola said that he based the portrayal of the Corleones on his own family. His words:

> I didn't know anything about gangsters, I had never met a gangster. I knew they were Italian-Americans so I just made them like my family in terms of how they ate, say. Also, New York Italians speak with a New York accent, they don't 'speaka lika dis'. So I just was true to what I saw with my uncles and my father. And although they were musicians, I used my own family.

It follows that Coppola's express wish was to render the IA community realistically also as regards their way of speaking. This is partly achieved in a number of scenes like the three scenes, one at the beginning of each episode, where all the characters are gathered: Connie's wedding in Part I, for which Coppola said he took inspiration from his own family's weddings, Michael's son's First Communion in Part II, and a party to celebrate a religious honour given to Michael in Part III. In all these scenes the characters alternate a New York American English accent with a dialectal form of Italian, which highlights their sense of belonging to the 'family'. From these scenes there emerges an image of the IA immigrants as a close-knit community, nostalgically linked to a far-off country unknown to many of them. This contributes to strengthen the IA stereotype since the scenes present several clichés, like the Italians' affection for the family, their love for music, opera, dance, food, and wine, as well as a band playing *tarantella* and all the guests singing Italian folk songs.

The use of the Italian language has a similar function in the scenes set in Sicily. The necessity to represent a foreign country where people do speak a language different from English, made Coppola ask his actors, many of whom are Italians or IAs, to speak Italian dialects. Yet, there is no *effet de réel*; the representation of Sicily is so pervaded by a sense of homesickness that Sicily is not perceived as a real place, rather as a place of memory, a sort of Arcadia inhabited by sheep and shepherds with men wearing *coppola* and *lupara* wandering undisturbed through the sunny fields. The sense of nostalgia for the homeland, its values, its religious traditions, its folk songs, and its language is a feeling all immigrants know well, but, seen on the screen associated as it is with a lawless country completely controlled by criminals, contributes to establish a direct connection between the criminal world and the Italian language, thus strengthening the stereotype of the IA gangster.

The flashbacks that in Part II show don Vito's past narrate events spanning from 1917 to 1925 and are set in New York where Vito works and lives and where his American Dream is frustrated by the secret society named the Black Hand (the first form of the Mafia). There all the characters speak only highly dialectal forms of Italian creating another *effet de réel*, as the protagonists are all first generation migrants living in a Little Italy inhabited by other Italians. Being these Italians all more or less involved in criminal activities, the Italian language cannot but be associated with violence and crime. Bondanella (2006, 928) has pointed out that these flashbacks show in detail the birth and growth of American organized crime starting from Italian origins.

Yet, there are also a number of scenes where the use of the Italian language, or better the switching from English to Italian, seems to have a different function and seems to prepare the audience for the violence that will follow. In Part I one of don Vito's associates, Luca Brasi, is brutally killed. Don Vito sends Brasi to infiltrate the rival family's organization and report back information. Brasi meets Sollozzo and Tattaglia, don Corleone's rivals, in a bar. The first words are spoken in English but Sollozzo soon switches to Italian as a more adequate way to come to an agreement, but soon afterwards Brasi is stabbed to one of his hands to prevent him from defending himself and garroted by an assassin.

Emblematic is the scene in Part I where Michael kills the rival Sollozzo to avenge the wounding of don Vito. They meet in a restaurant to make an agreement, but Michael has a plan to kill both Sollozzo and the corrupt police captain that supports him. The conversation, started in English, soon switches to dialectal Italian with the following words:

> S.: "Mi dispiace!".
> M.: "Sul serio?".
> S.: "Tu ai sapiri cachiddu ca successe tra mi e tu patri fu una cosa di
> business. Io ai un grosso rispetto pi tu patri, ma tu patri pensa all'antica.
> Iddu nu lo vo capiri che eo sono un uomo de onori".
> M.: "Non mi diri sti cosi. I sacciu".
> S.: "'o sai? E tu ai sapiri che eo ho aiutato a famiglia Tattaglia. Io credo che
> ci potemo mettere in accordo. Io voglio paci. E lasciamo perdere co tutti sti
> cazzati".
> M.: "Ma voggiu ca…".
> S.: "Che?".
> M.: "Come si dice? What I want, what's most important to me is I have a
> guarantee: no more attempts on my father's life".

Then Michael asks for permission to go to the toilet where he knows he will find a gun. When he is back Sollozzo switches to Italian again, but Michael kills him.

What is interesting here is that up to that moment Michael has been considered as a 'civilian' in the Mafia war, an outsider, not involved in the family business, a "nice college boy", as Sonny calls him. In his first appearance he is in US military uniform at his sister's wedding together with his wasp girlfriend Kay Adams to whom he is telling anecdotes informing her about his father's criminal life. But he also says: "That's my family Kay. It's not me". His non involvement in crime is often stressed throughout the first part of *The Godfather* also by Michael's use of the English language, but after killing Sollozzo and the policeman, Michael, as a classical tragic hero, can no longer contrast his Fate and is obliged to take his place in the family. The scene described above, therefore, can be considered as a real rite of passage and it is emblematic that when he is about to cross the line and enter the criminal world Michael speaks Italian; it is noteworthy, however, that he switches to English when he wants to assert his wish peremptorily since, as a second generation migrant, English is his mother tongue. Yet Michael's use of the Italian language seems a way to identify himself with his family and its behavioural norms, i.e. respect, honour, and revenge.

In the scenes where code-switching is associated with violence, therefore, the Italian language is not used as a neutral sociolect, as it is for the IA community, but as a sort of anti-language.

Defined by M.A.K. Halliday (1978, 265-275) as the language spoken by the anti-society, an anti-language is the secret jargon spoken by criminals, prisoners, members of subcultures and countercultures, whose function is to make the members of the anti-society identify themselves with the alternative social construction their anti-society proposes as a challenge to the mainstream. Despite its secrecy and obscurity, an anti-language is not completely separated from the natural language from which it originates. The differences between language and anti-language are mainly lexical, due to the phenomena of *relexicalization* and *overlexicalization*. The former consists in giving a new meaning to existing words, the latter results in lexical redundancy in those semantic fields that are central to the anti-society's values (Halliday 1978, 267).

The anti-language spoken by Coppola's mobsters is a mixture of English and Italian, for this very reason overlexicalized, with a few relexicalizations like *padrino, consigliere, caporegime, omertà, famiglia, onore*, Italian words used by the Mafia members with a meaning partly different from the one they have in standard Italian, particularly as regards connotation. But these differences are not evident to a non Italian speaker who can easily trace a direct connection between the Italian language and the Mafia world, which entails a generalization based on the idea that all those who can speak Italian, i.e. all immigrants of Italian ancestry, are mobsters.

It follows that, on the one hand, Coppola has succeeded in portraying interesting even charming characters, thus transforming the very genre of the gangster movie, but, on the other hand, his use of code-switching associated with violent actions cannot but bring the criminal's ethnicity to the fore, thus contributing to fixing the stereotype of the IA gangster in the audience's mind.

3. The outsider's gaze

The 1997 film *Donnie Brasco* directed by Mike Newell is an interesting case study. It is the transposition of the autobiographical book *Donnie Brasco: My Undercover Life in the Mafia* (1987) by the IA FBI agent Joe Pistone. The script written by Paul Attanasio narrates the undercover life of Pistone (alias Donnie Brasco) in the New York Mafia in the 1970s.

Donnie's process of infiltration in the criminal world passes through the learning of the behavioural and linguistic norms of the gangsters. Language, indeed, plays a major role in Joe's travel from the centre (the mainstream society Joe belongs to as an FBI agent, graduated at university, married with three daughters) to the periphery, a voyage underground during which Joe/Donnie is helped by Benjamin "Lefty" Ruggiero, a low level mafia killer who eventually becomes his friend, who teaches him what is acceptable and what is not among the mobsters. Such a teaching consists in a series of rules in the form of maxims – like "wiseguy don't carry his money in a wallet", "a wiseguy never pays for his drinks", or "wiseguys don't work on Mother's day" – that, on the one hand, portray the Mafia world ironically and, on the other hand, strengthen the *mafioso* stereotype by showing mobsters fixed in the role both criminal and mainstream society have assigned to them.

Newell's mobsters are not high-profile gangsters like Coppola's, they are ignorant criminals who speak English with a New York accent, enriched with swearwords and Italian insertions and tag-switching. Particularly interesting is the use of the phrase "yo capeesh", a calque of the American "you know", that is so strongly associated with IA speech that it has become the title of a book about IAs.[3]

This is the language Joe has to learn in order to be accepted in the mob. But *Donnie Brasco* is the story of a man living in two worlds and speaking two languages he cannot keep apart and at a given moment he identifies himself more with the mafia life than with his family life. Emblematic in this respect

---

[3] J. Caridi, *Yo Capeesh: A Guide to Understanding Italian Americans*, Lincoln, NE, Universe, 2002. Interestingly enough the slogan on the webpage advertising the book is "here's a book you can't refuse", which is a paraphrase of one of the most famous quotes from *The Godfather* and which cannot but strengthen the association between Italian-Americans and organized crime in the readers' mind.

is a scene where Joe and his wife, Maggie, are talking to a therapist to find a way to avoid divorce. When the therapist asks Joe what he is running from, he answers: "I ain't running from nothing", a sentence grammatically incorrect and spoken with a quite incomprehensible accent. Maggie's comment, "the man I met was a college man", is revealing of the role language has played in Joe's transformation. It is evident that the difficulty Joe finds in keeping his two identities apart is reflected in continuous code-mixing of the college English and the slang he has learnt in the New York streets.

The mobsters' slang in *Donnie Brasco* presents both characteristics of anti-languages. There are examples of overlexicalization, with Italian words used instead of their English equivalents or English phrases used as synonyms for other English phrases (like "friend of mine" for "connected guy" and "friend of ours" for "made guy") and relexicalization, of which the most famous is the phrase "forget-about-it" that is used by the mobsters with various different meanings determined by the situation in which it is used. It is Joe who explains this to his FBI colleagues who ask him "what's forget-about-it?". This is his answer:

> Forget-about-it is like [...] if you agree with someone, you know, like 'Raquel Welch is a great piece of ass, forget-about-it'. But then, if you disagree, like 'A Lincoln is better than a Cadillac?, Forget-about-it!'. But then, it's also like if something's the greatest thing in the world, like 'Mingia those peppers, forget-about-it'. But it's also like saying 'Go to hell!' too. Like, you know, like 'Hey Paulie, you got a one inch pecker?' and Paulie says 'Forget-about-it!'. Sometimes it just means forget about it.

The comic quality of the above dialogue is to be seen as another characteristic of anti-languages. In Halliday's words (1978, 286): "The obliqueness of meaning and form that makes them [the anti-languages] so effective as bearers of an alternative reality also makes them inherently comic". And it is not surprising that it is the outsider Newell who emphasises this aspect of the mob slang, whereas the insider Coppola prefers to indulge in the tragic quality of his characters who, in their voyage from the periphery to the centre of society, are obliged to lose part of their identity to conform to the new cultural and linguistic reality.

The character of the IA gangster is so appealing to the public that different genres, like comedy or even cartoon, feature IA gangsters, both at the cinema and on TV. Irrespective of genre, all mobsters are stereotyped and their speech, which actually functions as an anti-language, always plays a major role in this process. Although today IAs certainly belong to the mainstream, their stereotypical image of gangsters has been spread throughout the world and "Hollywood Italians continue to stand out as a group in the Hollywood pantheon, remaining far more 'ethnic' than their real counterparts" (Bondanella 2004, 12).

References

Donnie Brasco. 1997. Dir. Newell M. Perf. Pacino A., Depp J., Madsen M. DVD Mandalay Entertainement.

The Godfather. 1972. Dir. Coppola F.F. Perf. Brando M., Pacino A., Caan J. DVD Paramount, 2004.

The Godfather Part II. 1974. Dir. Coppola F.F. Perf. Pacino A., De Niro R., Duvall R. DVD Paramount, 2008.

The Godfather Part III. 1990. Dir. Coppola F.F. Perf. Pacino A., Garcia A., Mantegna J. DVD Paramount, 2008.

Applebaum S. "The Godfather is Back". Interview with F.F. Coppola, *The Scotsman*, September 9th 2009.

Bignell J. 2002. *Media Semiotics. An Introduction*. Manchester: Manchester UP.

Bondanella P. 2004. *Hollywood Italians: Dagos, Palookas, Romeos, Wise Guys, and Sopranos*. London: Continuum.

Bondanella P. 2006. "Gli italoamericani e il cinema". In Brunetta G.P. (ed.) *Storia del cinema americano*. Torino: Einaudi, 911-938.

Campagna S. 2001. "Voices from Bradistan. The Sense of Belonging in Multiracial Societies". In *Textus*, XIV, 2, 263-285.

Halliday M.A.K. 1978. *Language as Social Semiotic: The Social Interpretation of Language and Meaning*. London: Arnold.

Meyer-Scotton C. 1993. *Social Motivations for Code-switching: Evidence from Africa*. Oxford: Clarendon.

Zentella A.C. 1990. "Returned Migration, Language and Identity: Puerto Rican Bilinguals in Dos Worlds/Two Mundos". In *International Journal of the Sociology of Language*, 84, 81-100.

IRENE RANZATO

Sapienza – Università di Roma

Manipulating the Classics:
Film Dubbing as an Extreme Form of Rewriting

The choices of a translator shed light on the interplay between the translator's responses to expectations, constraints and pressures in a social context. Although forms of manipulation and censorship are more easily detectable under totalitarian governments, even in the most liberal and democratic contexts texts are rewritten until they are deemed acceptable to the poetics and ideology of the target culture. If the translated work that tries to take its place in the new context does not conform to the target audience's "horizon of expectations", its reception is likely to be rendered more difficult (Lefevere 1992).

Censorship can be defined as the review by an official authority of any material before dissemination. The concept of "horizon of expectations", a term employed by Jauss (1982, 24) to refer to the readers' general expectations on style, form, content etc. relative to the text in the translated new version, helps us to give shape to the more elusive, although more comprehensive, term of manipulation, as it defines the dialectical way a text is elaborated by the translator in a way that may respond to the expectations of the public, while it also defines the way the latter will interpret and judge it according to their own beliefs, biases and preconceptions. If these constraints bind the translator and the public from 'within', so to speak, at the same time prevailing target norms of a linguistic, translational, socio-cultural nature act as constraints from 'without'. Norms, rather than technical constraints, encourage translators and adapters to manipulate the text. Ideology but also, as Fawcett aptly writes, "human randomness and simple cussedness" (Fawcett 2003, 145).

The birth and growth of a successful dubbing industry were promoted in Italy by the fascist government (1922-1943) and understanding the complexities of the relationship of fascism to censorship is fundamental to understand the birth of the audiovisual industry in Italy and the evolution of practices and modes of the translation for dubbing.[1]

---

[1] For an exhaustive account of the relationship between cinema and fascism, see for example Brunetta (1975); Gili (1981); Talbot (2007); Ricci (2008).

When dubbing became technically viable in 1931, films were dubbed into Italian either in their original country or in Italy. But in 1933, the government prohibited the importation of films which had been dubbed elsewhere than in Italy. It was now possible for the censor to view the film in the original version and to 'suggest' the alterations in the dialogue that needed to be introduced in the dubbing so as to modify the 'unpleasant' sequences. With this policy the government achieved a greater control over the 'purity of the language', which added to the other, more overtly political, advantages: manipulation of content, deletion of unwanted references, freedom of adaptation and, in some cases, addition of more 'pleasant' references. The government could, from then on, exert without difficulty a linguistic control which aimed first of all at the disappearance of Italian dialects, regionalisms and accents in the final dubbed version. American films – the majority of the films imported – were to be dubbed in an 'abstract' Italian, thus contributing to the effort of cultural homogenization and regional uprooting which was one of the aims of fascism. From this point of view, as pointed out by Gili (1981, 35-37), the foreign film to be dubbed was a more flexible and controllable product than an original Italian film. The dubbed versions of foreign films gradually elaborated that 'middle language', suitable for "primary communicative functions" (Brunetta 1975, 427). All English language films were to be translated into 'pure' – that is, non-accented, non-dialect – Italian. If from the 1970s film dialogues lost much of their stiffness[2], still, the language of dubbing, as we can all hear, cannot and often is not concerned to convey all the linguistic subtleties of the original.

Italian adapters – an 'umbrella' term which can include up to three professionals: translator, adapter and even distributor – have used over the years various strategies of rewriting, creating texts that are sometimes quite distant from the original. Their treatment of the classics is generally not an exception.

It is, I believe, symptomatic of the attitude of our dubbing industry towards culture and literature, that literary and generally 'intellectual' references and quotations are often eliminated or manipulated – that is altered or expanded. From the plethora of instances from any period, an excerpt from one of Woody Allen's films best exemplifies this attitude. In *Manhattan* (1979), Mary is a 38-year-old woman speaking to the 17-year-old girlfriend of the much older male protagonist:

---

[2] It is not possible to trace here even an outline of the history of dubbing in Italy. It will be sufficient to say that in the 1970s we can register a remarkable, if not crucial, turning point in dubbing, when dialects started to appear in the productions of the big American companies. The first important film where characters speak Sicilian is *The Godfather* (Francis Ford Coppola, 1972). From then on, film dialogues have become less stiff and have been marked at times by expressions in dialect. So, since 1970, the linguistic gap between national production and foreign imported production has not been as wide as in the previous decades.

Manhattan, Woody Allen, 1979
ORIGINAL FILM DIALOGUE MARY: What do you do Tracy? TRACY: I go to high school. MARY: Oh, really. Really. Somewhere Nabokov is smiling, if you know what I mean.
ITALIAN ADAPTATION MARY: Tu che fai, Tracy? TRACY: Io faccio il liceo. MARY: Ma senti, senti, il liceo. Sembra talmente lontano il liceo.

And if 1979 seems far away, we can cite a more recent example: the film *Notes on a Scandal* (Richard Eyre, 2006), based on a screenplay by Patrick Marber, contains several literary references, including a direct reference to William Golding's *Lord of the Flies*. When describing the violent behaviour of teenagers in a classroom, one of the teachers says that "it's bloody *Lord of the Flies* in there". In Italian, the title of the book was translated with "È un pandemonio". A subtle reference to Joseph Conrad's *Heart of Darkness* was also ignored. Two classics of English literature were virtually suppressed in a film supposedly aimed at a cultured audience. The deletion or banalisation of 'intellectual' references is unfortunately a common practice in audiovisual translation into Italian. Translators act in this case on the basis of what I would define the 'presumed ignorance' of the target audience: the audience will presumably not understand the reference and will be confused by it. Highbrow has to become lowbrow by any means: by manipulating and suppressing contents in the source text and also by changing the balance among the various components of the original audiovisual text.

In the 1959 film version of Tennessee Williams's play *Suddenly, Last Summer*, directed by Joseph Mankiewicz, all references to homosexuality were diluted or deleted, and the same treatment was reserved to any sex-food metaphors and to the references to God. The heavy manipulation, for example, of the crucial lines of the film, when the protagonist, Catherine, explains that her homosexual cousin Sebastian chose the "blonds" and the "dark ones" as if they were dishes of an ideal menu, has altered the text in such a way that the blond and dark boys became with the Italian dubbing the more abstract North and South.[3] Many other examples show the need to 'sanitise' the sexually charged images of a ravenous and devouring nature. This kind of sex/food metaphors are constant

---

[3] A more thorough analysis, including various examples, of the dubbing of *Improvvisamente l'estate scorsa* can be found in Ranzato (2009).

through the film and the play and their omission dilutes the morbid sensuality of the story.

More interesting still for the present analysis are the less macroscopic ways of unsettling the balance of the original film. One of them is the manipulation of what we can call the prosody of the work through the translation of the phrase which is also the title of the play (and of the film): the words "suddenly, last summer", repeated continuously both by Mrs Venable and Catherine, are translated into Italian in a variety of ways ("l'altr'anno", "da un giorno all'altro", and similar expressions) and sometimes are completely omitted. In the original, the frequent repetition of these words has the effect of pathetically evoking the poem, the "summer song", that Sebastian, a deluded poet, delivered every summer after a nine-month gestation, until suddenly, last summer, he had left the page blank. By omitting this important repetition, the Italian version loses a text within the text: Sebastian's poem.

This particular form of rewriting which is dubbing, the last layer of an already multilayered text such as an adaptation usually is, does not simply suppress and alter contents, it also operates meaningfully on the rhythm and even musicality of a film. The narrative structure of this story, characterised by a crescendo of tension released by a few cathartic moments, is sensibly altered in the Italian version.

Another form of rewriting in audiovisual translation takes the form of an alteration of the idiolects. Williams' play could provide examples in this field too – from the rather vulgar Southern American accents of Catherine's mother and brother to the more refined monologues delivered by Elizabeth Taylor in the main role to the unmistakable upper class accent of Katherine Hepburn playing Sebastian's mother, Mrs Venable – but I would like to move on to another classic and to the characters of Brutus and Cassius in Shakespeare's *Julius Caesar* as adapted in the 1953 film directed by Joseph Mankiewicz. As David Daniell wrote in his introduction to the play, "linguistically, the thin, unsmiling, nervously-articulate Caius Cassius, a modern intellectual and anarchist, is also individually marked, particularly in a way that has not been noticed, for he shows a characteristic of using the most modern vocabulary. This is not absolute throughout the play, but it is notable. Again and again Cassius's words turn out to be first recorded in the mid-1590s or later" (Daniell 2003, 60). Daniell made a list of recent and very recent words (or recent in the special sense intended) used by Cassius, such as "gusty", "temper", "scandal", "banqueting", "buffet", "stemming", "creature", "lustre", "get the start", "majestic", "applauses", "bestride", "famed with", "jealous", "aim", "chew", "villager", "chidden", "humour", "trash", "indifferent". By contrast, Brutus's words are often ancient: "gamesome", "lack", "part", "quick", "spirit", "hinder" and so on, are all "solidly old" (Daniell 2003, 60-61). Daniell's interesting analysis parallels Cassius's 'speaking modern' to Iago's, thus characterising the 'speaking modern' as the idiolect of the villains in Shakespeare. Fascinating as this hypothesis is, what I would like to emphasize here is the fatal loss of such subtle, ingenious nuances in the Italian version, a difference of idiom in Shakespeare's play which was brought out quite effectively by James Mason as Brutus and John Gielgud as Cassius in Mankiewicz's film. The Italian faithful translation fails to respect this characterisation, failing to choose particularly 'contemporary' words for Cassius and putting on Brutus's lips expressions which are in fact quite modern:

Julius Caesar, Joseph Mankiewicz, 1953
ORIGINAL FILM DIALOGUE CASSIUS: Will you go see the order of the course? BRUTUS: Not I. CASSIUS: I pray you do. BRUTUS: I am not gamesome. I do lack some part Of that quick spirit that is in Antony. Let me not hinder, Cassius, your desires. I'll leave you. **ITALIAN ADAPTATION** CASSIO: Tu non vai a vedere le corse? BRUTO: Io no. CASSIO: Ti prego, va'. BRUTO: Non fa per me. Mi manca un poco del vivace spirito che ha Antonio. Non impedirò a te Cassio di andarci, ti lascio.

| **ORIGINAL FILM DIALOGUE**
BRUTUS: [...] Conceptions only proper to myself, Which give some soil,
perhaps, to my behaviour.

ITALIAN ADAPTATION
BRUTO: [...] Conflitti tutti personali miei che possono talvolta
adombrarmi la faccia. |

Note, in the second example, the translation of "conceptions" with "conflitti tutti personali miei", where the XIV century word "conflitti", from the Latin *conflictus*, is used here in the 'new' sense of psychology and thus certainly post-Caesar.

What becomes of these finely chiselled idiolects in the Italian translation? Obviously not much. Even if our adapters always and evidently rely on established published translations of these great texts, it is certain that the loss of colour in characterisation is immense and irreparable.

But if we think that Brutus spoke modern when he said "conflitti", what could we say of an adaptation totally conceived as to be aimed at a teenage audience, as in Baz Luhrmann's *Romeo + Juliet*?

This 1996 film was originally, clearly, aimed at the so-called MTV generation (young people born and bred on a diet of video-clip aesthetics), but it did so by way of a use of exclusively visual motifs. In the Italian version, the manipulation of the dialogues has the evident purpose to aim the product at an even younger, certainly less cultured target audience. I argue that this is actually one of the particular goals of adapters into Italian: to widen the target audience. Tonino Accolla, dubbing director and adapter of many Shakespearian films, tailored this product for teenage audiences. If the film in original puts Shakespeare's words in the mouth of the teenage idol Leonardo Di Caprio, the words are still unmistakably Shakespeare's. The minor cuts and deletions cannot change the fact that what we hear are Shakespeare's middle English words. Thus the audience of the film in the original version cannot be too uncultured, too lowbrow, or, hopefully, will be less so after viewing the film. English-speaking teenagers can hear Shakespeare's words practically unaltered in watching *Romeo + Juliet*, while Italian teenagers (and adults) hear a simplified Shakespeare: speeches that contain no asperities, with few outdated expressions.

Yet another important mode of rewriting in dubbing takes the form of unsettling the balance among the various elements of the audiovisual text (notably images, words and sounds). In the original *Romeo + Juliet* film, it is the images which help the audience understand, for example, Shakespeare's salacious remarks and jokes. The original film does not alter or simplify Shakespeare's words, it makes use of the images to give emphasis to the words. Images are used as a bridge to the exotism of Shakespeare's words but no attempt is made to translate Shakespeare into modern English. Images are there to make it modern. Dubbing intrudes and changes the balance between images and sounds:

Romeo + Juliet, Baz Luhrmann, 1996
ORIGINAL FILM DIALOGUE   BENVOLIO: Tell me in sadness, who is it that you love.   ROMEO: In sadness, cousin, I do love... a woman.   BENVOLIO: I aimed so near when I supposed you loved.   ROMEO: A right good marksman; and she's fair I love.   BENVOLIO: Rosaline! A right fair mark, fair coz, is soonest hit.   ROMEO: She'll not be hit with Cupid's arrow. She hath Diana's wit,   And in strong proof of chastity lives well armed.   BENVOLIO: Then she hath sworn that she will still live chaste?   ROMEO: She hath; and in that sparing makes huge waste.

ITALIAN ADAPTATION

BENVOLIO: Dimmi seriamente, di chi sei innamorato?

ROMEO: Seriamente, cugino, di una donna.

BENVOLIO: Ah, ho colpito nel segno quando ho detto che sei innamorato.

ROMEO: Hai fatto centro, ed è anche bella.

BENVOLIO: Quando il bersaglio è bello, cugino, si fa centro.

ROMEO: Ma io l'ho mancato. Non si fa vincere dalla freccia di Cupido,

né dall'assalto di occhi adoranti, né apre il grembo all'oro che seduce le sante.

BENVOLIO: Allora ha giurato di vivere in castità?

ROMEO: Sì, e questa economia è un grave spreco.

Benvolio's and Romeo's words on hitting the mark in this scene are underlined by the movements of their game of billiards. The sense of the words is exemplified by the thrusting movements of the players' sticks hitting the balls, so even if the words may sound 'exotic' to a contemporary audience, images are there to explain the meaning. The simplified Italian translation makes the visual explanation superfluous, even redundant (maybe even a little vulgar): the balance between images – the movements and expressions of the actors – and the words they utter is dangerously jeopardised:

Romeo + Juliet, Baz Luhrmann, 1996

ORIGINAL FILM DIALOGUE

FATHER LAURENCE: Our Romeo hath not been in bed tonight.

ROMEO: The last is true. The sweeter rest was mine.

FATHER LAURENCE: God pardon sin! Wast thou with Rosaline?

ROMEO: With Rosaline, my ghostly father? No.

I have forgot that name and that name's woe. […]

FATHER LAURENCE: What a ch'ange is here! Is Rosaline,

that thou didst love so dear,

So soon foresaken? Young men's love then lies

Not truly in their hearts, but in their eyes.

ROMEO: Thou chid'st me oft for loving Rosaline.

FATHER LAURENCE: For doting, not for loving, pupil mine.

ROMEO: I pray thee chide me not. Her I love now

Doth grace for grace and love for love allow. The other did not so.

FATHER LAURENCE: O, she knew well Thy love did read by rote, that could not spell.

ITALIAN ADAPTATION

FRATE LORENZO: Il nostro Romeo il letto non l'ha nemmeno visto.

ROMEO: È vero, ho fatto di meglio.

> FRATE LORENZO: Dio ci perdoni, sei stato con Rosalina?
>
> ROMEO: Con Rosalina? Mio caro padre, no.
>
> Ho scordato quel nome e quei tormenti. [...]
>
> FRATE LORENZO: Che novità è questa? E Rosalina, che amavi alla follia,
>
> l'hai già dimenticata? Tu mi vuoi fare pensare che non hai l'amore
>
> nel cuore ma dentro gli occhi.
>
> ROMEO: Tu non volevi che amassi Rosalina.
>
> FRATE LORENZO: La idolatravi, non era un amore sano, quello.
>
> ROMEO: Ti prego, non sgridarmi, colei che amo adesso consente
>
> e restituisce un amore sereno, l'altra non era così.
>
> FRATE LORENZO: Mah, quella sapeva che era un amore
>
> imparato a memoria, senza slanci.

Note here, as well as the translation of middle English into standard modern Italian, the addition of that little word, "(non) sano", to define Romeo's immoderate love. Again, a contemporary expression, an expansion to explain better, to make the audience understand better.

This simplifying, but also banalising, operation perfectly justifies the scream of sorrow and dismay of a teen-ager in the packed cinema where I saw *Romeo + Juliet* for the first time. At the end of the film, when both the protagonists are dead, the girl in the audience screamed: "Why did they make it end this way?! Is the director crazy?". This reaction demonstrates that Accolla's rewriting has hit its right fair mark, as Benvolio would say.

References

Brunetta G.P. 1975. *Cinema italiano tra le due guerre: fascismo e politica cinematografica*. Milano: Mursia.

Daniell D. 2003. "Introduction". In Shakespeare W. *Julius Caesar*. London: Arden Shakespeare, 1-147.

Fawcett P. 2003. "The Manipulation of Language and Culture in Film Translation". In Calzada Pérez M. (ed.) *Apropos of Ideology*. Manchester, Northampton: St. Jerome Publishing, 145-163.

Gili J. 1981. *Stato fascista e cinematografia: repressione e promozione*. Roma: Bulzoni Editore.

Jauss H.R. 1982. *Toward an Aesthetic of Reception*. Brighton: Harvester Press.

Lefevere A. 1992. *Translation, Rewriting and the Manipulation of Literary Fame*. London: Routledge.

Ranzato I. 2009. "Censorship or 'Creative' Translation? The Italian Experience from Tennessee Williams to Woody Allen to *Six Feet Under*". In Federici

F.M. (ed.) *Translating Regionalised Voices in Audiovisuals*. Roma: Aracne, 43-69.

Ricci S. 2008. *Cinema & Fascism, Italian Film and Society, 1922-1943*. Berkeley, Los Angeles, London: University of California Press.

Talbot G. 2007. *Censorship in Fascist Italy, 1922-43*. London: Palgrave Macmillan.

EMANUELE MONEGATO

Università di Milano

Photographing 7/7 dilemmas: *The Day After*
by Johannes Hepp and *People's Cinema*

> Certain works of contemporary art are designed to transmit trauma as directly as possible, to rub the spectator's face in the unspeakable and unimaginable. Mitchell (2005, 295)

This work aims at illustrating two unconventional case studies of contemporary post 9/11 pieces of art "rubbing the spectator's face in the unspeakable and unimaginable" (Mitchell 2005, 295) within the *topos* of terrorism representations. As a matter of fact, the title of my work includes all relevant aspects highlighted within this examination, starting from the peculiar meaning adopted by the polysemous expression *dilemma*: such a word is here to be considered in its Greek etymologic meaning of double proposition (*di-lēmma*) and not in its common use of mere problem or predicament involving no choice. A dilemma is, therefore, "a situation in which one has to choose between two (un)desirable things or courses of action"[1] that is, in my paper, either photographing the terror attack or surviving the catastrophe.

The time setting is clearly stated through the explicit reference to the terror attack of July 7th 2005, when 52 persons died because of a synchronized series of suicide acts, perpetrated by an Islamic fundamentalist[2] cell based in England.

---

[1] "Dilemma" Def. 1. In *Oxford Advanced Learner's Dictionary*. Oxford: OUP, 2001.

[2] This expression openly recalls Said's definition of the word 'fundamentalism': "fundamentalism (is) a word that has come to be associated almost automatically with Islam, although it has a flourishing, usually elided, relationship with Christianity, Judaism, and Hinduism. The deliberately created associations between Islam and fundamentalism ensure the average reader to see Islam and fundamentalism as essentially the same thing" (Said 2007, xvi). And that in this study the word 'Islam' associated with the concept of fundamentalism and terrorism is going to be used bearing in mind that: "(it) defines a relatively small proportion of what actually takes place in the Islamic world, which numbers a billion people, and include dozens of countries, societies, traditions, languages, and, of course, an infinite number of different experiences" (Said 2007, xvi).

The two analyzed cultural representations are explicitly referred to the tragedy of 7/7, although following the post 9/11 *topos* of artistic production linked to a catastrophic event and reshaping it in order to reproduce new perspectives of the London terror assault. As proved by the ongoing iconic cultural production making both direct and indirect reference to New York 9/11, "the most photographed disaster in history" (Kirshenblatt-Gimblett 2003, 12), it is possible to state that a terrorist attack at the heart of a city generates a cascade of cultural iconic representations linked to it. However, this paper aims at studying the relationship of photography and the terror attack of London 7/7 choosing two atypical representations of London Bombings and considering that day not simply a *Kodak moment* (Kirshenblat-Gimblett 2003; Munir and Phillips 2005), but also a visual event.

The label 'Kodak moment' usually "evokes amateur snapshot, candid images of everyday life or special events, not spectacular pictures [...] or the theatre of war taken by professional photographs with exclusive access to the action" (Kirshenblatt-Gimblett 2003, 14) shifting photography from a highly expert activity to an everyday life experience. On the contrary, as argued by Michel Foucault in 1970's and later reformulated by Mirzoeff (2002, 2005) while tackling the problematic relationship between events and visual studies, "the problem is at once to distinguish among events, to differentiate the networks and levels to which they belong, and to reconstitute the lines along which they are connected and engender one another" (Foucault 2000, 116). The culturalist approach of this study bears in mind what proposed by the French philosopher working, therefore, "by constructing around the singular event analyzed as process a 'polygon' or rather a 'polyhedron' of intelligibility, the number of whose faces is not given in advance and can never properly be taken as finite" (Foucault 1991, 76-77).

Modifying the definition of 9/11 as "the 'mother event', the pure event that concentrates in itself all the events that never took place" (Baudrillard 2002, 149), it is possible to state that 9/11 is the "visual mother event" of which 7/7 is a direct projection to be studied according to Foucault's declarations. Within this frame of knowledge, Johannes Hepp's post-photography and *people's cinema*[3] are going to be privileged field of study bringing to light two different faces of the "polyhedron of intelligibility" built around London 7/7.

In his essay *Art, Common Sense and Photography*, Victor Burgin states that the "the main thrust of photographic criticism these days is towards the consideration of photography as Art" opposed to "the issue of photography as an instrument of ideology" (Burgin 1999, 41). He develops these two apparently opposing trends defining the photograph as "a sign or, more correctly speaking, a complex of signs used to communicate a message" (Burgin 1999, 44). Within

---

[3] See http://news.bbc.co.uk/1/hi/in_depth/uk/2005/london_explosions/default.stm (last accessed August 2011).

the context of photography, opponents of this mutual relationship between art and ideology condemn such a kind of pictures as "manipulative", "that is to say, first, that the photographer manipulates what comes over the image; [and] second, that as a result his or her audience's beliefs about the world are manipulated" (Burgin 1999, 41). Referring to Hepp's post-photography, this essay considers the positive connotation of 'manipulated' since it opens up a new perspective on the representation of the terror attack, following Burgin's description of the strong link between digital operations and the essence of camera work both in terms of physical handling (cameras, films, lightning and digital devices are used to produce meanings) and political exploitation.

According to Shapiro (1988), in order to recognize the political rhetoric of photography, it is necessary "to look at photographic statements on the basis of their tendency to either reproduce dominant forms of discourse" or to look at them analyzing their "tendency to provoke critical, to denaturalize what is unproblematically accepted and to offer thereby an avenue for politicizing problematics" (*ibidem*, 130). Moreover, as he points out while making reference to the work of Barthes, Shapiro notes that:

> Applying his [Barthe's] more general notion of reading, viz. that no text can signify without the complicity of the reader, Barthes explores the reading of photographs, which is governed, he argues, by the set of social codes with which the photograph and viewer interact (*ibidem*, 128).

In such a political discernment Operator, Spectrum and Spectator (Barthes 1980, 10)[4] interact to establish and detect new meanings and political choices, conveyed through the manipulative characteristics of photography.

Although Susan Sontag recognizes the political element of photography, an art "commonly regarded as an instrument for knowing things" (Sontag 1973, 93), she suggests two different aesthetic criteria to evaluate a picture. Starting on the general assumption that photography "proposes a process of imagination and an appeal to taste quite different from that of painting" (Sontag 1973, 139), she points out two main factors setting the benchmark of iconic quality: *innovativeness* and *the quality of presence*. Innovativeness is the quality of imposing "new formal schemes or changes in the visual language" (Sontag 1973, 139), or the originality of new paradigms; while the quality of presence refers to the relationship between the

---

[4] According to Mirzoeff (2002) the formal distinction between Spectrum and Spectator proposed by Barthes (1980) is nowadays obsolete: as a matter of fact he ascribes these two categories the label of *visual subject*, "a person who is both constituted as an agent of sight (regardless of his or her biological capacity to see) and as the effect of a series of categories of visual subjectivity. During the modern period a two-fold visual subject was predicated by the disciplinary society. That subject added to Descartes' early modern definition of self – 'I think therefore I am' (Descartes) – a new mantra of visual subjectivity: 'I am seen and I see that I am seen'" (Mirzoeff 2002, 10).

aura a picture acquires through the passing of time and its exhibition in museums and galleries. However, as Pierre Bourdieu points out:

> Because the picture is always judged with reference to the function that it fulfils for the person who looks at it or the function which that viewer thinks it could fulfil for another person, aesthetic judgment relying explicitly on the recognition of 'genres', whose 'perfection' and range of application are conceptually defined. [...] It is within its participation within a genre that each individual photograph derives its purpose and its *raison d'être* (Bourdieu 1990, 89).

Without introducing a new iconic genre linked to international terrorism and 7/7 a general macroscopic division could be drawn between figurative representations produced while the bombing assault took place and its immediate aftermath or representations after a period of decantation and revision. Such a rigid distinction has driven scholars studying either artistic products created after the catastrophe and their relationship with reality, or live images of the disaster usually conveyed by the media (see Tulloch 2006; Rose 2007; Wells 2007); however, in this study, I am taking into consideration two peculiar representations which are difficult to be included into these two clear-cut categories.

Firstly, we have pictures of the terror attack taken directly from the survivors, grainy and blurred live images showing the catastrophe from its inner point of view. Within 45 minutes of the bus explosion in Tavistock Square, BBC website had received the first image of the damaged vehicle and by the end of the day about 1,000 mobile photographs and 20 amateur videos had been sent to the TV channel: mainly pictures of commuters lining or evacuating through the dark and yellow-lighted tube stations, men assisting casualties in the damaged trains and hellish portraits of tunnels and carriages (Scott 2005).

Iain Sinclair defines these pictures as a new way of representing "the age of extremity" (Sontag 1996)[5] we are currently living in:

> A new cinema requiring minimal light (and) no technical expertise – switch on and hold above your head like a torch –. The people's cinema of mobile-phone: careless and magical. [...] Mobile-phone reports are unauthored, without ego: the city as itself. At the moment of crisis, phones shift from being mere tools of convenience. They begin to create a poetry of unease (Sinclair 2005).

Sinclair's *poetry of unease* is created through the growth of a new form of reportage having as an Operator (Barthes 1980, 10) an amateur empowered thanks to the contemporary widespread of visual culture and digital technologies; as stated by John Ryley, executive editor at Sky News UK:

---

[5] "Ours is indeed an age of extremity. For we live under continual threat of two equally fearful, but seemingly opposed, destinies: unremitting banality of inconceivable terror" (Sontag 1996, 209-225).

The difference that mobile technology makes, it empowers ordinary people to show what happened as it happens, not a minute later or an hour later. So you are seeing the drama, the story unfolding (Scott 2005).

Not only "you are seeing the drama" but mobile phones and new technologies help registering the detailed vividness of flash photography (Brown and Kulick 1977) combining "elements of surprise, emotional intensity and consequentiality" (Kirshenblatt-Gimblett 2003, 16).

On the other hand, and far from recording the "story unfolding" as proposed by Kirsty Scott (2005), the German photographer Johannes Hepp portrays, in his multiple pictures, urban spaces becoming crystallization points in which social relationships and collective experiences are registered.

Defining his pictures as "archetypes of global insecurity" (http://www.johannes-hepp.com/) Johannes Hepp follows the emphatic relation among Operator, Spectrum and Spectator (Barthes 1980, 10) and the peculiar characteristics of photography highlighted by Susan Sontag:

All photographs are *memento mori*. To take a photograph is to participate in another person's (or thing's) mortality, vulnerability, mutability. Precisely by slicing out this moment and freezing it, all photographs testify to time's relentless melt (Sontag 1973, 15).

Making deliberate reference to the 1983 TV film *The Day After*, the artist has created a collection of digital panoramic images metaphorically conflating the crucial moment of terror attacks and the passage of time. The film depicts the results of a nuclear attack in terms of both physical and psychological reactions: the small town of Lawrence, Kansas, and its middle-class survived citizens tackle the aftermath of the nuclear explosion struggling to survive in a nightmarish atmosphere composed of murders, lootings, violence and moral decadence.

At the same level, Hepp describes us the grim atmosphere after an atrocity took place in twenty-six cities of the world (such as Paris, Jerusalem, Mumbai and Madrid, just to cite few examples) portraying the devastated areas either during a special anniversary or after few hours from the detonation, the mass murder or the terror attack. In the picture created after London Bombings of July 7th, Hepp creates an horizontal relationship among the persons and the urban background of Edgware Road "dissolving the solid and compact reality of everyday perception into an infinity of fleeting profiles like dream images, in order to capture absolutely unique moments of the reciprocal situations of things" (Bourdieu 1990, 76).[6]

Like all other composites created for *The Day After*, the picture describing the aftermath of Edgware Road is:

---

[6] Pierre Bourdieu states these words referring to the *temporal paradox* of standard photography, although they could be applied to Hepp's digital post-photography too.

[...] composed digitally and montaged together with anything up to 100 images, depicting incidents taken from different timeframes. Deliberately avoiding the notion of objectivity, 'The Days After' does not attempt to portray any illusions of reality, instead the work aims to raise an awareness of the symbiotic relationship between terrorism and the oxygen of publicity generated by media coverage – with innocent human beings providing the collateral (http://www.johannes-hepp.com/).

As Christopher Coppock, the director of Cardiff Photo Gallery, explains, the panoramic digital picture composed of 200 single images "reinforce the on-going narrative [...] [and] question our relationship to the notion of indiscriminate violence and bear witness to an era becoming historic: the era of terror" (*ibidem*). In his panoramic digital pictures, a peculiar *vernacular vision*[7] of the disaster is depicted through a documentary point of view. Hepp is inspired by battlefield paintings showing a "synchronic presentation of the military action"[8] which is similarly recreated in his digital manipulations where a "subjective and free composition of a large number of singular incidents" (http://www.johannes-hepp.com/press.html) is portrayed.

Recording the life of normal people in such previously damaged cities, Johannes Hepp focuses on the reborn life after a disruptive action more than on the spectacle of devastation (Virilio 2004); it is only through this artificial device that Hepp recreates either a mock world where terrors sites become memorials of the disaster, a kind of mausoleum where normal life will never come back, or a fake everyday life since, as stated by the photographer:

> The common images transmitted by the media have nothing to do with the sites I visited. [...] People are not really aware of how quickly normal life takes over again. I wanted to document those places and their people going about their daily lives. Trying to avoid anything spectacular! (http://www.johannes-hepp.com/press.html).

Although "trauma, like God, is supposed to be unrepresentable in word and image", as stated by Mitchell (2005, 295), it is possible to state that both the *poetry of unease* described by I. Sinclair and the multiple digital manipulation by Hepp could be ascribed to the different faces of the *polyhedron of intelligibility* proposed by Foucault (1991, 76-77) in order to report on unusual and catastrophic events. Therefore, these two peculiar narrations and their related trauma could take part in the building process of the cognitive structure, thanks to which a terror event like the London Bombings could be

---

[7] Vernacular watching takes place in the corner of one's eye, the passing detail that catches a glance or the sideways look at fellow waiter (Mirzoeff 2005, 30).

[8] For example, in his website, Hepp declares his tribute to the painting *Alexander Schlacht* by Altdorfer.

understood and studied under a culturalist point of view, together with all other representations constituting the different faces of the above-mentioned polygon.

References

9/11. 2006 [2002]. Dir. Jules and Gedeon Naudet. Paramount.

Barthes R. 1980. *Camera Lucida: Reflections on Photography*. London: Jonathan Cape.

Baudrillard J. 2002. "L'esprit du terrorism". In Hauerwas S., Lentricchia F. (eds.) *Dissent from the Homeland: Essays After September 11*. Durham: Duke University Press, 149-163.

Belpoliti M. 2005. *Crolli*. Torino: Einaudi.

Bourdieu P. 1990. "The Social Definition of Photography". In Bourdieu P. (ed.) *Photography – A Middle-brow Art*. Oxford: Polity Press, 73-95.

Brown R., Kulick J. (eds.) 1977. "Flashbulb Memories". In *Cognition*, 5, I, 73-99.

Burgin V. 1997. "Art, Common Sense and Photography". In Evans J. (ed.) *The Camerawork Essays: Context and Meaning in Photography*. London: Rivers Oram Press, 74-85.

Caruth C. 1996. *Unclaimed Experience: Trauma, Narrative and History*. Baltimore: The Johns Hopkins University Press.

Foucault M. 1977. "Nietzsche, Genealogy, History". In Bouchard D.F. (ed.) *Language, Counter-memory, Practice: Selected Essays and Interviews*. Ithaca (NY): WileyBlackwell, 139-140.

Foucault M. 1991. "Questions of method". In Burchell G., Gordon C., Miller P. (eds.) *The Foucault Effect: Studies in Governmentality*. Chicago: University of Chicago Press.

Foucault M. 2000. *Power: The Essential Works of Michel Foucault 1954–1984*, vol. Two. Faubion J. (ed.) London: Allen Lane.

Gillian R. 2009. "Who Cares for Which Dead and How? British Newspaper Reporting of the Bombings in London, July 2005". In *Geoforum*, 40, January, 1, 46-54.

Kirshenblatt-Gimblett B. 2003. "Kodak Moments, Flashbulb Memories: Reflections on 9/11" In *TDR*, 47, Spring, 1, 11-48.

McEwan I. 2001. "Beyond Belief". In *The Guardian*, November 12th.

Mirzoeff N. 2002. "The Subject of Visual Culture." In Mirzoeff N. (ed.) *The Visual Culture Reader*. London and New York: Routledge, 3-23.

Mirzoeff N. 2005. *Watching Babylon: the War in Iraq and Global Visual Culture*. New York and London: Routledge.

Mitchell W.J.T. 2005. "The Unspeakable and the Unimaginable: Word and Image in a Time of Terror". In *ELH* 72, Summer, 2, 291-308.

Munir K., Phillips N. 2005. "The Birth of the 'Kodak Moment': Institutional Entrepreneurship and the Adoption of New Technologies". In *Organization Studies*, 26, 11, 1665-1687.

Rose G. 2007. "Spectacle and Spectres: London 7 July 2005". In *New Formations*, 62, 1, 45-59.

Said, E.W. 2007. *Covering Islam – How the Media and the Experts Determine How We See the Rest of the World*. London: Vintage.

Scott K. 2005. "Victims Capture Unfolding Events on Mobile Phones". In *The Guardian*, July 9th.

Shapiro M.J. 1988. *The Politics of Representation*. Madison: The University of Wisconsin Press.

Sinclair I. 2005. "Theatre of the City". In *The Guardian*, July 14th.

Sontag S. 1973. *On Photography*. London: Penguin Books.

Sontag S. 1996. "The Imagination of Disaster". In Sontag S. *Against Interpretation and Other Essays*. New York: Picador, 209-225.

Tulloch J. 2006. *One Day in July – Experiencing 7/7*. London: Little Brown.

Virilio P. 2004. *Città panico – L'altrove comincia qui*. Milano: Cortina Raffaello Editore.

Wells K. 2007. "Narratives of Liberation and Narratives of Innocent Suffering: The Rhetorical Uses of Images of Iraqi Children in the British Press". In *Journal of Visual Communication*, 6, 55-71.

Web Sites
(last accessed August 2011)

http://www.johannes-hepp.com/

C. Bruna Mancini

Università della Calabria

Internet in a Cup, or a Cup of Internet: the Coffee-house Goes Online

1. Eighteenth-century coffee-houses and the public sphere

It is generally agreed that the first coffee house to open in London was established in 1652 by the Greek Pasqua Rose (or Rosée)[1], the servant of the rich merchant Daniel Edwards. Excited by the tasty and healing qualities of this exotic beverage, hundreds of curious Londoners flocked to Pasqua Rosée coffee-house, finding a place of male sociability and discussion. In fact, the 'respectable' and 'refined' ladies were not allowed to participate and they met at home, discussing and drinking tea. Within a couple of years, coffee-houses were springing up around London, becoming what Jürgen Habermas defines one of the primary locus of English bourgeois discourse, playing an important role in the formation of the so-called 'public sphere' as well as of the public and literary opinion. In fact, they were called "penny universities" because, for the price of a cup, customers of all social and political stripes could read the latest news and pamphlets, and participate in political as well as intellectual discussions; to the point that, in the satiric *A Character of Coffee and Coffee-house*, published in 1661 (M. P. 1661), the anonymous author declared that the coffee-house was dangerous to the Government, because "seeds of Sedition are here sown, & Principles of Liberty insinuated". In short, as we know, the coffee-house was the site of a sort of universal community which:

> hosted continuous conversation about public events and issues, encouraged the blurring of social distinctions we take for granted: between public and private, for example, or between the working and leisure classes, and especially between conversation and written texts. Texts – whether newspapers, pamphlets about current events, or printed books – were quoted extensively and became the basis for much of the public conversation, and

---

[1] England's first coffee-house opened in Oxford during the English Civil War.

(in turn) conversation and its colloquial and dialogic habits often migrated into print (Hunter 2006, 11).

2. Internet in a Cup: Coffee-houses and cyberspace

On the threshold of the New Millennium, when the Internet Era began, these spaces of communication and information exchanges seemed to be perfectly fulfilled by 'the Net of the nets'. As a matter of fact, on December 18th 2003, in an article of *The Economist* entitled "The Internet in a Cup", the journalist remarked:

> WHERE do you go when you want to know the latest business news, follow commodity prices, keep up with political gossip, find out what others think of a new book, or stay abreast of the latest scientific and technological developments? Today, the answer is obvious: you log on to the internet. Three centuries ago, the answer was just as easy: you went to a coffee-house. There, for the price of a cup of coffee, you could read the latest pamphlets, catch up on news and gossip, attend scientific lectures, strike business deals, or chat with like-minded people about literature or politics. [...] Like today's websites, weblogs and discussion boards, coffee-houses were lively and often unreliable sources of information that typically specialised in a particular topic or political whereas others provided foreign newsletters filled with coffee-house gossip from abroad.

Thus, in the eighteenth century, Europe's interconnected web of coffee-houses formed, in a way, the Internet of the Enlightenment era; but, with the due differences, of course. Because, obviously, in the twenty-first viewpoint. They were outlets for a stream of newsletters, pamphlets, advertising free-sheets and broadsides. Depending on the interests of their customers, some coffee-houses displayed commodity prices, share prices and shipping lists, century, while connected online, the conversations, debates, flirting, reading and games take place on a global rather than local environment, maybe under the recording eye of a CCTV camera. Unfortunately for too much time the 'cyberspace' – a quite vague term referring to the network which connects computers everywhere, all over the globe, as well as to 'the world in the wires', or better, all phenomena which may occur amongst or inside computers[2] – has been seen as the locuses of perversion and immateriality, of the disintegration of the human identity and interiority, the site where we could become – as Donna Haraway wrote in her "A Cyborg Manifesto" (1991) – "fabricated hybrids of machine and organism". The users, like

---

[2] "A space apart that of ordinary experience", created by the computer technologies (Koepsell 2000, 1).

zombies or 'cybernetic organisms', immobilized in front of the desktop PC, almost imperceptibly move the mouse selecting words from a displayed menu, slowly sliding into a new dimension: the space of alienation, of schizophrenia, of the transgression of boundaries between natural and artificial, mind and body, reality and simulation. But, as the cyborg's built-in androgyny, for Haraway, was a sort of victory for feminism, it is now time to (re)consider, without any fear, the possibility and the existence of new modes of communication, like the "high-speed communication networks" for example: a further (and maybe not the ultimate) development of the so called face-to-face communication. Instead of causing the decline of the traditional interpersonal relationships, they can promote a new way of interaction and of conceiving ourselves and the others. As a matter of fact, in her essay entitled "From City Space to Cyberspace" Jennifer S. Light observes that the use of the Internet often implies an interaction between individuals which can continue in everyday life, improving the physical as well as the social space surrounding us, pushing people to cross lines and mental borders; thus: "the Internet presents exciting opportunities to revitalize civic engagements in new ways" (Light 2006, 111).

Therefore, cyberspace could be seen, at all effects, as the latest evolution of the 'public sphere': "a postmodern analogue of the opportunity to enrich one's intellectual world offered by the eighteenth century coffee house" (Clayton 2004, 171). And to me this point seems to be also more important if we consider the use of the Internet in the contemporary coffee-houses, or better still, the cybercafés. In *London's Coffee Houses. A Stimulating Story*, Antony Clayton recalls that, as the Internet grew from a military tool to an academic resource and then rapidly became a global phenomenon, shrewd business minds realised that high street shops offering instant high-speed access to the World Wide Web and email would be in great demand, at least until the technology became cheaper and more portable (*ibidem*, 171). Thus in the first cybercafés – such as the Cyberia at 39 Whitfield Street – customers paid to sit at the computer and drink a cup of coffee, soft drinks and snacks, celebrating the renaissance (or the revival) of coffee house culture. Nina Wakeford defines them as "a *translation landscape of computing* where the Internet is produced and interpreted for 'ordinary people' who consume time on the machines, and/or food and drink. [...] The business goal of management is to sell the Internet experience – using a computer to access the Internet in a café – as a product" (Wakeford 2006). Obviously, also other components of the context are important, such as: the décor, the environment (which had to be strictly female-friendly), the staff, the other customers, the food, the coffee, and "the combination of a series of familiar experiences (buying coffee, sitting in a café, observing norms of sociability, etc.) with the often more unfamiliar encounters with the computer".

3. The case of Starbucks

It is the case of the famous chain of coffee-houses named Starbucks (it seems, from the first mate in Herman Melville's *Moby Dick*). The first coffee shop of the chain was opened in the United Kingdom in 1998, on Chelsea's King's Road, and by July 2002 the distinctive logo of the green crowned mermaid with two tails[3] was on display outside 230 outlets in London.[4] At the beginning, the shops were not 'cabled', and all the success of the brand depended on a higher quality coffee, improved standards of interior decoration and store locations, and the so-called "Starbucks Experience": the leading philosophy of the Company, aiming at "Turning the Ordinary (coffee, life, relationships and so on) into Extraordinary". According to it, the customer is the center, the heart of each single decision made by the Company, in order to create a place where "a person will feel comfortable hanging out alone or with friends" (quoting one of the most famous slogans). In this sense, the members of the staff are carefully trained to prepare "a unique and personal experience for customers" (*ibidem*, 6) because each desire of the client has to be satisfied and he/she must interact in order to create exactly the coffee(house) he/she prefers. Thus, even if its 'repetitive construction' makes it a typical "non-place", in Marc Augé's definition (1992), it perfectly represents the 'third place' defined by the sociologist Ray Oldenburg in the book entitled *The Great Good Place* (1989): spaces, like pubs and coffee-houses, offering a place of 'decompression' between home and work, where people may meet as equals, where conversation may flourish, individuals may come in association with others and society may reap the benefit of such collective reasoning. In fact, the same Howard Schultz, the chairman and former owner of Starbucks, suggested that a Starbucks branch *might* play an important role in the civic function of the community, providing an emotionally warm space for the collective engagement in society.

A powerful symbol of these ambitions, in Markham Ellis' words, was seen in the encouragement coffee-house chains have given to wireless Internet: "by which means individuals using their own laptops can participate in the on-line 'community' of the Internet, all the while remaining oblivious of the living world around them" (2004, 256). Thus, in 2007, when Apple announced that there would

---

[3] The logo was based on an old sixteenth-century Norse woodcut: a two-tailed mermaid, or siren, encircled by the store's original name, Starbucks Coffee, Tea, and Spice. That early siren, bare-breasted and Rubenesque, was supposed to be as seductive as coffee itself.

[4] http://www.brandautopsy.com/2005/06/the_evolution_o.html (last accessed August 2011). In the first version, which was based on a 16th-century Norse woodcut, the Starbucks siren was topless and had a fully visible double fish tail. In the second version, which was used from 1987-92, her breasts were covered by her flowing hair, but her navel was still visible, and the fish tail was cropped slightly. In the current version, used since 1992, her navel and breasts are not visible at all, and only vestiges remain of the fish tails.

be wireless communication between the iTunes Store and Starbucks, via AT&T, the Web became part of the "coffee house experience". In 2008 Starbucks started a community website, named "My Starbucks Idea", designed to collect suggestions and feedback from customers. There, Schultz posted his proposals in order to renew the Company, John Moore replied with his Manifesto entitled "What Must Starbucks Do?"[5], and also the other users/clients took part in the discussion with their comments. In particular, they asked for "comfy places to engage in conversation" and the possibility to get free WiFi (and I'm quoting from a message posted by a client at this site): "Instead of giving me a dollar cup of coffee, give me some free WiFi. I'll pay more for the coffee". As a sort of reply, in May 2008 a loyalty program was introduced for registered users of the Starbucks Card offering perks such as free WiFi Internet access and free refills. Obviously, this new free WiFi effort showed how important wireless Internet could be for a coffee shop chain, because nowadays people need WiFi as much as they need caffeine.

And if in the end of his *The Coffee-House. A Cultural History*, Ellis declares that the sociability of the chain coffee bar has cut its links with the satiric, vengeful, transgressive crowd, on the verge of insurrection, which filled the old eighteenth-century coffee-houses, I would in turn recall the desire of the customers to participate as well as to criticize also the cybercafé as an institution: such as the many webpages devoted to the "Resistance to Starbucks", a way to dissent and fight against Globalization and the Capitalism it represents, for example; or else, the many parodies and imitations of its famous logo and coffees. Clearly, it's a very soft kind of rebellion, typical of the New Millennium, which recalls to me the surreal, silent, gratuitous revolutions described by J.G. Ballard in his last novels, *Cocaine Nights* (1996), *Super Cannes* (2000), *Millennium People* (2004), and *Kingdom Come* (2006). "A small revolution was taking place, so modest and well behaved that almost no one had noticed", he wrote in the incipit of his *Millennium People*. Maybe, as soft-regime prisoners living in borderless jails built by earlier generations of inmates, this is the only way in which we can react and break free (Ballard 2004, 139-140).

References

Augé M. 1992. *Non-Lieux. Introductions à une anthropologie de la surmodernité*. Paris: Seuille.
Ballard J.G. 2004. *Millennium People*. London: Harper Perennial.

---

[5] Available at http://www.brandautopsy.com/2007/02/what_must_starb-2.html (last accessed August 2011).

Clayton A. 2004. *London's Coffee Houses. A Stimulating Story*. London: Weidenfeld & Nicolson.

The Economist. 2003. "The Internet in a Cup", December 18th, available at http://www.economist.com/node/2281736?story_id=2281736 (last accessed August 2011).

Ellis M. 2004. *The Coffee-House. A Cultural History*. London: Weidenfeld & Nicolson.

Haraway D. 1991. "A Cyborg Manifesto: Science, Technology, and Socialist-Feminism in the Late Twentieth Century". In Haraway D. *Simians, Cyborgs and Women: The Reinvention of Nature*. New York: Routledge, 149-181.

Hunter J. 2006. "Couplets and Conversation". In Sitter J. (ed.) *The Cambridge Companion to Eighteenth-Century Poetry*. Cambridge: Cambridge University Press, 11-36.

Koepsell D.R. 2000. *The Ontology of Cyberspace: Philosophy, Law, and the Future of Intellectual Property*. Chicago: Open Court Publishing Company.

Light J.S. 2006. "From City Space to Cyberspace". In Crang M., Crang P., May J. (eds.) *Virtual Geographies. Bodies, Space and Relations*. London: Routledge, 11-36.

M. P. 1661. *A Character of Coffee and Coffee-House*, available at http://people.bu.edu/jschmidt/enlightenment/clark.pdf (last accessed August 2011).

Oldenburg R. 1989. *The Great Good Place: Cafés, Coffee Shops, Bookstores, Bars, Hair Salons and Other Hangouts at the Heart of a Community*. New York: Marlowe & Company.

Wakeford N. 2006. "Gender and the Landscapes of Computing in an Internet Café". In Crang M., Crang P. and May J. (eds.) *Virtual Geographies. Bodies, Space and Relations*. London: Routledge, 178-201.

Alphabetical List of Contributors to this Volume

Printed by Grafiche VD srl
Città di Castello (PG) – Italy
grafichevd@gmail.com